PROMISED LANDS

Volume 1: Subdivisions in Deserts and Mountains

PROMISED LANDS

Volume 1: Subdivisions in Deserts and Mountains

authors
Leslie Allan
Beryl Kuder
Sarah L. Oakes

research assistant
Elizabeth Hillyer

editor
Jean M. Halloran

an INFORM book

INFORM, Inc.
25 Broad St., NYC 10004

Copyright © 1976 by INFORM, Inc.
All rights reserved.

Published 1976

Library of Congress #76-46735

COMPLETE SET ISBN 0-918780-03-9
VOLUME 1 ISBN 0-918780-04-7

photographs by Beryl Kuder
maps and graphs drawn by Elizabeth V. Hillyer

INFORM is a nonprofit, tax-exempt organization, established in 1973, which conducts research on the impact of American corporations on the environment, employees, and consumers. INFORM publishes books, condensed reports, and newsletters. These seek to clarify and define the nature of some of today's most serious corporate social problems. They describe and evaluate programs and practices that industries could adopt to improve future social performance. INFORM's program is supported by subscriptions and contributions from foundations, corporations, financial institutions, universities, government agencies, and concerned individuals.

Preface

Now that we know that the surface of Mars resembles the bleakest stretches of Arizona, Utah, and Nevada desert, I suppose it's only a matter of time until we turn on the radio and hear something like this:

> Have you always dreamed of investing in land but thought all the best places were gone? Well, we have the investment for you! At VISTA DEL VIKING RANCHITOS you can get in on the ground floor of the biggest new development under the sun.... Located in the heart of Mars' most popular tourist area, VISTA DEL VIKING is the Big Country, the Wide Open Spaces, the Great Outdoors. It's 50 million miles from the crime and grime of Times Square, but just a short 15 minutes radio distance from all urban conveniences. For a retirement home...for a vacation cabin in an exciting new environment... or for a sound investment where property values can go as high as the clear pink sky...get 687 days of sunshine every year at VISTA DEL VIKING, where it hasn't rained in 600,000 years and the young at heart can spoon under two moons!

Those familiar with the problems of large-scale land subdivisions know that this example only mildly exaggerates the kind of claims being made for swamplands, alkali flats, and inaccessible mountaintops peddled as vacation paradises and investment bonanzas throughout this country and abroad.

The installment land-sales business bears little resemblance to the traditional and honorable real-estate transaction, where a well informed buyer deals on an even footing with a locally-based firm for a clearly identified parcel of land. Increasingly, the business has degenerated into an updated version of the old snake-oil racket, sold by the acre instead of by the bottle. Companies aim for volume sales, not development, and this goal has created a built-in incentive to over-promise; once the contract is signed and the paper is peddled to a finance company, the promoter's only incentive to carry through on promises is tough, persistent, even nagging regulatory efforts.

Those efforts have been lacking. And in their absence, any business that involves a large cash flow and big profits with little or no governmental policing invites the attention of well manicured front men for the most sordid criminal enterprises. The booming--one might say "land office"--business done by large-scale developers in the past decade is no exception. The savage murder of a Phoenix reporter turned a national spotlight on the infiltration of organized crime elements in my home state. Aggressive investigation has uncovered a widening stain of fraud, bribery, and violence, and the mass marketing of remote subdivision lands appears to be a prime vehicle for this corruption. To remove that blot will require determined regulation and dogged vigilance.

It may be too late to help many of those who have already been inveigled by the fast-talking, quick-buck artists. Even relatively reputable promoters face financial uncertainty when the lots have been sold and the promised improvements start to fall due. Countless thousands of "investors" wind up with a tiny patch of remote land, accessible only by a rutted dirt road, miles from electricity, water, and stores, or with their title clouded by tax liens or by others who were "sold" the same lot, or with recourse only to the shell of a bankrupt corporation.

Yet there is a legitimate need for "new towns," vacation developments, and retirement communities. Large subdivisions in now undeveloped areas will meet those needs only when we understand the vast complex of factors that go into creating a successful development and when we muster the political courage to demand that promoters deal responsibly with those factors.

This study is an important step toward those goals. INFORM's record of meticulous, comprehensive work, using inductive methods to find practical means to reach achievable ends, has earned widespread acclaim from citizen groups, governmental regulators, and industry alike. In this project, inspection and analysis of desert, wetland, and mountain subdivisions has yielded a solid basis of real-world information on which to base future development policies. Draft performance standards are based not on theoretical models, isolated cases, or impressionistic accounts, but on detailed study of major developments: their successes and their failures.

Where do we go from here?

At the federal level, INFORM's findings--documenting the pervasiveness of consumer and environmental abuses and slapdash planning--argue strongly for tightened restrictions on interstate land sales, bigger budgets and more aggressive attitudes for the Office of Interstate Land Sales Registration, and above all for federal aid to promote state and local land-use planning.

States are given the data needed to implement tough, substantive, and sensible subdivision controls. Counties--especially the small, rural counties that are the most common target for these developments--can find in this study the ammunition to counter the slick presentations, multicolored maps, heady projections, and unsubstantiated promises of operators seeking approval for "dream cities."

And for those entrepreneurs and investors genuinely interested in building viable, environmentally and economically sound new communities, this report contains both a warning--the errors of the past--and a road map to better results.

The time is late. As much as 40 million acres--more than the area of Massachusetts, Connecticut, Rhode Island, and Vermont combined--are already gone, tied up in checkerboards of confused title, complex legal proceedings, and haphazard development by individual lot owners. Land, as the promoters are so fond of reminding us, *is* a limited resource.

--MORRIS K. UDALL

Acknowledgements

The research, writing and production of this study required an extensive commitment from many people over the three years during which work was in progress. The authors would especially like to thank Joanna Underwood, INFORM's Director, who conceived of the project and gave us her guidance, enthusiasm and complete support throughout its course.

Without Jean Halloran, INFORM's Editor, who coordinated all the elements of our work and prepared the final manuscript, this volume would never have emerged as finished product. We owe Jean particular appreciation for her months of indefatigable effort. To Meg Vaillancourt, Jeanne Jacobson and Jean Schrier also go our thanks for their diligent research assistance. During the last months of this study, they answered a multitude of remaining research questions and rounded up hundreds of missing facts.

Many dozens of people across the country, during preparation of this volume, advised us, gave us access to their files, spent long hours being interviewed, and reviewed portions of the manuscript. While INFORM accepts full responsibility for the information and conclusions presented in this study, we owe each and every one of them a special debt of gratitude for the contribution of ideas, time and interest. For all their help, we thank: Dave Duboise, California Regional Water Quality Control Board; Harold Berliner; Joy Lane and Joe Fontaine, Project Land Use, Bakersfield, California· Richard Nuckles, Kern County Planning Commission; The Colorado Open Space Council; Charles Thomson, Southeastern Colorado Water Conservancy District; Ron

Simpson, Pueblo County Planning Department; Dave Hamernick, Arizona Office of Economic Planning and Development; Leonard Halpenny, Water Development Corporation; Winton Woods, University of Arizona Law School; James Altenstadter, Cochise County Planning Department; Gene R. Fontes; Randy Gaines, Santa Cruz County Planning and Zoning Department; Sally Rogers and Brant Calkin, Central Clearing House, Santa Fe; Katherine and Peter Montague, Southwest Research and Information Center, Albuquerque; Paul Sears; Paul Bloom and Phil Bishop, New Mexico State Engineer Office; Doug Fraser, New Mexico Environmental Improvement Agency; Robin Fletcher and Robert Weinstein, Florida Department of Environmental Regulation; Al Butzel, Berle, Butzel and Kass; Marshall Beil, Karpatkin, Pollet & LeMoult; Norman Cortese, Arvida Corporation; John Crowder, U.S. Fish and Wildlife Service; James W. Jones, Arnold and Porter; Frank Grad, Columbia University Law School, Edwin H. Clark II and Joyce Kelley, Council on Environmental Quality; Gordon Kennedy, Gladstone Associates; Alan Kappelar and John McDowell, Office of Interstate Land Sales Registration; Richard Marshall, Ray Brunson and Robert Davey, Horizon Corporation; Dave Mosena, American Society of Planning Officials; James C. Nicholas, Florida Atlantic University; Morton Paulson, *The National Observer*; Richard H. Pough, Natural Area Council; William K. Reilly and Robert Cahn, Conservation Foundation; Laurance Rockefeller, Natural Resources Defense Council; K. Wayne Smith and Don Strand, Dart Industries; Anthony Wolff; Rae Zimmerman, New York University.

We would also like to express our gratitude to many others who helped with fact gathering, checking and sorting for this volume: Kathy Brownback, Pedro Cantillo, Mary Eyster, Joel Katzman, Frances Mayer, Abigail Norman, Randy Piechochi, Cheryl Robertson, Debby Samad, Ron Smith, and Michael White.

We are also indebted to Administrators Pat Konecky and Margaret Reinfeld, for keeping INFORM functioning, and to our production and copy editor, Dan Smullyan; copy editor Patricia Eakins; production assistants Al Malefatto, Alice Schiller, Vincent Trivelli, and Stewart Herman; and magnificent typists Mary Maud Ferguson, Bill Funk, John Klingberg, and Bob Szwed for their help in producing this volume.

For the financial assistance that made this study possible, we would finally like to express our appreciation to the Rockefeller, New York, Norman, Shalan, and Robert Sterling Clark Foundations, and the J.M. Kaplan Fund.

PROMISED LANDS

Volume 1: Subdivisions in Deserts and Mountains

I. THE LAND SUBDIVISION INDUSTRY

1
Overview of the Industry

The retail land-sales industry is engaged in the subdivision, promotion, sale, and sporadic improvement of vast amounts of rural land throughout the United States. Although the industry began to take its present form in the 1950s, subdividing land is no newcomer to the American business world. Soon after the federal government was established, land speculators, as well as individual states, controlled so much acreage bordering existing settlements that the impoverished federal treasury had no market for its sole abundant resource.[1] But shortly thereafter, the first of numerous attacks of land fever began to afflict the American people. By the 1820s, both the federal government and individual speculators had amassed vast profits by retailing land parcels to a hungry public. When the speculative fever abated in 1837, many newly acquired paper fortunes disappeared in the general economic depression that ensued. This "boom and bust" cycle would recur time and again.

Such cycles, determined largely by broad swings in the nation's economy, have historically characterized the retail land-sales business. It is one which suffers or benefits from severely fluctuating profits, which influence the size and intensity of industry activity. When the general economy provides an optimistic weather report, retail land sales companies emerge from periodic hibernations as predictably as bears in spring. And, given the miasmic ills begrudgingly suffered by the country's increasing urban centers, retail land-sales firms do not have to search far to find large numbers of consumers eager to follow Will Rogers' oft-abused advice: "Buy land. They ain't making any more of it."

The most recent cycle of retail land-sales activity, during which the industry assumed its current form, began in the 1950s.

when suburban subdivisions became popular. At that time a few privately held firms ("probably no more than 100," according to Dorothy Tymon in *America is For Sale*[2]) began to mass-merchandise subdivided lots, principally on Florida's west coast, in its swamplands, and in California's remote arid regions. Selling by mail on the installment plan, these companies found a large, nationwide market for small lot parcels that could be purchased cheaply, even if sight unseen. The lure of potential profits through appreciation of land values clinched the sale for many buyers.

Some of these operations involved selling lots under water—or lots without water—and earned the retail land-sales business a tawdry reputation. Legal action was eventually taken against a few of those companies, like Gulf American Corporation and California Cities Development Company, which had engaged in the most blatantly fraudulent schemes during the late 1950s. But it was principally a depressed economy that caused a brief decline in retail land-sales activities in the early 1960s. Then, over the course of the next decade, from 1963 to 1973, as the economy promised ever-increasing corporate earnings and personal income, the retail land-sales business came to attract some of the country's largest public corporations.

In the late 1960s, according to *Business Week*, "close to 300 major companies used inflated shares from a booming stock market to acquire new land—and almost every other real-estate venture."[3] By 1971, 21 of the nation's 200 largest firms were involved in the sale and/or development of raw land.[4] These included such giants as ITT, Tenneco, Boise Cascade, American Standard, and Dart Industries.

Chief among the industry's attractions to large corporations were its accounting methods, whereby firms recorded the full value of a sale made on an installment contract immediately, even though actual income would be received only over ten years. When these accounting practices were altered in 1972, according to a 1974 *Business Week* article,[5] so that a company's financial statements had to reflect real income from installment sales, earnings from retail land-sales activity dropped an estimated 20% or more. Prior to this change in accounting practices, however, many large corporations eagerly came to drink from what a Boise Cascade executive described in 1969 as "the great earnings faucet in the sky."[6]*

---

*In 1969, Boise Cascade, primarily a paper company, sold $164 million worth of lots from 29 projects in California and the rest of the country. In 1972, following legal and financial difficulties, the company wrote off $200 million worth of real estate investments and eased out of the business.[7]

OVERVIEW OF THE INDUSTRY

With the entry of these major corporations, marketing methods changed. The industry's former reliance on the mail-order merchandising of raw land gave way to a more sophisticated marketing of a more appealing product. Most of the large companies undertaking retail land-sales activities in the 1960s promised "homesites" in "pre-planned communities" designed for retirement, vacation, or permanent use. Vast numbers of company-employed salesmen attacked urban markets throughout the world, often using high-pressure, hard-sell tactics. Exaggerated promises made to consumers about the value and uses of land resulted, partly because of "the tremendous incentives [companies] placed on salesmen."[8] A survey made by the American Land Development Association in 1973 for a study by the President's Council on Environmental Quality (CEQ) found that "over three-fourths of the salesmen in the industry are paid strictly on a commission basis."[9]

By 1973, the year that most observers mark as the peak of this latest retail land-sales cycle, the Housing and Data Bureau estimated that land-related activity comprised the country's third-largest industry, generating $1 out of every $7 of the gross national product.[10]

The subsequent energy crisis and severe economic recession have had a particular damaging impact on the retail land-sales industy. The $40 million Horizon Corporation is a case in point. Among the largest land-sales companies in the country, it currently holds a total of 441,000 acres of land at six new "communities in New Mexico, Arizona, and Texas, and a 25,000-acre parcel of undeveloped land in New York. In 1973, the company had gross revenues of almost $100 million. In its fiscal year ending May 31, 1976, gross revenues came to just under $40 million.[11]

Retail land-sales firms like Horizon had found easy credit and eager buyers during the "boom" of the 1960s. But many of these firms, both large and small, had put themselves in highly leveraged positions and could not endure the harsh economic conditions occurring between 1973 and 1976. However, as the economy restabilizes, the historic appeal of land ownership will reassert itself. If past trends hold true, consumers will resume former purchasing patterns. The director of the American Land Development Association, an industry organization formed in 1970 to monitor and improve industry performance, confirmed in September, 1976, that "land sales as well as home-building are on the rise again this year."[12]

Industry Size and Scope

The actual scope of the retail land-sales industry's operations in the United States, while clearly enormous, has never been precisely defined. Accurate figures on the number of companies, the volume of sales, the location of projects, the acres of land subdivided, and the number of lots marketed have simply not been tabulated by any agency, association, or person. Combining existing fragments of descriptive data can, however, at least suggest the actual features of this industry.

Retail land-sales firms range in type and size from privately held operations, mostly small in scope which only market locally, to large publicly owned corporations which market lots all over the world. A 1973 survey by the American Land Development Association found that 70% of its respondents were privately owned, and only 30% were either publicly owned or subsidiaries of publicly owned corporations.[13]

There is particularly little data on the activities of the large segment of the retail land-sales industry which is privately held, unless the private firms are engaged in interstate commerce. While 41 states now require all retail-land sales firms offering lots for sale within state borders to register their projects with a state agency, very few regularly monitor data on the number of acres subdivided or the number of lots offered.

As of 1969, public or private firms which market in interstate commerce subdivisions consisting of fifty or more lots, each less than five acres in size, must register their projects with the Office of Interstate Land Sales Registration (OILSR) in the U.S. Department of Housing and Urban Development. The President's Council on Environmental Quality has surveyed these filings and found that most developments are relatively large—averaging 1000 acres—while most lots marketed are relatively small—a quarter to one acre.[14] OILSR's computer print-out sheet for May, 1976, showed a total of 16,429 registered subdivisions. They comprise 8,877,889 lots on 17,256,818 acres (17 million acres is approximately the equivalent of the land areas of Massachusetts, Connecticut, Rhode Island, and Vermont combined). Unfortunately, these figures are far from precise. They include numerous duplicate filings and "an overcount of self-contained individual projects, since one or more filings (listed as a 'subdivision') may be made for different sections or plots of a project."[15]

On top of these problems of data organization, an official with OILSR's Department of Policy and Development Control recently confessed that their computer system has the habit of "adding in 8's" on an apparently random basis when computing lot figures. He noted that OILSR anticipates having a modified data-retrieval system by May, 1977.[16] Alan Kappelar, a high-ranking OILSR official, "estimated" in June, 1976, that approximately 6,200 individual subdivision projects were filed with OILSR, the majority by separate companies.[17]

OVERVIEW OF THE INDUSTRY

Richard L. Ragatz, the foremost authority for the statistical parameters of this industry, noted in a 1975 article that "the industry is still characterized by lack of data and insufficient information." Working with OILSR data computed for the five years through January, 1975, Ragatz found filings for all states but North Dakota and Rhode Island. He further found that the six states of Florida, New Mexico, Arizona, California, Colorado, and Texas showed the greatest concentration of subdivision activity. They had 73.1% of the 3.4 million lots, 80.4% of the 7.1 million acres, and 53.5% of the 5,500 filings then registered with OILSR.[19] (Florida and Texas alone accounted for 48% of all lots filed with OILSR.[20])

Ragatz' figures on the five states in which INFORM has studied sites show that during the five-year period to January 1974: Florida had 1,942,155 acres of land (27% of the total on file at OILSR) subdivided for sale via interstate commerce; New Mexico had 1,030,208 acres (14%); Colorado had 824,700 acres (11.5%); California had 622,329 acres (8.7%); and Arizona had 467,015 acres (6.5%).

This acreage (4,886,407 in total) was subdivided into 1,770,496 lots as follows: Florida, 919,672 lots; New Mexico, 342,341 lots; Arizona, 260,728 lots; California, 159,944 lots; and Colorado, 87,810 lots.[22]

As noted above, these figures do not include lots sold solely within state borders. The OILSR filings represent only a portion of the total retail land-sales activity in each state. Their limited scope is suggested by comparing 1974 OILSR data with 1974 data available from three states: Colorado, California, and Arizona.

While OILSR showed 315 individual filings for the state of Colorado by 1974, the Colorado Real Estate Commission released figures as of July, 1974, showing 1,079 Subdivision Developers Certificates on file.[23] While OILSR showed something over half a million acres subdivided in California for interstate sale by 1974, data compiled by the California Department of Real Estate for 1974 showed Subdivision Reports issued for almost two and a half million acres.[24]

The Arizona state data points up a similar range of differences. Where OILSR had 467,015 acres subdivided into 260,728 lots for interstate sale by January, 1974, a state inventory of Arizona's remote subdivisions (those lying outside incorporated land areas) indicated two to three times as much subdivision activity: 943,460 acres had been subdivided into 742,829 lots comprising 2,565 subdivisions.*

---

*While this report, undertaken by the Planning Division of the state Office of Economic Planning and Development, was published in 1975, initial data acquisition was made in 1973.[25]

OILSR filings give some indication of the minimum number, and geographic concentration, of subdivided properties being sold interstate in this country. But by themselves they fail to reflect the level of national retail land-sales activity. Richard Ragatz, nevertheless, hazarded a guess in his January, 1975, presentation of the OILSR figures. In 1973-1974, according to Ragatz, OILSR estimated that only about 40% of the subdivision projects required to register with its office had done so. (An official currently with OILSR claimed it "had a much better track record today."[26]) Figuring from that premise and using the figures then available from OILSR, Ragatz has suggested:

> Perhaps 9 million lots and 18 million acres have been subdivided since 1968, [which could mean] that the total standing stock is between 15 and 20 million lots and 35 to 40 million acres.[27]

The latter acreage amounts to 62,500 square miles, an area slightly larger than the whole state of Florida, and nearly 2% of the land area of the continental United States. The number of lots, assuming three residents per homesite, is enough for 45 to 60 million people to live on. This is more than enough lots for every man, woman, and child in the cities of Los Angeles, San Francisco, Chicago, Detroit, Boston, New York, Philadelphia, and Washington, and the entire state of New Jersey.

Industry Market

Whatever the general industry-wide figures may be, there are irrefutably many more lots in remote subdivisions than population or housing needs call for. This is especially true in such areas of concentrated subdivision activity as the Southwest. In the case of Arizona, for instance, one of the few states where county-by-county data is available, the total state population was 2,150,000 in 1974.[28] Of this population 75% resided in the Phoenix-Tucson metropolitan area.[29] According to a study made by Arizona's Office of Economic Planning and Development, by 1974 the population capacity† of subdivisions located in all

---

†Population capacity was figured using the 1970 census data showing three people per dwelling unit; each lot was assumed to hold one dwelling unit.

OVERVIEW OF THE INDUSTRY

fourteen of Arizona's counties was slightly larger--2,220,700--than the state's existing population.[30] In eight of the fourteen counties, subdivision population capacity in 1974 was greater than the projected county population for the year 2000. Mohave County alone contained 28% of Arizona's total subdivided acres and 24% of its lots.[31] That County's projected population for the year 2000 is 50,350; the population capacity of its subdivisions in 1974 was 439,700.[32] Only 6.5% of its subdivided lots contained a structure at that time.[33]

This 6.5% "build-out rate" for subdivided lots in Mohave County, Arizona, is in fact a good deal higher than the estimated national average. *Subdividing Rural America,* a Council on "Environmental Quality study released in 1976, reported that "industry sources" have estimated no more than a 2% to 5% build-out rate on lots sold throughout the country.[34]

This study pointed out that "one major cause" of the low build-out rate in remote subdivisions "is...that many lot owners buy for investment and never intended to use the property in the first place."[35] Another major cause, they found, stemmed from the fact that many lot purchasers "could not afford to build homes on their lots."[36] (Most lots are purchased on installment contracts which take as long as ten years to pay off; title to the land is seldom transferred to the lot buyer until the final payment has been made.)

A third cause of low build-out rates which the study alluded to is that purchasers often could not build if they wanted to.[37] As the CEQ study states, "failure to deliver promised site improvements is one of the major consumer complaints against recreational land developers."[38] The study confirmed that most lots are marketed totally unimproved--only access roads have been provided--or exist in a subdivision where the developer has made "no more improvements in the land than local land use regulations require."*[39]

Measured against the security provided by money invested at 6% interest in a bank savings account where the money will double in twelve years, the purchase of a remote subdivision lot for eventual appreciation is an extraordinary gamble. Yet according to a survey conducted for the CEQ study, 3.4% of America's households own a vacant "recreation" lot.[41] Such statistics indicate

---

*Ragatz remarked in 1974 that "...the [retail land sales] business is still one of merchadising the land. Most developers operate in this market from two to six years. Many make just enough improvements to get sales rolling and then get out."[40]

the large annual sales volume of the retail land-sales industry. But again precise figures are lacking. Ragatz noted in 1975 that it is "even more difficult" to estimate the industry's annual sales volume than it is to determine the number of subdivisions in the country.[42]

Sales Volume and Number of Firms

The first director of OILSR, who resigned in 1971 to join Horizon Corporation, estimated before his departure that the retail land-sales industry had an annual sales volume of between $4 billion and $6 billion.[43] The American Land Development Association (ALDA) reported that an estimated 650,000 lots were sold in 1970 for $5.5 billion, with the average quarter acre lot selling for $7,300.[44] These two figures have come to represent an outer limit of possible sales activity in the industry. The former figure in particular has been widely used by journalists. However, an OILSR official snapped in mid-1976 upon hearing it, "I defy anyone to find accurate statistics on the finances of this industry....$6 billion was an imaginary figure without proper verifying data."[45] He would not offer an alternate range.

The same difficulty arises in attempts to quantify the number of companies in the retail land-sales industry. According to Gary Terry, the Executive Vice President of ALDA, HUD's Office of Interstate Land Sales Registration estimated that there were "more than 10,000 non-urban subdivision developers operating in the United States in 1973." But, Terry added, "there's no way to verify that." Terry himself "estimated" that in 1976 about 2,000 firms were operating.[46] An OILSR official, however, felt that figure was "way too low." He suggested, emphasizing that it was "a very rough guess," that 10,000 to 12,000 firms were doing business in 1976.[47]

Once again, Ragatz' definition of the problem's parameters must suffice in lieu of hard data:

> The number of participants in [this] industry fluctuates in an exaggeraged manner due to frequent and severe changes in market demand, interest rates, and intensity of land-use controls and regulations....It is impossible to characterize the developers according to type, magnitude and quality of commodity produced, as is done in other industries.[48]

Regulation of the Industry

Serious allegations of consumer and environmental abuses accompanied industry activity throughout the 1960s. In response to the rising volume of complaints, Congress passed the Interstate Land Sales Full Disclosure Act.

This Act is the principal tool allowing federal oversight of the retail land-sales industry. It is designed to protect the consumer by requiring a company to disclose information about the project for sale. All companies engaged in interstate commerce (using the mails, national radio-TV networks, etc.) in order to sell or lease subdivision lots must register their projects with the Office of Interstate Land Sales Registration. Companies must file a detailed Statement of Record describing the units for sale. They must also submit a federal Property Report. This document, an abbreviated version of the Statement of Record, must be provided to all lot purchasers no less than 72 hours prior to their signing a sales contract. OILSR may act "in any U.S. district court to enjoin practices which violate the Act, such as sale of unregistered land, improper disclosure in a Property Report, or deceptive sales practices."[49] In addition, HUD may employ certain administrative procedures to suspend a developer's right to sell land.

OILSR's record in implementing the provisions of this Act has not been striking. The CEQ study points out that it was not until 1972, under its second administrator, that OILSR began "to effectively enforce the law."[50] At that time, following hearings in seventeen major U.S. cities into the consumer practices prevalent in the retail land-sales industry, OILSR's new administrator, George Bernstein, remarked, "Thousands of people each week are being misled or cheated when they buy lots for recreational, retirement, or investment purposes."[51]

But a new administrator was only a beginning. A report issued by the General Accounting Office in 1973 found that OILSR was not capable of adequately monitoring the industry, principally because of its small staff.[52] This evaluation remains generally true in 1976, although the addition of more staff and administrative reorganizations have improved OILSR's performance. Nevertheless, the work required simply to verify the Statements of Record and Property Reports for the 6,000 to 7,000 registered subdivision "communities" is immense; and during OILSR's first few years there was the additional problem that many developers required by law to file with the office were not doing so.*

---

*In 1974 OILSR set up an enforcement division which is currently staffed with about 25 people. It located an estimated several thousand unregistered developers, most of whom were subsequently required to register.[53]

OILSR was recently placed under the Assistant Secretary of Consumer Affairs and Regulatory Functions within HUD; it has a staff of 107 and an annual budget for the 1977 fiscal year of $3.2 million. It is still a small office to overview a sprawling industry. As of September, 1976, OILSR had initiated indictment of 13 companies and suspended sales at 746 subdivisions since its inception. Indicating OILSR's recently increased efficiency, the bulk of these suspensions--332--occurred during the last fiscal year of 1976.*[54]

The Federal Trade Commission (FTC) is the other federal agency currently involved in regulating consumer abuses in the retail land-sales industry. Under the provisions of the 1969 Truth in Lending Act (Regulation "Z"), the FTC may investigate and regulate the "unfair" or "deceptive" sales practices of any commercial firm. It may issue Cease and Desist Orders and may also sue for restitution to consumers who have been unlawfully deceived.

In 1971, the FTC began investigating the consumer practices of some of the largest corporations engaged in retail land-sales activities. To date it has issued complaints against six of these firms: Great Western United, Inc., GAC Corporation, Cavanaugh, AMREP, Horizon, and ITT Community Development Corporation. Investigations are proceeding against several other large firms. In at least two of these cases--those against GAC and ITT--a consent order has been issued. The other cases, however, may drag on through years of litigations before any concrete results ensue.

Beyond activities of OILSR and the FTC, the overview and regulation of subdivision development is today, as it has been in the past, principally a local matter. But despite an increased awareness of the potential long-term cost of hosting poorly planned, under-inhabited remote subdivisions, county governments throughout the country are generally ill-equipped to regulate subdivisions. They often lack specified authority, the staff, the knowledge, and the inclination. Where subdivision regulations of substance do exist, virtually all have been enacted within the last few years, after extensive subdivision activity has already occurred.

According to the CEQ study, in 1971 only 39% of the nation's counties had zoning regulations for their unincorporated areas;

---

*According to an OILSR official, the agency recently put representatives in the field to check the accuracy of federal Property Reports against the sites for which they are filed. In his opinion, the increased number of suspensions in 1976 resulted from this practice.[55]

OVERVIEW OF THE INDUSTRY 13

only 25% had subdivision regulations for those areas. Furthermore, "subdivision regulations" for many rural counties remain little more than "simple platting laws which only require developers to survey lot lines and roads, and file a plat at the county courthouse."[57]

Recently enacted legislation in various states currently provides for some regulation of the industry's development and environmental practices. An increasing number of states have mandated development of local subdivision regulations (based on state guidelines) within a certain time frame and/or have passed regulations controlling "developments of greater than local impact." In addition, several states have moved to define and regulate development in areas of critical concern such as wetlands, mountain slopes, floodplains and shorelines.

However, no federal legislation has directly addressed the need for environmental and development standards throughout the retail land-sales industry. Existing federal laws such as the Clean Air Act Amendments, the Water Pollution Control Act Amendments, the Coastal Zone Management Act, and the Flood Disaster Protection Act apply only indirectly to the environmental consequences of retail land-sales activities. The Scenic Rivers Association of Oklahoma (and others) attempted in 1975 to force preparation of Environmental Impact Statements when land sales firms register with OILSR, a requirement which might have led to improved environmental planning. But although a circuit court of appeals decided for the plaintiffs that a filing with OILSR constituted a "major federal action" that necessitated preparation of an Environmental Impact Statement, the Supreme Court reversed this decision in 1976.

The last cycle of significant retail land sales activity in this country proceeded into the 1970s with very little public scrutiny of its possible consequences until, in many cases, after the damage had been done. A general reluctance to impinge on property rights, traditionally, though not always practically, held to be inalienable, prevails. In particular a man's right to do as he wishes with his land has encouraged obedient observance of the No Trespassing signs erected by corporate bodies engaged in retailing land. The notion that substantive guidelines should be promulgated and enforced, thereby controlling the use of private land, has implied unfamiliar limitations on private activities by the public sector.

Information about this industry has issued principally from the publicity--good and bad--attending its selling activities. Keenly aware of the primordial appeal of land--particularly in a nation of urban dwellers, the large retail land sales firms have packaged their product in the context of the old frontier dream.

They have promised to provide the "new community" where life is beautiful and easy; and they have offered it for such low payments.

Speaking out, at equal volume, against this attractive image of the industry and its product have been the voices of those who have been deceived. But while their stories have been told and retold, and while others have viewed with alarm the practice of carving a major irreplenishable resource into irretrievable pieces for uncertain purposes, the fact remains that the industry and its effects still lack precise definition.

INFORM initiated its study three years ago to provide this definition by analyzing, in depth, the operations, problems, regulation, and options of a selection of the largest companies in the industry. The resulting site profiles, legal evaluations, and Guidelines for Consumer and Environmental Protection Practices presented in Volumes I, II and III of this study show not only the realities of the past, but the possibilities of a future wherein decades of abuses can be brought to an end.

2
Findings of the Study

INFORM has studied in detail the consumer and environmental impact of nine large retail land sales companies at nineteen subdivisions. All of these companies profess to be in the business of creating "new communities" at locations relatively distant from and free of existing urban concentrations and urban ills. Virtually all operate by mapping out roads, lots, commercial sites and common areas and then selling lots to individuals over a period of years via the installment plan. The implicit or explicit assumption in these transactions is that although the land may be "predeveloped" at the time of purchase, it will be ready for the buyer when the buyer is ready for the land.

This volume presents INFORM's findings on ten subdivisions being developed by six companies in the desert grasslands and mountains of the West and Southwest. (The remaining nine subdivisions, located in Florida, will be discussed in Volume II.) Of these ten subdivisions, three are located in New Mexico, three in Arizona, two in Colorado and two in California. The subdivisions are in varied terrains: some flat and arid, others green and mountainous. They are located in a part of the country where there is in fact an increasing population and and growth pressure. However, as the succeeding discussion and the individual profiles of the ten subdivisions show, these subdividers, by and large, are falling far short of fulfilling their promises in terms of actually creating "new communities." From both the consumer and environmental perspectives, their records are poor. Consumers are generally left with lots which years later are not worth what they paid for them. Careless environmental planning has either already caused or threatens to cause severe land and water resource degradation.

SUMMARY OF FINDINGS

Based on INFORM's examination of the operations of a representative sample of the nation's largest retail land-sales and subdivision companies, the industry is in radical need of reform. Among the most striking findings of INFORM's detailed analysis of the consumer and environmental impact of ten large-scale subdivisions in the West and Southwest are the following:

- While the companies involved all claim to be "new community developers" who are expressly marketing lots in subdivisions as "homesites," the majority of subdivisions are not assured the most basic prerequisites for human habitation: adequate water. The West and Southwest are water-short areas. Yet at only one of the ten subdivisions studied--Dart Industries' Bear Valley Springs in southern California--did the subdivider secure an adequate water supply prior to marketing lots. (Even in this case, the ability of the state agency from which Dart obtained water rights to fulfill its promises over the next thirty years is in question.) Two more subdivisions are in localities where water is sufficiently plentiful and legal restrictions sufficiently lenient that the subdivisions appear assured of water for the foreseeable future. At the remaining seven subdivisions, water shortages are either probable, imminent, or already occuring.

- An increasingly popular way of financing installation and maintenance of central water, central sewage disposal, drainage systems, and other basic improvements at subdivisions is through bonds issued by a quasi-governmental legal entity known as a "special service district." Such districts were employed at four of the ten subdivisions studied by INFORM. However, the potential for abuse of districts is great. In the initial stages of development, with the company in charge (and virtually no resident population), the district may issue large amounts of debt. Later on, as lot purchasers become landowners in the district, they are saddled with the burden of repayment. The land in the district is the ultimate collateral behind the bonds. Lot purchasers thus stand to lose their entire investment in the land if the bonds are not paid off. Such problems have already arisen at McCulloch Properties' Pueblo West subdivision in Colorado.

FINDINGS OF THE STUDY

- By and large, environmental planning at the subdivisions is poor. Seven out of ten subdivisions have subdivided and allowed building on highly hazardous land--near an earthquake fault, within the 100-year floodplain, and on very steep slopes. Six out of ten subdivisions planned for sewage disposal primarily by individual septic systems on small, quarter- and half-acre lots. This practice has led to pollution of waterways, contamination of water supplies, and expensive after-the-fact installation of central sewage disposal in other parts of the country. Seven of the ten subdivisions allocated less than 20% of the land to recreational and open-space purposes. One--the Horizon Corporation's 70-square mile Arizona Sunsites subdivision--as far as INFORM could discern, has allocated *no* land to open-space and recreational use, aside from a golf course.

The ten large-scale subdivisions studied are evidently not responding to a real need for new housing, nor, apparently, to any real need on the part of consumers to get away from existing urban ills. Sales began at these subdivisions between five and fifteen years ago, and at all but one of the youngest, thousands of lots have been deeded to purchasers. Yet very few lot owners have actually chosen to take up residence on their land. McCulloch Properties' Lake Havasu City subdivision in Arizona has the largest population of the ten. At Lake Havasu City, where the company has gone to great lengths (including importing the London Bridge from England) to attract industry and tourism and thus give the city an economic base, the ratio of dwelling units to deeded lots is 24 to 100. At the company's Pueblo West subdivision in Colorado, population 2,200, the ratio is 19 to 100. At every other subdivision studied the ratio was less than 5 dwelling units to 100 deeded lots. The least "built-out" subdivision is, in fact, one of the oldest. At the Horizon Corporation's enormous Rio Communities project south of Albuquerque, New Mexico, where sales began in 1961, the ratio of dwelling units to deeded lots is 1.6 to 100. At the rate it is going, this subdivision would not be fully occupied for several thousand years.

- Overall, INFORM finds none of the subdivisions to have taken adequate consumer and environmental protection measures. The sites which come closest are Bear Valley Springs and Tahoe Donner, both being developed by Dart Industries, Inc., in California. Yet even at those sites, instances of very poor environmental planning mar the record. At the other extreme are: AMREP's Rio Rancho, and Horizon's Rio Communities, both near Albuquerque, New Mexico; Horizon's Arizona Sunsites, in southeast Arizona; and GAC's Rio Rico in south central Arizona. These four subdivisions are notable for their almost total lack of consumer and environmental protection measures.

• While the companies all market lots either explicitly or implicitly as "investments" which are likely to appreciate in value, at not one subdivision studied by INFORM did such claims turn out to be true. At three of the subdivisions a purchaser might be able to resell a lot at or below the price paid for it, though not at a profit. At the other seven, there are so many lots on the market and/or the problems of the subdivision are so great, that the chances of reselling a lot even at a loss are very slim.

FINDINGS OF THE STUDY

SCOPE OF THE SAMPLE

The scope and thus the potential impact of the subdivisions studied by INFORM is very great. These ten western and southwestern projects alone cover half a million acres—830 square miles. Their projected populations total over 1.2 million people. Approximately 350,000 people have already bought lots at these subdivisions. (About a third of these individuals have completed all payments and are fully titled landowners; the remaining two-thirds are still paying off their installment contracts.)

Subdivisions

The subdivisions themselves range from large to enormous. The smallest project studied—Dart Industries' Tahoe Donner, located in California's Lake Tahoe resort area, covers 4,020 acres (6.3 square miles) and expects a population of 15,000 to 20,000. The largest subdivision, Horizon's Rio Communities, south of Albuquerque, New Mexico, covers no less than 242,000 acres (378 square miles). This exceeds the area of all five boroughs of New York City. Its projected population (assuming three persons per lot) is 516,000. If fully occupied, it would be the largest city in New Mexico and among the eighty largest cities in the nation.

Eight of the subdivisions, while making great use of recreational appeal in marketing efforts, are intended primarily for permanent, full-time residence. The other two subdivisions (Dart Industries' two California projects) are expressly recreational developments. However, while the Dart subdivisions anticipate substantially greater seasonal than permanent populations, they too expect to have significant full-time occupancy.

While it is extremely difficult to draw any hard and fast conclusions about what is an optimal size for a subdivision, it was the impression of INFORM's researchers that even the smallest of the subdivisions studied was unmanageably large. Indeed, as the Tahoe Donner profile shows, that subdivision's needs have simply overwhelmed local resources in terms of water- and sewage-disposal requirements. Such problems are a strong argument for proceeding with lot sales and site improvement in small, workable phases. The consequences of not doing so are discussed further under Environmental Protection, below.

TABLE 1: Subdivisions in INFORM Sample, Acreage & Projected Population*

STATE	SUBDIVISION	ACREAGE	PROJECTED POPULATION
New Mexico	Rio Rancho	91,000	300,000
	Cochiti Lake	6,300	44,000
	Rio Communities	242,000	516,000
Arizona	Arizona Sunsites	47,296	60,000
	Rio Rico	55,420	102,000
	Lake Havasu City	16,700	100,000
Colorado	Pueblo West	30,000	65,000
	Colorado City	9,900	50,000
California	Bear Valley Springs	26,000	15,000
	Tahoe Donner	4,020	19,500
	TOTAL	528,636	1,271,500

*Based on approximately three persons per lot.

Companies

The six companies marketing these subdivisions are all large, publicly held corporations. In addition to the 10 subdivisions studied in the 4 western states, they are marketing another 22 land projects, in 10 states. Three of the six companies are primarily land developers: AMREP, Horizon, and GAC. The other three are diversified companies with land-development subsidiaries: Dart Industries, Great Western United, and McCulloch Oil. The former two only entered the business in 1969-1970, by acquiring existing development companies.

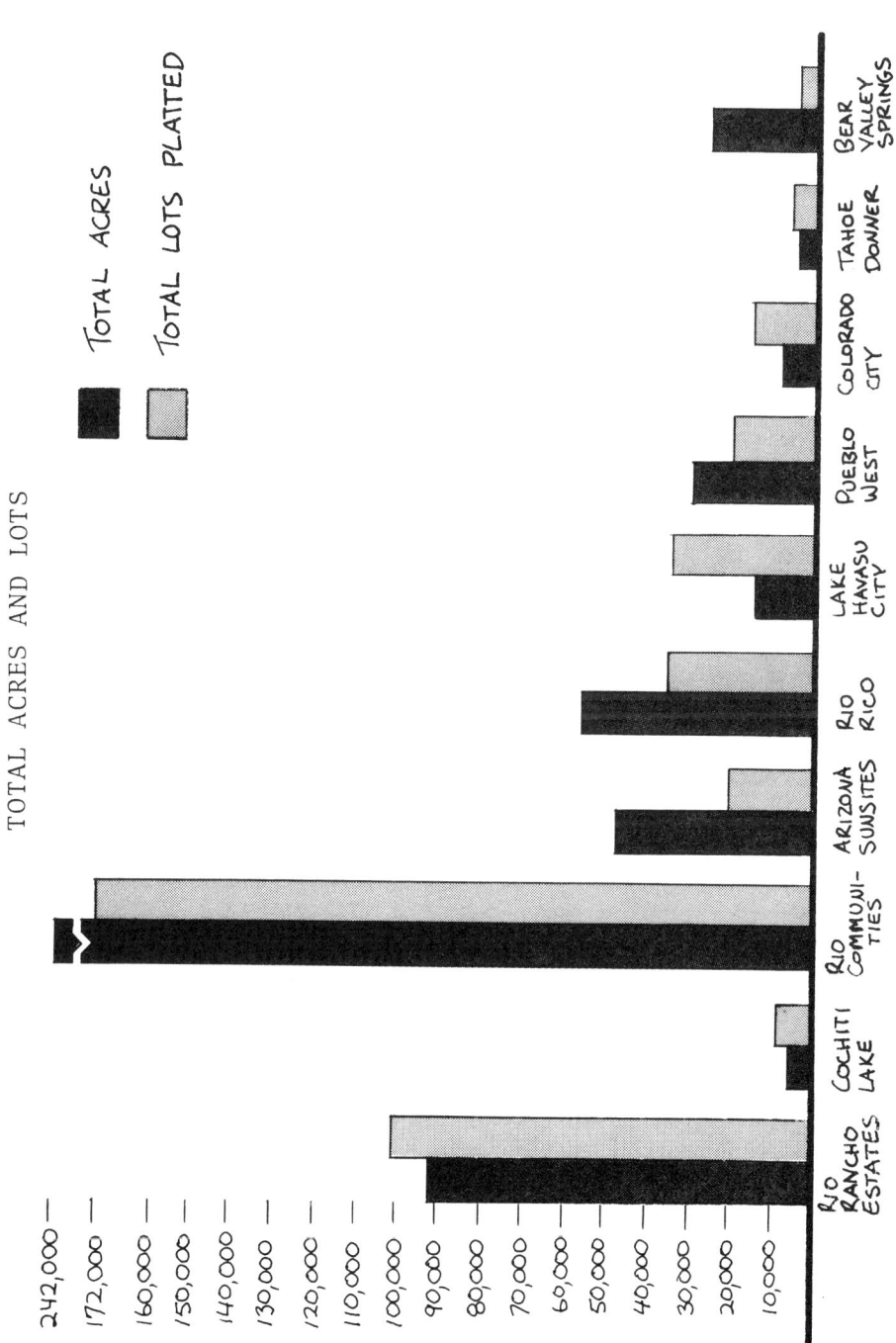

TABLE 2: Companies in INFORM Sample

COMPANY/ DEVELOPMENT SUBSIDIARY	SUBDIVISIONS IN INFORM STUDY	GROSS 1975 REVENUES (millions)	1975 NET INCOME (millions)	% SALES FROM LAND DEVELOPMENT
AMREP	Rio Rancho	$69.1	$1.7	--
Dart Industries/ Dart Resorts	Bear Valley Springs Tahoe Donnèr	$1,280.4	$78.9	0.8%
GAC	Rio Rico	N/A	N/A	--
Great Western United/ Great Western Cities	Cochiti Lake Colorado City	$508.4	$6.5	3%
Horizon	Arizona Sunsites Rio Communities	$56.1	$0.4	--
McCulloch Oil/ McCulloch Properties	Pueblo West Lake Havasu City	$124.3	$7.1	31%

It is now abundantly clear that company size is no guarantee of security to a lot buyer. All of these large companies have been hit hard by the industry-wide slump which began in 1973. The problems became sufficiently serious that in 1975 and 1976 GAC declared bankruptcy and Great Western decided to divest itself of its land-development subsidiary, Great Western Cities. While such difficulties can be of concern to shareholders, they can be a very serious problem for lot buyers, who are faithfully making monthly payments to the companies on the assumption that after ten years the company will convey both title and improvements. As the GAC Rio Rico profile indicates, a lot buyer who puts his faith in a financially shaky company may be faced with severe disillusionment.

FINDINGS OF THE STUDY 23

CONSUMER IMPACT

IMPROVEMENTS: BASIC SERVICES

Subdividers have sold lots as sites for vacations, retirement, or permanent homes, and at least implicitly as sound investments. But at most subdivisions studied, lots did not have the improvements which would make them habitable. Nor did lots at any of the subdivisions have any investment or resale value. Nonetheless, the companies studied are not taking many steps to ensure that lot buyers understand what they are buying, rather than simply engaging in fruitless land speculation. Only two of the subdivisions have even a moderately good record in terms of consumer impact: Dart Industries' Bear Valley Springs and McCulloch Properties' Lake Havasu City. Several subdivisions have exceedingly poor records. One, however, Horizon's Rio Communities--stands out from the others because the size and scope of its operations have magnified its impact on consumers enormously.

The most important function which a subdivider must perform, from the consumer's viewpoint, is to provide lots with the improvements that will make them suitable for building. It is basic services--central water, central sewage disposal, roads, drainage, and electricity, that make a piece of raw land a "homesite." They are also a prerequisite to the land's having any resale value. The Federal Trade Commission, among others, believes that for a subdivider to market lots as "homesites," without making such services available, constitutes fraud.

Unfortunately for the consumer, while all the subdividers studied by INFORM claim to be selling "homesites," the number which make adequate services available is meager. INFORM analyzed each of the ten subdivisions to see whether the subdivider had installed, or had made adequate financial guarantees and/or guarantees in purchase contracts for: central water to every lot; central sewage to all lots under one acre and lots unsuitable for septic systems because of soil conditions; solid-waste disposal at a sanitary landfill; paved roads to county standards; drainage adequate for handling the worst storm to be expected in a 100-year period; and electricity and telephone service. The results are not encouraging.

A total of 414,912 lots at these subdivisions have been platted (i.e., filed with the county prior to marketing) and 125,925 of these lots are fully paid for. Yet only 61,900 lots are "improved" with even two of these services (central water and one other service), and over half these "improved" lots are accounted for by one subdivision: McCulloch Properties' Lake Havasu City.

Only two of the subdivisions studied by INFORM made at least four of these six basic services available to every lot: Dart Industries' Bear Valley Springs and McCulloch's Lake Havasu City. At a third subdivision--Dart's Tahoe Donner--the company attempted to provide most of these services, but ran into severe difficulties with the local community when trying to find a water supply and an acceptable sewage-disposal method.

All of the remaining seven subdivisions still lack key improvements. At none of these does the purchase contract guarantee installation of these services by the date title is transferred. (Great Western Cities at Cochiti Lake does promise to have all site services available by the year 2020, presumably for the benefit of the purchaser's granchildren.) At only one subdivision, Cochiti Lake, has the developer used a surety bond or put money in escrow to insure that funds will be available to install services when they are needed. (Surety bonds or escrowed funds would be particularly useful given the vagaries of the economy and the financial instability evident in many of these companies.) About the only improvement a lot buyer in these subdivisions can expect with any certainty is a dirt road, and some are not even guaranteed that. Nor are buyers at nine out of ten subdivisions guaranteed a refund if promised improvements, whatever they are, are not forthcoming. (The only exception is GAC's Rio Rico, where a federal district court may require such a provision under the terms of a 1975 class-action suit settlement. However, since the company has now filed for Chapter X bankruptcy, it is questionable whether this requirement will benefit many consumers.)

In terms of actual future prospects for lot owners, the seven subdivisions where site services have been neither installed nor guaranteed fall into two categories: those where the individual purchaser is responsible for installing services, and those where this responsibility has been turned over to an independent, quasi-governmental entity. It is difficult to say which set of purchasers is in the worse predicament.

At Horizon's Rio Communities and Arizona Sunsites, AMREP's Rio Rancho, and GAC's Rio Rico, the only development that has occurred is in core areas where lots are not sold on the installment basis but on a conventional mortgage or cash basis for immediate building purposes.* Each of these showcase "cores" has

---

*At Rio Rico the court settlement of a class-action suit resulted in a court-imposed and supervised development schedule for lots outside the core area. However, GAC's subsequent bankruptcy has placed the implementation of this schedule in abeyance.

DEGREE OF IMPROVEMENTS

☐ TOTAL LOTS PLATTED
■ TOTAL LOTS IMPROVED

172,000	Rio Rancho Estates
100,000	
90,000	
80,000	
70,000	
60,000	
50,000	
40,000	
30,000	
20,000	
10,000	

Rio Rancho Estates, Cochiti Lake, Rio Communities, Arizona Sunsites, Rio Rico, Lake Havasu City, Pueblo West, Colorado City, Tahoe Donner, Bear Valley Springs

25

a central water system, a small central-sewage-treatment system, paved roads, and electricity and telephone service. Unfortunately, nowhere does the core area account for more than 2% of the lots. The owner of an outlying lot may be able to exchange his lot for a company-owned homesite in the core area. This exchange often involves an additional payment to the company for the land and some payment for the installation of utilities to his lot. Furthermore, there are no guarantees that lots will be available for exchange in the future. In each case, the amount of land set aside for exchanges is limited compared to the number of people who own lots outside the core area.

Alternatively, a lot purchaser at these four subdivisions can try to homestead on his original lot. He can install a well, septic system, generator, and radio-telephone at an approximate cost of $7,000. Attempting this may not always be possible, since New Mexico health regulations now prohibit simultaneous use of wells and septic systems on lots smaller than three-quarters to one acre.

Special Service Districts

At the three subdivisions--McCulloch Properties' Pueblo West and Great Western Cities' Colorado City and Cochiti Lake projects--problems for lot owners are different but hardly less severe. At these projects the subdividers have adopted various financing mechanisms to arrange for the installation of site improvements with the costs transferred to lot purchasers. The most common one, used by Great Western Cities at Colorado City and McCulloch at Pueblo West, is known as a "special district." State legislatures originally authorized creation of such districts to help property owners in existing communities or rural areas fund capital improvements such as irrigation systems. The retail land-sales companies subsequently adapted that purpose to establish a quasi-governmental entity which can issue bonds for purposes of extending a subdivision's basic utilities and services, often before any site residents move in. Lot purchasers would, by virtue of becoming the landowners in the district, acquire the legal obligation to repay the principal and interest on these bonds.

The potential problems of land subdividers using such districts are myriad. First, if the district issues large amounts of bonds in the early stages of development (when the subdivider

FINDINGS OF THE STUDY

is in charge), the resulting community can be saddled with an excessive debt. At Lake Havasu City, McCulloch used a district relatively successfully to finance extension of central water, roads, and drainage to almost all lots. The district has contracted so much debt, however, that the town cannot incorporate as a municipality. (The amount of bonds exceeds the municipal debt limit in Arizona.) In such situations, both the district fees which lot purchasers must pay to hook up to the systems and annual district taxes may rise. Because the land is the ultimate collateral behind the bonds, lot purchasers must pay these assessments or lose their entire investment. Hookup fees for water at the four subdivisions where special service districts have been formed by the developer (McCulloch's Lake Havasu City and Pueblo West, Great Western's Colorado City, and Dart's Bear Valley Springs) range from $100 at Bear Valley Springs to $490 at Pueblo West. Annual district assessments and taxes average several hundred dollars a year.

In order to keep district debt at a reasonable level, protecting lot buyers as well as bondholders, both Florida and New Mexico limit the debt of districts used in new community development to 15% and 5% respectively of the district's assessed value. This ratio for the districts INFORM studied, however, ranges from 32% to 72%.

Another problem with districts in subdivision development is that lot purchasers are often disenfranchised members, and thus have no say in district policies. At each of the four subdivisions noted below, lot purchasers become members of the district as soon as they sign the purchase contract for a lot. From then on they are obligated to pay annual district assessments. However, paying membership is not necessarily voting membership. Most state laws allow only those who are also district or county residents to vote in district elections. In most new subdivisions marketed on the installment plan, this means that it is at least ten years, and usually longer, before most district members and taxpayers have a voice in determining how much debt the district may incur or who will sit on its board of directors.

A third problem which can result from the use of districts, is that basic site services may not get extended due to a lot owners' revolt. Once control passes to lot purchasers, they may refuse to issue further bonds (as has happened at Pueblo West) or refuse to annex areas of the subdivision. At Colorado City, for example, the Water and Sanitation District simply refused to annex an extra 1,500 acres which Great Western added to the subdivision after the district was created and after control had passed into the hands of site residents. Although Great Western has marketed this land, the District is not obligated to extend water and sewer

TABLE 3: Special Service Districts at Subdivisions in the INFORM Sample

SUBDIVISION	DISTRICT NAMES	AUTHORIZED DEBT (Millions)	OUTSTANDING DEBT (Millions)	OUTSTANDING DEBT AS % OF ASSESSED VALUE	OUTSTANDING DEBT PER TITLED LOT OWNER
Lake Havasu City	Irrigation & Drainage District	$17.8	$14.1	32%	$ 916
	Sanitation District	$ 3.2	$ 2.5	N/A	$ 162
Pueblo West	Pueblo West Metropolitan District	$37.1	$12.7	72%	$3,165
Colorado City	Water & Sanitation District	$12.0	$ 2.9	68%	$ 391
Bear Valley Springs	Community Services District	$ 8.3	$ 3.5	N/A	$2,004

service to the lots. Great Western has been collecting a separate "water and sewer availability fee" in addition to installment lot payments from these purchasers, and so may have to undertake responsibility for the services itself or create another district.

In certain districts, services may also never be extended due to initial miscalculations by the developer. At Pueblo West, where site services are about 65% complete, miscalculations were numerous. Because the subdivider (McCulloch) erroneously assumed that water would be available from wells or a local nearby dam project, no money was budgeted for acquisition of water rights. When such action proved necessary, the district had to cut back on other parts of its program--a sewer system, drainage system, fire protection, streets, and parks. McCulloch also overestimated the rate at which people would move into the subdivision. This, together with unanticipated costs, has meant that the district has not had the income projected from water and sewage hookup fees. To make up for

FINDINGS OF THE STUDY

this deficiency, the district has had to quadruple the fees charged to hook up to water and sewer systems and substantially increase the taxes levied against all lot purchasers.

Given the complex ways in which districts function, it is not surprising that lot purchasers frequently fail to understand the obligations they incur when buying a lot in a subdivision with a district. At Pueblo West in particular, lot purchasers repeatedly commented that, "We thought the costs of development came out of the costs of the lots, which are high; but instead we found out that we picked up an additional burden, which we were not informed of."

The only subdivision in the INFORM sample which has used a service district somewhat responsibly is Dart Industries at Bear Valley Springs. At this project, the developer paid for the installation of all basic services and utilities, then deeded all but the water system to the district for maintenance and operation. The only bonds that the district had to issue were for the purchase of the water system. Thus, district assessments on lots pay for the continued management and operation of the project rather than excessive bond repayments. Nonetheless, assessments are $57 to $215 per year.

A variant of this kind of financing mechanism was developed by Great Western Cities for Cochiti Lake. Perhaps because New Mexico law significantly restricts the amount of debt that districts can incur, Great Western essentially incorporated the subdivision as a town under the political auspices of the Pueblo Indian government. This incorporation transferred to the town all responsibility for extending planned central water and sewage, paved roads, and drainage systems. It made the town responsible for collecting the funds for improvements. The town's taxpayers are, of course, lot purchasers.

Water Supply

The last, but by no means least, of the major problems involved with provision of basic services at these ten subdivisions in the West and Southwest is availability of water. Even if an adequate delivery system is installed, it is of little use unless there is water to flow through it.

As noted earlier, only three of the subdivisions--Dart's Bear Valley Springs, McCulloch's Lake Havasu City, and Horizon's Arizona Sunsites--appear assured of adequate water supplies for their projected populations. The other seven are in regions that are already very water short or have a water supply that is extensively legally appropriated. In these regions it is questionable whether there will be water available to meet the needs. The percentage of total population

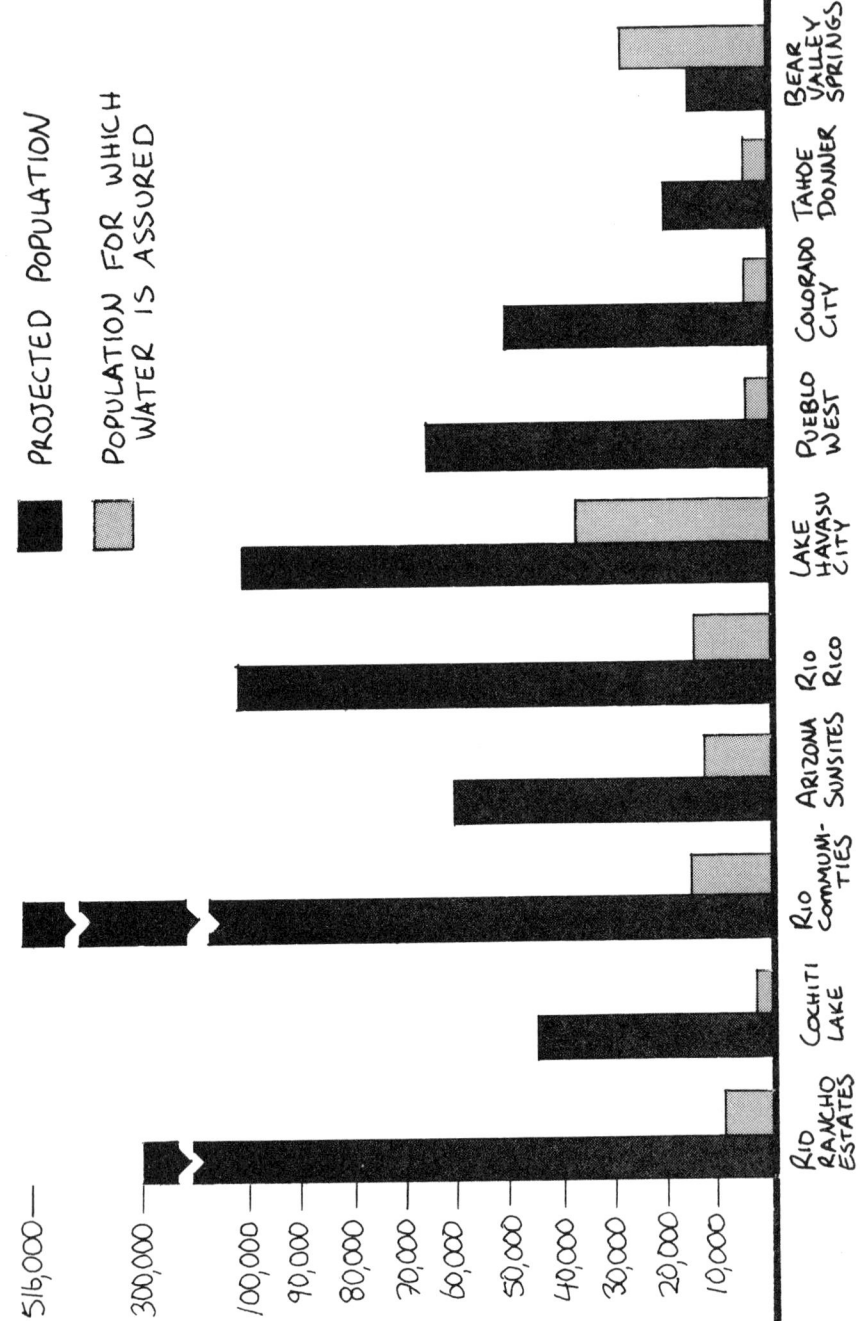

FINDINGS OF THE STUDY

for whom sufficient water has been secured ranges from just 3% to 20%

At the four subdivisions where outlying lot owners will most likely have to rely on individual wells in order to build, the water table ranges from only a few feet below the surface to a depth of more than 500 feet. As noted, these lots were also planned for sewage disposal by septic tank with no thought given to the possible consequent contamination of well water (or the possible upgrading of county or state environmental and health regulations that might prevent such practice and thus render lots useless.)

Other Services

Most of the subdivisions studied are highly dependent on surrounding towns, counties, and cities for various types of standard community services. Six of the subdivisions studied have permanent populations of between 100 and 1,000; the other four have between 1,000 and 10,000 people. Yet only one of the ten has its own police force (the rest depend on the county sheriff's department).

Nine out of the ten subdivisions are either wholly or in part dependent on volunteer fire departments. Only one (the largest) has a hospital on site. At the others, the nearest hospital is anywhere from 3 to 41 miles away. Only three of the subdivisions have their own facilities for solid waste disposal (i.e. sanitary landfill sites).

INVESTMENT VALUE AND COSTS

Many of the people who buy land in subdivisions do so for investment purposes, believing that their land will appreciate in value and to be resold later at a profit. Company advertising materials generally encourage this view. To measure the number of people who do buy for investment purposes, it is useful to compare the number of lots sold and deeded to purchasers at each subdivision with the number of lots that have actually been built upon. In every case, there are many more lots deeded to purchasers than there are homes. An extreme example is Rio Communities, begun in 1961, where over 48,000 lots are deeded but only 770 dwellings are constructed. While some of these property owners may be holding their land to build at a later date--perhaps upon retirement--it nonetheless is safe to assume that many of them bought the land in order to resell it.

Resale Market

INFORM examined the value of the land as an investment at each subdivision. No such value was found. At three of the subdivisions--Dart's Bear Valley Springs and Tahoe Donner and McCulloch's Lake Havasu City--the only resale market was at prices lower than the original lot purchase prices. At the other seven subdivisions there is no resale market at all. A particularly telling indication of the market's state was provided by a local realtor near Arizona Sunsites. He advises lot owners in their subdivision to advertise in their hometown newspapers. "I can't sell them locally...it's the only thing I can suggest," he says.

In some of these projects part of the reason for the lack of resale market was the developer's continually adding acreage to its landholdings to maintain an adequate inventory of lots. Rio Communities again provides a particularly glaring example. In 1969 and 1970 the Horizon Corporation more than doubled the site's original area by acquiring another 100,000 acres.

The always-increasing supply of lots for sale will continue to drastically exceed demand. In the competition for buyers, the development company, often equipped with a nationwide sales force and a large advertising budget, is most often the winner.

Costs

Far from being a source of profit to the consumer, these subdivision lots are often an unanticipated financial drain. Buying a subdivision lot on the installment plan frequently involves many hidden costs of which the consumer may only be dimly aware. These can add thousands of dollars to a basic price quoted by the salesman.

Lots sold on the installment plan at the subdivisions studied by INFORM range in price from as little as $1,000 for a quarter-acre residential lot at Rio Communities to $60,000 for a one-acre multi-family lot at Lake Havasu City. (In general, lots are between a quarter-acre and one acre in size, although lots as small as 1/25 of an acre, at Cochiti Lake, and as large as 80 acres, at Bear Valley Springs, are marketed.) In each case, on top of the lot's basic price, purchasers must also pay "interest," in reality a finance charge. It is calculated at a rate of between 5% and 9% annually, which can add between $207 (on the cheapest Rio Communities lot) to $28,085 (on the most expensive Lake Havasu City lot) to the purchase price. The rationale behind this charge is highly questionable. In all other transactions in which interest payments are required, they are for the use of something. For example, one

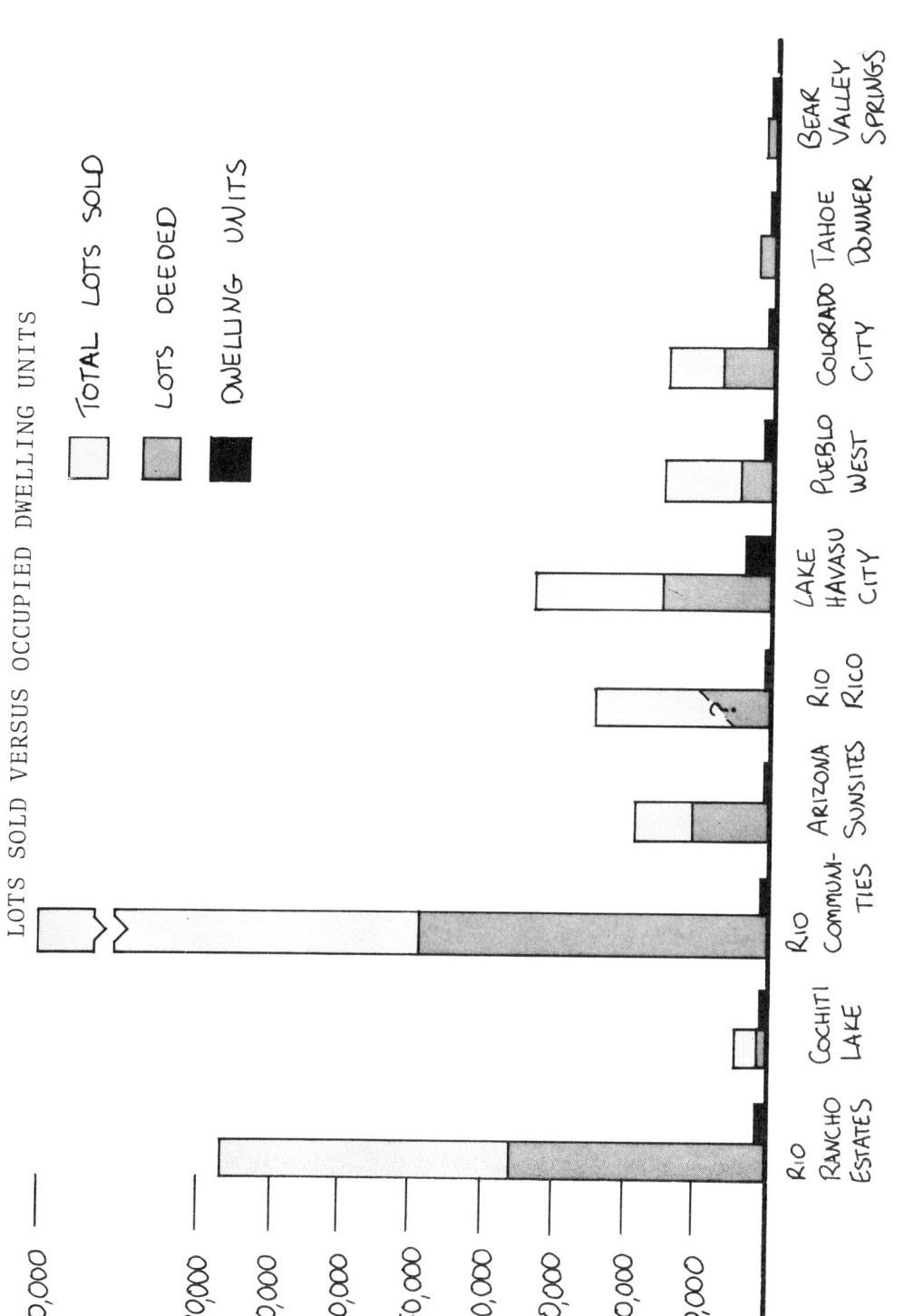

pays for the use of money in the case of a bank loan or the use of an appliance during the period that it is being paid for. Yet with the exception of subdivisions located in California and Arizona, where state law requires the deeding of lots to purchasers during the contract payment period, the consumer is not allowed to use or build on his property while paying off the installment contract. Since the subdivider has the use of the consumer's money during this period, the company might more logically _pay_ interest to the consumer.

The effective price, including finance charges, of the lots in the INFORM sample ranges from $1,207 to $88,085. The starting prices, including finance charges, for raw lots in the four subdivisions guaranteeing virtually no improvements (Rio Rancho, Rio Communities, Rio Rico, and Arizona Sunsites) range from $1,207 to $3,859. In each case, real estate brokers assured INFORM that similar, unimproved land was available outside the subdivision's confines at much lower cost. The starting prices (including finance charges) of lots in the subdivisions where the companies have made greater or fewer provisions for installation of basic services are between $4,300 and $11,700.

In addition to finance charges, lot buyers are often subject to a plethora of other assessments, some large and some small. These must be paid annually during the term of the contract. They may include property taxes (despite the fact that the lot buyer may not yet be the titled owner of the land), special service district assessments, bond reduction charges, recreation fees, property owners' association dues, and charges for improvements (called "betterment" fees or water and sewer availability or standby charges). These additional charges can add as little as $10 or $11 (as at Rio Rancho and Arizona Sunsites) or as much as $2,719 (as at Lake Havasu City) annually to a lot buyer's payments. This adds a total of between $100 and $26,800 to the lot price over a period of ten years!

Again, these annual assessments tend to be higher where the developer has made some provision for improvements than at those subdivisions where it has not. If at any time during the term of contract payments these assessments are not paid, the companies can consider the buyer in default, reclaim the lot, and retain all installment payments made to that point.

After paying the full lot price, "interest" payments, and annual assessments, a purchaser assumes title and finally has some equity at nine of the ten subdivisions. This is not true at Great Western United's Cochiti Lake subdivision. At this project, located on an Indian reservation in New Mexico, all a purchaser is actually "buying" is a lease. After the five- to fifteen-year period of installment contract payments is over,

FINDINGS OF THE STUDY 35

the purchaser must still make annual rental payments of between $188 and $1,600 for the remainder of the 99-year lease. Thousands of dollars later, when the lease expires ownership of the land and all improvements reverts to the Indians.

If a lot purchaser decides to build on his "homesite" after making all contract payments and assuming ownership (or lease), he may still have to incur substantial additional costs to obtain utilities. It is at this point that having bought a lot in one of the more expensive, high-assessment subdivisions would prove a better buy--provided, of course, that none of the possible exigencies described earlier have intervened to prevent extension of promised services. If all goes as anticipated, purchasers at the six subdivisions in the INFORM study planned for central water, central sewage disposal for lots under one acre,* paved roads, and drainage ditches, should eventually be able to connect to these systems, and/or install a septic system, for hookup fees and other expenditures of between $105 to $2,490. The latter cost is, of course, substantial considering the purchase price of the "improved" land and other assessments.

For lot owners at the cheaper, low-assessment subdivisions the cost of connecting to utility systems or otherwise finding a means of disposing of sewage, obtaining water and electricity, and communicating electronically with the outside world, would be astronimical. An individual septic system would cost $350 to $2,000, depending on soil conditions. The cost of a well could be $660 or as much as $26,640, depending on the depth of the water table. If the lot is smaller than the state or county minimum size for simultaneous use of wells and septics, central water lines must be extended. This cost would probably be close to the $15,840 per mile figure quoted for one subdivision. Generally electric line extension is also several thousand dollars a mile, so the lot owner would probably need to purchase a generator, which would cost about $3,500. A radio-telephone could add another $2,500.

Given the costs, it is little wonder that these lots have little or no resale value. The expense of using them for the sole purpose to which they are committed--residential use--is prohibitive.

---

*Not available at Lake Havasu City.

TABLE 4: COSTS OF LOTS SOLD ON THE INSTALLMENT CONTRACT AT SUBDIVISIONS IN THE INFORM SAMPLE

NAME	LOT PRICE	FINANCE CHARGE	TOTAL LOT PRICE	ADDITIONAL ASSESSMENTS (TOTAL OVER TERM OF CONTRACT)
Rio Rancho	$3,150–$25,000	$709–$8,035	$3,859–$33,035	$80
Cochiti Lake	$2,890–$6,290	$710–$2,581	$5,300–$16,371	$2,150–$9,750
Rio Communities	$1,000–$28,000	$207–$9,611	$1,207–$37,611	$136–$1,870
Arizona Sunsites	$1,800–$28,000	$348–$11,489	$2,148–$39,489	$110–$700
Rio Rico	$2,000–$12,000	$598–$4,584	$2,598–$16,584	$1,884–$3,780
Lake Havasu City	$6,000–$60,000	$1,794–$28,085	$7,794–$88,085	$1,520–$26,800
Pueblo West	$6,000–$55,000	$1,694–$21,313	$7,694–$76,313	$1,990–$19,020
Colorado City	$3,500–$12,000	$859–$4,924	$4,359–$16,924	$2,731–$5,514
Tahoe Donner	$9,000–$30,000	$2,691–$12,309	$11,691–$42,309	$3,550
Bear Valley Springs	$6,500–$25,000	$1,943–$10,258	$8,443–$35,258	$4,900–$15,300

SALES PRACTICES

The speculative acquisition of lots at these subdivisions is obviously not of financial benefit to consumers. Speculative purchases make it difficult for the company to plan the location and timing of service installation. Moreover, speculation is detrimental to the environment, since it results in the land being committed to a particular use--residential lots--prematurely and unnecessarily.

FINDINGS OF THE STUDY 37

In examining company sales policies,* however, INFORM found that they are generally designed only to sell as many lots as possible as rapidly as possible. Rather than taking steps to discourage speculation and encourage buying for actual use, the companies appear to do the opposite.

All of the companies sell lots "on time." At all but one subdivision, the company requires only a 10% downpayment on a lot--usually less than $1,000. Under current accounting rules, this percentage is the minimum required for the company to recognize the sale in its financial statements. (The exception is Pueblo West, where the required downpayment is 15%.) Purchasers usually have eight to ten years to finish payments, although Horizon Corporation, hard-pressed for cash, offers some two-year contracts at no interest. At three subdivisions the buyer may even take fifteen to twenty years to complete his payments.

All of the companies sell commercial, industrial and multi-family lots on the installment contract, clearly a speculative "investment" venture since few businesses that actually intend to utilize such lots would purchase them in this manner. The subdivision companies claim that by offering "easy contract terms" and a long payment period they are doing consumers a service. They say they offer many people the opportunity to buy land in the only way they can afford. While this claim is certainly true, subdividers are also subjecting consumers to considerable financial risk. It is difficult for a purchaser to assess his financial future over a ten-year period. With an installment land sales contract, should the purchaser become unemployed and be unable to continue his payments, he would lose the amount paid, despite the fact that, as previously noted, he has not had the use of the land during this period. Only GAC, under a Federal Trade Commission order, offers purchasers any substantial refund if they default on contract payments.

---

*Sales are currently suspended at two of the subdivisions studied at INFORM: at GAC's Rio Rico, due to the initiating of bankruptcy proceedings, and at Dart Industries' Tahoe Donner, pending resolution of problems with local authorities over hooking into a regional sewage treatment plant; AMREP's sale of lots in New York State has been suspended due to a criminal indictment. And at Great Western's Colorado City, sales are limited to lots in the core area on a cash or mortgage basis. However, at all these subdivisions the company has indicated that it intends to resume normal sales operations at some point. The analysis presented here reflects company policy at the time normal lot sales operations were halted.

Perhaps more serious is the fact that the company's financial difficulty during the ten-year contract payment period might result in the purchaser losing his investment. As GAC's bankruptcy shows, nothing is secure if the company goes under. Purchasers still paying off contracts are not necessarily even guaranteed receipt of title to their land, although this is considered likely. Chances for refunds, or obtaining promised basic services, are tenuous at best. Over a ten-year period the company could also change ownership or management, radically altering its development policies.

Were companies to conduct sales on a cash or conventional mortgage basis (as most do in their core development areas), or at least sell on installment contracts of shorter duration, the risk to the consumer would be diminished.

Only one company, Dart Industries, seems to be making any effort to limit speculative purchases. It is the one company that checks a purchaser's credit rating, perhaps because it has done the most to install site services. It is also the only company that generally allows purchasers to build on lots during the payment period. Dart requires lot purchasers to sign a statement that no promises were made about a lot's investment value. (This policy may have resulted from a recently settled class action suit by purchasers who claimed they were misled about Bear Valley Springs' investment potential.) Three of the companies, including Dart, claim to be attempting to limit speculation by limiting lot purchases to two without the express approval of management. However, the other three will sell purchasers as many lots as they are willing to buy.

Most of the companies take only minimal steps to ensure that a lot buyer is well-informed about a purchase. None of the subdividers requires an attorney's review of sales documents such as the contract and the property report. (The latter is generally a twenty to thirty page document full of complicated but highly important information detailing site finances, planned services, and mortgages, liens and easements. These facts are often expressed in unfamiliar legal terms.) Three companies claim to encourage such review, but this encouragement primarily consists of printing "seek professional advice" on the front page of the Property Report, as required by law.

In an effort to prevent poorly informed purchases, federal law requires companies to offer lot buyers a three-day period after receiving the Property Report to read the document, to consult a lawyer, and if desired, to cancel a sales agreement and receive refund of the downpayment. California requires a blanket fourteen-day "rescission period" after signing a sales

FINDINGS OF THE STUDY 39

agreement. The companies in the INFORM sample follow only the legally required minimums.

Besides a thorough reading of the contract and Property Report the most important prerequisite to an informed purchase is nan actual visit to the subdivision. Only Dart Industries and McCulloch Properties strongly encourage a pre-purchase site visit. Virtually all their sales transactions occur on-site. The other companies sell lots "sight unseen," often in distant parts of the country.

A final potential major problem associated with lot purchase on the installment contract is title protection. Title protection is not a problem at three of the subdivisions in the INFORM sample: Dart Industries' two California subdivisions and Horizon's Arizona Sunsites. At these sites, purchasers receive a "deed of trust" shortly after signing the purchase agreement. This deed of trust secures the title and gives the right to use the lot for the duration of all contract payments. At two more subdivisions--those owned by McCulloch Properties--the company offers a "deed of trust" if the buyer makes a downpayment of one-third of the basic lot price.

At the remaining four subdivisions* (and in some cases at the two McCulloch subdivisions), purchasers receive only a sales contract or agreement. Under this arrangement, the buyer agrees to make monthly payments for a period of years. At the end of the term, if payments have been kept up (and the company still exists), he will receive title. At these subdivisions it is therefore extremely important to protect the purchaser's right to title during the contract payment period. However, four of these six subdivisions do not even offer the most rudimentary protection: namely, recording the existence of the contract with the County Recorder's Office. (For the other two sites, Arizona's 1975 land sales law requires the subdivider to record the contract.) At one of the six--Horizon's Rio Communities-- the company does not even issue the contract in a form enabling the buyer to record it himself. Contracts in recordable form are contingent upon the buyer paying at least 25% of the lot price and meeting several other conditions.

Another way of protecting the purchaser's right to title during the contract period would be to put title in trust or escrow with a third party, to be released only to the lot buyer on completion of payments or to the company, if the buyer defaulted. Such action, now required by law in a few states, would protect the consumer in the event that the developer

---

*Protection of title is irrelevant at Cochiti Lake, since purchasers are only obtaining a lease.

became insolvent, since title to the land would be legally separated from the company's general assets. At three of the subdivisions title is placed in trust; at the other three—AMREP's Rio Rancho, Great Western's Colorado City, and Horizon's Rio Communities--title is not so protected.

FINDINGS OF THE STUDY 41

ENVIRONMENTAL IMPACT

Overall, the environmental practices of the ten subdivisions studied by INFORM have been poor in terms of both planning and actual development. Because of the limited development activity and populations at some of these subdivisions, the impact of this poor planning is still restricted to such effects as duststorms. (These are caused by the enormous networks of unpaved roads at these sites.) The subdivisions which already have several thousand people, however, are already causing more serious problems. Two-- McCulloch's Lake Havasu City in Arizona and AMREP's Rio Rancho Estates in New Mexico--have, for example, experienced damaging flash floods.

Surrounding areas suffer the effects of poor environmental planning of subdivisions--for example, through pollution of their streams. However, INFORM found that at the ten western and southwestern sites studied, present and future lot buyers may be those most penalized by the developers' failure to work within environmental constraints. It is the buyers themselves who will have to live with the monotonous rectangular street layouts, insufficient parks, eroding topsoil, clogged drainageways, flood damage, and polluted water supplies that result from poor initial environmental planning.

INFORM has evaluated each of the subdivisions from an environmental perspective to determine whether the company employed the basic minimal planning, land use, and water resource use practices necessary to prevent serious and often irrevocable environmental damage. The best overall records for environmental protection were compiled by Dart Industries' Tahoe Donner subdivision, located at the mountainous north end of California's Lake Tahoe resort region, and Great Western United's Cochiti Lake, on arid Indian land between Albuquerque and Sante Fe. A large part of the credit for good performance in the former case must go to environmental regulatory agencies, which in California are relatively strong, and to local citizens and county officials in the area who were exceptionally aware of and concerned with preserving the environment. All made significant demands on the company in the early planning and development stages.

These two subdivisions are the smallest of the ten studied (4,020 and 6,300 acres respectively) and are among the younger ones (sales began at Tahoe Donner in 1971, and at Cochiti Lake in 1970).

Although environmental protection efforts at none of the other subdivisions can be considered good, perhaps the worst practices were employed at one New Mexico and all three Arizona subdivisions: AMREP's 91,000-acre Rio Rancho Estates, which went on the market in 1961; GAC's 55,400-acre Rio Rico, where sales began in 1969; Horizon's 47,300-acre Arizona Sunsites, which began selling in 1961; and McCulloch's 16,700-acre Lake Havasu City, first sold in 1963.

PLANNING

The bulk of the decisions that will determine whether a subdivision will deface and despoil the landscape or blend peaceably with the natural environment are made at corporate headquarters, long before the first bulldozer arrives on the site. While the importance of planning for complete site basic services has been discussed above from a consumer protection viewpoint, such planning is also extremely important in terms of environmental protection. If individual household wells are sunk and septic systems installed throughout a subdivision, it becomes extremely difficult to monitor or control the subdivision's impact on the water table. Pollution and depletion of groundwater is likely. If no drainage system is installed, erosion and gullying may result. If no land is set aside for solid waste disposal, the new community may find itself, some years hence, with no place to dispose of its trash.

Unfortunately, only four of the ten subdivisions in the INFORM sample were master-planned for complete, adequate basic services (central water, central sewage disposal for all lots under one acre and lots with unsuitable soil conditions, a drainage system capable of handling the worst storm expected in 100 years and on-site solid waste disposal). These are Dart Industries' two California subdivisions, Great Western's Cochiti Lake, and McCulloch's Pueblo West.* (At the latter two, completion of these systems is by no means guaranteed.) Two more were planned for some of these services but not others; McCulloch's Lake Havasu City lacks central sewage disposal for most quarter- and half-acre lots, and Great Western's Colorado City was planned with a totally insufficient drainage system and no central sewage

---

*Tahoe Donner and Pueblo West have no on-site solid waste disposal site.

FINDINGS OF THE STUDY 43

system. (The latter was subsequently required by county health officials.)

The remaining four subdivisions--Arizona Sunsites, Rio Communities, Rio Rancho and Rio Rico--were, as noted under Consumer Impact, planned for no basic site services whatsoever outside their tiny "showcase" cores.

Another key element in sound environmental planning of a very large subdivision is phasing of development: dividing the subdivision into sections, and coordinating lot sales and extension of services so that both proceed together in an orderly fashion, section by section. Such phasing avoids sprawl and patchwork development, and saves the developer (or the special service district, as the case may be) the extreme financial drain of installing all site services at once. Not one of the ten subdivisions in the INFORM sample employed phased development. Dart Industries came closest to such planning, by extending all improvements and selling lots at each of its two California subdivisions in one giant phase. At each of the other eight subdivisions, lots have been sold over the entire site, and improvements installed, if at all, in an uncoordinated, relatively haphazard fashion. At Pueblo West, for example, central water lines have been extended to about 13,000 lots, and central sewage lines to about 7,900 lots. Roads have been bladed to all 19,800 lots in the subdivision (although fewer than 20% have been paved), and electric lines run helter skelter to serve the widely separated homes.

A third key element of environmentally sound planning is, perhaps surprisingly, good market research. None of the subdivisions studied by INFORM have grown at the rates originally projected by the development companies. McCulloch's Lake Havasu City, by dint of extravagant promotional efforts and infusion of an economic base by the parent conglomerate, has attracted the largest population, 10,000 people, but not the 20,000 predicted by the developer. At its current average annual rate of population increase, it would not achieve its fully projected population for about 100 years. At the other nine subdivisions it would take anywhere from several hundred to several thousand years, at the rate they are currently growing, before they achieve full "build-out." In all cases this failure to anticipate the real development rate has resulted in the needless disturbance of the environment--through cutting of roads--years before such disturbance was warranted by development pressures. Perhaps even more important is the fact that half a million acres of what was in most cases productive cattle-ranch-country is now committed to unproductive use for centuries. Cut up into tiny parcels, and bulldozed, mapped and sold, the chances of ever reassembling it for better planning are nil. More conscientious market research--assuming of course that the subdividers were in fact interested in the potential for real new community development and not just the potential for lot sales--could prevent this kind of non-land use.

Not only did the subdividers in the sample fail in the area of sound market research, they appear to have failed in the area of environmental research. Such research is necessary to plan for the sound layout and use of a site, and to coordinate the needs and impact of the subdivision with surrounding communities. An Environmental Impact Report was not prepared prior to the start of development for any of the subdivisions. Dart did hire a consulting firm to prepare one for Bear Valley Springs in 1972, in compliance with California's Environmental Quality Act. But by the time it was done only a few units remained to be developed, limiting the Report's usefulness.

LAND

While the site layouts and land allocations employed by some of the ten subdivisions in the INFORM sample are relatively sound and sophisticated, at most of the projects they grossly disregard the nature and limitations of the land.

Two subdivisions located in two very different environments--Dart's Tahoe Donner and Great Western's Cochiti Lake--have employed relatively sound designs. Streets are laid out in a curvilinear pattern following the terrain, and there is some clustering of homes. Both sites have left over 30% of the land undeveloped. At Tahoe Donner this includes land alongside two fast-flowing mountain streams. At Cochiti Lake it encompasses large drainage washes known as arroyos, common in the mesa country of the Southwest. In both cases, building in hazardous, flood-prone areas was avoided, and the site was provided with sufficient open and recreational space.

The other eight subdivisions studied reserved from 24% down to virtually none of the land as open space. Three of them--Horizon's Rio Communities, Horizon's Arizona Sunsites, and AMREP's Rio Rancho--have superimposed roads and lots in a rigid gridiron pattern on rolling hills, jutting cliffs, and sunken arroyos, in all or part of the subdivision. The booby prize belongs to Horizon's Arizona Sunsites, where INFORM researchers could find no evidence of any open space

FINDINGS OF THE STUDY

allocation at all aside from one golf course in the core development area.

All of the subdivisions encompassed some land which would be potentially hazardous to build on, such as landslide and earthquake-prone areas, floodplains and drainage washes, and very steep slopes. Only three of the subdivisions (Pueblo West, Rio Communities and Cochiti Lake) totally exclude development from such areas, either by setting the land aside as open space, or by making sure that each lot sold has some non-hazardous land to build on. In the latter case, building on the hazardous areas was prohibited through covenants and deed restrictions.

At the other seven subdivisions, various types of "natural" disasters are probable. Indeed, in some cases they have already occurred. Both Dart Industries' subdivisions are located in active earthquake zones; Bear Valley Springs in particular borders a major fault. Geologists say earthquake damage at both subdivisions is likely. Both subdivisions have also mapped lots on steep slopes (over 25%)- that would be particularly subject to slippage and movement in an earthquake.

Although located in a very dry part of the country, five of the subdivisions are, ironically enough, in danger of damage from flood. What little rain falls in the West and Southwest often arrives in torrential cloudbursts. This often leads to flash flooding. All of the subdivisions studied encompass arroyos and other natural drainageways and/or land in the 100-year floodplain of a river bed (i.e., the land that could be underwater at least once in a hundred years, or which has a 1% chance of being flooded in a given year). However, only half of the subdivisions have the lots mapped so as to avoid residential construction in these areas. At the other half of the subdivisions--McCulloch's Lake Havasu City, Horizon's Arizona Sunsites, GAC's Rio Rico*, AMREP's Rio Rancho, and Great Western's Colorado City--at least some lot buyers are in danger of moving in and at some point finding their house inundated.

Severe flood damage has already occurred at Lake Havasu City and Rio Rancho, the two subdivisions in the study which have substantial populations and building activity. At the former, after two exceedingly heavy thunderstorms in July, 1974, flood water roared through the downtown area causing

―――――――――――――――――――――
*While the company has reserved the 100-year floodplain of the Santa Cruz River as open space, it has not similarly reserved the arroyos on site.

three deaths, $3 million worth of damage to property, and $1 million damage to the site's drainage system. At Rio Rancho, during several thunderstorms in August, 1975, flood waters caused power failures at the subdivision and dumped silt on the downslope neighboring town of Corrales. This silt clogged a major drainage culvert, and storm water then backed up into Corrales' streets, yards and homes. Corrales residents have sued AMREP for damages.

The flood potential is heightened at most of these subdivisions by poorly designed drainage systems. Although at five of the subdivisions, including Lake Havasu City and Rio Rancho, systems were presumed to be designed to carry the runoff of the worst storm to be expected in 100 years, at the other five they are only designed for a five- or ten-year storm capacity. The latter five are Rio Rico, Arizona Sunsites, Colorado City, Cochiti Lake, and Pueblo West.

Few of these Western and Southwestern subdivisions are located on land which is critical, for environmental reasons, to society at large. (Such land includes wetlands, dunes and beaches, habitats of endangered species, watersheds and prime agricultural land.) Where the subdivisions have impinged on such areas, however, they have by and large not done a good job of minimizing their impact. Both Lake Havasu City and Bear Valley Springs were formerly the habitats of endangered or threatened species--pronghorn antelope and bighorn sheep in the former case, and the California condor in the latter. In a burst of exceptionally poor planning, Dart located a rifle range in the portion of the Bear Valley subdivision which the condor--a huge black bird in the vulture family whose population has been reduced to less than 100 birds--is most often known to frequent.

If a site is not well planned or well laid out, it becomes difficult to minimize the impact of subsequent development activity. If phasing had been employed at these subdivisions, it would not have been necessary to cut the dirt roads which are now serious sources of wind and water erosion. The sites in the INFORM sample are crisscrossed with 4,900 miles of dirt roads, enough to stretch from New York to San Francisco and most of the way back. Horizon's Rio Communities and AMREP's Rio Rancho are by far the biggest offenders in this regard. They account for 1,700 and 1,522 miles of unpaved roads respectively. The only non-offender is Dart Industries, whose two subdivisions have surfaced roads.

FINDINGS OF THE STUDY

WATER RESOURCES

Five of the subdivisions in INFORM's sample are located on or near major rivers: the Rio Grande, the Colorado, and the Arkansas. Three of the sites are directly adjacent to federally-funded dam projects designed for recreation, water storage and/or flood control. Another four subdivisions have streams and natural or artificial lakes on site. Only Arizona Sunsites is neither on nor near a surface water body. The potential impact of the subdivisions on water resources is thus great.

With the exception of Dart Industries, at its Tahoe Donner subdivision, no subdivider has a thorough and complete program for protecting water resources from pollution. INFORM gathered information on each of the subdivisions to determine whether its drainage system was adequately designed to prevent pollution of on-site and nearby water bodies from erosion and runoff. Only the drainage systems at Dart Industries' two California mountain subdivisions employ sediment traps and retention ponds, to catch the dirt, oil, fertilizers, animal excrement, and other pollutants in runoff before they end up in a waterway. These are also the only two subdivisions at which the developer has a program to replant and reseed areas where vegetation has been disturbed by construction work. Such revegetation holds soils in place and prevents water pollution by controlling mud and silt at its source. INFORM found one widely used measure for protecting waterways from erosion and runoff damage. Three out of of five subdivisons whose lands directly border waterways have established a greenbelt buffer zone, up to 100 feet wide, on either side of the waterway. These greenbelt areas not only prevent pollution (by filtering runoff before it reaches the water) but also generally provide attractive recreation areas.

As mentioned above, there is also a great possibility that excessive numbers of septic tanks at a majority of the subdivisions will pollute groundwater and eventually even nearby streams and rivers. Groundwater is the primary source of drinking water for eight of the ten subdivisions. While this fact should encourage greater precautions to preserve the quality of this resource, apparently it has not. As noted, five of the subdivisions were planned for individual septic systems on quarter- and half-acre lots. Such a concentration of individual sewage disposal systems has led to contamination of groundwater in many other parts of the country. At a number of these five subdivisions, county restrictions on the size of lot permitted to use septic tanks are gradually being tightened. However, some counties are loathe to retroactively apply such regulations to existing subdivisions.

Installation of central sewage treatment usually prevents water pollution from sewage discharges. However, if the treatment plant is not adequately designed, its effluent can become a pollution problem. Most of the small sewage treatment plants in the INFORM sample were meeting the 1983 goal of the federal Water Pollution Control Act namely, "no discharge" to a navigable waterway. These plants generally treat the sewage only from core development areas. Sewage receives primary and secondary treatment, and in most cases the effluent is used to irrigate a golf course. Such recycling of effluent keeps the golf course from using scarce water supplies and also provides a further level of natural sewage treatment. At two of the ten subdivisions--GAC's Rio Rico and Great Western's Colorado City--sewage treatment plant effluent is discharged directly into a nearby waterway.

At most of the sites studied by INFORM, the land itself is appropriate for development on some scale with adequate planning and development practices. It is the site's water resources that significantly limit the land's carrying capacity. If groundwater is withdrawn at a faster rate than it is renewed or recharged, the results can be serious. They can include increased mineralization, subsidence of the land, and long-term depletion of the water supply. INFORM surveyed the subdivisions to determine if they had any program for monitoring the quality and quantity of their groundwater, and whether they were depleting or degrading this resource. INFORM found that at three of the subdivisions (Rio Rancho, Cochiti Lake and Rio Communities, all in New Mexico) neither the subdivider nor anyone else was keeping track of the projects' effects on groundwater. At two more (Arizona Sunsites and Rio Rico), there were no indications that the subdivider was taking any steps to protect limited groundwater supplies from depletion. Only at Dart Industries' Bear Valley Springs is the company conducting continuous monitoring of groundwater quality and quantity under an arrangement to switch to another water source if there are signs of impairment.

FINDINGS OF THE STUDY 49

IMPACT OF GOVERNMENT REGULATION

Every one of the subdivisions studied by INFORM either has had, now has, or is about to have a major Federal Trade Commission (FTC) or class action suit pending against it. Some have both. At several sites, state attorneys general have also filed suit, and the federal office of Interstate Land Sales has conducted an investigation.

Yet in terms of concrete tangible results, all of the legal action has had remarkable little impact at the ten subdivisions studied. The actions have generally produced only two kinds of results: some consumers have received lot exchanges or small refunds; and companies have been forbidden to make certain misleading advertising and sales claims. The focus of most of these actions has been on truthful disclosures. As long as the company accurately describes its plans and practices, however poor they may be, the agency is satisfied.

No major agency or group has brought suit at any of those subdivisions because of environmental concerns. The U.S. Environmental Protection Agency in no way impinged on the activities of these subdivisions, except in granting permits for direct discharge of sewage plant effluent to waterways.

Some federal agencies, particularly various Bureaus within the U.S. Department of the Interior have, through their policies, actually encouraged large-scale, and ultimately irresponsible subdivision activity. The Department's Bureau of Indian Affairs encouraged the subdivision of Pueblo de Cochiti land. The Bureau of Land Management helped make the Lake Havasu City site available to McCulloch. The Bureau of Reclamation has cooperated with McCulloch's development activities at Pueblo West.

The only major legal action which has actually mandated a positive change in actual subdivision practices was the settlement of a class action suit against GAC. The settlement required GAC to undertake a program of phased extension of services at Rio Rico over a five-year period. Unfortunately, GAC's subsequent financial disintegration has probably nullified that gain.

The reason for the small effect of major suits is that the major regulatory agencies which oversee subdivision activities are authorized only to demand adequate disclosure of information. With such information, it is up to the buyer to beware.

The few cases where regulation has been effective have originated at state and local levels. The history of Tahoe

Donner provides the clearest example of the results of close scrutiny. It illustrates also problems that arise when agencies work at bureaucratic cross-purposes. Although the subdivider planned for sewage disposal by septic tank, the state Regional Water Quality Control Board insisted that the project tie into a central sewage treatment system. The subdivider planned to draw its water supply from a spectacularly beautiful glacial lake. However, the resultant lowering of the lake-water level aroused local citizens, and eventually prompted the state Land Commission to file suit. The company abandoned an already constructed $1.2 million intake system. Other agencies affected other aspects of the project. The Fish and Wildlife Service required the reservation of a deer migration corridor; and the Regional Water Quality Control Board required the restoration of a badly eroded ski run. Finally, when the local sewage treatment facility exceeded its capacity and further connections to the system were banned everywhere, including at Tahoe Donner, the state Real Estate Commission did not simply require the company to disclose this fact in the small print of its sales materials. Instead, it put a moratorium on further lot sales until the situation is resolved.

None of the other subdivisions have been subject to this kind of regulation. The two Colorado sites have run afoul of the state's water law. However, at other sites it is the county Health Department, if anyone, which has opposed poor practices--usually in its capacity of determining criteria for septic tank use. There is little systematic review of master planning; outside of California, no one requires preparation of an Environmental Impact Report prior to development.

Some of this is gradually changing. Colorado counties, for example, are now required to make sure that a subdivision has secured an adequate water supply before it gives permission to market lots. But if the INFORM sample is any indication, county governments, with whom effective regulatory authority now resides, have neither the expertise nor the will to have much impact on these gargantuan subdivision projects which have arisen within their midst.

Ultimately, the negative impact on the consumers of not developing these ten subdivisions as planned--involving the loss of millions of dollars--would probably be equalled by the negative impact on both consumers and the environment caused by their completion. For example, water supplies would have to be found and perhaps depleted, probably at great expense to site residents. Better initial planning is clearly needed to prevent similar situations from developing elsewhere in the future. Unless subdividers are willing to undertake this planning themselves--something which seems extremely unlikely based on INFORM evaluations--the answer will have to lie in increased regulation.

3

Guidelines for Consumer and Environmental Protection Practices at Large-scale Subdivisions

Over the last several decades, various individuals and institutions across the country have waged sporadic, defensive, and often losing battles against ill-conceived subdivision activity. Consumers have sued for fraud. Environmentalists have fought some of the worst affronts to the land. Regulators have sought certain changes in some companies' sales practices.

Yet, as this book documents, these efforts have had all too little impact on the practices of the industry. The efforts often come too late--after too many lots have been sold and too much land has been disturbed--for the damage to be repaired. Lot buyers, victims of a developer's failure to fulfill his promises, may spend years in court and still never receive full financial restitution. The land, sold off piecemeal and developed in an environmentally careless way, may never be able to be reassembled for better planning or use. Nor is the ineffectiveness of remedial efforts the only problem: often such efforts are not made at all. As the case studies of subdivisions in this book indicate, environmental and consumer abuses often go officially unrecognized and unopposed.

Clearly, better preventive action is needed. As a first step in this direction, this chapter describes a set of minimum consumer and environmental protection guidelines for large-scale corporate subdivision activity. If these guidelines were followed--either because they were adopted voluntarily by the companies, or because the law required adherence to their principles--the worst abuses of the irresponsible portions of the industry would be avoided.

This list of approximately fifty specific recommendations, compiled by INFORM, incorporates legal precedents and technical opinions gathered during a three-year examination of local, state, and federal laws regarding subdivisions; of relevant regulatory agency decisions; of the literature and expert opinions in the fields of consumer affairs, real estate, land-use planning, and water-resource protection; and of the practices of 9 major subdivision companies. Additionally, the guidelines have been reviewed by approximately 25 authorities in these fields. There is a guideline to address each of the major consumer and environmental abuses identified in INFORM's analyses of nineteen specific subdivisions.* For each guideline, the rationale for why it was chosen and what adherence to it would accomplish, is described. Precedents for each standard are also noted. Finally, if logical alternatives to a particular guideline exist, the arguments and precedents for the alternatives are also indicated.

Obviously, given the variety and complexity of large-scale subdivisions, these guidelines will neither cover nor apply in every situation. Nevertheless, when used together they constitute a sound and comprehensive set of minimum standards for responsible practice from which variations can be evaluated on their merits.

One further use of these guidelines is in providing a "yardstick" whereby consumers interested in buying land and citizens concerned about protecting natural resources can identify sound subdivision practice. INFORM has evaluated each of the nineteen subdivisions studied* according to these guidelines, and the results are described in Volumes I and II of this book under Conclusions.

The explanations of the guidelines are presented in two parts: Consumer Protection Practices and Environmental Protection Practices.

---

*Includes both the ten subdivisions analyzed in this volume and the nine Florida subdivisions described in Volume II.

SUMMARY OF GUIDELINES
FOR
CONSUMER AND ENVIRONMENTAL PROTECTION PRACTICES

CONSUMER PROTECTION

SALES

1. Conduct a credit check before allowing prospective purchasers to sign an installment contract.
2. Limit lot sales to no more than two homesites per purchaser.
3. Sell no industrial, commercial, or multi-family lots on an installment contract basis.
4. Require a cash downpayment of at least twenty percent on installment contracts.
5. Offer installment contracts of no more than five years' duration.
6. Structure installment contracts so that no interest is charged.
7. Actively encourage buyer to have an attorney or other qualified professional review the Property Report and contract.
8. Require a pre-purchase site visit.
9. Provide a fourteen-day rescission period in which a lot purchaser can cancel an installment contract and receive a refund of all monies paid.
10. Offer any purchaser who defaults on an installment contract a refund of all payments in excess of the company's reasonable costs, i.e., marketing and sales expenditures.
11. Include in the contract a provision for a full refund (with interest) if promised basic services are not available by the date specified.
12. Put contract payments in an escrow account or obtain equivalent surety bonding, for refund purposes until title is delivered and improvements are completed.

TITLE

1. Offer only lots which are "platted of record" at the County Recorder's Office.
2. Use a recordable contract, and record the sale at the County Recorder's Office.
3. Offer for sale only:

    Land to which the subdivider has title, unencumbered by a mortgage or other financial obligation

    OR

    Land encumbered by a mortgage which includes a release clause guaranteeing that lot purchasers will receive full title upon payment of all installments.

4. Upon signing of a purchase contract, either:

    Deed title to the purchaser

    OR

    Place title in trust or escrow under terms that fully protect the purchaser's property interest, and ensure that title will be deeded to the purchaser upon completion of all installment payments.

BASIC SERVICES

1. Install prior to sales, or guarantee in the purchase contract at a specified cost, the availability of the following by the date the purchaser is entitled to possession:

    Water of potable quality distributed via a central system capable of yielding at least 150 gallons per capita per day in the desert, 125 gallons per capita per day in the mountains, and 100 gallons per capita per day elsewhere for the foreseeable future;

    Central sewage collection and treatment for all lots under one acre and lots of any size which do not have proven adequate percolation rates and slopes and adequate distances from bedrock, water table, and surface waters for septic use;

    A drainage system sufficient to prevent flooding from a 100-year frequency storm;

GUIDELINES 57

> Solid-waste collection and disposal via a recycling system, incinerator, or sanitary landfill;
>
> Paved streets and roads built to county standards;
>
> Electricity and telephone service at standard cost.

2. Use escrow accounts or surety bonds (but not corporate performance bonds) to guarantee completion of promised services by specified dates to each lot.

3. Basic services are to be financed through bonds issued by a special service district only if the following safeguards are employed :

> The district's initial governing body includes one or more county representatives;
>
> The district's governing body is elected by all titled landowners on a one-man, one-vote basis (i.e., no voting on an acreage basis);
>
> The sum of the bonds issued is not more than two times what the developer has invested in basic services;
>
> The sum of the bonds issued does not exceed 15% of the assessed value of the land in the district at the time of issuance;
>
> The developer is a cosigner of all bonds.

ENVIRONMENTAL PROTECTION

PLANNING

1. Prepare a Master Plan, for review by county, regional, or state planning agencies, showing that the following will be accomplished:

> Provision of all basic services, i.e., central water supply, sewage disposal, solid waste disposal, roads, drainage, and electricity and telephone, as described in the Consumer Protection section of these guidelines;
>
> Development in five-year or shorter phases (extending basic services and restricting lot sales to a given section at a time with extension scheduled to coincide with completion of a majority of installment contracts);

>   *An anticipated build-out rate of 80% in ten years for each phase of development verified by market studies.*

2. Prepare an Environmental Impact Report, for review by government agencies if appropriate, which fully analyzes the proposed subdivision's possible impact on land, air, and water resources and describes the company's plans to minimize that impact. Such plans should meet or exceed the guidelines for protection of land and water resources outlined below.

<u>LAND USE</u>

1. Use a curvilinear or cluster but not a gridiron pattern of development.
2. Allocate at least 25% of total site acreage (exclusive of roads, paved areas, and canals) to natural open space or developed recreation areas.
3. Reserve from lot sales and development areas of critical environmental concern, defined as:

    Wetlands (tidal or freshwater)

    Dunes, beaches, and barrier islands

    Water sources (watersheds, aquifer recharge areas)

    Prime agricultural lands (Soil Conservation Service Category I)

    Habitats of endangered species or unique ecosystems

    Prime historical, archeological, cultural, aesthetic, or recreational resources.

4. Reserve from lot sales and development land which is hazardous for building, defined as:

    Subject to geological hazards (earthquakes, landslides)

    Subject to flooding (100-year floodplains, arroyos, other natural drainageways)

    Having a slope exceeding 25%.

5. Avoid major land alteration, i.e.:

    Blade roads only in areas scheduled for immediate development;

GUIDELINES

Devegetate only building and road areas;

Preserve existing topography.

WATER RESOURCE USE

1. Minimize and prevent water pollution from erosion and run-off, by:

    Providing a drainage system using adequate natural swales, sediment filters and traps, and retention ponds;

    Creating a buffer zone of at least 100 feet between lots and waterways (including wetlands);

    Replanting disturbed vegetation immediately.

2. Minimize and prevent water pollution from sewage by:

    Limiting septic systems to one-acre or larger lots with proven adequate percolation rates, slope, and adequate distances from bedrock, water tables and surface waters;

    Providing central sewage treatment with tertiary treatment or secondary treatment and land disposal.

3. Avoid major alteration of natural drainage systems by:

    Avoiding major stream channelization or alteration;

    Avoiding major wetland dredging and filling.

4. Use groundwater only up to the environmentally "safe yield," i.e., causing no salt water intrusion, increased mineralization, land subsidence, or long-term depletion of the groundwater.

Consumer Protection Practices

The main consumer problems related to large-scale subdivisions fall into three broad categories: (1) problems related to sales practices, i.e., sales tactics, installment-contract terms, refund provisions; (2) problems related to conveying title to the land; (3) problems related to providing basic services.

Numerous books, newspaper articles, court suits, and regulatory actions have attested over the past decade to the prevalence in the land subdivision industry of high pressure tactics, failure to deliver title to lot purchasers, and the sale of "homesites" which have no utilities whatsoever and no prospect of ever getting them. Anthony Wolff's *Unreal Estate,* Robert Cahn's *Christian Science Monitor* series, "Land in Jeopardy," Dorothy Tymon's *America Is For Sale,* Morton Paulson's *The Great Land Hustle*, and Vince Conboy's *Expose!* all document such consumer abuses. The Federal Trade Commission (FTC) states that it has received "thousands" of consumer complaints about the industry. The Office of Interstate Land Sales Registration (OILSR), the office within the U.S. Department of Housing and Urban Development charged with supervising the registration of subdivisions, presently receives about fifty consumer complaints a week and has received as many as two hundred a week in times of peak sales activity. Unfortunately, neither the FTC nor OILSR is equipped to follow up on the overwhelming majority of these complaints.

The INFORM consumer protection guidelines, grouped according to the three categories noted above,* indicate the

---

*The INFORM study has not addressed the issue of guidelines for adequate disclosure to the consumer in federal Property Reports and advertising. While complete, accurate disclosure of facts about a subdivision is extremely important federal requirements, as of the last two years, have become quite adequate in this regard with a few exceptions. Furthermore, disclosure requirements, while necessary, are not sufficient: as the recent report *Subdividing Rural America*, published by the President's Council on Environmental Quality, states, "The full disclosure technique on which most land-sales laws are based has not proven adequate as a means of stopping these [consumer victimization] abuses."[1] The INFORM guidelines were therefore drawn up to assure good company practices, not just full disclosure of poor company practices.

alterations and modifications of common retail land-sales practices which are necessary to avoid such complaints and abuses.

SALES

The sales practices of most large-scale land subdividers are designed to sell lots at a rapid rate, regardless of whether the consumer will receive fair value for his money, is well-informed about and can afford the purchase, or intends to make any real use of the land. Millions of consumers, lured by persuasive salesmen, long-term installment contracts, and small monthly payments, have bought land in subdivisions, convinced they were making a sound investment. All too often, this turns out to have been a mistake: the buyer discovers he cannot afford the payments and defaults, losing everything paid to that date. Several companies in the INFORM sample have extremely high default rates. Or, the buyer manages to make all payments, only to discover that the land has no resale value, utilities are not available, and the community has virtually no residents. At every one of the nineteen subdivisions studied by INFORM, local real estate agents reported that they can resell most lots, if at all, only at "hardship prices," i.e., prices below what consumers originally paid.

The potential for such consumer abuse can, however, be minimized by the use of sales policies, installment-contract terms, and refund provisions designed to discourage hasty, poorly informed buying, to encourage buying for real use rather than investment purposes, and to protect the lot purchaser in the event of the developer's reneging on his promises. These provisions will also help protect the environment, since the land, a valuable resource, will not be committed to residential use unless such use will likely be made of it.

1. *Conduct a credit check before allowing prospective purchasers to sign an installment contract.*

RATIONALE

A company's conducting a credit check would help protect a consumer from "getting in over his head" and later losing his investment through default. Most of the companies in the INFORM sample sell lots under ten-year installment contracts. However, few bother to conduct a credit check. Those companies with no intention of investing any money to improve already cheap land have little reason to find out if a purchaser can pay his installments. If the purchaser defaults, they keep all that he has paid and resell the lot. Generally, such companies have already sold his contract--at a significant discount--to a financing company anyway.

Those companies with a real product--land that they have developed--have more to lose by a purchaser's default and more to gain by checking his credit. If they have installed basic utilities and services, their "up-front" expenses have been greater. If the lot is not rapidly sold again, the company may incur a loss because the lot has reverted to inventory, where it is not producing income. In addition, the lot buyer's payments up to the time of default may not have been sufficient to cover the costs, such as salesman's commissions, incurred in marketing the lot.

In economic hard times the problem of default can become particularly serious; during the second quarter of 1974, for example, buyers at Great Western United's California City subdivision were defaulting at a faster rate, in terms of gross sales, than new lots were being sold.[2]

PRECEDENTS

Credit checks are a routine procedure among companies granting credit. They are conducted prior to the granting of bank loans or issuance of credit cards, for example, in order to weed out individuals who might not be able to repay the debt they incur. One banker familiar with the retail land-sales industry has taken the position that credit checks should definitely be undertaken if the company has any intention of selling its contracts to a finance company in order to raise cash. He concludes that "complete credit files should be established for every case sold on land contract" in order that the value of the contract, i.e., the likelihood that the consumer will continue paying, can be accurately judged.[3]

The American Institute of Certified Public Accountants uses several criteria to distinguish those companies that can record a sale as income immediately from those that can record only the actual installment payments as income. These criteria include appropriate credit checks.[4] Dart Industries administers a credit questionnaire to prospective lot buyers but is the only company in the INFORM study to do so.

2. *Limit lot sales to no more than two homesite lots per purchaser.*

GUIDELINES

RATIONALE

There is little disagreement about the fact that many subdivision lots are bought for speculation. Robert Cahn, in his *Christian Science Monitor* series, "Land in Jeopardy," describes a 28-year-old bachelor who had bought fifteen lots at five subdivisions. He was barely meeting his monthly installment payments, but was firmly convinced that the lots were a good investment for the future.[5] The Council on Environmental Quality report, *Subdividing Rural America,* cites various studies showing that between thirty percent and sixty percent of buyers have purchased for investment and that this speculation is a major cause of the very low build-out rate at most subdivisions. It also reports that industry sources estimate that about two houses are constructed for every hundred lots sold.[6]

Investment value, however, is almost always a mirage. According to *Consumer Reports*, GAC Corporation's own study showed that sales prices on Cape Coral lots rose only about ten percent in the ten years between 1960 and 1970. The same article quoted the President of the Urban Land Institute, Roy Drachman, as estimating that the money invested in unimproved land must double every five years just to meet the costs of taxes, interest, insurance, and inflation.[7] This seldom happens.

The former District Attorney of Nevada County was quoted in the *Christian Science Monitor* as estimating that the principal, interest, taxes, and assessments on a $10,000 lot in his county would total $19,460 over a ten-year period. If the buyer put the $1,000 downpayment and all monthly installments in a savings account paying five percent interest, he would have $30,464 after ten years. He stated that, based on these figures. "Just to break even, on resale, and allowing for 10 percent commission, the lot would have to increase in value 338 percent of the original price--unheard of in such subdivisions."[8]

The federal Office of Interstate Land Sales Registration takes such a dim view of the possibilities for profitable speculation at subdivisions that it requires all federal Property Reports to contain the following statement: "The future value of land is very uncertain; do NOT count on appreciation."

Speculation on subdivision lots is also considered highly undesirable by such authorities as the Task Force on Land Use and Urban Growth, a study group sponsored by the Rockefeller Brothers Fund, because it prevents the land, a valuable resource, from being put to good use, and because by dispersing ownership it hampers sound planning.[9]

The easiest way to limit speculation and purchase for "investment" value is to limit the sale of more lots than can actually be used. The purchase of more than one or two lots is, in fact, almost always for "investment," not use. Few families want to build more than one home in a subdivision or want more than two lots for more space or for their children.

PRECEDENTS

INFORM found no legal precedents for limiting sales to two lots per person. However, the sale of many investment lots so directly contradicts corporate claims of new community development and appears so unjustified from the point of view of valid consumer risk, that such a guideline seemed important.

3. *Sell no industrial, commercial, or multi-family lots on an installment contract basis.*

RATIONALE

Another form of encouraging land speculation, rather than use, is the sale of industrial, commercial, or multi-family lots on the installment basis on the grounds that the purchaser will have a valuable "commercial" property when the subdivision is built out. Generally these lots cost considerably more than single-family residential lots. Yet they have no greater chance of having any resale or investment value. In fact, in many subdivisions they have even less real value because the companies do not include them in any exchange option.

PRECEDENTS

The Federal Trade Commission recommended, in its March 1975 proposed order against Horizon Corporation, that the following statement be included in all of the company's promotional materials:

> The designation of lots as "single-family residential," "multi-family residential," or "commercial" is only the designation used by Horizon. There is no significant difference in the present or expected future value, if any, of lots having such different designations or locations. The future use of this land as designated is very uncertain--do not count on lots to be used as designated by Horizon.[10]

GUIDELINES

Since commercial and industrial properties almost never have investment value and, unlike residential lots, can rarely be used or exchanged, they should not be sold by installment contract. Moreover, since the development and use of these lots are key to new community growth, immediate not future use should be encouraged. Immediate use is not consistent with long-term installment contracts. Thus, such lots should be sold only on a conventional mortgage or cash basis.

4. *Require a cash downpayment of at least twenty percent on installment contracts.*

RATIONALE

The purchase of a $6,000 or $10,000 piece of real estate is a serious decision for most people. Writing a check for $300 or $500 and signing an agreement to pay $60 per month is far less serious. The smaller the downpayment, the less real the commitment, the more impulsive the purchase, and the greater the likelihood that the purchaser may default.

From the company's perspective, small downpayments are also not always beneficial. As was pointed out in Robert Cahn's *Christian Science Monitor* series, many installment land-sales companies operate with extreme deficit financing. The result is that,

> Because of the extraordinarily high promotion and commission costs in the industry, a downpayment of even 10 percent often leaves the developer in the hole financially even if he is selling the land for 50 times what he paid for it....
>
> Such deficit financing, especially for smaller, underfinanced developers, means that they are on a merry-go-round needing cash flow from volume sales to build the improvements promised to buyers, but losing money at the start for each lot sold....
>
> If the developer can hold out long enough, he can make millions. But he can also go bankrupt--and the resulting ghost subdivisions now litter many parts of the nation.[11]

PRECEDENTS

Because of a 1972 change in the accounting rules for the retail land sales industry, companies must now receive ten percent of the total lot sales price before they can "recognize" the sale on their financial statements. This minimum is "designed to provide an amount that would represent a sufficient equity commitment on the part of the buyer so that he could be expected to complete the remaining payments under the terms of the sales contract."[12] Because of the accounting rules, most companies studied by INFORM presently require a ten percent downpayment. However, many companies still experience a high default rate. A twenty percent downpayment should discourage much of the impulse buying that so often ends in default and a financial loss to the consumer.

5. *Offer installment contracts of no more than five years' duration.*

RATIONALE

An installment contract of only five years', rather than ten years', duration is desirable for the same reasons as a large downpayment. By increasing the buyer's monthly payments and bringing actual ownership into the foreseeable rather than the distant future, it may tend to reduce impulse buying, speculation, and the chances of default.

A further reason for utilizing a shorter, five-year contract period is that it reduces the consumer's financial risk. An installment contract is not a deed. The company retains ownership and rights to use the land for the duration of the contract. The purchaser owns nothing until he has completed his final payment and receives title. If he defaults, all payments are forfeited. If the company goes into bankruptcy or defaults on any mortgage it has on the land, the company may lose the land that the purchaser has been making payments on. The recent bankruptcy of GAC Corporation, one of the largest firms in the industry, illustrates the need to guard against this problem. As of mid-1976, it was not certain that lot purchasers who were in the middle of paying off contracts at the time bankruptcy was declared would ever receive title to their land.

Limiting the duration of the installment-contract period to five years (instead of ten) would reduce the period of the lot purchaser's risk.

Neither purchaser nor company would be as vulnerable to unpredictable, fluctuating long-term inflation rates and economic cycles. Both could do better financial planning, potentially reducing the chance of purchaser default (and forfeiture of all payments) or developer bankruptcy during the contract period.

PRECEDENTS

Most subdividers in this study offer ten-year contracts, although Deltona's vary between two and twelve years and AMREP's are of five to eight years' duration. A 1972 brokerage analysis singled out Deltona's five-year selling cycle of certain sites as "advantageous" since it "facilitates masterplanning."[13] GAC Corporation's Form 10-K Report filed with the Securities and Exchange Commission states that the company's contract cancellations declined in the several years up to 1974 due to "more restrictive sales practices [including]...increases in required downpayments, shortening of contract terms...."[14] (Obviously, however, such changes were not sufficient to stave off financial collapse.)

6. *Structure installment contracts so that no interest is charged.*

RATIONALE

The imposition of an interest charge on installment land-sales contracts is a practice uniformly adhered to by the land-sales companies studied by INFORM. However, it is not justified by conventional financial practice and serves to deceive the consumer about the real cost of a subdivision lot.

The theory behind charging interest on an ordinary consumer item, like a television or car bought on the installment plan or on bank loans, is that the consumer is paying for the use of something, namely the item or the money. In the case of installment land-sales transactions, however, the consumer obtains the use of nothing. He cannot use his land and does not even receive a deed until all payments are complete. A land-sales contract is in fact most similar to a purchase option or deposit arrangement, on which interest is not commonly charged.

Charging interest on land-sales contracts has the further detrimental effect of obscuring the real price of a lot: the amount quoted by the salesman plus five percent to eight percent interest per year. While the interest is tax deductible, it significantly raises the total cost of the lot. For a $6290 lot, the eight percent amounts to $2581 over the ten-year term of the contract. Use of this device can also lead to further consumer abuses. For example, many of the companies which allow a purchaser to exchange an outlying lot for an improved one will credit only his principal to the cost of the new lot.

PRECEDENTS

Alan Kappelar, a high-ranking official of the Office of

Interstate Land Sales Registration, told INFORM that, in his opinion:

> If the purchaser doesn't have title, and if he is restricted from use of the land during the term of the contract, charging interest on the contract is unreasonable.
>
> If the "real estate" had a "real value" and if there were a chance it would appreciate during the term of the contract, then an interest charge would be more acceptable. But of course, the kind of real estate that will appreciate is not sold under contract.
>
> If the companies did not charge interest, they wouldn't be able to sell their contracts to finance companies, and then they wouldn't have any cash. But this wouldn't be so bad. It would make them alter their financing and stop spending 35% to 40% of a lot's purchase price on promotion.[15]

An article in *Urban Lawyer* states:

> It is also interesting to note, aside from the questions of resale, that although most land sales installment contracts require the purchaser to pay monthly interest charges... on the purchase price, it would generally be more logical for the developer to pay interest to the purchasers....The developer is using the installment payments of the purchaser to fund his marketing and development activities, and would expect to pay interest for the use of such funds to any other lender.[16]

7. *Actively encourage buyer to have an attorney or other qualified professional review the property report and contract.*

RATIONALE

Real estate transactions are probably among the most complex undertaken by the average consumer. To make an adequate evaluation requires fluency in the languages of property and contract law. It requires knowledge of the product: the land's history (title), physical characteristics (topography, hydrology, geology), value, and usefulness. And it requires a full understanding of the terms of the agreement. Professionals would never close a sale without this knowledge; most average consumers are simply not equipped with it.

Frequently, retail land-sales companies sell lots at elaborate sales dinners held hundreds of miles from the subdivision. The movies and attractively designed advertising material presented often serve more to obscure than clarify the exact nature and cost of the "homesite" the consumer is purchasing. In such situations, it is particularly essential, yet extremely difficult, for the consumer to understand what he is being offered, and to fully understand the terms and costs of the transaction. The contract is often written in terms incomprehensible to the layman. And federal Property Reports, which the government requires that a consumer receive, are often very long and difficult to read.

A prospective purchaser should therefore be encouraged to seek the advice of an attorney or other qualified professional before signing anything.

With the help of a lawyer or real estate broker, the purchaser can learn from the federal Property Report and contract such crucial information as the condition of title to the lot, the existence of prior liens and encumbrances, his rights in the event of the company's bankruptcy, the subdivider's obligations to provide basic services, and the financial condition of the company.

PRECEDENTS

An article in the *Case Western Reserve Law Review* drew a parallel which well exemplifies the need for professional review of land-sales disclosure documents and contracts.

> Unlike the typical sale of lots, securities offerings before they reach the "public," filter through a superstructure of financial sophisticates (brokers and dealers) to whom the maze of prospectus information is presumably meaningful.[17]

The federal Office of Interstate Land Sales Registration requires companies to include a suggestion to "seek professional advice" on the front of each federal Property Report. New York state's Real Property Law specifies that if a purchaser's lawyer is not present when the contract is entered into, the buyer has special cancellation privileges.

8. Require a pre-purchase site visit.

RATIONALE

Buying any product sight unseen is very risky under any circumstances. Buying land sight unseen is particularly unwise. The value and usefulness of real property are determined by a great many factors including location, geography, availability of utilities and services, rates of growth, etc. While a potential purchaser cannot learn about all of these factors by visiting the site, without a site visit he will be almost totally uninformed.

PRECEDENTS

Iowa's Assistant Attorney General reported to a 1974 American Land Development Association meeting that "developers utilizing off-site marketing techniques bear responsibility for over 90 percent of the land sales complaints which [his] office has handled."[18] He recommended, in his speech, that:

> The first step that can be taken is to completely discontinue and abandon all off-site sales and rely solely on on-site sales. I make this suggestion dealing from my own experience where over ninety percent of the complaints we receive against land developers are complaints which allege the use of fraud, deception and misrepresentation in connection with sales presentations by companies selling via off-site sales methods. Naturally, even those companies who sell land only to people who have seen the land first still have problems but from my experience in handling several thousand land complaints these problems are of a nature that can be reasonably worked out while the problems caused by off-site selling can be only halted by severely restrictive legislation and massive prosecution.[19]

Land and Condominium Sales Registration, a study by the National Association of Attorneys General, states:

> The purpose of the Interstate Land Sales Full Disclosure Act was to control sales of land purchased sight-unseen. A substantial amount of testimony at the hearings on the Act concerned property being offered in remote states where the individual purchaser had no

> real opportunity for inspection. Many such
> offerings were in the swampy portions of
> Florida or Louisiana, or in the desert
> regions of Arizona or New Mexico.[20]

Significantly, the Act exempts subdividers from the requirement of preparing a federal Property Report if the land is free of all liens, encumbrances, and adverse claims and "if each and every purchaser or his or her spouse has made a personal on-site inspection of the real estate which he has purchased." It also exempts land with a home already completed or contracted to be completed within two years.[21]

In an article in the *Journal of Law Reform,* Robert Maxwell proposed:

> ...a requirement that the seller provide
> every potential buyer with an opportunity
> to see his lot, without cost, prior to sign-
> ing the agreement to buy. This would provide
> for fuller disclosure of the development's
> nature and would lessen the fraudulent devel-
> oper's incentive to offer land that is
> sufficiently distant that the purchaser is
> not likely to visit it prior to purchase.[22]

The American Land Development Association code of ethics includes an on-site visit. Representatives of both Dart Industries and McCulloch Properties, Inc. told INFORM that they encourage prospective purchasers to visit their subdivisions before buying in order to cut down on defaults. The federal Office of Interstate Land Sales Registration requires companies to include on the cover of the federal Property Report a suggestion to the consumer to "inspect the site...." At many of the sites studied it is common practice to have inspection tours for the sale of large industrial or commercial tracts.

Even with a site visit, a potential purchaser can be misled. According to *Land and Condominium Sales Regulations,* companies often use such practices as: separating husband and wife and then reporting to one that the other wishes to purchase; showing purchasers the wrong lot; transporting potential customers around the development in cars equipped with two-way radios which broadcast false sales.[23]

The state of Arizona requires subdividers to offer lot purchasers who bought sight unseen a six-month period in which they have the option of visiting the site and, if displeased, obtaining a refund. However, INFORM felt that the opportunities for deception and fraud by salesmen at distant locations were sufficient that a site visit should be mandatory, not optional.

9. *Provide a fourteen-day rescission period in which a lot purchaser can cancel an installment contract and receive a refund of all monies paid.*

RATIONALE

A rescission period is particularly important in situations where a lot purchaser has not consulted with an attorney or made a site visit. Potential purchasers are invited to dinner parties, wooed by movies, boat rides, and promises; encouraged by skilled and charming salesmen; and often misled about the documents they are signing. They need time--a mandatory recission period--to "cool off" and reconsider the purchase. During that time they may discuss it with a lawyer, investigate land values elsewhere, etc., as well as recover from any heavy sales pressures. Again, the better considered and informed the decision to buy, the smaller the possibility of fraud and default.

PRECEDENTS

Although the federal Office of Interstate Land Sales Registration presently mandates a three-day rescission period after receipt of a federal Property Report, many experts believe this is entirely inadequate. The Task Force on Land Use and Urban Growth, the study group sponsored by the Rockefeller Brothers Fund, recommended a rescission period of thirty days.[24] The Council on Environmental Quality study, *Subdividing Rural America*, recommends fourteen days.[25] Maryland's condominium law, unfortunately not applicable to lot sales, but directed at a similar problem, requires a fifteen-day rescission period. The California Subdivided Lands Act requires a fourteen-day rescission period for all "land projects" (remote subdivisions of the type studied by INFORM). The Federal Trade Commission order against GAC Corporation required the company to give purchasers a rescission period of ten business days as well as a completely filled-out cancellation form.[26]

10. *Offer any purchaser who defaults on an installment contract a refund of all payments in excess of the company's reasonable costs, i.e., marketing and sales expenditures.*

RATIONALE

Most retail land-sales companies presently retain all of a defaulting lot purchaser's payments as "damages." Such a practice is, however, highly unfair to the consumer, since real company damages generally amount to only a portion of the purchase price.

Obviously, land-sales companies must spend money to buy land, to market it, and to improve it. However, the company gives up neither the land nor improvements during the installment-contract payment period. As noted above, a lot purchaser buying on installments does not receive title to his lot, nor the right to use it, until all payments are complete. Thus, if a purchaser defaults, the company essentially loses only the costs incurred in marketing the lot. This is a considerable part of the purchase price. According to Form 10-K Reports filed with the Securities and Exchange Commission, the marketing and sales costs for the companies in the INFORM sample range from 25% (General Development Corporation) to 50% (McCulloch Properties, Inc.) of the total lot price. A 1973 survey conducted by the American Land Development Association found that 33% of the average gross sales in recreational land was spent on sales commissions, sales overhead, advertising, and promotion.[27] Nevertheless, were the company to return the balance of the consumer's payments after subtracting marketing costs, the lot purchaser would at least not have lost his entire investment, and the company would recoup its actual expenses. (The company will also have benefited from having the use of the lot purchaser's money for a period of years.)

PRECEDENTS

In complaints against GAC Corporation, AMREP, and Horizon Corporation, the Federal Trade Commission cited as an "unfair or deceptive act or practice" the inclusion in installment contracts of provisions stating that purchaser default entitles the company to retain all payments without reference to actual damages. It ordered GAC Corporation to make partial refunds to lot buyers who, in the past, defaulted on their contracts. The same FTC order required a different arrangement to be specified for all future sales contracts. According to a sliding scale, a purchaser who defaulted would be refunded between zero and approximately one third of principal, but not interest.[28]

11. *Include in the contract a provision for a full refund (with interest) if promised basic services are not available by the date specified.*

RATIONALE

Since improvements are implicitly part of the "product" a consumer purchases at a planned community and are almost always reflected in the purchase price, he should be guaranteed a refund if improvements are not available as agreed. This is especially important given the long contract periods at these subdivisions, during which circumstances affecting the developer's plans can change radically. At Dart Industries' Tahoe Donner subdivision, for example, changing community demands and regulatory requirements have resulted in the community's water and sewage disposal systems becoming unusable for a great many lots. Without these systems, a lot purchaser cannot build. His lot is virtually useless unless the problems are solved.

Two Federal Trade Commission complaints and one order all call for some sort of refund if services are not available.

The complaint against AMREP includes the provisions that if the company fails to provide sewerage, central water, and utilities to lots sold as homesites, it shall refund "all monies paid [by the purchaser]...plus 6% interest compounded annually."[29] The complaint against Horizon Corporation includes in the refund provision "all monies paid pursuant to the contract including monies paid to [the company], any improvement association, any municipal utility district, or to any third party, plus interest at the rate of 6% compounded annually," if promised improvements are not forthcoming.[30]

The FTC order against GAC Corporation required the company to exchange undeveloped lots at Golden Gate Estates for lots with an adequate supply of potable water, an adequate sewage system, and standard electricity and telephone service with the provision that, if no lots were available for exchange, the company had to offer the purchaser a refund of all monies paid under the contract.[31]

The Rockefeller Task Force on Land Use and Urban Growth recommends that federal and state legislation requiring subdividers to develop the land should include a provision entitling buyers to a refund with interest and damages if lots are not "fit for use" because they lack basic services.[32]

12. Put contract payments in an escrow account or obtain equivalent surety bonding, for refund purposes until title is delivered and improvements are completed.

RATIONALE

A great many circumstances can prevent the completion of a project even when the developer fully intends to improve all lots. Economic recessions, strikes, changes in environmental requirements, and lawsuits can all slow down or halt development. Purchasers can be left with unimproved lots; developers with no money to fulfill their commitments or to make refunds.

One way to at least partially insure that lot purchasers are protected from such events is to require subdividers to post a "surety bond" (in effect an insurance policy under which the subdivider pays a fee to an independent company which is then bound to meet his obligations in the event that the subdivider is financially unable to do so). Another form of protection is to require a subdivider to deposit sufficient funds or the purchaser's payments in a bank trust or escrow account, from which money can be withdrawn only to pay for improvements or provide refunds.

PRECEDENTS

Both of these protective procedures have been advocated by many authorities and regulators. The Rockefeller Task Force on Land Use and Urban Growth recommends, as insurance that subdivided lands will in fact become "functioning communities served by necessary facilities," requiring "that a portion of lot buyers' payments be deposited in escrow until the seller has fulfilled his obligations to the buyers."[33]

The Council on Environmental Quality study, *Subdividing Rural America*, recommends that state and federal governments should require financial guarantees that promised improvements will be installed.[34]

An article in *Planning*, the magazine of the American Society of Planning Officials, proposes requiring "the developer to deposit adequate development money with a reputable trustee each time he makes a sale," or posting "a surety bond from a reputable company, a common practice in the urban subdivision field."[35]

California requires large-scale subdividers to post bonds with the state or put purchaser payments in escrow until title is delivered. Iowa's Subdivided Land Sales Act also requires bonding or escrowing, but it covers only the sale of out-of-state land. Maryland's Horizontal Property Act, applicable unfortunately only to condominiums and not to lot sales, requires developers to put all deposits toward the purchase price in escrow and obtain a performance bond to insure completion of the project.

TITLE

When buying a sofa or a dishwasher, transfer of ownership is usually accompanied by physically transporting the object from the seller's premises to those of the purchaser. The buying of land, however, is accompanied only by the transference of pieces of paper, known as "deeds," and changing of notations in official record books. This gives a purchaser "title" to the land. Land is a peculiar commodity in other ways as well. It is common for certain kinds of "rights" to the land--such as the right to run a power line over it or the right to mine coal under it--to be sold apart from the land itself. Furthermore, title may be sold "encumbered" by certain types of claims: these can include mortgages, unpaid taxes, claims by spouses or creditors of previous owners, etc. These "encumbrances" obviously affect the value of title to the land, yet a neophyte in the area of real estate transactions may easily be totally unaware of them, or fail to understand the arcane legal terms used to describe them.

The potential for consumer abuse in this area is thus great. Some particularly unscrupulous subdividers have been known, for example, to sell the same piece of land on the installment contract to several different owners. Others more commonly sell land on which they are paying off a mortgage. If these companies default on their mortgage payments, title to the land might then belong to the mortgagee, i.e. a bank, rather than to the lot purchaser who is paying installments.

The following guidelines are designed to ensure that a consumer buying land in a subdivision actually receives his land and title (with or without various rights, as initially agreed). The subdivider should:

1. *Offer only lots which are "platted of record" at the County Recorder's Office.*

RATIONALE

Platting is the term used to describe the legal recording with the appropriate official body--usually called the County Recorder's Office--of the plan of a subdivision. Platting of a subdivision is accomplished by the filing of a "plat map"--a diagram of the lots and blocks into which the land is being divided. Platting is necessary to legally establish the existence and boundaries of lots, to prevent confusion in title and tax liabilities, and to register official permission for the described division of the land. Unless he is buying platted land, the consumer cannot be sure that the county will allow his lot to be created.

PRECEDENTS

California, New York, Arizona, New Mexico, and Florida are among the states which require all lots offered by subdividers to be "platted of record" prior to sale.

GUIDELINES 77

2. *Use a recordable contract, and record the sale at the County Recorder's Office.*

RATIONALE

Once a consumer has signed a purchase contract for a lot, it is important that there be an official record of his interest in the property, so that there is no chance that it might be sold to someone else. In a traditional real estate transaction, the time between the signing of the agreement for sale and the transference of the deed is relatively short. Therefore, only the deed is recorded. Its recordation gives adequate legal notice, makes the transfer final against other claims, and prevents any later deeds made to other buyers from having greater rights to the land.

Since an installment sales-contract payment period spans five, or more usually ten, years, the sales agreement itself must be recorded to perform the function of legal notice. Companies should draw up the contract so that it is in a form that is recordable. Furthermore, since many lot buyers live a considerable distance from the subdivision at the time they buy, it would be reasonable to expect that the company take care of the formality of actually recording the contract at the appropriate county office.

PRECEDENTS

The Florida Uniform Land Sales Practices Act requires all contracts for subdivisions marketed within the state to be in a recordable form. Arizona law requires that they actually be recorded, either by the owner, agent, or subdivider of the subdivision.

3. *Offer for sale only:*

> *Land to which the subdivider has title, unencumbered by a mortgage or other financial obligation*
>
> OR
>
> *Land encumbered by a mortgage which includes a release clause guaranteeing that lot purchasers will receive full title upon payment of all installments.*

RATIONALE

There are undoubtedly letters in the files of every state's Attorney General's office from purchasers who never received title to their land. This failure to obtain title can occur because the subdivider cannot fulfill the terms of his mortgage, because his creditors have a superior claim to the land, or because of other prior liens on the property. The title, and thus the purchaser's rights to the land, can be encumbered by unpaid taxes or assessments, leases, easements, or mineral rights.

Unfortunately, the Interstate Land Sales Full Disclosure Act offers purchasers no remedy "if the seller fails to provide either clear title to the land or promised improvements, so long as the seller makes no assurances as to these items in the Property Report."[36]

PRECEDENTS

In many states, including California, Florida, Iowa, and New York, a company may sell mortgaged land if the mortgage includes a "release clause." With such a clause, if the subdivider should fail to meet its obligations and the land should revert to the mortgagee, the individual purchaser can continue to make his installment payments to the mortgagee and receive his lot when all payments are complete. (In some cases the payment of an additional release fee may be required.) It should be noted that the right to release a single lot from a mortgage only ensures the purchaser title to his property; it does not assure either legal or physical access or any improvements which the subdivider may have promised.

Robert Maxwell, in an article in the *Journal of Law Reform*, suggested amendments to strengthen the Interstate Land Sales Full Disclosure Act. His suggestions include:

> A requirement of a release clause to assure that the buyer can obtain title to the property if the seller defaults on a blanket encumbrance, or an escrow arrangement for purchase monies until the title is released from the encumbrance. This would assure that the purchaser can obtain either title to his property or a refund of monies paid toward the purchase price in the event that the seller defaults on his obligations.[37]

GUIDELINES

4. *Upon signing of a purchase contract, either:*

   Deed title to the purchaser

   OR

   Place title in trust or escrow under terms that fully protect the purchaser's property interest, and ensure that title will be deeded to the purchaser upon completion of all installment payments.

RATIONALE

Given the shaky financial position of many land sales companies, it is important that title be protected during the installment contract period so that receipt will be assured at the end, even if the company should go bankrupt in the interim. One way to do this is to deed title immediately to the lot purchaser. (When this is done, the terms are usually such that title will revert to the subdivider if the buyer fails to meet installment payments; however, title is still in the consumer's name, an important legal protection). Another is to put the title in a trust or escrow account—that is, turn it over to a third party (usually a bank) for safekeeping, to be released only to the lot buyer when his payments are complete. In this way, title to the land is separated from the company's general assets, which may be distributed to creditors in a bankruptcy proceeding.

PRECEDENTS

Arizona law requires that title be either deeded to the purchaser or put in a trust or escrow account. California requires the same for all land which is not encumbered by a mortgage. Dart Industries follows the former practice on all its contracts; McCulloch Properties, Inc. deeds lots to purchasers who put down at least a third of the purchase price as a downpayment.

BASIC SERVICES

Even with title duly delivered, a subdivision lot is worth little to a consumer without such basic services as central water, central sewage disposal, roads, drainage, and electricity. Because of the importance of such services to the lot purchaser, and because of the considerable expense involved in their installation, their availability should be guaranteed both in purchase contracts and through surety bonds (or similar financial guarantees) posted with local governments. Further, while installation of these systems can be financed in various ways, the chosen financing should not burden lot purchasers with enormous additional hidden costs. A subdivider therefore should:

1. *Install prior to sales, or guarantee in the purchase contract at a specified cost, the availability of the following by the date the purchaser is entitled to possession:*

    Water of potable quality distributed via a central system capable of yielding at least 150 gallons per capita per day in the desert, 125 gallons per capita per day in the mountains, and 100 gallons per capita per day elsewhere for the foreseeable future;

    Central sewage collection and treatment for all lots under one acre and lots of any size which do not have proven adequate percolation rates and slopes and adequate distances from bedrock, water table, and surface waters for septic use;

    A drainage system sufficient to prevent flooding from a 100-year frequency storm;

    Solid-waste collection and disposal via a recycling system, incinerator, or sanitary landfill;

    Paved streets and roads built to county standards;

    Electricity and telephone service at standard cost.

RATIONALE

Retail land sales companies almost all advertise their product as "residential homesites and lots" in "developments and new communities." They sell lots at prices commensurate with these claims, i.e., considerably above the prices of raw, unimproved land nearby. To most consumers, these statements and prices imply the availability of basic services; that is, that water, sewage and solid waste disposal facilities, paved roads, drainage, and electricity and telephone service have been provided for by the developer. Regulatory agencies have concurred with this assessment. The Federal Trade Commission, in complaints against GAC Corporation, AMREP, and Horizon Corporation, has cited the representation of lots with no water, sewage or utilities as "homesites" as a deceptive and unfair practice. The FTC proposed order would prevent AMREP from advertising or selling any land as a usable homesite unless the company guarantees, within seven years of the date of the sale, adequate sewage disposal, a central water supply, and standard utilities.[38] The proposed order against Horizon Corporation would prevent the company from representing any land as a "community" unless it makes available to every lot paved roads, electricity, telephone service, and central water and sewerage "at no cost or nominal expense."[39]

There is, in fact, broad agreement among governmental agencies concerned with the industry that large subdividers marketing lots implicitly or explicitly defined as "homesites" should be responsible for providing basic services. The U.S. Department of Housing and Urban Development, in setting standards for new communities to receive funds under the Title X program, required electricity, telephone, paved streets, and central water and sewerage systems as a condition of funding. Colorado's model subdivision regulations, published in 1972, and Florida's Coastal Coordinating Council, an agency established to inventory and develop guidelines for Florida's coastal zone, recommend similar requirements.

The President's Council on Environmental Quality states, in its report *Subdividing Rural America*:

> The key ingredients of development quality are the adequacy of basic site improvements such as water and sewer systems, road and drainage systems, site design, and construction standards. Adequate project facilities lessen the extent of environmental impacts as well as the potential for negative fiscal impacts on local governments. ...Adequate development standards will drastically reduce premature recreational subdivision. Controlling development quality is also the surest form of consumer protection.[40]

Yet, when it surveyed 1,287 of the "recreational" subdivisions registered with the Office of Interstate Land Sales Registration, the Council on Environmental Quality found that nearly 70% of the projects relied solely on septic tanks for sewage disposal. Nearly 30% relied solely on wells for water supplies.[41] It also found that "at the time of filing with OILSR, less than half the projects had been approved for septic tanks by a public authority"; that roads had been accepted for maintenance by a public authority in only 18% of the projects; and that nearly 38% of the projects had no provision for solid-waste collection.[42] It further reported:

> Unimproved recreational subdivisions, which
> account for the majority of recreational land
> development which has occurred in the U.S.,
> generally make no more improvements in the
> land than local land use regulations require.
> Many attempt to avoid those areas with land
> use controls if at all possible. Expenditures
> by these developers for land improvements can
> run as low as $200 and $300 per lot.[43]

INFORM likewise found that a third of the nineteen subdivisions it studied do not guarantee paved roads to all lots; half do not guarantee a central water system; and two-thirds do not guarantee central sewage disposal.

The guidelines for provision of basic services at subdivisions are broadly aimed at guaranteeing that a lot buyer does have adequate services for his "homesite" by the time it is paid for, without incurring excessive expenses or financial obligations.* The Rockefeller Task Force on Land Use and Urban Growth advocated federal and state legislation requiring a subdivider's guarantee that any lot "be fit for construction of a dwelling" one year after the purchaser receives title. It defined fitness to include "suitable water supply," "lawful sewage disposal facilities," and safety (from danger of floods and rockslides). It concluded that "the seller...can much more readily install required facilities than can an individual buyer."[44]

The developer's installation of adequate basic services will not guarantee a fully functioning new community. This requires a sound economic base and many other favorable characteristics. But it will at least ensure a purchaser's lot is habitable, and that no undue burden will be placed on surrounding towns and counties to try and make up for the developer's deficiencies in the area of basic services.

---

*Although some subdividers specify that they will have services available within a certain period after a lot buyer requests them, it is more desirable that services be available by date of title transfer since (a) the developer will only be actively involved with the project for a certain period of time and might have left by the time the lot owner is ready to request his services and (b) this is consistent with a policy of actual and phased development, the value of which is described in the Environmental Protection Guidelines.

PRECEDENTS: CENTRAL WATER OF ADEQUATE QUALITY AND QUANTITY

The adequacy of the water system, an issue about which few people think to ask, is perhaps the most important consideration in buying subdivision land. To guarantee adequate water means to ensure that sufficient water is there, that the developer has the right to use it, and that it will be distributed via a central system.

The Council on Environmental Quality study *Subdividing Rural America* recommends:

> No subdivision plat should be approved...or lot sold until after the existence of a water supply adequate to support full build-out and permanent occupancy has been certified.[45]

The availability of water is a significant problem, however, in a growing number of areas of the country. Experts in New Mexico estimate that the state has barely enough water to meet existing agricultural, industrial, and domestic needs. These needs don't include projections for the state's one million acres of unoccupied subdivision lots. The New Mexico legislature has tried and failed for years to pass a law requiring subdividers to provide water.

The California State Water Project does not have the water to supply its year-2000 annual commitment of 4.3 million acre-feet. It hopes to discover new resources before then.[46]

Florida's water shortage is so severe that it precipitated a crisis conference in 1971 and enactment of four major land-use bills in 1972. Areas of the state have water rationing, and new developers are required to report on where they will get water. Several communities, including Pinellas County, have imposed building moratoriums until they solve their water-shortage problems. The Port Charlotte and Cape Coral subdivisions in southwestern Florida both suffer from severe water shortages, although they have achieved only a small percentage of their ultimate populations.

Not only must a developer locate an adequate water supply, but he must obtain legal rights to it. This is a particular problem in the West, where existing water supplies are often long since legally appropriated. Great Western Cities' Colorado City subdivision, for example, has been able to obtain legal rights to only enough water for a tenth of its lot owners.

Specific estimates of the amount of water needed per person per day vary according to the region, type of community, and who is doing the estimating. The National Association of Homebuilders reported average actual use figures of 123 gallons per capita per day in the West and 76 gallons per capita per day in the East in 23 surveyed residential communities.[47]

Noted Arizona hydrologist Leonard Halpenny uses figures of 180 gallons per capita per day in the desert and 125 gallons per capita per day in the mountains.[48] The Colorado Environmental Commission reported that Denver's per capita use of 204 gallons per day is higher than the national municipal average of 125 to 165 gallons per day.[49] D. A. Okun in *Water and Wastewater Engineering, Volume 1,* gives average residential use as 50 gallons per capita per day.[50] New York State regulations require community water systems in new subdivisions to be capable of delivering 100 gallons per capita per day of potable water if the system is not metered, 75 gallons per capita per day if it is metered.

Because of these variations, INFORM's requirement of at least 150 gallons per capita per day in the desert, 125 gallons per capita per day in the mountains, and 100 gallons per capita per day elsewhere seems a reasonable minimum. It may be adjusted according to local usage figures.

An adequate delivery system is as necessary as an adequate water supply. At present, the recommendations and requirements for central delivery systems vary widely across the country. But the trend is toward making them standard practice wherever a large subdivision exists.

The U.S. Public Health Service advocates the installation of public water systems in communities with lots two acres or smaller.[51] The New York State Department of Health regulations require public water-supply facilities for any subdivision having 50 or more lots or 200 or more persons. New Mexico's State Engineer (responsible for water allocation throughout the state) recommended, pursuant to the 1973 New Mexico Subdivision Act, county regulations requiring community water systems in subdivisions with more than 25 lots, any one of which is less than 10 acres. Colorado's model subdivision regulations also stated that a subdivider should supply water through a central system.

The Tahoe Regional Planning Agency Subdivision Ordinance requires subdividers to provide a central water-distribution system. It also requires them to demonstrate that their water supplier has the physical and legal capacity to supply the necessary water to the subdivision and has made a commitment to supply the water consistent with its existing and future commitments and demands. The National Association of Homebuilders' *Manual of Residential Water Supply Systems Development Standards* begins with the statement: "An adequate water supply system is an essential element of residential land development."

GUIDELINES

It defines an adequate system as one that provides safe, potable water under continuous pressure, that is capable of meeting reasonable fire-fighting requirements, and that is designed to meet present and appropriate future requirements.[52]

The alternative to a central water system, requiring each lot owner to drill an individual well, increases health hazards because most county health departments do not regularly test private-well water quality and because wells are often dug near septic tanks. Having to drill private wells may also prove to be a very expensive alternative for the consumer (adding up to several thousand dollars to his lot price) particularly in the Western states where water tables are very deep.

PRECEDENTS: CENTRAL SEWAGE DISPOSAL FOR LOTS UNDER ONE ACRE

The utilization of central, rather than individual sewage-disposal systems eliminates a great many problems before they are created. As is described in detail under Water Resource Use in the Environmental Protection Guidelines, the environmental impact, efficacy, and cost of individual sewage systems depend on a great many factors. These include soil conditions, slope, depth to groundwater, rainfall, numbers and size of lots, etc. Nevertheless, in high-density housing areas pollution and health problems from use of individual systems almost inevitably occur. In Long Island, New York, for example, septic-tank effluent from over 500,000 homes has contaminated groundwater with increased concentrations of synthetic detergents, chlorides, nitrates, sulfates, and phosphates.

Another problem with planning for septic-tank use in a subdivision is the real probability that local health regulations will change between the time a lot is sold and the time the buyer wants to build. This has **happ**ened at several subdivisions in the INFORM sample. If the minimum lot size for septic-tank use is increased, many lots become useless until a central sewage system is installed.

The National Association of Homebuilders, in its *Manual of Residential Sanitary Sewer Systems Development Standards,* states: "Sanitary sewer systems [i.e. central sewage systems] are essential in urban and suburban communities."[53] The Urban Land Institute's *Community Builders Handbook* recommends public sanitary sewer systems with septic tanks being used only as a last resort.[54] The Council on Environmental Quality study *Subdividing Rural America* recommends: "Septic tanks should not be considered acceptable as a permanent means of sewage disposal in high density subdivisions."[55]

The New York State Department of Environmental Conservation/ Department of Health regulations require a community sewage system for subdivisions with over fifty lots, Colorado's model subdivision regulations recommend that subdividers be responsible for providing a central sewage system. The Tahoe Regional Planning Agency Subdivision Ordinance requires subdividers to provide a central sewage system and a commitment from the sanitary sewage authority to provide treatment for the sewage of a built-out development.

Environmental and health considerations are the most important reasons for installing a central sewage-disposal system in a subdivision if lots are smaller than one acre and soil conditions are unsuitable for septic use. However, an argument for central systems can also be made on economic grounds. According to an analysis by the U.S. Department of Health, Education, and Welfare Public Health Service, a community sewerage system is normally justified by cost considerations in areas where the population density is 1,000 to 2,500 persons per square mile, or where lots are less than one acre in size.[56] INFORM's comparison of costs of individual septic systems and costs of hookup to a central sewage system at the nineteen subdivisions studied tends to confirm the Public Health Service's findings. All subdivisions had at least a small central sewage system serving lots of less than one acre in size. In only one case was it more expensive for a lot owner to hook up to the central system than to install a septic tank (provided, of course, that the utility company or developer had extended mains to the lot and the lot owner did not have to pay for line extension). In many cases, the hookup fee was considerably less than the cost of a septic tank.

PRECEDENTS: DRAINAGE SYSTEM ADEQUATE FOR 100-YEAR STORM

Drainage systems for subdivisions must handle surface runoff from both normal rains and more intense storms. In particular, they must be designed to accommodate the increased flows that result from the creation of impervious surfaces by development. U.S. Army Corps of Engineers studies have shown that imperviousness may vary from about 20% in low-density residential areas to about 90% in business-commercial areas.[57] At McCulloch's Lake Havasu City subdivision, an inadequately designed drainage system resulted in $4 million in flood damage during two extremely intense storms in July, 1974.

In its *Guide for Reviewing Subdivision Plans in Colorado* the U.S. Department of Agriculture Soil Conservation Service suggests that "The major [drainage] system...should protect the urban area from extensive property damage and loss of life due to flooding." It adds that it should "provide an outlet for floodwater resulting from the 100-year and storms of higher frequencies."[58] Systems can employ streets, gutters, land grading, open channels, and natural drainageways. (See Environmental Protection Guidelines for discussion of drainage systems.)

While a system capable of handling the worst storm expected in 100 years is generally considered optimal and is employed by Dart Industries, for example, at its two subdivisions studied by INFORM, there may be circumstances in which rigid adherence to such a criterion is not desirable. On some land, particularly low-lying lands or wetlands, a drainage system capable of preventing flooding from a 100-year-frequency storm is damaging to the environment. Florida requires only 10- and 25-year storm drainage, as anything more would severely lower the water table and harm both groundwater and surface water supplies.

PRECEDENTS: SOLID-WASTE DISPOSAL

According to the U.S. Geological Survey, "The disposal of more than 1400 million pounds of solid wastes in the United States each day is a major problem. This disposal in turn often leads to serious health, esthetic, and environmental problems."[59] The New York State Department of Health reports that accumulation of refuse in and around homesites may amount to 1,500 pounds per capita or more per year. The space required for landfill areas is about one acre per 10,000 population annually if materials are compacted to a depth of seven feet.[60]

Since local governments spend an estimated $3 billion each year on collection and disposal of solid waste--an expenditure second only to those for schools and roads--providing this service to new subdivisions can take a major toll on their budgets. Subdividers should thus plan for disposal via a recycling system (such as is now in operation at dozens of cities around the country), via an incinerator equipped with adequate air-pollution controls, or via a sanitary landfill, where each day's garbage is covered with several inches of dirt. If the latter is planned, sufficient acreage should be set aside to meet the long-term needs of the entire subdivision. A fourth alternative, disposal via an open dump, is not acceptable. Open dumps have been outlawed in Vermont and New Jersey because of the health, odor, and air-pollution problems they create.

PRECEDENTS: PAVED ROADS TO COUNTY STANDARDS

Subdividers almost always provide road access to a lot. However, the roads are often built to standards inadequate for the higher-density use of occupied subdivisions and often require extensive maintenance by counties, districts, or homeowners' associations.

Horizon Corporation, before it turned over road maintenance responsibility to the Rio Communities property owners' association, estimated that it would cost each absentee lot owner $50 per year to maintain the 1,700 miles of bladed road at the project.

For subdivisions of the type studied by INFORM, performance standards and maintenance requirements mandate that roads should at the very least be paved. County standards frequently do not require this. However, where county requirements are higher, roads should comply with those standards so that they will be eligible for acceptance and maintenance by the county.

PRECEDENTS: ELECTRICITY AND TELEPHONE AT STANDARD COST

In almost all areas electricity and telephone services are provided by independent utility companies rather than by subdividers. However, the subdivider should ensure that these utility companies will extend service to every lot at a reasonable cost. In sprawling remote subdivisions, the costs of extending utility lines to outlying lots can be prohibitive.

The Federal Trade Commission complaint against AMREP includes as a condition of a usable homesite "standard electricity and telephone service from a local utility...[which] will cost the lot holder only nominal hook-up and installation fees and customary and usual rates."[61] The FTC order against GAC Corporation requires the company to provide standard electricity and telephone service to lots in Golden Gate Estates within 180 days after receipt of written notice of a building permit, "at no initial cost to the purchaser other than nominal hook-up and installation fees."[62]

Placing utility lines underground is more desirable than stringing them aboveground. Underground wires are safer and less visually obtrusive, and they require less maintenance. Some counties now require wires to be underground.

2. *Use escrow accounts or surety bonds (but not corporate performance bonds) to guarantee completion of promised services by specified dates to each lot.*

RATIONALE

As was discussed earlier in these Guidelines, any one of a thousand things can happen to prevent even the best-intentioned developer from fulfilling his promises to lot purchasers. Some methods of countering such uncertainties are needed but are all too seldom employed. The Council on Environmental Quality found that out of 1,287 "recreational subdivisions" registered with OILSR, only 1.5% provided any financial guarantees that promised facilities would be constructed.[63]

Many states and communities require subdividers to post corporate performance bonds, to be forfeited if improvements are not made available as promised. However, such bonds are in effect only corporate IOU's and are of little value should the subdivider go into bankruptcy.

A far better type of guarantee is a surety bond, whereby some outside entity--usually an insurance company--agrees (for a fee) to provide funds to fulfill the subdivider's obligation if the latter is unable to do so himself. Escrow accounts-- whereby the developer puts a certain amount of money for each lot sold into a special account from which it can be withdrawn only to pay for the specified improvements--also provide a secure guarantee that promised improvements will be completed.

PRECEDENTS

According to New Hampshire's Assistant Attorney General, New Hampshire's lack of a provision requiring bonding or escrow for improvements has been a "major source of difficulties for consumers."[64]

Robert Maxwell, an advocate of stronger consumer protection against land-sales abuses, has suggested:

> a requirement that the seller provide a full performance bond for all improvements promised at the development through the Property Report or advertising. This would protect the purchaser from either a deliberately fraudulent developer or one whose weak financial position might cause him to default on the promised improvement.[65]

In settling a major class-action suit against GAC, a U.S. District Court ruled that the company had to establish and maintain the reserves "necessary to construct and complete the improvements and amenities" at specified projects according to a specified schedule of development.[66]

Colorado's model subdivision regulations recommend that no county approve a final plat map until the subdivider has submitted, and obtained approval for, an agreement guaranteeing construction of the public improvements shown in the plat documents. This agreement must include collateral sufficient for completion of the improvements in accordance with design and time specifications.

Both New York's Real Property Law and Florida's Uniform Land Sales Practices Act require bonding or escrow accounts of amount sufficient to complete promised improvements. However, both will allow posting of corporate performance bonds. Some Florida counties require a combination of corporate and surety bonding.

The Council on Environmental Quality study *Subdividing Rural America* recommends that developers either install promised facilities initially or guarantee completion via performance bonds or escrow accounts.[67]

3. *Basic services are to be financed through bonds issued by a special service district only if the following safeguards are employed:*

> *The district's initial governing body includes one or more county representatives;*
>
> *The district's governing body is elected by all titled landowners on a one-man, one-vote basis (i.e., no voting on an acreage basis)*
>
> *The sum of the bonds issued is not more than two times what the developer has invested in basic services;*
>
> *The sum of the bonds issued does not exceed 15% of the assessed value of the land in the district at the time of issuance;*
>
> *The developer is a cosigner of all bonds.*

RATIONALE

In an increasing number of states, enabling legislation provides for the formation of quasi-governmental entities, generally called "special service districts." These districts are authorized to provide one or more municipal-type services and to issue bonds and levy taxes to fund community improvements. In many cases, the special-service district statutes were originally enacted to provide a means by which rural landowners could join together to acquire the limited services needed by the community, services such as irrigation or drainage, without incurring all the financial and social obligations associated with municipal incorporation. However, in recent years the scope of services such districts have been authorized to provide has been expanded as developers have increasingly relied upon them to finance new community development. This often unanticipated application of special-service-district laws has given rise to a number of problems for consumers and states alike.

Although the type of bonds districts are empowered by law to issue varies, the type most frequently relied upon is a general-obligation bond secured by a lien against all land in the district and payable with interest over a period of not less than twenty years. Of the states included in the INFORM study, Arizona, New Mexico, Colorado, and Florida have laws authorizing the issuance of such bonds. Each of the states has been forced to deal with problems arising from their use in subdivisions.

The subdivider in the early stages of development, often controls the district because he owns most of the land. Problems arise when he decides to have the district issue millions of dollars' worth of bonds which lot purchases must eventually repay through taxes and special assessments. In those states where developers are not required to disclose to purchasers the amount of district debt, lot owners may be shocked to find themselves confronted years later with the alternative of repaying bond debt or losing their property. If the law does not limit the amount of indebtedness which may be incurred or the rate at which taxes may be levied by the district, the rate of taxation required to retire the bonds may even result in district insolvency. This problem reached such significant proportions in Colorado that in 1976 the state legislature enacted Senate Bill 44, commonly referred to as the "Special District Bail-Out Bill," to enable certain special districts to avail themselves of federal bankruptcy laws.[68] District insolvency ultimately creates a problem, not only for district residents, but for bondholders, who are possibly as unaware of the risks involved in special-district financing as the land purchasers are.*

Land purchasers may find themselves in double financial jeopardy. Subdivision lots are often sold at prices which reflect the improvements which are being provided by the special-service district; thus, lot purchasers may be paying twice for the same improvement--once when they buy the lot and once when they pay taxes and special assessments levied by the district to pay off the bonds.

Obviously, complete disclosure of existing and potential debt to the prospective lot buyer is one way to limit the worst abuses of special-district financing. Arizona requires subdividers to make such disclosures to the Real Estate Commissioner as part of the filing required under the state land-sales law but does not require that disclosure be made to purchasers.

Substantive measures clearly protect purchasers more effectively than disclosure. Of the states INFORM has included in this study, a number have incorporated into their statutes

---

*The SEC is presently investigating the possibility of fraud in the sale of special-district bonds for Pueblo West, in Colorado.

safeguards aimed at limiting or curtailing altogether the types of abuses noted above.

PRECEDENTS: SAFEGUARD FOR DISTRICT FORMATION

If initial formation of the district is permitted prior to the establishment of a significant population base, the district's initial governing board should include one or more county representatives. This would assure county input concerning district affairs which are of greater than local impact. It would also function as a control on the developer and on the amount of debt the board could issue. County officials are in a position to be aware of other taxes and assessments to which land in the district is subject. They would thus be able to assess realistically the feasibility of any proposed debt-repayment schedule. Arizona, New Mexico, and Florida have laws requiring county representation on special-service-district boards.

A firmer safeguard, but one which severely limits the use of districts, is to condition formation of the district on the vote of a specified number of electors who are titled property owners within the district. This would ensure that those who are responsible for the district debt have themselves determined that district formation is the best way to acquire improvements. In Colorado, prior to a 1969 amendment to the Special District Control Act which McCulloch Properties, Inc., was instrumental in passing, formation of a special district was predicated on the vote of 100 qualified voters in the district. The 1969 amendment added the alternative requirement that a district could be formed on the basis of the vote of 10% of the taxpaying electors of the district (property owners who need not be residents of the district). This amendment provided a loophole by which developers were able to establish and control metropolitan districts in Colorado before selling any lots.

PRECEDENTS: ONE MAN, ONE VOTE

As soon after initial formation of the district as possible, the district governing board should be elected on a popular--one person, one vote--basis by the vote of all titled landowners.*
This would ensure that control of the district, and thus the amount of debt, would fall directly into the hands of the lot buyers who will ultimately be responsible for repayment of the debt. Arizona, New Mexico, and Florida have structured their

---

*This guideline is predicated on INFORM's recommendation that title be transferred to lot owners at the time of the signing of the contract.

special-service-district laws applying to new community development to require election of the governing board by popular vote.

PRECEDENTS: DEBT LIMITED TO TWICE THE DEVELOPER'S INVESTMENT

District debt will be limited and speculative development discouraged if the developer is required to make an investment in the project significant in proportion to the debt new residents will ultimately have to repay. Under its Title VII funding of new communities, the U.S. Department of Housing and Urban Development gave guarantees for bonds if the ratio of bonded debt to developer's equity did not exceed 4 to 1.[69] Arizona limits the sum of the bonds issued by a district to no more than twice what the developer has invested in public improvements: INFORM has chosen that limit as its guideline.

PRECEDENTS: DEBT LIMITED TO 15% OF THE DISTRICT'S ASSESSED VALUE

A fourth safeguard, of value to both lot purchasers and potential investors in district bonds, is to limit the sum of the bonds issued to 15% of the assessed valuation of land in the district at the time of issuance. This would insure adequate collateral to secure the bonds. Florida has such a limit. New Mexico's law is even more restrictive, imposing a limit of 5%. California, on the other hand, allows the bonds to equal 200% of assessed valuation.

PRECEDENTS: DEVELOPER COSIGNS BONDS

A fifth safeguard would effectively prevent a developer from encumbering a newly formed district with a huge debt that it may not be able to repay. Florida requires the developer to provide financial assurance of the district's obligations by cosigning the district bonds. Thus, the developer's corporate assets as well as the land serve to guarantee the debt.

Other safeguards incorporated in the laws of some of the states studied are discussed in detail in Volume III of this study.

Environmental Protection Practices

The guidelines for environmental practices in the land subdivision industry fall into three categories: those related to overall subdivision planning; those specifically related to land-use practices; and those specifically related to water-resource protection practices.* Described here is a set of minimum standards designed to protect the environment from degradation by subdivision activity. Techniques are described generically, not on a brand-name basis.

For the most part, employment of these guidelines will protect the consumer as well, since a lot buyer inevitably pays a price for poor environmental subdivision planning. That price may range from the cost of replanting vegetation up to the cost of recovering from serious flood damage.

---

*Subdivisions also affect land and air resources by attracting automobile traffic. Certain methods of protecting land and preserving air quality, such as using cluster development and allocating sufficient open space, are discussed under Land Use. Other methods, such as using mass transit systems, were not included in these guidelines. Currently, vehicle-related air pollution is not a serious problem since most of the largely remote subdivisions studied have too few people and too little traffic to create one. However, none of the subdivisions in this study with large populations even have bus transportation around the site, and none indicated plans for the future use of mass transit to minimize automobile traffic and pollution.

In addition, subdivisions can affect the surrounding economic and social environment by taxing public facilities such as schools, roads, water systems, and public parks, or by introducing an urban population into a rural remote setting. These effects, while important, go beyond the scope of INFORM's study, which is confined to evaluating the direct impact of subdivisions on the physical environment.

PLANNING

Coordination of a new subdivision with the needs and capabilities of the surrounding area is key to sound environemental planning. To accomplish this, the careful review and approval of plans by a state agency or a state-created regional agency is needed. Such review and approval is now generally required at the county level for major new residential developments. However, the importance of broader supervisions has been recognized in a number of new state laws. All these laws share a common theme--the need to provide some degree of state or regional participation in the major land decisions that affect the use of our increasingly limited supply of land" and that are of more than local consequence.[1] The American Law Institute Model Land Development Code endorses this principle and calls for state oversight in decisions on "'categories of development which because of the nature or magnitude of its effect on the surrounding environment' are likely to present issues of state or regional significance."[2] Major new residential developments fall into this category.

Coordination and supervision of subdivision activity obviously necessitate preparation of documents for review which accurately reflect the developer's plans and probable impact. Florida, through its 1972 Environmental Land and Water Management Act, is one state which presently has broad review of subdivision environmental planning. To implement the law's goals, i.e., "to protect the natural resources and environment of the state" and to "facilitate orderly and well-planned development," the state requires "Developments of Regional Impact," a category in which most large land subdivisions fall, to submit plans and studies which allow comprehensive review of their plans by a regional planning agency.

Even if government supervision is minimal, a developer should do detailed advance planning to ensure that his development occurs in an orderly, environmentally sound fashion, compatible with local needs. Therefore, before altering the land in any way or marketing lots, a subdivider should:

1. *Prepare a Master Plan, for review by county, regional, or state planning agencies, showing that the following will be accomplished:*

    Provision of all basic services, i.e., central water supply, sewage disposal, solid waste disposal, roads, drainage, and electricity and telephone, as described in the Consumer Protection section of these guidelines.

Development in five-year or shorter phases (extending basic services and restricting lot sales to a given section at a time with extension scheduled to coincide with completion of a majority of installment contracts).

An anticipated build-out rate of 80% in ten years for each phase of development verified by market studies.

RATIONALE

There are thousands of "ghost" subdivisions in the United States--land which has been platted and sold but never developed. The Council on Environmental Quality study, *Subdividing Rural America*, reports that "as early as 1966 there were over 14 million vacant, single family lots in the U.S."[3] A paper presented in *The Appraisal Journal* in October, 1971, found that such premature subdivision has caused patchy patterns of land development as well as impairment of the natural environment, difficulty in reassembling the land for a better use, and waste of land due to use of small blocks and lots.[4]

The consumer problems that have resulted from a lack of coordination of installment lot sales with extension of services are legendary. If utilities are extended too soon, before residents have completed contract payments and are ready to build, there is no one there to maintain the systems. The residents of GAC Corporation's Cape Coral subdivision in Lee County, Florida, for example, who live in a seven-square-mile area, have found themselves responsible for maintaining the roads and drainage system that GAC prematurely extended over 105 square miles.

If services are installed too late, or not at all, lot purchasers also suffer. At Rio Communities, in central New Mexico, Horizon Corporation has sold approximately 160,000 lots but has extended services to less that 1% of them. The result is that many purchasers have finished payments on their lots only to find their "homesites" unusable because the cost of extending basic utilities would run to hundreds of thousands of dollars.

Developing in manageable phases, with extension of services and completion of contracts coordinated, is not only of benefit to the consumer. It is also the most environmentally sound way to proceed. It delays and prevents the unnecessary environmental disruption caused by bulldozing roads and laying utility lines before real development necessitates it. (Many subdividers presently cut dirt roads to all lots as soon as they begin marketing them, and then leave them to erode and deteriorate over the ten-year period during which the consumer makes his payments.) Phasing also limits the commitment of land to subdivision use until the time such commitment is needed.

Most installment contracts, and thus what phasing there is, now run for ten years. However, using a relatively short five-year development time-span is necessary and desirable for several reasons. Vulnerability to unforeseen events, including changes in economic conditions, is reduced. Subdividers will be more able to accurately assess real demand and the costs of development. They and local governments will be better able to foresee and plan for the impact of the proposed population on community facilities and services.

Most important from an environmental point of view, a shortened time span will combat the premature commitment of land to what may become dated environmental knowledge and planning principles. This has become a particularly thorny problem in Florida, where thousands of acres of coastal and inland wetlands were sold to consumers during the 1960s with the promise that by the time the consumer finished paying, the company would have dredged and filled, converting them into dry land. The intervening years have brought new understanding of the extremely valuable environmental functions wetlands serve (described in more detail below), and regulators are seeking to halt the dredging and filling. The effect of one such recent regulatory decision at Deltona's Marco Beach subdivision in Florida may be disastrous for the company. It may have to refund millions of dollars to purchasers of swamp-land lots.

Obviously, the commitment of land, a valuable resource, to a particular use should not be undertaken unless it is clear that the use is necessary and will not cause significant environmental damage. In the case of most of the subdivisions studied by INFORM, neither the plans for services, the need for the subdivision, nor the timing of development was seriously evaluated either by the company selling lots or by any governmental agency. As a result, the land is often inalterably defined for a use it cannot or will never have. Unless such poor land-use decisions are to be repeated, better planning must become the rule.

PRECEDENTS: PROVISION OF BASIC SERVICES

In a few states, regional planning agencies do review subdivision plans to determine the adequacy of services and their compatibility with the local environment.

The Tahoe Regional Planning Agency, established to evaluate new development in the California/Nevada Lake Tahoe area, issued a detailed Subdivision Ordinance in 1972. The Ordinance requires developers to provide a central water distribution system, a central sewage disposal and treatment system, adequate drainage, and, generally, underground electricity and telephone lines.

One of the six factors which Florida regional planning agencies are instructed to consider in reviewing a subdivision, or other type of "Development of Regional Impact," is whether the developer will "efficiently use or unduly burden" water, sewer, solid waste-disposal, stormwater-drainage, power-supply, and transportation facilities. Florida has not developed any standards for what levels of service should be available at a subdivision.

Basic minimums for adequate levels of each of these services are described in detail, along with the rationales for why they were chosen, earlier under Basic Services in the Consumer Protection Guidelines.

PRECEDENTS: DEVELOPMENT IN FIVE-YEAR PHASES

The Task Force on Land Use and Urban Growth, a study group sponsored by the Rockefeller Brothers Fund, endorses the desirability of both phasing and a shortened time span for sales and development activity:

> We anticipate that one common result [of the implementation of its recommendations] will be a reduction of the long waiting periods between time of lot purchase and time of lot use. This result...seems highly desirable from every standpoint: to subdividers who may then adjust their planning to real needs and to a market that does not depend on high pressure sales practices; to buyers who will then run less risk of holding property that is unusable and unsaleable; to local governments, which will be able to consider subdivision registrations simultaneously with plans for provision of facilities and services; and, finally, to lenders, who will be able to make loans against real development projects where values will be less likely to evaporate as buyers walk away from contracts they got into under pressure.[5]

The U.S. Department of Housing and Urban Development (HUD) included among the factors it would consider in granting assistance to new communities under the Title VII program:

> Balanced phasing of all elements of the physical plan and program (including housing, industry, utilities, commerce, circulation systems, resource management of undeveloped

> land, institutions, open space and special
> innovative features) on a schedule compatible
> with economic feasibility and geared to the
> timing of land acquisition, development and
> disposition.[6]

One HUD-funded development, Flower Mound, Texas, established a schedule of four approximately four-year phases in which to develop its 6,150 acre area; another, Jonathan, Minnesota, utilized five five-year phases for its 8,150 acres.

According to Professor James A. Clapp, in most well-designed new towns growth is usually allowed to reach a certain level of completion in one or two neighborhoods before others are opened up for development.[7]

In settling a class action suit against GAC Corporation, the court ordered the subdivider to bring basic services (streets, water, sewer, drainage) to specified neighborhoods, in its Poinciana and Rio Rico subdivisions, according to a series of deadlines extending through 1985.[8] This was, in effect, court-ordered phasing.

Most of the large subdivisions studied by INFORM engage in a minimal form of phased development: they have a small "core" area to which all basic services were extended upon initiation of the project. Unfortunately, however, there is rarely phasing or extension of basic services to the rest of the project.

It should be pointed out that this guideline is not intended to discourage the long-term planning that is required for new community development. Rather, it is only intended to limit the physical alteration and retail sale of land to five-year time spans, so that long-term plans can be periodically adjusted to changing conditions and knowledge.

PRECEDENTS: 80% BUILD-OUT RATE WITHIN 10 YEARS

A developer's proving that there is a need for the project is no less important than his plans for services. Market studies are the most practical method of showing such a need. Florida suggests that "Developments of Regional Impact," including subdivisions, supply market studies along with their "Application for Development Approval," for use in determining whether the development should be allowed as planned. It also asks the developer to present "the justification for the need of the proposed development in the region."[9]

If there is indeed a need for the subdivision, lot purchasers will begin building on their lots soon after they have finished their payments and obtained basic services. An 80% build-out rate within ten years could be expected if there were a genuine demand for housing in the subdivision and if lot sales and development occurred in five-year phases. Subdivisions in the Tahoe Regional Planning Agency's jurisdiction in California must show 85% build-out of all vacant parcels before the Agency will allow them to market new areas.[10]

2. *Prepare an Environmental Impact Report, for review by government agencies if appropriate, which fully analyzes the proposed subdivision's possible impact on land, air, and water resources and describes the company's plans to minimize that impact. Such plans should meet or exceed the guidelines for protection of land and water resources outlined below.*

RATIONALE

Land development of any sort radically changes the environment. The impact of these changes can be severe, extensive, and in many cases, unanticipated. For example, when GAC Corporation's predecessor drained hundreds of thousands of acres to create dry ground at its Golden Gate Estates subdivision in southwest Florida, it seriously impaired not only the ecology of the Big Cypress Swamp, but the water supply of an entire region.

The preparation of an Environmental Impact Report requires the developer and his engineers to study and consider environmental factors that might otherwise be overlooked or ignored.

PRECEDENTS

Environmental Impact Reports have been required for federally funded or permitted projects since the passage of the National Environmental Policy Act in 1969. The states of Washington and California now require similar reports for subdivisions. The Tahoe Regional Planning Agency Land Use and Subdivision Ordinances also require developers to submit detailed "Land Capability Reports" or "Information Reports" showing the anticipated impact of a project on the area's resources.

Florida's Environmental Land and Water Management Act requires that an extensive environmental impact report be prepared for any "Development of Regional Impact." The states of Maine and Vermont require that subdividers' applications for development permits include reports on potential environmental impact.

LAND USE

Observation of certain basic guidelines for land use can prevent land resources from being degraded by subdivision activity. Where land is developed, its disturbance should be minimized. Some types of land, such as wetlands, for a variety of reasons, should not be developed at all. Guidelines for environmentally sound subdivision land use practices are as follows:

1. *Use a curvilinear or cluster but not a gridiron pattern of development.*

RATIONALE

Massive networks of straight subdivision roads superimposed over deserts, plains, and hills scar the landscapes of the American Southwest. In Florida, the same rectangular webs, augmented by drainage canals, cross lowlands, swamps and grasslands. These grids of streets, blocks, and lots--monotonous to the eye and disruptive to the environment--are uniform regardless of the natural terrain.

The visual result of such planning at Rio Rancho Estates in central New Mexico was graphically described in the *New Mexico Review:*

> AMREP's main roads run straight across the countryside, up and down hills, over slopes and down into and across arroyos, in total and callous disregard for the character of the landscape as it might relate to future development. Where the main roads encounter ...easements [railroad rights of way, gas pipeline, and electric transmission lines], and where residential streets encounter major arroyos, they angle abruptly and then continue as straight lines beyond these obstacles. The result is a vast gridwork interrupted by crazy quilt patches of angled streets.[11]

There is no need to employ a gridiron street and lot layout. Curvilinear plans allow for curving roads and more oddly shaped lots which conform to natural contours. Cluster plans (by far the most sophisticated) allow dwelling units to be grouped on smaller lots, leaving the remaining land undivided for common use. (Unfortunately, traditional zoning and density limits can impede the use of cluster planning.)

A State of California report on *Environmental Impact of Urbanization on the Foothills and Mountainous Lands of California* notes that "the grid pattern of development violates many standards of good urban planning and efficient land use" in mountain projects. "Curvilinear street alignment permits fitting of streets to the terrain...problems of erosion are minimized, and more natural vegetation can be retained."[12] The President's Council on Environmental Quality says, "The simple clustering of houses alone can reduce the amount of air pollution from automobiles by 20 to 30 percent."[13] It also points out that gasoline and energy consumption are likewise reduced.

Curvilinear and cluster development can also be more economical to the developer by reducing the lengths of roads, utility lines, and sewer and water mains. A U.S. Department of Interior publication entitled *Where Not To Build: A Guide for Open Space Planning* notes that using a grid plan, 94 lots would require 12,000 feet of streets and utilities; using a curvilinear plan the same number of lots would require 11,600 feet; and using a cluster plan, just 6,000 feet.[14]

PRECEDENTS

A New York State Department of Health publication, *Planning the Subdivision as Part of the Total Environment,* lists a grid street pattern as an example of "poor planning" and a curvilinear street pattern as an example of "good planning."[15] It shows how, for one sample tract, by switching from a grid to a curvilinear layout on the same parcel of land, the number of lots could be increased slightly (while maintaining the same average size) from 156 to 169; the total length of streets required could be reduced from 5,850 feet to 4,050 feet; and the total cost of basic improvements could be reduced by approximately 30%.

The Costs of Sprawl, a study sponsored by the Council on Environmental Quality and the Department of Housing and Urban Development, compares conventional and cluster development and finds that the latter can reduce the cost of roads by 14% and of utilities by 33%.[16]

2. *Allocate at least 25% of total site acreage (exclusive of roads, paved areas and canals) to natural open space or developed recreation areas.*

RATIONALE

Inadequate open space is a serious problem in many of the nation's urban and suburban areas. The report, *Where Not to Build*, points out that if this problem is to be avoided in new

GUIDELINES 103

and growing communities, open space must be a prime determinant of planning.[17]

Open space, besides its obvious aesthetic and recreational appeal, serves many valuable ecological functions. It provides a habitat for wildlife. Its vegetation buffers noise and serves as a natural air pollution filter, absorbing carbon dioxide and other pollutants and giving out oxygen. Its soils absorb rain and run-off, lessening flooding potential. Preservation of open space is often necessary to preserve natural drainage courses such as arroyos, creeks, and swampy areas, which function as natural water-purification and dispersion systems.

Recommendations vary as to how much acreage in a new residential area should be allocated to open space. In many cases, the location of the project and the characteristics of the land itself can determine the appropriate amount. Areas of critical environmental concern and hazardous areas (fully described later in these guidelines) are unsuitable for building but ideal as open space.

At its Bear Valley Springs subdivision in southern California, Dart Industries has reserved 24% of the site as natural open space. Yet the topography--approximately 66% of the land is extremely steep slopes--indicates that more of the site should have been left undeveloped. Similarly, in its plans for the Myakka Estates subdivision at Port Charlotte, Florida, General Development Corporation allocated 30% of the land to open space. However, county planning surveys indicate that 50% of the land should be designated for conservation, and 5% to 10% for preservation. If the company had followed these environmental constraints, 55% to 60% of Myakka Estates would be natural open space.

In other cases, there can be standard allocations based on acreage or population: for example, 10 acres of parks and 100 acres of natural open space per 1,000 urban population.[18]

PRECEDENTS

Where Not To Build suggests that new development areas should have "10% in parks and recreation, and 10% in other green space and utility and multiple-use space, as a minimum."[19] It notes that Reston, Virginia, acknowledged to be a model of community planning, left 22% open space. Jonathan, Minnesota, a similar new town project, allocated 28%. The Rocky Mountain Center on the Environment recommends that at least 30% of the land in a new subdivision be left as parks or natural open space;[20] and a report to the California Department of Fish and Game suggests that "on large subdivisions within important wildlife habitat areas...the lots should be clustered so that at least 50 percent of the gross area is retained as permanent open space."[21] (The subdivision of an important wildlife habitat might itself be questionable.)

Given these variations, it would seem that at least 25% of a site--and possibly more depending on the land topography and area--should be allocated to parks and open space.

3. Reserve from lot sales and development areas of critical environmental concern, defined as:

    Wetlands (tidal or freshwater)

    Dunes, beaches, and barrier islands

    Water sources (watersheds, aquifer recharge areas)

    Prime agricultural lands (Soil Conservation Service Category 1)

    Habitats of endangered species or unique ecosystems

    Prime historical, archeological, cultural, aesthetic, or recreational resources.

RATIONALE

The subdivision and development of areas of critical environmental concern has already cost individuals, governments, and corporations untold millions. Although the federal government has passed some laws to protect environmentally critical lands, such as the National Coastal Zone Management Act and the Fish and Wildlife Coordination Act, a great deal more needs to be done.

Until the last two decades, all land was "developable." Swamps could be drained, hills and forests leveled, beaches reinforced, rivers diverted. Virtually no land, except that in designated parks and forests, was considered of greater value to society-at-large than to its owner. Recently, however, economists, planners, and natural scientists began to tally the cost of this ethic. They found that certain lands are of significant benefit to society because of their critical role in large ecosystems; that the large-scale subdivision and development of these lands has cost far more than we can afford; that frequently, in the case of subdivisions, future site residents also suffer from the disturbance and inappropriate use of these areas. Those who found themselves in the path of Hurricane Camille, for example, learned the hard way the price of building on Florida's and Alabama's dunes and beaches.

PRECEDENTS: WETLANDS

The values of of wetlands--tidal or freshwater swamps, marshes, submerged grassbeds, etc.--are almost universally acknowledged by scientists, planners, and regulators. (See chapter on Wetlands in

Volume II of this study.) They serve as essential links in the marine food chain, as wildlife habitats, and as flood protection and water purification areas.

The U.S. Department of the Interior stated in regulations adopted under the Fish and Wildlife Coordination Act:

> There exists a national recognition that wetlands and shallow water habitats have such high ecological and social values as to admit of their destruction or degradation only where there is no question that the public interest demands it.[22]

The Florida Coastal Coordinating Council recommends no modification of marine grassbeds except in cases of overriding public interest; and no development of coastal marshes or mangrove swamps which are greater than 40 acres in size. It strongly discourages development of freshwater swamps and marshes. Unfortunately, this recommendation has not been translated into law in Florida.

The Conservation Foundation publication, *Coastal Ecosystems*, includes wetlands and tidelands among vital areas which should be immune from virtually all types of use.[23] Ian McHarg, noted planner, recommends "recreation" as the only appropriate use of marshes.

The Tahoe Regional Planning Agency Land Use Ordinance defines recharge areas and poorly drained wetlands (marshes, streams, floodplains, meadows, and beaches) as "lands that should remain in their natural condition."

New York State has passed both tidal and freshwater wetlands acts designed to "preserve, protect and conserve" these resources. Anyone engaging in virtually any action which might alter or affect a wetland must obtain a state permit before proceeding. Massachusetts, North Carolina, Connecticut, Georgia, Maryland, Delaware, Florida, Washington, and Virginia all have some form of wetland-protection legislation.

Given the positive effects for society of preserving wetlands, and the potential negative effects on the consumer of developing them, wetlands should not be subdivided for residential homesites.

PRECEDENTS: DUNES, BEACHES, BARRIER ISLANDS

Dunes, beaches, and barrier islands, besides having enormous recreational advantages, constitute a valuable buffer zone between man and the sea. As outlined in *Coastal Ecosystems*, beaches absorb flooding, and can take the brunt of hurricanes. Dunes--covered with special forms of vegetation--both hold the shore intact against wind and water erosion and provide a barrier to storm waves which would otherwise go cascading inland. Dune vegetation is extremely strong in the face of wind and sea. However, it is extremely vulnerable to man, losing the ability to maintain itself if the dune is disturbed by being bulldozed, shoveled, ridden over, or even frequently walked upon. Barrier islands--elongated seafront islands formed by ocean currents and waves--also stabilize the shore and absorb flood waters. In addition, they often contain valuable wetlands.[24]

The Conservation Foundation includes all three-dunes, beachfronts, and barrier islands--among the "vital areas" which should be immune from virtually all types of use. It has compiled an inventory of Atlantic and Gulf Coast barrier islands and barrier beaches, and has stated that "without extraordinary engineering efforts, most barrier islands are unsuitable for human habitation." It also reported that the Federal Insurance Administration "'strongly discourages any development of barrier islands because of the significant dangers to life and property from flooding.'"[25]

Florida's Beach and Shore Preservation Act prohibits construction within 50 feet of the mean high water line, a point usually well down on the active and valuable dune portion of the beach. The state's critical beach erosion problems indicate that this setback requirement is inadequate.

The Florida Environmental Land Management Study Report recommends no development be undertaken within 25 feet of the demonstrable dune line or 150 feet from the mean high water line.[26]

The Tahoe Regional Planning Agency Shoreline Ordinance prohibits the construction of housing on the lake shoreline. California's Coastal Zone Commission regulates all development within 1,000 feet of the state's coastline.

New Jersey's Coastal Area Facilities Review Act requires state permits for subdivisions between roads and shorelines. Wisconsin and Minnesota have set minimum state standards for county regulation of shorelands development.

PRECEDENTS: WATER SOURCES

Recognized sources of fresh water supply are also exceedingly valuable to society, whether they are watersheds which drain into reservoirs or areas where aquifers--underground geological formations which carry water--are recharged with new water. The state of California defines both watersheds and aquifer recharge areas as being of statewide "critical concern."[27] Planner Ian McHarg recommends as appropriate uses for aquifer recharge areas, "agriculture, forestry, recreation, industries that do not produce toxic or offensive effluents."[28] (Housing is excluded from this list.)

In July, 1974, Florida designated the Green Swamp an "area of critical state concern." Under the state's Environmental Land and Water Management Act, this subjects the swamp to stringent land-use controls, because of its value as a natural water supply and purification system. Other recognized watershed and groundwater recharge areas should similarly be reserved.

PRECEDENTS: PRIME AGRICULTURAL LANDS

Prime agricultural lands, in a period of rising food prices at home and increasing food shortages worldwide, should be reserved for farming. Ian McHarg states, "Mere market values...do not reflect the long-term value or the irreplaceable nature of these living soils....Excellent soils lost to agriculture for building can finally only be replaced by bringing inferior soils into production." He recommends that, "In principle, U.S.D.A. Category 1 soils should be exempted from development (save by those functions that do not diminish their productive potential."[29] The Rockefeller Task Force on Land Use and Urban Growth includes "unique and highly productive farmland" among its categories of land which should remain free of development.[30] California includes among its lands of "critical concern" for which guidelines to regulate development should be formulated:

- All land which can be rated as Class I or II in the Soil Conservation Service land use capability classifications;

- Land which supports livestock used to produce food and fiber and which has an annual carrying capacity equal to at least one animal unit per acre as defined by the U.S. Department of Agriculture; and

- Land which produces agricultural products whose annual value has been at least $200 per acre for three of the past five years.[31]

Over 30 states have enacted some form of preferential tax assessment for agricultural land in an effort to reduce the economic incentives to sell farms for development.

PRECEDENTS: HABITATS OF ENDANGERED SPECIES, UNIQUE ECOSYSTEMS

Endangered species--whopping cranes, Florida panthers, alligators, et al.--are by and large endangered because of their incompatibility with man and his creations. Society's concern for maintaining these disappearing creatures was indicated by passage of the 1973 National Endangered Species Act. This pledges the United States to "conserve to the extent practicable" species deemed endangered. More than 100 birds, mammals, reptiles, and fish species are currently listed as endangered or threatened by the U.S. Department of the Interior. The Act states as one of its purposes, "To provide a means whereby the ecosystems upon which endangered and threatened species depend may be conserved." It also provides for citizen suits to enjoin any federal agency from permitting any project which would modify the critical habitat of a species so listed. Since modification and/or eradication of its natural habitat is tantamount in most cases to eliminating an animal from an area, subdivision and sale of lots in such areas would not conform with the spirit of the law and might be subject to citizen lawsuits.

The Adirondack Park Agency's Model Local Land Use Controls recommend as a general guideline: "Locate development and other intensive human activities so as to protect the location and habitats of rare and endangered terrestrial wildlife species and allow for the continuing propagation of these species."[33] California has included among its areas of critical concern lands which "support breeding grounds and/or principal concentrations of species declared to be rare and endangered."[34]

Unique ecosystems were listed as "areas of critical environmental concern" during U.S. Senate hearings on the Coastal Zone Management Act. The North Carolina Coastal Zone Management Act of 1973 stipulates that areas containing uniqe or fragile ecosystems which are not capable of withstanding uncontrolled development may be included among "areas of particular public concern." The Tahoe Regional Planning Agency Land Use Ordinance defines areas with "fragile flora and fauna" as "lands that should remain in their natural condition."

PRECEDENTS: PRIME HISTORIC, ARCHEOLOGICAL, RECREATIONAL, AESTHETIC, OR CULTURAL RESOURCES

Finally, certain environments are valuable because they constitute prime historic, archeological, aesthetic, recreational, or cultural resources. These areas, whose identification involves many subtle and qualitative judgments as well as quantitative factors, are perhaps the most difficult to clearly define. Yet they constitute national treasures which may tend to be undervalued in the rush to develop. Such areas may easily be adversely affected by subdivision activity. For example, the Council on Environmental Quality study, *Subdividing Rural America*, reports that subdivisions near or within public parks and forests "create a number of major administrative and environmental problems for public land managers." These problems include interfering with public land acquisition programs by inflating prices, creating solid waste problems, taxing the recreational capacity of the parks, reducing wildlife habitats and migration routes, and increasing fire hazards and traffic loads.[35]

GUIDELINES

California includes among its areas of "critical concern" a site which "has yielded or may be likely to yield information considered by qualified professionals in archeology, history or architecture as important to pre-history or history, or as symbolic of the work of a master craftsman."[36] The U.S. Department of Housing and Urban Development defines sites listed on the *National Register of Historic Places*, compiled by the U.S. Department of the Interior, as worthy of attention.

The Tahoe Regional Planning Agency Subdivision Ordinance requires that subdivisions be planned so as to preserve areas of special natural beauty and important vistas. The Agency's Grading Ordinance prohibits grading, filling, or clearing in any areas with historic or prehistoric ruins or monuments.

Vermont's subdivision permit procedure requires subdividers to show that their projects "will not have an unduly adverse effect on scenic, historic or irreplaceable natural areas."[37]

It should be noted that it is generally possible for the above areas of critical environmental concern to be included within a subdivision's boundaries, so long as such areas are reserved as open space and protected in such a fashion that they can continue to serve their original and most beneficial function.

4. *Reserve from lot sales and development land which is hazardous for building, defined as:*

> *Subject to geological hazards (earthquakes, landslides)*
>
> *Subject to flooding (100-year floodplains, arroyos, other natural drainageways)*
>
> *Having a slope exceeding 25%*

RATIONALE

Certain types of land are unsuitable for housing. Attempts to build on them are often damaging to both the environment and the eventual residents. These lands should therefore either be excluded from subdivision or reserved as open space.

The consequences of developing hazardous areas are serious. They range from the devastation wreaked by the San Francisco earthquake of 1907, a consequence of building on or near a geologically hazardous area, to the many millions of dollars in flood damage caused annually to buildings in the 100-year floodplain.

PRECEDENTS: GEOLOGICAL HAZARD AREAS

While many cities have been built in areas subject to geologic hazards, the consequences for human life and society's resources have by and large been very great. Given recent advances in scientific understanding of the probability of such events, a subdivider making choices today as to where to site a new community should avoid such geological hazard areas.

The California Division of Mines and Geology is mapping, for the entire state, lands subject to earthquake shaking, volcanic eruptions, tidal waves, fault displacement, landslides, subsidence, erosion, and expansive soil. The state includes, among its areas of "critical concern," the areas the Division rated "high severity" for these hazards. These included:

- land which could expect earthquake shaking equivalent to a Modified Mercalli Intensity of IX or X within the next 200 years (plus many lesser earthquakes);*

- areas which have experienced volcanic eruptions, or damage from eruptions, in historic time;

- areas which have experienced recurrent damage from tidal waves in historic time;

- areas traversed by faults known to have moved within the last 200 years;

- areas in which subsidence has occurred;

- areas which have a high incidence of landslides according to the U.S. Geological Survey "Map Showing Relative Amounts of Landslides in California";

- areas which have lost 6.4 or more acre-feet of soil per square mile per year;

- areas mapped as "high" in soil expansiveness by the U.S. Soil Conservation Service.[38]

The Tahoe Regional Planning Agency Subdivision Ordinance prohibits building on lands subject to landslides, avalanches, or earthquakes, unless environmentally sound corrective measures can limit the hazard.

PRECEDENTS: FLOOD-PRONE AREAS

Areas subject to flooding should be reserved from development for similar reasons. Most authorities cite the 100-year floodplain as land which should specifically not be developed.

---

*The Modified Mercalli Scale measures the intensity of an earthquake in terms of actual ground shaking on a scale of I to XII. The other commonly used measure of earthquake severity, the Richter Scale, measures the actual energy of a quake on an open-ended scale. The largest recorded quakes have measured approximately 8.9 on the Richter Scale.

Areas in this floodplain have a one-in-a-hundred or greater chance of being inundated during any given year, or, stated another way, their flooding is expected once in every hundred years.

As planner Ian McHarg and others point out, floodplains often make ideal recreational and open-space areas and should be reserved as such. This would especially hold true for large subdivisions, where broad land-use planning is possible.

The Federal Flood Disaster Protection Act was signed into law on December 31, 1973. It requires all towns in "flood-prone" areas to prohibit development in flood-prone districts or to require that construction be adequately flood-proofed or built above the flood level. Without so doing residents and businesses cannot qualify for mortgages or other loans for construction from banks or the federal government, and for federal flood insurance. It defines flood-prone as lying in the 100-year floodplain. In regulations pursuant to this Act, the Adirondack Park Agency's Model Local Land Use Controls recommend that no buildings and structures in the 100-year floodplain be used for human habitation. Colorado's model subdivision regulations recommend against any building in a 100-year floodway.

The Tahoe Regional Planning Agency Subdivision Ordinance prohibits the construction of buildings in the 100-year floodplain.

PRECEDENTS: EXCESSIVE SLOPES

Steeply sloping land is not only often beautiful, but generally unsuitable for building. It is difficult and expensive to build safely on such land, and the environmental effect of disturbing the existing vegetation and soil may be highly detrimental. Slopes are frequently expressed as a percent: a 10% slope is one which drops 10 feet over a 100-foot horizontal distance. A U.S. Department of Agriculture, Soil Conservation Service *Guide for Reviewing Subdivision Plans in Colorado* points out that certain kinds of vegetation, including "trees, shrubs, grasses and plant cover on very steep slopes," which it defines as a 50% grade, "are almost irreplaceable once they are destroyed."[39] Ian McHarg states that maintaining natural plant cover on steep slopes is central to solving the problems of flood control and erosion. One of his "development principles" is that "Valley walls, and all slopes of 25% or greater should be prohibited to development and should be planted to forest cover."[40]

Steep slopes also present a fire hazard to a potential resident; a fire on a 30% slope will spread four times as fast as it would on the level.[41] Colorado's model subdivision regulations recommend that each lot must have at least half the lot, or half an acre, for which the slope does not exceed 15%.

The Tahoe Regional Planning Agency Land Use Ordinance stringently limits development on steep slopes by restricting the percentage of impervious surface allowed. In an area with a slope of greater than 30%, only 1% of the land may be covered with impervious surfaces (i.e. roofs or paving). For land with slopes of 9% to 30%, the Ordinance limits impervious surface covering to between 5% and 20%, depending on erosion and runoff potential.

INFORM has used McHarg's figure of 25% as a guideline for the upper limit of slope of land which can be subdivided and sold as lots. Steeper land should be reserved as open space.

5. *Avoid major land alteration, i.e.:*

> *Blade roads only in areas scheduled for immediate development;*
>
> *Devegetate only building and road areas;*
>
> *Preserve existing topography.*

RATIONALE

All land alteration activity creates the potential for wind and water erosion. When trees are cut and land is bulldozed, there is nothing to hold the soil in place. Consequent erosion wastes valuable and productive topsoil, pollutes streams and lakes with silt, and can cause serious flooding by clogging drainageways.

At many subdivisions, land alteration activity may be considerable. Roads may be bladed over the entire site as soon as sales commence. In fact, New York's Real Property Law virtually mandates this practice by requiring that there be road access to every lot offered for sale in the state. The subdivider blades the roads and then often leaves them to erode and deteriorate over the years while installment contracts are paid off. In desert grassland subdivisions such as AMREP's Rio Rancho and McCulloch's Pueblo West, bladed roads have seriously aggravated dust storms. In hilly terrain, water-erosion problems are exacerbated if large cuts are made to accommodate roads to steep slopes.

Many studies have commented on the adverse impact of blading roads in subdivisions. A California study states, "Of the activities associated with urban development, the construction of roads has the most serious impact on the soil mantle. Exposure of soil during the construction period can result in sediment production equal to 10 times the normal rate from cultivated lands, 200 times that from grassland, and 2,000 times that from forest land."[42]

GUIDELINES 113

Bladed roads are a particular problem in arid regions. Deserts and grasslands have a fine layer of soil that resists erosion until it is broken by vehicles. When it is broken, however, wind and water erosion create serious dust storms and sedimentation problems. In New Mexico, officials estimate eroding subdivision roads annually create 700 million tons of blowing dust, enough to "cover Albuquerque one foot deep."[43]

PRECEDENTS: BLADE ROADS ONLY IN IMMEDIATE DEVELOPMENT AREA

The U.S. Department of Agriculture, Soil Conservation Service notes:

> Land grading [for roads and other purposes] causes many problems when not performed correctly or when areas are too large. Grading should proceed no further ahead of actual development than is absolutely necessary. Top soil should be replaced to aid revegetation which should be established as soon as possible.[44]

INFORM recommends that road building should be undertaken along with other aspects of phased development (such as installing the water and sewerage systems) no more than two years before a majority of lot purchasers in a section are scheduled to complete their contract payments. At that time roads should be paved.

PRECEDENTS: DEVEGETATE ONLY BUILDING AND ROAD AREAS

Removal of vegetation, except when absolutely necessary to build structures or roads, is similarly to be avoided. The U.S. Department of Agriculture points out that good vegetative cover is the most permanent and effective way to control wind erosion, as it reduces wind speed and prevents the direct wind force from reaching erodible soil particles. The U.S. Environmental Protection Agency states as a principle of controlling water pollution at any construction site, "preserve established vegetation to the maximum extent."[45]

The Florida Coastal Coordinating Council noted that natural vegetation retards runoff and retains soil moisture, prevents shoreline and wind erosion, absorbs excess nutrients, purifies the air, and provides a habitat for birds and animals. It therefore recommends no unnecessary ground clearing, especially in shoreline areas and on slopes. Vegetation of any kind should be left until just before construction is to begin, and only the minimum area required for operations should be disturbed at any one time. Likewise, a California study of subdivision activity states that, "Good construction practices include protecting existing vegetation...and clearing only those areas necessary."[46] The Tahoe Regional Planning Agency Subdivision Ordinance requires the maximum possible preservation of existing natural vegetation and a plan for revegetation. The Agency's Grading Ordinance requires a permit for clearing vegetation over an area exceeding 1,000 square feet.

PRECEDENTS: PRESERVE EXISTING TOPOGRAPHY

Reconfiguration of topography--large-scale grading or cut-and-fill work--is usually undertaken to create level areas for roads or buildings. By its very nature it is a poor environmental practice as it removes topsoil and destroys vegetation. The Adirondack Park Agency's Model Local Land Use Controls state as a general guideline: "Minimize excavation, cuts and fills and site grading by employing to advantage existing topographic features."[47]

The Tahoe Regional Planning Agency Subdivision Ordinance requires subdividers to preserve natural topography by planning for the "minimum feasible amounts of land coverage and the minimum feasible disturbance of soil and site by grading." It prohibits massive grading or land alteration by terracing. It also limits road construction with the requirement that "Road alignment should follow natural terrain and no unnecessary cuts and fills or tree removal should be allowed to create additional lots or building sites."[48]

The Agency's Grading Ordinance requires permits to be obtained prior to altering more than 200 square feet of land if the excavation work to be done is over four feet deep or fill work is over three feet. The Ordinance requires subsurface investigation for cuts or fills over 20 feet high or for fills on slopes greater than 16%. It also requires that all grading, filling, and clearing operations "preserve, match or blend with the natural contours and undulations of the land."[49]

WATER RESOURCE USE

According to the U.S. Geological Survey, "of all land use changes affecting the hydrology of an area, urbanization is by far the most forceful."[50] It alters water use, storm-water drainage and runoff, ground- and surface water quality, and groundwater recharge. These alterations can have disastrous consequences for future subdivision residents. Homeowners at McCulloch's Lake Havasu City, for example, suffered $3 million worth of damage from flash floods in 1974, due to poor planning which disrupted natural drainage patterns.

The adverse consequences of ill-planned subdivisions may also affect society-at-large. As noted above, GAC Corporation's draining of a portion of the Big Cypress Swamp in Florida in order to subdivide the land has contributed to water shortages in the entire region.

The extent of urbanization's effects can be limited and controlled, however, by careful subdivision planning and development. INFORM's guidelines to mitigate the impact of subdivisions on water resources are as follows:

1. *Minimize and prevent water pollution from erosion and runoff, by:*

    Providing a drainage system using adequate natural swales, sediment filters and traps, and retention ponds;

    Creating a buffer zone of at least 100 feet between lots and waterways (including wetlands);

    Replanting disturbed vegetation immediately.

RATIONALE

Subdivision activity potentially both increases the volume of water which will "run off" from the site, and pollutes it with dirt and chemicals. In California, erosion from Dart Industries' Tahoe Donner subdivision so polluted an excellent local trout stream as to ruin the fishing there for several seasons. At nearby Lake Tahoe, according to the Council on Environmental Quality study, *Subdividing Rural America*, 48% of the sediment entering the lake comes from erosion of subdivision roads.[51]

The volume of runoff depends on the percentage of area covered by roofs, streets, and other impervious surfaces; the amount and intensity of rainfall; and the slope of the land, type of soil, and vegetation. The U.S. Geological Service (USGS) estimates that in a subdivision consisting of 6,000- to 15,000-square-foot lots, 40% of the land is covered with impervious surfaces.[52] The California Department of Fish and Game reports that one out of six acres in mountain subdivisions is rendered impervious, and "The impact of 100 acres of nearly impervious surface per square mile of land is sufficient to double or triple the normal peak runoff following a heavy rain storm."[53] Increased peak runoff reduces groundwater recharge and enlarges stream channels to accommodate the flows, thus devegatating the banks and potentially increasing erosion.

The USGS reports that urbanized or developing areas can yield 1,000 to 100,000 tons of sediment per square mile per year compared to 200 to 500 tons from unurbanized basins.[54] This

eroded dirt can cause a public health hazard by transporting bacteria and chemicals into a water supply; may plug channels and drains causing flooding; may alter streams and water bodies; may increase water treatment and street maintenance costs; and may reduce or destroy the ability of receiving water bodies to support fish or plant life because of the water's turbidity.
Besides sediment and silt, urban runoff from streets, pavements, parking lots, lawns, etc. also contains fertilizers and pesticides, leaves and grass cuttings, animal excrement, gasolines and oils. The President's Council on Environmental Quality indicates that "stormwater runoff is a major source of water pollution in urban areas," becoming more important than sewage once basic treatment facilities (85% BOD removal) are built.[55]

In preventing or limiting water pollution from erosion and runoff at subdivisions, a sound goal would be to ensure that the water draining from a subdivision into any water body should be the same in quantity, and at least as good in quality, after development as it was before development. The Conservation Foundation, in *Coastal Ecosystems,* advocates that any development in areas that drain into coastal waters must not significantly change the natural rate of flow, nutrient or salinity regimes, turbidity, temperature, or oxygen concentration of the coastal waters.[56] The U.S. Environmental Protection Agency's predecessor, the Federal Water Pollution Control Administration, published criteria in 1968 generally advocating the same standard.[57]

PRECEDENTS: ADEQUATE DRAINAGE SYSTEM

A well-designed drainage system is of greatest importance in preventing water-quality degradation. Since increasing the amount of impervious surface increases runoff and flood peaks, subdivision drainage systems must accommodate a higher volume than pre-existing natural drainage, and must be designed to capture pollutants as well.

Certain types of structural controls can easily capture mud and sediment. The U.S. Environmental Protection Agency cites the following as "commonly used" methods of controlling water pollution from erosion:

• gravel inlet filters (gravel beds which capture sediment);

• sediment traps (straw bales, sand bags, stones or other materials placed across a stream channel, temporarily detaining running water and allowing sediment to settle);

• sediment basins or impoundments (larger versions of traps in which runoff is diked to create a pond).[58]

The U.S. Soil Conservation Service, the U.S. Geological Survey, the South Florida Regional Planning Council, and the California Resources Agency all recommend roughly the same measures, plus the use of swales (grass-lined drainage ditches) instead of paved gutters or storm sewers. Replacing storm sewers with swales both decreases the rate of flow and permits natural absorption and purification processes to take place.

The Tahoe Regional Planning Agency Subdivision Ordinance requires subdividers to protect and preserve existing natural drainage channels. Drainage systems must not increase off-site erosion and must release water at least as clean as it was before development. The Agency's Grading Ordinance lists as potential erosion control requirements: sedimentation controls (desilting basins), retention and detention areas, multiple discharge points, and physical erosion control devices. It also requires dust-control measures in any area where land is filled or cleared.

PRECEDENTS: BUFFER ZONE

Grasslands, woodlands, and floodplains are natural water purifiers. Preserving these areas as greenbelt buffer zones along streams, wetlands, and other water bodies provides a filter to remove sediments and pollutants from urban runoff. The land reduces the speed of the runoff's flow and absorbs nutrients.

Ian McHarg recommends leaving 200 feet of natural greenbelt along both sides of streams.[59] *Residential Development in the Mountains of Colorado* recommends that developers "incorporate streams in greenbelt corridors of at least 100 feet on each side of the stream."[60] The California Department of Fish and Game also recommends preserving a 100-foot-wide swath on either side of a waterway.[61] The Tahoe Regional Planning Agency Grading Ordinance prohibits grading, filling, and clearing (except for roads and utilities) within a stream buffer zone of unspecified size or in the 100-year floodplain. INFORM has adopted the 100-foot buffer zone between a waterway and subdivision lots as a reasonable minimum guideline.

PRECEDENTS: IMMEDIATE REVEGETATION

Natural vegetation is a primary soil stabilizer. It reduces the eroding impact of wind and water, and its roots hold soils in place. As noted previously, limiting devegetation to an absolute minimum is basic to controlling erosion from disturbed land. Immediate revegetation is equally basic.

The Adirondack Park Agency's Model Local Land Use Controls recommend "seeding [disturbed land] to provide an effective cover crop during the first growing season."[62] The Soil Conservation

Service adds that "areas exposed to erosion for long periods of time before the recommended season of the year for permanently planting them should be protected by an interim or temporary cover. Such protective cover can be established from annual grain crops such as wheat and rye."[63] A California state report recommends that construction be timed to coincide with conditions suitable for rapid reestablishment of vegetation on denuded areas. It suggests "protecting existing vegetation during the construction phase and...the reestablishment of vegetation at the first opportunity on stripped areas."[64]

A U.S. Environmental Protection Agency publication on controlling pollution from construction activities recommends planting fast-growing annual and perennial plants for interim soil stabilization and long-lived perennials for permanent stabilization.[65]

The Tahoe Regional Planning Agency Grading Ordinance requires immediate revegetation and even considers this step of sufficient importance to warrant a revegetation performance bond being posted, to be held until the vegetation has survived for three years.

2. *Minimize and prevent water pollution from sewage by:*

Limiting septic systems to one-acre or larger lots with proven adequate percolation rates, slope, and adequate distances from bedrock, water tables and surface waters;

Providing central sewage treatment with tertiary treatment or secondary treatment and land disposal.

RATIONALE

Sewage is the other major potential source of water pollution from subdivisions. Septic tanks--individual disposal systems--literally dispose of families' sewage in their own backyards. In a septic system, liquid wastes are piped into an underground tank from which they are gradually dispersed into the ground. Septic systems thus depend on the absorption and filtration capacity of the soil to purify sewage. Septic tanks fail if the land is too steep, the water table too high, the layer of soil above bedrock too shallow, or the soils too cemented. In such cases, unabsorbed contaminants, including fecal organisms, "leach" into the groundwater or seep along and through rocks into ground- and surface waters. When hundreds or thousands of septic tanks are constructed on quarter- or half-acre subdivision lots, the potential for pollution problems is vastly increased.

According to *Septic Tanks and the Environment*, a report written for the Illinois Institute for Environmental Quality, an estimated thirteen million septic tanks are in use in the United States, serving approximately fifty million people.

GUIDELINES

As is noted in this report:

> These septic systems are considered by many people to be an acceptable method of sewage disposal in unsewered areas. In contrast, most experienced public health engineers agree that the septic system, in most instances, is an unsuitable waste disposal technique, and that frequently its use results in contamination of soil, groundwater and surface waters, and constitutes a public health hazard....
>
> Even with proper tank design and installation, the effectiveness and acceptability of a septic system depends almost entirely upon the soil characteristics....Pollution of groundwater, leading to contamination of wells, is an almost routine occurrence in areas employing septic systems.
>
> Estimates of the number of septic tanks performing inadequately range up to 50% of those in use today. These malfunctional systems constitute a severe public health hazard and a major source of contamination of the environment.
>
> Septic tanks have been linked for many years to pollution of groundwater and wells, surface soil, and rivers and lakes which lie adjacent to septic tank installations. Outbreaks of typhoid fever, gastro-intestinal infection, infectious hepatitis and infant methemoglobinemia have been traced to malfunctioning septic tank systems, often coupled with improperly sited and constructed private wells. Many public health workers feel that the most critical environmental effect of septic systems is contamination of private wells. In addition, nutrients released from septic systems which drain into surface waters contribute a significant quantity of fertilizer material to these waters, and can promote their rapid eutrophication. The total evidence available, circumstantial and otherwise, indicates that septic systems today exert a significant detrimental effect upon environmental quality.[66]

The U.S. Geological Survey estimates that contaminated water must move through unsaturated soil at least 100 feet in order to be adequately purified; therefore no septic system should be installed closer than 300 feet to a channel or watercourse. But even this minimum setback does not prevent dissolved phosphates, chlorides, and nitrates from degrading stream waters.[67]

The Conservation Foundation comments:

> In a rural setting, with the proper soil and location, septic tanks are a reasonable way of handling wastes and returning them to the earth. However, they contaminate ground waters by seepage of nutrients, bacteria and viruses. As rural areas grow, the subdivision of open space into small acreage plots (1/2 to 5 acres) brings more people, more wastes, and more septic tanks into closer proximity, and the cumulative effects of septic tank drainage fields are uncertain.[68]

Septic tank leaching has contaminated the groundwater underlying much of Long Island, N.Y. The Rockefeller Task Force on Land Use and Urban Growth reports that in a Pennsylvania county with 12,000 subdivided lots, soils in about half the areas are unsuitable for individual sewage systems and some water supplies are already contaminated.[69] In one rural county outside Washington, D.C., 27% of drinking water wells were found to be polluted from septic leaching.[70] The Conservation Foundation reports that septic tanks and related individual underground disposal systems are a major source of pollution of coastal waters when installed along shores.[71]

PRECEDENTS: LIMITATIONS ON SEPTIC TANKS

The best method of preventing water pollution from septic tanks is to utilize central sewage treatment. A University of Colorado study, *Residential Development in the Mountains of Colorado*, states simply that for that area, "Septics should be phased out...because of the minimal treatment accomplished."[72]

According to *Septic Tanks and the Environment*:

> [T]he consistently poor performance of septic tanks in densely populated suburbs, subdivisions and other fringe metropolitan areas indicates that waste disposal alternatives are required to replace the septic tank system in these unsewered areas....
>
> ...

> Most authorities agree that septic systems are
> suitable only for isolated properties or in
> very small subdivisions where the population
> density is strictly limited and where soil
> conditions are suitable for effective absorption....According to one author, septic tanks
> should never be allowed for use in settlements
> with more than one family per acre. Even this
> may be too dense a population if soil and
> groundwater conditions are not ideal....
>
> Individual septic tank systems should always
> be considered a temporary means of sewage
> disposal when installed in subdivisions or
> large developments which are destined to
> become congested communities....
>
> Mississippi will not approve individual residential sewage disposal systems of any type in
> new subdivisions, additions to existing subdivisions, or undeveloped portions of existing
> subdivisions, unless the establishment of a
> community sewage system is economically
> unfeasible....[Louisiana] has resolved that
> every effort should be made by all health
> officials to prevent use of individual sewage
> disposal facilities in land developments
> involving urban size lots, unless it can be
> clearly demonstrated that the individual
> facilities are temporary and will be replaced
> with proper community-type facilities within
> a short period of time.[73]

New York State Department of Environmental Conservation/Department of Health regulations require a community sewage system for subdivisions with over 50 lots; and as noted above, Colorado's model subdivision regulations also recommend that the subdivider be responsible for providing a central sewage system.

The Tahoe Regional Planning Agency Subdivision Ordinance requires subdividers to provide a central sewer system and a commitment from the sanitary sewage authority to provide treatment for the sewage of a built-out development.

Florida allows the use of septic tanks until the density of a subdivision unit reaches 50%. At that time, the developer, or more accurately, the residents, must install a central sewage system.

INFORM has used as a reasonable guideline that a subdivider should always provide central sewage treatment to all lots smaller than one acre. For lots larger than that, central sewage treatment may also be necessary, unless the Soil Conservation Service has determined that the soils have only "slight limitations" for septic tank use, or unless the subdivider has conducted equivalent testing and found that the soils on each lot one acre or larger:

- have adequate percolation rates;
- are a safe distance from bedrock and the highest seasonal groundwater table (definitions of "safe" vary from 4 feet, according to Arizona and the Soil Conservation Service, to 8 feet, according to Colorado, to 13 feet, according to an Arizona Public Health engineer);
- are 300 feet from the nearest body of water or 150 feet from the upper boundary of a floodplain.

Even if these criteria are met, the cumulative effect of many septic systems may eventually degrade ground- or surface water. In such cases, and in subdivisions where septic tanks are allowed as a temporary waste-disposal system, the after-the-fact installation of a central sewage system will be much more costly than would be original installation.

PRECEDENTS: TERTIARY TREATMENT OR LAND DISPOSAL

Central sewage-treatment plants should provide tertiary treatment (biological treatment and nutrient removal) or the equivalent. The latter would consist of secondary (biological) treatment coupled with spray irrigation, evaporation-percolation ponding, or other land disposal of treatment-plant effluent.

Land disposal is clearly favored by most authorities. A California Department of Fish and Game survey reports, "Direct discharge of sewage treatment plant effluent to surface waters should be discouraged because such discharges usually cause noxious slimes and other growths to develop in the stream. Discharge to land is preferable."[74]

In 1971, a California Department of Public Health report found that "the record of performance for mountain area sewage disposal systems...clearly demonstrates that systems which employ land disposal are much more reliable than systems which discharge effluent directly to mountain waters.[75] The Department has had as its goal the elimination of all direct discharge of sewage effluent into mountain streams, lakes, and reservoirs.

The Conservation Foundation *Water Quality Training Institute Kit* reports that while there may be some unknown long-range environmental consequences from land disposal of effluent, the advantages of such disposal argue strongly in its favor. These include the fact that effluent gets the equivalent of advanced treatment and water and chemicals are returned to the environment for reuse. "Where it is feasible, application of wastewater to the land can return the nutrients to the soil as fertilizer, build up the soil's humus content, produce saleable crops, and possibly recharge the local groundwater supply."[76]

The major drawback to land disposal of effluent, the cost of the land, is not as serious in new subdivisions as it is in existing municipalities. According to the Conservation Foundation, 130 acres of well-vegetated land with minimum slopes (3% to 6%) can handle land disposal of the treated sewage of 10,000 people.[77] Likewise, the engineering firm for one of the subdivisions in the INFORM study reported that an 18-hole golf course can absorb one million gallons of water a day, an amount equal to the sewered effluent of a population of 10,000.[78]

Florida's Department of Pollution Control requires all sanitary waste-disposal facilities discharging into state waters to provide advanced waste treatment (tertiary) or alternate effluent disposal (i.e., no direct discharge into water bodies) as deemed necessary and ordered by the Department.

3. *Avoid major alteration of natural drainage systems by:*

   Avoiding major stream channelization or alteration;

   Avoiding major wetland dredging and filling.

RATIONALE

While minor water impoundments are not a significant environmental problem, the major alteration of natural drainage systems by rerouting or damming streams and rivers or dredging and filling natural wetlands has had disastrous consequences for the nation's waters.

Extensive channelization or alteration of stream courses increases the flow of water, raising the flood potential downstream. It also decreases the effectiveness of natural purification processes, leading to deterioration of the quality of receiving waters. For example, after Florida's 102-mile Kissimee River was straightened and shortened, at a cost of $30 million, into a 58-mile canal, it was discovered that the river drained 30,000 to 40,000 acres of marshland that were essential to purifying the water which feeds Lake Okechobee. The lake therefore began to deteriorate, a serious problem since it is the main reservoir for the water supplies of Miami and Palm Beach. This situation finally required that the Kissimee be returned to its original marshy, meandering condition at a cost of $88 million.[79]

The Conservation Foundation describes the best subdivision storm-drainage system as one which most nearly simulates natural drainage. It advocates no alteration of any drainageway by realignment, bulkheading, filling, impounding, or any other process that shortcuts the natural rate or pattern of flow.[80] A statement prepared by Charles Wharton, a biologist at Georgia State University, for Congressional hearings on Dredging, Modification and Channelization of Rivers and Streams in 1971, has documented the adverse impacts of channelization on: wildlife and fish resources, floodplain forest resources, groundwater levels, flood prevention, natural water purification, soil maintenance, and the valuable river and swamp ecosystems.[81] According to the U.S. Geological Survey, severe sedimentation problems occur when natural stream or channel flows are altered by realignment, fill, or construction. The Califronia Department of Fish and Game reports that "realignment and channelization of permanent streams is extremely destructive to fish life and should be avoided."[82]

PRECEDENTS: AVOID ALTERATION OF STREAMS

The Tahoe Regional Planning Agency Subdivision Ordinance prohibits any environmentally damaging alteration of natural streambeds. The Agency's Grading Ordinance prohibits stream alterations unless the work will not substantially change the natural flow or harm the environment.

New York State requires a developer planning any major alteration of a stream, including any dredging, changing of its course, or damming of waters to obtain a permit from the state's Department of Environmental Conservation. In order to receive a permit, the project must not cause "unreasonable, uncontrolled or unnecessary" environmental damage in terms of soil erosion, water pollution, etc.

PRECEDENTS: AVOID DREDGE AND FILL

Dredging and filling, the process by which submerged or frequently flooded wetlands are raised to a level adequate for building, destroys the vital economic, environmental, aesthetic, and recreational resources of tidelands and estuaries described above.

The Conservation Foundation recommends that: "Wetlands and tidelands are not to be filled, drained by ditching, canalized for access, or preempted or altered for other purposes, except when there is no alternative to serve public needs."[83] The U.S. Fish and Wildlife Service has consistently stated that dredging and filling to create waterfront property has had one of the most adverse effects on the nation's valuable estuaries of any of man's activities. New York State has strong laws to protect both tidal and freshwater wetlands. These laws regulate, via a permit system, virtually any activity which directly or indirectly affects wetlands. The Tahoe Regional Planning Agency Shoreline Ordinance prohibits dredging within the water or shore zone of the lake, and limits filling to cases where it is beneficial to existing water quality or shore zone conditions.

Under Section 404 of the 1972 Federal Water Pollution Control Act, the U.S. Army Corps of Engineers may not grant permits for any dredge or fill activity in tidal or inland wetlands adjacent or connected to navigable waters if the dredging and filling would cause substantial ecological harm. In one of the first major decisions under the law, the Corps in 1976, after a five-year controversy, denied the Deltona Corporation a permit to dredge approximately 3,000 acres of productive coastal wetlands at its southwest Florida Marco Island subdivision.

Once again, what is bad for the environment is also bad for the consumer. According to the Corps of Engineers, the only buildings on filled land which are safe from hurricane tide destruction are those on fill 20 feet above sea level. Those at ground level can easily be demolished by a tidal surge.

4. *Use groundwater only up to the environmentally "safe yield," i.e., causing no salt water intrusion, increased mineralization, land subsidence, or long-term depletion of the groundwater.*

RATIONALE

Both in heavily populated Eastern states, where water supplies are subject to ever-increasing demands, and in Western states where the legal rights to surface water were long ago claimed by early landowners, groundwater is a critical resource. Aside from certain "closed" aquifers--underground geological formations in which water was trapped and held eons ago--groundwater is also largely a renewable resource.

Groundwater can be renewed locally from rainfall seeping into the ground. It can also be replenished from water carried underground through an aquifer formation from a distant location. A certain amount of water can thus generally be withdrawn from the ground without reducing the quality or quantity of water available. However, there are problems in determining the amounts of water that are safely available for use.

Many aquifers and water basins have not yet been surveyed. The water supply in others is constantly diminishing as drainage and development alter recharge areas. For example, the water level in wells in some coastal areas of New Jersey has dropped more than 100 feet during the past few decades.[84] Subdividers should not only do hydrological studies on the extent of groundwater resources, but should continuously monitor the impact of their withdrawals on water levels.

Subdivisions in coastal areas can pose special problems. Excessive withdrawals of water from coastal aquifers can result in salt water's moving inland to replace withdrawn freshwater. This has been a particular concern in Florida, where saltwater intrusion has already imperiled freshwater supplies in many coastal counties. A Florida Geological Survey and U.S. Geological Survey leaflet on saltwater intrusion in Broward County reports: "The primary threat to the invaluable freshwater resources of the county is intrusion of salt water into coastal streams and into subsurface water-bearing materials." The salt water has intruded because of the combined effects of drainage canals and "the lowering of freshwater levels near the coast as a result of large withdrawals of ground water [from municipal well fields]."[85]

A final problem is that intensive withdrawals of shallow groundwater can also cause soils to compact and the land to subside. According to the U.S. Geological Survey, the land in the Santa Clara Valley in California has subsided 3 to 8 feet in the last 40 years because of groundwater withdrawals.

According to *The New York Times*, the most dramatic subsidence has been occurring in the San Joaquin Valley in California. Over the last several decades, in some areas, the Valley has subsided nearly 30 feet.[86]

PRECEDENTS

Many planners and government agencies are concerned about subdivisions drawing on groundwater at a rate which would exceed an environmentally "safe yield," defined in the Environmental Impact Statement for the Dart Industries' Bear Valley Springs development as "the quantity of water which may be pumped annually without causing a long term decline in the water table or adversely affecting the ability of the basin to absorb and transmit water."[87] A University of Colorado study, for example, has estimated that in the Front Range area of the state, only one inch per acre--the equivalent of 75 gallons per day--of the annual recharge is available to wells for use. "A density of one person per acre [or one family per four acres] will thus be provided a safe yield from wells."[88] Subdivisions on the Front Range with lots smaller than four acres would ultimately have population densities that would exceed the available subsurface water supply. The study recommends that subdivision regulations ensure the safe yield density.

A New York State Department of Health publication on subdivision planning and the environment recommends that "before surface or groundwater supplies are planned and developed, dependable information must be obtained on the quality and safe yield of the present sources and on any conditions which may affect the yield at some future date."[89]

Florida's Development of Regional Impact application requires an analysis of available surface- and groundwater supplies and the demand of the proposed project on them, in order to determine the project's impact on water resources.

The Southwest Florida Water Management District defines, in delineating areas of "Water Use-Caution," those areas where aggregate water uses "detrimentally exceed or threaten to exceed...or impair, the renewal or replenishment of such waters or any part of them." The District requires a permit for any withdrawal of 100,000 gallons per day (adequate for 1,000 people) in declared basins. It will deny the permit if the withdrawal of water will cause a lowering of surface water levels more than one foot and groundwater table levels more than three feet or will significantly induce saltwater intrusion.[90]

Since it is generally future site residents whose long-term freshwater supply would be most endangered by excessive withdrawals of groundwater and consequent decline of the water table, it is doubly important that a new subdivision use groundwater only up to the environmentally safe yield.

II. SUBDIVISIONS IN DESERT GRASSLANDS

1
The Desert Grassland Environment

The desert grasslands of the American Southwest form a relatively small, but ecologically interesting, vegetative zone. Two factors, topography and climate, determine their nature.

Desert grasslands occur in an area of the United States geographically defined by the Rockies to the east and the Pacific coastal range to the west. Between these parallel chains extends a thousand-mile rain-starved area, sometimes referred to as the Intermontane Region. Topographically, this diverse area is characterized by numerous mountain chains--some with peaks as high as 9,000 feet--rising abruptly off desert floors.[1]

While subregions within this area--such as the "cold" Great Basin desert in the Northwest and the hotter saguaro cactus deserts of Arizona and New Mexico--have their own identifiable character and specific biotic communities, they all share, at their lower elevations, an extremely arid climate. This results principally from a "rain shadow" that is cast over the entire region by the mountain chains to the east and west.* Consequently, the average

---

*Air currents coming off the Pacific Ocean are forced to rise abruptly along the coast by the Cascade and Sierra Nevada Mountains. The increasing altitude cools the air, condensing its moisture and creating rain on the Pacific side of the slopes. As the currents descend the leeward side of the mountains, moving down the interior plateaus of this Intermontane Region, the air becomes warmer, lighter, and drier. When these currents meet the rising warm air from the desert floors, the high dry winds characteristic of arid and semi-arid environments result. Along the region's eastern border, the Rocky Mountains similarly take the moisture from the air currents moving up from the Gulf of Mexico.

rainfall is about ten inches a year.[2] (Some areas receive significantly less and other areas, generally at higher elevations in the mountains, receive considerably more rain.)

Precipitation rates do not solely determine a desert environment. Temperature, evaporation rates, capacity of the soil to retain moisture, and seasonal precipitation patterns are important determinants as well. Nevertheless, precipitation rates do provide a rough point of demarcation. Areas receiving less than ten inches of rain a year exhibit in inverse proportions more and more of the surface characteristics of "true desert" regions. These include the dominance of sparsely distributed "xerophytic" (from the Greek word *xeros* meaning dry) plants, such as cactus, sagebrush, and creosote bush, especially adapted to survive arid conditions; encrusted fragile topsoils and barren rocky terrain; sandy, dry stream channels; and, in certain areas where precipitation is extremely low, wind-blown, rolling sand dunes. Regions where the annual rainfall exceeds ten inches exhibit proportionate increases in vegetative covering. With twenty to forty inches of rain a year, a full ground cover of the herbacious perennial known to the nonspecialist as "grass" can exist without interruption.

In all environments, a combination of climatic and topographical factors encourages the dominance of one form of vegetation over others. The vegetation, in turn, determines the nature of the animal forms dependent on it. Broadly speaking, six principal biotic groupings, called "biomes," cover the earth: desert, grassland, deciduous forest, conifer forest, tundra and tropical. In between these broad ecological units exist numerous intergradations where wildlife and vegetation from adjacent biomes mingle.[3] Desert grasslands, as their name implies, are one such intergradation, or transition zone. They share features of both the desert and the grassland biomes without being fully one or the other. Consequently, one can say that desert grasslands are "the most arid of all the North American grassland regions,"[4] or, conversely, that they are the wettest of the various desert regions.

In regions with an annual precipitation range of ten to forty inches, where the environment is still too arid for forest growth, grasses will predominate over other vegetation forms.[5] The different grass species (over a hundred have been identified) range from the tall and mixed grasses that once blanketed America's prairies and require twenty to forty inches of rain a year, to the shorter grasses characteristic of the more arid Great Plains and Rocky Mountain foothills. Where rainfall drops to below seventeen inches a year, the grass mantle is consequently sparser, resulting in a biotic community which extends from Colorado's mountain plateaus and foothills through parts of Arizona and New Mexico, into western Oklahoma and Texas.[6] These lands contain the country's

THE DESERT ENVIRONMENT 133

most arid prairies, many of which stretch along the upper margins of the Southwest's deserts at elevations of 1,000 to 5,000 feet.[7] The grassland biome as a whole is exceptionally vast geographically, and remarkably diverse in the types of grasses adapted to its range of climatic conditions. The desert grasslands form a relatively small zone within this larger unit.

Desert grasslands, like their prairie relatives to the east, support a highly varied wildlife community which is severely affected by subdivision and development. The principal wildlife group is the herbivores, predominantly rodents such as mice, ground squirrels, and jack rabbits, which find grassland soils and the desert shrubs well suited to their defensive needs. Other herbivores include mule deer, whose populations are declining, and the pronghorn antelope--the swiftest of all North American mammals--which used to exist in the millions and is now seldom sighted at all.

Among the carnivores of the desert grassland are reptiles, birds, and mammals. These animals control the herbivorous rodent population. Dominant reptiles are lizards and snakes. Birds of prey include hawks and owls. Mammals include foxes, raccoons, porcupines, skunks, coyotes, cougar, and bobcats. The threatened jaguar was at one time occasionally sighted among the upper reaches of Arizona's southernmost desert grasslands, but no news of its presence has been reported for many years.

Six of the ten subdivisions examined in this volume are located either on desert grasslands in the Southwest, or on very similar short-grass lands in the Colorado foothills. Horizon's Rio Communities, AMREP's Rio Rancho Estates, and Great Western Cities' Cochiti Lake are located in central New Mexico, among elevated grassland foothills extending from the southern extremity of the Rocky Mountain range. Horizon's Arizona Sunsites and GAC's Rio Rico are located in southeast Arizona, where desert grasslands extend along the elevated rim of the Upper Sonoran Desert. McCulloch's Pueblo West is located at the edge of foothills along Colorado's Rocky Mountains.

In all these areas, a transitional desert-grasslands zone forms a broad belt around the lower slopes of mountain ranges whose presence assures them an annual average of ten to seventeen inches of rain.* A seventh subdivision, McCulloch's Lake Havasu City,

---

*While the desert floor adjacent to a mountain range may receive as little as 4 inches of rain in a year, precipitation at the mountains' summits may amount to 50 inches a year. Accordingly, as C.J. Hylander notes in his study of life zones and wildlife communities: "In many of the southwestern mountains one can travel ecologically a distance of 5000 miles--equivalent to the distance from the Rio Grande to Hudson Bay--while actually traversing only three miles up the mountain side."[9]

averages less than five inches of rain a year. It is located on an edge of the Mohave Desert that juts across the Colorado River into western Arizona.

Though the term "desert grassland" does not suggest a terrain with any particular value in its natural state, the land is a more valuable natural resource than is commonly thought. It in fact includes many millions of acres of range for a significant portion of the country's cattle industry. As so often happens, however, when a new factor--such as man and his livestock--is introduced into an ecologically stable community, desert grasslands are undergoing a significant, and deleterious, alteration.

For over a hundred years, desert grasslands have been evolving into strictly desert environments because of a gradual but persistent invasion of desert vegetation into the ecological niche formerly occupied by grasses. Xerophytes such as the prickly pear cacti, the cane cacti, and various chollas, plus numerous desert shrubs--principally mesquite, but also creosote bush, catclaw, brittlebush, ocotillo and many others--have taken over vast expanses of the Southwest's desert grasslands.[8] These and other undesirable plants such as snake weed and burroweed, which have accompanied the larger shrub invasion, are of no nutritious value to range animals. This desert vegetation is avoided by most herbivores and is easily disseminated by rodents and livestock. As the woody shrubs and xerophytes begin to form an upper story of vegetation, the moisture supply for the existing grass cover is significantly reduced, diminishing the grasses' reproductive ability. The invading vegetation establishes itself with large spaces between individual plants or plant groupings, and the intervening ground cover of grasses slowly disappears. Over time, the increasing dominance of desert vegetation severely affects soil stability. It renders the land more vulnerable to progressive deterioration from the severe climate, and promotes the gradual development of a true desert biome.

Until recently, it was generally assumed that a combination of overgrazing and an increase in climatic aridity was causing the disappearance of previously dominant grasses. A more current theory, espoused by R. R. Humphrey* at the University of Arizona, and others, suggests a third factor. This factor, formerly indigenous

---

*Humphrey documents this persistent evolution by referring to two studies made at an experimental 53,000-acre range located at the base of the Santa Rita Mountains, south of Tucson, near GAC's Rio Rico subdivision. In 1904, more than half the range had been documented as "grass dominant"; by 1954, when he reexamined it, grasses covered only the foothill regions and occupied less than one fifth of the total."[11]

to desert-grassland regions but eliminated by settlement and grazing, is "fire." Humphrey notes that the semi-arid grasslands of the Southwest were never unbroken expanses of grass as were the prairies further east. Being transitional zones, they tolerated limited woody shrubs--along washes or on rocky shallow soil areas-- and small numbers of invading xerophytes from adjacent desert areas.[10] The woody shrubs were much more vulnerable to lethal damage by fire than the perennial grasses. Thus, recurring natural fires may have checked the further incursion of xerophytes on desert grasslands.

Humphrey suggests that the elimination of this one control factor--natural fires--combined with overgrazing and climatic shifts, effectively destroyed the tenuously established demarcation lines between deserts and desert grasslands.[12]

As noted, without ten to twenty inches of rain annually, grasses cannot maintain their dominance over neighboring plant species better adapted to arid conditions. When other factors such as roads and housing developments, as well as the absence of fires, diminish the extent of the absorptive ground cover, normal precipitation patterns cause considerable damage.

Perhaps surprisingly, desert-grassland regions are prone to flooding. They receive much of their moisture in prodigious summer downpours, which can produce up to ten inches of rain within an hour.[13] Although these intense storms (sometimes referred to in southeast Arizona as "the summer monsoons"[14]) are infrequent and short-lived, they strain drainage systems and absorption capacities wherever they occur. An ample grass cover helps immensely to reduce flooding by intercepting much of the rain for its own use. However, even less intense summer storms generally produce more moisture than can be absorbed in the brief storm period. The principal conduits for the remaining water, or "runoff," in desert-grassland areas are "arroyos," dry washes which have been cut through the mountains' foothills and the deserts below. These wide, sandy stream beds suddenly fill with rushing water after intense storms. When they are unable to contain the surge of water flowing down from higher elevations, they overflow, producing the "flash floods" common to southwestern regions.

Another less common type of overflow occurs across alluvial fans* at the base of mountains, or across "the bajadas" (the lower plains), below. These lands flood to shallow depths with waters that have found no specific channel for their course. Such

---

*Alluvial fans, which lie at that juncture where the mountain slopes merge with the desert lowlands, are distinctive geologic ripples, created by wedges of debris and sediment spilled from the mountain peaks. They often have a desert-grassland cover.

"sheet flooding" can cover wide swaths of relatively flat land, often as large as a hundred square miles.[15]

Both flash- and sheet-flooding problems can be severely aggravated by subdivision activity unless proper precautions are taken. By covering the land with roads and houses, development decreases the amount of permeable soil and vegetative cover by 20% to 90%, depending on the pattern and density of development.[16] To prevent severe flooding when runoff increases, the excess must be channeled into retention areas or large waterways which can absorb it. Unfortunately, many of the desert-grassland subdivisions in the INFORM sample have no special provisions for drainage; some even have lots in arroyos and areas prone to sheet flooding.

A related problem aggravated by subdivision development is erosion. Grasses have several special characteristics that protect ground areas subject to extreme wind and rain. The visible portion of the grass is but a small portion of the whole plant. The underground root system may extend as deep as five feet into the soil.[17] Two principal grasses found in semi-arid upland environments, Blue Grama and buffalo grass, have extensive root systems. Buffalo grass roots branch out a few inches below the surface into a fibrous network especially adapted to absorb water quickly from brief storms. These root networks knit the soil into a stable web that resists erosion, a process that is particularly important on the hilly terrain of most desert grasslands. When grasses are removed by road or housing construction, high winds and brief torrential downpours easily strip away valuable topsoil. Increased runoff, from impervious surfaces, attacks the land. An inch of soil that required a hundred years to accumulate can be blown or washed away in a summer afternoon's cloudburst.[18] There ensues a cycle of land degradation wherein the desert grasslands are ineluctably transformed into the dramatic but less "useful" landscape of the Southwest's deserts.

The most serious and far-reaching problem attending man's continued settlement in desert-grassland environments is the proportionate scarcity of water for his various needs. Lack of rain and high runoff rates create a severely limiting factor affecting all forms of life in this region. The residential, agricultural, and recent industrial development occurring throughout the Southwest has already necessitated, and sometimes been the result of, massive and costly water diversion projects. These transport supplemental water from other areas to the large rain-starved sections of the region. Out of their historic struggle with this fundamental limitation, many Southwestern states (including Arizona, New Mexico, and Colorado) have evolved a body of water laws which specify who has the right to exactly how much water. To persons from wetter regions, the "doctrine of prior appropriation," which establishes "senior" or first rights to the use of water, can be a confounding discovery. Outside of the Southwest, the right to use water generally resides in the ownership of riparian lands. Water on or under the land belongs to the landowner for whatever use he chooses. In most Southwestern states, however, an individual (or company, or city) must acquire a legal right to a specified quantity of water for a specified use. Use is defined by one of four categories: domestic, municipal, industrial, or irrigation. Those whose rights were established prior to those of others have first claim to an existing water source.*

The recent purchase of land contiguous to a stream or river does not assure its owner the right to use that water. Nor does a title to land automatically convey the right to use a well. (In Colorado, an underground water source tributary to a river is considered river water even though emanating from a ground source.) In fact, a landowner may or may not find a supply of water to which he can establish (or buy) a right. If he can establish rights, they will be junior to those who preceded him, and senior to those following him.

Several of the desert-grassland subdivisions studied by INFORM, where plat maps were recorded prior to state requirements demanding proof of adequate water, ignored this "water rights" system: They acquired the land, but not the appropriate legal rights to water. Now they may never be able to acquire sufficient rights to supply 100 to 200 gallons of water a day to the thousands of individuals who have purchased lots. Many of these purchasers are from Eastern and Midwestern urban areas where water is still plentiful, and thus would not imagine that their developer cannot provide an adequate water supply.

In order to circumvent the demanding legalities and cost of acquiring rights to surface waters, some of the desert-grassland subdivisions in Arizona and Colorado have tried to use another water source, one which in these states was not subject to strict regulations.† Drilling deep wells hundreds of feet beneath the surface, developers tried to tap into non-tributary, underground water bodies. As a result of various geological formations, vast water bodies,

---

*This question of "prior rights" assumes great significance in areas where existing waters are over-appropriated, such as along the Arkansas River in Colorado. More rights to its water have been recorded than the river can supply. Thus, those with junior (i.e., less prior) rights can find themselves without a water source.

†Colorado, however, passed laws regulating the use of this water source in 1965, and again in 1973.

called aquifers, exist at different levels beneath the earth's surface, and extend across large areas, sometimes the size of a whole state. Certain aquifers are not recharged by surface water flows. The use of their water is analagous to mining an irreplenishable resource. Other aquifers lying closer to the earth's surface, where the soil is permeable, are recharged by rainfall and surface flows. These are vulnerable to pollution from improperly functioning septic systems and contaminated runoff. Underground formations are a principal source of water in much of the Southwest.

Since World War II, the Southwest has needed large amounts of water for farming and urban use. A fully built-out subdivision with 60,000 residents requires approximately 10,000 acre-feet of water a year (3.3 billion gallons based on 150 gallons per person per day) with no industrial use. One square mile of land under irrigation uses twice as much water as the same area subdivided for residential use. If pulled from closed, impermeable aquifers, this water never returns to its original source. Even if it is withdrawn from a rechargeable aquifer, the amount used can exceed the amount returned. There are now numerous instances of recorded declines, or "drawdowns," in aquifer water levels throughout the Southwest. Yet only very recently have states recognized the necessity of monitoring these declines, and no standards yet exist for determining "safe yields." Where aquifer drawdowns already exist, further massive withdrawals will obviously significantly shorten the aquifer's life-span.

There is a further problem in subdivisions using aquifer water. The chemical quality of water from underground formations varies greatly. Some aquifers have high levels of radioactivity and/or minerals. McCulloch's Pueblo West subdivision near Pueblo, Colorado, for example, has sunk nineteen wells into different levels of the underlying aquifer. Only six have produced enough water with a low enough mineral content to be rendered potable through treatment. A developer in a desert-grassland environment who intends to draw from an aquifer cannot assure adequate quality water to lot purchasers without extensive testing prior to lot sales. Nor can he assure adequate quantity, as aquifer yields vary extensively from one depth and location to another.

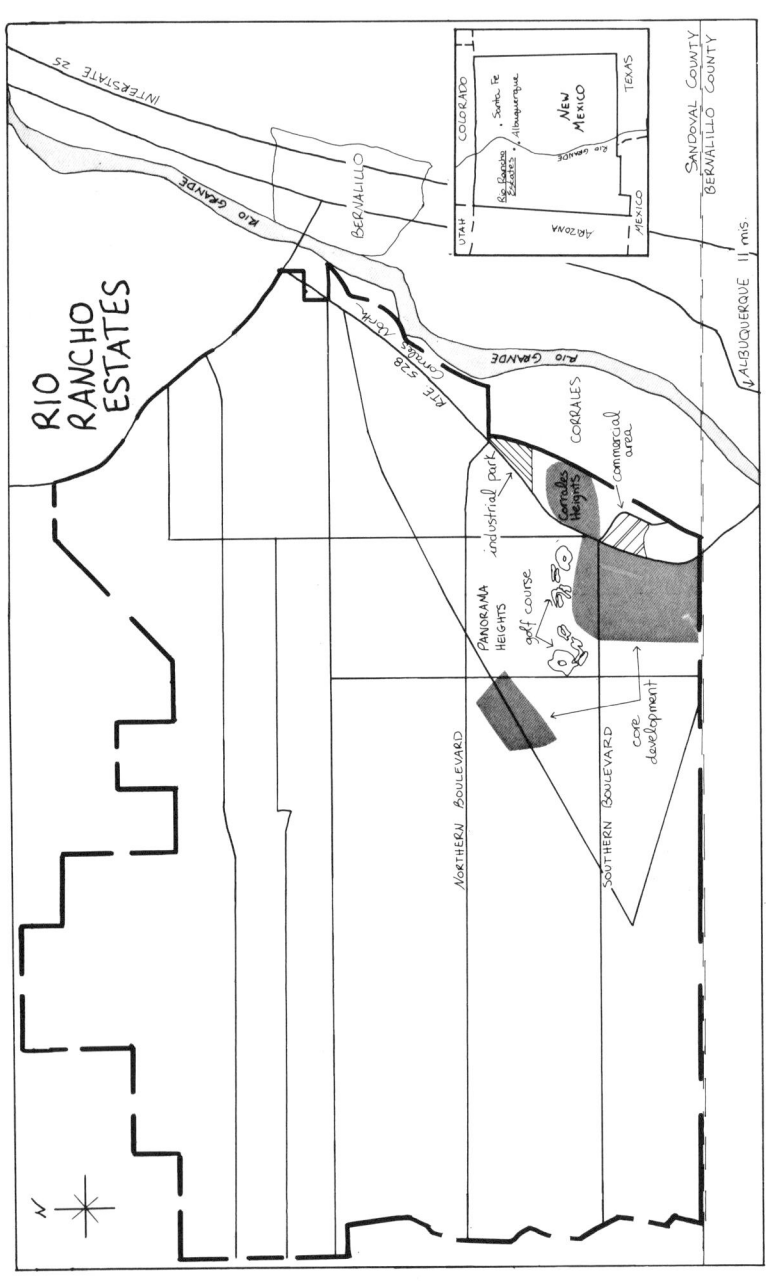

2

Rio Rancho Estates

Rio Rancho Estates is one of the largest subdivisions in New Mexico and one of the most widely marketed in the nation. It's approximately 91,000 acres¹--about 142 square miles--of semi-arid, rolling cattle range are located eleven and a half miles northwest of Albuquerque on the West Mesa of the Rio Grande.* Since 1961, lots at the subdivision have been agressively sold in 37 states using such inducements as free dinners, television advertising, movies and slide shows.² The basic message at the promotional events is the same: leave the crowded city behind. "Come get away" to the spacious West to "a glorious place to live, with dramatic views of the Skyline of Albuquerque... plus distant mountains, mesas and canyons sweeping the horizon for 70 miles in almost every direction."³

Should an unwary consumer buy a lot at Rio Rancho the extent to which he leaves urban amenities behind may come as a shock. Fifteen years after sales began, approximately 98% of the

---

*Both Rio Rancho Estates, Inc. and its parent company, AMREP Corporation refused throughout the course of this study to communicate with INFORM. Rio Rancho is thus one of just three subdivisions--out of a total of nineteen studied by INFORM--for which the company did not verify the accuracy of the facts. Facts may therefore be outdated or inconsistent.

subdivision's 100,000 lots still lack water, sewage-disposal facilities, electricity, or telephones: any improvements, in fact, besides dirt roads.* Further, AMREP Corporation, the development company, provides no guarantees that these services will ever be available. The cost of extending just electricity and telephone lines is over $10,000 per mile: an amount obviously prohibitive to virtually all lot owners.[5]

Both environmental- and consumer-protection practices at Rio Rancho Estates are very poor compared to those at other subdivisions analyzed by INFORM. The site was planned, sold, and developed--although development has been minimal--with virtually no attention paid to the capacities of its land and water resources. This disregard has already resulted in serious flooding and erosion problems, dust storms, and the lack of sufficient water rights for the entire projected population.

For a purchaser who has bought land at Rio Rancho on the basis of its investment potential, the outlook is bad. There is very little possibility of his lot increasing in value, or even being resalable at its purchase price. The site's population growth, a necessary factor in creating value via market demand for lots, has been relatively small. Although over 77,000 lots have been sold, only 5,100 people have moved to the site.[6] This population is three times that of the Horizon Corporation's gargantuan Rio Communities just to the south of Albuquerque (see chapter on Rio Communities) but it is less than 2% of Rio Rancho's ultimate population. At the present average annual rate of population increase, it will be at least 900 years before all 300,000 people have arrived at the site.

Because of the contrast between its development obligations and its sales messages, AMREP has recently become the object of two major legal actions: a Federal Trade Commission (FTC) complaint and an eighty-count federal criminal indictment for fraud.†[7] Both allege that the company used unfair and deceptive practices to sell lots, misrepresenting their value and usefulness as homesites or investments. As a result of the federal indictment, sales of Rio Rancho lots have been suspended in New York since October 28, 1975. The company has denied the charges in both actions.

---

*AMREP's 1975 Status Report on Rio Rancho Estates designates the "immediate building area" (lots supplied with utilities) as Corrales Heights and Panorama Heights. These consist of 1,194 lots and 387 lots respectively. The total of 1,581 improved lots represents less than 2% of the subdivision's 100,000 lots.[4]

†In July, 1976, a superseding indictment was filed in the U.S. District Court, Southern District of New York.

If the FTC complaint is upheld in administrative hearings and the federal appellate courts, AMREP will be required to significantly alter its sales, advertising, and development practices in compliance with the terms of a final cease and desist order. If it is found guilty of the allegations in the indictment, AMREP, two of its subsidiaries, and seven of its officers and directors could be subject to fines and imprisonment. Neither action offers direct relief to the thousands of people who have already bought lots. However, if the FTC is successful in its administrative action, it can file a new civil action in state or federal court to seek refunds for consumers. The process from complaint to restitution will take many years.

Regional Context

Rio Rancho is located in Sandoval County. Despite its proximity to Albuquerque, the County, much of which belongs to the Pueblo and Navaho Indians, is historically poor and undeveloped. AMREP has long advertised Rio Rancho as the natural beneficiary of Albuquerque's growth. Yet, while Albuquerque grew from a city of 201,000 in 1960 to one of 243,000 in 1970,[8] its population is still smaller than that projected for Rio Rancho Estates. In addition, as of 1972, there were eight major subdivisions within thirty-five miles of Albuquerque, all expecting to benefit from its highly touted expansion. Just four of these projects had a total projected population of 600,000.*[9]

AMREP paid an aggregate price of $17.9 million, or $196 per acre for the Rio Rancho site.[10] Its predecessor company, Great Sweet Grass Oils Company (renamed American Realty & Petroleum Company, and later AMREP Corporation), purchased the first 54,000 acres in 1961 for about $178 per acre.[11] According to *The New Mexico Review*, AMREP then offered the land for sale at about $1,495 per acre.[12] By February, 1971, the price was up to $3,070 per acre,[13] and by December, 1974, it had reached $7,000 to $11,400 per acre.[14] Yet nothing had happened to the land outside the core area to change its value, and there was no resale market to warrant the rise in price per acre. In fact, ten years after the original purchase, AMREP was able to buy another 31,000 acres for virtually the same price: $180 per acre.[15]

From its original size of 55,000 acres, planned for 65,000 dwellings, the site has gradually been enlarged by the acquisition of additional parcels of land. Presumably new land was needed to maintain AMREP's inventory of lots to sell. Purchas-

---

*Population projections were not available for the other four.

ers after March, 1969, bought with the impression that the project would eventually consist of 72,500 lots.[16] Those who bought after August, 1969, were told that the project would have approximately 85,000 lots.[17] After February, 1970, the projected figure was given as 93,000 lots.[18] By the end of 1974, there were over 100,000 lots at Rio Rancho Estates.[19] This continuing expansion is a problem for lot buyers who expect that Rio Rancho Estates is, in fact, as AMREP President Howard Friedman characterized it, a "new city....a planned community with its own economy and industry."[20] According to recognized planning concepts, a master-planned development includes a predetermined acreage and grows at a reasonable rate to a pre-established optimum population. Rio Rancho Estates seems to have been conceived with none of these constraints.

THE OFFERING: LAND AND IMPROVEMENTS

LAND

Physical Characteristics

The land at Rio Rancho Estates is characteristic of much of central New Mexico: dry, low-yield, cattle range, about a mile above sea level, criss-crossed with arroyos (deep gullies) formed by flash-flood waters rushing to the Rio Grande. As described in *The New Mexico Review*, Rio Rancho Estates "rises in rolling slopes and low hills between the branching arroyos, giving the tract a spectacularly crumpled appearance when viewed from the air in a low sun angle."[21]

Status of Development

There is a stark distinction between the developed and undeveloped areas of Rio Rancho Estates. The built-up area, with sections known as Corrales Heights and Panorama Heights, is a suburban first-home development of over 5,100 people.[22] In October, 1975, it had 1,806 homes and apartments, 34 miles of paved roads, two elementary schools, an industrial park employing 262 people, a recreation-community center, a medical clinic, and a shopping center.[23]

The undeveloped area, on the other hand, consists of about

RIO RANCHO ESTATES 145

The edge of Rio Rancho's developed "core."

90,000 acres of desert grassland. This acreage has been subdivided, decades and probably centuries before it will be used, into thousands of one-half- and one-acre lots. Defining these lots are more than a thousand miles of bladed dirt roads which are rapidly blowing away in the dry seasons and washing away during summer rains.

As of the end of 1975, about three-quarters--76,916--of the lots marketed since the subdivision's inception were sold or under purchase contract.[24] Yet, assuming three residents to a lot, at the present average annual rate of increase, it will be between 900 and 1,000 years before all lots are actually occupied.

Basic Services

A major focus of both the FTC complaint and the U.S. Attorney's indictment is the implication inherent in AMREP's sales pitch that its lots will be usable as homesites. In fact, AMREP accepts no responsibility and has made no arrangements for providing basic services. It has set aside no money in trust or escrow for the extension of water, sewage disposal, solid-waste disposal, drainage, electricity, gas, or telephone service to any lot or unit outside the core areas of Panorama Heights and Corrales Heights.[25] For owners of land in outlying areas, AMREP's responsibilities end with blading a dirt road and staking a lot to locate its corners. Rio Rancho is among the six subdivisions of the nineteen in the INFORM sample* which guarantees so little in the way of services.

It would be economically difficult, if not impossible, for anyone to live on a lot outside of the core areas. As mentioned, the cost of extending utilities (electricity, water, sewage disposal, and telephone) to outlying lots is prohibitive. Even in the core area, only some lots have paved streets and utilities in place. For others, addition of these basic services can add $1,500 to the cost of a lot.[26]

Although AMREP's lot prices implicitly reflect the value of improved land, the federal indictment alleges that:

> • [the company] had not and [was] not improving with water, utilities, and other customary amenities the "homesite" and "commercial" lots being sold.[27]
>
> • in the overwhelming majority of cases utili-

---

*Includes both the ten subdivisions in Volume I of this study and the nine Florida subdivisions analyzed in Volume II.

ties were many miles away from the lots sold and offered for sale;[28]

- it was not practical or economically feasible for the persons to be defrauded [purchasers] to drill wells for water or to extend utilities to their lots;"[29]

- The [company] was only placing utilities in company-owned building areas [wherein lots] which had utilities were only available by means of the "exchange privilege" to "homesite owners" who were ready to build a home.[30]

If the provisions of the FTC-proposed order were effected, AMREP would have to print on the contracts for all of these lots,

- This completely undeveloped land is being sold "as is." Electricity, water, sewer and telephone service are not planned for this subdivision and may be impossible for you to obtain at a reasonable cost. Your lot will be accessible, if at all, only by unpaved roads which will not be maintained. The use of such roads may be impossible without maintenance. Your lot has virtually no use at present or in the foreseeable future.[31]

AMREP would also have to stop advertising, offering, contracting for, or selling, "any land represented in any manner as being usable now or in the future as a homesite, unless" it promises to make available, within seven years of the date of the sale: a septic tank or central sewage system, central water, and standard electricity and telephone service, all at reasonable extension and hookup fees. Failure to provide these services would require a refund of all payments and 6% interest.[32]

There are no special service districts on the site, nor does the company claim that aid-in-construction extension of utilities, where the lot owner "aids" the utility company, is a reasonable option. (See chapter on Rio Communities.)

AMREP has set aside land for schools, parks, recreation, and other public use, but its only disclosed commitment is that it "may deed [these areas] to a governmental entity or lot owners association."[33] As of December, 1974, AMREP was voluntarily maintaining common facilities without assessing residents and intended to do so at least until August, 1975. It has no obligation to continue doing so, however, and it explicitly assumes that lot owners will form an association "to which they will pay dues sufficient to maintain such common facilities and pay for any other responsibilities assumed by such association."[39] Purchasers must pay taxes on their land. Taxes on land under contract are apportioned at about $10 per year, which the company collects from purchasers and pays to the County.

Water

Throughout much of the arid Southwest, it is water that gives land its value. Without it, no development and no urban growth can occur. In New Mexico, with the exception of water drawn from individual domestic wells, the ownership and use of this resource is a legal right determined by water law and court decisions, and administered by the State Engineer Office.

At Rio Rancho Estates, adequate water is currently supplied to the core development areas via a central system. But the New York State Offering Statement* makes it clear that the company does not promise to provide similar service to the thousands of lots outside the core areas: "The possibility exists that no water service will be available to many of the lots for an indeterminate number of years, until sufficient homes are built to render it economically feasible for the utility to expand the system. No representation or warranty is made that such service will ever be installed or rendered...."[35]

The absence of a central water supply is one of the most serious potential problems for the vast majority of Rio Rancho lot purchasers. Although New Mexico water law allows individuals to drill wells and withdraw up to three acre-feet of water per year (an amount more than adequate for normal household needs),† State Environmental Improvement Agency regu-

---

*New York State requires the development company to issue a report disclosing pertinent consumer information on lots offered for sale.

†Although this amount is considered more than adequate for normal households, prohibiting individual wells in large-scale subdivisions has been debated during several New Mexico legislative sessions. A law to that effect, however, has not yet been passed. In 1973, the State Engineer Office, pursuant to the New Mexico Subdivision Act, recommended that all counties promulgate regulations requiring central community water systems in new subdivisions. Sandoval County was one of the six counties--out of 32--that did not adopt this recommendation.[36]

lations issued in 1973 now prohibit such wells on lots smaller than three-quarters of an acre if septic tanks are to be simultaneously used for sewage disposal.[37] According to the federal criminal indictment, "the overwhelming majority of 'homesite' lots at Rio Rancho Estates are 1/2 acre."[38] The lack of a guaranteed central water (or sewage) system thus renders "the overwhelming majority" of Rio Rancho Estates lots completely useless as homesites until one or the other utility is extended.

There are economic as well as legal obstacles to the use of individual wells. New York Offering Statements for Rio Rancho Estates disclose that private wells must be dug to depths of between 400 feet and 850 feet at a cost of $10 to $18 per foot. This would cost a total of $4,000 to $15,000.[39] The indictment charges that some wells must be drilled to depths of 1,480 feet.[40]

Rio Rancho makes no offer to pay the costs of drilling a well, nor does it reimburse or refund the purchase price to lot owners who cannot dig a well or who dig "dry wells" and cannot find water under their lots. A purchaser's only recourse is to exchange his lot for one in the developed area, an option that is riddled with exceptions and other costs. (See discussion under Consumer Protection.)

AMREP's federal Property Reports are very misleading in their description of water availability. While observing that Rio Rancho lies over the Santa Fe Formation--the acquifer that supplies water to the entire Middle Rio Grande Basin, including Albuquerque--and that "the results of test pumping indicate that an adequate water supply is available for Rio Rancho Estates as a fully developed community,"[41] they make no mention of the following: all the ground and surface water in the acquifer and basin is fully appropriated by other users; the company must purchase the rights to this water and obtain the approval of the New Mexico State Engineer to use it; the water must be delivered via a central system, the extension of which will be prohibitively expensive to most lot owners.

Company advertising perpetuates similar misconceptions. One ad, quoted in the federal indictment, reads "Rio Rancho Estates is blessed with an abundance of soft delicious water--more than enough to fill every community need--which runs through one of the finest water systems in the entire Southwest."[42]

Only in its Consolidated Statement of Record, a multi-volume document on file at the Office of Interstate Land Sales Registration (OILSR) in Washington, D.C., does AMREP disclose that the New Mexico Public Service Commission will not grant it any franchise rights extending beyond the area within which there will be a demand in the near future.

Rio Rancho's central water system is operated by the Albuquerque Utilities Corporation, an AMREP affiliate. The system has six wells and storage facilities for 3.25 million gallons.[43] The water is chlorinated before entering the distribution system and, according to the Environmental Improvement Agency, is of "pretty good quality...about the same as in Albuquerque."[44] The Albuquerque Utilities Corporation has a State Engineer permit which authorized the withdrawal of 3,450 acre-feet of water in 1974. The subdivision actually used 2,526.53 acre-feet in that year.[45] According to its current water diversion schedule, the company's allocation will increase to 6,832 acre-feet by 1982, an amount adequate for 11,360 people at the current per capita use rate.* In 1983, and thereafter, the company's allocation drops to 1,540 acre-feet unless additional water rights are secured.[46] For residents of the core development area, hookup to the central water system costs $250, plus a $15 deposit.

Sewage Disposal

AMREP has arranged for sewage disposal at Rio Rancho Estates in the same manner as for a water supply. Central facilities serving core area lots are good. They provide tertiary treatment for 500,000 gallons of waste per day and were designed for potential expansion to a capacity of 2 million gallons per day.[47] However, since AMREP makes no guarantee that the central sewage system will ever be extended to the rest of the site, most individual homeowners will have to rely on septic tanks or equivalent systems.

Unfortunately for lot owners, septic tanks may no longer be allowed in many areas of the site because of the 1973 state Environmental Improvement Agency regulations. These regulations limit septic tanks to one-half- to three-quarter-acre lots with central water and three-quarter- to one-acre lots with individual wells. If the soils have "severe limitations" for septic tank use, the regulations prohibit individual sewage-disposal systems altogether. (Soil capacity is determined by soil depth to bedrock or water table, slope, percolation rate, and flooding potential.)[48]

AMREP has not conducted percolation tests to determine the suitability of the soils on each lot. The individual lot owner must pay for these tests himself in order to get a septic tank permit. If unsuitable soils are indicated, he will not be permitted to build a home. If a lot is smaller than the state minimum,

---

*The current average per capita use rate, 477 gallons per person per day, is very high. Engineers generally cite 150 gallons per day as an amount adequate for meeting a person's needs in an arid climate.

the owner may apply for a variance. The state has granted such variances, but there is no assurance that it will continue to do so. Finally, the state might require central sewer systems for all or some multi-family or commercial lots.[49]

The estimated cost of a septic system is $500 to $900 depending on the size of the home. The 1974 cost of connection to the main sewer line in Unit 16 was $450 for a lot with an eighty-foot frontage. For larger lots, the owner paid an additional $5.25 per front foot.[50]

Solid Waste

Three private companies collect garbage and trash from the core areas of Rio Rancho and dispose of it at an open dump several miles to the north.[51] There is no solid-waste collection or disposal service outside the core areas.

Roads

In conformance with its policy of providing access to every lot via an unpaved road, AMREP has constructed 1,485 miles of compacted dirt, clay, or caliche roads and, in the core area, 34 miles of paved road.[52] The roads are built to county standards, and have been accepted for maintenance by Sandoval County. At present, however, Rio Rancho Estates maintains the roads. Its road maintenance crew and facilities are larger than those of the County.

According to Paul Sears, author of several articles on Rio Rancho, much of this mileage is presently not being kept up, and road maintenance could eventually become a serious problem for the County.[53] Sandoval County standards do not require any surfacing, and AMREP has indicated no plans for paving the existing dirt roads.

Drainage

Rio Rancho's drainage system was not well planned and has already proved inadequate. AMREP claims, in its disclosure statements, that lots at Rio Rancho Estates do not require corrective drainage work beyond normal grading, side ditching, and culvert installation.[54] The company's only warnings about possible drainage problems are that: "many of the lots are burdened with drainage ditches which cut through various portions of [the lots]" and that "there is a deep and wide arroyo cutting through the property and certain lot owners may have to travel an additional distance around the arroyo to get to a main road."[55] The company has neither made arrangements nor accepted responsibility for constructing any additional drainage system.[56]

AMREP's disclosures may mean little to purchasers unfamiliar with the terrain along the Rio Grande. To New Mexicans, they mean that the site plan was superimposed on the land with little attention paid to important natural drainage features or to the changes in channels and capacities that will accompany urbanization. Although Rio Rancho's former engineer claims that the system will handle the runoff from a 100-year storm, it has already failed to do so.

AMREP indicates in its Statement of Record filed with OILSR that although there is no present need for artificial drains, storm sewers, or flood-control channels, these facilities may be required when large numbers of homes are built.[57] In fact, these facilities proved necessary much sooner than expected. According to the U.S. Department of Agriculture, Soil Conservation Service, as the core development area became built up, it began to experience severe flooding. (See discussion under Environmental Protection.) AMREP tried to rectify the situation by installing some storm sewers. However, this after-the-fact solution was also poorly designed. Discharged runoff from the storm sewers overflows onto property downslope of the subdivision. The owners of this property have filed suit against AMREP, charging that the company's drainage system has damaged their land.[58] As of mid-1976, the suit was still pending.

Rio Rancho's on-site and downslope flooding is clearly a problem of AMREP's own making. According to Paul Sears, when the company platted the land, it consulted neither the Corrales Watershed District nor the parent Central Rio Grande Soil and Water District. The Corrales Watershed District was established to design and construct a drainage system that would protect low-lying areas below the West Mesa from major arroyo flooding. The original plan, designed before AMREP arrived, did not anticipate the increased runoff associated with development.

AMREP interfered with the Corrales District's watershed drainage plan by acquiring some of the land needed for dams and diversion channels and refusing to grant easements for its use unless the District helped it solve on-site flood problems. Site construction and development activities have increased runoff and sedimentation to such an extent that the District's aim is now to get the arroyos at the east end of Rio Rancho Estates' properties to stop dumping water and silt on Corrales.[60]

Any solution to Rio Rancho's drainage problems will prove costly. AMREP is currently trying to join the District to help defray these costs.[61]

Utilities

Electricity, gas, and telephone services are promised only to the Corrales Heights and Panorama Heights core development areas. The Public Service Company of New Mexico, the Southern Union Gas Company, and the Mountain States Telephone Company will extend service beyond these areas only if the number of new buildings makes extension economically advantageous.[62]

The costs to individuals of extending utility lines to outlying lots are excessive: $8,000 to $12,000 per mile for electricity with a possible refund "in whole or in part" over time from revenues received if more people tie into the power line;[63] and $2,112 per mile for telephone service with no refund offered regardless of the number of additional connections made.[64]

Utilities are above ground in Panorama Heights and underground in Corrales Heights. According to the Public Service Company of New Mexico, all future electric lines will be placed underground.[65]

COMMUNITY AND RECREATIONAL FACILITIES

Since the developed area of Rio Rancho Estates is only eleven and a half miles from Albuquerque, residents have access to that city's schools, hospitals, churches, shopping facilities, and transportation. The site itself also has extensive community facilities compared to other subdivisions studied by INFORM. Facilities include a shopping center, four churches, a post office, a motel, two community centers, a private golf course and country club, two elementary schools, a medical clinic, and private doctor and dentist. Six Sandoval County deputy sheriffs (paid by AMREP) and a volunteer fire department protect site residents. There is regular, though infrequent, bus service from Rio Rancho Estates to Albuquerque, leaving from the development's southeast entrance.

ENVIRONMENTAL PROTECTION

From an environmental standpoint, AMREP's planning of Rio Rancho Estates has been extremely poor. This apparently is not due to any ignorance on AMREP's part with regard to the value of sound environmental planning. The following "Pledge," made in the mid-1960's, first appeared in an advertising brochure entitled "Rio Rancho Estates--Your Investment in the Future." It has been reprinted as recently as 1972, appearing in the company's annual report for that year.

THE AMREP PLEDGE
(April 24, 1965)

AMREP Corporation pledges that its community development projects will be so planned and constructed as to preserve the natural beauty of their surroundings.

This pledge is a commitment to transform our properties into balanced communities of homes, schools, churches, commercial centers and industrial parks with a generous balance of greensward and recreation areas, and with permanent safeguards against the blighting of the countryside and the pollution of atmosphere and water which have despoiled so much of the pristine natural splendor of our country.

This pledge is a commitment that all AMREP developments will emerge as communities enriched by the natural beauty of their environment, preserving for our descendants the purity of the sparkling rivers and crystal lakes around us, and of the air and sunshine above." [66]

As far as INFORM could determine from available data, the planning and development of Rio Rancho Estates violates virtually every aspect of this pledge. Perhaps the most serious shortcoming in AMREP's treatment of the environment has been its failure to design an adequate drainage system for Rio Rancho. This failure has already--with less than 2% of the lots occupied*--resulted in arroyo washouts, flooding, and siltation both on the site and downslope in the town of Corrales.

PLANNING

Rio Rancho Estates' physical layout took no cognizance of the natural terrain on which it was to be placed. The development company, in fact, appears to have little interest in more advanced planning concepts. By contrast, Horizon's Rio Communities, also located in central New Mexico's dry, arroyo-crossed cattle range, and also initiated in 1961, has, at least in those areas mapped in recent years, tried to fit its roads, lots, and open space to the natural terrain.

---

*As noted earlier, there are approximately 1,800 dwelling units and 100,000 lots.

AMREP has simply superimposed predetermined grids over rolling hills and branching arroyos. In the words of Paul Sears, author of many articles on New Mexico's vast subdivisions,

> AMREP's main roads run straight across the countryside, up and down hills, over slopes and down into and across arroyos, in total and callous disregard for the character of the landscape as it might relate to future development. Where the main roads encounter... easements [railroad rights of way, gas pipelines, and electric transmission lines], and where residential streets encounter major arroyos, they angle abruptly and then continue as straight lines beyond these obstacles. The result is a vast gridwork, interrupted by crazy quilt patches of angled streets.[67]

Sears criticized AMREP's approach to open-space planning on the same grounds. "AMREP locates parks, not where they are needed to serve neighborhood areas, but wherever AMREP has land it can't market."[68] Thus, instead of well-conceived parks and open space, Rio Rancho has reserved for such purposes: the major arroyos; the 10% or 15% of the land that is too rough to use for building sites; and small irregular parcels of land left over after units have been subdivided into the requisite number of one-half- and one-acre lots.[69]

The company would not disclose and INFORM could not determine how much of the site is actually allocated to open space. It was not clear whether all the miscellaneous pieces of open land together total the overall 25% recommended by most planners. (See Environmental Guidelines.)

Only within the core area, where utilities are extended as needed, does AMREP employ even a semblance of phased development. In the remaining 98% of the site there are no planned completion dates for any basic services other than dirt roads, and these are bladed everywhere, regardless of whether they will be used. This alteration of the land has caused serious sandstorms and gullying. Lots are sold with the same disregard. AMREP was not required to, and thus did not, prepare an Environmental Impact Report for use in planning the subdivision.

LAND

Environmentally, the Rio Rancho site is appropriate for a certain amount of residential development. It contains no valuable water-related resources (estuaries, wetlands, etc.), no habitats of endangered species, and no prime agricultural lands. It does, however, have areas that, because of natural hazards, are unsuitable for building. AMREP has largely ignored these constraints by subdividing and selling land in arroyos and other flood-prone areas. The site, like the rest of the Middle Rio Grande Valley, is also subject to moderate earthquakes. The impact of this hazard can be lessened by special building techniques.

Flooding and Erosion

Flooding is a serious threat in arid regions where sudden summer thunderstorms can drop much more rain than the soils can immediately absorb. Excess waters flow downhill in the arroyos and gullies toward the nearest body of water. In the Albuquerque area, during peak summer floods, the major arroyos draining into the Rio Grande can temporarily carry more water than the river itself.

Under natural conditions, with topsoil and vegetation to absorb and slow this runoff, the arroyos are usually adequate to carry the water. If floods occur, nothing much is damaged. With development, however, water courses change and impermeable surfaces--compacted clay or dirt roads, paving, roofs, etc.,--replace vegetation and topsoil. This causes the amount, speed, and direction of runoff to increase. Such increased flows, although they last but a short time, can be more than the arroyos can handle. As a consequence, water overflows or washes out arroyo banks, often flooding formerly safe areas.

Rio Rancho Estates lies on a mesa west of the Rio Grande. The land slopes down to the river at a rate of about 500 feet per mile (10% slope).[70] It is criss-crossed with minor arroyos that feed into several major arroyos.

AMREP has platted and sold lots on land subject to overflow and flooding from both major and minor arroyos. As indicated in its disclosure statements, the company has sold lots with arroyos running right through them. In addition, AMREP's practice of stripping the topsoil from hundreds of miles of roads and hundreds of acres of building sites to reach the impenetrable hard caliche sublayer has had the predictable effects of increasing runoff and erosion and altering flow patterns. This has in turn added to the danger of flood in Corrales. AMREP's systems to carry surface runoff from the developed areas of Units 11 and 16 are badly de-

Erosion damage at Rio Rancho.

signed and do not follow natural drainage patterns. Culverts are clogged, and, from the beginning, both units have experienced runoff and siltation problems.[71] According to the New Mexico Environmental Improvement Agency, there are no sediment traps or siltation basins to help prevent these problems.[72]

In August, 1975, the subdivision and adjacent properties suffered the consequences of AMREP's poor drainage plans. Several thunderstorms caused severe flooding, power failures, and arroyo washouts in Rio Rancho Estates and the neighboring community of Corrales. Surface water washed hundreds of cubic yards of silt down from the top of the Rio Rancho mesa to the town downslope. The silt clogged and then collapsed a major culvert, creating a dam which diverted the floodwaters to streets, yards, and homes.[73]

Years before this dramatic event, in an article published in *The New Mexico Review*, Paul Sears had already charged AMREP with consistently failing to take important flood-control precautions that would have prevented serious drainage and flooding problems both on site and downslope.[74] Sears reported that AMREP did not take into account the inability of the arroyos to contain the increased flows that result from development, that it failed to consider the effect of its construction activities on areas downslope from its mesa, and that it had not recognized the need for undeveloped overflow lands or water-retention areas.[75] As mentioned earlier, the company is now belatedly trying to join the Corrales Watershed District, hoping for its help in solving Rio Rancho's problems.

WATER RESOURCES

As there are no water bodies on site except for an artificial lake at the golf course, there is little potential for the degradation of surface water quality.

A small 500,000 gallon-per-day sewage-treatment plant serves the core section of Rio Rancho Estates. According to the state Environmental Improvement Agency, it is one of the best in New Mexico.[76] This plant employs an activated sludge process followed by sand filtration and treatment with a disinfectant. The treated effluent is disposed of via spray irrigation and leaching from a holding pond. No sewage effluent is directly discharged into a water body.

The rest of the site, however, is designated for septic-tank use, a plan which threatens degradation of groundwater quality. Unlike that in coastal states, most land in New Mexico does not have obvious limitations on the use of such systems: the water table is deep; soils generally sandy and pervious. In 1962, and again in 1971, the New Mexico Department of Health rendered the opinion that the Rio Rancho Estates site was generally satisfactory for individual sewage-disposal systems constructed in accordance with the standards it had established.[77] Nevertheless, the Department did elaborate on some problems that might limit septic-tank use. These included the presence in some places of impervious layers six to eight feet below the surface, and in one area, a surface layer containing eight feet of red clay that would necessitate using seepage pits instead of tile leaching fields. The Department's letter of opinion recommended that leaching pits be kept shallow, "otherwise the combination of many individual sewage disposal systems and individual wells can result in contamination of the water supply. This could cause difficulty in the entire subdivision."[78]

The Department's opinion, generally approving the use of individual sewage systems in such numbers and over such a large area, seems to have been both premature and unwise. It was based on data from five holes drilled somewhere on the original 55,000-acre site,[79] and it was rendered before the Soil Conservation Service had done detailed studies of soil and drainage conditions. As has been discussed, in 1973, the state Environmental Improvement Agency issued much stricter subdivision regulations. These limit septic tanks to one-half- to three-quarter-acre lots with central water and three-quarter- to one-acre lots with individual wells. If soils are found to have "severe limitations," septic tanks are prohibited altogether.[80] These regulations make it highly unlikely that the more than 100,000 septic tanks planned for Rio Rancho Estates will all receive the permits required for construction. However, tens of thousands of such systems could still be installed if a central water system were extended.

The ultimate impact of Rio Rancho Estates' water use on groundwater in the Rio Grande Basin has not been determined. In New Mexico, the granting of a State Engineer's well permit is contingent upon the user's demonstrating that he will not impair the existing water supply. AMREP has submitted hydrological studies for each new well at Rio Rancho. The State Engineer has verified the company's claims with its own investigations and has granted the additional permits.[81] However, while the central system's water use is monitored and regulated by the State Engineer Office, the hundreds of individual wells planned for the property fall outside its jurisdiction. Their impact on the groundwater is thus indeterminable.

CONSUMER PROTECTION

AMREP's consumer practices are poor, conforming to only one of INFORM's twelve Sales Guidelines. (Dart Industries, by contrast, follows eight.) The company's policies have prompted two federal legal actions charging fraud and misrepresentation. AMREP was also the only company in this study consistently to refuse any communication with INFORM.

Sales

According to the New York Offering Statement, as of December 24, 1974, basic prices for half-acre undeveloped single-family lots at Rio Rancho Estates ranged from $3,500 to $5,700 excluding interest.[82] As might be expected, single-family lots in the developed areas, not available on the installment basis, cost more: prices started at $6,450.[83] Commercial and multiple dwelling lots were priced from $3,150 all the way to $196,550![84] Again, this extremely high (the highest anywhere in the INFORM sample) upper limit was for lots in the developed area. Elsewhere the maximum was about $25,000. Contracts averaged seven years with 5.7% to 8.5% interest. The minimum downpayment required was 10%.[85]

AMREP would not disclose to INFORM any information about its sales practices and policies. However, based on the allegations in the criminal indictment and the Federal Trade Commissions complaint, AMREP does not attempt to protect purchasers from high pressure salesmen or to discourage speculation. In fact, both legal actions allege the opposite: that the intent of its sales practices is to misrepresent, conceal, and defraud.[86]

AMREP does not investigate a purchaser's credit standing, it sets no limit on the number or type of lots an individual may buy on the installment basis,[87] and it makes no attempt to encourage outside review of sales documents by an attorney or professional realtor.[88]

An INFORM researcher who attended an AMREP sales dinner in the fall of 1973 confirmed that high-pressure sales tactics and exaggerated claims were employed to sell lots. When the researcher finished consuming her veal parmigiana and tried to leave, the salesman assigned to the table at which she was sitting repeatedly urged her to sign a contract on the spot and even went so far as to assure her that the skiing in the nearby Sandia Mountains, one of the subdivision's selling points, was available "all year round."[89] The New Mexico tourist bureau suggested that perhaps the AMREP salesmen meant water skiing, since the snow-skiing season extends only from November to April.[90]

Refunds

In accordance with OILSR regulations, AMREP offers purchasers 72 hours after reviewing a Property Report in which to cancel a contract and receive a refund of all money paid. After this period, if a purchaser defaults on a contract, AMREP retains all payments. The FTC-proposed order recommends a ten-business-day rescission period and the inclusion of a cancellation form with every contract.[91] INFORM, following the California precedent, recommends a fourteen-day rescission period.

The FTC complaint characterized as unfair the company's practice of retaining all payments when purchasers default.[92] Under similar circumstances, the Commission required GAC Corporation, in a final order issued in March, 1974, to refund to past purchasers any excess over the cost of real damages and to retain only partial payments from future defaulting purchasers.[93]

In accordance with New Mexico law, AMREP gives purchasers six months in which to take a company-guided tour of the site and to request a refund if dissatisfied. This provision would seem to give a dissatisfied customer an "out." But the FTC alleges that it is unfair because the company "actually uses these tours to sell purchasers more land and to discourage such purchasers from exercising their cancellation privilege."[94] The only other conditions on which AMREP will refund a purchaser's payments are: if the company cannot convey free and clear title; if Shell Oil Company enforces its oil and gas rights and damages the lot; or if a purchaser wishes to exchange his lot for a developed lot and no developed lots are available.[95]

According to the FTC-proposed order, in the event that all promised improvements (i.e., a dirt road and staked corners) were not completed within six months of the date specified on the contract,[96] AMREP would be required to refund all purchaser payments plus 6% interest compounded annually or offer a lot of equal price and size for exchange. It would also, as mentioned earlier, prohibit the company from advertising or selling as a homesite, any land not guaranteed central water, sewage disposal, standard electricity, and telephone service at a reasonable cost.[97]

Title Protection

What a purchaser receives on the installment contract at Rio Rancho estates is not a fully protected right to title. Lots are platted with Sandoval County and contracts are recordable, but AMREP does not record the contract for the purchaser.[98] Thus, the most minimal protection--notifying the county clerk that someone has a financial interest in the land--does not exist. If the purchaser does not record his lot himself and AMREP or Rio Rancho Estates, Inc., should go bankrupt, the purchaser "would become a general creditor of the [company] and could lose part or all of his investment."[99] Without this protection, liens recorded subsequent to the date of the contract could have a prior right to the land as could any subsequent purchasers or creditors of anyone with an interest in the land.[100]

AMREP does not put purchaser's payments or title to the lot in trust or escrow. All funds go into the company's general account. The result is that there is no guarantee that sufficient funds will be available to fulfill even AMREP's meager obligations or promises.

As of December, 1974, AMREP owned fee title to at least the 86,000 Rio Rancho lots it was then marketing in New York State. Other parts of the property, Units 20 through 26, were encumbered by "purchase money deeds of trust" held by the First National Bank of Albuquerque. These mortgages have clauses releasing lots to individual purchasers upon full payment of their contracts.[101]

Certain "exceptions to the deed"--restrictions, easements, and reservations--may apply to property purchased at Rio Rancho. Previous owners or independent companies may have rights to the minerals, oil, and gas under a particular lot. Utility companies may have reserved part of a lot as an easement for pipelines or wires. As required by law, AMREP discloses in the federal Property Reports the easements and reservations affecting portions of the site. It does not, however, indicate the specific lots to which they apply. Unless a purchaser checks the records in the Office of the County Clerk of Sandoval County, he will not know what restrictions, if any, affect his lot.*

Costs

At many of the subdivisions in this study lot purchasers must make substantial additional payments to property-owners associations and various special service districts. While still paying for their lots on the installment plan, they must also pay property taxes to the counties in which their land is located. These purchasers, buying lots at "improved prices," pay once for improvements in the basic lot sales price and again in service-district assessments. (See chapters on Pueblo West and Colorado City.) At Rio Rancho, however, this is not the case. There are no special service districts, and the only annual assessment is a property tax averaging $10 per year. Lot purchasers thus pay only once for an "improved lot." Of course, they receive none of the basic services such as central water, central sewage, drainage and roads that constitute the "improvements" implicit in the inflated basic lot price. Because the developer takes no responsibility for either providing basic services or establishing community mechanisms for their provision, lot owners must eventually face this financial burden themselves.

---

*New York Offering Statements do disclose which mortgages, restrictions, and reservations apply to which lots, so that a careful New Yorker does have the information he needs in this regard.

As originally planned by AMREP, a lot owner choosing to inhabit an outlying lot would have to pay, in addition to the $3,500 to $5,700 he pays for the undeveloped land, $4,000 to $15,000 for a well and pump, and $500 to $900 for a septic tank. If he wished to have electricity and telephone service as well, lines could be extended at a cost of $12,000 and $2,110 a mile, respectively.[102] Since the state of New Mexico now prohibits wells and septics together on half-acre lots, a lot owner might have to pay to have central water or sewer lines extended to his lot. Judging from the costs at other subdivisions, this could add from several thousand to several hundred thousand dollars to the owner's expenses.

It is clear that the cost of moving into most of the lots at Rio Rancho is prohibitive. Virtually the only option open to the owner of an outlying lot is to attempt to resell or to exchange it for one in the developed core area.

Resales

AMREP's policy of continuing to acquire land to expand its inventory of lots virtually eliminates the possibility of resale on the open market. In fact, the market for Rio Rancho Estates lots is so depressed that at a recent, highly touted auction held in August, 1975, by a private entrepreneur (Rocky Mountain Land Auction Co.), only 60 of the 300 lots listed were sold. Prices ranged from $800 to $1,500 for a half-acre lot, considerably lower than AMREP's current prices. Most of the lots were sold to builders who planned to exchange them for lots in the developed area where they would then construct houses.[103]

Most lot owners are not even this lucky in finding buyers for their lots. The Better Business Bureau of New Mexico summarized the resale problem at Rio Rancho in a letter to INFORM:

> The major problem [with Rio Rancho] and the one few people take into consideration,...is resale. The vast majority of real estate firms in Albuquerque will not list this land because of the distance involved and the lack of a resale market. Resale is virtually impossible.[104]

The New York Offering Statement officially warns purchasers that:

> Lots may also be purchased for speculative purposes but such purchasers are warned [that] resale for a profit may be difficult for a number of years in view of the fact that water and utilities may not be available to certain

> lots for an indefinite number of years; that a percentage of the purchase price paid is...for use in advertising and development; and that in trying to make a resale, the purchaser may be competing with the company which has thousands of lots to sell.[105]

The FTC complaint and the federal indictment both charged AMREP with false advertising and promotional claims misrepresenting the resalability of Rio Rancho Estates lots. The indictment added that

> ...there had been virtually no resale market for these lots throughout the entire fourteen-year history of this scheme and artifice to defraud; [and] that most purchasers wishing to resell their lots would not be able to sell them at all....[106]

Exchanges

Given that the vast majority of lots are neither usable nor negotiable, the only option open to many consumers is an exchange. AMREP offers purchasers the right to exchange one unimproved lot for another of equal value in a unit where utilities are available. The right of exchange extends for only five years after the date of the contract signing.[107] There are also a great many limitations to this exchange "privilege." Purchasers can only exchange "a single residential lot for one residential building lot of comparable value." In practice, this means a smaller lot. They must retain any undeveloped acreage in excess of one-half acre and they must agree to immediately build a home on the property they receive.[108] Furthermore, owners of commercial or multi-family lots are not eligible for this option at all. The Federal Trade Commission proposed that AMREP preface this exchange offer with the statement:

> A SUBSTANTIAL NUMBER OF PURCHASERS WHO EXCHANGE FOR BUILDING LOTS OBTAIN A SMALLER PARCEL OF LAND IN EXCHANGE FOR THE VACANT LOT, AND ALSO PAY A SUBSTANTIAL AMOUNT OF MONEY FOR THE EXCHANGE. IT IS THE COMPANY'S POLICY TO ENCOURAGE SUCH UNEVEN EXCHANGES.[109]

As of June, 1974, there were only 1,200 unsold residential lots that were improved with a water system and utilities.[110]

Legal Status

As noted earlier, both a Federal Trade Commission Complaint and a federal criminal indictment filed with the U.S. District Court, Southern District of New York are pending against AMREP as a result of its practices at Rio Rancho. The FTC held hearings in the sumer of 1976. The U.S. Attorney's suit is scheduled to go to trial in the fall of 1976. Neither action will give any redress to the tens of thousands of people who have already bought lots at the subdivision, nor will they require the company to pay refunds to past purchasers. Should the government win, however, the company would have to substantially reform its sales and development practices.

---

*The FTC held hearings in the summer of 1976. The U.S. Attorney's suit is scheduled to go to trial in the fall of that same year.

ENVIRONMENTAL CHECKLIST

<u>Overall environmental protection record:</u> POOR

Does the subdivider:

PLANS	Plan for complete basic services?	NO
	Phase lot sales and extension of services?	NO
	Get 80% build-out in 10 years of each section marketed?	NO
	Prepare an Environmental Impact Report?	NO
LAND	Use a curvilinear or cluster design?	NO
	Retain 25% or more open space?	?
	Reserve from lot sale and development the following areas of critical concern:	
	wetlands?	--
	dunes and beaches?	--
	water sources?	--
	prime agricultural lands?	--
	habitats of endangered species?	--
	prime historical, archaeological, cultural, aesthetic, or recreational resources?	--
	Reserve from lot sale and development the following areas hazardous for building:	
	geological hazard areas (earthquake, landslide)?	--
	flood-prone areas (100-year floodplains, arroyos)?	NO
	areas of slope exceeding 25%?	?
	Blade roads only in immediate development areas?	NO
	Clear only for buildings and roads?	YES
	Preserve existing topography?	YES
WATER RESOURCES	Design the drainage system to control erosion?	NO
	Retain 100-foot buffer zone around water bodies?	--
	Replant disturbed land immediately?	NO
	Limit septic systems to one-acre or larger lots with adequate: percolation rates, slope, and distance from bedrock, water table and surface waters?	NO
	When utilizing central sewage disposal, provide tertiary treatment (or secondary and land disposal)?	YES
	Avoid major stream alteration?	--
	Avoid major wetland dredging and filling?	--
	Use groundwater only up to the safe yield?	?

NOTE: See chapter on "Guidelines" for more complete explanation of items on Checklist.

RIO RANCHO ESTATES 167

CONSUMER CHECKLIST

Overall consumer protection record: POOR

Does the subdivider:

SALES	Conduct a credit check on lot purchasers?	NO
	Limit lot sales to two per purchaser?	NO
	Sell only residential, i.e., no industrial, commercial or multi-family lots on installment contracts?	NO
	Require a cash downpayment of 20% on all sales?	NO
	Limit duration of installment contracts to 5 years?	NO
	Charge no interest on installment contracts?	NO
	Encourage attorney review of sales documents?	NO
	Require a pre-purchase site visit?	NO
	Allow a 14-day rescission period in which purchaser can obtain a refund for any reason?	NO
	Offer a partial refund if purchaser defaults?	NO
	Guarantee a refund, with interest, if promised services are not made available by date specified in contract?	NO
	Escrow contract payments, or provide equivalent surety bonding, for refund purposes?	NO
TITLE	Offer only platted lots?	YES
	Offer a recordable contract, and record the sale?	NO
	Offer unmortgaged land, or land mortgaged with a release clause, only?	YES
	Upon contract signing, deed title to purchaser, or place title in trust?	NO
BASIC SERVICES	Guarantee, or have available, to each lot:	
	central water, of adequate quantity and quality?	NO
	central sewage disposal, as necessary?	NO
	drainage system, adequate for 100-year storm?	NO
	solid waste disposal, via adequate method?	NO
	roads, paved, to county standards?	NO
	electricity and telephone?	NO
	Guarantee completion through escrowing or surety bonding?	NO
	If services are financed through special service district bonds, employ them only if:	
	initial governing body includes a county official?	--
	elections include all landowners on one-man, one-vote basis?	--
	sum of bonds is less than twice the developer's investment in basic services?	--
	sum of bonds is less than 15% of the assessed value of land in the district?	--
	developer co-signs all bonds?	--

COST OF LOTS BOUGHT ON THE INSTALLMENT PLAN

LOT PRICE

basic price (½ - 1 acre)*		$3,150 - $25,000
finance charge (5.75% - 8%)		$709 - $8,035
	Total	$3,859 - $33,035

ADDITIONAL ANNUAL ASSESSMENTS DURING TERM OF CONTRACT

improvement association		0
special service district		0
property taxes		$10
	Total, per year	$10
	Total, 8 years	$80

ONE-TIME COSTS FOR SERVICES

lot survey		0
water		? - $26,640
well	$4,000 - $26,640	
central extension	N/A	
central hook-up	$250	
sewage		$500 - $900
septic system	$500 - $900	
central extension	N/A	
central hook-up	$450	
electricity ($8,448 - $12,000/mile)		$8,000 - $120,000
telephone ($2,112/mile)		$2,000 - $20,000

*Includes industrial, commercial, and multi-family lots.

170 PROMISED LANDS

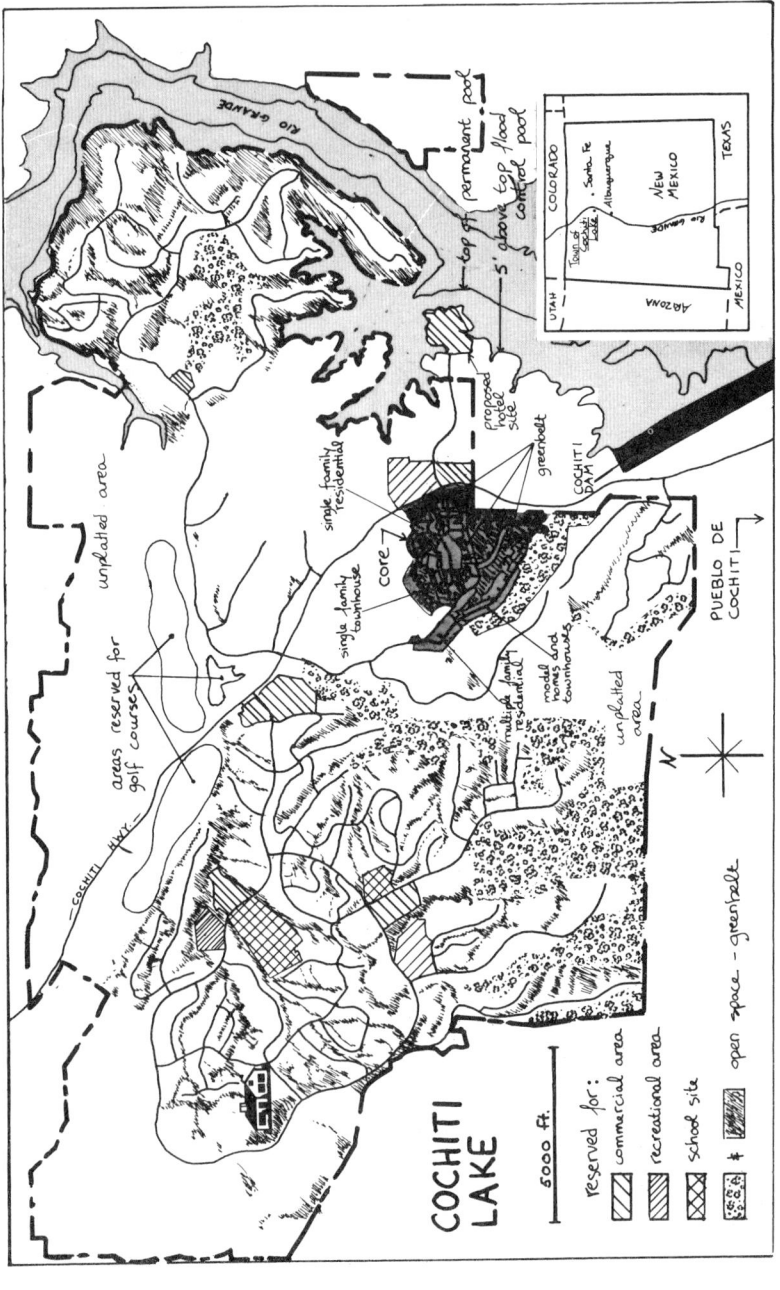

3
Cochiti Lake

The "Town of Cochiti Lake" occupies 6,300 acres of the Pueblo de Cochiti Indian Reservation. Located in an isolated stretch of north-central New Mexico, 41 miles south of Santa Fe and 49 miles north of Albuquerque, this Great Western Cities' subdivision is characterized by a complex past and an uncertain future. Its most significant "natural" feature and primary recreational focus is Cochiti Lake, a controversial $91 million Army Corps of Engineers dam and lake project that will almost certainly be too small to be shared by the cities of Albuquerque and Santa Fe and the "Town's" projected population of 44,000.

There is virtually nothing simple about the Town of Cochiti Lake. Unlike the transactions at the other eighteen subdivisions in the INFORM study,* what an individual receives on the installment plan at Cochiti Lake is not title to the land, but rather the right to lease it for 99 years. At the end of this period, the land and improvements revert to the Pueblo de Cochiti. Sublessees can expect to pay at least $30,000 and possibly as much as $150,000 just to lease the land. Yet despite these excessive costs, they build up no equity. In fact, they have no firm assurance of even being able to use their land for almost half the term of the lease because Great Western Cities guarantees no improvements until December 31, 2020. The burden of providing the entire $28 million necessary to create the Town of Cochiti Lake, whose population as planned would equal that of Santa Fe, falls upon the sublessees themselves.

---

*Includes both the ten subdivisions in Volume I of this study and the nine Florida subdivisions analyzed in Volume II.

Legally, the Town is a morass of issues, documents, agreements, and cases, many of which are unresolved, and which together govern all aspects of development. The most important of the unresolved issues is whether the subdivision will have any water. The most important of the documents is the Town Charter, attached as an amendment to the Master Lease for the property. In an unprecedented legal maneuver, this Charter effectively transferred all development, construction, and maintenance responsibility from Great Western Cities to the lot sublessees, establishing a government whose authority goes far beyond that of an ordinary town and in some respects supercedes that of the state of New Mexico. This authority includes unlimited taxing powers.

Even disregarding its legal entanglements, the subdivision's very future is now in doubt because of financial factors. Great Western Cities has suffered serious financial reverses since its incorporation seven years ago. Its parent company, Great Western United, decided in May, 1975, "to undertake an orderly disposition of Great Western Cities by sale, or otherwise."[1] The impact of this decision on sublessees is unknown.

Cochiti Lake is the newest of Great Western's three subdivisions. It is, however, the only one to have been planned and developed by the corporation, a conglomerate whose primary business is beet sugar. (The company's other two projects, California City and Colorado City, were laid out by the California City Development Company before Great Western acquired it in 1969. (See chapter on Colorado City.) The site's layout is relatively good from an environmental standpoint. Lots and streets conform to the natural terrain, some building lots are clustered, a generous amount of open space has been allocated, and there has been minimal alteration of the land. While the site's profuse archeological resources will undoubtedly suffer severely from development, this negative impact was virtually unavoidable once the Army Corps of Engineers made the decision to build the dam, and the Indians, greatly in need of supplementary income, decided to invite a subdivider to locate next to the lake.

While Great Western's environmental planning is good, its consumer policies are among the poorest in this study. They conform to only one of INFORM's twelve guidelines for responsible consumer practice, and have been the object of legal actions by the Federal Trade Commission and several state governments.

Regional Context/ History

The Pueblo de Cochiti Indians on whose land the subdivision is located date back to prehistoric times. They have occupied the present site for 700 years, weathering Coronado's expedition in 1540, Spanish settlement in the 1600s, a revolt in 1680, the Roman Catholic Church in the 1700s, and the U.S. government and tourists in the 1800s and 1900s. However, like many New Mexico Indian tribes, the present-day Cochitis are terribly poor. They suffer from a low standard of living and chronic unemployment. Until recently, the tribe's primary source of income was the leasing of land for agricultural purposes. It also worked a small amount of irrigated farm, orchard, and grazing land. As of February, 1974, only 512 members of the tribe lived on the Pueblo lands, although jobs generated by the dam and subdivision projects were bringing more back.[2]

The Cochiti Lake subdivision's peculiar sales status arises from the fact that although the land has been owned by the Pueblo since the days of Spanish dominion, federal law prohibits the Indians from selling it. The law does, however, allow the Pueblo to lease its lands for up to 99 years for public, religious, educational, recreational, residential, or business purposes. Leases must be approved by the Secretary of the Interior. At the end of the 99 years, leased land and all improvements made on it revert to the Indians unless a new lease is negotiated.

The subdivision came into existence as a direct result of the creation of Cochiti Lake. The Lake, originally an Army Corps of Engineers project, was designed to control floods, reduce sedimentation and aggradation of the Rio Grande, and to increase the potential for the development of fisheries downstream. The dam and reservoir system which formed the Lake was authorized by three separate water-resource acts passed by the U.S. Congress between 1960 and 1964: a 1960 Flood Control Act authorizing construction of the dam (the last of a four-dam comprehensive flood-control program for the Rio Grande and its tributaries); the 1962 San Juan-Chama Transmountain Diversion Project Act authorizing the transport of water from the Colorado River Basin across the Continental Divide; and a special 1964 Act which brought the water and dam together by authorizing the use of San Juan-Chama water to create a permanent recreational lake on the Pueblo de Cochiti land. Construction began on February 11, 1965.

According to the *New Mexico Review*, the Cochiti Indians had minimal say in the dam project.[3] They were simply advised by the Corps of Engineers that the dam would flood 260 acres of cultivated land and several thousand more acres of low-value rangeland and rugged canyons. Having had little to do with initiating the project, the Cochiti decided to do something about gaining some benefit from it. In 1964, the Pueblo de Cochiti Tribal Council asked the Bureau of Indian Affairs in Albuquerque to study development options for its lands adjacent to the planned dam and lake. The Bureau hired a consulting firm which reported the obvious concerning any development of the site: first, that it should emphasize the recreation potential of the lake; second, that it would have an indeterminate effect on the Cochiti's culture and lifestyle; and third, that it would require outside capitalization.[4] On November 16, 1965, nine months after dam construction began, the Corps of Engineers and the Pueblo de Cochiti entered into an agreement whereby the tribe granted the Corps a perpetual easement on 4,069 acres of land for $145,200.[5] The agreement was accompanied by a "Memorandum of Understanding" which outlined the responsibilities of the Corps and the Pueblo for constructing and maintaining public recreational facilities on land adjacent to the lake.

Then, in early 1967, the Bureau of Indian Affairs issued a prospectus virtually advertising the Cochiti land for lease as a site for recreational development. The California City Development Company, at that time being sued for fraud, deceit, and misrepresentation by California City property owners, responded.[6] It proposed to develop a town of 50,000 people by subleasing lots to individuals on installment contracts. On April 15, 1969, the company's president, Nathan K. Mendelsohn, and the Governor of the Pueblo signed the first of many documents, a "Master Lease" between the Pueblo and the California City Development Company. The Lease was for 7,500 acres at the northern end of the Pueblo on the west side of the Rio Grande. This tract was adjacent to the land held by the Corps of Engineers for public recreational use and access to Cochiti Lake. The Department of the Interior approved the Master Lease on April 17. In June, the proposed development became a project of Great Western Cities, Inc., when Great Western United, a Colorado conglomerate composed at the time of Great Western Sugar Company and Shakey's (Pizza) Incorporated, acquired California City Development Company and 36 related corporations for $28.7 million in Great Western United stock.*[7] The president of California City Development Company became, for a short time, president of the newly formed subsidiary corporation.

Not everyone was pleased by the agreement between the Indians and California City Development Company. Both dam and subdivision have come under serious criticism.

In February, 1974, the Corps of Engineers issued a Final Environmental Impact Statement (EIS) for the dam. (The law requiring such statements was passed in 1969.) At the time of issuance, con-

---

*The other Great Western Cities' subdivision, Colorado City, is profiled in the Mountain Ecology section, Chapter I.

struction had been underway for nine years, $64 million had been spent, and the project was over 73% complete.[8] The Statement pointed out that the dam would transform eight miles of the fast-flowing Rio Grande into a stillwater lake. This stretch of river, coursing through White Rock Canyon, was one of New Mexico's last remaining white-water areas, and was used for river rafting. The Statement also reported that the dam and lake would make accessible, and possibly cause the flooding of, what were previously remote and hard to reach sections of the Bandelier National Monument, an area which had been proposed for inclusion in the National Wilderness Preservation System.

Many of the public comments on the EIS showed New Mexicans' concern with these environmental problems. They also expressed the suspicion that the Corps might be spending $91 million of public funds to build what amounts to a private lake for private development interests.

Great Western has made extensive use of the lake in its promotional efforts, advertising the "Town" as "the home of the 7-Day Weekend" where "swimming, sailing and fishing will lie at the base of the new community." Even the Corps acknowledges that the company has utilized "lakeside living and water oriented recreation...as prime promotional incentives and [that] there is little doubt the complementary presence of the lake does influence potential customers."[9] Unfortunately, the lake may not be large enough to serve both the population of north-central New Mexico and the Town of Cochiti Lake. The flooded area will extend eight miles upstream into the canyon, but the area suitable for recreational use will be just one-and-a-half miles long and a half mile wide.[10] Because of the canyon walls, only 5 of the 21 miles of shoreline will be accessible. This deficiency combined with an inadequate surface area* will severely limit the lake's recreational capacity.

The availability of water is also a problem. Filling the lake will depend on water imported from the Colorado River system. "The size and the aesthetic and recreational value of the lake could be adversely affected by judicial, administrative, or congressional action regarding the San Juan-Chama Diversion Project...or by drought conditions."[11] In the latter case the water would be sent to Albuquerque.

There is also a shortage of recreational land near the lake. When the original dam project was expanded to include a recreational lake, the Corps of Engineers planned to use 900 acres of Pueblo de Cochiti land and 640 acres of U.S. Forest Service land for public recreation. However, three factors intervened: the Cochiti

---

*According to the EIS, in fifty years, sedimentation will double the surface area and raise the pool level 25 feet.

Indians reduced the amount of land they would make available to 304 acres; the Corps discovered that it could not fund projects on Forest Service lands; and the Forest Service announced that it had no funds to develop the land itself.[12] Thus, only 304 acres are now set aside for use by an eventual 1.6 million people per year.[13] The Corps acknowledged that "without [the Forest Service lands], overcrowding and resultant degradation of environmental quality... may occur during peak use-days."[14]

The EIS tries to convince the reader that everyone will have equal access to the lake, and that it is unlikely that residents of the subdivision, despite the opportunity offered by proximity, will monopolize its use. It acknowledges, however, that usage limitations may have to be imposed and access controlled. This inevitability was more accurately summarized by a U.S. Department of the Interior field representative. In a letter objecting to speedboating on the lake, he noted that the 320 acres considered safe for water skiing would accommodate, at the most, sixteen boats. He also stated that, "with over a million visitors projected for the reservoir, a city of over 50,000 located adjacent to the shores, and the close proximity of the Albuquerque metropolitan area, extreme congestion and conflicting demands for the resource is a certainty."[15]

Despite all these problems, by the time the EIS was issued, the project was too far along to stop or postpone. The only possible options were for the Corps to continue as planned or to complete the dam for flood- and sediment-control purposes only, eliminating the permanent recreation pool. Many environmentalists favored this latter option because, as the EIS pointed out, the recreational development would have a far more damaging impact than the dam itself on the cultural, historic, aesthetic, and ecological resources of the site. However, it was the recreational potential of the permanent pool that offered the only chance for the Pueblo de Cochiti tribe to make any economic gains in exchange for the loss of its land. And it is the lake that serves as Great Western Cities' primary marketing tool.

There are considerations other than the environmental side effects of the dam and subdivision. Obviously, the Town of Cochiti Lake will have a significant impact on the Pueblo de Cochiti. The primary question is whether the economic advantages which may accrue to the tribe will balance the cultural disadvantages. There are specific provisions for Indian employment and training in the Master Lease between the Pueblo and Great Western Cities, and the Governor of the Pueblo wrote, in a letter appearing in the March 4, 1974 issue of *Newsweek,* that every Cochiti member who wants to be employed on the dam and development now has employment. According to an article in *The New Mexican,* the Cochitis expected their median

To the left, the Cochiti Dam and Lake; at center, irrigated agricultural land.

per capita income to rise from the 1971 level of $1,800 to a 1978 level of $4,000 to $5,000, by which time Great Western Cities predicted that it would employ Cochitis in 230 full-time and 114 part-time jobs.[16] The tribe may also try to augment its economic base by exercising an option in the Master Lease permitting it to franchise gas and electric service and provide fire and police protection to the subdivision.

The Cochiti Indians' fortunes and future are thus closely tied to the subdivision's growth. While they received only $145,200 for the 4,069 acres leased by the Corps, the Master Lease requires Great Western Cities to pay the Indians a minimum annual rental fee of $50,000 made up of 5% of basic lot sublease prices, 0.5% to 15% of gross receipts of businesses, at least 20% of annual residential-lot rental payments, and 5% of the funds in the Improvement Trust Fund.[17] Obviously, if the subdivision or Great Western Cities fails, there will be no rentals or receipts.

The Corps noted in the EIS that the value of land near its reservoir projects usually increases significantly, but neglected to mention that any such benefit of this increase will accrue mainly to Great Western Cities and sublessees. It reported, without any documentation, that "Great Western Cities' development will represent maximum economic development to the Cochitis" although "it is possible that there may be an accelerated loss of cultural heritage of these historically significant people unless an awareness of these desirable values is maintained."[18]

THE OFFERING: LAND AND IMPROVEMENTS

LAND

Physical Characteristics

Cochiti Lake's geography is similar to that of much of the Rio Grande Valley. Dry, rolling rangeland, sparsely vegetated with grasses and desert shrubs, and dissected by numerous steeply sloping arroyos and gullies. The climate is dry and hot in the summer, cold in the winter, and moderately windy in the spring. The area gets most of the little precipitation it receives during violent summer rainstorms.

Status of Development

When Great Western Cities unveiled plans for Cochiti Lake in July, 1970, it announced an ambitious set of goals. The subdivision would, according to the company: "accommodate a population of 50,000 sometime between the years 1980 and 2000; be built with a construction expenditure of more than $200 million; become 'the first truly planned community with complete dedication to environment and ecology'; give New Mexico a new market with a buying power of more than $100 million a year; provide 150 jobs in Great Western operations alone, including 120 jobs for residents of Cochiti; utilize an annual recreation budget of $500,000 or more; and pay Cochiti Pueblo rentals in excess of $1 million a year within the next decade."[19]

Great Western Cities originally arranged to lease 7,500 acres. It planned to exercise successive options, at 18-month intervals, on 1,000-plus acre tracts which would be developed as "a series of nucleated Pueblo-type communities and Rancho estate areas" for permanent and second-home residents.[20]

Great Western began subleasing lots in August, 1970. According to a September, 1971, article in *The Albuquerque Tribune*, in the first year of development the company invested $1.1 million in capital improvements at Cochiti Lake. This included $750,000 for model homes and houses, $114,000 for a sales and information center, $239,000 for roads, water systems, and sewer systems, and $30,000 for an overlook tower and access road.[21]

Since 1970, the initial corporate optimism has been greatly tempered. In April, 1972, Great Western's lease was amended to delete a 1,000-acre tract and some additional sacred lands from the company's options. This reduced the total acreage of the project to 6,300 acres and the projected population to 44,000.*

Even more important, Great Western Cities has suffered serious financial reverses in the past few years. According to an August, 1974, Great Western United Proxy Statement/Prospectus, "As of the present time, Great Western Cities has not been able to obtain financing for commercial or recreational construction, but has been able to obtain some funds to finance residential construction."[22] In fiscal year 1974, the company suffered an operating loss. It had a 40% cancellation rate at Cochiti Lake (and an overall cancellation rate of 64% at all three of its projects). It also cut its sales force by nearly 50%.[23] In May, 1975, Great Western United decided to "sell, to divest, or otherwise dispose of [Great Western Cities]."[24] The impact of this decision on sublessees cannot be determined, but it is unlikely that the Pueblo de Cochiti will have the funds or expertise to develop the project itself.

As of early 1976, Great Western had platted 4,154 of its 6,300

---

*The amendment also allowed Great Western to exercise sub-options on parcels smaller than 1,000 acres without recording a plat map with the Cochitis and the Secretary of the Interior.

acres. Of the approximately 9,200 lots on this land, it had sublet 4,887. Only 491 of these were fully paid for, since most installment contracts run for ten years.

The subdivision, now six years old, is still a very long way from achieving the population of 44,000 originally projected in 1972. No more than a hundred dwelling units have been built. They house the 147 residents of the Town of Cochiti Lake.

TOWN GOVERNMENT

Because it is on Indian land, every possible aspect of the Cochiti Lake project is defined and determined by legal agreements. The legal issues involved are precedent setting and fascinating to lawyers, but are a Gordian knot to laymen. A Memorandum of Understanding between the Army Corps of Engineers and the Pueblo de Cochiti governs the construction and maintenance of public-use recreational facilities associated with the lake. A Master Lease governs Great Western Cities' possession, development, and subleasing of the land. A Town Charter written by the Pueblo and appended to the Master Lease establishes governmental authority and responsibility over the project and transfers all development obligations from Great Western Cities to the sublessees. A lawsuit brought by the New Mexico Attorney General and the stipulation which concluded the suit establish the extent of state jurisdiction over most aspects of the project. Several other lawsuits, involving other Pueblo lands, leave important issues, such as the site's water supply, unresolved. In addition, virtually everything that is done on or to the land is overseen and reviewed by the Pueblo de Cochiti Council, the Bureau of Indian Affairs, and the Secretary of the Interior.

The most important of these legal arrangements to a potential site resident, and perhaps the most intriguing to lawyers as well, is the Town Charter. Described by the *Albuquerque News Chieftain* as unique and without precedent in American law, the Charter is a document written by Indians to allow non-Indians to govern non-Indians. It can be viewed as a mechanism to insure proper land use, zoning, and governance in a subdivision which the developers and Indians consider exempt from state laws. Or as the *Albuquerque News Chieftain* suggested, it can be viewed as an "unparalleled attempt to incorporate a town before a single house is built... [which] effectively prevents residents...from organizing their own town government at some future date."[25] An *Albuquerque News* columnist called it "one of the most audacious moves ever attempted in the political history of the U.S."[26]

The Charter defines the Town of Cochiti Lake as a political subdivision of the Indian Pueblo, just as a normal town is a political subdivision of the state. It establishes a five-member governing body, the Assembly, and describes its appointed boards, advisory agencies, and executives. It dictates that the first assembly group will be appointed by Great Western Cities, but that when the population of the subdivision reaches 300, three of the appointees will be replaced by members elected by the residents. At the next regular election (regular elections are held every other year in April) the other two appointees will be replaced by elected members. Assembly members hold office for four years. After six years of development, they are still Great Western appointees.

The Charter thus established a government which, for the foreseeable future, is synonymous with Great Western Cities. It gave this government virtually unrestrained authority and in so doing, it allowed a private corporation to bypass many of New Mexico's laws and most of its governmental agencies: the New Mexico Subdivision Act, the Municipal Code, the state taxing authorities, the office of the State Engineer, the State Construction Industries Board, the Environmental Improvement Agency, and others.

Under the original terms of the Charter, the Assembly had the following extraordinary list of prerogatives. It could: levy and collect ad valorem property taxes, use taxes, sales taxes, payroll taxes, and general and special assessments; issue subpoenas; appoint all town officials including the mayor, attorney, engineer, building inspector, police chief, and fire chief, and prescribe their duties; grant indeterminate franchises for all public utilities; collect Improvement Trust Fund payments from sublessees; adopt ordinances and building and construction codes (subject to limitation by Great Western's master plan and specifications); operate parks and recreational facilities; make and enforce land-use regulations through zoning power; and issue bonds to be repaid by any source of funds.

The Assembly was limited only by those restrictions forbidding it to contract for any expenditure over $5,000 without the approval of the Pueblo Council and, when necessary, the Secretary of the Interior; and those forbidding it to authorize any contract payable by the Improvement Trust Fund without certification by the Trustees of the Fund.[27]

The *Albuquerque News Chieftain* speculated that the virtually unlimited taxation powers given to the new city government by the Town Charter could "sink the town far into indebtedness long before many property owners actually take up residence."[28] This assumption of overwhelming governmental authority contributed to making Great Western Cities the object of a lawsuit. In December, 1970, the New Mexico Attorney General filed suit against then Acting Secretary of the Interior Fred J. Russell and other department officials for approving a town charter which attempted to place non-Indians outside the state's legal and administrative jurisdiction.[29] In the suit, the state Attorney General asked the court to determine whether an Indian Pueblo had the legal authority to create a town without complying with the provisions of the state Municipal Code. The state's concern in filing the suit was greater than just Great Western's sweeping assumption of powers. It also focused on the worrisome possibility that other Indian lands might become prime sites for "sovereign towns" exempt from state taxes, state laws, and state enforcement.

In the normal course of legal events, the Secretary of the Interior would have answered the complaint and the case would have gone to court for settlement of the primary question. A local newspaper opined at the time that resolution of the legal status of the subdivision was of such importance to New Mexico (which has nineteen potentially subdividable Pueblo as well as Navaho and Apache lands) and other states with Indian reservations that the case would undoubtedly end up in the Supreme Court. However, in a very peculiar political maneuver, the Secretary of the Interior never even filed a response, nor did the case go to court. The suit was settled six months after it was filed, in June, 1971, by an out-of-court stipulation. This was signed not by the defendants, but by Great Western Cities, which was not even a party to the suit. Even more peculiar, the stipulation did not address the primary question of the Town's legality. Indeed, as a result of the stipulation, the state Attorney General's dismissal of the suit (with prejudice) barred the state from any future direct challenge to the Town's legality.

The settlement itself involved simply Great Western Cities' concession to limited state authority over certain aspects of the project in exchange for New Mexico's dropping the suit. Great Western agreed to comply with state law in all areas except water rights and planning and platting, at least until the courts ruled otherwise. It accepted state authority over construction activities, crime, and the levying and collection of property and business taxes. Since the stipulation was not signed by either the Pueblo de Cochiti or the Secretary of the Interior, it did not represent their concessions to the principles of state jurisdiction.

New Mexico's Attorney General subsequently re-challenged federal authority over non-Indian development activities on Indian lands by filing suit against another subdivision: the Colonias de Santa Fe development located on land belonging to the Pueblo de Tesuque.[30] In this case, the U.S. District Court for New Mexico initially decided that the state and county did have jurisdiction with respect to planning and platting, construction, sewage disposal and the protection of water quality, the levying and collection of property and gross receipts taxes, and the sale of alcohol.

However, a higher court ruled that the case had been brought prematurely on grounds that the subdivision in question had not yet filed and obtained approval of an Environmental Impact Statement when the lower court made its decision. Had the original decision been maintained, it would have been applicable to Cochiti Lake, and could have caused it considerable difficulty. Although Great Western, under the terms of the stipulation, has been voluntarily complying with most state laws, it has never complied with the state subdivision law, which requires that plats be submitted for county approval before sales begin. Should subsequent litigation resolve the issues in the state's favor, Great Western might be forced to suspend lot sales from existing plats and refund payments to sublessees.[31]

COSTS

Individuals who choose to sublease land at Cochiti Lake become subject not only to an extraordinary collection of governing authorities, but to a dizzying variety of continuing costs as well. According to the August, 1974, Great Western United Proxy Statement/Prospectus, depending on lot size, a purchaser must initially pay a basic "sales" price of between $2,890 and $6,290 for lots ranging from 1,900 square feet (a miniscule 1/25 of an acre) to two acres. The average sales price is $4,473. Interest on these prices ranges from 5% to 8%. In addition, the 1975 federal Property Report on the project discloses that a sublessee must pay an "offsite improvement charge" to the Improvement Trust Fund (to provide funds for promised streets, utilities, water, and sewage disposal) of $1,700 to $7,500. The annual rental costs $66 to $510 for the first five years or until a structure is built, $144 to $1,200 for the next five years, and $188 to $1,600 thereafter (plus $48 for each additional residential unit on the lot). There are also recreational fees amounting to $60 yearly which Great Western Cities will use to meet its obligations (specified in the Master Lease) to install a marina and boating facilities. Added to these charges are Sandoval County taxes of $40, a Town lease tax of $10 to $50 per year, and school district assessments. If he chooses to build a home on the lot, the purchaser must pay $50 in Town lease taxes, $930 to $1,020 in central-sewage and water hookup fees, and $150 to $470 for gas and telephone hookup. On the one percent of lots with slopes over 25% he will also have to pay $500 to $2,000 for corrective work.

Since neither Great Western Cities nor the Town government promises to provide basic services to lots before December 31, 2020, a sublessee may in fact be paying $16,870 to $82,020 simply for the right to lease 1/25 of an acre to two acres of raw land for the next 44 years. By the end of the 99-year period of the lease, an unused lot would "cost" a whopping $30,280 to $159,420. A lot with a home would cost considerably more. But in either case there would be no resale value, since after 99 years ownership reverts to the Indians (unless the lease is renewed).

There is not even any assurance that a resident's costs will be limited to those mentioned above. There seems to be no limit to the amount for which a sublessee might ultimately be liable. The improvement charge has already increased from $950 in 1970 to its current $1,700 to $7,500 level, and according to the August, 1974, Proxy Statement/Prospectus:

> Great Western Cities believes that the funds generated from the improvement charges are presently insufficient to serve the long-range purposes of the [Improvement] Trust. Great Western Cities is able and intends to increase these charges...[and]believes that, with increases from time to time in both the off-site improvement charge and in the assessments, funds deposited in the Trust...will be sufficient to meet Great Western Cities' obligations with respect to the construction or funding of off-site improvements. It is reasonable to anticipate that an increase in charges and assessments may depress the rate of sales.[32]

In addition, according to the 1975 federal Property Report: the monthly recreation fee and annual rental can be increased in May, 1984, and every five years thereafter in response to fluctuations in the Consumer Price Index; in January, 1984, the Trustee of the Cochiti Lake Improvement Trust Fund can levy a special assessment of $140 per year; and each year the central water and sewer-extension fees increase 5% as a result of inflation.

BASIC SERVICES

Cochiti Lake is one of seven (out of nineteen) subdivisions in the INFORM sample master-planned for complete basic services: central water, central sewage (to 90% of the site), roads, drainage, and utilities. However, not all of these systems will be built to the minimum standards outlined in the INFORM guidelines, and none is guaranteed before the year 2020. Indeed, there is some question as to whether water may even be available to the subdivision. Furthermore, Great Western Cities is not responsible for paying the cost of improvements. It seems to consider itself responsible for nothing beyond the planning of the site.

The California City Development Company sold the project to the Pueblo de Cochiti on the basis that it had the financial capability to develop a major recreational and residential resource. Great Western Cities sold the project to several thousand purchasers on the same basis. Yet the underlying truth, explicitly stated for the first time in the 1975 federal Property Report, was that the total bill for development would be shouldered by the sublessees. The Report reads:

> THE DEVELOPER ESTIMATES THE COST OF COMPLETING THE ROADS, WATER, AND SEWAGE IN THIS SUBDIVISION TO BE OVER 28 MILLION DOLLARS. IT WILL BE YOUR RESPONSIBILITY, ALONG WITH OTHER SUBLESSEES, TO PAY FOR THE INSTALLATION OF THESE FACILITIES THROUGH THE CHARGES LISTED.... IF INADEQUATE FUNDS ARE AVAILABLE, THE DEVELOPER MUST ADVANCE FUNDS TO THE EXTENT NECESSARY TO PROVIDE THE FACILITIES. YOUR ATTENTION IS DIRECTED...TO THE FINANCIAL STATEMENTS FOR INFORMATION RELATIVE TO THE DEVELOPER'S FINANCIAL CAPABILITY.[33]

The sublessees, therefore, through their Improvement Trust Fund and recreational payments, were to pay for the installation, operation, and maintenance of the water and sewer systems, streets, lighting and gas extensions, drainage and flood-control systems, recreation center, equestrian center, and camping and picnic areas.

This transfer of responsibility from development company to lot sublessees was accomplished through the same Town Charter, appended to the Master Lease, that established the government of Cochiti Lake.

Before it was amended, the original Master Lease specifically required Great Western to spend $7.5 million by 1979 on development. This figure was broken down as follows:

- $5,250,000 for "off-site" improvements (streets, drainage, water system, sewers, street lighting, power, gas, and landscaping).

- $2,250,000 for "on-site" improvements (motel-restaurant complex, commercial area, swimming pool and game area, riding stable and facilities, indoor sports and recreation building, picnic and camping facilities, marina, homes, apartments, and mobile homes). Many of these facilities are for lakeside public use and service, and were part of the Pueblo's responsibility under the Memorandum of Understanding with the Corps of Engineers.

The Master Lease also required Great Western to fulfill the following, general but seemingly substantial, obligations:

- "to furnish or cause to be furnished" all municipal services including water, sewage, streets, drainage, utilities, schools, parks, etc.;
- to post corporate surety performance bonds guaranteeing the completion of any improvement;
- to set up an interest bearing escrow or trust account carrying 115% of the cost of improvements and advance the required funds if necessary;
- to develop the land in accordance with specified schedules;
- to take over the Cochiti's rights and obligations to the Corps of Engineers established in the November, 1965, Memorandum of Understanding.

By amending the Lease to include the Town Charter, Great Western and the Pueblo de Cochiti effectively transferred all these general development obligations from the company to the Town of Cochiti Lake. It is now the Town, i.e., the sublessees, which will furnish all services, operate the escrow account, develop the land, and fulfill the Cochiti's obligations under the Memorandum of Understanding.

The amendment thus reduced Great Western Cities' legal obligations to only the construction of the $7.5 million of specified "on-site" and "off-site" improvements to land that, as of May, 1974, it had already subleased for $24.7 million.[34] In practice, Great Western is constructing a core area with funds from the Improvement Trust. The sublessees will develop the rest of the site at a cost of approximately $28 million.

The Town of Cochiti Lake will install basic services on a very vague and long-range schedule. Installation will be done "as the need is established."[35] It will fund all improvements with the money sublessees pay into the Improvement Trust Fund. This money is escrowed, so at least it cannot be used for any other purpose. Some lots may not be connected to sewer-collection and water-distribution systems nor have paved streets or access to utilities until 2020.

Moreover, although the Town pays for all basic services and facilities, Great Western still determines when, and to which lots and units, services will be provided. According to the federal Property Report, the company will make decisions based on the availability of Improvement Trust funds and the need for additional improvement lots. At present, six years after development began, utilities are extended to only 359 lots--half of the 718 lots in the initial development area--and are actually hooked up only to the 100 existing residences.

No refund is offered if services are not made available. However, if a sublessee has completed all his payments and wants to build before services are available to his lot, he "may trade [his] property...for a like property...[with services] from the developer's inventory, in the initial development area, as long as such inventory is available, provided the property is developed with a residence."[36] These lots "may" have higher selling prices, higher annual rentals, and higher taxes. Of course, if enough people trade, they may not be available at all.

Water

One of the most complex and crucial of the legal issues at Cochiti Lake is whether the subdivision is entitled to enough water for its needs. In the Master Lease, the Pueblo agreed to provide sufficient water for domestic and municipal (though not industrial) use. Conservative estimates of the ultimate demand, when the subdivision is fully developed (using the figure 100 to 150 gallons per person per day*) are 4,900 to 7,400 acre-feet per year. Whether or not the Pueblo actually owns the rights to the necessary amounts of Rio Grande Basin water will be determined by the courts.

In New Mexico, use of surface water and groundwater in designated basins (including the Rio Grande Basin) is overseen by the courts and administered by the State Engineer Office. The courts determine the nature and extent of water rights, based on the long-standing doctrine that the first landowner to put the water to beneficial use has senior rights over those who follow. Later users must take what is left or buy and transfer senior rights. The State Engineer Office administers the purchase and transfer of water rights through permits and court decrees.

Until recently, Pueblo Indian lands were assumed to be exempt from state jurisdiction, including water law. In 1908, the Supreme Court ruled that in granting Indians their reservations, Congress or the Executive endowed them with prior and paramount rights to all water originating on, bordering, or crossing their land. This decision, known as the Winters Doctrine, legally reserved for the Indians sufficient water to forever irrigate and sustain their reservation lands. (The extent of Winters rights is not yet fully settled by court decisions.)

In 1966, however, the New Mexico State Engineer initiated a federal court action (State of New Mexico v. Aamodt et al.) to determine the nature, priority, and extent of Pueblo Indian rights to water in the Rio Grande and its tributaries. The action was based

---

*Company figures on current rates of use average a very high 446 gallons per person per day. However, this figure may reflect increased water use for construction activities.

on an assertion that since Pueblo lands are not reserved by the federal government, but rather owned outright by the Indians under the terms of the Treaty of Guadelupe Hidalgo, the Winters Doctrine does not apply. This case, although directly involving only four northern Pueblos on the Rio Tesuque tributary of the Rio Grande, potentially affects all Pueblos drawing Rio Grande water, including the Pueblo de Cochiti.

The court's final decision will determine whether New Mexico's Pueblos are governed by the state's water rights doctrine of "prior appropriation for beneficial use," or by the Winters Doctrine reserving sufficient water for present and future needs. If the former is decided, the Pueblos will have rights to only that amount of water they have historically used for irrigation, which could be a major limitation on the development potential of their lands. If the latter applies, they will be exempt from state water law and have an overriding right to the amount of water they need. The Pueblo de Cochiti is not a party to this suit, but the outcome is of direct importance to all sublessees, because it may determine whether the Pueblo has rights to enough water to supply the population of the subdivision.

In late 1974, the U.S. District Court ruled in State of New Mexico v. Aamodt et al. that the Pueblos are governed by New Mexico's law of prior appropriation. The U.S. government appealed the decision and the case is pending in the 10th Circuit Court. If, as some suggest might happen, non-Indians with Rio Grande water rights join the suit, it will take years to resolve and may become the most complex case in U.S. history.

The Pueblo de Cochiti has historically used very little water for irrigation and agriculture. If the final court decision establishes that the Pueblo has rights only to what it has used, the Town of Cochiti Lake will have to try to purchase sufficient additional rights. But as the company itself has noted, there is "no assurance...that Great Western Cities will be able to purchase the water for future development of the Project on favorable terms"[37] or "that anticipated water resources will be available to serve the requirements of the total anticipated population of the subdivision."[38]

To provide water for the initial development area, Great Western Cities purchased rights to 510 acre-feet per year. (These rights, transferred to the subdivision by a State Engineer's permit, are not related to the Pueblo's water-rights claim in the Aamodt case.) The company claims that this amount of water should be adequate for 1,020 homes or 2,000 people. Water-distribution facilities extend to 359 lots in the initial development area.

Sewage

As is the case with other services, the Town of Cochiti Lake plans eventually to extend a central sewage system to all lots, "except where on-site sewage disposal is permitted by local and state health agencies,... A staged sewer system is planned, consisting of on-site sewage disposal such as septic tanks, seepage pits or evapotranspiration systems initially (at sublessee's expense) followed by public sewers as development and densities dictate" (also at sublessee's expense).[39]

Great Western Cities reported to INFORM that some areas of the project have received tentative approval to use individual sewage systems until the central system is extended. Eventually the central system will serve 90% of the lots and individual systems will serve the remaining 10%. Some of the lots using septics may be as small as a half-acre. The INFORM guideline recommends a one-acre limit. The existing central system is extended to 359 lots and hooked up to the 100 existing residences.

Solid Waste

A private contractor collects solid waste and disposes of it at a sanitary landfill on the site.

Roads

A paved access road to the dam and subdivision has been completed. The Town is responsible for constructing and maintaining all other roads (to its own and the Pueblo's standards) using funds from the Improvement Trust. Great Western is supposed to determine the need for roads. However, it has not established a schedule or plan for completion, and there is no assurance that roads in the project will be completed before December 31, 2020.

As of early 1976, there were eleven miles of paved road in the core area. None of the eighty miles outside the core area had been paved, but all main roads in the project were graded, and most residential streets were staked or bladed.

According to the 1975 federal Property Report, "Finished street conditions will be reached through a phased development approach that may begin with graded or graveled roads to be followed by either a double penetration oil coat or asphalt paving when required by use. Partial width roads are also probable until widening is made necessary by increased usage."[40]

Drainage

As of 1975, the company had no program in effect to control soil erosion, sedimentation, or flooding. The 1975 federal Property

Report stated that, "Erosion and flooding could result in property damage and could create a health and safety hazard."[41] As with other basic services, the Town of Cochiti Lake will install a system of artificial drains, culverts, and flood-control channels "when the need therefor exists."[42] Great Western indicated to IN-FORM that parts of its drainage system (culverts and pipes) are designed to handle flows from a 50-year storm, and parts (downdrains and structures) are designed for a 10-year storm. Most planners advocate using a drainage system capable of handling a 100-year storm (see Guidelines).

Electricity and Telephone

Utilities are made available to the developed area by Southern Union Gas Company, Public Service Company of New Mexico (electricity), and Mountain States Telephone. They are to be extended when the Town, the utility company, and Great Western Cities determine that there is a need. As is the case with most subdivisions, "in portions of the development located a substantial distance from existing telephone and electric lines the cost of obtaining these services and gas at the present time is prohibitive."[43] According to the 1975 federal Property Report, hookup in the developed area costs $100 to $150 for gas and $57 (four-party line) to $321 (private line) for telephone. There are no hookup fees for electricity if the extension is less than 110 feet from an existing line. Utility lines at the site will be underground.

COMMUNITY AND RECREATIONAL FACILITIES

The Cochiti Lake subdivision is extremely isolated. There are an elementary school and minor shopping facilities six miles away, but all other services and facilities--shopping, high school, doctors, dentists, and hospitals--are 38 to 48 miles from the site in Bernalillo, Santa Fe, and Albuquerque. The nearest public transportation to these towns is "approximately 16 miles from the subdivision at the Santo Domingo junction where [three bus companies] make regularly scheduled flag stops ten times daily."[44] Under the terms of the Town Charter, the Town government is responsible for establishing departments to furnish fire and police protection and parks and recreation services. Currently, a volunteer fire department and two county deputy sheriffs protect the site.

The Town of Cochiti Lake is in the Bernalillo Municipal School District. By November, 1970, all the schools within reach of the Town--the elementary school at the Pueblo de Cochiti six miles from the subdivision and the junior and senior high schools 38 miles away in Bernalillo--were enrolled to capacity. Great Western Cities has set aside land for school sites within the subdivision, but the question of how school construction will be financed remains unresolved. The state provides school bus transportation.

On-site recreational facilities include a swimming pool, tennis courts, a small games area, and a riding stable. However, the most significant recreational feature of the area is the adjacent Cochiti Lake. The 1,240-acre reservoir, completed in May, 1975, is Great Western Cities' prime drawing card. But the controversy surrounding the almost inevitable overuse of the lake indicates that the drawing card may turn into, as environmentalists angrily phrased it, "an extremely overcrowded, highly regulated, potentially dangerous...recreation slum."[45]

The responsibility for developing the 304 acres of land leased for public recreation was originally divided between the Pueblo and the Army Corps of Engineers. The Corps was to construct basic facilities including trails, parking areas, camping and picnic areas, roads, boat ramps, comfort stations, a water system, electric power, and overlook shelters. The Pueblo was to maintain and operate these facilities with the understanding that it could charge reasonable fees for use of the facilities but not for use of the lake itself. The Pueblo also agreed to build a marina, a country store and concession area, and a gas station by 1970; and a swimming pool or beach, riding stable, and restaurant-motel-lounge for public use by 1975.[46] As was mentioned earlier, the Pueblo, in the Master Lease, transferred all of its construction, maintenance, and operation responsibilities to Great Western Cities.

As of October, 1975, Great Western Cities had completed some picnic areas and the recreation and equestrian centers, and the Corps of Engineers had half finished the public-use area. Great Western Cities, however, had not begun the marina, swimming pool, beach, or restaurant-motel-lounge complex and was just breaking ground for the country store and concession area. The company reported in the 1975 federal Property Report that, although these improvements are the obligation of the developer, there is no financial assurance that they will be completed. Moreover, state permits required to build the marina had not been obtained and might not be obtainable. The Property Report summarizes, "It has not been determined what the extent of any of the facilities will be in that they are not definitely described in the Master Lease."[47]

ENVIRONMENTAL PROTECTION

Because the public has had very limited access to the Cochiti area, its canyons, rangeland, wilderness areas, and archeological ruins have been untouched for eons. The U.S. Army Corps of Engineers in its Environmental Impact Statement (EIS) on the dam stated: "the impact of this development will be as environmentally significant, if not more so, as that of the dam and lake,"[48] and that "urbanization brought on by private development may overshadow and ultimately diminish the ecological and aesthetic gains of the [dam] project."[49]

While suitable for development on some scale, the land is far from ideal for a subdivision of this size. Much of it is steeply sloping, water is in short supply, and it is subject to moderate earthquakes. The decision of the Pueblo de Cochiti, the U.S. Department of the Interior, and the development company to house 44,000 people on this site was thus highly questionable.

That basic decision aside, however, Great Western Cities has subdivided the site in a relatively sound manner with regard to environmental concerns. Development is clustered, and building is restricted in hazardously sloping and flood-prone areas. The site is planned for central sewage disposal which will minimize the pollution of groundwater from septic systems.

The company's major shortcomings, in terms of the environment, have been its insufficient erosion-control methods. Dirt roads have been bladed throughout most of the subdivision, sometimes decades in advance of use, giving them many years in which to wash out or blow away. Furthermore, no particular drainage or flood-control measures are in use to prevent eroded silt from washing into the lake.

PLANNING

The master plan for the Town of Cochiti Lake is well designed. Great Western Cities hired planning consultants Sasaki-Walker, one of the nation's most respected firms, to take charge of its preparation. Their plan stresses the preservation of natural terrain by locating apartments and townhouses on ridges, detached houses on slopes, and ranchettes on rough lands. There are no gridiron road patterns. Roads follow land contours, and arroyos are left as natural water courses. Utilities are to be laid underground. Cochiti Lake is the only site of the nineteen studied by INFORM to include

Clustered development at Cochiti Lake avoids building in arroyos.

cluster development in its planning. Thirty percent of the total acreage is allocated to open space, and a more than adequate 5% is allocated to developed recreational space. Of the rest of the land, 51% will be single-family, 10% multi-family, and 2% commercial lots. The site will have no industry.

The company has not employed phased development. The only specific completion date for services outside the core area is December 31, 2020. But in order to comply with consumer-protection requirements that lots be accessible to purchasers, Great Western has bladed or graded about eighty miles of road 45 years in advance of the promised completion date of all other services. In addition, the company did not utilize an Environmental Impact Statement in planning the site. One being prepared by the Bureau of Indian Affairs has been "put on the back burner, and is not yet available to the public."[50] The Corps of Engineers' Environmental Impact Statement on the Cochiti dam gives only a cursory discussion of the potential impacts of the residential development.

LAND

The site includes three types of land considered hazardous for building: land with a slope exceeding 25%, land in a 100-year floodplain, and land in an earthquake zone. All of these hazardous areas have been subdivided. However, lot covenants and restrictions prohibit sublessees from constructing a building on slopes greater than 25% and in a 100-year floodplain. Using what it calls the envelope concept, the planners laid out the site so that all lots have at least an area of sufficient size for building that is not on hazardous land. This building site is "enveloped" by steeply sloping or flood-prone land which cannot be altered by construction. Thus, although privately owned, the land will be preserved from development.[51]

According to the 1975 federal Property Report, fewer than 1% of the lots with a slope of 25% or greater will require any corrective work before house construction.

The earthquake hazard is unfortunately one which could not be overcome by good planning. It does not, however, appear to be overly severe. According to the 1975 federal Property Report "the majority of [the] State of New Mexico...is classified as being in Seismic Zone II by the International Conference of Building Officials. Moderate earthquakes can occur causing structural damage. There have been no tremors in the past five years in the Cochiti Lake area. The last major earthquake in New Mexico [which] occurred in 1927...was centered over 200 miles south of Cochiti Lake."[52]

The site includes no habitats of endangered species or environmentally valuable water-related lands (aquifer-recharge areas, watersheds, or swamps). It does, however, have one area of critical environmental concern: archeological ruins. Perhaps the greatest environmental threat of both the subdivision and lake is that posed to these ruins.

The lands which will be flooded, subdivided, and made accessible to boaters contain a profusion of archeological sites. The Museum of New Mexico, which prepared two incomplete surveys of the threatened sites for the Corps, estimates that there are at least 550 of them as old as 3,000 and 5,000 years and that over half of these will be affected by increased visitor impact.[53] Great Western Cities reported to INFORM that it has neither subdivided nor offered for sublease any archeological sites. But, according to the Environmental Impact Statement, this will probably not insure their preservation. The Statement notes that:

> ...Three [of the archeological sites] have been excavated; but the likelihood that the remainder can be salvaged before they are destroyed by development is slim...

And further that:

> ...On those lands already leased for development, protection of known sites from the residents alone cannot be insured by the lessor or by the lessees. Planning is such that those sites not actually threatened by construction will be entirely surrounded by house lots.[54]

WATER RESOURCES

The surface-water quality in the Rio Grande Basin, although it varies widely, is relatively high in the river above Cochiti. But the Environmental Impact Statement predicts: "Continued population growth, gradual development of presently rural areas, and institutional and legal constraints may together slowly cause serious water quality management problems."[55] There are three major towns upstream from Cochiti which might create problems: Taos, Espanola, and Santa Fe. If the Town of Cochiti Lake develops as planned, it will probably be added to the list of offenders.

The greatest threat to water quality at Cochiti Lake is pollution caused by erosion and runoff from the developing Town. The area is subject to intense thunderstorms that can produce flash floods. With steep slopes and sparse vegetation, much of which has been destroyed by overgrazing, heavy rains have little opportunity to seep into the ground. Instead, the water rushes down the arroyos, carrying silt.

Development will exacerbate this situation by decreasing permeable surfaces, loosening and exposing soils during construction, and adding urban pollutants like oil to the runoff. The Corps' Environmental Impact Statement for the dam notes that much of the runoff will be discharged into the lake. The U.S. Forest Service added that since the soils on the site are sensitive and relatively infertile, stabilization measures adequate to prevent serious erosion will be difficult and expensive.

Despite this erosion potential, Great Western Cities, as mentioned earlier, has taken few preventative steps. According to the 1975 federal Property Report, it has no program to control soil erosion, sedimentation or flooding, or to reseed disturbed areas. It has, however, avoided clearing the land of vegetation or significantly altering the topography. It has also left a 100-foot "green-belt" buffer zone between developed land and the lake, except near a few lots at the north end of the site, and in an area where it is planning to build a hotel. These measures should help limit erosion.

Company plans to prevent water pollution from sewage are generally good. All existing homes are hooked up to a central system which is scheduled to serve 90% of the site. Secondary treatment of sewage is provided by an activated-sludge facility and holding pond, the effluent from which is disposed of via evaporation and percolation. The Town system will also handle, by agreement, the sewage from the public-use areas around Cochiti Lake.

Portions of the site have been approved for septic tanks until the central sewage system is extended. Because of the steep slopes, these systems might cause some pollution problems. There are also a few half-acre lots which will permanently use septics. To fully insure that there will be no pollution from septic-tank leaching, most planners and regulators recommend that their use be limited to lots of one acre or larger (see Guidelines).

Virtually no information is available concerning the possible effects of the subdivision on the groundwater resource: whether the amount drawn from site wells will increase its mineral content or salinity, or whether its continued use will cause any long-term depletion of the water table. The Corps' Environmental Impact Statement reported that it did not know whether the land disposal of sewage effluent described above would alter the chemical concentration of substances in the groundwater to any significant degree. Great Western Cities has not obtained any engineer's report or hydrological survey.

COCHITI LAKE   197

CONSUMER PROTECTION

Although Great Western United's environmental planning at Cochiti Lake is relatively good, the company has not been similarly responsible toward the consumer. From a strictly financial standpoint, a lot at Cochiti Lake is not a good buy. Costs are unusually high. Yet virtually all the sublessee receives for his money is the benefit of Great Western's planning efforts. The company provides the consumer with neither permanent title to the land--the consumer "buys" only the right to sublease it for 99 years--nor with improvements. At other, comparably-priced subdivisions, such as Dart's Bear Valley Springs, the developer provides both.

Great Western United adheres to only one of INFORM's twelve guidelines for responsible sales practices. (By contrast, Dart follows as many as eight.) Great Western's sales practices have made it the object of a Federal Trade Commission (FTC) order. Further FTC action against the company is expected soon.

Sales

Currently, all that is offered for lease on installment contracts is unimproved land located outside the core area. In order to lease an improved lot, the sublessee must obtain a mortgage and build immediately.[56]

As mentioned earlier, lots range from 1,900 square feet (1/25 of an acre) to two acres in size with a basic "sales" price of between $2,890 and $6,290. Beginning in 1974, the required downpayment on contracts was increased from 6% to 10%, with the balance of the basic price and 5% to 8% interest payable over five to fifteen years. The additional costs of leasing a lot, discussed earlier in this chapter, can total up to $150,000 over the 99 years of the lease.

Despite such high costs, Great Western has not taken many steps to ensure that prospective sublessees know what they are getting into. The company does not investigate a sublessee's credit, limit the number of lots an individual may lease, limit leases of commercial or multi-family lots on installments, or use an independent closer. Taking these measures might have lowered the company's fiscal-year-1974 cancellation rate of 40%. It would also have protected many sublessees from either taking on too heavy a financial burden or succumbing to high-pressure sales methods.

On the positive side, the company reported to INFORM that it advises sublessees to have an attorney review all documents and that it encourages site visits before contracts are signed. The

August, 1974, Proxy Statment/Prospectus stated: "Management believes that most purchasers visit the Project before or shortly after they purchase."[57] Since approximately 50% to 60% of the sublessees at Cochiti Lake are New Mexico residents, and since lots are offered out-of-state only in Illinois, it may be assumed that many of those who sign contracts have seen the project.

Refunds

Great Western's refund policies are highly inadequate from a consumer-protection point of view. In accordance with the requirements of the Office of Interstate Land Sales Registration, sublessees are given only 72 hours after receiving the Property Report to rescind their contract without losing their payments, a period which, considering California's fourteen-day period and INFORM's guidelines, is much too short. In the event of a sublessee's default after the initial rescission period, Great Western Cities retains all payments and restores the lot to its inventory. The Pueblo de Cochiti likewise retains all rental payments. Some but not all contracts offer a refund to sublessees who cancel following a site visit within six months of the date of contract signing.

Failure to pay county taxes and any special assessments that might be levied constitutes a default under the terms of the contract and it too can result in termination of the sublease and restoration of the lot to the company's inventory. Since no improvements are promised until December 31, 2020, the question of whether Great Western offers a refund in the event that improvements are not completed on schedule is rather moot; except, perhaps, for a very young sublessee. The youngsters may be interested to know, however, that no such refund is offered.

Title Protection

Since Cochiti Lake lots are leased rather than purchased, sublessees do not get title to the land nor do they build up any equity. Their interest in the subleased property is, however, protected. Lots are platted with the Pueblo de Cochiti and Sandoval County. The sublessee's contract is recordable and Great Western records each with the Pueblo. The company also records a memorandum of the sublease agreement with the County to put it on record, but the sublessee himself is responsible for recording his actual contract with the County.

The Cochiti Indians are better protected than lot purchasers in the event of Great Western Cities' bankruptcy or default. The Master Lease specifies that if Great Western fails to develop the core area according to schedules and plans, it must increase its guaranteed minimum rental to the Cochitis by 50% until it completes the improvements. Furthermore, if Great Western defaults on rental payments or fails to submit a bond for improvements, the Cochitis and the Secretary of the Interior can sue, take over any not-yet-subleased property and lease it, and terminate their agreement with the company. If the lease is cancelled, Great Western is liable for $500,000 in liquidated damages, and the Cochitis can continue to collect all payments directly from the sublessees. In the case of the company's bankruptcy, the Cochitis are the first preferred creditor.

According to Great Western, if the company defaults on its lease, the Pueblo de Cochiti will recognize the sublessee's interest and fulfill Great Western's obligations. However, minimal as these obligations are (see discussion under Basic Services)--totaling only $7.5 million worth of development--it is nonetheless questionable whether the Pueblo would have the wherewithal to fulfill them. Indeed, it was for just this reason that it brought in Great Western in the first place. Thus, the Pueblo's promise to fulfill company obligations is of little assurance to sublessees.

Resale Value

Should a lot sublessee have second thoughts about continuing his sublease and want to sell it to someone else, the prospects for doing so are dim. Great Western Cities set up a lot-resale program at Cochiti. However, it conceded in its 1974 Proxy Statement/Prospectus that this program has had "no significant effect to date, [that] there presently are limited markets for resale of land; [and that]...such sales are made at prices substantially lower than Great Western Cities' current offering prices."[58] In addition, as of early 1976, the company still had 2,146 acres to plat and sublease in competition with resales. Future lot resales look even dimmer. Barring a renewal or extension agreement, all land and improvements are scheduled to revert to the Pueblo de Cochiti with the expiration of the lease in 2068. As such the passage of time can only serve to diminish whatever value the land may have.

Legal Status

Great Western Cities' sales activities have been the object of a number of legal actions. During 1970 and 1971, the Federal Trade Commission (FTC) investigated the company's recruiting, sales, and advertising practices. It alleged that these "practices...had the tendency to mislead and deceive customers as to the investment potential of lots, growth potential of areas in which subdivisions are located, costs to purchasers beyond purchase price of lots, income to be made by salesmen, and rescission rights."[59] The FTC issued a cease and desist order, which primarily required the company to fully disclose to buyers that Cochiti lots are in fact a sublease, not an outright purchase, and to fully disclose the sales price and finance charges.[60]

In 1974, the FTC alleged that Great Western Cities had violated certain terms of the order. The Commission and company are now negotiating a settlement which may involve refunds of approximately $4 million to lot purchasers at Great Western's three subdivisions, and development expenditures of approximately $16 million.[61]

COST OF LOTS BOUGHT ON THE INSTALLMENT PLAN

LOT PRICE

basic lease price (1/25 - 2 acres)*		$2,890 - $6,290
finance charge (5% - 8%)		$710 - $2,581
off-site improvement charge		$1,700 - $7,500
	Total	$5,300 - $16,371

ADDITIONAL ANNUAL ASSESSMENTS DURING TERM OF CONTRACT

rental		$66 - $1,600
years 1 - 5	$66 - $510	
years 5 - 10	$144 - $1,200	
years 10+	$188 - $1,600	
recreational fee		$60
county taxes		$40
town taxes		$10 - $50
	Total, per year	$176 - $1,720
	Total, 10 years	$2,150 - $9,750

ONE-TIME COSTS FOR SERVICES

lot survey		0
water		$430 - $520
well	0	
central extension	$360 - $450	
central hook-up	$70	
sewage		$500 - $1,500
septic system	$800 - $1,500	
central extension	0	
central hook-up	$500	
electricity		N/A
telephone		$57 - $321
gas		$100 - $150

*Includes industrial, commercial, and multi-family lots.

ENVIRONMENTAL CHECKLIST

Overall consumer protection record: GOOD

Does the subdivider:

PLANS	Plan for complete basic services?	YES
	Phase lot sales and extension of services?	NO
	Get 80% build-out in 10 years of each section marketed?	NO
	Prepare an Environmental Impact Report?	NO
LAND	Use a curvilinear or cluster design?	YES
	Retain 25% or more open space?	YES
	Reserve from lot sale and development the following areas of critical concern:	
	wetlands?	--
	dunes and beaches?	--
	water sources?	--
	prime agricultural lands?	--
	habitats of endangered species?	--
	prime historical, archaeological, cultural, aesthetic, or recreational resources?	NO
	Reserve from lot sale and development the following areas hazardous for building:	
	geological hazard areas (earthquake, landslide)?	--
	flood-prone areas (100-year floodplains, arroyos)?	YES*
	areas of slope exceeding 25%?	YES*
	Blade roads only in immediate development areas?	NO
	Clear only for buildings and roads?	YES
	Preserve existing topography?	YES
WATER RESOURCES	Design the drainage system to control erosion?	NO
	Retain 100-foot buffer zone around water bodies?	YES
	Replant disturbed land immediately?	NO
	Limit septic systems to one-acre or larger lots with adequate: percolation rates, slope, and distance from bedrock, water table and surface waters?	YES†
	When utilizing central sewage disposal, provide tertiary treatment (or secondary and land disposal)?	YES
	Avoid major stream alteration?	--
	Avoid major wetland dredging and filling?	--
	Use groundwater only up to the safe yield?	?

*This land has been subdivided, but cannot be built upon due to lot covenants and restrictions.

†Some lots under one acre may be permitted to use "temporary" septic systems.

NOTE: See chapter on "Guidelines" for more complete explanation of items on Checklist.

COCHITI LAKE   203

CONSUMER CHECKLIST

Overall consumer protection record: POOR

Does the subdivider:

<table>
<tr><td rowspan="12">SALES</td><td>Conduct a credit check on lot purchasers?</td><td>NO</td></tr>
<tr><td>Limit lot sales to two per purchaser?</td><td>NO</td></tr>
<tr><td>Sell only residential, i.e., no industrial, commercial or multi-family lots on installment contracts?</td><td>NO</td></tr>
<tr><td>Require a cash downpayment of 20% on all sales?</td><td>NO</td></tr>
<tr><td>Limit duration of installment contracts to 5 years?</td><td>NO</td></tr>
<tr><td>Charge no interest on installment contracts?</td><td>NO</td></tr>
<tr><td>Encourage attorney review of sales documents?</td><td>YES</td></tr>
<tr><td>Require a pre-purchase site visit?</td><td>NO</td></tr>
<tr><td>Allow a 14-day rescission period in which purchaser can obtain a refund for any reason?</td><td>NO</td></tr>
<tr><td>Offer a partial refund if purchaser defaults?</td><td>NO</td></tr>
<tr><td>Guarantee a refund, with interest, if promised services are not made available by date specified in contract?</td><td>NO</td></tr>
<tr><td>Escrow contract payments, or provide equivalent surety bonding, for refund purposes?</td><td>NO</td></tr>
<tr><td rowspan="4">TITLE</td><td>Offer only platted lots?</td><td>YES</td></tr>
<tr><td>Offer a recordable contract, and record the sale?</td><td>YES</td></tr>
<tr><td>Offer unmortgaged land, or land mortgaged with a release clause, only?</td><td>--</td></tr>
<tr><td>Upon contract signing, deed title to purchaser, or place title in trust?</td><td>--</td></tr>
<tr><td rowspan="13">BASIC SERVICES</td><td>Guarantee, or have available, to each lot:</td><td></td></tr>
<tr><td>   central water, of adequate quantity and quality?</td><td>NO</td></tr>
<tr><td>   central sewage disposal, as necessary?</td><td>NO</td></tr>
<tr><td>   drainage system, adequate for 100-year storm?</td><td>NO</td></tr>
<tr><td>   solid waste disposal, via adequate method?</td><td>YES</td></tr>
<tr><td>   roads, paved, to county standards?</td><td>NO</td></tr>
<tr><td>   electricity and telephone?</td><td>NO</td></tr>
<tr><td>Guarantee completion through escrowing or surety bonding?</td><td>YES</td></tr>
<tr><td>If services are financed through special service district bonds, employ them only if:</td><td></td></tr>
<tr><td>   initial governing body includes a county official?</td><td>--*</td></tr>
<tr><td>   elections include all landowners on one-man, one-vote basis?</td><td>--*</td></tr>
<tr><td>   sum of bonds is less than twice the developer's investment in basic services?</td><td>--*</td></tr>
<tr><td>   sum of bonds is less than 15% of the assessed value of land in the district?</td><td>--*</td></tr>
<tr><td></td><td>   developer co-signs all bonds?</td><td>--*</td></tr>
</table>

*The incorporation of the "Town of Cochiti Lake" effected the same financing authority as the formation of a special service district would have. The results are discussed under Town Government in the chapter.

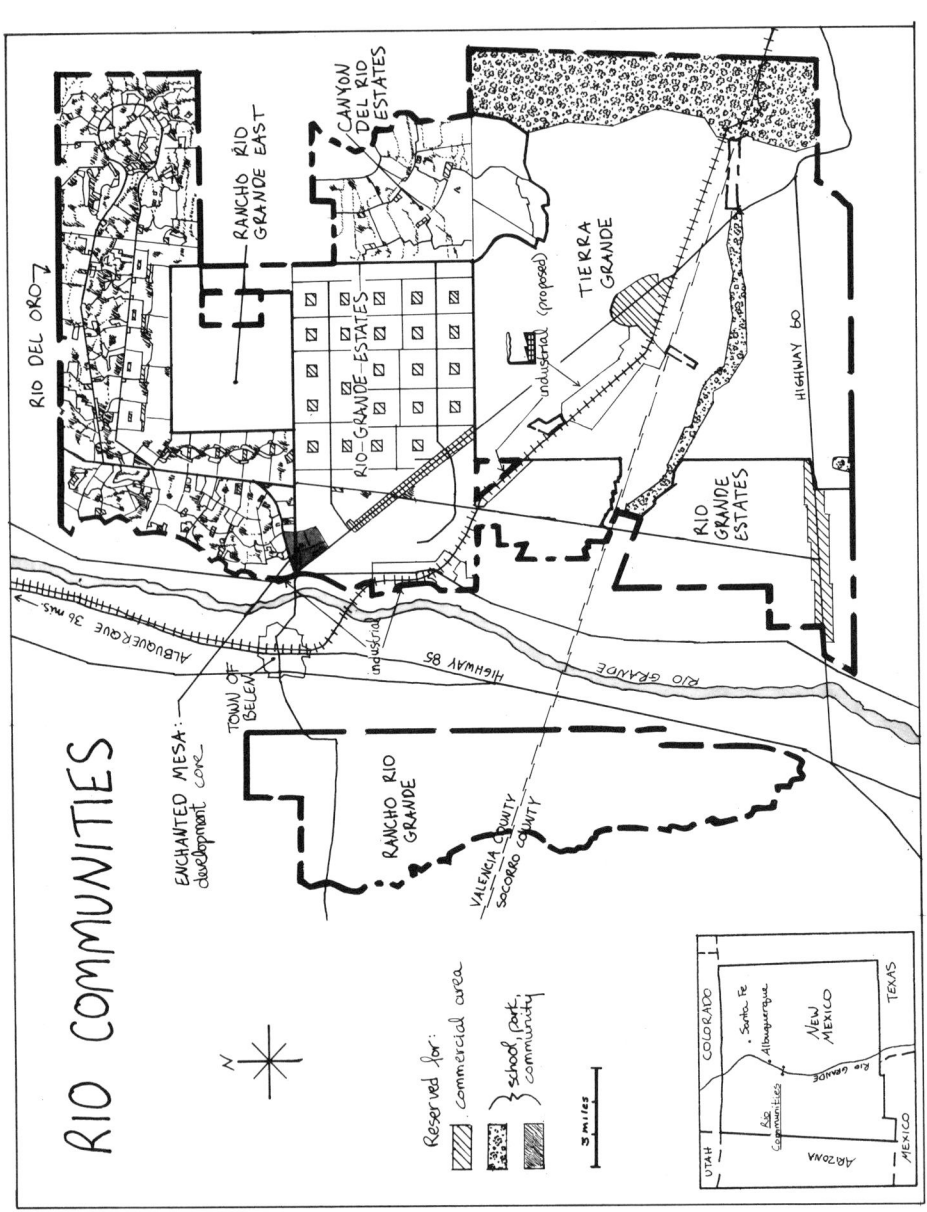

4
Rio Communities

The Horizon Corporation's Rio Communities subdivision is more than twice as large as any other among the nineteen studied by IN-FORM.* Indeed, covering as it does 400 square miles of dry, cattle-grazing land in New Mexico's Valencia and Socorro Counties, it may be the largest subdivision in the United States.† But in all its area, Rio Communities can boast no outstanding economic or recreational resources, and land there has been marketed primarily on the basis of its potential value as a beneficiary of Albuquerque's "explosive growth."[1] In the face of Rio Communities' sheer physical enormity, Albuquerque's boom becomes a faint pop.

Rio Communities begins 36 miles south of downtown Albuquerque, stretching further south for about 24 miles on either side of the Rio Grande. Horizon has subdivided this land into 172,000 lots, enough to absorb the entire population of Albuquerque and then some.▽ Yet there is little reason for residents of Albuquerque or

---

*Includes both the ten subdivisions in Volume I and the nine Florida subdivisions analyzed in Volume II.

†As there is no central private or government clearinghouse for such statistics, it is impossible to say whether this is, in fact, the nation's largest subdivision. However, in the entire course of its three years of research, INFORM came across no project of comparable physical scope.

▽Horizon gives the population of the Albuquerque metropolitan area, in the above brochure, as 350,000. Assuming an average of three residents per lot, Rio Communities' 172,000 lots could house 516,000 people.

anyone else to move to Rio Communities. Both Horizon's environmental planning and consumer practices are mediocre to poor compared to those at other subdivisions in this study. The older portions of the subdivision--almost half the total acreage--were laid out in a monotonous gridiron pattern with virtually no land allocated for parks or recreational use. Perhaps even more important to the potential resident is the fact that lots come with no improvements except a dirt road. Water, sewage disposal, and utilities must all be installed at the owner's expense. For a lot lying many miles from the developed "core" area, the costs would be prohibitive: up to half a million dollars, according to a federal Property Report.*[2]

By 1975, fifteen years after Horizon began marketing the site, many lot purchasers and the Federal Trade Commission (FTC) had come to the conclusion that the sales practices used at Rio Communities constituted fraud. Purchasers filed a $100 million class action suit, and the FTC a complaint.[3] In the words of the latter, "Lots [at Rio Communities] are of little value to purchasers as investments and little use as homesites."[4]

The FTC proposed a "cease and desist" order, and the parties to the class-action suit proposed a settlement. These together would somewhat modify Horizon's sales policies. However, neither would require the one thing which would give lots some significant value, namely the extension of central water and other basic services.

Thus, outside the core development area--which comprises less than 1% of the subdivision's acreage--for the foreseeable future, Rio Communities is likely to remain raw New Mexico grassland. The subdivision presently has just 1,790 residents. It has the longest estimated time span before full occupancy--several thousand years-- of any subdivision in this study.† Land is held in small parcels by tens of thousands of lot owners. It is to date "improved" by only 1,700 miles of dirt road, and it looks no different now than it did fifteen years ago when Horizon began selling it. The land's owners can neither use their lots, nor sell them, even at prices lower than they paid, and those who have not yet finished paying off their contracts--perhaps a hundred thousand people--will undoubtedly find themselves in the same predicament, when they too become "homesite" owners.

---

*The U.S. Department of Housing and Urban Development, Office of Interstate Land Sales Registration (OILSR), requires the development company to issue a Property Report giving important consumer information on the lots offered for sale.

†Includes both the ten subdivisions in Volume I of this study and the nine Florida subdivisions analyzed in Volume II.

Regional Context

Rio Communities is in an area of heavy subdivision activity. Besides this site, whose 242,000 acres lie south of Albuquerque, Horizon owns Paradise Hills, a 13,000-acre subdivision to the north of the city. There are also AMREP's Rio Rancho Estates, covering 91,000 acres, and Great Western Cities' Cochiti Lake, a 6,300-acre recreational subdivision. (See chapters on Rio Rancho and Cochiti Lake.) Horizon's promotional materials describe a study which projects a possible population in a three-county area around Albuquerque of 467,800 to 531,400 by the year 2000, a 37% to 56% increase over the 1970 population. Yet Rio Rancho and Rio Communities alone have enough lots to house, at a rate of three people per homesite, 816,000 people. The city of Belen, across the Rio Grande from Rio Communities' "Enchanted Mesa" core development area, is a sleepy ranching and agricultural town of about 6,000.* Belen is principally distinguished by being the main east-west switching yard for the Santa Fe Railroad.

History

The Horizon Corporation, formed in 1959, holds nearly half a million acres of land in Arizona, New York, and Texas, in addition to New Mexico. (See chapter on Arizona Sunsites.) Most of this land has been marketed both nationally and, until 1974, internationally, as part of six separate subdivisions. At the height of its marketing success in 1972, the company had a sales force of 1,651 and made most of its sales--as it stated in its 1975 Form 10-K Report filed with the Securities and Exchange Commission--"to people who do not see the land before they buy it."[5]

Horizon began marketing lots at Rio Communities in 1961. Its early sales materials stressed the prospects for immediate growth, population increase, and financial gain. Horizon distributed a 1964 brochure, entitled *HOW TO SUCCESSFULLY INVEST IN REAL ESTATE*, which counseled people that:

> •...real estate investment...[is] one of the safest, surest ways of increasing your capital and preserving your income.
>
> •A well-chosen site--in the path of population expansion, near main access roads, etc.,--that is not yet fully developed can bring a 25% or higher return on your money in relatively short order. Moreover, the safety of your capital is

---

*The greater Belen Chamber of Commerce Community Audit places the 1974 Belen/Rio Communities population at 7,900.

> almost guaranteed by the fastastic demand for
> land in the Southwest and the intrinsic value
> of real property.
>
> • Subdivisions, particularly in growth areas in
> the earliest stages of development, or even
> beyond development, will undoubtedly continue
> to grow at a rapid clip.[6]

As government agencies began to examine sales materials more closely and to regulate more stringently the unequivocal use of investment as an inducement to purchase, Horizon moderated its message. In a 1972 brochure it counseled people to purchase land in the "predeveloped period" when "the price of land is still relatively low. Long term population growth is clearly predictable and planning for future development is starting to get underway....With very few exceptions, the predevelopment stage is precisely the best time for people with moderate resources to buy land."[7]

Even today, Horizon advertises Rio Communities as "a carefully planned cluster of communities growing so rapidly that they seem to have emerged like a mirage."[8] However, it generally includes qualifiers such as the following:

> The extent to which Horizon's Rio Communities
> will benefit from anticipated area growth will
> depend upon industrial growth in eastern Valen-
> cia County, highway and mass transportation
> systems which may evolve in the future, the
> market's perception of the desirability of the
> community as a preferred location for resi-
> dence, business and industry, the availability
> of natural resources and other presently unpre-
> dictable factors.[9]

In fact, the project is composed of seven vast parcels of land, considered separate but barely distinguishable even by name: Rio Grande Estates, Rancho Rio Grande, Rancho Rio Grande East, Tierra Grande, Rio del Oro, Canyon del Rio Estates, and Enchanted Mesa. As of May, 1975, three of these areas had been pulled off the market because they were almost totally sold out. But lots in Rio del Oro, Tierra Grande, and Canyon del Rio Estates--138,000 acres--were still offered for sale on the installment basis.*[10]

---

*Horizon Corporation was among the most cooperative companies in the INFORM sample. It provided a wealth of statistics and documents on Rio Communities. Unfortunately, since the enormity of the site makes accuracy difficult if not impossible, the data provided are not consistent.

Enchanted Mesa lots, developed and usable, were offered for cash with the provision that purchasers begin constructing a home within 90 days.[11]

The disparity between Horizon's sales messages and the reality of its projects finally caused legal trouble. In the early 1970s the Federal Trade Commission began an investigation.* On March 17, 1975, the Commission issued a lengthy complaint alleging that the company used "unfair and deceptive practices" in selling lots at Rio Communities and three other sites: Paradise Hills, Horizon City, Texas, and Waterwood, Texas. The complaint and a proposed cease and desist order alleged that Horizon misrepresented the usefulness and value of lots as investments or homesites, did not accurately portray the extent of current and proposed development, and was misleading with regard to the possibility of resale. It further stated that:

> [Horizon's projects] consist primarily of vacant acreage with limited industrial, commercial, shopping and recreational facilities; limited amenities; and limited public services. In substantially all instances the only building which has occurred or in most instances is likely to occur in each property is in areas reserved by [the company]. The amount of such building is insignificant in relation to the total acreage of each property and the length of time [the company] has been offering for sale and selling lots located within each property.[12]

Horizon denied all material allegations and intends to contest the complaint. The case will be heard first by the Commission and may ultimately be decided by the federal appellate courts. In its defense, it asserts, among other things, "That the purchase of Horizon's land, at the prices for which [it] is offered for sale, is a desirable expenditure of discretionary assets for either investment or use over a long term of years...."[13]

If the FTC is successful and the proceedings result in a final cease and desist order, Horizon may have to stop designating lots as homesites unless the improvements and utilities that would make them usable are provided during the contract period. It may also have to begin refunding money to defaulting purchasers, and provide a ten-day "cooling off" period after contracts are signed. Furthermore, in the event of such a ruling the FTC can institute a new civil action in state or federal court to seek refunds

---

*The FTC has also investigated several other companies studied by INFORM, including GAC, ITT, AMREP, and Great Western Cities.

or restitution for past consumers. The process from complaint to restitution will take many years.

Also in 1975, Horizon agreed to settle a $100 million class-action lawsuit brought against it by purchasers of lots at Rio Communities and Horizon City, Texas. The class alleged that the value of lots was considerably less than the sales price, and that Horizon "made deceptive and misleading oral and written representations and utilized deceptive and misleading sales practices and materials which violated the provisions of the Interstate Land Sales Full Disclosure Act and constituted common law fraud."[14]

The proposed settlement agreement covered 46,000 purchasers who bought lots at the two subdivisions between October 31, 1971, and February 28, 1975.[15] Unlike the September, 1974, settlement of the class-action suit against GAC Corporation, under which that company agreed to make available $4.5 million in contract credits, pay $500,000 in partial refunds to defaulted purchasers, and adhere to a five-year development schedule, Horizon's proposed settlement provided very little. The only refund provision was that already established by law: if purchasers had not been given the federal Property Report, they were eligible for a full refund. All other "restitution" was via certain lot exchange programs described in detail under *Consumer Protection* in this chapter.

THE OFFERING: LAND AND IMPROVEMENTS

LAND

Physical Characteristics

The land at Rio Communities is virtually all semi-arid, desert grassland. It lies near, but does not actually abut, the Rio Grande. Six of the seven "communities," including the core area, lie east of the Rio Grande. The seventh, a 33,682-acre parcel, is west of the river.

Most of the site is relatively flat, rising gradually to the steeper slopes of the Manzano Mountain foothills to the east. The site's elevation ranges from 4,800 to 6,000 feet above sea level. Like much of the land in New Mexico, that of Rio Communities is heavily dissected by a network of natural drainageways known as arroyos. These are normally dry, but during summer cloudbursts they fill with rainwater flowing from the mountains to the river and become raging torrents.

Status of Development

Despite minimal actual development at Rio Communities, lots have sold well. In the three oldest of the seven "communities,"--Rio Grande Estates, Rancho Rio Grande, and Rancho Rio Grande East--lots are now virtually all sold out. Horizon purchased these sites from one landowner in 1960 at the bargain price of $9.50 an acre. Over 65,000 lots were marketed during the 1960s. Prices which started at $200 for one acre and $700 for five acres by 1975 had risen to $700 for a one-acre lot and $28,000 for a "parcel."[16]

In the three newer "communities"--Tierra Grande, Canyon del Rio Estates, and Rio del Oro--50% to 85% of the total 100,000 lots have been sold. Purchased in 1969 and 1970 from several different owners, the land in these areas cost Horizon more than its earlier purchase: $75 to $100 an acre.* One-quarter- and one-third-acre lots now sell for $1,000, with "parcels" of indeterminate size selling for up to $50,000.[17]

The seventh area, Enchanted Mesa,† is the only identifiable and actual "community." It consists of 2,180 acres--less than one percent of the total site--and is subdivided into 3,600 lots.▽[18] Horizon has retained ownership of much of this land, offering it since 1974 at prices ranging from $3,500 to $12,000 per lot.[19] Only those wishing to build a home immediately may purchase, or obtain by exchanging an outlying lot, a lot in the Enchanted Mesa area. Horizon's capital investments in Rio Communities between 1960 and 1975 total $23 million. Since there is little development elsewhere, most of this must have been spent in Enchanted Mesa.[20]

In the site as a whole, Horizon still has between 12,000 and 20,000 lots on the market. This inventory exceeds the total number of lots at several of the subdivisions in the INFORM study.∆ It has already sold approximately 160,000 lots, more than the total number of lots at eighteen sites in the study. Of these lots, 48,000 are fully paid for and deeded to their purchasers. Yet Rio Communities currently has a resident population of only 1,790 peo-

---

*Prices available only for Rio del Oro and Canyon del Rio Estates.

†The Enchanted Mesa section includes the Vista del Rio mobile-home park and the Playa Verde golf-course development area.

▽Only 1,319 acres subdivided into 2,682 lots are platted.

∆In a notebook of facts prepared for INFORM, Horizon reported on one page that 160,000 of its 172,000 lots are sold or under contract for sale. On another page, it reported that there are at least 20,714 lots unsold: 13,195 in Rio del Oro; 5,291 in Canyon del Rio; and at least 2,228 in Tierra Grande.[21]

RIO COMMUNITIES: STATUS OF DEVELOPMENT

Name	size lots (acres)	# acres platted	# lots offered	# dwellings	% sold out	basic services
Enchanted Mesa (core & exchange)	¼ - 1	2,180	2,680 - 3,600	770	?	available (except water in Unit 1)
Rio del Oro	¼ - ½	43,280	87,970	0	85	available on aid in construction basis only
Canyon del Rio	¼ - 5	14,845	11,025	0	52	not available—Units 1-9; Units 10-12 aid in construction basis only
Rancho Rio Grande East	2½ - 5	18,685	?	0	99	available on aid in construction basis only
Rancho Rio Grande	2½ - 80	24,080	5,415	0	99	none
Rio Grande Estates	½ - 1	52,150	60,296	0	93	none
Tierra Grande	5 - 40	67,215	5,572	3 (model homes)	21-59 (depending on area)	none

ple. By contrast, the other two subdivisions in the INFORM sample of comparable size and age--Cape Coral (144,000 lots) and Port Charlotte (196,750 lots), both in Florida--have attracted populations of 25,000 and 39,000 respectively. (See chapters in Volume II of this study.)

The prospect of Rio Communities ever acquiring a substantial population, much less of achieving full build-out on all its 172,000 lots, is extremely remote. The subdivision has virtually no economic base, it offers no particular recreational opportunities, and it is just one of many subdivisions in the area which could offer "bedrooms" to participants in Albuquerque's highly touted boom.

Horizon's President Sidney Nelson stated in a 1974 address to the New Mexico Press Women's Association, "I would hope that a community developer, like Horizon, could be accepted as performing in the public interest, too. We believe that what we are doing is a needed public service in solving pollution and growth problems."[22] Yet Rio Communities' present growth rate suggests a very limited need for the subdivision. A February, 1972, Horizon promotional brochure lists the site as having 369 dwelling units. By early 1976, this had increased to just 770 units, an addition of only about 100 units a year. If Rio Communities were to continue to grow at the same average annual build-out rate exhibited over the first fifteen years of its existence, it would take 3,350 years for all of its lots to be fully occupied.

BASIC SERVICES

Horizon accepts no responsibility, has made no arrangements, and has set aside no money in trust or escrow for any basic services.[23] It provides no water, sewage disposal, solid-waste disposal, drainage, electricity, gas, or telephone service to any lot or unit outside the core development area: an area which includes Enchanted Mesa, the Playa Verde golf-course development, and the Vista del Rio mobile-home park. Furthermore, all of the 3,600 core-area lots are not fully developed. Horizon reported to INFORM that central water lines have only been extended to about 650 lots and central sewer lines to about 168 lots.

Horizon's failure to promise any basic services places Rio Communities among the seven out of nineteen subdivisions in the INFORM sample at which a lot purchaser is not guaranteed even a paved road. The 99% of the site outside of the Enchanted Mesa area may be usable only if lot owners or improvement associations provide all utilities and services. Horizon explains this rather straightforwardly in its Form 10-K Report, a document unfortunately seen by few people except financial analysts.

> The "laying out and planning" of a project or a community is not analogous to the "development" of a project or a community. The fact that any particular project has been laid out and planned by the Company does not insure its development. Except for limited "immediate development" areas in certain projects, the only improvements which the company generally obligates itself to provide are fronting access roads, which in certain cases are paved and in other cases are not paved, although other improvements are sometimes supplied.[24]

In some areas, services are offered on an "aid-in-construction" basis, in which the lot owner "aids" the utility company by paying all costs of extending service from existing lines in excess of what is economically feasible for the utility. The amount spent by the lot owner can be refunded from revenues earned, if other users move in and use the utility line within five years. However, this arrangement is beyond the means of most individual lot owners.

The cost of extension depends on the demand, the size of the area to be served, and the distance from the existing system. Horizon reported to INFORM that extension of electricity costs $4,000 to $5,000 per mile and that extension of telephone lines costs approximately $6,200 per mile.[25] However, its estimates of utility extension costs vary widely in its 1975 federal Property Reports for different "communities." Extension of electricity ranged from $3,000 to $9,500 per mile; extension of telephone lines ranged from $8,000 to $33,000; and extension of central water lines was approximately $15,840.[26] These costs totaled $572,500 to extend water mains, electricity lines, and telephone lines to the most remote lot in Canyon del Rio Estates, 15 miles from the developed core.[27]

If the provisions of the FTC-proposed order were effected, Horizon would be required to print on the sales contracts for most of its sites:

> THIS COMPLETELY UNDEVELOPED LAND IS BEING SOLD "AS IS." Electricity, water, sewer and telephone service are not planned for this subdivision and may be impossible for you to obtain at a reasonable cost. Your lot will be accessible, if at all, only by unpaved roads which will not be maintained. The use of such roads may be impossible without maintenance. Your lot has virtually no use at present or in the foreseeable future.[28]

There are no special service districts on site. The presumed source of all site improvements is Rio Communities' two property-owners associations: the Horizon Communities Improvement Association and the Tierra Grande Improvement Association. These organizations were set up to "develop the common good and social welfare" of residents at Rio del Oro, Enchanted Mesa, Canyon del Rio Estates, and Tierra Grande. The associations, to which all purchasers and owners of lots in these "communities" belong, are empowered to make and increase assessments,* borrow money, and spend money. They can also establish and enforce liens, covenants, conditions, and restrictions on the land; extend, operate, maintain, and repair utilities and services; manage and control community use of these services; and sell or dispose of these services and facilities.[29]

There are three serious problems inherent in Rio Communities' associations. The first is that they have the authority to provide site improvements, but are not obligated to do so. According to Horizon Vice President Richard Marshall, no funds were spent in the first two years of either association's existence except for administration.[30]

The FTC has alleged that this authority-without-obligation arrangement is unfair because lot purchasers, while they are required to pay annual assessments to the association, are given no guarantee that these funds will be spent for the improvement of their lots.[31] The FTC's proposed order would prohibit Horizon from requiring a purchaser to join or make payments to any improvement association which is not legally obligated to provide or make all basic services available to his lot by the time his installment payments have been completed.[32]

The second problem with the associations is that the annual assessments cannot possibly cover the costs of constructing and maintaining all site facilities. The associations are empowered to provide: parks and recreational facilities and services; drainage systems; streets, roads, curbs, gutters, landscaping, and lighting; sewage and garbage collection and treatment; any mass-transit facilities; public-utilities systems for electric power and natural gas; communications systems; social, cultural, educational, or recreational buildings; hospitals and clinics; libraries; traffic-control systems and parking lots; facilities for animal rescue and shelter; and zoos, playgrounds, bowling alleys, tennis courts, and other miscellaneous recreational facilities.[33] In 1974, the $13 to $50 an individual paid in annual fees totaled $2.6 million. Of this

---

*The percentage increase in assessments is not to exceed the increase in the U.S. Bureau of Labor Statistics consumer price index.

total, Horizon paid $400,000.[34] Such fees cannot possibly cover the costs of both constructing and maintaining a "city" twice the size of Albuquerque. In fact, based on estimates made by Great Western Cities for its Cochiti Lake subdivision, the cost of providing basic services to a 6,300-acre development would be $28 million. Rio Communities is 38 times as large. (See chapter on Cochiti Lake.)

The third problem with the associations is that their broad powers are in effect vested with Horizon rather than with the lot owners. This is because the company's position as the largest landowner gives it the largest single block of votes. Thus, although it is legally limited to a maximum of one vote less than 50%, Horizon will undoubtedly continue to constitute a controlling interest for a great many years.

The associations are governed by boards of directors. As of the end of 1974, four of the five members of the Horizon Communities Improvement Association board were Horizon officials. The fifth was a resident appointed by the other four.[35] The Director of the Association acknowledged to an Albuquerque newspaper that "the vote of the directors is tantamount to total control," but he added that since the company officials know what is going on, they are the best source of input.[36] Board members are elected at annual meetings by mailed ballots. A term on the board lasts five years.

The *Albuquerque Journal*, in a December 19, 1974, editorial, called the Horizon Communities Improvement Association "an exaggerated example of taxation without representation, except in this case, the oppression comes from a private corporation rather than an agency of government."[37] It suggested establishing a review board consisting entirely of purchasers or providing proportional purchaser representation on the board of directors.

Water

In an arid region like the Southwest, water is the crucial determinant of land value. Without adequate supplies of water, no development and no urban growth can occur. Horizon has not assured Rio Communities of an adquate water supply, it has not verified the quality and purity of groundwater at the site, and it has made no arrangements to provide water to lots outside the core development area.

A small existing central water system, operated by the Rio Grande Utility Company, a Horizon subsidiary, supplies water to 650 lots. Because this actual development is so minimal, there have been no water-supply problems to date. However, should the site's population potential ever be realized, water problems could be serious. In its 1975 federal Property Reports, Horizon straightforwardly discloses the extent of its concern about the water supply and the consequences of its potential inadequacy.

> The developer has not obtained an engineer's report or a hydrological survey indicating the source and quantity of water in the subdivision and accordingly there is no assurance that a sufficient quantity of water will be available to serve the anticipated population of the subdivision.[38]

In New Mexico, as in most arid, western states, the ownership and use of water is a legal right determined by water law and court decisions. These matters are administered by a state agency, the State Engineer Office. Horizon does not have sufficient legal water rights for the ultimate population of Rio Communities. In its 1975 federal Property Reports for Rio del Oro and Canyon del Rio Estates, Horizon reported that it:

> ...has purchased water rights to serve only the population of the existing development [approximately 1,790 people] and five years anticipated growth thereof. The population is estimated to be 10,000 people. Additional water rights will have to be acquired in the future to serve a population in excess of that number of people. Such additional rights are currently available but there is no assurance of future availability.*[39]

According to the New Mexico State Engineer Office, Rio Communities has rights to 2,690 acre-feet of water per year (2.4 million gallons per day) and used 680.19 acre-feet (607,500 gallons per day) in 1973.[40] The Belen Chamber of Commerce describes Rio Communities' water system as having a capacity of 933,000 gallons per day.†[41]

---

*Given the subdivision's growth rate thus far, it is likely to be considerably later than 1980 before Rio Communities has a population of 10,000.

†In answer to INFORM's questions about its water rights, the company responded: "Horizon's water rights acquisition program began in 1961; the amounts, prices and other information are company proprietary." However, it did state that Rio Communities was using 216,666 gallons of water a day, one-third of what the state said it was using. It also reported that the capacity of its water system is 500,000 gallons per day, about half of what the Belen Chamber of Commerce said it was.

The lack of a central water supply is potentially one of the most serious problems for many Rio Communities lot purchasers. Although New Mexico water law allows individuals to drill wells and withdraw up to three acre-feet of water per year,* state Environmental Improvement Agency regulations issued in 1973 now prohibit such wells on lots smaller than three quarters of an acre if septic tanks are used for sewage disposal.[42] Horizon has not planned a central sewage system, yet a great many lots at Rio Communities, including all those in Rio del Oro, are smaller than this minimum size. These lots will be completely useless as homesites until a central sewage or water system is extended. Commercial and multi-family lots will be equally useless unless owners either purchase water rights or extend a central water system, since the three acre-feet allowance applies only to individual domestic water use. In Horizon's words, "You will not be permitted to use individual water systems and water will not be available to your lot until the central water system has been completed."[43]

Unfortunately, "the central water system" is available only if lot owners pay for aid-in-construction extension. As previously described, the distances involved make this an economically impossible alternative: the estimated cost of extension, at $3 per foot, to the most remote lot in Rio del Oro is $340,000.[44]

There are also economic constraints on the use of individual wells. Wells cost between $660 and $3,850 depending on the depth of the water table. In Rancho Rio Grande, the "community" located on the west side of the Rio Grande, wells are even more expensive. Because the tract is on a high plateau, the depth of the water table in some of the units is greater than 500 feet. Horizon states in a 1972 advertising brochure that in this area, "development contemplated by a user should be of a scope to make a central water system or extension of a municipal [such as Belen's] economically feasible,"[45] i.e., don't buy unless you are a developer planning to re-subdivide, build homes, and install central water. These costs were obviously not taken into consideration during site planning. While it might actually be possible to engage in development of this scope on some of the eighty-acre tracts which Horizon has of-

---

*Although it has been debated during several New Mexico legislative sessions, a law prohibiting individual wells in large-scale subdivisions has not yet been passed. In 1973, the Office, State Engineer, pursuant to the New Mexico Subdivision Act, recommended that all counties promulgate regulations requiring central community water systems in subdivisions with more than 25 lots any one of which was smaller than ten acres. Valencia and Socorro Counties were among the six counties--out of 32--that did not adopt this regulation.

fered for sale in Rancho Rio Grande, it is highly impractical on the two-and-a-half- to five-acre lots which compose much of the "community."

Sewage

Horizon planned that virtually all lots at Rio Communities would employ individual sewage-disposal systems: septic tanks. There is a very limited central-sewage collection system now in use in the core development area. It services 168 quarter-acre lots and mobile homes. Operated by Horizon's Rio Grande Utility Corporation subsidiary, the system has a 100,000 gallon-per-day-capacity package plant which treats 35,000 gallons per day.

Although Horizon reported to INFORM that the number of lots planned for connection to a central sewage system is indeterminate until state environmental legislation is completed, its federal Property Reports unequivocally state:

> Sewers are not presently available. The developer has made no provision for the installation of a central sanitary sewerage system nor has the developer made any provision to set aside any money to fund the installation of such a system.[46]

The planned reliance on septic tanks renders a great many Rio Communities lots useless as homesites. In the 1960's, the New Mexico Department of Health, now the Environmental Improvement Agency, generally approved the use of septic tanks for residential lots at Rio Communities. Its regulations then permitted the use of such systems on quarter-acre lots with central water and on half-acre lots with wells.[47] However, since 1973, the Agency's regulations have limited septic systems to one-half- to three-quarter-acre lots with central water and three-quarter- to one-acre lots with individual wells. If the soils have "severe limitations" for septic-tank use, as determined by soil depth to bedrock or water table, slope, percolation rate, and flooding potential, the regulations prohibit septic systems altogether.[48]

The consequences for lot owners of these new regulations are disclosed in Horizon's 1975 federal Property Reports. One pertinent piece of information is that lot owners can get septic-tank permits (prerequisite to building permits) only after having percolation tests done. If these tests indicate unsuitable soil conditions, the health department will not issue a septic-tank permit, and the lot may not be used until a central sewage-disposal system is extended. If a lot is smaller than the three-quarter- to one-acre minimum size, as many Rio Communities lots are, its owner may apply for a variance. The federal Property Reports state that although the health department has granted such variances it will not necessarily continue doing so. Finally, owners of multi-family and commercial lots may be required to provide a central sewage system or individual package plant.[49]

As is the case with all other basic services, the construction and extension of a central sewage system beyond the core area will be the responsibility of the Horizon Communities Improvement Association or individual lot owners. At present, septic systems or individual package plants cost between $350 and $1,250. There is no charge for hookup to the central sewage system.

Solid Waste

Three independent companies provide solid-waste collection services to the core development area. Wastes are disposed of in the Valencia County sanitary landfill.

Roads

Unpaved roads built to company rather than county standards are the only basic service which Horizon promises to provide. Accordingly, the company has bladed 1,700 miles of dirt roads--enough to stretch from Albuquerque to Buffalo, N.Y.--while constructing only 14.3 miles of paved roads. Yet, incredible as it seems, Horizon has still to construct 58% of the roads planned for Canyon del Rio, 89% of the roads planned for Rio del Oro, and 81% of the roads planned for Tierra Grande. The company admits that, except for units of Tierra Grande, no bond, escrow, or trust arrangement guarantees completion of these roads.

Road maintenance may become a problem. In a 1972 advertisement, Horizon stated that "road maintenance is subject to the availability of equipment, regular programming of schedules, the discretion of the maintainer, and the availability of funds."[51] In 1976, Horizon reported to INFORM that although Valencia County has accepted maintenance responsibility for nearly 900 miles of Rio Communities' roads, it does not actually provide this service. Horizon maintains the roads in the "core development area and some adjacent land"; the improvement associations will maintain the roads in their areas; but no one currently maintains the roads in the rest of the site.

Drainage

The entire Rio Communities site is dissected by major and minor arroyos: deep, wide gullies which carry rainfall from the Manzano Mountains to the Rio Grande. Besides providing roadside ditches and easements, Horizon has not elaborated on this natural drainage system, nor has it installed any artificial channels or storm sewers in the undeveloped areas of the site.[52] In its 1975 federal Property Reports, the company states that "erosions and flooding could result in property damage and could create a health and safety hazard."[53] The improvement associations are responsible for elaborating on and maintaining natural drainage.

The Federal Trade Commission charged that the drainage easements at Rio Communities limit the amount of land a purchaser can actually use. It alleged that Horizon's failure to disclose their nature, location, size, and significance constitutes a deceptive act or practice. Horizon, however, maintains that with the exception of some large (e.g., forty-acre) tracts in Tierra Grande, no parcels have drainage easements running across or through them. In the company's words, "The land has been engineered so that drainage runs across common ground for the most part. There are a few acres throughout Rio Communities where drainage easements run on the borders of some properties, but the most this should take up is 12 feet on the very edge of the property line. It's difficult to see how this would limit the use of a piece of property."[54]

Horizon's claims are probably true in the newer "communities" of Rio del Oro, Canyon del Rio, and Tierra Grande. There, on the basis of engineering studies, arroyos and other natural drainageways sufficient to accommodate the runoff from a 100-year storm were set aside as park areas. However, it seems unlikely that lots in the oldest "communities"--Rio Grande Estates, Rancho Rio Grande, and Rancho Rio Grande East--are free of drainage easements or arroyos subject to flooding. These areas were platted in the early 1960s in a rigid gridiron pattern with little attention paid to natural features. (See discussion under Environmental Protection.)

Electricity and Telephone

As of March, 1975, the Rio Communities core development area had 700 telephone connections and 26 miles of gas mains.[55] The utility companies (Southern Union Gas Company, Mountain States Telephone, and Public Service Company of New Mexico) will extend service to areas outside the core only on an aid-in-construction basis. The 1975 federal Property Reports warn just how outrageously expensive extension of these services to lots without intervening development might be. Bringing electricity to the most remote lot in Rio del Oro would cost $120,000. To the most remote lot in Canyon del Rio Estates, the cost would be $142,500. Extension of telephone lines to these remote lots would cost $120,000.[56]

Horizon reminded INFORM that the cost of extending utilities could be shared by many lot owners. It also suggested alternate options available to an outlying-lot owner such as trading his lot for one closer to the core, or installing a generator and a radio telephone. A generator would cost $3,500, and a radio telephone, $2,500. The company added that, "A less expensive system now being used by several remote lot owners in Rio and Tierra Grande involves use of Citizens Band radio to a micro-wave relay, which patches into the local telephone system. Base unit cost is $250."[57] Utility lines are placed both above and below ground, depending on the area.

COMMUNITY AND RECREATIONAL FACILITIES

Rio Communities has very limited community and recreational facilities. The Enchanted Mesa core development area has a 26-man volunteer fire department; one church; and a few small stores. Its one industry, a Cannon Craft louvered-shutters manufacturing plant, employs 45 people. For other jobs, as well as for schools, public transportation, police protection, doctors, dentists, and a hospital, the residents of Rio Communities must rely on the resources of Belen, New Mexico, the town of 6,000 people 3 miles northwest of Enchanted Mesa, or on those of Albuquerque, 36 miles away. A bus line connecting Rio Communities with Belen and Albuquerque has been proposed by the Road Runner Bus Company.

Compared to many subdivisions, Rio Communities offers few recreational amenities. There are two community centers and a nine-hole public golf course. There is also a private country club which has a swimming pool, tennis courts, and another nine-hole golf course. Membership fees are $350 initially and $35 per month. The provision and maintenance of any current or future community recreational facilities is the responsibility of the improvement associations.

ENVIRONMENTAL PROTECTION

The land at Rio Communities is not exceptionally valuable or critical in terms of the region's ecology. Nevertheless, the development practices used there, particularly prior to the 1970s, leave much to be desired. Relative to those at other subdivisions--such as the nearby Cochiti Lake subdivision--Horizon's practices at Rio Communities are poor.

PLANNING

Rio Communities was described by site manager Lamar Hanson as "a massive parcel of land master-planned for a full city with all the city facilities."[58] But even on paper, this statement could be construed as true for no more than half the site.

There is a very noticeable difference between the layouts of the older and newer "communities." As delineated on the company's promotional land-use plan, the older areas--Rancho Rio Grande East, Rio Grande Estates, and Rancho Rio Grande--are laid out with very little concern for natural topography or the realistic needs of a community. Lot units and blocks are all rectangles superimposed on the asymmetry of the land, ignoring its curves and valleys. Virtually the entire length of property along both sides of the state roads that traverse the site is designated as commercial land, guaranteeing that if the tract is ever actually developed to any significant extent there will be miles of neon-lit "strips." Furthermore, in the entire 95,000 acres, only one tiny area is designated on the map as park or community space.

The plans for the newer areas--Rio del Oro, Canyon del Rio and Tierra Grande--are quite different. They were master planned by the noted firm of Victor Gruen Associates. In these "communities" at least some land use conforms to the topography. Space has been allocated for parks and "greenbelts" (mostly brown in this dry climate), arroyos have been left in their natural states, and "strips" have been avoided by centralizing commercial and multi-family use areas.

INFORM could not accurately determine the amount of land reserved for permanent open space at Rio Communities. Horizon variously reported the figure 21,000 acres, or 8.7% of the site's acreage, and 43,560 acres, or 18%.[59] INFORM was able to confirm that 14,500 acres, located on the steeper slopes of the Manzano Mountains at the eastern edge of the site, were designated in the master plan as a park. But all these estimates are less than the 25% open-space allocation advocated by most planners. By contrast, 30% of the Cochiti Lake subdivision has been reserved for open space. However, given the fact that after 15 years, more than 99% of the site is still empty, the amount of land planned as open space cannot be considered the site's major problem.

Horizon also reported to INFORM that 40% of the site is planned in a gridiron pattern, 30% in a curvilinear pattern, and 30% in a cluster pattern.

Phased development, the most sensible and careful way of extending a community, has almost no role at Rio Communities. Lots have been sold all over the 400-square-mile site, and it is Horizon's policy to blade a road to any lot by the time it is paid for. The company reported to INFORM that it constructs such roads only to conform with a New York State law requiring that purchasers have physical access to their lots. It stated that, "Environmental interests often oppose these roads as 'unused' and damaging to terrain; however, the developer has no control over the matter. It would be less expensive for the developer not to build such roads until demand for them was sufficient."[60] The developer does, however, have control over where it sells lots and whether it sells them before there is a sufficient demand. Controlling sales in this manner would be the best way to promote sound land use.

The only semblance of phased development, and one that is vastly out of scale with the total size of Rio Communities, is Horizon's practice of retaining acreage throughout the project. This land surrounds the existing core development area of Enchanted Mesa, and future "core development areas" in Tierra Grande,* Rio del Oro, and Canyon del Rio. Horizon retains this acreage to provide lots for "future growth" and to maintain an inventory of "developable" lots to exchange for those of outlying-lot owners who want to build a home. While such a policy has the desirable effect of insuring that home-building will proceed outward from a "core," it also insures that the economic benefits of this growth accrue to Horizon rather than to lot owners waiting for an opportunity to resell. Horizon reported to INFORM that in an effort to prevent speculation it has not revealed the size or location of the Canyon del Rio core area. Nor has it revealed its plans for any of the areas.

LAND

Apart from its limited water resources, the Rio Communities site is generally appropriate for development from an environmental standpoint. It contains no valuable water-related resources (estuaries, wetlands, etc.), no habitats of endangered species, and no prime agricultural lands. The site's only areas of environmental concern are its archeological ruins. According to company advertising materials which promote the archeological interest of the site, artifacts and signs of an ancient village have been found and "arrowheads are almost commonplace on the property." The company reported to INFORM that it is preserving an area of Rio del Oro currently being explored by a University of New Mexico professor. The research, which Horizon and the Horizon Communities Improvement

---

*Horizon refers to its few model houses in Tierra Grande as an existing second core development area. INFORM researchers do not concur because the houses are not occupied and no additional buildings are planned.

Isolated model home at Rio Communities.

Association are supporting with grants, labor, and security, has uncovered "several notable finds." Horizon has also "presently excluded" from subdivision activity a local landmark--El Cerro Hill--which is of important religious significance to the Isleta Indians.

The Rio Communities site does have areas that, because of natural hazards, are unsuitable for building. The land is crisscrossed with arroyos, there are slopes exceeding 25%, and like the rest of the Middle Rio Grande Valley, in which it is located, it is in an earthquake zone.

As mentioned, Horizon has set aside the steepest areas of the site--the Manzano Mountain foothills--as a park. In the newest "communities" it has also designated arroyos as greenbelts and equestrian trails. In the older "communities," it prevents building on arroyos by designating drainage easements. The lots in Tierra Grande seem most affected, having drainage easements ranging from thirty to a thousand feet in width. Lots with a gross area of 5 acres can thus be reduced to a 3.6-acre usable area.[61] One reason the lots in Tierra Grande are as large as they are (5 to 40 acres) may be to accommodate these easements.

WATER RESOURCES

The drainage system at Rio Communities is not adequate to control erosion and urban runoff either on or below the site. As quoted earlier, the 1975 federal Property Reports warn that "erosion and flooding could result in property damage and could create a safety and health hazard."[62]

According to Paul Sears, in a *New Mexico Review* article entitled "How to Ignore a Flood," Horizon made no provision for managing arroyo flooding and runoff until 1969, platting most or all of Rancho Rio Grande and Rio Grande Estates, as well as part of Rio del Oro, without benefit of drainage studies.[63] In 1969, however, after landowners downslope of AMREP's nearby Rio Rancho subdivision sued that company for damage from floods and erosion, Horizon hired an engineering firm to study the drainage requirements for the 23,400 acres in Rio del Oro that were as yet unsubdivided. The firm was instructed to try to keep Horizon's expenses to a minimum. In March, 1970, it concluded that "excavated earth channel sections and existing natural arroyos...[are] the most economical way of transporting storm runoff...the only immediate problem for Horizon Corporation consists of assuring the required easement widths are set aside."[64]

According to *The New Mexico Review*, Horizon's cost constraints led to several compromises. One of these is that streets dip to cross arroyos rather than being carried over them on bridges. This is a dangerous practice considering the high velocities of floodwaters. Another is that there are inadequate outlets to the Rio Grande. As Paul Sears concluded in his article:

> No doubt exists,...that even with the beginnings of development at Rio del Oro, floodwaters from the tract will have to be conveyed safely into the Rio Grande. Horizon, by failing to establish specifications and related costs for the necessary outlet, has again shortchanged "investors" in its land, to say nothing of the hypothetical future residents and taxpayers of Rio del Oro.[65]

To the extent that they are adequate, in the portion of Rio del Oro to which the study applied, runoff is carried by natural water-courses. Corridors have been set aside for future construction of supplemental channels, and streets will carry local runoff to the maximum extent possible. However, since there has been virtually no elaboration on natural drainage, it may be presumed that retention ponds and sediment traps, which could prevent sediment and pollution from damaging land downslope and reaching the Rio Grande, have not been employed. The company also has no program for revegetating disturbed areas, a measure which could prevent erosion.

The potential also exists for a significant amount of pollution from sewage. If virtually all of Rio Communities were constructed as planned, with septic tanks and individual wells serving hundreds of thousands of lots, serious pollution and contamination could result. The implementation in 1973 of new state Environmental Improvement Agency sewage-disposal regulations lessened this potential by limiting the simultaneous use of septic tanks and individual wells to lots three-quarters to one acre in size. At the same time, it made the use of many of the site's lots contingent upon the installation of central water and/or sewage systems, improvements far beyond the means of individual lot owners.

The existing, small (100,000-gallon-per-day) sewage-treatment plant, serving 168 lots, operates at 35% of its capacity. It provides secondary treatment via an activated-sludge system. This method is considered an adequate level of control.

There is no indication that Rio Communities is depleting the site's groundwater resources. However, the company has no program for monitoring its depletion. The subdivision's impact on groundwater in this water-scarce state is thus unknown.

CONSUMER PROTECTION

Although Horizon's consumer practices are poor, the company was one of the most cooperative and candid in the INFORM sample. Its sales practices conform to the barest minimum required by state law. For example, the company does not have a consistent grace period for buyers who default: i.e., those who fail to promptly pay their monthly installments, improvement-association charges, and property taxes as billed by Horizon. Only in New York, where it is required by state law, does the company give purchasers a sixty-day grace period (with certified or registered mail notification) to catch up on payments before they forfeit their investment.[66] In constrast to Dart Industries, which seems to go to considerable lengths to discourage speculation and provide usable homesites, Horizon appears to have made speculation a cornerstone of its sales program.

Sales

As noted above, the Federal Trade Commission, in a legal proceeding that will probably not reach a final resolution for many years, has charged Horizon with fraudulent and deceptive sales practices. Among the abuses enumerated in its complaint against the company are the following: misrepresenting the purpose of sales dinners; disseminating promotional materials which purport to offer unbiased advice on real-estate purchases; using outdated testimonials to imply the company's good reputation; giving purchasers insufficient time to examine property reports; using contracts which employ incomprehensible language and small print; and implying in its sales "pitch" that it is urgent to buy a lot immediately before the price increases or a desired lot is sold to someone else.[67]

The actual lots which Horizon is selling at Rio Communities range in size from one-quarter acre to forty acres. Their prices vary from $1,000 to $28,000, depending on their location and projected usability. According to a salesman on the site, one-quarter- to one-acre lots in the Enchanted Mesa core area cost $3,500 to $5,500; lots in Playa Verde, the development area adjacent to the golf course, cost $4,500 to $12,000. In Canyon del Rio and Rio del Oro, defined by Horizon as "predeveloped areas," lots sell for $1,000 to $1,800. Lots in more remote outlying areas are even less expensive: $800 an acre in Rio Grande Estates, and $700 to $800 an acre for "ranch-size" lots (five to forty acres) in Tierra Grande.[68]

Enchanted Mesa lots, where basic services are available, are not sold on installment contracts. Anyone buying on installments is buying in the 99% of the site where the only improvement offered is a dirt road. Contracts are for periods ranging from two to nine years, with an average payment period of eight and a half years. Interest rates on the unpaid principal of the contract range from 5% to 8%. The minimum downpayment required is 10%. However, in certain situations, as noted in the 1975 federal Property Report, customers may make an initial deposit of only 5% provided an additional 5% is included in the first monthly payment.[69]

Horizon makes no guarantee that what purchasers receive for their money will be usable, valuable pieces of land. Its sales practices generally reflect a lack of concern about whether decisions to buy are careful and informed or whether purchasers are financially capable of meeting the terms of the contract they sign. In a report to INFORM, the company stated that it encourages prospective purchasers to visit the site before buying a lot. However, it disclosed in its 1973 Form 10-K Report filed with the Securities and Exchange Commission that "...most of Horizon's sales are made to people who do not see the land before they buy it."[70]

Horizon does not run credit checks on purchasers. It reported to INFORM that it has done so in the past, but that credit checks "did absolutely nothing in turning up factual economic data about the customer! They were, in short, unreliable." The company claims that when company salesmen make sales presentations in a customer's home, they are provided with an indication of the purchaser's capabilities and status.[71]

Horizon does not limit the sale of commercial and multi-family lots to businesses that put them to actual use. Nor does it require an independent closer or buyer's attorney to be present at a sale.

Indeed, of the seven INFORM guidelines for sales practices which would effectively limit speculation and prevent purchasers from getting in over their heads, Horizon adheres to only one: it currently limits purchasers to one lot without special approval of the vice president of sales and marketing.

Refunds

In accordance with Office of Interstate Land Sales Registration (OILSR) regulations, Horizon offers a purchaser 72 hours after seeing the Property Report in which to cancel his contract and receive a full refund. The Federal Trade Commission proposed order recommends a ten-business-day rescission period and inclusion of a cancellation form with every contract. INFORM, following the California precedent, recommends a fourteen-day rescission period.

Horizon explained to INFORM that, in practice, purchasers have a period of 21 to 30 days in which to change their minds, because a signed contract must travel a complex route within the corporation (from salesman to customer service to inventory manager to Horizon officer) before being returned to the customer with Property Reports and other disclosure information. The purchaser has the requisite 72 hours from the time he receives the well-traveled contract to cancel the sale.

After the rescission period, if a purchaser defaults on a contract, Horizon has the right to, and generally does, retain all payments. It also may sue for damages. The company says that it judges each case on its own merits and has on occasion made refunds to purchasers. However, the Federal Trade Commission complaint characterized the company's regular practice of retaining all payments in excess of reasonable damages as unfair.[72] Under similar circumstances, the Commission required GAC Corporation to make partial refunds to purchasers who default on payments.

Although the sales message and use of the terms "community" and "development" imply that services are or will be available, Horizon neither promises nor offers to provide water, sewage disposal, solid-waste disposal, paved roads, drainage, or electricity and telephone service to any lot outside of the core development area. If the company is not able to provide the two "improvements" it does promise--a dirt access road and the staking of one corner of the lot--it will refund the purchaser's payments and reclaim the lot. However, if the lack of other basic services renders the lot useless, it offers no refund, even if no improved lots are available for exchange.

The only other time a refund is made is when a buyer requests one immediately following a company-guided site tour on which it has been determined that the property was misrepresented at the time of sale. This tour must be taken during the first year of the contract. However, the purpose of encouraging visits seems to be to sell purchasers additional land. According to a sales representative at Rio Communities, 225 of the visitors to the site during July and August, 1974, had purchased during the previous year. Of this total, only 8 requested refunds, while 106 bought additional property.[73]

The Federal Trade Commission complaint alleged that Horizon's requiring an immediate request for a refund following the guided tour was unfair. It proposed that purchasers be given three days after a site visit to request a refund.

Title Protection

Purchasers at Rio Communities are not legally assured of acquiring title to their lots. Although lots are platted with the counties, Horizon writes its contracts in a recordable form only in

those states where it is required to do so. Elsewhere, contracts
can be made recordable with the counties only by the issuance of an
Addendum. Horizon will not issue this Addendum for a purchaser unless: he has paid 25% of the lot price; he makes a written request;
all his rescission rights, including the one-year site-inspection
period, have lapsed; and he agrees by executing the Addendum that
Horizon's affidavit will be conclusive proof of his default or forfeiture.[74]

The complexity of these requirements probably assures that
most purchasers do not record their contracts. This means that the
most minimal protection--notifying the county clerk that someone
has a financial interest in the land--does not exist. Without it,
if Horizon defaults or goes bankrupt, the buyer is subject to losing his lot and investment. In addition, the purchaser's interest
in the land may be secondary to that of any subsequent recorded
claim, to creditors of anyone with a prior interest in the land,
and to liens recorded subsequent to the date of the contract.

There are currently liens on the property, but they are subordinate to the interests of the purchaser provided he remains fully
compliant with the purchase-contract terms. Neither purchaser's
payments nor title to lots is held in trust or escrow. All funds
go into the company's general account. The result is that there is
no guarantee that the funds will be available to fulfill even Horizon's meager obligations.

Costs

While Horizon paid between $10 and $100 per acre for its land,
the purchaser, buying a lot ranging from a quarter acre to forty
acres in size, may find his investment rising into many thousands
of dollars. This includes the sales price of the raw land as well
as other related costs. The Federal Trade Commission charged as
unfair Horizon's practice of presenting a lot price as complete
when it does not include the costs of basic services.

Horizon explains the difference between the price it paid for
the land and the price it charges in the following manner:

> There are many factors involved in establishing
> this difference: the cost of surveying, conducting topographical studies, hydrologic studies and other engineering studies called for in
> the purchasing, masterplanning and subdividing
> of such sized tracts; other costs involved in
> the purchase, such as title fees, transfer fees
> and recording fees; the costs we incur by paying for property that is set aside for greenbelts, roadways, utility easements and community

sites; the costs we incur by deeding land over
free and clear to one of the Horizon Communities Improvement Associations, such as the Horizon Community Improvement Association of New Mexico or the Tierra Grande Improvement Association, or dedicating it for use as school or
church sites.

Then, too there is the cost of sales, the
cost of advertising, promotion, actual selling
and afterwards, customer service. And finally,
there is the tremendous cost of bringing a
property to market in full compliance with the
federal, state and local regulations designed
to protect the consumer and ensure environmental quality within the development.[75]

This explanation does not mention the cost of making the land usable for homesites. The lot purchaser is expected to pay this himself.

Expenses at Rio Communities include an annual assessment to either the Horizon Communities Improvement Association ($13 to $26 per year) or the Tierra Grande Improvement Association ($20 to $50 per year). There are also Valencia or Socorro County property taxes ($3 to $170 per year, depending on size, location and type of lot). Annual assessments during the 8½-year contract period could thus add as much as $1,870 to the basic purchase price of a lot. Another expense is accrued in staking the lot to locate its boundaries. In Canyon del Rio, this can cost $90 to $240; in Rio del Oro, $35; and in Tierra Grande, $150 to $240. Beyond these costs for the land itself, all costs of such basic improvements as would make the land usable--roads, sewage disposal, water, electricity, and telephone service--are additional. For pioneers or homesteaders, who choose to live outside the core area, and whose lots are sufficiently large (three-quarters to one acre) that the state will allow simultaneous use of a well and a septic system, a quasi-habitable homesite may be obtained with the following installations: a well and pump, costing $660 to $3,850; a septic tank costing $350 to $1,250; an electric generator costing $3,500; a radio-telephone $2,500; and bottled gas.[76] The installation of these utilities would thus total between $8,055 and $11,340.

A less adventurous lot purchaser who wishes to live in a more conventional suburban fashion may be able to trade an outlying lot for one in the core area. The only kind of exchange allowed is the trading of one single-family residential lot (i.e., not commercial, multi-family, or any other kind) for another of similar size, provided one is available. Construction of a home must begin within ninety days and must be completed within three months. The purchaser who chooses to exchange his lot must still pay the costs of extending utilities to the lot line, a charge which averages $2,200[77] and can run as high as $4,000[78] depending on a lot's size, its distance from existing lines, and the availability of the service. The company does not guarantee that improved lots will be available for exchange. As of mid-1976, there were approximately 500 lots available in trade-in areas. Horizon considered this an adequate inventory.

Resales

According to local realtors interviewed by INFORM, inquiries from out-of-state landowners about the possibilities of reselling the lots they own at Rio Communities are received at an average rate of five or six a week. The realtors say there is no resale market. In fact, those in the town of Belen generally will not even list property in Rio Communities because they assert that the lots cannot be located (they are staked only at one corner) and are over-priced. Ranch land in the area sells at $40 to $60 per acre and irrigated land is sold for $2,600 to $3,100 per acre. Since Horizon's land sells at a minimum of $700 an acre, is frequently priced at $7,500 an acre, and is not in the irrigation conservancy, local people are not interested.

Horizon states in its Property Reports that it makes no representation of the availability of a resale market and has no resale or repurchase program. The proposed Federal Trade Commission order would require Horizon to state further in all sales, advertising, and promotional materials:

> You should consider the purchase of land very risky. The future value of this land is very uncertain--do not count on an increase in its value. It has not been possible for purchasers of land from Horizon to resell the land at a profit. Purchasers usually have been unable to resell the land at all.[79]

Legal Status

The litigation surrounding the Federal Trade Commission's complaint against the company, as noted above, may be in the courts for many years. The class action suit, however, was settled in August, 1975. Horizon agreed in the settlement to make three minor changes in its consumer practices: to speed up its road-building and lot-staking programs; to cast its votes in favor of turning over road-maintenance responsibility to the Improvement Associations; and to include the following statement in all sales contracts:

THE PURCHASE OF ALL LAND ENTAILS RISK. THE FUTURE OF THIS LAND AND YOUR ABILITY TO RESELL IT ARE UNCERTAIN BEING SUBJECT TO MANY MARKET FACTORS. THE FUTURE POPULATION GROWTH OF THIS SUBDIVISION AND THE SURROUNDING AREAS CANNOT BE PREDICTED. THE SELLER OBLIGATES ITSELF TO PROVIDE ONLY LOT STAKING AND UNPAVED STREETS. THE AVAILABILITY AND COST OF SERVING YOUR LOT WITH CENTRAL WATER, SEWAGE DISPOSAL, ELECTRICAL POWER OR TELEPHONE SERVICES CANNOT BE ASSURED. SEE THE PROPERTY REPORT FOR IMPORTANT INFORMATION CONCERNING THESE AND OTHER MATTERS.[80]

The settlement required Horizon to do very little in terms of relief for past lot purchasers. Those who could prove, via a lengthy, rather cumbersome questionnaire, that they had been misled or given insufficient information were eligible for one of three exchange options. Under each of these options, any purchaser with enough legal training to understand the explanation of his alternatives could exchange an unsalable, unimproved lot for what will almost certainly also be another unsalable, unimproved lot.*

Under the first option, a purchaser could exchange a remote outlying lot--in what is euphemistically called the "National Sales Area"--for a different remote outlying lot with a current selling price 20% higher than that of his lot. Or he could choose to keep his lot and receive a second lot worth 20% of the current selling price of his lot. Neither choice represents an improvement for the purchaser; since regardless of Horizon's selling price these outlying lots have no resale value. Horizon chose the lots for exchange.

The second option appears to offer more. A purchaser could exchange his lot for a lot in the development area, although not without a considerable additional expense. He was required to pay the difference between the original sales price of his lot (not the current selling price) and the appraised value of the exchange lot. The difference was to be paid by extending the term of his contract

---

*Past purchasers were given the option to exclude themselves from the settlement to pursue individual suits. However, only if a purchaser specifically requested exclusion from the class before January 5, 1976, was he free to pursue individual action against Horizon. If a purchaser filed a claim, regardless of whether it was allowed, the claim operated as a complete release of all future claims against Horizon pursuant to a lot purchase. If the purchaser took no action, his non-action also operated as a complete release of all claims. The court did not decide whether the class-action settlement would bar any future Federal Trade Commission lawsuit seeking consumer refunds or restitution.

rather than by increased monthly payments. He also had to pay the cost of improvements or $4,000, whichever was less. This amount had to be secured by the purchaser's personal note, and be paid either in cash within thirty days or in 36 monthly installments with 7.5% interest. Indeed, the only difference between the second option and the exchange privilege a purchaser automatically receives upon signing a contract was that in this case the buyer was not under any obligation to build immediately on the lot taken in exchange.

Horizon made approximately 450 lots at Rio Communities available for this second option. Some of the lots were fully improved: with water and sewer lines; gas, electricity, and telephone service; and paved roads and curbs. If all goes well, others may be improved within one year after the final judgement approving the completion of the claims procedure (including appeals). However, Horizon is under no obligation to extend the improvements. If the utility companies (several of which are owned by Horizon) are not willing or able to extend them, they will be granted another two years in which to do so. If after these two years, they are still not willing or able, Horizon will refund the improvement costs, cancel the outstanding personal note, and have no further obligation to install any improvements. It seems, in other words, that purchasers who chose this option were extending Horizon a guaranteed $4,000 loan to improve the lot without any commensurate guarantee from the company that this would be done. In effect they may have exchanged an unimproved outlying lot for an unimproved lot in the core area.*

Under the third option, a purchaser could exchange a remote outlying lot for a lot in a designated area "either adjacent to or in close proximity to existing development areas." Again, if the exchange lot had an appraised value greater than the original sales price of his lot (not the current selling price), the purchaser had to pay the difference in price by extending the term of his contract. As in Option Two, Horizon is not obligated to improve these lots. The company selected for Option Three 2,800 lots in Rio del Oro Units 63, 64, and 65.

Horizon set aside 6,975 lots for Options Two and Three. If

---

*A further catch is that the lots in Option Two are not registered with OILSR because Horizon does not sell lots in the core development area on installment contracts. As the result of a legal technicality, if the court decides that these lots must be registered with OILSR, Horizon may not have to make them available for exchange. If anyone challenges their exemption from OILSR registration requirements, Horizon also has the right not to exchange them, to wait until the court makes a decision on the challenge, or to try to register the lots before making any exchanges.

this number is not adequate for all successful claimants, those who do not receive lots in exchange can try to get a contract credit for the unpaid principal balance of their contracts, i.e., they would not have to make any further payments on their contracts, except for those constituting interest. However, there is a major catch. As noted above, anyone hoping to get an exchange under this program must prove he or she was misled. The instructions, given in the Notice of Class Action Settlement, list, as examples of possible material misrepresentation or omission, statements about price, value, appreciation, income value, location or accessibility, resale market, financial stability, and the dependability of Horizon. According to the Settlement, purchasers can only get the contract credit if they can prove a misrepresentation that is not covered by any of the items on this list. It is difficult to imagine any form of misrepresentation which does not fall into one of these categories.

Horizon set aside $2 million for contract credits. In the unlikely event that successful claims exceed this amount, each claimant will receive a prorated credit which, rather than being applied now, will be applied when the amount left to be paid on the contract equals the amount of the credit.

A settlement committee of one Horizon attorney and one class-action attorney decides the validity of each claim. If these two cannot decide, the court will.

Nearly a year after the Class Action Settlement, Horizon was again sued. In June, 1976, the State Attorney General in Arizona filed suit against the company, alleging violation of Arizona's Consumer Fraud Act.

In August, 1976, the State Attorney General in New Mexico filed a suit in conjunction with the State Commissioner of Securities. This suit alleged that Horizon's sale of Contracts for Deed was "unconscionable" in light of the disparity between the sales prices for the lots and their real value; it further alleged that Horizon had violated New Mexico's Security Registration Act by not registering land sold as an investment and offered through an exchange privilege with the state Securities and Exchange Commission. If the court upholds this latter allegation, the company would be required to allow rescission of all contracts sold between 1974 and 1976.

COST OF LOTS BOUGHT ON THE INSTALLMENT PLAN

LOT PRICE
    basic price (¼ - 40 acres)* $1,000 $28,000
    finance charge (5% - 8%) $207 - $9,611
                                                    Total $1,207 - $37,611

ADDITIONAL ANNUAL ASSESSMENTS DURING TERM OF CONTRACT
    improvement association $13 - $50
    special service districts   0
    county taxes $3 - $170
                                   Total, per year $16 - $220
                                   Total, 8½ years $136 - $1,870

ONE-TIME COSTS FOR SERVICES
    lot survey $35 - $240
    water $660 - $340,000
        well $660 - $3,850
        central extension   0 - $340,000
        central hook-up   0
    sewage $350 - $1,250
        septic system $350 - $1,250
        central extension   N/A
        central hook-up   0
    electricity $3500 - $142,000
        generator $3,500
        line extension   0 - $142,000
    telephone $2500 - $120,000
        radio-telephone $2,500
        line extension   0 - $120,000

---

*Includes industrial, commercial, and multi-family lots.

ENVIRONMENTAL CHECKLIST

Overall environmental protection record: POOR

Does the subdivider:

PLANS	Plan for complete basic services?	NO
	Phase lot sales and extension of services?	NO
	Get 80% build-out in 10 years of each section marketed?	NO
	Prepare an Environmental Impact Report?	NO
LAND	Use a curvilinear or cluster design?	NO
	Retain 25% or more open space?	NO
	Reserve from lot sale and development the following areas of critical concern:	
	wetlands?	--
	dunes and beaches?	--
	water sources?	--
	prime agricultural lands?	--
	habitats of endangered species?	--
	prime historical, archaeological, cultural, aesthetic, or recreational resources?	YES
	Reserve from lot sale and development the following areas hazardous for building:	
	geological hazard areas (earthquake, landslide)?	--
	flood-prone areas (100-year floodplains, arroyos)?	YES*
	areas of slope exceeding 25%?	YES
	Blade roads only in immediate development areas?	NO
	Clear only for buildings and roads?	YES
	Preserve existing topography?	YES
WATER RESOURCES	Design the drainage system to control erosion?	NO
	Retain 100-foot buffer zone around water bodies?	--
	Replant disturbed land immediately?	NO
	Limit septic systems to one-acre or larger lots with adequate: percolation rates, slope, and distance from bedrock, water table and surface waters?	NO
	When utilizing central sewage disposal, provide tertiary treatment (or secondary and land disposal)?	YES
	Avoid major stream alteration?	--
	Avoid major wetland dredging and filling?	--
	Use groundwater only up to the safe yield?	?

*Arroyos are reserved or designated as drainage easements.

NOTE: See chapter on "Guidelines" for more complete explanation of items on Checklist.

RIO COMMUNITIES

CONSUMER CHECKLIST

Overall consumer protection record: POOR

Does the subdivider:

<table>
<tr><td rowspan="13">SALES</td><td>Conduct a credit check on lot purchasers?</td><td>NO</td></tr>
<tr><td>Limit lot sales to two per purchaser?</td><td>YES</td></tr>
<tr><td>Sell only residential, i.e., no industrial, commercial or multi-family lots on installment contracts?</td><td>NO</td></tr>
<tr><td>Require a cash downpayment of 20% on all sales?</td><td>NO</td></tr>
<tr><td>Limit duration of installment contracts to 5 years?</td><td>NO</td></tr>
<tr><td>Charge no interest on installment contracts?</td><td>NO</td></tr>
<tr><td>Encourage attorney review of sales documents?</td><td>NO</td></tr>
<tr><td>Require a pre-purchase site visit?</td><td>NO</td></tr>
<tr><td>Allow a 14-day rescission period in which purchaser can obtain a refund for any reason?</td><td>NO*</td></tr>
<tr><td>Offer a partial refund if purchaser defaults?</td><td>NO</td></tr>
<tr><td>Guarantee a refund, with interest, if promised services are not made available by date specified in contract?</td><td>NO</td></tr>
<tr><td>Escrow contract payments, or provide equivalent surety bonding, for refund purposes?</td><td>NO</td></tr>
</table>

<table>
<tr><td rowspan="4">TITLE</td><td>Offer only platted lots?</td><td>YES</td></tr>
<tr><td>Offer a recordable contract, and record the sale?</td><td>NO</td></tr>
<tr><td>Offer unmortgaged land, or land mortgaged with a release clause, only?</td><td>YES</td></tr>
<tr><td>Upon contract signing, deed title to purchaser, or place title in trust?</td><td>NO</td></tr>
</table>

<table>
<tr><td rowspan="14">BASIC SERVICES</td><td>Guarantee, or have available, to each lot:</td><td></td></tr>
<tr><td>   central water, of adequate quantity and quality?</td><td>NO</td></tr>
<tr><td>   central sewage disposal, as necessary?</td><td>NO</td></tr>
<tr><td>   drainage system, adequate for 100-year storm?</td><td>NO</td></tr>
<tr><td>   solid waste disposal, via adequate method?</td><td>NO</td></tr>
<tr><td>   roads, paved, to county standards?</td><td>NO</td></tr>
<tr><td>   electricity and telephone?</td><td>NO</td></tr>
<tr><td>Guarantee completion through escrowing or surety bonding?</td><td>NO</td></tr>
<tr><td>If services are financed through special service district bonds, employ them only if:</td><td></td></tr>
<tr><td>   initial governing body includes a county official?</td><td>--</td></tr>
<tr><td>   elections include all landowners on one-man, one-vote basis?</td><td>--</td></tr>
<tr><td>   sum of bonds is less than twice the developer's investment in basic services?</td><td>--</td></tr>
<tr><td>   sum of bonds is less than 15% of the assessed value of land in the district?</td><td>--</td></tr>
<tr><td>   developer co-signs all bonds?</td><td>--</td></tr>
</table>

*Company claims de facto, 21-day rescission period.

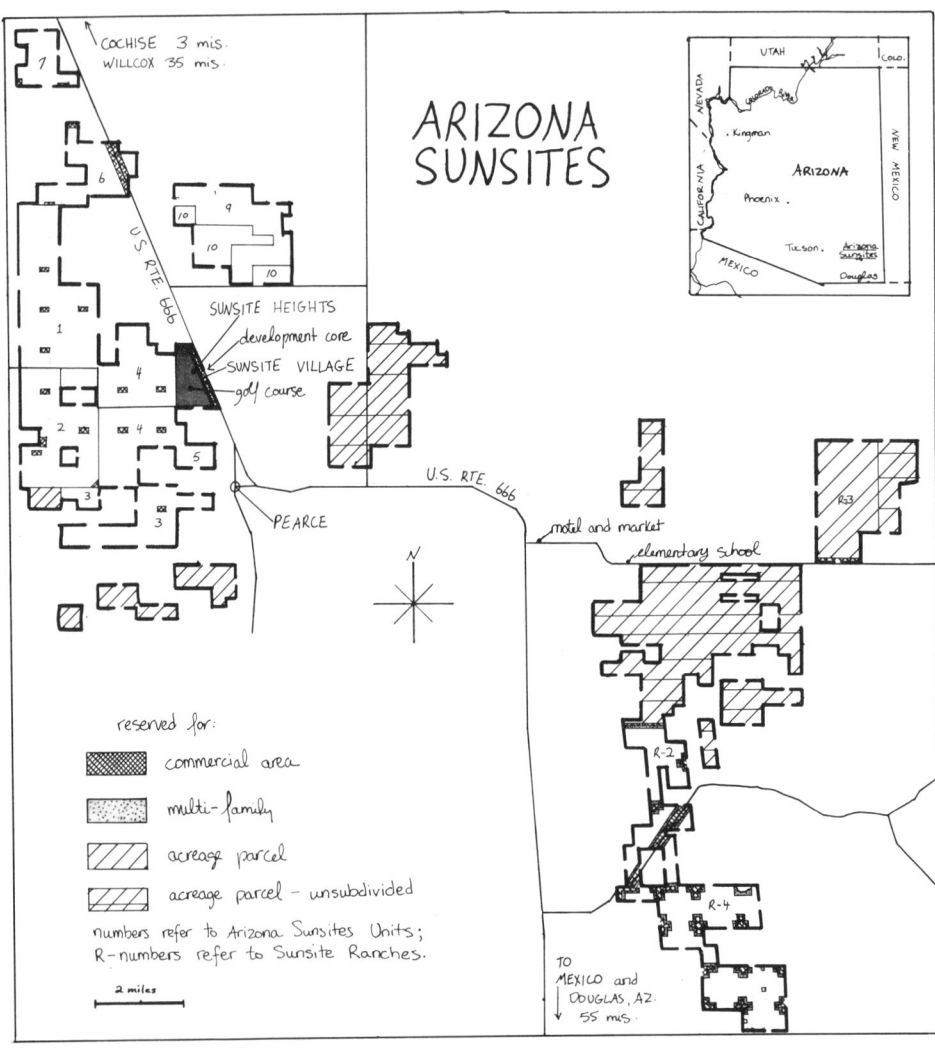

5
Arizona Sunsites

Horizon Corporation's Arizona Sunsites, in the southeastern corner of the state near the Mexican border, consists of ten separate, disconnected parcels of land totaling almost 50,000 acres. It is indeed a remote subdivision--Tucson, the nearest major city, is more than ninety miles away--and Cochise County in which it is located is rural and undeveloped, consisting predominantly of high quality rangeland, mountains, and desert. Despite being fifteen years old, Arizona Sunsites is largely empty.

Horizon Corporation, formed in 1959, holds nearly half a million acres of land in Arizona, New Mexico, Texas, and New York. Most of this land has been marketed both nationally and, until 1974, internationally as part of six separate subdivision developments. At the height of its marketing success in 1972, the company had a sales force of 1,651[1] and made most of its sales--as it stated in its 1973 Form 10-K Report filed with the Securities and Exchange Commission--"to people who do not see the land before they buy it."[2]

Horizon's consumer and environmental planning for Arizona Sunsites may be categorized by one word: poor. Perhaps because the company recognized that the approximately 20,000 lots marketed at the site would probably never be occupied, it made few plans for site services. It made no provision for supplying the 98% of the subdivision which lies outside the presently developed "core" area with water, sewage disposal, electricity, telephones, or drainage--indeed, with anything except dirt roads. Only two others of the nineteen* subdivisions studied by INFORM--Horizon's Rio Communities and AMREP's Rio Rancho, both also huge desert grassland

---

*Includes both the ten subdivisions in Volume I of this study and the nine Florida subdivisions analyzed in Volume II.

241

projects--offer as little in the way of basic improvements. Extending basic services from the core development area to one of the more remote Arizona Sunsites lots could cost a "homesite" owner over $135,000 (see discussion under Consumer Protection).

The land Horizon picked to develop was not as ecologically fragile as some of the wetland areas other firms have developed in Florida. However, Horizon ignored those environmental constraints that do exist at Arizona Sunsites: in choosing the site, it disregarded the fact that the groundwater was already being overdrawn by existing users; in laying out a relentless gridiron of lots, it overlooked the fact that much of this land lies in an area subject to flash floods; and in allocating space, it set aside no land for future park or recreational use.

Ninety-five percent of the lots at Sunsites are sold due to Horizon's heavy national promotional efforts. The land has no local resale value, nor has it many inhabitants. With a population of just 850, Sunsites has the slowest annual average-population growth rate of the older subdivisions in the INFORM sample. For many Arizona Sunsites lot purchasers, who were lured by references to the land's "potential for long-term appreciation,"[3] or who succumbed to high-pressure encouragement to build in a thriving new community, the progress of Horizon's fifteen-year development effort at the subdivision must be distressing. To the Federal Trade Commission, the gap between Horizon's promises and reality was sufficiently wide that it issued a complaint against the company in 1975 alleging unfair and deceptive sales practices.

Regional Context

Cochise County, home of Arizona Sunsites, experienced negative growth--its population consistently declined--for several decades prior to 1954.[4] In that year, the U.S. Army decided to make Fort Huachuca, located in the County's southwest corner, the permanent site for its Electronic Proving Ground. In 1971, the Army added an intelligence school to the base. These events, which reversed the County's downward population trend, have concentrated many of its approximately 75,000 people in the southwestern corner, between the Fort Huachuca-Sierra Vista complex and the copper mining and smelting towns of Douglas and Bisbee.[5]

Horizon's land holdings are not located near this urbanized activity. They stretch 34 to 52 miles north of the town of Douglas. The nearest town of any size to Arizona Sunsites is Willcox (about 30 miles away). With a population of 2,568, it is the County's farm and grain equipment center.[6] The Sunsites area itself has at present no economic base, virtually no commerical or industrial development, and hardly any residential development. Most of the construction of its 342 dwelling units has occurred in the last four years. Only 2% of Sunsites' five-acre-and-under lots have been, or are being, improved with central water, sewage systems, roads, electricity, and telephone service (see discussion under Basic Services). None of the lots marketed in parcels over five acres will be improved by Horizon.

Consistent figures reflecting the amount of land owned by Horizon under the name "Arizona Sunsites" are hard to come by. In a 1971 study of Cochise County's environmental services requirements, the Planning Division of Arizona's Department of Economic Planning and Development indicated that the site consisted of three blocks of land which totaled 34,000 acres: Arizona Sunsites (16,000 acres), Sunizona (8,000 acres), and Sunsite Hills (10,000 acres). These blocks of land represented the largest private land development in Cochise County.[7] In 1975, the company's New York Offering Statement* for the development used 47,296 acres as the cumulative figure. During the same year, a Horizon official gave INFORM a site area total of 44,000 acres.

While Arizona Sunsites is the largest land-sales project in Cochise County, it is by no means the only one. Cochise County is distinguished among Arizona's fourteen counties in that a large proportion of its total area--39%--is under private ownership.†[8] Much of this has been subdivided: the County ranks third in total number of subdivided lots. By 1974, according to the state's Department of Economic Planning and Development, the County had a population capacity, based on the number of subdivided lots, of 254,600.[9] The projected county population for the year 2000, however, is only 116,950.[10]

The year 1961, when Horizon began marketing Sunsite lots, and the years immediately following, were a time of open season on land

---

*New York State requires the development company to issue a report disclosing pertinent consumer information on lots offered for sale.

†The fact that only 15% of Arizona's total land area is privately owned, implying that land is in extremely short supply in the state, has unfortunately become one of the most frequently abused statistics in the repertoire of the state's many land peddlers. The State Land Commissioner, Andrew L. Bettwy, has pointed out "that the 15% of Arizona that is privately owned and available for development represents 11.1 million acres of land, which is nearly equivalent to the combined land areas of New Jersey and Maryland together." Mr. Bettwy added that "if the population density were ten persons per acre, as it is in Nogales, Arizona, the 11.1 million acres would be enough land for 110 million people to live on, while Arizona's population in 1974 was just over 2 million."[11]

in Cochise County.* During this period, the County had no planning commission, no subdivision regulations, and no county engineer, all of which have since been added over Horizon's objections.[12] But until very recently, the regulatory pressures which could be brought to bear on Horizon were minimal. Like many other subdividers in Cochise County, Horizon was selling much of its land (at least 13,000 acres) in 40-acre parcels.[13] Land parcels of this size were exempt from compliance with existing county subdivision regulations.

When the County Planning Commission passed new regulations requiring that parcels of 36 acres or more be approved for sale by the County Subdivision Committee, Horizon, in early 1975, sued. The company maintained that the County lacked authority for such action and called the regulations illegal and unconstitutional. The Planning Commission and Board of Supervisors simply wanted to assure that lots, even of this size, had been staked and surveyed, and that purchasers were provided with physical (i.e., road) as well as legal access to the land. Horizon's complaint was not upheld in Superior Court, but the company has appealed the decision. As of early 1976, the Appeals Court had not handed down an opinion.[14]

THE OFFERING: LAND AND IMPROVEMENTS

LAND

Due perhaps to the stricter regulatory climate impinging on all large land-sales companies, Horizon recently clarified for the Securities and Exchange Commission, if not for the lot purchaser, what had been a convenient ambiguity between its land-subdivision (i.e., lot-sales) activity and land-development practices. In its 1973 Form 10-K Report, the company stated:

> Part or all of the particular projects are laid out and planned to become, at some undetermined future time, self-contained communities.[15]

However,

> The laying out and planning of a community is not analogous to the development of a project or a community. The fact that any particular

---

*Horizon made its first filing on Arizona Sunsites with the Arizona State Real Estate Department on December 20, 1961.

project has been laid out and planned by the Company does not insure its development. Except for "limited *immediate* development" areas in certain projects, the only improvements which the Company generally obligates itself to provide are fronting access roads, which in certain cases are paved and other cases are not paved, although other improvements are sometimes supplied.[16]

Physical Characteristics

The latter elaboration accurately describes Horizon's operational approach to its Arizona Sunsites land holdings. These holdings stretch northeastward in non-contiguous blocks starting on the west along the lower foothills of the Dragoon Mountains and continuing east toward the Sulphur Springs Valley floor. The terrain is gently rolling, proceeding from an elevation of 4,100 to 4,800 feet. Vegetation consists principally of desert grasses.

Status of Development

Of the total acreage, slightly over 41,317 acres are platted and recorded with the County. Most of this subdivided acreage is marketed in Arizona and as many as fifteen other states, depending on the states' regulations.[17]

Approximately 600 acres, three-quarters of which is platted, comprise what Horizon terms "the limited immediate development area." According to the company's two 1975-amended federal Property Reports on Arizona Sunsites, this core area contains 445 lots to date.* A portion of these (155 lots) are restricted to commercial use and are identified as belonging to Sunsite Village. The remainder (290 lots) are identified as belonging to Sunsite Heights and are restricted principally to single-family residences, though some may be used for multi-family or commercial purposes. Though the Property Report makes no mention of it, a company official explained that Horizon has designated this land as a "compulsion area." This means that the lots can be purchased only under an arrangement which obligates the buyer to build within a certain specified time (in this case, ninety days) following purchase.[18] The federal Property Report does not define the size of these lots. However, a company official stated that they are just under one-quarter acre in size.[19]

---

*The U.S. Department of Housing and Urban Development, Office of Interstate Land Sales Registration (OILSR) requires the development company to issue a Property Report giving important consumer information on the lots offered for sale.

The remainder of the lots (slightly over 20,000 in number) are offered for sale at prices of $1,800 to $28,000 on an installment plan. They are divided by Horizon, according to size, into three categories: "Sunsites Units 1-10," "Sunsite Ranches," and "Acreage (or Bulk) Parcels."

Geographically, however, these units fall into many more than three block areas.* Sunsites Units 1-6 and Unit 8, consisting of 12,527 three-quarter-acre and one-and-a-half-acre lots, lie west of the Village-Heights core development area, and thus west of U.S. Route 666.† Unit 7, subdivided into 837 three-quarter-acre lots, lies about eight miles to the north. Units 9 and 10, comprising approximately 4,362 half-acre and three-quarter-acre lots, lie to the east and on the other side of U.S. Route 666. Units 1-10 together total 17,306 lots.

Horizon's second type of offering, "Sunsite Ranches Units," includes 3,024 lots ranging from two-and-a-half to five acres in size. These form nine separate land units scattered across the valley floor and the lower foothills of the Dragoon Mountains. According to a Horizon 1970 land-use map, 241 of these lots fall within an area that is principally National Forest. Horizon prohibits industry, manufacturing, and commercial businesses on them.

Horizon's third category of land offering, the "Acreage (or Bulk) Parcels," consists of seven scattered blocks of "unsubdivided" land totaling about 12,802 acres. According to the Director of the Cochise County Planning Department, Horizon had at one time planned to subdivide one portion of this acreage into a 200-acre immediate-development area consisting of one-acre parcels, to be called Sunsite Hills. When the county engineer requested a full drainage report from Horizon it turned out that there was a serious flood hazard from Ashton Creek in a significant portion of the area under consideration and that the area was unsuitable for intensive residential development.

Horizon then decided to market the land in 40-acre parcels, which were exempt from all state, county and/or federal regulations. Horizon filed a federal Property Report in 1973 listing 230 40-acre parcels for sale. It noted that the developer promised no facilities other than unsurfaced roads which would be constructed but not maintained; that the parcels would not be staked or surveyed; and that the County made no assurance that it

---

*Information on Horizon's lot arrangements at Arizona Sunsites has been compiled from company site-plan maps and the federal Property Reports.

†Except for a tiny portion of Unit 6, which straddles U.S. Route 666.

would permit the use of individual septic systems. When, in 1975, the Cochise County Board of Supervisors passed regulations requiring Horizon to record a map survey, stake lots, and provide public-roadway easements of adequate width and suitable location, before it would approve the sale of 40-acre lots, Horizon went to court.* However, by the time the County's position was upheld in the Supreme Court, Horizon had complied with the regulations.[20]

Approximately 33,000 of Arizona Sunsites' 47,296 acres have been sold.† Out of approximately 21,558 lots offered,▽ 10,500 have been conveyed by free and clear title to purchasers. Yet despite these sales, there is as yet very little at Arizona Sunsites to substantiate Horizon's assertion, in one of its recent promotional brochures, that "Arizona Sunsites is not just another aimless tract of land with an uncertain future."[21] The company's further claim that "Arizona Sunsites is rapidly taking on the look of a complete community, carefully shaped by [Horizon's] master plan"[22] is simply not borne out by looking at the progress and quality of "development" underway now for fifteen years.

As mentioned earlier, while Arizona Sunsites encompasses 47,296 acres, Horizon is improving only about 600 acres, those in the Sunsite Village-Heights area adjacent to U.S. Route 666. The 1975 federal Property Report states that as of October, 1975, 310 homes in this development area and 32 homes in the outlying area were occupied. The population at Arizona Sunsites, including children, was about 850. In addition to its water, sewage, and utility systems which will be discussed below, this core area contains the project's recreational, community, and commercial services. None of these services, however, is extensive.

A company official described the project as "a bedroom community to Willcox."[23] However, with less than 3,000 in population

---

*Horizon withdrew all of its bulk parcels from the market in January, 1975, though a substantial portion had already been sold. The Director of the County Planning Department explained that company statements in the federal Property Report were not in compliance with local regulations.

†Apparently, sales have been low and/or cancellations high in the last three years, probably at least partly due to the economic recession. This figure for acreage sold, approved as accurate for December 31, 1975 in a communication to INFORM, was also the figure the company reported in both its 1974 and 1973 Form 10-K filings.

▽While this figure is the one used by company officials in a 1975 communication to INFORM, a federal Property Report on Arizona Sunsites, filed October, 1975, lists 20,775 lots.

and no major employment attractions itself, Willcox can hardly be expected to need a 60,000-person bedroom. This is probably the main reason for Arizona Sunsites' slow growth to date. If the site continued to attract population at the rate it has in its first fifteen years, it would not be fully occupied for 900 to 1,000 years.

BASIC SERVICES

Horizon purports to market "homesites" everywhere in the Arizona Sunsites project except on its bulk-acreage parcels. However, the basic services which are a prerequisite for homesite use are made both physically and financially accessible only in, and close to, the core development area which amounts to approximately 2% of the site. It has not promised to provide such services to the rest of the site, nor has it put up corporate or surety bonds to guarantee their installation. According to figures derived from the 1975 federal Property Reports, the costs to an individual lot purchaser of extending basic services would be astronomical. Central water (mandatory for about half of all lots due to County regulations) alone could cost up to $105,600 for the most distant lot. Extension of electricity could add $24,744, telephone $3,850, and installation of a septic tank $700, to the unlucky outlying-lot owner's expenses.

The new 1975 federal Property Report on Arizona Sunsites takes commendable steps towards forewarning the prospective purchaser of this fact.* In bold red letters under "Warning" at the very beginning of the Report it states:

> The property in Arizona Sunsites Units 1-10 and Sunsites Ranches is totally undeveloped. Horizon Corporation will not develop any of this property except to provide dirt roads. The extension of all utilities to your lot will be at your expense and will be in addition to the purchase price of your lot. The cost of extension may be extremely high and perhaps economically unfeasible.[24]

However, Horizon's advertising materials convey a far different impression: that of a functioning, fully-serviced new community.

---

*Unfortunately, earlier Property Reports filed by the company on Arizona Sunsites with OILSR omitted such information.

ARIZONA SUNSITES

Water

A central water system, supplied and managed by a Horizon-owned public utility called the Clear Springs Water Company, presently delivers water to approximately 310 homes within the Village-Heights core area and to some of the 32 homes outside. The connection charge is $3 per front-foot; the owner of a 100-foot by 100-foot lot would thus pay $300. According to recent company data, this system has a delivery capacity of 1.87 million gallons per day, enough for approximately 12,480 people at standard rates of use in dry climates (150 gallons per person per day). Current daily usage amounts to 204,687 gallons per day. The water comes from seven wells that draw on a portion of the large alluvial deposits underlying the County.

The 1975 federal Property Report states that an estimated 1.64 million acre-feet of water is available under the lands in Arizona Sunsites and that the anticipated water use in 2073 will be 1.03 million acre-feet.* However, the Report adds that "the developer does not undertake to extend water lines to any particular lot or area. There is no development plan for the subdivision other than in Sunsite Heights and Sunsites Village;...."[25]

The basic water problem at Arizona Sunsites, at least for the 98% of the lots which lie outside the core area, is thus not one of quantity but rather of practical accessibility. About 50% of all lots--namely the 11,344 lots in Sunsites Units 4-10, all of which are three-quarter to one-half acre in size--must connect to the Clear Springs Water Company central water system because of their size. The Arizona Department of Health Services has limited the simultaneous use of a well and an individual septic system to lots of one or more acres. These Sunsites lots will certainly have to rely on the latter type of sewage system for the foreseeable future, and thus will be ineligible to use wells for water. Therefore, as the 1975 federal Property Report notes, lot owners will have no way of obtaining water "in advance of the extension of the central system."[26]

The cost of extending the main line to a lot, whenever it may occur, must be borne by the lot purchaser. This is no small matter. The Property Report warns with bold underlining: "<u>The cost of line extension to the most remote lot from existing service is estimated at current costs to be $105,600.00.</u>"

Owners of the 4,779 lots in Units 7, 9, and 10 may encounter a further problem in obtaining central water, not mentioned in the Property Reports. Units 7, 9, and 10 form two separate land blocks

---

*One acre-foot of water amounts to 326,000 gallons and is sufficient water for 2,100 persons for one day based on an average 150-gallons-per-day consumption rate.

which are not contiguous to the area where the present water system exists. The intervening land is not owned by Horizon. INFORM could not determine whether these areas will have to establish their own individual delivery system or whether the Clear Springs Water Company has obtained rights-of-way to lay pipe.

Owners of another 30% of Sunsites' lots--the 6,379 one-and-a-half-acre lots in Sunsites Units 1-3--may elect to drill a well, if they prefer, in lieu of using the central water system. The cost of a complete well, including the installation of a pump,* has been estimated at between $2,200 and $4,700.[28]

The remaining 3,024 lots in Sunsite Ranches Units, all over one acre in size, are to use their own wells for water.

Water quality may also prove to be a problem at Arizona Sunsites. According to the 1975 federal Property Report, chemical and bacterial analysis tests have been performed on the water from the company's existing wells. These tests indicate that the water is approved for domestic use, but that the high levels of iron and fluoride in the water require mixing. The Property Report further notes, "The developer has not obtained a letter or report from a cognizant health officer on the quality and purity of water."[29]

The 1971 *Environmental Services Needs Study* for Cochise County noted that the quality of "raw water at its source varies [throughout] the county from soft to highly mineralized to completely impotable."[30] Such variety is determined both by natural causes and by agricultural water use. The federal Property Reports state that there is no assurance that the untested water underlying Arizona Sunsites will be "of acceptable quality."

Sewage

Only 210 homes in the Village-Heights core area and a few in the outlying area are currently served by the central sewage system. This system, provided by the Clear Springs Water Company, has a design capacity of 50,000 gallons per day. (This is sufficient for approximately 500 persons based on a 100-gallon-per-person-per-day usage rate.) In 1975, the system was processing 15,000 gallons per day. According to the federal Property Report, new users must pay a $50 connection charge.

This same Property Report states that the state Health Department has approved all remaining lots--98% of the site--for individual septic-tank systems which are estimated to cost $700. However, prior to the construction of septic tanks, the Cochise County Sanitarian must issue an installation permit. The Property Report adds that there is no assurance that such a permit will be issued. New

---

*If the pump is to be powered by electricity, however, the lot owner may have further extraordinary costs.

County regulations passed in January, 1975, impose a one-acre limitation on septic-system use, even with no well on the property. They further require soil-percolation tests (which lot owners must pay for) based on borings made every acre, instead of every five acres as was previously the custom. It was, however, the County Sanitarian's opinion that these regulations would not be applied retroactively. He also felt that the sandy-loam nature of the soil at Arizona Sunsites, and the depth of the water table--ranging from 150 to 600 feet below surface level--indicate positive conditions for the use of septics.[31]

If the county regulations are enforced, the central sewage system will have to be extended, again at additional cost to individual lot owners.

Solid Waste

Garbage is presently disposed of at the County sanitary-landfill site. Regular pickup service is available in the core area.

Roads

Six of the nineteen subdivisions studied by INFORM failed to guarantee or provide lot purchasers with the most basic improvement--a paved road to their lots built to county standards. Arizona Sunsites was one of these. As noted in Horizon's 1974 Form 10-K Report, unpaved fronting access roads are "the only improvements which the company generally obligates itself to provide" throughout a project. These roads "...are not necessarily built to the standards of, or maintained by, the County or other governmental entity, [thus] the Company has maintained certain of these roads as it has deemed in its own best interest without generally having a contractual obligation to do so."[32] As implemented at Arizona Sunsites, this basic policy has resulted in the blading and grading of approximately 550 miles of dirt roads installed in grid fashion throughout the project and in the construction of 10.5 miles of paved roads in the Village-Heights area.

The federal Property Report warns that while the developer currently maintains the roads throughout Arizona Sunsites, "it does not commit itself to continue maintenance for any period of time." Consequently, a lot purchaser may be required to pay at least $50 per mile for maintenance between his lot and the nearest county, state, or federal road, unless other owners along his road also contribute to maintenance costs.

If the roads are not maintained, the Report adds, they will "become unusable in a short period of time." The Report further notes that the roads in the Sunsite Ranches Units (comprising a total of 3,024 lots) are actually *easements* (i.e., the lot owner retains ownership of the land specified as an easement for road use), and that the County will not maintain road easements, irrespective of the quality of the road construction. Owners of lots in these units have no choice but to always maintain their own roads.

While very thorough in its review of the ominous financial implications for the lot purchaser of Horizon's road-maintenance practices (which vary according to lot category), the October, 1975, federal Property Report is incomplete in one respect. It states that in the Village-Heights core area, "the County has accepted certain of the streets for maintenance." However, the Director of the Cochise County Planning Department emphasized that the County has agreed to accept the paved roads for maintenance only when they are constructed to county standards as defined in the County Subdivision Regulations. Not all roads at Arizona Sunsites have met these standards, although Horizon is attempting to improve the roads in the core area to meet required specifications.[33] The Property Report further notes that the County will maintain roads it has accepted only "after there is occupancy thereon."

Drainage

The site's drainage system is presently inadequate in the core area, and virtually nonexistent outside it. The federal Property Report states at one point: "Drainage facilities will consist of the use of natural drainageways and drainage ditches constructed as a part of the road system." At another point it makes clear that the developer has no program in effect to control soil erosion, sedimentation, and flooding throughout the entire subdivision, and that "erosion and flooding could result in property damage and could create a health and safety hazard."[34] A reader must deduce that such drainage facilities as do exist are not sufficient to forestall the possibility of flooding. According to the Cochise County Planning Director, Horizon has recently begun constructing its drainage system within the Village-Heights area to county standards, as is required if the County is to assume the costs of road maintenance.[35] The drainage system is presently maintained by Horizon, but as the federal Property Report warns, the company makes no commitment to continue doing so.

A 1971 U.S. Soil Conservation Service report on the 94-square-mile Black Diamond Peak Watershed, which encompasses parts of Arizona Sunsites, gives evidence that the minimal existing drainage system is inadequate to prevent flooding in a 100-year storm.[36] The report was particularly concerned about flooding from the Noonan Canyon Wash, which "traverses Sunsites [the core area] in a northeasterly direction" as a "broad, rather obscure swale."[37] It reported that the only existing protection against the sheet flooding that can result from the overflow of this or other shallow swales in the area consists of Treasure Road, with only a three-year storm capacity, and a bladed Vee ditch with a five-year storm capacity. Flood waters rushing down Treasure Road soon encounter Highway 666 which acts as an impoundment dike downstream of Sunsites. Any overflow from it or the Vee ditch will thus spread along both the roadway and the Village-Heights core development area.[38] (See discussion under Environmental Protection.)

Electricity and Telephone

Underground electric lines presently exist in the Village-Heights development area, and some lines have been extended outside it. The Sulphur Springs Valley Electric Cooperative, Inc., a public utility, provides electricity. The Property Report emphasized with underlining the following: "The most remote lot with relation to existing electric service is four miles away. The extension cost based on $1.20 per foot over 500 feet would be $24,744.00; however such an extension is subject to negotiation."[39]

The federal Property Reports also warn prospective purchasers that, "There is no assurance telephone service will ever be available to your lot," and add that extension to the most remote lot could cost $3,852.[40]

COMMUNITY AND RECREATIONAL FACILITIES

Despite Arizona Sunsites' remoteness from existing urban centers, Horizon has arranged for few local community services. Police protection is provided by the county sheriff's office, located in Bisbee, 50 miles distant. Sunsites Units 2, 4, 5, 6, and parts of 1 and 3, and the Village-Heights core development area are provided year-round fire protection, according to the latest Property Report, but the rest of the property is not protected. Primary schools are 3 to 9 miles away from residences; the nearest high school is 22 to 27 miles away. The nearest doctor, dentist, or hospital is even farther--28 miles away. Sunsite Village "has limited shopping facilities" and a small post office. There is no public transportation from Sunsites to any other location.

Recreational facilities are also limited. A golf course, tennis courts, and a swimming pool are available on a membership basis ($125 initiation fee, and $15 monthly fee). The 1975 federal Property Reports warn that "The developer is not committed to continued operation and maintenance of the above-named facilities. Therefore there is no assurance that these facilities will be available for [the buyer's] use in the future."[41]

There is no industry or major source of employment within the entire project and no indication of any interest on Horizon's part in encouraging such.

ENVIRONMENTAL PROTECTION

Any discussion of the environmental effects of Horizon's Arizona Sunsites development must of necessity be speculative. Actual development is currently, and will be for the foreseeable future, confined to less than 2% of the total land area: approximately 1 square mile out of 68. Beyond some small degree of expansion around the Village-Heights neighborhoods, the harsh realities of development costs, as well as the lack of any real economic base for the community, render further intrusions upon the land unlikely. Consequently, most of the more than 47,000 acres will probably remain in their present condition except for the continued erosion resulting from the miles of bladed roads now cutting through them. Ultimately, a vegetative covering may grow over those roads which have not suffered excessive erosion, but not before the land has been left with permanent scars and gullies.

PLANNING

Insofar as they have been put into effect, Horizon's environmental planning and development practices have been very poor. The development was laid out in a rectangular gridiron pattern in total disregard of natural topography, flood potential, or regional availability of groundwater. As far as can be determined from company literature and its "Land-Use Plan" map, aside from two golf courses and one public park in the core area, no land whatsoever has been set aside for parks, recreation, or natural open-space areas. (This is a far cry from the 25% open-space allocation recommended by reputable planners and utilized at several of the nineteen subdivisions studied by INFORM.*) Land was allocated to commercial use wherever major highways cross Sunsites property, encouraging neon-lit "strip" development. About the only instance of good environmental planning at the site is the placement of electric lines underground in the core development area.

*Includes the ten subdivisions in Volume I and the nine Florida subdivisions analyzed in Volume II of this study.

LAND

Unlike many Florida wetland subdivisions, Horizon's Arizona Sunsites is located on land which can tolerate residential development. It contains no areas of critical environmental concern. However, as mentioned, portions of the site are in danger of flash and/or sheet flooding and are thus inappropriate for lot use. Horizon's "Land-Use Plan" ignored this fact.

In a 1971 report on the Black Diamond Peak Watershed (which includes portions of Arizona Sunsites) requested by the Cochise County Board of Supervisors, the U.S. Department of Agriculture, Soil Conservation Service (SCS), noted that the natural terrain in the watershed area presents a "deceptive picture as to the safety from floodwaters."[42] The reasons for this have to do with the nature of the drainageways: rather than well defined or deeply incised washes, they are indistinct broad swales. The study concluded that "...extensive damage could result if homes or other structures are constructed in the swales," and noted "several areas of immediate concern."[43]

The first is Sunsite Village and Sunsite Heights which are traversed by Noonan Canyon Wash. The report states unequivocally that proposed northward development of the Village-Heights community could result in "severe damage."[44] The second area of concern is Sunsites Unit 7 where proposed development will traverse another shallow swale known as Big Draw. This swale has a drainage area of 25.03 square miles. A third area of concern involves Sunsites Units 9-10 where proposed development will traverse a portion of the 165-square-mile drainageway for Turkey Creek. The study states that, "Severe damage could result if these areas are developed."[45]

The specific program recommended by the Soil Conservation Service for flood protection in the region, including portions of Arizona Sunsites, has proved too costly for the County to undertake ($2.26 million was the estimated amount the County would have had to spend in addition to federal assistance).[46] Other less costly measures that could forestall the development of flood-prone areas in the future--such as county identification of 100-year flood lines, and strong county ordinances for flood prevention--have not yet been implemented.[47]

On the basis of the SCS report, the County did submit the whole Sunsites development area to the U.S. Department of Housing and Urban Development Flood Insurance Administration (FIA) for flood designation. According to the Cochise County Planning Director, the FIA designated twelve areas in Cochise County as flood-prone (i.e., lying in the 100-year floodplain) and listed Sunsites among them. However, due to an unexplained error in its mapping, the demarcated area described by HUD as "Sunsites" is well to the south of the Village-Heights area now undergoing development, and close to the old ghost town of Pearce.[48]

Only one of the suggestions made by the SCS has been even partially put into practice. In its report it concluded that certain types of flood-proof construction should be incorporated into the existing development of the Village-Heights area for future protection.[49] While this was not done for the then existing community, an SCS official told INFORM that the Sunsites Homeowners' Association, after discussing these flood hazards with the SCS, has caused new homes in the area to be built on 18-inch raised slabs.[50]

In contrast to reassurances offered in Horizon's October, 1975, Property Report,* lot buyers at Arizona Sunsites are faced with the definite possibility of infrequent but potentially dangerous floods, whether in the Village-Heights core development area, or in the outlying units. Because of the deceptive nature of the terrain and the relative infrequency of serious flooding problems (there hasn't been a major flood in the Sunsites area since 1968), neither the residents in the Sunsites core development area nor the County itself has tried to organize a flood-control district. There is not, as yet, a flood-identification program, nor are there 100-year floodplain regulations. However, if development increases, roads and houses will create widespread impermeable surfaces. These will be unable to absorb storm runoff and the need for flood-control measures will then become both more apparent and more difficult to implement.

---

*In answer to question 8d in the federal Property Report: "List all existing or proposed unusual conditions relating to the location of the subdivision and to noise, safety or other nuisances...," Horizon states:

> [No portion of the lots for sale] are covered with water at any time during the year other than water that might stand during a heavy rain. The subdivision is not in any area designated to be flood-prone as identified by the Federal Insurance Administration, U.S. Department of Housing & Urban Development.
>
> The area of the subdivision has not been *formally* identified by any federal, state, or local agency as being in an area subject to a special natural hazard [emphasis added].

Although the above statements are accurate, they obscure the real state of affairs.

WATER RESOURCES

There are no surface water bodies at or near Arizona Sunsites aside from the intermittently flowing washes described above. Thus, there is no potential for degrading surface-water quality. There is, however, a potential for affecting groundwater.

While underground water sources seem capable of supplying all potential Arizona Sunsites residents, the long-term regional implications of intensive water withdrawals have not been considered by many state or county officials, and certainly not by Horizon Corporation.

According to the first part of a recently completed Arizona Water Commission study, groundwater provides the major water source for Cochise County.[51] Due to the large amount of water required to irrigate its agricultural lands--335,000 acre-feet in 1970[52]--the County suffers from the second-highest ratio (4.2:1.0) of depletion to supply of all the counties in the state.[53] Based on 1970 figures, the County's annual renewable water supply amounts to 85,000 acre-feet, while its annual consumption is 353,100 acre-feet. Thus, it has an annual overdraft of 268,000 acre-feet.[54]

A 1971 *Environmental Services Needs* study for Cochise County noted that "Large groundwater withdrawals have caused declines in the water table of between 25 and 75 feet in most areas.... Since continual overdraft will eventually cause serious problems for the area, it is certain that future water needs for the county will have to be met by supplemental sources."[55] Changes in use habits or water laws may also be necessary, according to the State Water Commission study.[56] If Arizona Sunsites achieves its potential resident population of 60,000 or so, its water needs will surely aggravate the already existing overdraft problem.

The groundwater level below Arizona Sunsites ranges from 100 to 700 feet.[57] This distance is generally considered adequate protection against pollution from septic-tank-sewage leaching. A noted Arizona hydrologist confirmed that the depth of the water table at Arizona Sunsites should preclude any problems from septic-tank use.[58]

However, with a full resident population Arizona Sunsites would have approximately 11,346 lots of less than one acre (with approximately 34,038 residents) using septic systems. This would be contrary to the County's new minimum-lot-size restrictions, and the INFORM guideline. A county sanitarian has indicated that permits will "probably" be granted the Sunsites lots upon application and the above law not applied retroactively.[59] This is certainly not an optimal situation from an environmental point of view.

As mentioned, company data supplied to INFORM indicates that the existing sewage-treatment plant which presently serves the

Village-Heights core-development area has a 50,000-gallon-per-day capacity (large enough for about 500 to 700 people) and provides secondary treatment by means of holding and oxidation ponds. No effluent is discharged to a waterway. The Arizona Sunsites drainage system has not been designed to capture mud, silt, and other pollutants from urban runoff.

CONSUMER PROTECTION

Horizon's consumer practices at Arizona Sunsites are among the worst in this study. Horizon does not guarantee any of the six minimum basic services (central water, central sewage, adequate drainage, paved roads, solid-waste disposal, electricity and telephone) that would make lots usable. By contrast, thirteen of the nineteen subdivisions studied by INFORM guaranteed, or had already provided, at least one of these services to all lots, and one subdivision had provided five out of six. As for Horizon's title and sales practices, consumers are afforded only those protection measures required by law, and the company has been the object of legal actions alleging deception on its part.

Sales

Given what little the company has to offer at Arizona Sunsites, it would not be surprising if grandiose claims were needed to sell lots. As noted, the Federal Trade Commission (FTC) alleged in a complaint in 1975 that Horizon had engaged in unfair and deceptive sales practices. A former Horizon salesman who claimed to have attempted, prior to 1972, to combat such practices within the corporation, said that he knew of "hundreds of cases" of salesmen making fraudulent statements. The salesman, who had been with Horizon for six years, described such techniques in a letter to the federal Office of Interstate Land Sales Registration:

> One experience occurred where there were two men operating as a team. If they experienced any difficulty in a quick close, one of the partners would address the closer and say, "Why don't you let this man have the lot next to the oil well. I don't think that the guy we talked to earlier has enough money to swing it." The customer...in this case signed up. In another

ARIZONA SUNSITES

Above, typical Arizona Sunsites residential area. Below, showcase core area development often pictured in advertising materials.

similar case they were having difficulty closing a prospect who wanted income property and balked at the closing. The partner said to the closer, "Why don't you let this man have those lots next to the six-story apartment building." (Center of a barren desert). These kind of men are constantly highlighted as outstanding and successful men which all other salesmen should follow. At the same time the corporation home office issued notices that if men get caught misrepresenting they will be fired. The corporation executives know of the illegal practices ...[but] do not complain or reprimand them [the salesmen] unless the cancellations reach an excessively high amount.[60]

Whether or not being the object of an FTC complaint will prod Horizon into substantially and permanently altering its sales methods remains to be seen. One distinct improvement, however, is Horizon's 1975 federal Property Report on Arizona Sunsites, required by new OILSR regulations. Unlike previous property reports, it gives thorough and explicit information on most questions relevant to the consumer, including where improvements are and are not available.

One of the few omissions from the 1975 Property Report is the following important fact: lots in the core Village-Heights area, where real development is in progress, are not available for purchase on an installment basis. In order to purchase one of these lots, which is in truth an "improved lot" and not merely a subdivided section of raw land, the purchaser must make his payment on a cash or mortgage basis. He must agree to commence building a home within 90 days of the sale's closing, and complete construction within 120 days thereafter. Horizon sells only unimproved homesites, with no services other than dirt roads, on an installment-contract basis at Arizona Sunsites.

Most of the lots offered for sale are between a quarter-acre and five acres in size. Prices for these lots range from $1,800 to $21,800.* Forty-acre parcels are sold for up to $28,000.

According to company data sent to INFORM by Horizon, installment purchases paid off over ten years require a miminum downpayment of 10% of the lot purchase price plus an interest charge of 4% to 8% per annum depending on the amount of the downpayment. Ninety-day or two-year contracts do not require interest payments.

---

*These prices include multiple-family and commercial lots as well as single-family ones.

The 1975 New York Offering Statement notes that a discount allowance of 5% (up to a maximum amount of $600) "may be allowed for the purpose of encouraging personal inspection of the subdivision" for up to one year from the date of the Agreement for Deed. Unfortunately, the value of this policy in terms of encouraging the consumer to make an informed purchase is undercut by the fact that he cannot make the inspection alone. To get the discount, the personal inspection must include a company-guided tour, which gives the company the opportunity to encourage the buyer to make further land purchases. However, after the tour, a sufficiently determined purchaser may cancel his sales agreement "for any reason," and, provided he does so between the second and sixth month following the agreement date, he may receive a full refund of all monies paid.*

If the buyer does not make the trip, he has only the maximum three-day (not fourteen days as required in California) rescission period presently required under federal law. No provisions have been made to refund a buyer's money should he default during the term of his contract on any of his payments due. This could include delinquencies on property taxes which range from $10.52 to $69.98 annually, as well as installment payments. The federal Property Reports warn that Horizon may resell the property or sue the contract holder for the balance due "plus costs of this suit."[61]

Indeed, the only way a buyer can get any money back after the six-month visitation period is to sue for misrepresentation or fraud. The state of Arizona requires subdividers to obtain surety bonding to cover any damages awarded in such suits. However, the amount of surety bonding Horizon has been required to obtain--just $100,000 to cover three subdivisions in the state--is extremely small compared to its total sales at these sites.

There is no indication that Horizon conducts a credit check on prospective lot purchasers, imposes any limitation on the number of residential lots a purchaser may buy, or limits the sale of commercial or industrial lots to individuals. Nor does the company seem to encourage the purchaser to review his contract and property report with an attorney. All of the above would serve to protect the consumer by discouraging him from speculation or spending beyond his means.

Title Protection

By virtue of the new 1975 Arizona sales law, the purchaser's right to title to an Arizona Sunsites lot is fully protected. The land Horizon offers for sale at Arizona Sunsites is not free and clear of all financial obligations. There are mortgage liens on

---
*None of the above New York Offering Statement information is available in the federal Property Reports on Arizona Sunsites.

all the Sunsites Units plus Ranches Unit 3, and there are option agreements on Ranches Units 2 and 4. However, all these encumbrances are subordinate to the interests of a purchaser who has fully met the terms of his sales agreement.

All lots offered for sale are platted with the County, so that there is an official record of their existence.

In the six months between the filing of its May and October, 1975, federal Property Reports on Arizona Sunsites, Horizon altered its sales contracts so that the contracts would be in recordable form. Furthermore, under its newly modified sales policy, sales will be by Deed. The purchaser must sign a Deed of Trust and a Deed of Trust Note for the balance of the purchase price when the lot is bought on an installment program. This good arrangement is similar to a mortgage. Horizon will record this Deed within sixty days provided payments due are current. The changes eliminate the possibility of third parties or creditors of anyone having an interest in the land acquiring title to the property without an obligation to deliver a Deed to the purchaser. Even more important, they allow the purchaser to use his lot during the ten or so years he is paying for it.

All the lots are subject to zoning-type restrictions as to their use, and certain specified lots are subject to drainage, utility, and road easements which are noted and described in appendixes to the Property Report.

Exchanges

Included in the Arizona Sunsites sales agreements are two types of lot-exchange provisions. First, up to the time of delivery of Deed, the full principal paid on one lot may be applied to any other lot within the subdivision that is *not* "located within any designated building area." In other words, the buyer has the option to trade one unimproved lot for another unimproved lot. The only conceivable advantage this offers the buyer is the possibility of receiving in trade a lot whose location is nearer to the core development area of Sunsite Village-Heights. Such a lot might be improved sooner than a lot located miles from existing development. But, as the federal Property Report notes with bold underlining:

> ...since there can be no assurance as to the future availability of lots in general, or to lots of an equal exchange value, you may not be able to exercise the exchange provision or such an exchange may result in the purchase of a higher priced lot which in turn would increase your monthly payment.[62]

The second exchange provision included in the Arizona Sunsites sales agreement pertains to single-family residential lots which have been conveyed by Deed to a purchaser. These lots may be exchanged for a similar-sized lot "in any building exchange area within the same development" (the buyer is not informed that at Arizona Sunsites this is the Village-Heights area only). The buyer does not have to pay an increased price for the improved lot, but he must agree to begin building within 90 days and complete construction 120 days thereafter.

In addition, "...current utility costs to the lot line and proportionate street improvement costs are to be paid for by the purchaser at the time construction is to commence, or shall be included in the cost of the house if purchased from the developer."[63] The Property Report does not elaborate on these costs. However, the 1975 New York Offering Statement notes that "The cost of lot improvements in the building exchange area, including water, power, natural gas, and telephone to the lot line, is presently $400 [plus] $300 to $350 for paving dependent upon the lot size."[64] Thus, the Arizona Sunsites lot buyer who decides to exchange a piece of raw land for a truly improved homesite must build immediately, plus pay an additional $700 to $750 for his improvements, exclusive of any sewage-disposal system. This is certainly much cheaper than trying to bring improvements to a homesite in an outlying area, which could cost up to $135,000, as noted earlier.

Resale

Rather than exchange his raw land for other raw land, a lot owner may wish to resell his lot. Unfortunately, the prospects for doing so are extremely slim. The 1975 federal Property Report provides several pertinent warnings as to the possible resale value and market for Arizona Sunsites lots. At the beginning, in bold red letters, the Report states:

> There is no assurance that your lot will increase in value. Such an increase will depend on factors like the extension of utilities into your area and the building of houses. Therefore, future development and appreciation of land rests solely on you and other lot purchasers, not the developer.[65]

Under "Special Risk Factors," at the end of the Report it warns:

> The future of land is very uncertain; do NOT count on appreciation.
>
> Resale of your lot may be subject to the developer's restrictions, such as limitations on

posting of signs, limitations to the rights of
other parties to enter the subdivision unaccompanied, membership prerequisites or approval
requirements, or developer's first right of refusal.

You should consider the competition which you
may experience from the developer in attempting
to resell your lot and the possibility that real
estate brokers may not be interested in listing
your lot.[66]

A local real estate dealer noted that if a lot is not located
in the Village-Heights area, his agency will not even list it. "I
can't sell them locally because people know what the situation is
[in terms of the lack of improvements and cost of installing them].
The only thing I can suggest to them is that they try to advertise
in their home-state papers."[67]

In the core development area the resale price is determined by
the lot's proximity to the golf course and the nature of the home,
though there is competition from Horizon in that the company is
still selling lots in this area.

Legal Actions

A further matter which may, as stated in the 1975 federal
Property Report, "materially affect lot purchasers" at Arizona Sunsites is the as yet unresolved dispute between Horizon and the Federal Trade Commission. The FTC issued a general complaint against
Horizon on March 17, 1975, alleging, in detail, its use of unfair
and deceptive sales practices, involving misrepresentations about
availability of utilities, resale possibilities, etc., to induce
the public to purchase its land. A settlement between the two parties has not been reached; Horizon denies the allegations. The FTC
has stated that if the final determination of the proceedings results in a cease and desist order, it may seek "consumer redress
for all purchasers of lots from Horizon during the period commencing March 17, 1972."[68]

A year later, in June, 1976, Arizona's State Attorney General charged Horizon with violating Arizona's Consumer Fraud
Act. In August, 1976, New Mexico's State Attorney General filed
suit in conjunction with the State Commissioner of Securities,
alleging that Horizon's sales program was "unconscionable" in
view of the disparity between the sales prices for the lots and
their real value; it further alleged that Horizon had violated
New Mexico's Security Registration Act by not registering land
it sold as an investment and offered through an exchange privilege with the state Securities and Exchange Commission.

COST OF LOTS BOUGHT ON THE INSTALLMENT PLAN

LOT PRICE

    basic price (¼ - 40 acres)* $1,800 - $28,000
    finance charge (4% - 8%) $348 - $11,489

                                              Total $2,148 - $39,489

ADDITIONAL ANNUAL ASSESSMENTS DURING TERM OF CONTRACT

    property owners association   0
    special service district   0
    property taxes $11 - $70

                             Total, per year $11 - $70
                             Total, 10 years $110 - $700

ONE-TIME COSTS FOR SERVICES

    lot survey   0
    water $2,200 - $105,600
       well $2,200 - $4,700
       central extension   0 - $105,600
       central hook-up $300
    sewage $700
       septic system $700
       central extension   N/A
       central hook-up $50
    electricity ($1.20/foot)   0 - $24,744
    telephone   0 - $3,852
    road maintenance ($50/mile)   N/A

---

*Includes industrial, commercial, and multi-family lots.

ENVIRONMENTAL CHECKLIST

Overall environmental protection record: POOR

Does the subdivider:

PLANS	Plan for complete basic services?	NO
	Phase lot sales and extension of services?	NO
	Get 80% build-out in 10 years of each section marketed?	NO
	Prepare an Environmental Impact Report?	NO
LAND	Use a curvilinear or cluster design?	NO
	Retain 25% or more open space?	NO
	Reserve from lot sale and development the following areas of critical concern:	
	wetlands?	--
	dunes and beaches?	--
	water sources?	--
	prime agricultural lands?	--
	habitats of endangered species?	--
	prime historical, archaeological, cultural, aesthetic, or recreational resources?	--
	Reserve from lot sale and development the following areas hazardous for building:	
	geological hazard areas (earthquake, landslide)?	--
	flood-prone areas (100-year floodplains, arroyos)?	NO
	areas of slope exceeding 25%?	--
	Blade roads only in immediate development areas?	NO
	Clear only for buildings and roads?	YES
	Preserve existing topography?	YES
WATER RESOURCES	Design the drainage system to control erosion?	NO
	Retain 100-foot buffer zone around water bodies?	--
	Replant disturbed land immediately?	NO
	Limit septic systems to one-acre or larger lots with adequate: percolation rates, slope, and distance from bedrock, water table and surface waters?	NO
	When utilizing central sewage disposal, provide tertiary treatment (or secondary and land disposal)?	YES
	Avoid major stream alteration?	--
	Avoid major wetland dredging and filling?	--
	Use groundwater only up to the safe yield?	NO

NOTE: See chapter on "Guidelines" for more complete explanation of items on Checklist.

ARIZONA SUNSITES

CONSUMER CHECKLIST

Overall consumer protection record: POOR

Does the subdivider:

<table>
<tr><td rowspan="12">SALES</td><td>Conduct a credit check on lot purchasers?</td><td>NO</td></tr>
<tr><td>Limit lot sales to two per purchaser?</td><td>NO</td></tr>
<tr><td>Sell only residential, i.e., no industrial, commercial or multi-family lots on installment contracts?</td><td>NO</td></tr>
<tr><td>Require a cash downpayment of 20% on all sales?</td><td>NO</td></tr>
<tr><td>Limit duration of installment contracts to 5 years?</td><td>NO*</td></tr>
<tr><td>Charge no interest on installment contracts?</td><td>--</td></tr>
<tr><td>Encourage attorney review of sales documents?</td><td>NO</td></tr>
<tr><td>Require a pre-purchase site visit?</td><td>NO</td></tr>
<tr><td>Allow a 14-day rescission period in which purchaser can obtain a refund for any reason?</td><td>NO</td></tr>
<tr><td>Offer a partial refund if purchaser defaults?</td><td>NO</td></tr>
<tr><td>Guarantee a refund, with interest, if promised services are not made available by date specified in contract?</td><td>NO</td></tr>
<tr><td>Escrow contract payments, or provide equivalent surety bonding, for refund purposes?</td><td>NO</td></tr>
<tr><td rowspan="4">TITLE</td><td>Offer only platted lots?</td><td>YES</td></tr>
<tr><td>Offer a recordable contract, and record the sale?</td><td>YES</td></tr>
<tr><td>Offer unmortgaged land, or land mortgaged with a release clause, only?</td><td>YES</td></tr>
<tr><td>Upon contract signing, deed title to purchaser, or place title in trust?</td><td>YES</td></tr>
<tr><td rowspan="14">BASIC SERVICES</td><td>Guarantee, or have available, to each lot:</td><td></td></tr>
<tr><td>   central water, of adequate quantity and quality?</td><td>NO</td></tr>
<tr><td>   central sewage disposal, as necessary?</td><td>NO</td></tr>
<tr><td>   drainage system, adequate for 100-year storm?</td><td>NO</td></tr>
<tr><td>   solid waste disposal, via adequate method?</td><td>NO</td></tr>
<tr><td>   roads, paved, to county standards?</td><td>NO</td></tr>
<tr><td>   electricity and telephone?</td><td>NO</td></tr>
<tr><td>Guarantee completion through escrowing or surety bonding?</td><td>NO</td></tr>
<tr><td>If services are financed through special service district bonds, employ them only if:</td><td></td></tr>
<tr><td>   initial governing body includes a county official?</td><td>--</td></tr>
<tr><td>   elections include all landowners on one-man, one-vote basis?</td><td>--</td></tr>
<tr><td>   sum of bonds is less than twice the developer's investment in basic services?</td><td>--</td></tr>
<tr><td>   sum of bonds is less than 15% of the assessed value of land in the district?</td><td>--</td></tr>
<tr><td>   developer co-signs all bonds?</td><td>--</td></tr>
</table>

*Some contracts of two years are offered with no interest charges.

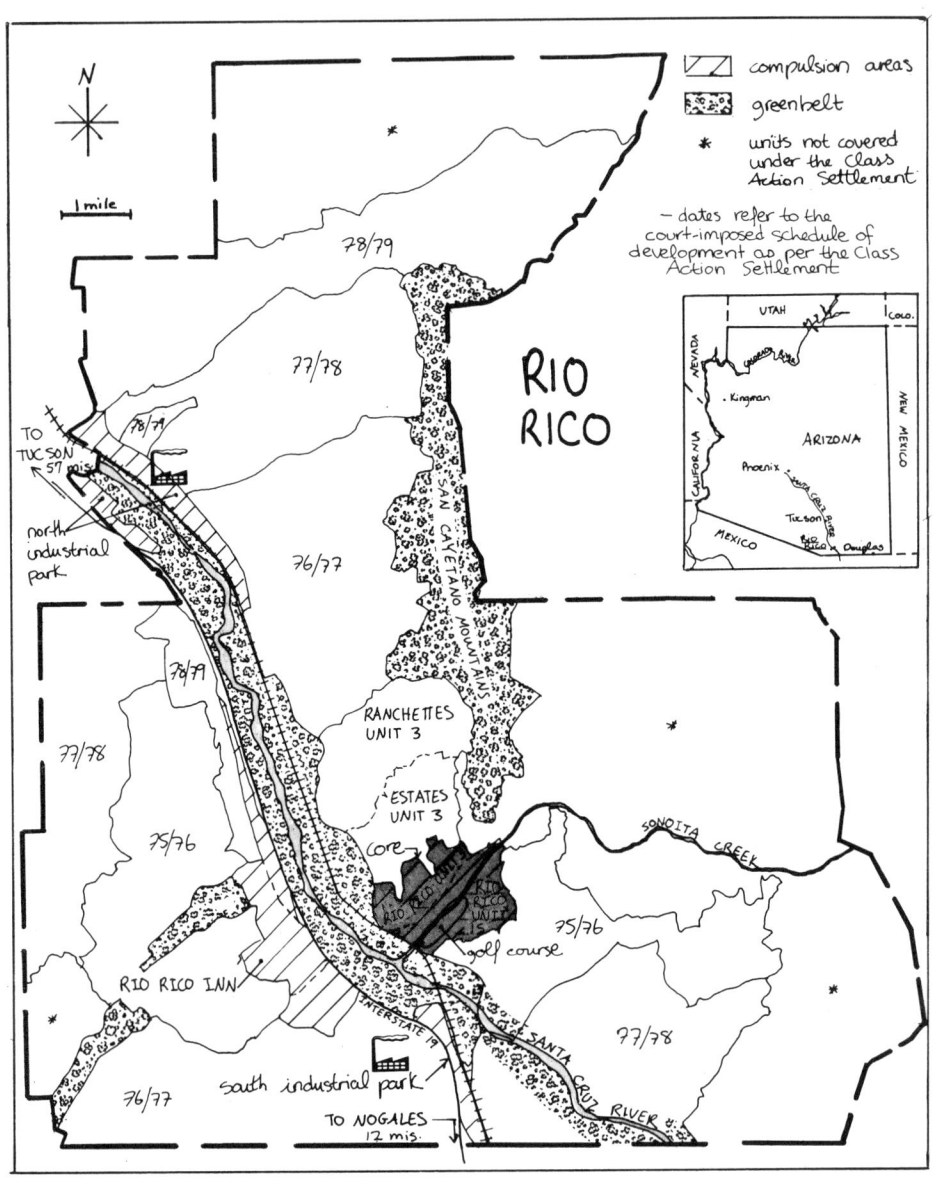

6
Rio Rico

In many ways, GAC Corporation's lot-sales operation at Rio Rico* typified the kind of marketing sleight of hand practiced by many of the least responsible retail land firms. The subdivision's nearly 86 square miles of sparse, Arizona desert-grassland--located in the southeastern corner of Arizona twelve miles north of Nogales and the Mexican border--was sold primarily out of state on the installment plan to customers who had never seen what they were buying. Lots were advertised as "homesites," when many had no improvements at all, not even a dirt road. The site was promoted as a "preplanned community," when very little attention was given to the installation of services or to the projected population's possible impact on the environment.[1] The land was offered on the basis of its "investment" value when it had virtually none.

Many land-subdivision companies have operated in a similar fashion for years. They purchase a remote tract of land at a price reflecting remoteness and lack of development. Then they sell lots at inflated prices, receiving income from installment payments. But they do little to promote real development or give value to the land by providing improvements. For the $400 million GAC Corporation, this profitable house of cards collapsed late in 1975.[2] GAC started marketing Rio Rico lots in 1969; by the early 1970s certain of its more deceptive sales practices began to receive national publicity. Several major

---

*Apart from granting an initial interview, GAC Properties, Inc., refused throughout the course of this study to communicate with INFORM. Rio Rico is thus one of just three subdivisions--out of a total of nineteen studied by INFORM--for which the development company did not verify the accuracy of the facts.

269

suits alleging misrepresentation and fraud were launched. At about the same time, the nation entered a period of economic recession.

Rio Rico and GAC's other land operations suffered a drastic drop in sales, at a time when the company was over leveraged and badly in need of income. Among many financial demands placed upon it were those resulting from the settlement, in late 1974, of a class-action suit filed on the behalf of approximately 20,000 lot buyers at Rio Rico. Under the terms of this settlement, GAC agreed to install central water, roads, and other improvements to a significant portion of the subdivision according to a five-year, court-supervised development schedule. Installing these improvements would have required large and unanticipated cash outlays on the company's part.

In early 1976, GAC found itself unable to meet the long-term debt obligations due its bondholders. Consequently, both GAC Properties, Inc., and the parent company, GAC Corporation--owner of seven land-development projects and once the nation's largest installment land-sales company--filed with the courts under the Federal Bankruptcy Act for protection against creditor lawsuits. By mid-1976, GAC had accumulated $218 million worth of development commitments at its various land-sales projects. Court-appointed trustees responsible for the reorganization of GAC's finances stated that "...in order to preserve the economic viability of [GAC and its subsidiary] companies for the benefit of customers and creditors..." they would try to reduce development commitments by $70 million.[3] If the trustees' plan is approved by the court, the company will "simply not develop as much property as it is committed to develop under its contracts with customers."[4]

As of 1976, approximately 25,000 people owned, or were in the ten-year process of paying for, land at Rio Rico. What impact GAC's poor planning and final declaration of bankruptcy will have on them is not yet known. Clearly, the company will not be taking as active a role in turning this village of 700 into a thriving city of 180,000 as was once projected. In the face of its dubious finances there are no longer any legal assurances that the company will keep to its court-imposed development schedule, or continue conveying title to purchasers who keep up their installment payments. An attorney for the plaintiffs in the class-action suit cautioned against purchasers making payments to an insolvent company and expecting it to provide improvements to their lots. As to which of the company's many creditors and development obligations will get priority, he noted: "The situation is in the hands of the courts."[5]

RIO RICO

History

GAC Properties, Inc., described in a 1971 news article as, "perhaps the best known and largest developer in both Arizona and the world,"[6] is one of many subsidiaries of the GAC Corporation. The latter, in the course of its rise, from 1933 to the end of 1971, acquired and managed large interests in "the fields of finance, insurance, land sales and community development, construction, utilities and resort development and operations."[7]

In 1969, GAC expanded its real estate and community development activities through a merger with the Gulf American Corporation. This company's Florida land holdings* had been marketed throughout the United States and in sixty foreign countries, using immensely profitable but unethical tactics. When Gulf American Corporation ran out of dry land to market, it added to its sales inventory some 300,000 water-covered acres in Big Cypress Swamp, and piloted prospective buyers over these lush-appearing lots in a helicopter.[8] Ultimately, such practices caused the Florida Land Sales Board to charge the company with five counts of fraud. In the course of its subsequent legal problems, Gulf American's earnings dropped from $11.5 million to $2.9 million whereupon GAC, whose financial star was then rising, acquired it.[9]

As a result of this merger, GAC inherited two sizable properties in southern Arizona. One of them was Rio Rico: 55,420 acres of desert grassland, rough-hewn mountains, and prime grazing land, that formerly belonged to a Spanish Land Grant ranch known as Baca Float. According to the county tax assessor, Gulf American originally bought the property in 1964 for approximately $57 an acre.[10] By 1971, an acre of land at Rio Rico brought an average of $3,000 on the installment sales market.[11]

In 1972, a GAC administrative vice-president testified to the success of the sales practices used at Rio Rico during the previous three years by noting that the subdivision now had 26,000 contract holders.[12] That year, however, marked the end of GAC's climb to fortune. A severe decline in contract sales began at Rio Rico, as well as at the company's other "developments." Contract cancellations increased markedly, reaching the point where lots being returned to inventory exceeded new sales. In its 1974 Form 10-K Report, filed with the Securities and Exchange Commission, GAC listed as under contract or deeded to purchasers at Rio Rico 2,700 fewer acres than it had in 1972. Financial reports also showed that the company's income from

---

*Two of GAC's Florida subdivisions, Cape Coral and Poinciana, are analyzed in Volume II of this study.

installment land sales had dropped from $63.5 million in 1973 to $19.5 million in 1974.[13] Among the numerous causes of this decline was publicity concerning the vastly inflated prices of Rio Rico's undeveloped "homesites." The publicity was generated by a tax dispute between GAC and the state of Arizona. In 1970, as reported in a more recent *Arizona Daily Star* article, "GAC told the Arizona State Property Tax Appeals Board...that those lots in Rio Rico selling for $5,000 were worth only $185 each."[14] This startling fact came out when GAC went to the Board to appeal the Santa Cruz County tax assessor's valuation of the total Rio Rico acreage. GAC had said the land "is currently being used for grazing purposes and should be appraised as all other comparable grazing land."[15] It therefore placed a $4,836 cash value on all of Rio Rico's acreage. The County tax assessor had placed a $517,889 cash value on the land, based, he wrote, "on a [lot] price list submitted by GAC with suitable allowances for lack of offsite improvements." He added further that, "Approximately 9,000 lots have been sold out of GAC subdivisions in the six months preceding January 1, 1970."[16]

On June 10, 1970, the state Board upheld the County's valuation. In the course of the hearing that preceded this ruling, GAC offered the "future-use" concept of pricing as an explanation for the vast disparity in valuation. According to this concept, which is a rule of thumb in the retail land-sales industry, the value of a lot itself at the time of purchase is substantially less than the contract price; not surprising inasmuch as a purchaser is initially buying little more than raw grazing land. Ostensibly, however, a lot's value increases during the course of installment payments, the assumption being that this ten-year period will see the addition of basic community improvements such as roads, water, and sewage systems.

While it used the concept of future use to justify its high prices at Rio Rico, it also admitted that a lot price of $5,000 included $2,500 in promotional costs, as well as the cost of improvements. At the same time, the company acknowledged that improvements would not be available for at least ten years.[17] (In the seven years since lot sales started at this site, over 95% of the lots have remained unimproved. Furthermore, 1975 federal Property Reports* pertaining to certain Rio Rico units state that essential services such as water delivery cannot be requested for twelve years following the date of contract.)

---

*The U.S. Department of Housing and Urban Development, Office of Interstate Land Sales Registration, requires the development company to issue a Property Report giving important consumer information on the lots offered for sale.

At about the same time as the tax dispute emerged, it also became widely known that the land at Rio Rico had no resale value. A December, 1971, *Arizona Daily Star* article on land developers in the state, using as its source a GAC Prospectus available to company bondholders but not to Rio Rico lot purchasers, noted the following admission:

> The prices at which [GAC] Properties sells land under installment contracts do not reflect the current market price for cash purchases of comparable-developed or undeveloped land. There is no significant resale market for installment land contracts.[18]

Four years later, new federal Property Reports for specific Rio Rico Units did mention among "Special Risk Factors" that: "You should consider...that real estate brokers may not be interested in listing your lot."[19] A local broker interviewed in 1974 affirmed: "We can't move parcels that are eight to ten years away from development."[20] Another bluntly remarked, "There might be buyers for *improved* lots, but we haven't sold any."[21]

Inevitably, GAC's widespread practice of marketing what is basically raw land at an extreme mark-up* came under fire. One former salesman for both Gulf American and GAC said, in a 1971 interview with Tom Pew, Editor of *The Troy News*, that, "Gulf American may have a new parent company, but the old sales team is still using the old ways of selling the land."[23] A local realtor told the same journalist, Rio Rico "is a purely speculative project, a forced proposition, with sales made primarily to out-of-state people who don't know what they're getting into."[24]

GAC's Form 10-K Reports list sixteen different court or regulatory actions filed against the parent company and/or its subsidiaries between 1971 and 1975. Five of these actions specifically mention GAC's Rio Rico land-development project.

In 1971, both the Rhode Island Department of Business Regulation and the California Real Estate Commission brought charges against the company, alleging misrepresentation and fraud in the promotion and sale of lots at Rio Rico.†

In April, 1972, a $100 million class-action lawsuit was filed on behalf of an estimated 20,000 Rio Rico property owners.

---

*GAC's president and chairman acknowledged to *The New York Times* in 1973, "The assessed value of the land at the time our customer purchases it may be less than five percent of the selling price."[22]

†California charged GAC with luring state residents to a Las Vegas, Nevada, hotel where the company could then promote Rio Rico lots.

It charged GAC with numerous offenses including fraudulent sales activity and violations of the federal securities acts and the federal Interstate Land Sales Full Disclosure Act.

In December, 1973, the Office of Interstate Land Sales Registration (OILSR) filed a notice of proceedings against GAC for failing to adequately disclose adverse financial information in its Property Reports. In March, 1974, the Federal Trade Commission (FTC) issued a complaint and order against the company "alleging numerous misrepresentations, [and] unfair and deceptive sales practices..."[25]

The settlements of these (and other) legal and regulatory proceedings vastly altered GAC's marketing methods. They also both directly and indirectly affected lot purchasers at Rio Rico. According to the Director of the Santa Cruz County Planning and Zoning Department, in 1974, GAC "stopped its fraudulent practices."[26] One practice that was discontinued was the sale of Rio Rico lots sight-unseen to out-of-state residents. Following the settlement of the class-action suit the company began improving a small portion of the site with central water, roads, and electricity.

By the time GAC responded to pressure and modified its practices, it was all but too late. On October 15, 1975, OILSR officially suspended the sale of all land at Rio Rico (as well as at GAC's Poinciana and Cape Coral sites in Florida) until the company adequately disclosed to prospective land buyers what it had bluntly stated in a recent report to its shareholders: that "a perilous financial condition [exists] which could affect development plans at some projects."[27] In 1975, GAC filed new federal Property Reports on certain Rio Rico Units. These Reports incorporated some of the marketing reforms that resulted from preceding legal and regulatory actions against the company. They were filed in spite of the fact that no installment-contract lots have been marketed at Rio Rico since 1974.

In early 1976, GAC Properties, Inc., and the parent GAC Corporation filed under Chapters XI and X respectively of the Federal Bankruptcy Act. (Under Chapter XI, a company may continue to operate protected from creditor lawsuits while it attempts with court supervision to work out an arrangement on its debt. Under Chapter X, one or more trustees are appointed by the court to appraise and reorganize the debtor's business operations.) One of the court-appointed supervising attorneys involved in these proceedings commented that "This will probably be one of the most complicated bankruptcy cases in a long time."[28]

Regional Context

If the court-appointed trustees are unable to maintain development activities at Rio Rico, Santa Cruz County will be among the project's many victims. The subdivision is the County's largest single taxpayer. It provides fully one-third of the taxes collected.[29] A worried County official remarked in 1974 that the worst thing that could happen with regard to Rio Rico would be for GAC to go bankrupt. The County would then have to take over the project, and as the official explained, "the County doesn't have the money."[30]

Santa Cruz County is located in Arizona's southeast corner along the U.S.-Mexico border. It is the smallest county in the state, encompassing approximately 1,245 square miles and, with 17,000 people as of 1976, it has the third-lowest population.[31] In 1971, before being overwhelmed by its troubles, GAC had projected populations for Rio Rico alone of 4,742 by 1975 and 20,000 by 1991.[32] It even went so far as to project an ultimate total of 180,000 residents. As of early 1976, however, Rio Rico's population was about 700.

More than half the people in Santa Cruz County live in Nogales, the county seat, which lies twelve miles south of Rio Rico. Nogales is primarily a processing and distribution point for Mexican-raised produce bound for U.S. and Canadian markets. Approximately forty produce-distributing companies work out of the area. These firms and a growing tourist industry common to Southwestern border towns make Nogales the focus for the County's much-desired economic growth.

Except for this small urban area, the County is rural and undeveloped. It is characterized by high mountains, rolling rangelands, and semi-arid desert valleys. Approximately 60% its land area is publicly owned. It either belongs to the state or is part of the Coronado National Forest. The Arizona Office of Economic Planning and Development has noted in a study of the County that much of the remaining private land is "being held by land-development enterprises for speculation purposes and possible future development. Livestock grazing is only an interim use for this land."[33]

Despite the persistent invasion of mesquite and other woody shrubs more characteristic of true deserts, the foothills of Santa Cruz County provide "some of the best grazing lands in the County."[34] GAC has subdivided and sold a large chunk of such land at what Arizona's Office of Economic Planning and Development optimistically termed in 1974, the "totally preplanned community" of Rio Rico.[35]

THE OFFERING: LAND AND IMPROVEMENTS

LAND

Physical Characteristics

Rio Rico is situated 57 miles south of Tucson in a semi-arid valley formed by the San Cayetano Mountains on the east and the Atacosa Mountains on the west. The property extends for about fourteen miles along both sides of the Santa Cruz River at an elevation of 3,300 to 3,800 feet. The River, which is the County's principal waterway, flows south into Mexico, wanders back across the border six miles east of Nogales and continues northward until it feeds into the Gila River near Phoenix. It is in its northerly course that it bisects the Rio Rico site. Much of the 86-square-mile GAC property lies in the relatively flat riverbed. Its boundaries are located 10 to 12 miles away in the mesas and foothills of the surrounding mountains.[36]

Status of Development

As of August 1, 1974,* with the exception of scattered recreational and promotional facilities (such as the Rio Rico Inn), the site's only improvements were in the units defined as "Rio Rico Urban." None of the approximately 1,500 acres in these "urban" units (about 3% of the subdivision's 55,427 acres) were ever marketed under installment contracts. Known as "compulsory building areas" (where house construction must begin within twelve months of lot purchase), they comprise the project's "core."

Even in this "core" area, however, development has fallen short of expectations. As of August, 1974, GAC had improved only 552 acres of the total 958 scheduled for improvements. The other 406 acres were under development, i.e., "utilities, roads, drainage work and other site preparation [would] soon be completed."[37] The core area was ultimately to have been divided by use as follows: 545 acres, residential; 46 acres, commercial; 149 acres, industrial; and 218 acres, recreational.

In its original design, GAC expected to plat approximately 34,012 lots[38] zoned for single-family, multiple-family, commer-

---

*Rio Rico lot owners and purchasers-under-contract were notified of the proposed settlement of the class-action suit against GAC on August 1, 1974.

Aerial view of a portion of Rio Rico.

cial, industrial, and community use.* Lots at Rio Rico were marketed in four development categories: Urban lots, Villa lots, Estate lots, and Ranchette lots. The first category, where the core area was to be located, were marketed on a cash or mortgage basis. All the others were available through installment contracts. These land offerings ranged in size from 6,000 square feet (about one seventh of an acre) in Rio Rico Villas to over twenty acres in the Ranchettes.

Currently, about 700 persons reside at the subdivision, all of them in the core area's Urban Unit 3. Across the Santa Cruz River from this Unit, next to Interstate 19, lies a 544-acre commercial area, much of which remains undeveloped. The Rio Rico Inn, a $4 million, 200-room motel which GAC constructed in 1971, dominates this area from its position atop a 4,000-foot mountain. At a lower elevation, a 12-acre shopping center offers a supermarket, a savings and loan service, and office space. Both Urban Unit 3 and the developed portion of this commercial area are serviced by central water and central sewage systems. Utility lines in these sections have been placed underground.

At the southern end of the development, bordering Interstate 19 and the Southern Pacific Railroad (both of which run north/south through the subdivision) lies Rio Rico's 233-acre South Industrial Park. According to the County's planning director, as of April, 1976, most of this acreage was sold, but there were only about twenty tenants.

Various recreational facilities, located throughout the development, also have complete utility service. These facilities include a community-recreation center (equipped for basketball, tennis, swimming, baseball, and handball), a playground, and a park. Facilities for riding, trap and skeet shooting, and camping are suitably situated in the unsubdivided 3,000-acre River floodplain between Urban Units 3 and 4. Also in this area are a community-development center, which houses a U.S. Post Office, space for religious, civic, and social activities, and GAC's sales office.

As of mid-1976, GAC's recent filing for bankruptcy had not had a severe impact on Rio Rico. The County tax assessor confirmed in April, 1976, that GAC had paid all taxes due.[40] The court-imposed development program appeared to INFORM to be proceeding nearly on schedule, with, according to one of the court-appointed trustees for the company, almost $2 million

---

*The number of lots used above is a 1973 GAC figure. The August, 1974, Notice of the Class Action Settlement against GAC stated that "the project consists of approximately 31,800 lots...."[39]

spent on improvements at Rio Rico thus far in 1976.[41] A July, 1976, article in the *Miami Herald* reported that GAC has 78,000 customer contracts which provide the company with a cash flow of "about $4 million a month from persons throughout the U.S. and abroad...."[42] Attorneys for GAC assured INFORM that contract payments are being used for the installation of improvements at Rio Rico and other sites, as well as for daily company expenditures. They added that since money is currently being spent for site improvements (rather than escrowed as would normally occur in such a case) the courts, and the trustees assigned to manage the parent company, are under a greater obligation to protect the equity of Rio Rico lot purchasers in forthcoming court decisions establishing creditor priority.[43] The trustees, who are drawing up an operational plan to be approved by the courts, have stated that it is their intention (subject to approval by the court) "to continue operation of the companies as ongoing businesses...."[44]

However, should GAC's cash flow decline, or should the court ultimately give priority status to any of GAC's many other creditors, Rio Rico lot purchasers who are still making contract payments and whose titles were not escrowed could lose their equity. For those who own their lots there will be no legal recourse available through which to obtain GAC-promised improvements.

The continued installation of services and improvements is, of course, essential for Rio Rico's growth. This growth has been minimal to date. Based on the average annual rate of population increase during its first seven years, it could take 750 years for the 24,800 lots already sold to become occupied. Populating the total 34,000 platted lots could take an additional several hundred years.

Furthermore, according to the July, 1976, *Miami Herald* article, the trustees' plan for GAC's continued operation calls for a major "swap program" in which purchasers will be invited to exchange their contracted lots for others in subdivisions "now under development or which are scheduled for development in the next 10 years."[45] As the plan is still in the process of being devised and must ultimately be approved by the court, it is impossible to say what awaits Rio Rico's many buyers.

BASIC SERVICES

Fewer improvements are guaranteed to lot purchasers at Rio Rico than at any of the nineteen subdivisions studied by

INFORM.* GAC failed to install services upon initiating sales, and given its current fiscal status, the chances of it ever fully doing so are slim. GAC's original development plan for Rio Rico was essentially the same as that used at most large installment-lot-sales projects. The subdivision was divided, for development purposes, into two distinct sections: a very small "core area" and a vast "outlying area." Lots in the core area had to be purchased on a cash or mortgage basis. Buyers there had to start constructing homes within a relatively short period of time. It appears likely that all of Rio Rico's core-area lots will eventually be improved with a central water-and-sewer system and paved roads.

The vast majority of the subdivision's lots, however--97% of its total land area--are in the outlying, completely unimproved, section. Although lots in the Estates, Ranchettes, and Villas Units were sold as "homesites," many of them are not even accessible by conventional vehicles.

In the Deeds of Reservations and Restrictions appended to its Property Reports, GAC stated that these outlying lots would be provided with central water, electricity, and in certain cases sewer lines, "as and when required by the appropriate governmental authorities."[46] Eventually governmental authorities--in this case the federal courts--did demand the phased installation of improvements. In September, 1974, GAC attained a virtually unique status among installment-land-sales companies. In settling the class-action suit, it agreed to follow a radically reorganized, court-appointed, court-supervised schedule of development.

The settlement agreement divided Rio Rico's outlying area into two parts. By 1980, the bulk of the Units, approximately 40,087 acres subdivided into 24,993 lots, was scheduled to have central water, central sewage-disposal (in those Units not approved by the Arizona State Board of Health for septic tanks), paved roads (except in the Ranchette Units), a drainage system, and access to electricity.† The most distant outlying Units

---

*Includes both the ten subdivisions discussed in Volume I of this study and the nine Florida subdivisions analyzed in Volume II.

†Completion dates were specified as:[47]
    1975: Ranchettes Unit 3; Estates Unit 3
    1976: Ranchettes Unit 14; Estates Units 4, 6, 7, 9, 10
    1977: Ranchettes Units 4, 5, 17; Estates Units 8, 13
    1978: Ranchettes Units 7, 9, 10, 11, 12, 18;
           Estates Unit 11; Villas Unit 16
    1979: Estates Units 14, 16; Villas Units 10, 11, 12, 13, 14

(Villas Unit 9, Estates Unit 12, and Ranchettes Units 13, 15, and 42) and the Urban Units were excluded from the court-supervised schedule of development. Purchasers of lots in these excluded outlying Units were offered lots in "the more compact area surrounding the central core of Rio Rico"[48] on an exchange basis. This right had to be exercised within a specified period.

By insisting on this improvement schedule and by offering a lot-exchange option, the court hoped to bring about "a consolidation of all purchasers nearer the central core...[whereby] the likelihood of there being a substantial community development at Rio Rico in a much shorter time would be greatly enhanced."[49]

Soon, however, problems with the settlement began to develop. Beginning in February, 1975, GAC was to have filed with the court an annual report "showing that the scheduled improvements as of the preceding October 31 have been completed" in accordance with the settlement agreement.[50] The court could at that time approve deviations from the schedule or establish further conditions. If GAC was found to have violated the conditions, the court could order it to refund all principal and interest paid on contracts relating to the lots affected. According to attorneys for the plaintiffs in the class-action suit, as of April, 1976, GAC had not submitted any annual reports, and the court had taken none of its possible actions.[51]

The settlement agreement further stipulated that "GAC will establish and maintain the reserves applicable to such improvements...."[52] Counsel for the plaintiffs stated recently that there is no way of knowing whether GAC has done this,[53] but the company's 1975 federal Property Reports on Rio Rico state that it has not.

Most crucial, of course, is the effect GAC's filing under Chapter XI of the Federal Bankruptcy Act will have on company funds and on the development schedule in general. Had the court required GAC to place funds for this purpose in escrow (rather than simply to maintain reserves), as the plaintiffs originally demanded, completion of Rio Rico's development would be considerably less in doubt than it is today.

GAC's 1975 federal Property Reports on Rio Rico disclose that no money has been put aside for the installation of utilities and that the company is under no obligation to provide such service until twelve years after the date of contract signing. These Property Reports cover all the Units included under the court-supervised schedule of development (and due under that schedule to be totally improved by 1980). This apparent conflict in schedules remains unexplained. Counsel for the plaintiffs in the class-action suit were unaware of GAC's 1975 OILSR filings.

The question of who, among GAC's many creditors, has a priority right to its shrinking but ongoing cash flow is one of utmost significance to lot purchasers at Rio Rico. As mentioned earlier, the courts will ultimately establish an order of priority, but no one can say exactly when their final decision will be handed down. At present, funds for improvements come primarily from the receipt of installment-contract payments and the collection of several special fees. As noted in the 1975 federal Property Reports and applicable Deeds of Restrictions, all lot owners at Rio Rico must help finance the installation of basic services through payment of a "betterment fee." One month after he receives his deed, a lot owner begins making mandatory monthly contributions of $10 which continue until he has paid a total of from $954 to $1,700, depending on the location of his lot. Payments thus continue for eight to fourteen years, unless the utility lines are installed sooner, in which case the full balance must be paid immediately.

In addition, according to the same Deeds of Restrictions, once a lot owner receives title, he must pay a $5-per-month maintenance fee "for the sole purpose of maintaining community improvements within the entire subdivision."[54] This charge is not to begin before 1980.

Failure to pay the betterment and maintenance fees for a period of ninety days automatically gives GAC a lien against an owner's lot.[55] Both fees are subject to escalation.

Until the court has completed its reorganization of GAC's finances, it is impossible to determine whether or not the company will be able to install basic services at Rio Rico to the full extent required. To date, the company has met the court's requirement for the first phase of development. Improvements at Rio Rico Estates Unit 3 and Ranchettes Unit 3 were to be completed by the end of 1975. By early 1976, water mains were in place in these two Units, and twenty miles of roads had been graded, thirteen of which were paved. Access roads in Estates Unit 3 were paved. Those in Ranchettes Unit 3 were paved only where the grade exceeded 15%. According to a Santa Cruz County planning official, other roads throughout the Ranchettes Units will probably never be paved.[56] He indicated that property owners in these Units can "presumably" receive service within two weeks of filing a request.[57]

Water

GAC planned to provide water, via a central system, to all Rio Rico lots. However, the 1975 federal Property Reports reveal inconsistencies within this plan. They warn that the company set aside no money for the system's completion, and that, while it has stated its intention to extend water lines within ninety days after a lot owner receives a building permit and requests service, such requests may not be made "prior to 12 years after date of contract," i.e., two years after completion of all payments. (This does not conform to the court-ordered schedule.)

The 1975 Property Reports state unequivocally that there will be an adequate water supply, drawn from "a series of wells" to be drilled along the Santa Cruz River. These will be of sufficient capacity "to sustain the entire community when all the lots have been developed."[58] There is reason to question the accuracy of this statement. Rio Rico's sole water source is the groundwater in the Upper Santa Cruz Basin. This Basin, which extends beyond Santa Cruz County, is also the only source of water for the cities of Tucson and Nogales. Due to treaty arrangements between Mexico and the United States, most research on the Basin has been carried out by the International Boundary and Water Commission. Its findings are classified. The Arizona Water Commission, however, has recently completed a state-wide inventory of water resources and uses which notes that the Upper Santa Cruz Basin suffers an annual depletion of 204,000 acre-feet.[59] This overdraft "is a problem which is becoming more severe as municipal and industrial demands increase."[60] Furthermore, the Water Commission points out that while the state as a whole uses 1.7 times its annual dependable supply of water (i.e., more surface water and groundwater than is annually recharged), Santa Cruz County (which does not include Tucson) is using 2.6 times its annual dependable supply.[61]

In 1974, the Deputy Director of the Santa Cruz County Environmental Health Department stated that the aquifer from which Rio Rico draws its water supply would remain adequate for another 100 to 200 years. He pointed out, however, that unless costly treatment facilities were used, a serious problem could result from the poor quality recharge returned to the aquifer.[62]

Reflecting the unknowns surrounding Rio Rico's long-term water supply, the 1974 class-action settlement agreement stated:

> The parties are in disagreement as to the adequacy of proven water supplies to meet the potential demand if GAC continues to sell individual lots pursuant to installment contracts for Deed in certain units at the Rio Rico project.[63]

Under the terms of the settlement, GAC agreed not to sell on an installment basis any lots in Villas Unit 9, Estates Unit 12, or Ranchettes Units 13, 15, 16, and 19, without first obtaining court approval (based on evidence of an adequate water supply).

The only exception to this ruling would exist in the event that 10% or more of the contract-holders in these remote Units* neglected to exercise their previously described exchange option.⁶⁴

At present, a central water system operated by Citizens Utilities Corporation serves the approximately 250 housing units in Rio Rico's "urban" core. The site's commercial and industrial facilities are also serviced by this system which consists of four wells--two of which are temporary--with a combined capacity of 2.16 million gallons per day. The wells provide enough water for approximately 14,400 people (at 150 gallons per person per day). The system includes a 381,000-gallon storage tank.⁶⁵

Between $465 and $623 of each lot owner's "betterment fee" payments is for the extension of central water lines to his or her lot. As of April, 1976, lines were extended to approximately 500 lots in Urban Unit 3, Estates Unit 3, and Ranchettes Unit 3. Water service was also available in the South Industrial Park, the shopping area, the golf course area, and at the Rio Rico Inn. The site uses an average of approximately 150,000 gallons of water a day.⁶⁶

Sewage

Only about 10% of Rio Rico was planned for hookup to a central sewage system. As mentioned earlier, Citizens' Utilities Corporation operates a system for the disposal of sewage in the Urban core areas. According to the 1975 federal Property Reports all lots in Villas Units 5, 12, and 13 will ultimately be included in this system.† Lot owners must pay $596 for the extension of lines to their lots, but the 1975 federal Property Reports' warning with regard to other utilities also applies here: lot owners must wait twelve years from the date of contract signing before they can request service.

The other 90% of Rio Rico was planned for individual sewage-disposal systems. If the entire community were occupied, there would thus be at least 29,000 septic tanks in use at the site. The 1975 federal Property Reports state that the cost of installing an individual sewage system ranges from $900 to $2,000.

The Reports further disclose that although Rio Rico's lots

---

*Villas Unit 9 and Estates Unit 12 are currently registered with OILSR for installment sales but lots are not being marketed.

†A County Health Department official reported to INFORM in April, 1976, that only the core-area Units, Ranchettes Unit 10, and the shopping center would be on a central sewage system. The rest of the site would have septic systems.⁶⁷

have been generally approved for septics by the Arizona State Health Department, they must also receive individual approval from the County Environmental Health Department (whose decisions can be overruled on the state level). The Deputy Director of the County Environmental Health Department indicated in 1974 that he was stricter than his predecessor in approving septic-tank permits. He observed that soils at Rio Rico vary almost every five feet, changing from sand to rock to clay, and that "many lots will have problems."[68] In 1971, he had ruled that in high-density areas septic tanks must be limited to lots of 21,000 square feet (one-half acre) or larger. In his opinion the state's general approval of individual systems at Rio Rico "should be looked at again."[69]

In April, 1976, a County Health Department official affirmed that the County was considering, but had not yet established, a minimum lot size and percolation standard for septics.[70] According to the County's engineer, "Even a 5,000-square-foot lot [one-sixth acre] can easily get a septic-tank permit if it passes the percolation test."[71]

As of January, 1976, sewage lines had been extended to 455 lots, and there were 213 homes connected to the system. The treatment facility, a small predesigned package plant offering secondary-level treatment, operates at 60% of its capacity. It currently processes approximately 75,000 gallons per day of sewage.[72]

Solid Waste

GAC has not set aside a site for solid-waste disposal. At present, solid-waste collection is available only in Urban Unit 3. Refuse is disposed of in a County-maintained sanitary landfill.

Roads

In April, 1976, the only paved roads at Rio Rico were those in Urban Unit 3, those in Estates Unit 3, those with a grade of more than 15% in Ranchettes Unit 3, and those going to the Inn, the commercial area, and the golf course. This represented a total of 19.47 miles of paved road. Another 135 miles of roads had been graded. Much of the site, however, remained accessible only by four-wheel-drive vehicles.[73]

As a means of assuring that GAC would honor its promise to construct roads and stake lots at Rio Rico, the County required the company to post $11 million in corporate obligation bonds (basically corporate IOUs). These bonds are all but worthless today. GAC claimed that it intended to pave and maintain roads

in all Units except the Ranchettes until the County accepted
them for maintenance. But according to recent federal Property
Reports, it set aside no funds for either construction or maintenance. The County will accept maintenance responsibility for
all roads that meet its specifications within one year after
their completion and inspection date. At present only the roads
in Urban Unit 3 have been accepted.[74]

Drainage

Santa Cruz County had no drainage requirements for subdivisions when Rio Rico was platted.* It is not surprising then
that GAC has paid little attention to the site's drainage problems. A written agreement regarding Rio Rico's drainage, made
in 1969 between GAC and the County planning & zoning director,
states only that most drainage will be carried in natural water
courses, and that culverts or dips sufficient to carry the runoff from a ten-year storm will be constructed where these water
courses cross roadways.[75] The present County Engineer interpreted this as meaning that GAC "can do pretty much what it
wants to."[76] Referring to the company's actual drainage installations he added, "There is really no drainage in detail. There
are some culverts, small pipes, concrete inlets and outlets by
the roads, and sometimes a concrete apron to channel flow."[77]

Because Rio Rico's hills are sparsely vegetated, rainwater
tends to flow unchecked down canyons and into arroyos, often
at high speeds. As described by the engineer, "The entire
county is an arroyo, and all erosion material eventually goes
into the Santa Cruz River."[78] A County planning official noted
that GAC and property owners have constructed, "not always at
GAC's expense," drainageways on some of the individual lots.[79]
The company has not, however, built any retention areas or settling ponds to handle runoff before it enters the River. There
has been no bonding or escrowing of funds for a drainage system,
despite the recommendation of most planners that a developer
construct one capable of handling the runoff from a 100-year
storm.

Electricity and Telephone

Electricity will be supplied by Citizens Utilities Corporation. The cost of extension ranges from $489 to $517 subject to
adjustment, and is included in the "betterment fee." Telephone

---

*The County Board of Supervisors intends to establish County
drainage standards this year, but since they will not be retro-
active, Rio Rico will be exempt from them.

service will be supplied by Mountain Bell Telephone Company. How much lot owners will be charged for extension is not known. No request for electric or telephone service can be made until twelve years after the date of contract signing.

COMMUNITY AND RECREATIONAL FACILITIES

Police protection is provided by the County Sheriff's Office. Fire protection is available for the core area from a local rural fire department.

Rio Rico has a primary school and a junior high school but the nearest senior high school is located almost forty miles away. Bus service is provided by the school district. According to the County tax assessor, school-district taxes jumped 20% to 30% between 1974 and 1975, to meet the costs of busing and otherwise serving school children residing at Rio Rico.[80]

For medical and dental facilities, residents must travel thirteen miles to Nogales. There is, as mentioned, a small shopping center on the site; Nogales provides more extensive services. Public bus transportation to the site is available from Tucson in the north and Nogales in the south. There is an airport at Nogales.

ENVIRONMENTAL PROTECTION

GAC's environmental-protection practices have been poor. Should Rio Rico ever achieve the densities of population once projected for it by the developer, the environment would almost certainly be severely affected. The principal impact would be on water resources, an extremely valuable commodity in this water-short region. In addition to putting more stress on an already overdrawn aquifer (an underground, water-bearing geological formation), Rio Rico's plans rely heavily on the use of septic tanks for sewage disposal. Because of the site's location over the Upper Santa Cruz Basin's principal recharge area, the widespread use of this method could seriously pollute both underground water and the Santa Cruz River.

PLANNING

Rio Rico was designed and laid out in a curvilinear pattern, which allows some accommodation of development to natural topographical features. Information on how much of the site's total acreage has been allocated for open space is not available. In the small core area, according to the Notice of the Class Action Settlement, 218 out of 958 acres have been reserved for this use. This amounts to 23%, very close to the 25% advocated by respected planners. The company has also set aside approximately 3,000 acres of land (5% of the whole site)--on either side of the Santa Cruz River and along Sonita Creek, which cuts through the core area--for future recreational purposes. This land is currently used as irrigated farmland.

Although GAC did not intend to use phased development at Rio Rico, it has been forced to do so under the terms of the 1974 Agreement of Settlement. The subdivision has thus become one of the few in the INFORM sample where phased development is being employed. As noted above, services are due to be extended (if GAC can continue funding development costs) to about 70% of the site, on a Unit by Unit basis, between 1975 and 1980. This will avoid blading roads and stringing wires across Rio Rico's vast acreage long before there is any possibility of their use.

As far as INFORM could determine, GAC currently has no plan for extending services, phased or otherwise, to the remaining 30% of the subdivision; this in spite of the fact that thousands of lots have been sold in these areas.

The company was not required to, and did not, prepare an Environmental Impact Report for use in planning at Rio Rico.

LAND

The Rio Rico site is inappropriate for large-scale development in three respects: it is a recharge area for the region's groundwater; it contains numerous steep slopes; and it includes areas subject to flooding. GAC has taken no steps to minimize any of these hazards except to a certain extent that of flooding.

As discussed earlier, Rio Rico is situated directly over a portion of the main recharge area for the Upper Santa Cruz Basin. But the subdivision is by no means alone in drawing its water from this source. Tucson, approximately sixty miles to the north, and a number of other cities in the region depend on it as well. As a result, the aquifer is already being overdrawn at a rate of about 204,000 acre-feet a year. Development at Rio Rico will cover over much of the permeable surface through which rainfall can percolate into the ground. This could potentially decrease the quantity of water finding its way back into the aquifer. Development may also seriously pollute this water, especially if, as is now planned, site sewage is disposed of almost totally by individual septic tanks.

The slope of much of Rio Rico's land presents a second severe problem. The site ranges in elevation only from 3,300 to 3,800 feet, but its topography varies widely. Reports filed by GAC with the Arizona Real Estate Department in 1971 indicate that one Unit contains "sharp ravines in the southeast and easterly part,"[81] and that another contains "hilly [land] in the northwest portion with a canyon intersection...."[82] A 1971 New York Offering Statement* discloses that "sloping skyline" lots have a 15% slope and that "hillside lots" have a 35% slope. A significant proportion of the lots covered by the Offering Statement fell into these two categories. Such steep grades approach or even exceed the 25% maximum advocated by noted planners.

Where roads in Ranchettes Unit 3 have a grade of over 15%, GAC has spot-paved them. However, the County Engineer fears that, "there will [still be] problems on the steeper roads. They will erode: especially those north of Urban Unit 3 where grades are steep."[83]

GAC has made some real effort to deal with the site's third potential problem: that of flooding. The company's predecessor, Gulf American Corporation, consistent with its predilection for underwater lot sales, had platted lots not only alongside the riverbed, but in it as well.[84] When GAC acquired Rio Rico in 1969, it immediately abandoned such plans, redrawing the project's development lines to avoid building on the 100-year floodplain, which was defined by a 1969 U.S. Army Corps of Engineers study made at the request of Santa Cruz County. About 3,000 acres located in the site's fourteen miles of River valley have been withheld from lot sales and development.[85] The Deputy Director of the County Environmental Health Department remarked that "GAC has done a good job of leaving the flood prone area free."[86] GAC's Director of Public Relations at Rio Rico, however, stated in 1974 that the company might sell this land, depending on "future water right matters at some future time."[87]

---

*New York State requires the development company to issue a report disclosing pertinent consumer information on lots offered for sale.

WATER RESOURCES

Pollution from sewage at Rio Rico is already considered a problem by one state official. It could easily get worse. The few occupied homes are connected to a central sewage system. A plant provides secondary treatment, via an activated sludge process, but its effluent is discharged directly into the Santa Cruz River. (Most subdivisions in this study dispose of effluent through spray irrigation of a golf course or other land areas. See Guidelines.) An official with the State Health Department, Division of Water Quality Control, was concerned about the discharge into the River, stating in 1974 that "the only reason Rio Rico is getting away with its effluent discharge in this manner is because the town of Nogales is too."[88] Since the Santa Cruz River has a seasonal flow, during dry spells when it would normally disappear its only flow is effluent from these towns' sewage-treatment plants.

With approximately 90% of Rio Rico's 34,000 lots planned for septic tanks, sewage leaching from individual systems could add significantly to the problem of water pollution in the future. According to the County's Deputy Director of Environmental Health, while three-quarters of a septic tank's effluent may evaporate, the other quarter will drain either into the aquifer or into the River. This would contribute to a degradation of groundwater quality. An early state *Board of Health Bulletin* reported the issuance of new regulations prohibiting the approval of septic tanks as the predominant sewage-disposal method in "planned communities" (the term which GAC used to describe Rio Rico in all of its marketing efforts).[89] According to the Deputy Director of the County Environmental Health Department, however, these regulations were of little importance since the Arizona Attorney General ruled them unenforceable. Rio Rico thus received state approval for septic-tank use.[90] Counties in Arizona now have the power to establish sewage-disposal regulations for subdivisions, but Santa Cruz County has not yet availed itself of this authority.

As noted previously, GAC has made no specific provisions to prevent erosion and runoff from polluting the groundwater or the Santa Cruz River. Its rudimentary drainage system does not include sediment traps or retention ponds where pollutants could settle out or decompose. The company has no revegetation program to prevent erosion in construction areas. Its preservation of the floodplain, however, does provide a buffer zone between the developed area and the Santa Cruz River.

CONSUMER PROTECTION

As of early 1976, the sale of Rio Rico lots via installment contracts had been halted for over a year. Core-area lots, available for cash or on a traditional mortgage basis, were still offered for sale as of August, 1976. GAC officials at Rio Rico were unresponsive to all of INFORM's inquiries and would not say when or whether the company ever intended to resume selling lots in outlying Units. However, by virtue of the FTC's demands, the class-action Agreement of Settlement, and Arizona law, if GAC ever resumes installment-contract sales, its practices will be slightly better than those of most of the companies in the INFORM sample.

In the meantime, through its declaration of insolvency, GAC has defaulted on its most basic obligation to consumers: that of maintaining a viable company long enough to fulfill the promise it has made--both implicitly and explicitly--to provide the purchaser with a functional homesite in a self-sufficient real community

Sales and Title Protection

Lots at Rio Rico range in size from under one-quarter acre to over twenty acres. Until sales were halted in 1974, they were being offered at prices ranging from $2,000 to over $12,000. A purchaser of any Rio Rico lot outside the core area acquired his lot via a Contract For Deed issued upon his making a small downpayment (generally 10%) on the purchase price. All lots offered for sale were platted of record with the County, as required by Arizona law. Legislation passed in 1975* also requires the developer to record the contract. This latter measure protects the purchaser's equity in the event of the company's bankruptcy and gives his right to the land priority over that of subsequent liens.

Thousands of Rio Rico lot purchasers are still paying off contracts signed before sales were stopped in 1974. The terms of these contracts extend for up to ten years, during which time the purchaser pays monthly installments including 6.0% to 7.5% interest on the principal. He must in addition reimburse GAC annually for its payment of the lot's property tax. In 1974, this amounted to $9.17 per $100.00 calculated at 18% of the as-

---

*Arizona's 1975 Land Sales law is analyzed in Volume III of this study.

sessed market value. The purchaser pays no other additional costs during the term of his contract.

Upon payment in full (including taxes) a purchaser is currently issued a Warranty Deed which he must record with the County. At that time, title should be conveyed to him free and clear of all encumbrances, except restrictions, reservations, and easements of record. The court, in determining creditor priority, could legally transfer this land to others, but such a decision is unlikely according to attorneys involved with the bankruptcy proceedings.

Due to the lack of cooperation from company officials at Rio Rico, INFORM could not determine whether GAC had placed title to the property in trust prior to Arizona's 1975 sales law requiring such action. There are no blanket mortgages or liens on the property which might otherwise interfere with the lot purchaser obtaining title upon full payment.

Refunds

Before the August, 1974, issuance of the FTC consent order, GAC could cancel those sales contracts it held to be in default* without offering any refund. While both the consent order and the class-action settlement affected GAC's treatment of default, the impact of these rulings may be negated by the company's recent filing for bankruptcy.

Under the terms of the FTC consent order, GAC agreed to "cease and desist from the use of various sales practices." It also agreed to revise its sales contracts and provide "a ten-day unconditional cancellation privilege" after a contract is signed during which time the buyer may cancel the sale and receive a full refund of monies paid.[91] Under Arizona's new law, should sales at Rio Rico ever resume, a purchaser who buys his lot sight-unseen will have six months in which to visit the site and demand a refund if desired.

The consent order further required GAC "to refund to buyers who defaulted on land contracts between June 30, 1968,† and August 12, 1974, any payments beyond the downpayment and the first thirty standard monthly installments."[93] Many purchasers were

---

*A purchaser was in default if payments were sixty days in arrears, and less than 30% of the contract balance had been paid. Under Arizona law, if 50% or more of the balance had been paid, the purchaser had nine months to clear up his delinquency before the company could declare him in default.

†This date was chosen because GAC's records prior to that date had been routinely destroyed.[92] Since Rio Rico started sales in 1969 all its lot purchasers were covered under this ruling.

excluded by these provisions. Those who defaulted in the first thirty months of their contracts received nothing.[94] Likewise, purchasers who were current in their contract payments as of the date of the consent order, but defaulted thereafter, would receive nothing. The FTC determined that, since GAC had pledged all contracts current as of that date as security for bonds and bank loans, changing the refund provision would change the security's value. For defaulting purchasers who signed contracts after August 12, 1974, the FTC required GAC to give refunds according to a complicated formula. Under this formula, the maximum possible refund would be about 40% of the purchaser's total payments.

Defaulting lot purchasers fared less well under the class-action settlement. Refund provisions and procedures applied solely to members of the "Rio Rico Class," defined as "all persons who during the period of June 1, 1969 through May 31, 1974 entered into Contracts for Deed or Agreements for Deed for purchase of lots in Rio Rico, Arizona."[95] Excluded from the Class were any persons who had signed contracts subsequent to May 31, 1974, purchasers of commercial property, purchasers of lots in the core area of Rio Rico, and purchasers with cancelled contracts who had paid no more than $100.[96]

In order to receive relief, members of the Class had to file a claim no later than November 15, 1974. They then had to prove to a special master court that they had been "defrauded in connection with the purchase of a Contract for Deed or Agreement for Deed to undeveloped land...."[97] GAC's 1974 Form 10-K Report, filed with the Securities and Exchange Commission, states that only 7,000 out of 44,000 eligible Rio Rico lot purchasers filed such claims.[98] Those whose claims were allowed, and whose contracts were in default or cancelled, were given a refund of "the excess principal payments on (their) previous contract over the first $100.00 of principal paid."[99] (Under the terms of installment contracts the earlier payments consist only of interest due on principal so that payment on the principal balance does not begin for some time.) The settlement established a $500,000 limit to fund all claims. If the aggregate exceeded this limit, GAC could reduce each individual claim proportionately.[100] Those whose claims were allowed, and whose contracts were current, were to receive a credit equal to 20% of the principal of the contract price, provided--as was the case--that the total number of allowed claims totaled no more than 25% of the total number of current contracts involving members of the class.[101]

The Agreement of Settlement further stipulated that GAC will be required to refund all principal and interest to Rio Rico lot owners (those who have completed payments and received titles) if central water service is not available to their lots by the date established in the court-ordered development schedule or if it is not provided within 180 days after the owner's receipt of a building permit and request for such service. In addition, GAC agreed that the court could require it to refund all interest and principal received on Rio Rico contracts if it failed to meet the full development schedule. Due to the company's filing for bankruptcy, those individuals now entitled to refunds must make their claims with the bankruptcy court and wait for that court to determine creditor priorities. This will be a lengthy process.

Resales and Exchanges

Rio Rico lots located outside the small developed core area have never had any resale value. As mentioned earlier, Villas Units 5 and 9, Estates Unit 12, and Ranchettes Units 13 and 15 were described as being "extremely difficult to develop at this time due to the distance from the core of the city...."[102] Thus certain members of the Rio Rico Class who chose to continue making contract payments for lots in these areas were encouraged under the Agreement of Settlement to trade their lots for others "in a unit which will be developed at an earlier date...and which will be in a more compact area surrounding the central core of Rio Rico...."*[103]

The court intended, through this provision, to ensure that by 1980, all members of the Class would have lots developed by GAC.[105] Unfortunately, the company's fiscal disintegration may prevent this from happening. Despite GAC's many promises to a naive public, it appears increasingly unlikely that the company can make Rio Rico's desert grasslands bloom into the "planned community" lot buyers hoped would emerge.

---

*If over 10% of the eligible lot purchasers in any of the five specified Units requested exclusion from the provision, GAC was given the option to retract the exchange offer in that Unit, and to instead install water and roads "at the times set forth in the Contracts for Deed."[104]

COST OF LOTS BOUGHT ON THE INSTALLMENT PLAN

LOT PRICE

    basic price ($\frac{1}{4}$ - 20+ acres)* $2,000 - $12,000
    finance charge (6% - 7$\frac{1}{2}$%) $598 - $4,584

                                                Total $2,598 - $16,584

ADDITIONAL ANNUAL ASSESSMENTS DURING TERM OF CONTRACT

    betterment fee (max. $954 - $1,700) $120
    maintenance fee $60†
    property tax (assessed $9.17/100, $33 - $198
               18% of m.v.)

                            Total, per year $213 - $378
                            Total, 10 years $1,884 - $3,780

ONE-TIME COSTS FOR SERVICES

    water   0
        well   -
        central extension   0
        central hook-up   0
    sewage $500 - $2,000
        septic system $900 - $2,000
        central extension $500 - $596
        central hook-up   0

    electricity   0

    telephone   N/A

---

*Includes industrial, commercial, and multi-family lots.
†Begins in 1980.

ENVIRONMENTAL CHECKLIST

Overall environmental protection record: POOR

Does the subdivider:

PLANS	Plan for complete basic services?	NO
	Phase lot sales and extension of services?	NO
	Get 80% build-out in 10 years of each section marketed?	NO
	Prepare an Environmental Impact Report?	NO
LAND	Use a curvilinear or cluster design?	YES
	Retain 25% or more open space?	?
	Reserve from lot sale and development the following areas of critical concern:	
	wetlands?	--
	dunes and beaches?	--
	water sources?	NO
	prime agricultural lands?	--
	habitats of endangered species?	--
	prime historical, archaeological, cultural, aesthetic, or recreational resources?	--
	Reserve from lot sale and development the following areas hazardous for building:	
	geological hazard areas (earthquake, landslide)?	--
	flood-prone areas (100-year floodplains, arroyos)?	NO
	areas of slope exceeding 25%?	NO
	Blade roads only in immediate development areas?	NO
	Clear only for buildings and roads?	YES
	Preserve existing topography?	YES
WATER RESOURCES	Design the drainage system to control erosion?	NO
	Retain 100-foot buffer zone around water bodies?	YES
	Replant disturbed land immediately?	NO
	Limit septic systems to one-acre or larger lots with adequate: percolation rates, slope, and distance from bedrock, water table and surface waters?	NO
	When utilizing central sewage disposal, provide tertiary treatment (or secondary and land disposal)?	NO
	Avoid major stream alteration?	--
	Avoid major wetland dredging and filling?	--
	Use groundwater only up to the safe yield?	NO

NOTE: See chapter on "Guidelines" for more complete explanation of items on Checklist.

RIO RICO 297

CONSUMER CHECKLIST

Overall consumer protection record: POOR*

Does the subdivider:

SALES	Conduct a credit check on lot purchasers?	?
	Limit lot sales to two per purchaser?	?
	Sell only residential, i.e., no industrial, commercial or multi-family lots on installment contracts?	NO
	Require a cash downpayment of 20% on all sales?	NO
	Limit duration of installment contracts to 5 years?	NO
	Charge no interest on installment contracts?	NO
	Encourage attorney review of sales documents?	NO
	Require a pre-purchase site visit?	NO
	Allow a 14-day rescission period in which purchaser can obtain a refund for any reason?	YES
	Offer a partial refund if purchaser defaults?	YES*
	Guarantee a refund, with interest, if promised services are not made available by date specified in contract?	YES*
	Escrow contract payments, or provide equivalent surety bonding, for refund purposes?	NO
TITLE	Offer only platted lots?	YES
	Offer a recordable contract, and record the sale?	NO
	Offer unmortgaged land, or land mortgaged with a release clause, only?	YES
	Upon contract signing, deed title to purchaser, or place title in trust?	NO
BASIC SERVICES	Guarantee, or have available, to each lot:	
	central water, of adequate quantity and quality?	NO
	central sewage disposal, as necessary?	NO
	drainage system, adequate for 100-year storm?	NO
	solid waste disposal, via adequate method?	NO
	roads, paved, to county standards?	NO
	electricity and telephone?	NO
	Guarantee completion through escrowing or surety bonding?	NO
	If services are financed through special service district bonds, employ them only if:	
	initial governing body includes a county official?	--
	elections include all landowners on one-man, one-vote basis?	--
	sum of bonds is less than twice the developer's investment in basic services?	--
	sum of bonds is less than 15% of the assessed value of land in the district?	--
	developer co-signs all bonds?	--

*Installment contract sales were suspended in 1974. Evaluations reflect policy at that time. See details of Federal Trade Commission and class action suit settlements in chapter.

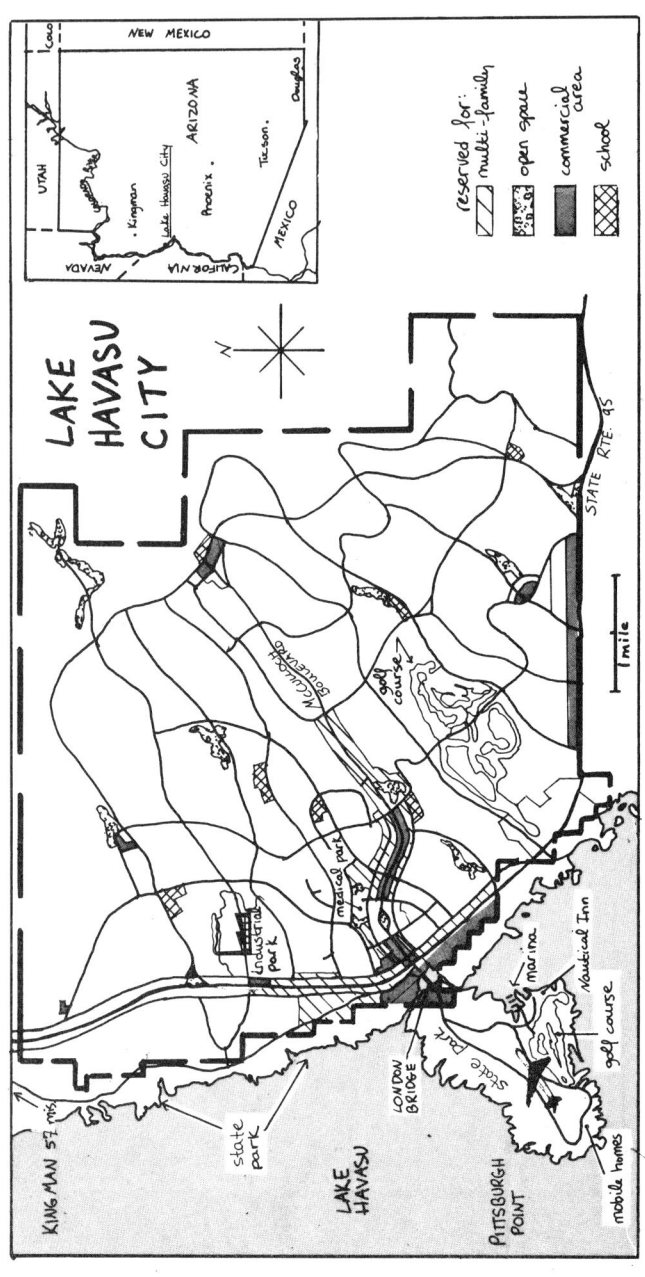

7
Lake Havasu City

Halfway down the western edge of Arizona, on desert land along the lower Colorado River, lies a solitary bustling "city" of almost 10,000 people. This apparent mirage is in fact Lake Havasu City. It was the first of eight land-development projects begun by McCulloch Properties, Inc. (MPI), a subsidiary of the McCulloch Oil Corporation. The 26-square-mile site, home mainly of antelope and bighorn sheep until McCulloch's arrival in 1963, is separated by a thin strip of state parkland from 45-mile-long Lake Havasu, a federal Bureau of Reclamation dam project.

Robert P. McCulloch, Sr., Chairman of the Board of McCulloch Oil Corporation, and C. V. Wood, Jr., President, clearly intended Lake Havasu City to be a real development, as opposed to a speculative lot-sales operation. However, in order to sell homesite lots, and at the same time to avoid the tremendous "front-end" expenditures which real development normally requires, McCulloch employed methods which ranged from the flamboyant and ingenious to the questionably legal.

A new community developer must usually make two major investments: in land and in improvements. McCulloch managed to minimize both. He bought the land for Lake Havasu City at bargain prices from the government, in a complicated deal involving both the state of Arizona and federal agencies. Most of the site's 16,700 acres had previously been part of a national wildlife refuge.

Major improvements--roads, central water, drainage, and a highly limited central sewage system, now all almost entirely completed--were paid for through bonds issued by specially created districts. Since site residents, not the development company, must pay back the districts' bonds, this maneuver effectively transferred a major part of the cost of improvements from the company to buyers of Lake Havasu City lots.

Although its performance on provision of basic services is relatively good, MPI's environmental and sales practices at Lake Havasu City are poor, relative to INFORM's guidelines and to the performance of other companies in this sample. An especially acute problem at the site is flooding. The subdivision's original drainage system has proven inadequate to handle the sudden and torrential storm runoff from the neighboring Mohave Mountains. In the early 1970s, the subdivision suffered $4 million worth of damage from flash flooding. Even if site residents avoid direct damage, their financial liabilities are sure to increase as the Irrigation and Drainage District attempts to rectify the system's inadequacies while at the same time repaying principal and interest on its outstanding debt.

Nevertheless, McCulloch has accomplished something at Lake Havasu City which all the developers in this volume profess to do, but which in reality they have failed to bring about. The company has created a viable new community. Most site services are complete, and the community has been given some economic base, mainly by bringing in other parts of the McCulloch Oil empire, and by promoting tourist attractions.

Prompted by these developments and by MPI's intense promotional efforts (including importation of the London Bridge), residents have moved into this desert outpost faster than into most subdivisions in this study. Although growth has not occurred at the rate anticipated by MPI, Lake Havasu City is still the only site studied by INFORM* which at present annual rates of growth would achieve full build-out in less than a century. Consumers, sold the dream of living in a "planned new community," are for once seeing that dream approach reality.

Regional Context

Lake Havasu City is one of only three population centers in Arizona's sparsely populated Mohave County, an area larger than the states of Massachusetts and Connecticut together.[1] Typically Southwestern in terrain, its rugged mountain chains rise abruptly from hot desert valleys and deeply gorged canyons. Its dramatic scenery is familiar to, and attracts, many out-of-staters, who visit the tourist and recreational facilities located along Lake Mead, the lower Grand Canyon, and the 265 miles of state and federal land bordering the lower Colorado River.

The County's resident population, despite having tripled between 1960 and 1970, is still very small. Arizona's Office of Economic Planning and Development (OEPD) estimated that in 1973, 36,755 people lived permanently in the County. Slightly over

---

*Based on the sixteen sites at which sales began in 1971 or before, described in this volume and Volume II of this study.

14,000 of these live in the vicinity of Kingman, Mohave's county seat and only incorporated municipality, which is located 57 miles northeast of Lake Havasu City.

Despite its severe aridity and remoteness from major employment centers, Mohave County has experienced significant subdivision activity over the last decade. Only 15% of the County's land is in private hands (almost all of the remainder is federally administered). Fully a fifth of that has been subdivided. The County has over 200,000 platted lots which, based on an average of three people to a lot, gives it an existing population capacity of 600,000 persons. Yet the Mohave County Planning and Zoning Department projects a population in 1990 of only 115,000.[2] Other Arizona state offices estimate as few as 41,941 residents by that date.[3]

History

Against this background, Lake Havasu City's establishment as a viable residential community is especially notable. Just thirteen years ago, the site's only residents were Chihuahuan and Sonoran antelope herds (today the former is classified as a "threatened" species and the latter as "endangered"), desert bighorn sheep (another threatened species), desert mule deer, feral horses and burros, and the numerous freshwater fowl such as cormorants, herons, and sandhill cranes which used the lakeshores as a major nesting area.

In 1938, the U.S. Department of the Interior's Bureau of Reclamation built the Parker Dam on the lower Colorado River, thereby creating Lake Havasu, to provide water for southern California. Twenty years later, Robert P. McCulloch, Sr., whose industrial empire was then centered in Los Angeles, was seeking a testing site for his outboard motors. Lake Havasu appeared to offer an ideal location. It even had an old Air Force airstrip built during World War II on a peninsula jutting into its waters.

According to MPI's promotional material on Lake Havasu City, McCulloch promptly purchased 3,530 acres on the peninsula, which was known locally as Pittsburgh Point, "establish[ing] a fully-equipped testing facility, an extensive boating marina, and the City's pioneer homes, a 100-unit mobile home park."[4] As the story continues, five years later, "On August 2, 1963, McCulloch Properties, Inc., purchased at public auction from the State of Arizona the only city-size parcel of land available for private development adjacent to Lake Havasu. Together with the land previously acquired for the test facilities, the site of Lake Havasu City thus now comprises 16,630* acres."[5]

How this city-size parcel of federal land became available for

---

*In company data this figure is generally rounded off to 16,700.

private development is a complicated and interesting story, though not the sort that is publicized in advertising brochures. In 1941, the federal Bureau of Reclamation had deeded the Lake and contiguous lands to what is today the Department of the Interior, Fish and Wildlife Service. They were deeded specifically for the protection of local wildlife. The Havasu Lake National Wildlife Refuge was subsequently established along the Lake and on both sides of the Colorado River. Today, 41,000 acres of this Refuge still lie directly to the north of Lake Havasu City.

However, the future site of Lake Havasu City and the adjoining land directly adjacent to the lakeshore were transferred in 1963 from the Fish and Wildlife Service to the Bureau of Land Management and earmarked for "recreational" use. This was accomplished following negotiations between the U.S. Department of the Interior and agencies from the California, Nevada, and Arizona state governments to establish a land-use plan for the lower Colorado River Valley. According to MPI's promotional material on Lake Havasu City, the final plan reserves the 265-mile stretch of the Colorado from Hoover Dam in Nevada to the Mexican border for long-range public and recreational development. The objective is to ensure that the area's natural beauty remains available for the enjoyment of the West's fast-growing population. Unfortunately, the Lake Havasu region of the River may prove to have little wildlife in it. Today, only six miles of Lake Havasu's shoreline are still a wildlife refuge, and a Fish and Wildlife Service official recently noted that "private development lands are right up against that area."[6]

The transfer of land from the Wildlife Refuge to the Bureau of Land Management was only the first step towards McCulloch's acquiring the site. The next required Arizona's cooperation. Arizona is one of four states in the union* which is still authorized (under terms of the State Enabling Act granting it statehood in 1912 and Article 10 of the Arizona Constitution) to select lands from federal land holdings to be placed in trust for the "beneficial use" of the state's population. About 9.6 million acres--over 13% of Arizona's state-land area--are currently so held by the State Land Department.[7] Approximately 180,000 acres still remain for the state to select. Arizona's Land Commissioner is responsible to the "beneficiaries" of this trust--i.e., the common schools, universities, and certain original state institutions--for the management, development, and disposition of these lands. Under certain circumstances he may sell, lease, or exchange lands "for the greater benefit of the beneficiaries."[8]

Shortly before McCulloch's purchase of the Lake Havasu City land, the state of Arizona requested and received that acreage from

---

*New Mexico, Utah, and Colorado are the other three.

the Department of the Interior Bureau of Land Management for State Trust lands. This was done "clearly because McCulloch wanted it,"* according to a former *Arizona Republic* reporter who had researched Lake Havasu City's origins. There remained significant obstacles to McCulloch's obtaining it, however. Title 37 of the Arizona State Code placed specific limits on the amount of Trust lands classified as "agricultural" or "grazing" that the state could market in one sale. In the former case the limit was 160 acres, and in the latter, 640 acres. The state Land Commisioner, however, reclassified the 13,100 acres subsequently purchased by McCulloch from "grazing" to "commercial." Simultaneously, the state Attorney General issued an opinion exempting Trust lands classified as "commercial" from acreage limitations.† The full 13,100 acres was then, as required, put up at "public" auction on August 3, 1963, in order to create a market wherein a "fair price" could be established. But according to an MPI official interviewed in 1974, "The guy heading the other group of bidders had a heart attack the night before the auction, and McCulloch paid about $72 an acre for it."[11] (The California Real Estate Commission's records indicate that McCulloch paid $973,416, or approximately $75 an acre.)

As the former *Arizona Republic* reporter noted, by allowing the land to be auctioned in such a large block, the state excluded other bidders without the resources of a large corporation from competing. And, while $75 an acre might appear fair value for raw desert land (even when next to a large lake), subdivision activity in Mohave County was such, he said, that similar land was bringing as much as $500 an acre. Consequently, he added, "In my opinion the state (and thus its public) really didn't get a fair value in the sale; I always felt it was a bad deal for the state, but of course there were others who felt differently."[12]

---

*A recent *New York Times* report on land-sales activities in Arizona quotes a former administrative assistant to the then Secretary of the Interior, Stewart L. Udall, as stating: "I think it was pretty well known in the department beforehand that in this big disposal of land, the only people in a position to bid on it would be the McCulloch Company."[9]

†The present state Land Commissioner, Andrew P. Bettwy, has stated that such exceptions will not be made in the future and that Trust land which qualifies for commercial classification will have the same 160-acre limitation for sale as agricultural lands. "To my knowledge it is the first and only time that a parcel in excess of this limit was sold by the state," he noted recently to a *New York Times* reporter.[10]

McCulloch's own promotional material on Lake Havasu City indicates that it was encouraged and assisted by both the federal government and the state of Arizona in pursuing this development enterprise. The Lower Colorado Land Use Plan, which represents a joint venture between the Department of the Interior and the states of Arizona, California, and Nevada,* was signed by the Secretary of the Interior on June 3, 1963, three months before McCulloch purchased the major portion of Lake Havasu City's acreage from Arizona at "public auction." Yet in a booklet entitled *Today's Story of Lake Havasu City* (copyright 1972), MPI reproduces a land-status map (Figure 11) from the "Lower Colorado Land Use Plan." The map, dated June 3, 1963, diagrams then "existing" and "proposed" land uses along the upper sections of the Lower Colorado River Valley. It clearly shows "Lake Havasu City" in the "existing" category, in spite of the fact that McCulloch had not yet acquired the 13,100 acres.[13]

MPI copy appended to this map emphasizes that additional land was also used to benefit McCulloch's development, stating that "surrounding recreational land is being *preserved* by the State of Arizona and the Federal Government...and this enhances property values at Lake Havasu City."[14] (Emphasis added.) The booklet continues:

> As part of [this Lower Colorado River] Land Use Plan, [another] 13,000 acres of Lake Havasu frontage immediately adjacent to Lake Havasu has been leased by the Department of the Interior to the State of Arizona for development as a State Park and recreation area. It is literally at the "front door" of the city.[15]

This park provides 23 miles of public shoreline along the Lake, and a buffer zone of 1,000 feet to 1 mile between the Lake and the City's private property.[16]

On some of the acreage, however, the state's efforts have gone well beyond "preservation." The Arizona Parks Department, under whose jurisdiction the state placed the federally leased land, has sublet 1,080 acres (including portions but not all of Pittsburgh Point, the area of McCulloch's original 1958 purchase) to McCulloch's development company for fifty years. According to this arrangement, MPI agreed to spend at least $800,000 on developing public-use facilities.[17] MPI and others have, in fact, spent much more than that. MPI invested $700,000 in a 68-unit Nautical Inn, which was used principally by McCulloch's "fly-ins," prospective buyers flown in weekly by MPI to tour the development site, until

---

*According to the Yuma, Arizona office of the Bureau of Land Management, Nevada is no longer participating in the plan.

1974, when MPI sold the Inn. (A company sales official recently indicated to INFORM that it was sold because, "We were informed that we couldn't hold our sales operations on State land any more."[18]) MPI has sublet portions of the 1,080 acres to several other private contractors who constructed the Lake Havasu Marina, and the Crazy Horse Campground. Several public beaches have also been created on the peninsula.

Recently there has been one more instance of successful negotiations between federal and local agencies to the benefit of Lake Havasu City. According to the *Lake Havasu City Herald*, the combined efforts of the Mohave County Supervisor and the staff of U.S. Representative Sam Steiger resulted in another land reclassification. The Department of the Interior Bureau of Land Management categorized approximately 1,300 acres just south of the City's boundaries as a "Special Activities Recreation Area." Under this new classification, the Bureau of Land Management leased the land to Mohave County. The County in turn agreed to "work out a management arrangement with the Havasu Recreation Association,"[19] a planning and administrative committee of the Lake Havasu Irrigation and Drainage District. This District, discussed below, functions for all intents and purposes as Lake Havasu City's governing agency.

The McCulloch team is uniquely skilled both in its land dealings and in promoting its own projects. In 1968, Bob McCulloch, Sr., devised what is surely the most elaborate promotional scheme in the history of an industry already noted for promotional extravaganzas. Attending another "public auction," he purchased from the City of London its famous London Bridge for $2.4 million. At a cost of over $5 million, he had it transported, block by block, the 10,000 miles to Lake Havasu City. There the Bridge was reconstructed (several feet shorter in order to have stones from the Bridge to sell to tourists) over desert sand. The sand was later dredged so that water from Lake Havasu could flow under the Bridge. An elaborate ceremony marked the opening of the Bridge and an adjoining International Resort Center replete with Tudor-styled shops and an English Pub. This grand gesture generated nationwide publicity for the subdivision, including an NBC Network "Special" run May 7, 1972--repeated on prime time August 8, 1972--starring such luminaries as Jennifer O'Neil and Rudolf Nureyev.[20]

The Bridge's relocation and construction is described in promotional literature as, "The fulfillment of the original Master Plan to make Lake Havasu City a self-sustaining community."[21] Such flamboyance marks the spirit behind Lake Havasu City's promotion and development to date. The subdivision's master-planner, C. V. Woods, was a major planner of Disneyland. He was quoted in an article on Lake Havasu City as distinguishing between his two jobs as follows: "In an amusement park you have to keep people happy for

The London Bridge, a prime tourist attraction at Lake Havasu City, imported block by block from England by McCulloch at a cost of $2.4 million.

five hours; now the problem is to keep them happy for a lifetime."[22]

Despite the intemperate climate (Astroturf has been used in place of grass by the few residents who insist on reminders of wetter climes), despite the City's total dependence on individual automobiles (no other mode of transportation exists within the City's limits), even despite a lack of employment opportunities beyond what the nascent business community and industrial base can provide, MPI has sold almost all of Lake Havasu City's lots. Purchasers are slowly taking up residency. With a slight tinge of bravado, a company official recently stated, "No, the recession didn't hurt us; folks came out here to escape urbanitis."[23]

THE OFFERING: LAND AND IMPROVEMENTS

LAND

Physical Characteristics

Except for the proximity of Lake Havasu and the Colorado River, which offer splendid recreational resources, MPI chose to place its first community development in an unlikely topographical location. Situated along the alluvial fans stretching out from the Mohave Mountains, it appears at first view to hold little that is hospitable to life. Its desert climate permits only small shrub growth to develop, and that very sparsely. Its brown, sandy soil and deep gullies are littered with rocks and boulders that have washed down in the course of storms. Numerous drainageways cut east-west across the site from its upper elevation of 1,250 feet down to Lake Havasu's shores at 450 feet.

Temperatures are hot. According to the California Subdivision Report on Lake Havasu City, temperatures of 121°F in the summer and 20°F in the winter are on record,[24] although the 1975 federal Property Report* lists a summer high of 108°F and a winter low of 40°F. The area receives approximately five inches of rain annually (a tenth of that generally received in New York City), often in torrential cloudbursts that allow little of the rain to be

---

*The U.S. Department of Housing and Urban Development, Office of Interstate Land Sales Registration (OILSR), requires the development company to issue a Property Report giving important consumer information on lots offered for sale. Similar reports are required by many state land sales registration agencies including the California Department of Real Estate.

absorbed by the soil. Where vegetation is minimal and the desert's topsoil is disturbed by development activity and human use, these storms can create serious erosion problems. The federal Property Report also warns that "winds are common in arid regions resulting in occasional dust storms."

Status of Development

Fully 15,383 of Lake Havasu City's 16,700 acres of land have been recorded and platted with Mohave County.* This acreage is subdivided into 33,514 lots. The vast majority--28,356--are quarter-acre single-family residential homesites. The site is largely sold out. Only about 640 to 740 of the platted lots remain to be sold. Another 160 or so have not yet been platted for sale.[26] The majority of the quarter-acre single-family lots were sold for $6,000 to $9,000. A few--724 surrounding a private golf course-- were sold for $13,000 to $30,000.

In addition to single-family lots, the site includes 3,600 multi-family, 40 motel, 500 mobile-home, and approximately 1,600 commercial and industrial lots. Approximately 400 acres on the northern side of Lake Havasu City adjacent to State Route 95 have been set aside as a Science and Industry Park. Its principal tenant is the McCulloch Industrial Complex for manufacturing chain saws and engine parts which employs 1,400 persons. About ten boat manufacturers and several other businesses have also located there.[27]

Lake Havasu City's proposed population is approximately 60,000 persons, according to the community prospectus on Lake Havasu City issued in 1973 by the Arizona Office of Economic Planning and Development. However, based on an average of three persons per lot, existing single-family residential lots alone could accommodate a population of 85,000.

While almost all lots are sold at Lake Havasu City, and about half--approximately 15,000--are fully paid for and deeded to the purchasers, people have not moved in at officially expected rates. The community prospectus includes a chart of population projections for Lake Havasu City prepared prior to 1973 based on information received from McCulloch Oil concerning plans to move manufacturing operations to Lake Havasu City. The chart forecasts a 1975 population of 17,300 and a 1976 population of 20,300.[28] Despite available recreational resources and incipient industrial growth, as of November, 1975, about 10,000 people (including a considerable number

---

*According to the engineering firm keeping statistical data reports on development progress at Lake Havasu City, the 1,317 unrecorded acres are being held by MPI for sale in large acreage parcels to outside subdividers. Two 20-acre parcels have already been sold and developed by companies other than MPI into townhouse units.[25]

of children) were living there.

The 1975 federal Property Report for the site notes that 2,267 dwellings are completed or under construction, in addition to 29 townhouses, 172 condominiums, and 1,293 apartment units. There are also 298 commercial structures and several industrial structures. Approximately 3,467 of these units are currently in use for residential, commercial, or industrial purposes.*

If the City continues to grow at the annual rate it experienced during its first decade, the site will not be fully occupied for about another hundred years. This is, however, the shortest time frame to full occupancy of any subdivision in the INFORM sample. Several subdivisions, at their present growth rates, would not achieve their full projected populations for several thousand years.

BASIC SERVICES

Many of the "land developers" in this study appear on close examination to have had limited intentions of engaging in real development. MPI, on the other hand, clearly meant from the start for Lake Havasu City to be more than simply a lot-sales program based on colorful planning maps. But providing real development in a community the size of Lake Havasu City creates tremendous "front-end" costs. Chief among these is the cost of installing basic services. An astute and skillful businessman, McCulloch approached this problem by utilizing--and in practice modifying--existing legal instruments to provide for the creation of "special districts," thereby significantly diminishing the financial burden confronting his development company.

This particular use of special districts appears to be McCulloch's trademark as a land developer. In Colorado, where an existing Metropolitan District Act was inadequate for his needs, McCulloch engineered the passage of specific amendments which enabled him to finance Pueblo West's development in a similar, though less successful manner. (See chapter on Pueblo West.)

An old, vaguely worded Arizona statute provided the vehicle for McCulloch to defer a major portion of Lake Havasu City's development costs onto its future residents. This statute was originally enacted to help farmers finance irrigation systems by providing for the legal establishment of special "irrigation and drainage districts," authorized to issue tax-exempt bonds.

Using an Irrigation and Drainage District to help finance the development costs of a new community was an original idea on McCulloch's part. A noted state hydrologist familiar with Arizona land

---

*Based on the number of water meters installed as of December 3, 1975.[29]

developments remarked, "As far as I know this is the only time a developer has gone this route.* McCulloch had a smart lawyer who figured it out for him."[30]† The former *Arizona Republic* reporter quoted earlier adds, "McCulloch took advantage of laws--he's a good businessman, a real dreamer and ruthless--but he never actually violated them, as far as I could find out."[31]

One month after the acquisition of Lake Havasu City's land from the state, McCulloch established the Lake Havasu Irrigation and Drainage District complete with a company-appointed three-man board of directors. One of the three was Lake Havasu City's planner, C. V. Woods, now President of McCulloch Oil Corporation, who remained on the board until December, 1975. The manager of the District, who was appointed by this original board, previously held the position of legal advisor to the Arizona State Land commissioner, and was formerly assistant to the State Attorney General whose decision on selling state commercial land made Lake Havasu City possible.[33] McCulloch placed under the District's jurisdiction Lake Havasu City's 16,700 acres and about 1,800 of the 13,000 acres of federal land bordering the Lake and leased by the federal government to Arizona. ∇ (The state established the Lake Havasu State Park on this land in 1965, shortly after construction began at Lake Havasu City.)

The powers legally vested in the Lake Havasu Irrigation and Drainage District are extremely broad. They include the right to:

a. Purchase or acquire water rights.

---

*It is probably the last time a developer can "go this route" as well. When McCulloch subsequently tried to establish an Irrigation and Drainage District to finance municipal improvements for another of his land developments in Arizona--Fountain Hills near Phoenix-- the League of Cities and Towns challenged such a broad use of this act in court and was upheld. Arizona has since passed a General Improvement District Act which, as of 1973, allows for use of "new community" special service districts. However, their powers and actions are closely regulated.

†McCulloch worked closely with the California bond attorneys Wilson, Jones, Morton and Lynch. According to the Nader report on land use in California, they initiated the practice of using special districts to finance the municipal improvements in large-scale land developments with publicly subsidized bonds in the 1950s.[32]

∇Discrepancies in the exact number of acres within the Irrigation and Drainage District exist. The manager of the District remarked that he usually uses an 18,000-acre figure but others use 18,500.[34]

b. Acquire or lease real estate when necessary.

c. Construct, acquire or purchase canals, ditches, reservoirs, water, water rights, and rights of way necessary for the use of the District.

d. Provide for construction, operation and control of plants for distribution and sale of electrical energy.

e. Make appropriations of water for irrigation and power purposes.

f. Establish tolls or charges for service of irrigation, domestic water, electricity and other commodities.

g. Provide the District with water, electricity and other public conveniences and necessities [which include the construction and surfacing of the basic access roads throughout the District].[35]

In order to execute the above and thereby carry out the development program, voters of the District (who must, by law, have resided in Mohave County for ninety days and own land in the District) approved the issuance of $7.14 million in general obligation bonds. This was done in January, 1964. Since actual construction work did not begin at Lake Havasu City until August, 1964,[36] the residents who authorized the District's original debt were clearly McCulloch associates, and not the future lot buyers who have to assume liability for this debt. As the years passed and the costs of the District's development obligations increased, further bond authorizations were voted. By November, 1975, the District's debt authorization had increased to $17.83 million--32% of its 1975 assessed value.* Approximately $14.1 million of this amount has actually been issued in general obligation bonds which fall due up until the end of the 1990s.

The Lake Havasu Irrigation and Drainage District is responsible for construction and maintenance, both within Lake Havasu City proper and on a portion of the state-leased land within its boundaries, of three kinds of basic services: (1) a central water system to serve the entire community; (2) a major road system throughout the District area; and (3) a community drainage system. The District is also responsible for maintaining, but not for building, "in-tract improvements." A "tract" may hold from under ten to up

---

*Arizona law limits the debt liability of an Irrigation and Drainage District to 60% of its assessed value after the improvements are complete. New Mexico and Florida limit district debts to 5% and 15% respectively of assessed value.

to several hundred individual lots. MPI is responsible for initially installing unpaved roads and water lines within (but not between) these units.*

This distinction between MPI's "in-tract improvements" and the District's improvement responsibilities was an important one for prospective lot purchasers. It is completely obscured in Lake Havasu City's federal Property Report which refers to MPI as "the Developer," who "subject to acts of God, strikes, national material shortages and other similar type causes beyond its control" has "a planned construction program generally spanning a period of four years" for the installation of "in-tract" improvements.[37] The term "in-tract" is never defined.

In fact, the Irrigation and Drainage District, a separate legal entity from MPI, carries the major development responsibility for the community. Its costs are funded by District fees placed on each lot. These now average $40 a year for a half-acre lot, but may increase. If the District had not been able to finance and service the subdivision with an adequate water supply or access-road system, such "in-tract improvements" as were provided by MPI would be of dubious use. The Lake Havasu Irrigation and Drainage District is referred to in the Property Report as "the legal entity authorized to install the major roadways" as well as "the primary water system" but it offers no schedule of development or commitment of completion. Nor does it indicate that the District's debt liabilities, which the lot purchaser assumes, are financing the construction of basic improvements which the lot owner may presume he pays for in the purchase price of his land.

Actually, as the following information indicates, the Irrigation and Drainage District has so far provided Lake Havasu City with a fairly good system of basic services. The exceptions are the lack of a central sewage system for most of the site, and a less than satisfactory drainage system, which the District is now attempting to upgrade. But the prospective purchaser, who was probably unfamiliar with both the term "in-tract" and the financing mechanisms of special districts, receives no help from the Property Report in understanding either of these matters.

In addition to its principal role in the development of McCulloch's community, the Lake Havasu Irrigation and Drainage District has functioned since its inception as the city's governing agency. There is currently considerable interest on the part of community residents in making Lake Havasu City an incorporated municipality, and thus eligible--it is hoped--for state and federal assistance in

---

*Those lot owners on the central sewage system provided by the Lake Havasu Sanitary District must undertake the cost of the required sewage laterals themselves. MPI does not provide these.

various ways. However, Arizona law presently limits the ratio of bonded debt to assets in an incorporated municipality to less than the current ratio within the districts at Lake Havasu City. Not too surprisingly, the Irrigation and Drainage District Director told INFORM in July, 1975, that "steps are being taken to encourage amendment of the existing state law prohibiting our incorporation."[38] Upon further discussion in February, 1976, he noted, "there is now a bill before the state legislature to increase the debt-asset ratio allowed municipalities."[39]

Water

A central water system has been built by the Irrigation and Drainage District. It presently provides water for all Lake Havasu City residents and tourists as well as for the City's several industries and many commercial facilities. As of early 1976, the District had installed 3,467 individual water meters and laid 375 miles of water line.[40] While there is no guaranteed date of completion for Lake Havasu City's water system, the District expected the entire system to be completed by July, 1976. The main water lines are presently extended beyond current lot use.[41]

The town's water supply was obtained through another special arrangement with a government agency. The Irrigation and Drainage District negotiated a contract with the Bureau of Reclamation--which has jurisdiction over the Colorado River--for withdrawal from the Colorado of up to 14,500 acre-feet of water per year.[42] This is equivalent to about 13 million gallons of water a day. The contract between the Bureau of Reclamation and the District was executed in November, 1968, to run for a ten-year period. At the end of this time the contract will be reviewed and renegotiated for a larger or smaller amount of water based on the City's use patterns over the decade. Under contract terms water diverted from the river by underground pumping and wells is considered river water.

To date, the District draws water for its population of 10,000 from nine wells with a daily capacity of approximately 8.4 million gallons. Water consumption has varied, according to seasons, between 3.5 million gallons per day and capacity output (a range of 350 to 840 gallons per person per day).[43] Thus, while there appears to be no present water shortage at Lake Havasu City, there might be one when the town's population grows to between 15,000 and 37,000, if average usage does not decrease. At that point, at current use rates, the District's needs would exceed its allocation.

Of course, given sufficient funds from the District to continue expanding the supply system and given continued government cooperation, sufficient water should be obtained. The District's contract with the Bureau of Reclamation is up for renegotiation in 1978.*

The quality of the present system's water is fair; it has minor undesirable traits. The Arizona State Health Department has found it slightly above the recommended limits in soluble solids and sulphates.[44] A California Subdivision Report on Lake Havasu City states, "Although the water supply has been approved by the Arizona State Department of Health, the fluoride ion content of the water exceeds the maximum allowable under the standards set by the California State Department of Health."[45] (Arizona's recommended limit is listed in the above-mentioned Report as "variable.")

In 1975, the District began to draw water directly from the Colorado River. Since its saline content would have required treatment to make it suitable for domestic use, it is presently being used primarily for irrigation purposes.

District water charges borne by the lot purchaser include a $110 fee for a service connection to the District's main line and for installation of a water meter.

Sewage Disposal

Lake Havasu City's central sewage system will serve about 1,136 (4%) of the site's 28,356 single-family quarter- to half-acre residential lots, approximately 3,641 multi-family, commercial, and industrial lots, and also an unspecified portion of another 2,850 lots. Thus, of the subdivision's 33,514 lots, about 80% will be left dependent on individual septic tanks. Such a high concentration of septics, particularly in the area of a large water body, is generally considered undesirable. It poses a risk of contamination to groundwater and surface-water bodies. However, state authorities claim the sand and gravel characteristic of Arizona soil provides such good filtering action that "septics are a very minute source of pollution."[46]

The federal Property Report confirms that septic-tank use has been approved by the Arizona State Health Department. However, it does not mention that the County requires a permit before a septic system can be installed. Nor does it note that Mohave County has a somewhat arbitrary approval method that could pose serious problems

---

*The allotted amount of water could supply the domestic water needs (but not industrial or commercial) of approximately 86,000 persons based on a standard consumption rate of 150 gallons per person per day. However, current consumption is much higher, on a per capita basis, no doubt due to heavy water use by industry, and, seasonally by tourists.

for certain lot owners if the County chooses in the future to take a stricter view of environmental matters. Mohave's chief sanitarian stated that the County approves the use of septic systems in the subdivision on a "general interim" basis. Then when the individual lot owner comes in to apply for his permit, his lot is checked to see if it lies "too near" the Lake, or has too high a water-table level.[47] While the state allows four feet between the bottom of the septic system and the water table, Mohave County feels four feet is inadequate protection against pollution and requires twelve to thirteen feet. What might be considered "too near" the Lake has not been uniformly determined. If a lot were judged unsuitable for septic use, the unfortunate applicant could find himself owner of an essentially unlivable "residential lot." There is, however, no indication this has occurred to date.

Of the 1,136 single-family residential lots planned for Lake Havasu City's central sewer system, 724 are in an area known as Improvement District 1 (not to be confused with the Irrigation and Drainage District). Improvement District 1 provided the financing for Lake Havasu City's initial showcase-development area, built around the City's golf course within a nine-month period in 1964. The homes on these lots were financed with Federal Home Administration assistance, a prerequisite of which is a central sewage system.

Construction of the central system began toward the end of 1964. At that time, MPI established yet another district, the Lake Havasu Sanitary District. This enabled the company to obtain federal funds amounting to 75% of total cost to finance construction of the system's treatment plants. The Sanitary District comprises only 4,087 acres (6.4 square miles) and is authorized to issue $3.24 million of general obligation bonds. To date it has issued $2.50 million of its authorization. The treatment system consists of a large plant which can treat 1.25 million gallons of sewage per day, and two satellite plants which can handle an additional 25,000 and 50,000 gallons per day respectively. As of July, 1976, the Sanitary District had 987 sewer connections.

The federal Property Report identifies for the buyer those lots scheduled to use septics and those scheduled to use the central sewer system. It indicates that installation of an individual septic system may cost lot purchasers from $500 to $700.

Initial hookup to the central system may cost $175. In addition, the Sanitary District has imposed an ad valorem tax of $1.29 per $100 of assessed value on lots within its jurisdiction. (On a lot assessed at $4,000 this would amount to $52 annually.) The Sanitary District may in the future, if it chooses, impose a stand-by fee on those lots where the line is available for connection but not yet in use. The Property Report adds that lot owners in the Sanitary District are "responsible for all necessary lateral lines," but gives no cost estimates. A Sanitary District official stated that the District is obligated to run its main lines to within five feet of a property line. The lateral line runs from this main to the home. The official stated that he did not know the cost per foot of this extension. The Sanitary District has never scheduled a completion date for the whole system, but the sewer mains are extended beyond presently needed capacity.

Solid Waste

Refuse collection is adequately handled by a private firm at a cost of $36 a year per residence. Garbage is disposed of at an 80-acre sanitary-landfill site leased from the Bureau of Land Management and maintained by the Lake Havasu Sanitary District.

Roads

As of March, 1975, the Irrigation and Drainage District had paved 312.9 miles of basic access road and graded another 80.5 miles. These roads are constructed to District specifications and are maintained by the District, which can support such costs with much less difficulty than could Mohave County.

Drainage and Flood Control

MPI's relatively good record in providing basic services to Lake Havasu City residents is somewhat marred by recurrent problems with its drainage system. Given the location of the City's 26-mile area on the slope between the Mohave Mountains and the Lake into which their runoff drains--sometimes quite fiercely--Lake Havasu city faced flood dangers from its inception. Subsequent development activity which filled in some of the 90 miles of washes, or arroyos, providing natural drainage channels for storm runoff added to the preexisting hazard.[48] MPI did recognize the general problem. The company, in fact, took the initiative in planning a drainage system which could handle a storm defined as being of 100-year intensity. It did so despite the fact that no state or county laws regulated such matters at that time. (Even today no regulations prohibit building in or near washes, although Arizona law does require subdivisions to design drainage systems to handle storms of 50-year intensity.[49])

Unfortunately, problems arose in defining the 100-year storm level. A private engineering firm hired by MPI determined that the 100-year storm level at Lake Havasu City was 1.6 inches of rain within an hour. This figure was verified by other private consulting firms. When development began in 1963, Lake Havasu City's drainage system was designed according to this standard. The figure was not, however, unanimously accepted as adequate, even at that time. An employee of the U.S. Department of Agriculture Soil Conservation Service who was familiar with Lake Havasu City's original system stated in an interview that the maximum runoff standards used in engineering the system were considered by many to be too low. According to this account, MPI dismissed outside objections to its drainage plans. It ignored recommendations that the system include retention storage in the hills above the City and fewer right-angle turns in the washes relied on for flood channeling. By 1965, when Mohave County required county approval of subdivision plans, MPI had already constructed the backbone of its system relying on compacted-dirt reinforcement of selected washes. County engineers subsequently required MPI to build wider washes in developing tracts. But when these were constructed, many fed into the original, narrower washes which then overloaded during storms.[50]

Serious flooding occurred during storms in 1970, 1971, and 1972. Then, two exceptionally intense storms in the summer of 1974 caused such severe damage that the original 100-year storm criterion used in the drainage system's design had to be reconsidered. During these storms, which occurred within a few days of each other in July, 1974, 2.5 to 4.5 inches of rain fell on Lake Havasu City within one to one-and-a-half hours. Three deaths occurred, sixteen cars were swept away, water lines burst, and paving was destroyed. All told, an estimated $1 million worth of damage was done to Lake Havasu City's Irrigation and Drainage District. Another $3 million of damage was done to other property throughout the City area.

In 1975, in response to this devastation, the Lake Havasu Irrigation and Drainage District undertook four separate drainage-system improvement-and-repair projects. The largest of these cost $775,000.[51] According to the District's manager, much of the work was part of ongoing efforts to upgrade the system to meet a new 100-year storm criterion of 2.5 inches of rain within an hour. The District has begun to grade and widen portions of its ninety miles of natural-wash channeling. It has also reinforced many of the sharp turns along the washes to keep their banks from flooding out again.

In addition to District work, the U.S. Army Corps of Engineers is presently beginning to rehabilitate those portions of the drainage system which qualified under the federal Flood Control Emergency Act as a disaster area. This work will entail only "replacement in kind," i.e., repair of the system rather than expansion and improvement, though an officer with the Corps of Engineers stated that the Corps was going to recommend to the District that it increase its nominal use of rip-rapping, i.e., stone linings for drainageways.[52] Under the requirements of the law, the Corps will make annual inspections in the future to assure that repaired areas

Eroded drainage wash in 1974.

have been properly maintained. Maintenance of the whole drainage system is one of the District's many obligations at Lake Havasu City, and, as seen, one that even occasional inclement weather conditions can make very costly.

With regard to the Irrigation and Drainage District's current efforts, a Soil Conservation Service employee recently expressed a qualified skepticism about their overall effectiveness. He noted that significant structural improvements had been made, particularly around bridges and roads. But he questioned the stability of the material--basically compacted dirt--used throughout the system.[53]

The discussion of flood problems in the most recent federal Property Report on Lake Havasu City (November 28, 1975) is inadequate, and occasionally even misleading. The Report notes that while the U.S. Army Corps of Engineers has stated that portions of the subdivision are located within a 100-year-floodplain, "the subdivision has been planned and engineered to eliminate flood hazard, including a 100-year flood, by the construction of various graded flood-control channels."[54] Elsewhere it adds that "The Developer has a program to control periodic flooding...and the plan has been approved by appropriate officials responsible for the regulation of land development."[55] This latter addendum seems quite misleading, since the County officials it presumably refers to have not yet concerned themselves with either defining 100-year storm levels or with drainage systems designed to handle such. Statements elsewhere in the Property Report suffer from acute understatement. While they assert that "erosion and flooding could result in property damage and could create a health and safety hazard," this notice is preceded by the assertion that "the arid nature of the subdivision" precludes any need for "the use of temporary [retention] basins" (such as those originally recommended by some critics of MPI's early drainage plans).[56]

In addition, a lengthy paragraph informs the purchaser that the federal Flood Insurance Administration of the U.S. Department of Housing and Urban Development has determined that the subdivision is eligible for flood insurance under the National Flood Insurance Act of 1968, and that such insurance is mandatory for any persons requesting mortgage loans from federally regulated lending institutions.

Thus while the Irrigation and Drainage District seems to be making a conscientious effort at present to improve the drainage system, the community is not yet adequately protected and lot buyers are not made adequately aware of this fact.

Utilities

According to the 1975 Property Report, electricity will be extended to a lot upon request at no cost to the buyer. The Citizens

Utility Company will extend its lines up to 1,000 feet at no charge. MPI has agreed to pay any costs of further extensions. However, the federal Property Report notes that the developer has not set aside any special funds for this purpose.

The Citizens Utilities Rural Company plans to extend telephone facilities to all lots at Lake Havasu City by December, 1976. There is no cost to the lot purchaser for this extension either. All utility lines, unfortunately, are above ground except in the original core area around the golf course.

COMMUNITY AND RECREATIONAL FACILITIES

In keeping with McCulloch's original plan when he first envisioned this desert city, numerous elaborate recreational and resort facilities are now centered around Lake Havasu itself. They have made the community a principal focus for outdoor tourist activities in the area. By 1973, the City had 11 motels with 514 accommodations.[57] As noted above, it also has numerous campgrounds and the London Bridge tourist center.

The existing overbalance in the leisure-industry sector of Lake Havasu City's economy, while of benefit to the 500 or so locally established small businesses, has concerned those considering the community's future viability. The need for more light industry to buttress and stabilize its year-round economy is widely acknowledged. MPI has continued its efforts to draw additional manufacturing plants to the City's Science and Industry Park. At present, McCulloch Oil's chain-saw and engine-parts factory provides the principal source of local industrial employment. It employs approximately 1,400 persons. A 1974 magazine article mentioned, however, that "the city's future still depends upon the goodwill and financial strength of the McCulloch empire...." It added the reminder that "if one hundred and fifty miles of isolation gives a lot of physical security [from the myriad ills besetting America's older urban centers] it also means an undercurrent of economic instability." If something should go awry with the community's economic base, "the surrounding desert would not be able to pick up much of the employment slack."[58]

Such possible long-range problems notwithstanding, the City does boast a large retinue of municipal services. For its approximately 2,500 children, there are two elementary schools, one junior high school, and a high school. There is also a community college, and a library with 13,000 volumes. Medical care is available from numerous doctors and dentists residing in the community, and there is a 34-bed hospital. At least five state and county government service agencies are located in the City.

An on-site branch of the County Sheriff's Office provides police protection for residents. Fire protection is provided by a volunteer fire department, which has two local stations and is funded by a special Fire District.

The one service conspicuously lacking at Lake Havasu City is any kind of public transportation, even for the school children.

Lake Havasu City's development was based on a presumption of abundant resources and general economic affluence. How development will progress in a less expansionary era--one of tight money, less accessible mortgages, inflated construction costs, and generally reduced economic means--is a major question. The project manager at Lake Havasu City recently described one of his principal tasks as keeping the community's employment growth equal with the population growth.[59]

ENVIRONMENTAL PROTECTION

Overall, environmental planning at Lake Havasu City has been relatively poor. The subdivision eliminated a valuable wildlife habitat. Development was not phased, so that many areas have been disturbed far ahead of an arriving population necessitating it. Development was planned for areas subject to flash floods, areas that should perhaps have been left as open space. Plans for site drainage, for protection of surface-water and groundwater supplies from pollution, and for recreational and open space all fall short of INFORM's guidelines.

PLANNING

While the basic street and lot design of the community is an adequate curvilinear pattern, other aspects of site layout were not well considered. Only about 13% of the site's 16,700 acres is set aside for recreational or open-space use.* Much of this consists of drainage washes. According to the company, the only developed recreational areas are 255 acres of golf courses and 10 acres of tennis courts, less than 2% of the site.

---

*INFORM calculation, based on company-supplied figures on total allocation to roads, washes and open space, and length and width of road areas.

Once again, McCulloch has counted on public resources to meet its subdivision's needs. The 13,000-acre state park, bordering portions of the community, guarantees both open space and recreational facilities to City residents. The park area also functions as a buffer zone from 1,000 feet to a mile wide between the Lake and private development on Lake Havasu City's land.

This parkland does not entirely substitute for the absence of adequate neighborhood park, recreation, and open-space areas. Most planners recommend setting aside about 25% of a subdivision for open-space and recreational purposes (see Guidelines).

To the dismay of the Irrigation and Drainage District, which must install basic services throughout the community, development has not proceeded in scheduled phases. Titled lot owners may request servicing for residential construction anywhere within the community.

No Environmental Impact Report was prepared for use in planning the site.

LAND

The development of Lake Havasu City has already produced two major adverse environmental effects. Both are directly attributable to McCulloch's choice of this site--which includes areas hazardous for building and areas of critical environmental concern.

Located in a sparsely vegetated desert valley, the town, as noted above, sits atop alluvial fans--basically large silt deposits--which have washed out of the neighboring Mohave Mountains, in a region subject to torrential cloudbursts. In such an environment, it is difficult to design a totally flood-proof drainage system. According to an officer with the U.S. Army Corps of Engineers, "Really, the whole problem is caused by development directly on the alluvial fans. When there is a heavy runoff...it has to be channelized and what you have at Lake Havasu City are soft-bottom channels and soil material that is highly erodable."[60]

It is especially important, given such hazardous topography, that areas of building activity be defined by the natural constraints of the land. Yet an official with the U.S. Department of Agriculture, Soil Conservation Service stated that when development first began, such considerations were ignored at Lake Havasu City. "Things have improved since the first day," he added. "Initially there was building going on anywhere--in the hazardous drainage areas as well."[61] Even today, according to the Corps of Engineers officer, "Some yards and buildings are right up against the edge of the washes,"[62] which may erode and subside in a severe storm.

The manager of Lake Havasu City's Irrigation and Drainage District confirmed that "a number of large washes come down through the community from the higher elevations to the lake."[63] As roads continue to be paved, and houses built throughout the site, the loss of permeable surface area will aggravate flooding and drainage problems by increasing the speed and amounts of storm runoff these washes must carry. Despite the Irrigation and Drainage District's recent attempts to upgrade existing drainage channels following the severe storms of 1974, the effects of inadequate planning, including lack of retention ponds, will remain.

A second unfortunate effect of Lake Havasu City's location has been disruption and loss of a former wilderness area and wildlife refuge. The Lake Havasu City land area lies in Region III of the Arizona Game and Fish Department, which over the last decade has lost much public land and wildlife habitat to "lien selection by the State Land Department and subdivision development." The herds of desert bighorn sheep, desert mule deer, and pronghorn antelope throughout this Region have declined significantly. According to an Arizona Game and Fish Department official, the antelope, which has been classified as an "endangered species," is on the brink of extinction as a result of man's intrusion into its habitat range, and the bighorn sheep is classified as "threatened" for similar reasons.

Along the Lake shore, treetops not covered by the flooding from the Parker Dam formerly provided nesting habitat for heron, cormorants, sandhill cranes, egrets, marsh birds, ducks, and even snow geese. These waterfowl have disappeared from Lake Havasu City's area of the Lake. This was a result of the Bureau of Reclamation's determination, shortly after McCulloch acquired the Lake Havasu City land, that the trees were hazardous to boaters and should be removed. For similar reasons, the Bureau also removed underwater logs and obstructions which formed a primary fisheries habitat in the Lake, despite the "major disagreement" expressed by the state Game and Fish Department. One of the major promotional activities sponsored by MPI was an annual boat race, and much of Lake Havasu City's recreational development has focused on boating.

WATER RESOURCES

Given the value of water resources in dry desert regions, one might think that at Lake Havasu City McCulloch would take special pains to preserve water quality, but this has not been the case. No efforts have been made to control the flow of silt into Lake Havasu (and the Colorado River) from erosion and run off. The land has been heavily bulldozed in some areas, disturbing the soil and making it more erosion-prone. And if Lake Havasu City achieves its population capacity of 60,000, a significant increase in silt (from construction) and toxic pollutants (from auto, fertilizer, pesticide use, etc.) running into the Lake will certainly occur.

Lake Havasu City's use of Colorado River water (via its wells) will also inevitably further tax the quality of this already overused resource. The River is currently suffering from excessive salinity.

While all commercial and industrial lots will be on a central sewage system as discussed above, all but a small portion of the 28,356 quarter-acre single-family lots are planned for septic use. There is no one-acre limitation on size of lots permitted to use septics. Even with the good percolation provided by the soil, and the park's buffer zone between the Lake and the community, such intensive use of septics is undesirable. An official of the Lake Havasu Sanitary District acknowledged that at some point in the community's growth, "The government will probably require a central sewage-treatment system for the whole area. Then we'll have to do what other communities in the country do and set up improvement districts."[54] This shortsighted approach, of course, defers the financial burden of a central system onto taxpayers and residents, after the latter have already installed and paid for their individual disposal systems. It may also delay installation until after pollution problems cause serious damage.

The existing sewage-treatment plants (see discussion under Basic Services) provide adequate disposal for the businesses and few houses they serve. The sewage receives secondary treatment and is disposed of by evaporation and percolation from settling ponds and by irrigation of the golf course.

CONSUMER PROTECTION

Sales

Single-family primarily quarter-acre homesites, now almost entirely sold out, have been offered at from $6,000 to $34,000, with most in the $6,000 to $9,000 range. Lots designated for apartments and duplexes, ranging in size from a third of an acre to one acre, have sold for $9,000 to $60,000. Industrial and commercial lots, up to one acre in size, have been offered for from $19,000 to $40,000. Such prices are high in view of the fact that the buyer received no guarantee of basic services even upon completion of his lot payments. However, roads, drainage, and water, though not sewage, have generally been extended.

Sales of lots are made via an installment contract of eight to ten years' duration. They require a 10% minimum downpayment and subsequent monthly payments which include an interest charge of 6% to 9%.

MPI's sales practices are poor. They conform to only one of INFORM's twelve guidelines in this area. (Other companies in the INFORM sample conform to as many as eight.) No special provisions for refunds or a rescission period beyond those required by state and federal regulations exist. If a purchaser defaults on contract payment, the 1975 federal Property Report on Lake Havasu City warns that his losses will include not only all contract payments made to date but also any taxes and/or assessments paid, "plus the cost of improvements placed on the property, if any."[65]

With the exception of encouraging a site visit, the company makes virtually no attempt to encourage an informed purchase, to prevent lot speculation, or to prevent lot purchasers from "getting in over their heads" financially. MPI conducts no credit check on prospective purchasers; it makes no special attempt to get a prospective buyer to go over the sales contract or Property Report with a lawyer. It places no restrictions on the number of lots an optimistic purchaser can buy (including industrial, commercial, and multi-family lots) on an installment basis. This lack of restrictions does nothing to quell speculation in hopes that such lots will have higher resale values in the future.

Such hopes are, in fact, totally unfounded. An investigation by the California Real Estate Commission indicated that Lake Havasu City lots are fundamentally overpriced. Under California law this office reviews the pricing of all out-of-state land marketed in California to determine if it is being sold at a "fair, just and equitable" value. In the case of Lake Havasu City, the Real Estate Commission determined that it could not "accept the original sales price as accomplished by the subdivider's sales presentation [as reflecting] the market value for lots being appraised."[66] It required, following a court determination in its favor, that MPI reduce lot prices on certain Lake Havasu City lands marketed in California.

The Real Estate Commission noted that "In many instances, original buyers in the subdivider's sales presentations could leave the guided group, contact a local broker, and purchase a comparable property for hundreds of dollars less."[67]

MPI's sales policies have encouraged Lake Havasu City lot buyers to see their lots before purchase. But the company tour guides who smoothly shepherd prospective purchasers around the tour route firmly but tactfully block any efforts by individuals to diverge from the preassigned tour paths. Consequently, few of McCulloch "guests" are even aware that lots costing significantly less tha those marketed by the company are available on a resale basis fr other real estate agents in the community.

One local real estate agent confirmed that his office never saw any of the "fly-ins" because of McCulloch's perpetual and de liberate supervision of the groups' itinerary.[68] He added that agency had about 1,500 Lake Havasu City lots listed for resale, owners of which expected to make a resale profit of $2,000 to $3,000. However, most of the lots which first sold for $6,000-- "sky-high" price according to the agent--end up being listed for resale at $3,500. "Even then," he said, "they move very slowly. In 1972, a California Real Estate Commission appraiser noted in report that "the resales of the lots may more accurately portray market value than does the original sale of the lots from the ne subdivided units."[70]

Even the Arizona Office of Economic Planning and Developmer admits in its community prospectus on Lake Havasu City that "Cor struction and land acquisition costs at this remote site are way out of line with other state-land costs. They are even slightly higher than those in the state's major metropolitan areas."[71]

Additional Costs

Lots at Lake Havasu City are clearly sold for prices that r flect improved land value. However, a lot purchaser must pay an nual special assessments to the Irrigation and Drainage District to an Improvement District, and to the Sanitary District, if his lot lies within their boundaries, for the improvements which the entities supply to the community. Such assessments can increase his costs by several hundred dollars a year. And he must pay th during the term of his contract, before he legally owns his lot, well as after receiving title to it. Should a purchaser default during the eight to ten years of his contract payments, all asse ment payments are forfeited, in effect becoming a donation to th financing of Lake Havasu City's improvements.

The annual assessments established by the Lake Havasu Irrig tion and Drainage District have increased dramatically as the co munity's development and population have grown. In 1966, the Di trict charges all lot owners at Lake Havasu City between $1.15 a $9.40 annually, depending on the size and type of their lots. I 1973, according to a Property Report, the charge was $60.64 per acre, or $30.32 for the majority of residential lots under one acre. By 1975, the rate had risen to $39.12 a year for the aver half-acre residential lot. The California Real Estate Commissio estimated that "these assessments will gradually increase to $91 [per acre] in 1980-81 and thereafter gradually reduce to $17.92 [per acre] in 2000-01."[72]

Purchasers of lots located in the Lake Havasu Sanitary District must pay an ad valorem tax in addition to the above assessment. The 1975 federal Property Report asserts that this tax is $1.29 per $100 of the lot's assessed value. The Property Report further explains that a lot's assessed value at Lake Havasu City is computed by the County for its property tax rolls on a basis applicable to "*unimproved* [emphasis added] residential and commercial property." The County figures its tax on the basis of 18% of 70% of the lot's sales price. Thus the current Sanitary District ad valorem tax on a Lake Havasu City residential lot lying within its boundaries might be as low as $13.93 on a $6,000 lot or as high as $270.90 on a $30,000 one.

Certain Lake Havasu City lots are located in the above two Districts and also in Improvement Districts 1, 2, or 3. However, only Improvement District 1 contains single-family residential units. Lots in this District are charged an annual tax of $0.81 per $100 of assessed value. This would add from $18.95 on a $13,000 lot, to $170 on a $30,000 lot, to the taxes of the several hundred residents of this District.

In addition to district taxes, property taxes (including school, County, and Fire District taxes) of $10.48 per $100 of assessed value are levied on Lake Havasu City lots. This cost might range from $113.18 to $2,200.80 per residential lot. Thus the total annual tax burden for a residential-lot purchaser at Lake Havasu City, both before and after taking title to his land, may range from $152 to $2,680.*

One might argue that McCulloch's astute reliance on the financing powers of districts to fund the massive front-end costs of development is a practical and convenient method for a developer to finance large-scale land developments. But it would be hard to construe any defense for the arrangement of power vested in the Lake Havasu Irrigation and Drainage District. As has been discussed, a lot buyer under contract must pay the Irrigation and Drainage District assessment or be held in default. Yet the District's voting regulations do not allow him to participate in any District elections or decisions. He can vote in a District election only after taking title to his lot and residing in Mohave County for ninety days. He is thus a disenfranchised taxpayer with no voice in such crucial matters as deciding who sits on the District's Board, who is to be its manager, and how much debt it shall

---

*For purchasers of lots in mobile-home tracts there is one more assessment: $14 a month ($168 a year) to the Lakeview Property Owners' Association.

incur. Few lot buyers will become residents until they have completed ten years of installment payments. Thus the District's resident-voting requirements, established under the state law pertaining to Irrigation and Drainage Districts, allows the developer to control District policy for many years without assuming any financial liabilities.

Title Protection

While Lake Havasu City lot buyers may not be sure of what their land will really cost or when services will be available, the few who have purchased lots after June, 1975, can be certain of one thing. By virtue of Arizona's 1975 sales law, their right to title is fully protected during the contract period. All lots are platted with Mohave County. As of June, 1975, MPI also records sales contracts, i.e., Real Estate Purchase Agreements, with the County within sixty days of their execution.

A purchaser does not receive title to his lot until all payments plus taxes and assessments due on the contract have been made. However, title is placed in trust in the interim.* The one exception to this practice occurs if the buyer's initial downpayment amounts to one third of the sales price. In this case MPI deeds the property to the buyer immediately. (The deed is then subject to a promissory note secured by a Deed of Trust, which is recorded by the subdivider, an arrangement similar to a mortgage.) Under either of these arrangements, the purchaser is protected against third parties' acquiring title to the property free of any obligation to deliver the deed.

There are no blanket encumbrances or liens on the Lake Havasu City property which might prevent a lot purchaser from obtaining title to his lot. However, a June, 1974, federal Property Report-- though not the 1975 Property Report--explains that the existing ownership arrangements could possibly affect the purchaser's right to specified improvements on his lot. The land at Lake Havasu City is not owned outright by McCulloch Properties, Inc. It is held in a trust while MPI purchases it. Should MPI default on its purchase payments, the terms of the trust guarantee that a lot purchaser will receive title upon completion of all payments. However, the trust does not guarantee that all improvements which McCulloch promised the purchaser will actually be completed.

Various zoning regulations and architectural controls define lot use. The purchaser's deed also includes numerous restrictions

---

*The 1975 Property Report does not inform a purchaser that title to his lot is placed in trust. However, this is required by state law and was confirmed by the company to be its policy.

and reservations, easements, and rights of way. The 1975 federal Property Report describes these restrictions but does not tell the buyer which ones affect his particular lot.

Legal Status

Up to 1976, Lake Havasu City was one of the few subdivisions in the INFORM sample to have had no legal difficulties in the course of its life. Then in June, 1976, an insurance company (Affiliated FM Insurance Co. of Rhode Island) filed claim against the Lake Havasu Irrigation and Drainage District, MPI, and related engineering firms for the recovery of payments, in the amount of $757,701, made to parties damaged by the severe floods in 1974.

In the fall of 1976, according to the *New York Times*, the McCulloch Oil Corporation became the target of several investigations by federal, state, and local bodies of possible improprieties in its land development projects, including Lake Havasu City. These investigations are being conducted by the Securities and Exchange Commission, the Federal Trade Commission, the Office of Interstate Land Sales Registration, the Arizona State Attorney General's Office and the Pueblo County District Attorney in Colorado. Each investigation, according to the *Times*, is focusing on whether irregularities existed in McCulloch's "acquisition, development, or marketing of projects."[73]

ENVIRONMENTAL CHECKLIST

Overall environmental protection record: POOR

Does the subdivider:

PLANS	Plan for complete basic services?	NO
	Phase lot sales and extension of services?	NO
	Get 80% build-out in 10 years of each section marketed?	NO
	Prepare an Environmental Impact Report?	NO
LAND	Use a curvilinear or cluster design?	YES
	Retain 25% or more open space?	NO
	Reserve from lot sale and development the following areas of critical concern:	
	wetlands?	--
	dunes and beaches?	--
	water sources?	--
	prime agricultural lands?	--
	habitats of endangered species?	NO
	prime historical, archaeological, cultural, aesthetic, or recreational resources?	--
	Reserve from lot sale and development the following areas hazardous for building:	
	geological hazard areas (earthquake, landslide)?	--
	flood-prone areas (100-year floodplains, arroyos)?	NO
	areas of slope exceeding 25%?	--
	Blade roads only in immediate development areas?	NO
	Clear only for buildings and roads?	--
	Preserve existing topography?	NO
WATER RESOURCES	Design the drainage system to control erosion?	NO
	Retain 100-foot buffer zone around water bodies?	--
	Replant disturbed land immediately?	--
	Limit septic systems to one-acre or larger lots with adequate: percolation rates, slope, and distance from bedrock, water table and surface waters?	NO
	When utilizing central sewage disposal, provide tertiary treatment (or secondary and land disposal)?	YES
	Avoid major stream alteration?	--
	Avoid major wetland dredging and filling?	--
	Use groundwater only up to the safe yield?	--

NOTE: See chapter on "Guidelines" for more complete explanation of items on Checklist.

LAKE HAVASU CITY 331

CONSUMER CHECKLIST

<u>Overall consumer protection record</u>: FAIR

Does the subdivider:

SALES	Conduct a credit check on lot purchasers?	NO
	Limit lot sales to two per purchaser?	NO
	Sell only residential, i.e., no industrial, commercial or multi-family lots on installment contracts?	NO
	Require a cash downpayment of 20% on all sales?	NO
	Limit duration of installment contracts to 5 years?	NO
	Charge no interest on installment contracts?	NO
	Encourage attorney review of sales documents?	NO
	Require a pre-purchase site visit?	YES
	Allow a 14-day rescission period in which purchaser can obtain a refund for any reason?	NO
	Offer a partial refund if purchaser defaults?	NO
	Guarantee a refund, with interest, if promised services are not made available by date specified in contract?	NO
	Escrow contract payments, or provide equivalent surety bonding, for refund purposes?	NO
TITLE	Offer only platted lots?	YES
	Offer a recordable contract, and record the sale?	YES
	Offer unmortgaged land, or land mortgaged with a release clause, only?	YES
	Upon contract signing, deed title to purchaser, or place title in trust?	YES
BASIC SERVICES	Guarantee, or have available, to each lot:	
	central water, of adequate quantity and quality?	YES
	central sewage disposal, as necessary?	NO
	drainage system, adequate for 100-year storm?	NO
	solid waste disposal, via adequate method?	YES
	roads, paved, to county standards?	YES
	electricity and telephone?	YES
	Guarantee completion through escrowing or surety bonding?	NO
	If services are financed through special service district bonds, employ them only if:	
	initial governing body includes a county official?	NO
	elections include all landowners on one-man, one-vote basis?	NO
	sum of bonds is less than twice the developer's investment in basic services?	?
	sum of bonds is less than 15% of the assessed value of land in the district?	NO
	developer co-signs all bonds?	NO

COST OF LOTS BOUGHT ON THE INSTALLMENT PLAN

LOT PRICE
    basic price (¼ - 1 acre)*　　　　　　　　　$6,000 - $60,000
    finance charge (6% - 9%)　　　　　　　　　$1,794 - $28,085
                                      Total　　$7,794 - $88,085

ADDITIONAL ANNUAL ASSESSMENTS DURING TERM OF CONTRACT
    Irrigation & Drainage District　　　　　　$20 - $78
    other districts　　　　　　　　　　　　　　0 - $441
        sanitary　　　　$14 - $271
        improvement　　$19 - $170
    (#1, 700 lots)
    property taxes
        (county, school & fire)　　　　　　　　$113 - $2,200

                        Total, per year　　$133 - $2,719
                        Total, 10 years　$1,520 - $26,800

ONE-TIME COSTS FOR SERVICES
    lot survey　　　　　　　　　　　　　　　　0
    water　　　　　　　　　　　　　　　　　　$110
        well　　　　　　　　　　0
        central extension　　　0
        central hook-up　　　　$110
    sewage　　　　　　　　　　　　　　　　　　$175 - $700
        septic system　　　　　$500 - $700
        central extension　　　0
        central hook-up　　　　$175
    electricity　　　　　　　　　　　　　　　0
    telephone　　　　　　　　　　　　　　　　0

*Includes industrial, commercial, and multi-family lots.

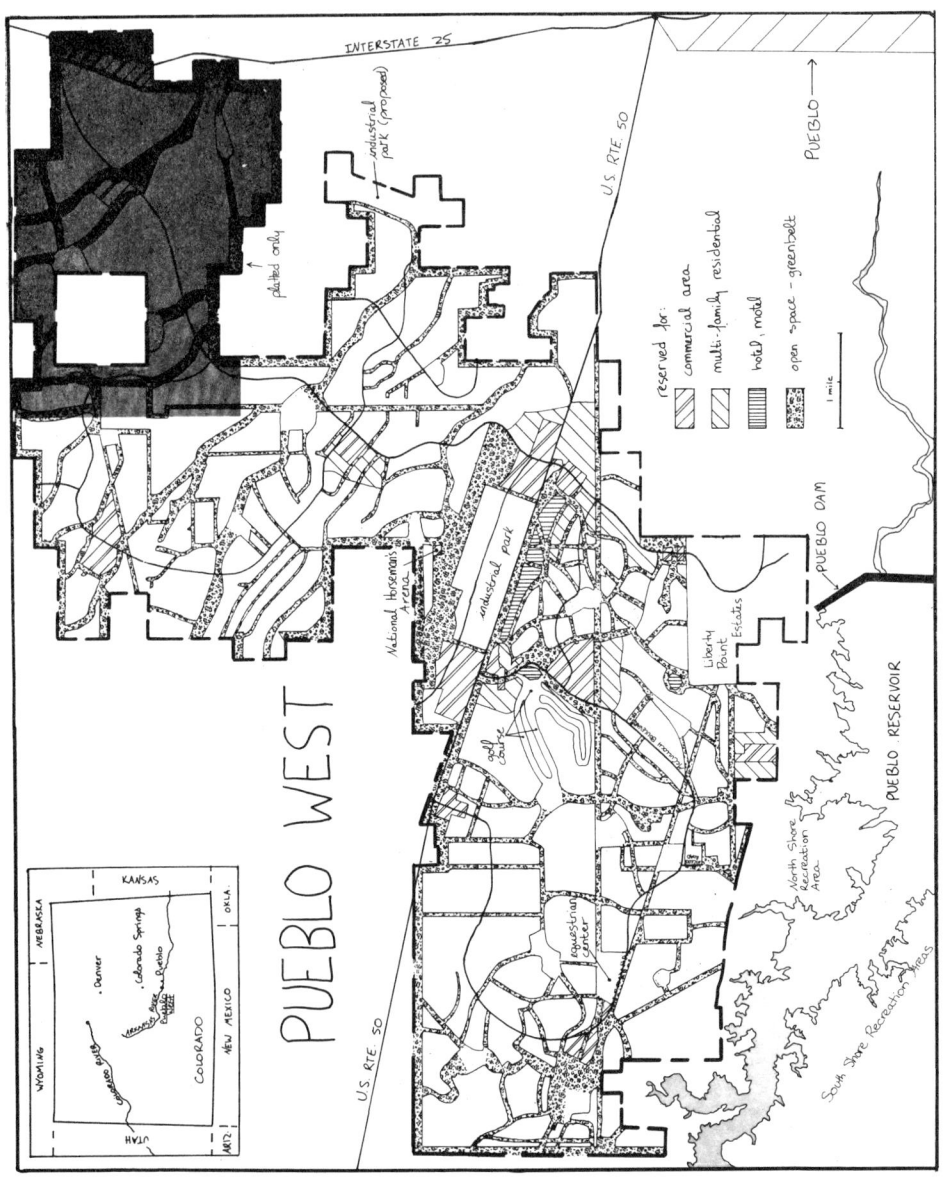

8
Pueblo West

Few consumers have ever heard of a legal mechanism known as a "special service district." Even fewer understand how such districts work. Practically none are aware of the possible pitfalls of using them in new community development.

Lot buyers at Pueblo West, however, can no longer claim blissful ignorance on this subject. Pueblo West now stands as a virtual object lesson on the enormous hazards and nearly insoluble problems the irresponsible use of such districts can create.

Pueblo West, located six miles northwest of the city of Pueblo, Colorado, is the second and largest of eight land-development projects currently under construction by McCulloch Properties, Inc. (MPI), a subsidiary of the large conglomerate McCulloch Oil Corporation. It covers 30,000 acres (47.5 square miles) of arid grazing land at the southern end of Colorado's "Front Range" urban corridor. Like McCulloch's relatively successful first venture, Lake Havasu City (see chapter on Lake Havasu City), Pueblo West borders recreational lands adjacent to a dam and reservoir built by the U.S. Department of the Interior's Bureau of Reclamation. Sales began in 1969, and the project is now approximately 85% sold out. Unlike Lake Havasu City, however, Pueblo West is poorly supplied with basic services, and it is questionable whether they will ever be fully available.

The subdivision's problems with obtaining basic services are virtually all traceable, one way or another, to McCulloch's creation and use of the Pueblo West Metropolitan District. The initial Service Plan for Pueblo West was modeled after Lake Havasu City's. There, a special district was successfully used

335

to finance major subdivision improvements: central water, road, and drainage systems.

By using this special-district device, McCulloch divided the financial responsibility for installing improvements between its own corporate complex and the subdivision's lot purchasers. A district is a quasi-governmental entity empowered to issue tax-exempt bonds for certain purposes. By becoming landowners in a district, lot purchasers become legally obligated to repay its bonded debt.

Unfortunately, McCulloch's success at Lake Havasu was not to be repeated. With McCulloch's adroit promotion and guidance, amendments to Colorado's Metropolitan District Act were passed which permitted the establishment, prior to the start of sales, of a multi-purpose service district similar to the one McCulloch had employed in Arizona. However, the planning for Pueblo West's development was based on two erroneous assumptions.

One assumption was that the Pueblo West Metropolitan District would be able to obtain a water supply adequate for the subdivision's projected population. A sufficient water supply--a matter of paramount importance for large subdivisions located in semi-arid sections of the country--was not confirmed prior to initiation of sales. Subsequent Colorado subdivision regulations would have prevented this omission.* An adequate water supply has yet to be secured.

The second erroneous assumption was that the subdivision's population would grow at a relatively rapid rate. Were Pueblo West to achieve a population of 65,000 in the fifty years following the start of sales, as originally projected, its residents could perhaps tolerate the District's extending a $37 million debt, the amount allotted under the District's Service Plan for the land's improvement. However, this projection left little margin of error for the wayward buffetings of an unpredictable economy. Given progress to date, achievement of the projected population is doubtful. Based on the average annual rate of increase so far, it will be about two hundred years before the full population arrives. As a result, the Pueblo West community will either be dependent for many more years on the financial resources of the McCulloch Corporation or have to do without

---

*Colorado's subdivision regulation law, passed in 1972, demands that Colorado's counties require from subdividers evidence, such as proof of ownership of water rights or documents showing feasibility of providing water, that "a water supply of sufficient quality, quantity, and dependability will be available" prior to county approval of the project.[1]

essential, promised, basic site improvements. This situation is assuredly one that neither lot purchasers, the District, nor MPI finds comfortable.

MPI's environmental planning at Pueblo West was only slightly better than its planning for basic services. Its record is mixed: some good steps were taken, such as using a curvilinear design, while others, such as proper erosion controls, were not. Relative to INFORM's guidelines and to the practices of other subdivisions in the INFORM sample,* MPI's sales practices are poor.

Regional Context

Colorado's State Deputy Engineer, charged with administering state water resources, recently remarked that "the only thing more valuable than gold in Colorado is water."[2] The Continental Divide, which runs through the Rocky Mountains, traverses the state from north to south, splitting it into two different water-resource regions. Two-thirds of Colorado's surface-water supplies issue from the mountains' western slopes. These mountains cast a "rain shadow" over the foothills and plains to their east, thereby limiting annual precipitation in eastern Colorado to under eighteen inches.[4]

Severe water-supply problems have developed in eastern Colorado over the last decade. The state has experienced dramatic population growth and industrial development along a narrow strip of the semi-arid eastern plains. This Front Range area, as it is called, runs along the edge of the Rocky Mountain foothills from Fort Collins in the north to Pueblo in the south. It holds over 80% of Colorado's 2.4 million population and almost all of its rapidly expanding industry.[5] When the water needs of this urban corridor are added to those of Colorado's agricultural and mining industries, the demand far exceeds the capacity of the state's legally available surface-water supplies.†

---

*Includes both the ten subdivisions in Volume I of this study and the nine Florida subdivisions analyzed in Volume II.

†Eighteen states share in the use of Colorado's waters. Interstate compacts and Supreme Court decisions determine each state's allocation from Colorado's principal river basins: the Upper Colorado River Basin, the South Platte Basin, the Arkansas Basin, and the Rio Grande Basin. Colorado is entitled under these laws to only about one-half of its total stream production.[6]

It is thus not surprising that one of the principal initial attractions to McCulloch of the Pueblo West area was the then-planned $63 million Pueblo Dam and Reservoir. Located four miles south of Pueblo West's center, the Dam and Reservoir are part of a massive U.S. Department of the Interior, Bureau of Reclamation water-management project. Recently completed, they provide the terminal water-storage point in a multi-purpose effort to alleviate the water shortage facing certain Front Range communities. This effort, known as the Fryingpan-Arkansas Project, was authorized by the U.S. Congress in 1962 for the diversion, transportation, and storage of water from Colorado's Fryingpan River Valley on the western slope of the Rocky Mountains to the state's Arkansas River Valley in the east. According to the Bureau of Reclamation, the Project was specifically designed to "provide municipal, industrial and irrigation water, flood protection [and] water recreation opportunities [which would] stimulate related short and long term economic activity to communities of the Arkansas River Valley."[7]

The scope and expense of the Project are awesome. Congress authorized $170 million in 1962 for the necessary construction. But ten years later, according to McCulloch's promotional material for Pueblo West, costs had increased to $265 million, and work still remained to be done.[8] When complete the Project will include: six dams and reservoirs, eighteen diversion structures, ten tunnels, two canals, two power plants, eleven pumping stations, and two municipal and industrial water-delivery conduits totaling 266 miles in length.[9]

The city of Pueblo is one of the Project's principal beneficiaries. The Project, on which actual construction began in 1964, will enable the Pueblo city region to increase its participation in the urban and industrial development under way to its north. With a current population of over 100,000, the city is Pueblo County's single industrial center and is the county seat. Its population has increased 40% since 1950, while the population in the County's rural and predominantly ranching sectors, on the other hand, has slightly declined.[10]

In 1965, about the time that McCulloch initiated its land dealings in the Pueblo area, the U.S. Congress passed the Federal Water Project Recreation Act. As described in a Bureau of Reclamation publication, this Act "established the authority for the acquisition of land and construction of specific facilities for recreation and fish and wildlife enhancement in connection with water resource development projects."[11] Together with other legislation, this Act enabled the Bureau of Reclamation to begin acquiring the 18,012 acres in the Pueblo area necessary for the construction of both the Pueblo Dam and

Reservoir and the accompanying recreational facilities.[12] The Reservoir's North Shore Recreation Area now shares a common boundary with McCulloch's community; as stated by the Bureau of Reclamation, the area is "readily available to the residents of Pueblo West for day-use, boating and fishing."[13]

The Draft Environmental Statement on the Fryingpan-Arkansas Project, issued by the Bureau of Reclamation in accordance with the requirements of the 1969 National Environmental Policy Act, explains that MPI considered the water-sports arena which would be created by the construction of the Pueblo Dam and Reservoir "one of five major factors for selecting the present site of Pueblo West."[14] MPI's promotional literature emphasized this factor.[15] However, it is more than likely that another one was the water that could be pulled from the Arkansas River, which would be supplied by the Bureau of Reclamation's diversion of west-slope waters flowing into the Pueblo Reservoir. (See discussion under Water.) Such an approach had provided water to McCulloch's first community at Lake Havasu City in Arizona,* and McCulloch had little reason to suspect that the productive relations evidenced between that project and the Bureau of Reclamation would not aid a second McCulloch land-development operation in another state.

The Final Environmental Statement on the Pueblo Dam and Reservoir published by the Bureau of Reclamation in 1972, three years after McCulloch started sales at Pueblo West, confirms the positive relationship existing between McCulloch's second land project and this federal agency. Pueblo West is frequently described in this document as "a unified residential-recreational-light industrial community with a 21st-century concept of spacious country living."[16] The subdivision is acclaimed throughout the Statement as a model example of the kind of benefits provided to the region by construction of the Dam and Reservoir. The National Parks Service, one of the government agencies that reviewed the Draft Environmental Statement, explicitly requested that the phrase "a 21st century concept" be deleted, stating that "[the Final Environmental Statement] should be objective and factual and should avoid use of such phrases that are typically used by real estate promoters."[17] However, the Bureau of Reclamation retorted: "The term '21st century concept' is locally used and was therefore incorporated into the author's style of writing. It was not deleted because it is an appropriate descriptive term."[18]

---

*A contract signed by the Bureau of Reclamation and Lake Havasu City's Irrigation and Drainage District provides that community a substantial supply from the Colorado River water in the Lake Havasu Reservoir.

Unfortunately for lot purchasers, the legalities and politics of water supply in Colorado proved different from those in Arizona, the cooperation of federal agencies notwithstanding.

History

In the 1960s, land subdivision became big business in Colorado. The climate throughout the state was expansionary and pro-growth. There was no state overview of land-use matters. Pueblo County, like other counties in Colorado, not only lacked regulations controlling subdivision activity, but saw little need to introduce such "impediments to growth." Many large ranch-owners who were not then actively profiting from subdivision activities were simply "holding" their land waiting for values to further increase.

According to a former Regional Planning Director for Pueblo County, the city of Pueblo was then surrounded by three very large "speculator ranches." These effectively controlled the land market around the city's fringe. The purchase by McCulloch (and the Bureau of Reclamation) of the old Nicholls ranch for development delighted city and county officials. McCulloch's arrival forced an opening in the region's traditionally monopolistic land-use patterns and assured the city of Pueblo that it would have a suburban residential zone. "Nobody thought at that time to ask questions [about possibly negative impacts of such a development]," the same Regional Planning official noted. "Then when some of us began to, things had gone too far; the climate of opinion was so pro-growth we couldn't be heard."[19]

By 1969, when development and sales actually began at Pueblo West, McCulloch should have completed all the steps necessary to ensure the smooth realization of Pueblo West's future development. Given Pueblo's cooperative socio-political climate, McCulloch had but one reason not to anticipate that Pueblo West would emulate, even exceed, "the successful growth pattern" of Lake Havasu City.[20] The Southeastern Colorado Water Conservancy District (SCWCD), which was responsible for the delivery of Fryingpan-Arkansas Project waters to member communities, had warned McCulloch that its plans for Pueblo West's water supply were poorly researched and unrealistic. But, according to an SCWCD official, the warnings were summarily dismissed and McCulloch proceeded to launch its lot-sales program.[21]

To meet the high front-end costs entailed in transforming 30,000 acres of scrub rangeland into "improved" lots suitable for homesites, some means of outside financing (separate from the McCulloch Corporation's assets) was desirable. Consequently, in 1968, before any of Pueblo West's lots were platted with the County, McCulloch initiated certain preliminary actions designed to facilitate its use of a Metropolitan District at Pueblo West.

Colorado's Metropolitan District Act--adopted in 1947 and amended in 1965 and 1969--was one of several Colorado laws which enabled landowners to finance specified community needs (such as water and sewer facilities) through issuance to the general public of long-term tax-free general obligation bonds.* As its name implies, the Metropolitan District was granted, through its enabling act, the largest range of municipal powers of all of the various types of districts. But from McCulloch's point of view in 1968, the Colorado law posed several minor problems and contained one very major obstacle to the course of action the corporation wished to pursue in developing Pueblo West. Certain wordings in the law, if left unchanged, would have effectively prevented McCulloch from using a Metropolitan District at this initial stage when Pueblo West's development schedule was most pressing. (Around this time, the U.S. Department of Interior's Bureau of Reclamation had finalized its plans for the public-use recreation areas surrounding the Pueblo Reservoir, and McCulloch and the Bureau would soon begin to negotiate the access route to the North Shore Recreation Area, which now bordered Pueblo West.)

Unlike Arizona's Irrigation and Drainage District Act, which was interpreted in 1963 (though not later) so as to enable McCulloch to establish a broadly powered municipal services district at Lake Havasu City before lots had resident owners, Colorado's Metropolitan District Act was tightly worded. It specifically required that a Metropolitan District be initiated by a petition signed "by not less than one hundred of the taxpaying electors of the district who were registered and qualified to vote at the last general election."[23] Thus, as the law stood in 1968, a developer could not legally establish a Metropolitan District prior to the occupation (i.e., development) of a land area.

In 1969 this law was amended, enabling McCulloch to form the Pueblo West Metropolitan District before starting the community's sales program. The sponsors of and lobbyists for Colorado's House Bill 1280, which affected these amendments, have minimized McCulloch's involvement in this process. However, correspondence from the Denver law firm of Akolt, Shepherd, Dick & Rovira (then representing McCulloch's interests in Colorado) to the head office of MPI in Los Angeles indicates just how direct McCulloch's influence was.

A letter dated February 13, 1969, addresses the principal impediment to McCulloch's use of the law as it was then written, stating:

---

*Today there are over 800 special districts in Colorado, some of which are in serious financial straits.[22]

> Because of some practical problems concerning the landowners and electors involved in your project we thereupon suggested an amendment which would allow non-resident property owners to vote in all elections including the incorporation election. This suggestion has already been incorporated in Section 5 of this bill.[24]

The proposed new legislation was appended to the letter with the comment:

> You will find the amendments suggested by you have been included in this bill together with other legislation which was initially desired by the bonding company [for Pueblo West's Metropolitan District] and other existing metropolitan districts.[25]

The letter closes with the reassurance that:

> We will continue all reasonable activities to promote its passage and to keep it flowing....We have put an emergency clause on it so that it would go into effect immediately upon the Governor's signature [as] this might help you with your "timing."
>
> When the bill gets a number we will advise you of same in the event you might have other sources of help within the Legislature.[26]

According to District officials, the amending legislation was drafted by a bond attorney named Wilson, who was a partner in the bond firm of Wilson, Jones, Morton & Lynch of San Mateo, California.*[27] MPI had worked with this same firm to establish the Lake Havasu Irrigation and Drainage District back in 1963, and the firm has served as bond counsel to the Pueblo West Metropolitan District since its establishment. *Politics of Land*, a Nader study group report on land use in California, points out that this bond firm originated the use of special

---

*Several years after the Pueblo West Metropolitan District was established, the District initiated proceedings with the California Bar Association to disbar Wilson on grounds of unethical conduct and conflict of interest stemming from his authorship of Bill 1280 prior to serving as the District's bond counsel, but no action ensued.[28]

districts to finance improvements for undeveloped sites in the 1950s. At that time it helped establish what became the debt-burdened Estero Municipal Improvement District at Foster City, California.²⁹

Bill 1280 was introduced in the Colorado House on March 3, 1969. Within three weeks, it passed 58 to 0. Two months later, on May 6, it passed the Senate 33 to 0; Governor Love signed it into law on July 9.

The day the amending bill passed the Senate, McCulloch's Denver law firm sent MPI's Los Angeles office a letter summing up the satisfactorily completed legislative effort and informing McCulloch officials:

> ...it would generally appear that you are safe now in using the Metropolitan District approach for your service plan....We have also thanked, in our name and yours, friends and lobbyists who helped us lobby this bill through.³⁰

It is generally held in the Pueblo area that Tom Farley--a close friend and former business partner of Tom Healey, who helped arrange McCulloch's purchase of Pueblo West's land--expedited the quick passage of the amending legislation through the House in his capacity as House Minority Leader, a position he had held since 1967.³¹ Farley has denied any improper activities. Shortly after Bill 1280 was signed into law, he became legal counsel to both MPI and to the legally separate but McCulloch-controlled Pueblo West Metropolitan District.* He retained these two positions until 1974, when he sought the Democratic nomination for Governor and was dismissed by the District's board. His past involvement with McCulloch and the establishment of Pueblo West's Metropolitan District soon became political issues in that campaign.

The new amendments to Colorado's Metropolitan District Act expanded the municipal services such a District could provide commensurate with a Service Plan which McCulloch's engineering firm had ready to print as soon as the law passed.† (One former

---

* A main road in the northeast section of Pueblo West was named Farley Avenue.

† As was pointed out by a former county commissioner, MPI's engineering firm in California, Trico International, Inc., issued this Service Plan in May of 1969. The plan assumed that the entity financing the estimated costs and delivering the defined services to Pueblo West would be a "Metropolitan District."

power was eliminated--that of police protection.) More importantly, the amending legislation eliminated the requirement under the old law that a petition to incorporate a district (i.e., legally organize it) "be signed by not less than 100 of [the resident] taxpaying electors of the district." In the newly amended law the required petition had to be signed "by not less than ten per cent or one hundred of the taxpaying electors of the district, whichever number is smaller" and the definition of "taxpaying elector of the district" was revised to include both "resident(s) and non-resident(s)."[33] With the addition of a few sentences, Colorado's law thus permitted McCulloch (or any other developer) to establish a Metropolitan District comprising totally undeveloped land and to undertake an extensive range of improvements with unlimited funds* borrowed from the public--to whom Pueblo West's future lot owners, rather than McCulloch, would be legally responsible.

The Pueblo County Commissioners approved the Service Plan for Pueblo West's Metropolitan District on July 10, only one day after the Governor signed House Bill 1280 authorizing the District. This highly technical document described at length the District's long-range financing projections and scheduled delivery of basic services to Pueblo West's lots. Colorado statutes call for hearing notices and hearings to allow adequate public study and review of such a plan; in this case these procedures were clearly pushed through perfunctorily. Had the County Commissioners examined the Service Plan more thoughtfully at that time, the County itself, future lot owners, representatives of the District, and McCulloch's development company might all have been saved many future trials and tribulations.

One month after the Plan's approval, Tom Farley appeared as counsel for McCulloch before a Pueblo district judge to win approval (as required under law) of the petition to organize the Pueblo West Metropolitan District. A former member of the District's board said of this procedure:

> Twenty people voted for the formation of the District. Sixteen of them were members of the Denver law firm [which assisted McCulloch in the writing and passage of House Bill 1280]. The other four were made up of two officers

---

*Florida has recently prohibited special service districts from issuing bonds in excess of 15% of a district's assessed valuation. Colorado places no such limitation on its Metropolitan Districts, which may issue as much debt as their voters authorize.

Pueblo West's development has not been phased.

of Trico Engineering...and their wives. Each
of these individuals had been deeded a piece
of Pueblo West property before the election.[34]

Once the petition was granted, the Pueblo West Metropolitan District was "legally" formed. According to the former board member, a five-man board of directors was appointed on September 19, 1969. This first board consisted of two Trico officers, one of their wives, and two partners from McCulloch's Denver law firm. It was not until 1973 that someone not associated with McCulloch was voted onto the board.[35]

The next month the voters of the District authorized the District to issue bonds up to the amount of $37,075,000. This debt, to finance development needs, was allotted as follows:

- Water: $15,890,569
- Sanitation: $12,271,899
- Roads: $6,238,643
- Traffic and safety control and devices: $121,949
- Parks and recreation: $458,271
- Fire protection: $1,111,660
- Properties, buildings, and equipment: $982,000.[36]

The authorizing vote was cast by many of those who had requested formation of the District. According to a former member of the District's board, three no-votes cast by Pueblo West property owners from Pueblo "were contested and thrown out. All others were yes-votes cast as absentee ballots. After this initial bond election those persons who had been deeded Pueblo West property [by McCulloch] returned it to McCulloch. None of them owns land in Pueblo West today, and, in fact, most have never seen Pueblo West."[37]

The amount of debt authorized in 1969 for Pueblo West's Metropolitan District is more than four times that originally authorized for the Lake Havasu Irrigation and Drainage District and almost double the debt currently extended by the latter. Yet Lake Havasu City's current population (and thus its tax base) is five times the population of Pueblo West. The debt authorization for Pueblo West's Metropolitan District also exceeds what MPI had invested in Pueblo West as of January, 1976. While available figures show that McCulloch has so far expended approximately three times more than the District on improvements at Pueblo West, the Service Plan still calls for the

District's expenditure of another $27 million in improvements over the next four years.*[38]

As of June, 1976, the Pueblo West Metropolitan District had an outstanding debt from principal and interest on issued bonds amounting to $12,663,257. This outstanding debt is approximately 72% of the District's assessed value, which amounts to $17.5 million.[40] Certainly the existing Pueblo West community cannot support any major increases in its District's debt, but without further increases, or McCulloch's assistance, there will be few funds to finance continued installation of basic services.

As a consequence of the various irremediable actions taken during 1968 and 1969 by Colorado's legislators, by Pueblo County officials, and by McCulloch's entourage, Pueblo West's lot owners and its District representatives have had to shoulder, with openly declared resistance and irritation, unanticipated financial and administrative burdens. As one local realtor put it in 1976, Pueblo West is still "suffering fantastic growing pains."[41]

THE OFFERING: LAND AND IMPROVEMENTS

LAND

Physical Characteristics

The Nicholls ranch--over 33,000 acres in size--had been owned for more than thirty years by a Dallas, Texas, family. Its boundaries extended down to and along the north shore of the Arkansas River, though most of its land consisted of flat, parched scrub range extending back from the bluffs overlooking

---

*According to the District's 1976 Bond Statement Series A, "...the total outlay for improvements in the community [amounts to] $88,708,393 since the District's opening in the fall of 1969. Total capital expenditures include the following:

MPI	$34,992,452
The District	$ 7,213,731
Private utility companies	$ 6,043,600
Building permit valuations	$23,452,860
Equipment and inventory	$17,005,750

The 1976 District Budget calls for the District to spend another $3,333,252--some of which cost will be undertaken by McCulloch.[39]

the river valley. It was recently described by a local utility contractor as "desert land with a little sagebrush and a few rattlers."[42] Rain is infrequent: precipitation averages less than twelve inches annually, though winter snowfall may amount to thirty inches. Temperatures range from a high of 92°F to a low of 15°F.[43]

Pueblo West's portion of this land begins near the foot of the eastern slopes of the Rocky Mountains. It varies in altitude from approximately 4,600 to 5,500 feet. Long stretches of flat, treeless terrain are intercut by numerous dry washes. The western portions shift to rolling, desert-shrubbed hills with massive rock outcroppings. These jut through the thin, dry topsoil to provide dramatic scenic contrasts as well as opportunities for pollution of the groundwater from storm runoff and sewage leaching. According to a local realtor, when McCulloch began to purchase this land, it was so overgrazed that "there wasn't enough grass on it to raise a goat."[44]

The subdivision is bisected east-west by U.S. Highway 50 and touches on Interstate 25. The Interstate runs north-south, connecting the city of Pueblo with the other principal Front Range cities: Colorado Springs, Denver, and Fort Collins. Though the McCulloch land forms one contiguous unit, several small blocks within it are held by others, including the state of Colorado.

Available figures for Pueblo West's total acreage vary considerably. Company data sent to INFORM indicate that the total acreage currently owned is 30,000, a figure consistent with the District's 1976 Bond Statement's reference to 30,455 acres in the District. However, figures published in prospectuses issued by McCulloch Properties Credit Corporation, in Official Bond Statements for the District, and in the 1972 Revised Service Plan range from 30,984 to as high as 34,000 acres.[45]

Whatever Pueblo West's exact total size, approximately 27,500 of its acres have been subdivided into 19,873 lots. Of these, about 12,000 are residential, of 1 to 5 acres in size each; another 3,600 residential lots are under 1 acre each. The prices of these lots range from $6,000 to $17,000. There are also 2,000 multi-family residential lots, priced at up to $55,000; 1,200 commercial lots; 45 motel lots; and 600 mobile-home lots.[46]

According to the most recent company data supplied to IN-FORM, about 85% of the platted lots (16,945) are sold.* Of

---

*The 1976 Bond Statement, Series A states that 18,227 lots have been sold at Pueblo West. The difference in the figures reflects either an error, or a very high cancellation rate on purchase contracts between January and April, 1976.[47]

these, 4,000 have been completely paid for and deeded to purchasers.

A 783-mile network of roads threads through Pueblo West's acreage. A total of 668 miles of this road system have not been paved. These miles of exposed dirt surfaces contribute to the severity of occasional dust storms and to the further erosion of Pueblo West's poor-quality land.

The nascent Pueblo West business community includes a bank, a few small light industries, and the headquarters for a local utility. It also includes the $1.5 million, 81-unit Pueblo West Inn, built by McCulloch principally for the use of "fly-ins," persons flown to the community by MPI.

Despite its high lot-sales figure, as of early 1976, Pueblo West had only 2,200 residents. Approximately 680 building permits for residences had been issued, an increase of 122 over 1974.[48] This slow build-out rate--about a hundred residences a year--falls far below company projections. Given Pueblo West's average annual rate of population increase, it will take approximately 200 years for the community to achieve its full projected population of 65,000. Nevertheless, the rate of development is considerably more rapid at Pueblo West than at most of the subdivisions in the INFORM sample. Several of the subdivisions studied by INFORM--such as Horizon's Rio Communities and GAC's Rio Rico--will not, at their present growth rate, achieve full population for at least 1,000 years.

BASIC SERVICES

Several of the developers in the INFORM sample have assured buyers of lots in their "new communities" no improvements but a dirt road. McCulloch, on the other hand, while not guaranteeing central water, central sewage, roads, drainage, and electricity in the purchaser's contract, does state in its federal Property Reports* that these services will be available. As noted above, however, McCulloch has passed the responsibility for providing a major portion of these services over to the Pueblo West Metropolitan District. The District is empowered to acquire, operate, and maintain: a domestic water system; a sanitary sewer system (to all lots less than one acre in size); surface- and stormwater drainage; fire protection; street paving, curbs, gutters,

---
*The U.S. Department of Housing and Urban Development, Office of Interstate Land Sales Registration (OILSR), requires the development company to issue a property report giving important consumer information on the lots offered for sale.

culverts, bridges, sidewalks, lighting, and traffic and safety controls; and parks and recreational facilities.[49]

MPI retains the responsibility for installing so-called in-tract improvements. The 19,873 lots currently platted at Pueblo West are divided into 120 "tracts," each of which holds anywhere from 4 to 509 lots. Most of these lots connect to the primary water mains, to sewer mains (where applicable), and to major road arteries. McCulloch finances the secondary "in-tract" construction work. According to the 1974 federal Property Report, this work will be completed either four years from the date when McCulloch records the lot with Pueblo County or within ninety days after the buyer's receipt of a building permit and application for water services. (The buyer could not apply for water services until he or she had received title-- usually ten years after signing the original purchase agreement.) The federal Property Report does not contain any schedule for completion of the District's development responsibilities.

It now appears doubtful whether the District will be able to make good on its share of McCulloch's promises to Pueblo West's lot purchasers. While some of the work is fairly advanced--the sewage system is 80% complete, for example--other basic tasks, like building a drainage system, have barely been tackled. Furthermore, the District faces two serious problems. One is finding a sufficient source of water for the domestic system. (See discussion under Water.) The other is finding the money to pay for everything for which McCulloch has made it responsible.

Among its other burdens, the Pueblo West Metropolitan District is a victim of poor planning by McCulloch's engineering firm, Trico Colorado, Inc. Less than two-and-a-half years after the County's approval of Trico's Service Plan for the District, the Plan underwent significant modification. Trico's April, 1972, Revised Service Plan contained four alterations. First, allocated funds were cut from each of the Plan's seven development categories (although the budget total for the District's full development responsibilities at Pueblo West remained at the originally authorized $37,075,000). Sewerage funding was cut the most--by $6,571,899. These cuts were effected to enable creation of an eighth, formerly ignored, category--Water Rights--requiring an estimated additional expenditure of $8,455,000, an amount added to the $15 million already allocated in the first Service Plan for supplying Pueblo West's water needs. Second, the site's total population estimate was revised downward from 65,000 in the year 2020 to 40,000, projecting fewer people ultimately to carry the District's debt.* Third, the four phases of site construction originally envisioned were abandoned. Fourth, the cost of the planned sewerage system, based now on the District's receipt of a 60% grant-in-aid from the federal government, was recomputed.[50]

According to a former member of the District's board, abandoning the original plan of phasing development with sales has created particular problems for the overtaxed District.[51] Under the 1969 Plan, Phase I, which consisted of 14,310 acres-- all the Pueblo West land south of U.S. 50 and a small portion of contiguous land just to its north--was to be "fully improved to its maximum potential" between 1969 and 1979.[52] The land in Phases II, III, and IV would be sold "in acreage blocks of not less than 5 acres for the buyer's ultimate resubdivision...."[53] Its use would "be restricted...until predetermined dates [1980, 1985, and 1990] when utilities and improved roads will be provided."[54] "Probably," the former board member said, "lots in Phase I sold so well that McCulloch decided to open up the other phases. [McCulloch's cash-flow needs may also have prompted this decision.] Now we have 50 square miles with buildings going up everywhere. It's very expensive to extend water and sewer lines like this, helter-skelter."[55]

Trico's 1972 Revised Service Plan called for the District to complete all its development responsibilities by 1980, stating that the District "has determined that the phased development program originally contemplated...was not in the best interest of the public or the District."[56] However, the former board member pointed out that this 1972 revision of the original Service Plan was undertaken at a time when the District's board was still composed entirely of McCulloch and Trico members.

From the financial perspective of Pueblo West lot purchasers today, very little of either Service Plan was actually in the best interests of the public or the District. According to a Pueblo West resident in 1974, lot purchasers "have been burdened with doing a substantial amount of the community's development without being forewarned....We thought the costs of development came out of the costs of the lots, which are high; but instead we found out that we picked up an additional burden, which we were not informed of."[57]

This theme of disillusioned discovery was reiterated to INFORM by numerous District landowners. The District's current lawyer explained, "The problem is that it is implied to the lot purchaser that the improvements are in. The purchaser doesn't understand that he's retiring the District's debt."[58]

---

*McCulloch data sent to INFORM in 1976 projects a final population of 65,000 for Pueblo West, but without a target date.

The 1974 federal Property Report filed on Pueblo West does describe the District, list its numerous obligations, and discuss the amount of its authorized debt. It also states, "This debt will be retired from revenues from service charges (primarily from the sale of water and sewer service charges) and funds derived from ad valorem property taxes."[59] However, the Property Report does not inform a purchaser that the District is (and was in 1974) having serious problems meeting its financial obligations to its bondholders. A former member of the board noted in 1974 that at that time the District's financial exigencies demanded that "we not issue any further bonds, and not spend money extending roads and water to remote areas. McCulloch had promised HUD that four years after a tract was opened up the roads and utilities would be in, but some areas had no people so we stopped honoring it--we'll put in utilities when the people are in."[60] (The District's subsequent negotiations with McCulloch tempered the definitiveness of these resolutions.)

The federal Property Report does not, moreover, inform the buyer that as part of the District property, his lot serves as legal collateral for the District's debts, i.e., that the District's indebtedness constitutes "a perpetual [and first] lien" on all property in the District.[61] Finally, the federal Property Report does not inform the buyer that if service and use fees are insufficient to "provide for the payment of all District expenses, including payment of operating and maintaining water and sanitary sewer systems and other public works and the maturing principal of and interest on the bonds [outstanding], the District has a mandatory duty to levy an annual ad valorem tax [essentially a property tax]--*without limitation as to rate or amount*" (emphasis added), as the Bond Statement notes.[62]

Furthermore, disclosures in a federal Property Report have less impact on most potential buyers than the lot-salesman's declarations. According to a District official interviewed in 1974, salesmen tell purchasers that "the cost of a lot includes all utilities, services, etc."[63] Another lot owner noted that "the salesmen work on a straight commission, so they'll say anything to sell a lot....You're led to believe that lots cost so much because the utilities are in."[64]

As those concerned with Pueblo West's future have discovered, using a multi-service district to finance and construct initial improvements for a totally undeveloped site of this size entails considerable risk. If the financial apparatus on which the whole community relies for its principal improvements is not to break down, a large tax base must be rapidly established within the community. Such a tax base has not developed at Pueblo West.*

So far McCulloch has been reluctantly assisting the District. In June, 1973, McCulloch agreed to advance almost $4 million for bond principal and interest repayment due from 1977 to 1986 (related to purchase of water). The understanding is that between 1979 and 1989 the District will reimburse McCulloch for the principal only.[65] In 1975, McCulloch advanced another $500,223 to the District for payments of bond principal due and contributed $203,427 for interest due.[66]

There is no guarantee, however, that it will continue to make such contributions. In 1975, negotiations between McCulloch and the District were begun "as to which party was responsible for the cost of certain capital improvements made and to be made within the District."[67] As of the end of 1975, the parties had not reached an agreement on this question. The District then threatened to take McCulloch to court over the original formation and debt authorization of the District but in fact took no legal action.[68] For its part, McCulloch agreed to underwrite the District's projected 1976 operating deficit of $121,000. It also agreed to guarantee repayment of "interest and principal maturities on the outstanding portion of the proposed 1976 Series A of general obligation bonds"[69] if the district could not do so from its revenues over the 20-year life of the issue.† "If McCulloch didn't assist us every year," a lot owner interviewed by INFORM stated, "we'd have to double our tax rate, and it's already very high. Our tax base is so low we're going to tax ourselves out of existence unless we get a lot of building in the next five years."[71] From McCulloch's point of view, as a company official commented in early 1976, "The District's responsibilities are in the Service Plan, and the District didn't want to accept what's in there; now [following lengthy negotiations] it has agreed to."[72] The District, which has had three different managers in the last few years, several board resignations, and, recently, a board recall initiated by its members,

---

*One reason for Lake Havasu City's avoidance of Pueblo West's problems, aside from the promotional extravaganzas showered on it by McCulloch, may be that Lake Havasu City is designed for a much higher population density. The same tax base will bear the costs of funding improvements for an area nearly one-half Pueblo West's size, i.e. 18,000 acres at Lake Havasu City as opposed to 30,000 acres at Pueblo West.

†The debt service (8%) on the $675,000 in bonds issued by the District--March, 1976--brings their total cost (payable annually to 1995) up to $1,481,800.[70]

has found its position astride increasingly conflicting interests a difficult one.

Water

As of mid-1976, Pueblo West still faces serious problems with the quantity and quality of its water supply. Obtaining water is proving extremely expensive: the Pueblo West Metropolitan District is spending close to $7 million just to acquire rights to a surface-water supply.[73] While McCulloch is currently helping the District with some of these costs, as noted, it is not legally obligated to continue doing so.

In the first Service Plan for the District, McCulloch anticipated that water for Pueblo West's initial residents would come from wells, tapping local groundwater. According to that Plan, McCulloch hoped ultimately to purchase surface water from the Southeastern Colorado Water Conservancy District (SCWCD), which delivers Fryingpan-Arkansas Project water to stipulated members. Obtaining water from either of these sources has proved far more difficult, however, than McCulloch or its engineering firm envisioned.

Although Pueblo West was annexed to the SCWCD in February, 1971, it was clear that water would not be obtainable from the Water Conservancy District in the foreseeable future. According to the resolution adopted by the SCWCD's board of directors including Pueblo West in the District, Pueblo West will "not be eligible to purchase Fryingpan-Arkansas Project water until after all other eligible purchasers have been satisfied although Pueblo West could rent space in Pueblo Reservoir for such other waters they may acquire." The resolution added that "if the Arkansas Project is altered or enlarged, McCulloch Properties, Inc. will be eligible to participate as will all other eligible beneficiaries within the District."[74]

Commenting on the region's overall water shortage, a SCWCD official affirmed in early 1976:

> This year we [the SCWCD] have 10,000 acre feet of water to sell; and we have applications for over 39,000 acre feet. Pueblo West is so junior [in its water rights] that it just couldn't get project water from us; and it found this out rather late.[75]

The 1972 Revised Service Plan for Pueblo West's District therefore indicated that the District would be sticking to the alternative of obtaining water from wells. The Plan stated:

> The District is continuing its groundwater
> development program, and it is expected that
> the present sources of water supply will
> adequately serve the District's needs for
> the next 25 years.*[76]

Relying on local groundwater, however, has created serious practical and financial difficulties for the District, for the community, and for McCulloch. These problems could have been avoided had McCulloch's initial hydrological research and planning been more thorough and realistic.†

An SCWCD official has recently described how McCulloch decided that groundwater would adequately supply Pueblo West in spite of warnings to the contrary:

> They [Robert McCulloch, Jr. and C. V. Woods] came to Pueblo some time in 1968 and proposed taking tributary waters from the Arkansas River and pumping them from the ground. That's what they'd done at Lake Havasu City--extracted river water from the ground. I tried to tell them they couldn't do that here. For one thing, the topography and hydrology around Pueblo Reservoir is not the same as along the Colorado River. Furthermore, in Arizona they permit the use of pumps along a river. We don't. I told them that our water laws, and the whole issue of water availability, was very different in this state, but, of course, they thought they could ignore this. I talked to various company people a number of times and tried to warn them. Finally McCulloch officials told me, right here in my own office, that I was small potatoes compared to what they could do--that they could go to the legislature and

---

*This new Service Plan projected a population of 15,000 at Pueblo West in 1997.

†The 1972 Revised Service Plan explains that this decision, which was incorporated into the 1969 Service Plan for the District, had been based on "the geological reports of the District's consultant."[77] However, the first Service Plan for the development of Pueblo West was published before the District had even been established, at which time any geological consultants were surely working for McCulloch.

>   get the laws amended. (They hadn't researched
>   Colorado's water laws, or its availability.)
>   The problem is that the water just isn't
>   here--we're overappropriated now, like we
>   were then.[78]

In Colorado, all water "tributary" to a river, including underground water, is allocated according to a system of water rights wherein first priority for its use is given to those with the oldest (most senior) rights.

Because of Colorado's increasingly rigorous regulation of its surface water and tributary groundwater, the Pueblo West Metropolitan District has had to sink very deep wells which would draw on the Dakota Aquifer--an underground water-bearing stratum, or layer, which is not tributary to any river. The water from this Aquifer varies greatly in quality. The Draft Environmental Statement for the Bureau of Reclamation's Fryingpan-Arkansas Project warned that desalinization would be necessary before water from deep aquifers in the Pueblo area could be used.[79] Pumping this water from deep wells has proved expensive, and the Pueblo West Metropolitan District has had to build costly treatment plants to remove iron and manganese from its groundwater. In addition, the portion of the Dakota Aquifer underlying Pueblo West produces not only poor-quality water, but very little of it.[80]

According to data from McCulloch, and Trico Colorado, Inc. (Pueblo West's engineering firm), the District has drilled nineteen wells to date.* Only six have produced enough high-quality water--following treatment by three plants--to provide Pueblo West with a central supply.[82] The general manager of Trico recently explained that "it was economically unfeasible to treat the water from the thirteen unused wells because of its poor quality."[83] In addition, under legislation passed in 1973, Colorado's State Engineer has imposed a limit on the amount of water each operating well may pull from a non-tributary aquifer.[84] Trico states that the capacity of the District's six operating wells, which provide the sole water source for Pueblo West's existing central system, "is 600,000 to 800,000 gallons per day depending on different variables having to do with the draw-down censors on the wells. These shut the pumps off at a certain point of withdrawal."[85] (McCulloch company data submitted

---

*The Revised Service Plan states that eighteen wells had been drilled at that time. Another was to follow in 1973 and four others in 1973-74.[81] The District has not been able to meet this schedule.[81]

to INFORM used the 600,000 gallons per day figure.)* Thus, Pueblo West's existing water system is sufficient, with no supplementary industrial uses, for a population of only 4,000 people using an average of 150 gallons per person per day. Yet the community's projected population is 15,000 in 1997 and 65,000 when fully built-out. A Trico general manager succinctly summarized Pueblo West's unhappy state of affairs. "Groundwater," he said, "simply can't support this community--not ultimately."[87]

Shortly after the 1969 Pueblo West Service Plan was published, McCulloch apparently recognized that its "geological consultant" might have reported overly optimistic projections of site groundwater supplies and that another source should be sought. As early as 1970, according to a *Rocky Mountain News* article, Tom Farley, who as noted was then the lawyer for McCulloch and the Metropolitan District, started "negotiating with a group of Crowley County farmers called the Twin Lakes Reservoir and Canal Company on behalf of Pueblo West for [surface] water rights."[88] His negotiations were successfully completed in 1972. The Revised Service Plan for Pueblo West's District explained that:

> To assure an adequate long-term water supply for the District, it has become apparent that the District should at this time purchase additional transmountain water....This purchase... will require the expenditure of approximately $5.4 million plus interest.†[90]

By means of this expenditure Pueblo West obtained the right to 5,618.41 shares of the Twin Lakes Reservoir and Canal Company's west slope water, according to an official with that company. He explained that since a share normally averages 1.2 acre-feet

---

*The 1976 Bond Statement Series A grossly misrepresents the permissible supply capability of Pueblo West's water system by stating, "To date, 19 production wells, capable of producing 1,965 gallons of water per minute, have been completed by the District. Six of the wells are connected to three treatment plants."[86] This statement generates the conclusion that all nineteen wells are in use and that the per-day production capacity of Pueblo West's water system is 2,829,600 gallons--approximately 4.7 times more than the existing wells can, or are legally allowed, to produce!

†A former member of the District's board cautioned in July, 1976, that this figure does not reflect the full costs of purchase and delivery, which were still "unknown."[89]

of water a year--although the amount of water a share obtains
can vary according to seasonal water flow--Pueblo West has an
annual allotment of 6,724 acre-feet. This amount is adequate
for a population of 39,000 at 150 gallons per person per day.
Under the terms of the agreement with Pueblo West, its shares
were purchased under contract for up to fourteen years, with
payments beginning in 1974.* During the fourteen-year period,
the sellers have first right to the water's use each year if
they request it by a certain date. Upon the District's completion of payments in 1986, Pueblo West will have first right.[93]

Several problems complicating the District's actual use of
this water are mentioned in neither McCulloch's nor the District's published materials. First, most of the Twin Lakes Company's water rights are designated agricultural rights. Under
Colorado law, water rights are classified according to use, and
agricultural water cannot be used for municipal purposes. The
water company has been in court for several years trying to get
a "change-in-use" that would render its water rights "municipal."
For some of the company's rights, the change has been granted,
but the U.S. Forest Service is contesting the change for other
company-owned rights. "There's just not enough water out here,"
the company official said, "there's a battle all the time."[94] If
the court does not grant the change, Pueblo West could find itself with some portion of its dearly bought surface water legally available only for farming.

However, the major problem with the surface water Tom
Farley acquired for the District is its potential total cost,
which includes the expense of transporting it from the Pueblo
Reservoir, where the District may store it, to the community of
Pueblo West. The 1974 federal Property Report states that Mc-
Culloch "has agreed to advance up to $6,685,000 to the Pueblo
West Metropolitan District *for the purchase of water rights*
[emphasis added]...of which $706,800 was paid in 1973. [Accord-
ing to the 1975 Prospectus for McCulloch Properties Credit Corporation, the District paid another $694,000 in 1974.] Of the
$6,685,000, $5,151,000 is repayable by the District commencing
in 1979 and is secured by the water rights."[95]

This amount may not meet the additional cost of transporting the water. During the four years that followed publication
of the Revised Service Plan, the Metropolitan District and Mc-

---

*There is a discrepancy between the existing figures describing
the exact number of shares purchased. The 1972 Revised Service
Plan states that negotiations were for 5,280 shares.[91] The 1976
Bond Statement Series A states that 5,381.08 shares were purchased.[92]

Culloch tried to devise a means of avoiding the construction of their own individual delivery system for this water. The 1972 Revised Service Plan discussed the possible options:

> ...we have provided funds [in the budget] for a direct lake intake, the pumping equipment, and transmission lines necessary [to deliver the] water to the District and the construction of a treatment plant within the District. This portion of the program, totalling $1,635,000, may never be used in this manner since it is quite probable that the District will enter into an agreement with the city of Pueblo Water Board or the Conservancy District that will provide for the treatment and transmission of water on a joint venture basis.[96]

Whether Pueblo West has to construct an independent system or can participate in a joint venture, the cost will be high. The question remains undecided whether McCulloch or the Metropolitan District will bear the greater portion of this cost. In an effort to prod the District to undertake this responsibility, McCulloch has guaranteed an $800,000 grant towards whatever option the District chooses.[97]

As of 1976, the city of Pueblo had not agreed to a "joint venture." The District has, however, recently received permission to include its water in another joint transmission system, the ninety-mile Fountain Valley conduit line for the Fryingpan-Arkansas Project water being delivered to Colorado Springs and four other local communities in the Southeastern Colorado Water Conservancy District. But the Fountain Valley line, which has already been rerouted by the Bureau of Reclamation to run through Pueblo West, will have to be enlarged for several miles to carry Pueblo West's water. This enlargement, plus the additional pumping required, would raise the cost involved for all participants, who must share the cost burden equally.[98] Needless to say, the other participants are not eager to carry the extra charges. According to a Bureau of Reclamation official, the pipeline cost was previously estimated at $40 million without including Pueblo West's water. The Bureau is now drawing up new cost estimates.[99] When they are finalized, the Metropolitan District will have to study them, compare them to the cost of other alternatives, and decide what it wants to, or can, do.

Negotiations between the District, the four SCWCD communities, and the Bureau of Reclamation have been under way since 1972 over this matter of water delivery. According to an official with the SCWCD, Pueblo West's water problems present "...a really desperate situation that simply never should have been."[100] It is the opinion of this Conservancy District that "for economic reasons, in all probability...[Pueblo West] will not participate in using that [Fountain Valley conduit] line."[101]

While McCulloch has lost some major skirmishes in its various water battles at state and local levels, it still has its old allies on the federal level, and so it may have one more option for transporting its surface water from the Pueblo Reservoir up to Pueblo West. The District may be able to obtain a long-term loan at low interest through the Bureau of Reclamation to aid in the construction of its own pipeline system. A Bureau of Reclamation official explained, "Our principal objective is to deliver water for irrigation needs, but under the Fryingpan-Arkansas Project authorization act, as well as under reclamation law, we can fund the construction of facilities for the development of municipal water supplies."[102] A former member of the board of the Pueblo West Metropolitan District pointed out, "There is [already] a tap in Pueblo Dam that might be available to us."[103] If the other alternatives currently under consideration by the District prove to be costly, the Bureau's offer may be the one Pueblo West can't refuse.

The Pueblo West Metropolitan District has been able to handle the simpler problem of installing the community's internal water-delivery lines better than it has the complicated issue of water supply itself. Aided by McCulloch's financial assistance, line extension has proceeded at a relatively fast pace. According to data from McCulloch and from Trico Colorado, Inc., 264 miles of water lines have been laid, serving approximately 65% of the total community. The major portion has been installed in the land area south of U.S. 50, the area which comprised Phase I in the 1969 Service Plan. Of the 777 building permits issued at Pueblo West as of December 31, 1975, 708 are for homesites which have water connections to the District's central system.

The cumulative cost to the Pueblo West lot owner for water delivery is considerable. The 1972 Revised Service Plan recommended a "water connection charge of $140 per single-family residence...."[104] But as of January 1, 1976, the District had to charge $490. This cost is scheduled to increase annually until it reaches $750.[105] (In contrast, the same charge at Lake Havasu City is $110.) In addition, a purchaser must pay a monthly "readiness-to-serve charge" of $1.50 as well as $0.85 per thousand gallons of water used. Two years after water lines are installed, the District charges all lots--whether titled, purchased under contract, or still owned by McCulloch--an annual fee of $24.

In spite of Pueblo West's overall water-supply problems, its District agreed under an "interim arrangement" made with the Bureau of Reclamation in 1975 to supply water to the Pueblo Reservoir's North Shore Recreation Area.[106] One of several recreation areas planned around the Reservoir, the North Shore was the first to be completed. It lies adjacent to Pueblo West's southern boundary. (See discussion under Roads.) Before this area opened in 1975, the Bureau of Reclamation paid Pueblo West's District to construct a two-inch water line from the community's water system to the federal land.* The District can interrupt this supply if it interferes with Pueblo West's needs and according to a former District board member, the North Shore Area "will pay a little more [than Pueblo West] for the water it uses."[107] The Bureau's project manager added that the Pueblo West District will provide water only until the Bureau can "consummate its contract with the city of Pueblo to tie into its water lines."[108] However, this transfer to Pueblo city water is expected to cost several million dollars, funds the Bureau of Reclamation has still to request from the U.S. Congress.[109]

In view of the range of complicated issues relating to Pueblo West's water supply, it is surely a gross oversimplification to assert, as does the federal Property Report for Pueblo West, that "Water is available to the subdivision and the supply is adequate to serve the anticipated population."[110] Apparently, McCulloch salesmen have also made misleading statements about Pueblo West's water supply. In 1976, Southeastern Colorado Water Conservancy District officials told INFORM that Pueblo West's salesmen had frequently exaggerated to many prospective purchasers the importance of the District's membership in the SCWCD. "They used us so heavily--and there wasn't any basis in fact for what they were saying. It wasn't fair to the people buying at all."[111]

Sewage

The 1972 Revised Service Plan calls for the District to develop a central sewage system comprised of three secondary-level treatment plants. The system is to service 7,893 lots--encompassing about 25% of Pueblo West's 30,000 acres[112]--including all residential lots under one acre in size and all

---

*The open portion of the North Shore Recreation Area has been turned over to the Colorado Division of Parks for management and administration, but the federal Bureau of Reclamation funds and installs improvements as Congress appropriates money for the project.

commercial, all industrial, and all multi-family residential lots. As with the development plan of Pueblo West's water system, MPI is to install the "in-tract" sewer-collection lines (i.e., subsidiary, but not major, mains) for the serviced lots within four to ten years from the date of a tract's recordation or sale. As of March, 1976, the District had extended a hundred miles of primary sewer lines to 6,500 lots, making its system about 80% complete. Of the approximately 700 buildings at Pueblo West, 400 are currently serviced by the central sewage system.

The first of the three planned "activated sludge process" plants went into operation in January, 1972. It is designed to treat the sewage from homes on 3,500 acres and to process 150,000 gallons per day; it currently treats an average of 80,000 gallons per day.[113] The plant effluent is already used to irrigate the community's golf course,* and surplus effluent will be sold to agricultural users as an extra source of revenue for the District.[115]

The cost to resident property owners of connecting to the central sewage system has risen dramatically in the last four years. This cost increase indicates once again the difficulty confronting a District whose population is disproportionately small compared to its development obligations. In 1972 the District charged $125 for a sewer connection;[116] in 1976 the charge had risen to $585. (The 1976 charge at Lake Havasu City amounts to $175.) In addition, the District charges all lots (titled, under contract, or not sold) a $16 "availability of service" fee when sewer facilities have been available for over two years, and there is a monthly sewer charge, not to exceed $10 maximum, for single-family residences.

For the 75% of Pueblo West lots which will not be serviced by the central system, septic tanks constitute the only option. An individual septic system at the site costs between $450 and $1,500, depending on whether the County Health Department allows a conventional system to be installed or requires a more sophisticated one to handle drainage problems within the lot.

Solid Waste

No special provisions have been made by McCulloch for solid-waste disposal at Pueblo West. Regular commercial pickup

---

*According to the 1972 Revised Service Plan for the Metropolitan District, "an 18 hole golf course will use up to one million gallons per day, which is the sewered population equivalent of 10,000 people."[114]

service is available at a $4-a-month charge. A landfill is maintained by the County.

Roads

"The roads are a big problem out at Pueblo West," an official with Pueblo County's Air Pollution Control Division recently remarked, "and as it grows it'll get worse, unless they can keep up with the paving."[117] To date, 782 miles of road have been cut through Pueblo West's 30,000 acres, but only 115 miles are paved. Another 238 miles are "gravel improved," and 429 miles are "graded."

Following the basic master plan for the community's development, McCulloch intended to install the in-tract roads within either four or ten years of a tract's recordation or sale. The District was made responsible for installing the subdivision's main traffic arteries and for maintaining all of Pueblo West's roads (subdivision and in-tract) until accepted by Pueblo County for maintenance.

Because of its overextended financial situation, the District has told McCulloch that it cannot maintain the roads.[118] Consequently, McCulloch has undertaken this job while pressing the County to accept the roads for County maintenance. But the County, which has its own financial problems, is loath to do so, at least partly because the roads were not built to present County standards.

Some Pueblo West roads have been accepted for maintenance in the past by the County Road Commissioner, but since they were not accepted by the Board of Commissioners, the County insists they were not legally accepted. Negotiations to determine who must maintain Pueblo West's roads have been in progress for some time and have been intensified by a McCulloch threat to take the County to court.[119]

A secondary issue involving roads at Pueblo West highlights once again the long-term cooperative relationship between McCulloch and the Bureau of Reclamation. Back in June, 1970, when the initial contract for the construction of Pueblo Dam was awarded, the County made an agreement with the contractor that Nicholls Road--a County road running through the old Nicholls Ranch--would be the haul road used to carry construction material for the Dam. This agreement stipulated that the contractor would improve the road. "For some reason," according to one of Pueblo's County Commissioners,"the contractor's mind was changed and other [non-County] roads through Pueblo West [i.e., Metropolitan District roads] were used for this purpose, and then paved."[120]

In 1975, the Bureau of Reclamation used the availability of road access through Pueblo West into the adjacent North Shore Recreation Area to justify completing and opening this park space prior to another area on the other side of the Pueblo Dam, ten miles closer to the city of Pueblo.[121] The latter "Arkansas Point" park is scheduled to open in 1976. But, according to the Bureau of Reclamation's project manager, "Our priorities for development remain on the Northern area. There will be a fairly minimal level of development at Arkansas Point for the next few years."[122] (Most of the approximately $5 million the Bureau of Reclamation has spent to date for Pueblo Reservoir recreation facilities has been expended on the North Shore Area adjacent to Pueblo West.)[123]

Drainage

Pueblo West's drainage system is currently inadequate. According to company data sent to INFORM, the little work done to date has provided an interim system only designed for a five-year storm capacity. Many planners recommend designing drainage systems to handle the flows from a 100-year storm (see Guidelines) and McCulloch indicated to INFORM that it hopes that the system will "ultimately" be upgraded to that level.

Electricity and Telephone

Two different private utility companies supply electricity to Pueblo West. The cost of extending service to an unserved lot will depend on its distance from existing lines and on type of terrain new lines must traverse.

Telephone service is supplied by Mountain Bell, but according to the 1974 federal Property Report, "There is no schedule for telephone installation... [and] costs are borne by Buyer."[124] In this situation a lot purchaser whose lot is not near existing telephone lines could find the cost of installation prohibitive.

According to MPI, electric and telephone lines have been extended to about 25% of all lots.

COMMUNITY AND RECREATIONAL FACILITIES

Like the site's basic services, Pueblo West's community and recreational facilities are feeling the pinch of inadequate financial resources. Police protection, originally part of the Metropolitan District's list of responsibilities, was eliminated from that list by the 1969 amendments to Colorado's Metropolitan District Act. Consequently, the responsibility fell to the County Sheriff's Office, which for a time was unable to provide adequate protection. Sporadic vandalism at the community led to the formation of a vigilante group. As of mid-1976, the Sheriff's Office had increased its supervision of the area, and the crime rate has since declined.[125]

Fire protection still falls under the District's aegis, but financial and other problems have led to reliance on a volunteer station located in the center of the District. In 1973 the District's fire-protection efforts did result in a reduction in the cost of residential fire insurance.[126]

A primary school for 600 students opened at Pueblo West in 1974. Enrollment in 1975 was 213. Other schools are located about ten miles from the site.

The city of Pueblo, approximately ten miles from the community's center, maintains two hospitals and has numerous medical and dental services.

A small shopping center is located on the site. The community's proximity to Pueblo provides residents with access to other retail stores.

No public transportation is currently available between the city of Pueblo and Pueblo West. The former has airline and bus service.

Much of the area left as open space for drainage purposes is planned for equestrian trails. (Two separate riding centers are located on Pueblo West land.) There is a golf and tennis club owned and built by MPI, and the District is nearing completion of a 21-acre park, which includes a community swimming pool.

ENVIRONMENTAL PROTECTION

One problem in protecting the environment at Pueblo West is that little attention has been paid by anyone to the potential short- or long-term environmental effects of Pueblo West's growth. The U.S. Army Corps of Engineers pointed out in its review of the Bureau of Reclamation's Final Environmental Impact Statement on Pueblo Dam and Reservoir that "since...Pueblo West was sited because of its proximity to Pueblo Reservoir, the statement might be strengthened by acknowledging the environmental impact of the community of 60,000 people."[127] The Bureau of Reclamation responded:

> The discussion acknowledges that Pueblo West
> and other developments* may result in pollu-
> tants being introduced into the reservoir
> via storm drainage. This is not anticipated
> to be a significant problem due to the arid
> climate, the natural desert theme of the
> area, and high water rates discouraging
> residential lawn establishment. Increased
> air pollution, solid waste problems, and
> aesthetic impairment will occur to some
> degree as a high plains grassland area is
> converted into urban developments. Pueblo
> West is a good example of a new master-
> planned city which is a unified residential-
> recreational-light industrial complex with
> a "21st century" concept of spacious country
> living.[128]

In fact, McCulloch's record in the area of environmental protection, as in the area of extending basic services, is mixed. While it has made some good decisions in terms of the basic layout of the site, it appears to have simply not considered problems of environmental impact such as wind erosion from unpaved roads, and water pollution from runoff and septic tanks.

PLANNING

One of the principal environmental problems at Pueblo West results from McCulloch's failure to phase development or cluster buildings. Pueblo West now has more than 600 miles of unpaved roads spread over the entire subdivision. The District's difficulty in maintaining these roads was not foreseen. Nor was the dire effect of the region's climate on them considered. The high winds characteristic of this region have not only caused erosion but created bad dust storms. As indicated above, the Air Pollution Control Division in Pueblo County considers these unpaved roads "one of the biggest problems" in the area.[129]

Most planners recommend that 25% of a site be left for recreation, parks, and open-space use. McCulloch's allocation of just 16% of the total acreage at Pueblo West for such uses is inadequate, although it is better than the allocations of some other subdividers in this study. In addition, included

---

*This reference is to the so-called Liberty Point development, which has been incorporated into Pueblo West.

in the 16% open, park, and recreation space are approximately
65 miles of natural drainageways, many of which are dry washes.
Leaving these undisturbed is a sound practice. Regarding
McCulloch's general planning process for this subdivision,
no environmental impact report was required and none was
prepared.

LAND

The Pueblo West site contains no areas of critical environmental concern and only one type of area which is hazardous for building: the drainage washes noted above, which are preserved as open space. Pueblo West will thus create no problems due to building on inappropriate lands. INFORM also found no evidence of unnecessary devegetation or alteration of topography at Pueblo West apart from the blading of roads.

WATER RESOURCES

There is, however, the potential for Pueblo West to adversely affect local water resources, primarily the quality of the water in the Pueblo Reservoir. A U.S. Department of Agriculture Soil Conservation Service official in Pueblo pointed out that most of Pueblo West's land area consists of rolling plains, and intense rainstorms are infrequent.[130] Runoff is thus not likely to be extremely heavy. However, no holding ponds have been built or other measures taken to minimize the flow of eroded dirt and other pollutants from Pueblo West into the Pueblo Reservoir below it. McCulloch also appears to have undertaken no program for replanting vegetation in disturbed areas to prevent erosion.

Pueblo West's major adverse impact on water resources may result from the developing community's heavy reliance--almost 12,000 lots--on individual septic systems for sewage disposal. According to a County health official, about 10% of the land area at Pueblo West is markedly unsuited for conventional septic use. Rock outcroppings and a thin soil mantle will likely result in the leaching of sewage into the groundwater below.[131] Prior to Colorado's 1972 subdivision regulations, lots smaller than one acre were allowed to-use septic systems, and a few were installed at Pueblo West.

The County health official stated that there had been some failure among existing systems.[132] (A 1971 letter from the County Health Department to the Colorado State Department of

Health noted that there had been observed instances of effluent coming to the surface from improperly installed leach fields.)[133] The State Department of Health has assured some regulation of septic-tank use by characterizing about 75% of the Pueblo West site "a designated area."[134] This means that each lot owner must obtain approval of the use and location of an individual system from the County's Health Department before it can be installed. The system must also be designed by a licensed engineer.

As mentioned above, the Colorado State Engineer presently regulates Pueblo West's use of groundwater to prevent overdrafts.

CONSUMER PROTECTION

McCulloch's consumer protection practices at Pueblo West are poor compared to those at other subdivisions in the INFORM sample. While McCulloch advertises Pueblo West as a new community, promotes its lots as homesites, indicates in its property reports that central water and other basic services will be available, and prices the lots accordingly, it nevertheless provides no guarantees that these services will ever be extended to all lots. As discussed earlier, a mechanism for installing the major water, road, sewer, and drainage systems has been created in the form of the Pueblo West Metropolitan District. However, this independent quasi-governmental entity is not legally bound to fulfill McCulloch's promises.

By contrast, Dart Industries, another subdivider in the INFORM sample, completed virtually all improvements at its Tahoe Donner and Bear Valley Springs developments at its own expense within five years after it began marketing lots.

Sales

For the most part McCulloch's sales policies are designed neither to discourage speculation nor to ensure that a lot buyer is well informed about his or her purchase. Although McCulloch encourages potential buyers to visit the site before buying a lot (one of INFORM's recommended consumer-protection practices), the company takes none of the other eleven steps recommended in INFORM's guidelines for consumer protection (see Consumer Checklist, Sales). Dart--again by contrast--employs up to eight good consumer practices at each of its subdivisions.

McCulloch sells all of its lots by installment contract, as do most retail land-sales companies. Its contracts call for downpayments of approximately 15% of the total purchase price, followed by monthly payments comprising the balance, with 6% to 9% interest. Payments are made over a ten-year period. While the 15% initial downpayment is actually higher than the 10% required by most subdividers studied by INFORM, it is still lower than the INFORM guideline of 20%, which would further tend to limit speculation.

Once a lot-sales contract is signed, McCulloch will not refund any payments unless required to by law. The only refund or rescission option available to purchasers is thus one required by state regulations, or the three-day rescission right following a buyer's receipt of the Property Report, as mandated by federal law but considered inadequate by INFORM.

After the three-day rescission period has elapsed, the buyer who defaults forfeits everything he has paid, including any fees or ad valorem taxes paid to the Pueblo West Metropolitan District. Nonpayment of the latter, when due, also constitutes default. Further, the lot buyer's payments are not escrowed, an action which would ensure that if a refund were necessary, the money would be there to return.

The list of INFORM-recommended practices which McCulloch has further failed to observe includes the following: the company conducts no credit check on prospective purchasers to be sure they can handle the investments they plan to make. It places no limitation on the number of residential lots purchasers can buy and none on buying commercial or industrial lots for "investment" purposes. The company does not encourage an independent closer or a buyer's attorney to be present at the contract's signing in an advisory capacity, nor does it encourage the purchaser to review his contract and federal Property Report with any attorney "unless," according to McCulloch, "the subject arises prior to the buyer visiting the site."[135] All of these practices not adopted by McCulloch would ensure better informed buyers and encourage lot purchases aimed at real use of the resource rather than at wishful speculation.

Title Protection

The purchaser's title to the land he is buying on an installment contract at Pueblo West is not fully protected. Although all lots offered for sale are platted with the County, the installment contract is not in a recordable form, so there is no way of recording the buyer's interest in the property with the County. MPI does place title in trust during the payment period, affording the buyer some protection, although it is not transferred until all payments are completed.

The consumer does have the option of entering into a less hazardous, more equitable purchase agreement. If he puts a third of the purchase price down, MPI will transfer title immediately in an arrangement similar to a mortgage. Under such an arrangement, the purchaser is able to use the lot during the contract period and is protected against losing title in the event of subdivider bankruptcy.

While the deeds conveying title are encumbered by restrictions and easements, the latter will not "affect the Buyer's beneficial use and enjoyment of his property," according to the 1974 federal Property Report.[136]

Costs

Prices for Pueblo West's lots range from $6,000 to $17,000 for the one- to five-acre parcels; $10,000 to $35,000 for the commercial lots; and $9,000 to $55,000 for the quarter- to one-acre multi-family residential lots. The multi-family lots are some of the most expensive in the INFORM sample. Industrial lots sell for about $15,000 an acre.

Contract payments on a Pueblo West residential lot include annual taxes even though a purchaser has not received title to his lot. These taxes are based on the improved value reflected in the lot's purchase price. Up until 1976, Pueblo County assessed Pueblo West lots at 30% of 30% of the sales price. Starting this year they will be assessed simply at 30% of the sales price.* The tax rate is $110.51 or $112.86 per $1,000 of assessed valuation depending on the lot's location in one of two school districts at Pueblo West. Thus, on a $6,000 lot a purchaser under contract in 1976 will have to pay taxes of about $200 annually (as opposed to $88.40 in 1973). Over the ten-year term of an installment contract, these tax payments add $2,000 to the basic purchase price.

Included in the general tax rate is the Metropolitan District's ad valorem tax imposed on all lots in the District.

As noted previously, if water and sewer services are extended to a lot, a lot purchaser, as well as a titled lot owner, must pay an annual availability fee of $24.00 and $16.00

---

*However, according to an official at the County Assessor's Office, platted lots which have not been sold, on which McCulloch must pay the tax, are assessed at a lower (unspecified) rate until 50% of all the platted lots in a tract are purchased under contract. Then McCulloch's lots are also assessed at their improved value.[137]

respectively, starting two years after the service becomes available. These fees are charged even if service is not used. As noted above, another $490.00 and $585.00 must be paid for water and sewer connections when use is desired.

Inasmuch as a purchaser is not allowed to use his lot until receipt of title and may not vote in District elections until he is a titled property owner and a resident of Colorado, these extra costs incurred during the term of a contract payment are essentially all part of the lot's price from a purchaser's point of view. Thus a $6,000 lot for which water and sewer service are available actually costs $9,400 on a ten-year installment contract, excluding interest charged on the $6,000 base price.

Resales and Exchanges

As is evident from the preceding discussion, Pueblo West's lots are priced at "improved" values whether or not they have water and other basic facilities. A local real estate agent noted in 1974 that compared to prices in Pueblo, the cost of a Pueblo West lot was "grossly inflated."[138] Consequently, Pueblo West's lots have little resale value. The amended 1974 federal Property Report warns the purchaser under SPECIAL RISK FACTORS:

> YOU SHOULD CONSIDER THE COMPETITION WHICH YOU MAY EXPERIENCE FROM THE DEVELOPER IN ATTEMPTING TO RESELL YOUR LOT AND THE POSSIBILITY THAT REAL ESTATE BROKERS MAY NOT BE INTERESTED IN LISTING YOUR LOT.[139]

A local realty agent interviewed by INFORM late in 1974 confirmed the need for this warning. McCulloch, which still had approximately 15% of its lots to sell at Pueblo West in 1976, "will do all sorts of things to keep a purchaser from knowing about any resale market. Many purchasers are willing to sell at a loss just to have someone take over their payments on the lot but can't find buyers. A lot of agents have stopped taking listings," she added.[140]

Legal Status

As noted earlier, Pueblo West's lots are sold as "homesites" with no guarantees that they will ever receive the improvements such as central water, central sewage disposal, paved roads, electricity, and telephone service that would make them truly habitable. The U.S. Federal Trade Commission has categorized this sales practice as fraudulent in complaints issued against GAC Corporation, Horizon Corporation, and AMREP Corporation (see chapters on Rio Rico, Rio Communities, and Rio Rancho).

Perhaps because McCulloch deferred the principal responsibility for the provision of basic services at Pueblo West to a Metropolitan District, McCulloch had avoided major legal actions until very recently. According to an Offering Circular for McCulloch Properties Credit Corporation, "...the FTC served a civil investigative demand upon McCulloch [in March, 1974] to produce data regarding its selling practices. McCulloch complied..." and no action ensued.[141] However, as of mid-1976 it appeared that McCulloch's halcyon days at Pueblo West may be numbered. According to INFORM data, the Office of Interstate Land Sales Registration, the Federal Trade Commission, and the Securities and Exchange Commission have all launched investigations focused on McCulloch's land-sales, financing, and development practices at this site. In addition, and serving perhaps to catalyze the above-mentioned federal actions, the Pueblo District Attorney impaneled a Grand Jury in early 1976 to hear charges pertaining to McCulloch's possible irregular use of the Pueblo West Metropolitan District.

COST OF LOTS BOUGHT ON THE INSTALLMENT PLAN

LOT PRICE

    basic price (¼ - 5 acres)* $6,000 - $55,000
    finance charge (6% - 9%) $1,694 - $21,313

                                                        Total $7,694 - $76,313

ADDITIONAL ANNUAL ASSESSMENTS DURING TERM OF CONTRACT

    property owners association   0
    district assessments & taxes $199 - $1,862
    water availability fee $24
    sewer availability fee $16

                            Total, per year $199 - $1,902
                            Total, 10 years $1,990 - $19,020

ONE-TIME COSTS FOR SERVICES
    lot survey   0
    water $490 - $750
        well   -
        central extension   0
        central hookup $490 - $750
    sewage $450 - $1,500
        septic system $450 - $1,500
        central extension   0
        central hookup $585
    electricity   N/A
    telephone   N/A

---

*Includes industrial, commercial, and multi-family lots.

ENVIRONMENTAL CHECKLIST

Overall environmental protection record: FAIR

Does the subdivider:

PLANS	Plan for complete basic services?	YES
	Phase lot sales and extension of services?	NO
	Get 80% build-out in 10 years of each section marketed?	NO
	Prepare an Environmental Impact Report?	NO
LAND	Use a curvilinear or cluster design?	YES
	Retain 25% or more open space?	NO
	Reserve from lot sale and development the following areas of critical concern:	
	wetlands?	--
	dunes and beaches?	--
	water sources?	--
	prime agricultural lands?	--
	habitats of endangered species?	--
	prime historical, archaeological, cultural, aesthetic, or recreational resources?	--
	Reserve from lot sale and development the following areas hazardous for building:	
	geological hazard areas (earthquake, landslide)?	--
	flood-prone areas (100-year floodplains, arroyos)?	YES
	areas of slope exceeding 25%?	--
	Blade roads only in immediate development areas?	NO
	Clear only for buildings and roads?	YES
	Preserve existing topography?	YES
WATER RESOURCES	Design the drainage system to control erosion?	NO
	Retain 100-foot buffer zone around water bodies?	--
	Replant disturbed land immediately?	NO
	Limit septic systems to one-acre or larger lots with adequate: percolation rates, slope, and distance from bedrock, water table and surface waters?	YES*
	When utilizing central sewage disposal, provide tertiary treatment (or secondary and land disposal)?	YES
	Avoid major stream alteration?	--
	Avoid major wetland dredging and filling?	--
	Use groundwater only up to the safe yield?	YES

*Septics are limited to lots of one acre or larger. However, there have been problems associated with slope, and bedrock.

NOTE: See chapter on "Guidelines" for more complete explanation of items on Checklist.

PUEBLO WEST 375

CONSUMER CHECKLIST

Overall consumer protection record: POOR

Does the subdivider:

SALES	
Conduct a credit check on lot purchasers?	NO
Limit lot sales to two per purchaser?	NO
Sell only residential, i.e., no industrial, commercial or multi-family lots on installment contracts?	NO
Require a cash downpayment of 20% on all sales?	NO
Limit duration of installment contracts to 5 years?	NO
Charge no interest on installment contracts?	NO
Encourage attorney review of sales documents?	NO
Require a pre-purchase site visit?	YES
Allow a 14-day rescission period in which purchaser can obtain a refund for any reason?	NO
Offer a partial refund if purchaser defaults?	NO
Guarantee a refund, with interest, if promised services are not made available by date specified in contract?	NO
Escrow contract payments, or provide equivalent surety bonding, for refund purposes?	NO
TITLE	
Offer only platted lots?	YES
Offer a recordable contract, and record the sale?	NO
Offer unmortgaged land, or land mortgaged with a release clause, only?	YES
Upon contract signing, deed title to purchaser, or place title in trust?	YES
BASIC SERVICES	
Guarantee, or have available, to each lot:	
central water, of adequate quantity and quality?	NO
central sewage disposal, as necessary?	YES*
drainage system, adequate for 100-year storm?	NO
solid waste disposal, via adequate method?	NO
roads, paved, to county standards?	NO
electricity and telephone?	NO
Guarantee completion through escrowing or surety bonding?	NO
If services are financed through special service district bonds, employ them only if:	
initial governing body includes a county official?	NO
elections include all landowners on one-man, one-vote basis?	NO
sum of bonds is less than twice the developer's investment in basic services?	YES
sum of bonds is less than 15% of the assessed value of land in the district?	NO
developer co-signs all bonds?	NO

*Service not guaranteed in contract, but lines have been extended to 80% of lots under one acre.

III. SUBDIVISIONS IN MOUNTAINS

1
The Mountain Environment

Each of the nation's approximately 35 major mountain ranges has its own unique personality and physiognomy, imparting a great variety of landscapes to the general term "mountain lands." The gentle Appalachian Highlands; the great wall of Rocky Mountains rising off the plains; innumerable staccato ranges stretching south down the thousand-mile-long plateau west of the Continental Divide; and the far west's Cascade, Sierra Nevada and Coastal Range mountains all present a broad diversity of temperatures, precipitation patterns, and habitats. Regardless of its geographic location, each single mountain in whichever range wears a marvelous cloak, intricately woven and dominated in design by a dramatic display of vertically arranged life zones circling it from base to peak like ribbons. Running down like unifying threads through all the zones on each mountain are the streams and creeks and rills that feed the rivers of the lowlands.

These many life zones, the area and location of which are determined by temperature patterns, "...provide environments for more varied populations than ever could exist on the prairies or in the deserts."[1] On a western mountain, "a thousand feet in altitude equals a horizontal distance of six hundred miles at sea level....one can travel ecologically a distance of 5,000 miles--equivalent to the distance from the Rio Grande to Hudson Bay--while actually traversing only three miles up the mountain side."[2] The variety of life zones found on western mountains can be illustrated by proceeding up the north slope of a 12,000-foot mountain west of the Rocky Mountain range. Below an altitude of 2,000 feet, minimal rainfall creates a desert environment. The dominant vegetation, hardy xerophytes such as mesquite, creosote bush, and cactus belongs to the lower Sonoran Life Zone.

From 2,000 to 4,500 feet, in the foothills, slightly more rainfall encourages a semi-arid desert-grassland environment. The vegetation in this Upper Sonoran Life Zone includes hardy desert grasses, sagebrush, and some woody desert shrubs in the more arid areas, and willows and aspens in moister valleys.

The Transition Life Zone extends from 4,500 feet to 6,500 feet. It is a border zone of grasses merging into conifer woodlands of stunted pinon pine and juniper. This zone separates the mountain's warmer, arid base from its colder and wetter upper slopes.

The richest montane environment extends from 6,500 to 10,000 feet. Enough precipitation falls in this Boreal Life Zone to support thick evergreen forests of Douglas Fir and Ponderosa Pine, blending into forests of Engleman Spruce and Alpine Fir. The environment of this zone is the coldest in which forests can develop.

At about 10,000 feet, the upper edge of the Boreal Life Zone merges gradually into the tundra vegetation characterizing the Arctic-Alpine Life Zone. The trees become smaller and more scattered until the dominant vegetation becomes non-woody plants such as lichens, mosses, and grasses. Alpine regions are exceptionally vulnerable. One pass with a motor vehicle or ten days of walking erodes an ecosystem that takes one hundred to five hundred years to restore itself.[3] Above this zone, snow and ice form a perpetual ground cover.

Each of these major life zones has its own discrete wildlife community. Lakes, streams, creeks, and ponds contribute to the variety of habitats at all elevations. "Almost every yard, and certainly every mile in the downhill course of a river offers a different habitat for...aquatic...creatures...."[4] Many mountain animals live within one zone; others live in different zones in different seasons. Elk and deer, for instance, descend in winter from high-altitude to lower-altitude forests, taking with them some of the larger predators such as cougars, wolves, and coyotes.

The vegetation of a mountain is crucial. It not only supports the distinct wildlife communities, but protects the slopes from excessive loss of soil, or erosion, a process which is naturally encouraged by a mountain's incline and by the harsh climate along its upper slopes. Erosion is particularly serious in the sparsely vegetated mountain lands of the Southwest.

Plants, with their extensive root systems, increase soil permeability; falling plant debris contributes humus to the soil. Both functions help prevent soil compacting, which increases runoff volumes and consequent erosion. By buffering the impact of falling rain and holding the soil to the slope, vegetation protects the watershed formed by a mountain's drainage system from siltation and flooding.

Most importantly, mountain vegetation helps rain and snow infiltrate the soil and percolate into groundwater supplies. On a healthy, fully vegetated slope free from gashes and gullies, the plants and the underlying soil bed may retain as much as 60% to 65% of precipitation.[5] However, when precipitation exceeds the soil's absorption tolerance, the stability of the slope is threatened. Hazards such as landslides, mud flows, flooding, and subsurface soil shifting (ground slumps) can have serious consequences on downslope development areas and water resources. While natural factors, such as heavy snow melts, seismic activity, and heavy rains can generate these hazardous conditions, the principal offender, of late, has been man. Negligent development practices frequently disturb the many important fuctions of vegetation, with potentially dangerous consequences. Such practices are coming to be recognized by states and regional agencies as hazards in themselves.

The retention of water is crucial to the mountains' function as the nation's principal watersheds. The mountains' high elevation cools the air currents rising above them and generates precipitation in the form of snow and rain.* Much of this precipitation winds its way downhill in streams and creeks, which feed the major rivers that run through more arid lands at lower altitudes. Indeed, all the great rivers in America originate in mountain areas except the Mississippi, which begins in the lowlands of Minnesota.[7] A portion of the precipitation also seeps through fissures in the rocks into underground rivers, which often flow for many miles before joining surface waters or underground aquifer systems.

The state of Colorado, where the Rocky Mountains form the Continental Divide and split the nation as well as the state into two separate drainage basins, has been called "the mother of rivers."[8] Its snow-capped peaks generate stream systems which produce an average of sixteen million acre-feet of "virgin flow" annually.†[9] These peaks hold the headwater of the

---

*In Colorado, for example, average annual precipitation is sixteen inches. However, the state's mountain regions receive over fifty inches annually, while its arid areas can receive as little as seven inches.[6]

†One acre-foot is equal to 326,000 gallons.

Colorado, Platte, Rio Grande, and Arkansas Rivers. Eighteen states share the use of Colorado's mountain flows,[10] which, as fresh-running streams of great appeal, have lately drawn millions of people into mountain areas formerly travelled by very few. The American Society of Planning Officials has said of environmentally sensitive areas such as mountains:

> The wise use of these areas will help preserve the natural flow of clean water from uplands into adjacent surface water and into groundwater reservoirs; the unwise use will result in more erratic flow of dirtier water into lakes and rivers, and, in turn diminish and pollute groundwater resources.[11]

Mountains often contain "areas of critical environmental concern" which cannot tolerate insensitive development. Their watersheds, habitats of endangered species, freshwater wetlands, shorelines, and prime archaeological, aesthetic, or recreational resources are all highly valuable to society-at-large. Mountains also contain certain lands unsuitable for building because of consequent hazards to the environment and to the eventual residents. Lands subject to earthquakes, landslides and flooding or lands with excessive slope function best as open space.

Man has traditionally enjoyed and used, but sometimes badly abused, the resources of the mountains. The American Indians ventured up into the mountains' higher slopes only on occasion, for rituals and mystical communion with the gods. Immigrating Europeans saw the mountain wilderness simply as a barrier to expanding trade routes and settlement patterns. Trappers collected furs and pelts, miners prospected, and timber companies leveled the forests to provide fuel and lumber to a burgeoning population.

Each of these "development" activities occasioned further extensions of roads, railroads, and settlements through mountain areas. However, until recently the elevation of many mountain ranges, particularly those in the West, served to protect them against the excessive encroachment by human beings. Permanent mountain settlements were generally situated on plateaus and in valleys at lower elevations, where gentler terrain provided agricultural and grazing land. While these settlements--small local villages and large farms and ranches--modified and altered the natural character of the lower slopes, they did not destroy the integrity of the foothill environment. Moreover, vast portions of the upper slopes remained remote wilderness--penetrated infrequently and temporarily by a few hardy sportsmen, curious naturalists, and aggressive explorers.

Since the late 1950s, however, the nation's fragile mountain environments have been subjected to increasingly intolerable population pressures. An urban, affluent society has "discovered" the mountains. Hunting, fishing, camping, hiking, river-rafting, snow-mobiling, and especially skiing have attracted millions of vacation and weekend visitors.* Rough, sparsely scattered, "winter cabins" infrequently used by determined outdoorsmen have given way to new housing patterns. Wherever lakes, streams, or peaks offer recreational possibilities, a trend towards high-density development has encouraged the superimposition of a modern urban environment on the nation's mountain regions.

Poor rural counties rich in remote and undeveloped lands have encouraged the growth of a recreation-tourist industry. They have constructed the roads and tunnels necessary to make mountain regions accessible and have approved plans for subdivisions.

Despite often scarce water supplies, many large ranches in lower mountain valleys have been subdivided into numerous lots. As a study undertaken by the state of California in 1971 points out, "Much of the current urban growth is occurring in the foothills and mountains adjacent to the cities."[13] This sort of intensive subdivision and development activity in western foothills with an altitude range of 3,000 to 6,000 feet can affect a large and diversified range of ecosystems. At higher altitudes, small mining towns have been reborn as popular vacation ski centers with subdivided lots sprawling from the cores of old towns. Man's intrusion into these higher elevations has significantly taxed the environment and disrupted many wildlife habitats.

Subdivision activity can tear up large areas of mountain lands. Careless construction practices which strip slopes of the vegetative cover that holds the soil in place invariably cause serious erosion problems. Precipitation, no longer checked by absorptive material, attacks the mountain's slopes and carries increasing loads of sediment into downstream water bodies. The large areas of impervious surfaces created by paving and soil compaction increase the speed and amount of

---

*Between 1950 and 1970 annual attendance in state park systems increased more than 300% (from slightly over 100 million to almost 500 million); annual visits in the national park system increased more than 400%--from about 40 million to almost 200 million.[12]

run-off causing streams to alter their flow pattern and often flood adjacent land. Fish and wildlife habitat is destroyed. Distant lowland areas may suffer from land-, or mud-slides initiated by the erosive forces underway in the hills above them.

The reliance on septic systems for sewage disposal in mountain subdivisions particularly threatens regions beyond the immediate area. Mountain soils are often inappropriate for the use of septic tanks. Rock outcroppings and compacted soils encourage leaching of inadequately filtered sewage into surface- and groundwater bodies. The purity of the mountain watershed is violated, and polluted water fills the reservoirs for distant urban regions.

A few states are now beginning to establish development regulations and programs designed to prevent these consequences and to protect what are increasingly recognized to be areas of "critical environmental concern." However, these programs are only in their infancy, beset by legal challenges, and still involved in defining their scope. They have yet to make a significant mark on the land subdivision industry.

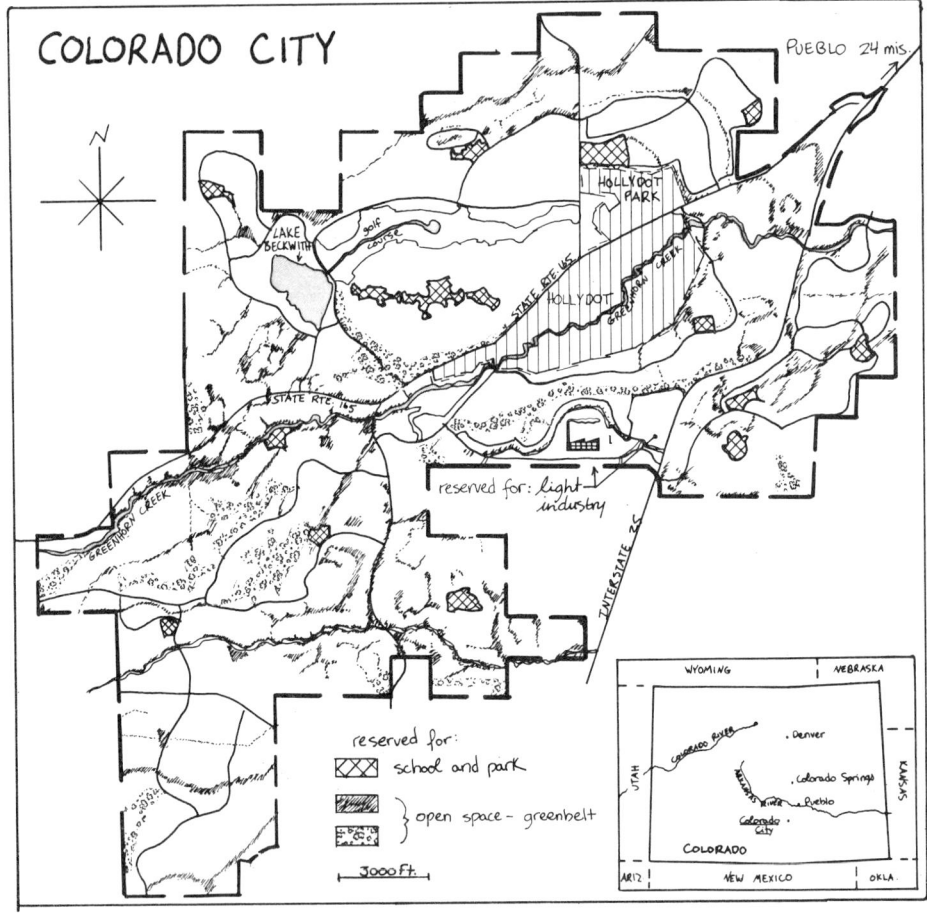

2
Colorado City

In terms of physical site characteristics and regional economic climate, Colorado City enjoys a more attractive location for community development than many of the subdivisions in the INFORM sample.* This subdivision, a relatively small one by sample standards, covers 9,900 acres of land (15.5 square miles) and is situated in a grassy valley in the foothills of the Rocky Mountains. It is only 24 miles southwest of the city of Pueblo at the southern end of Colorado's fast-growing "Front Range" urban corridor.

Unfortunately for the 14,000 or so individuals who have bought lots at this subdivision during the last thirteen years, three key ingredients to its success as a sound and viable new community are missing.

The first missing ingredient is water. Proper legal rights to enough water for the subdivision's full projected population--extremely important in this semi-arid region--were not secured by the site's original developer, a clever and notorious subdivision entrepreneur named Nathan K. Mendelsohn. Although promotional materials promised "plenty of water,"[1] Colorado City today has rights to only enough water for 4,100 people, about a tenth of its projected 35,000 to 70,000 population. The subdivision's prospects for getting all the water it needs are negligible.

The second missing ingredient at Colorado City is sufficient capital for site improvements. Great Western United, a large

---
*Includes both the ten subdivisions in Volume I of this study and the nine Florida subdivisions examined in Volume II.

conglomerate whose main businesses are sugar and pizza, bought
out Mendelsohn in 1969, acquiring Colorado City and two other
subdivisions, California City and Cochiti Lake.* But Mendelsohn,
and subsequently Great Western Cities, the conglomerate's newly
formed land-development subsidiary, abdicated a large portion of
their responsibility for installing a water system, sewage system, roads, drainage, or recreational facilities. Early in Colorado City's history most of these responsibilities were turned
over to two quasi-governmental entities set up by the developer,
a Water and Sanitation District and a Recreation District. These
Districts can raise money to finance improvements by issuing
bonds, but the obligation for repayment rests with the landowners in the Districts, i.e., with the lot purchasers themselves.
Not surprisingly, given the site's small tax base, the Water and
Sanitation District has issued only $2,815,000 of its $12,000,000
authorized debt, and the central water and central sewage-disposal systems have been extended to only 10% to 15% of the lots.

A third and final missing ingredient is good planning.
While Great Western Cities (GWC) appears to have gone to some
lengths to do sound environmental planning at Cochiti Lake,
which was just in the planning stages when the company acquired
it from Mendelsohn, it has not made similar efforts at either of
the two older subdivisions, California City and Colorado City.
The latter community has relatively little open space, has lots
located on steep slopes and flood-prone land, and has no erosion-control program. Relative to INFORM's guidelines and to the
performance of other subdividers in the sample, planning for
sound environmental and consumer practices is poor at Colorado
City.

---

*Mendelsohn started several land projects that lacked adequate
water supplies. Early in his land-sales career, the California
State Public Utilities Commission charged him with not providing
water to subdivided lots he had sold "on the guarantee that
there was...water available [and] at reasonable rates."[2] Mendelsohn's fraudulent sales practices at California City capped
his notoriety. This subdivision was one of the grander schemes
perpetrated in the late 1950s against gullible buyers. Covering
a 186-square-mile area 85 miles north of Los Angeles, it boasted
only 922 dwelling units sixteen years after its inception. Yet
39,000 lots had been sold for over $183,000,000.[3] California
City was described in 1969 in a California State Attorney General's report, excerpted in a Nader study, as offering "unpaved
roads to nowhere."[4] The abuses associated with this development
ultimately brought about major revisions in California's land-subdivision laws.

COLORADO CITY

Lacking these three crucial ingredients, Colorado City has yet to become the "new community" described in Great Western Cities' promotional material.[5] Although the subdivision is nearly 80% sold out and Great Western has ceased marketing its lots on the installment plan, only 370 housing units have been constructed. At this rate, it will be hundreds of years before the subdivision actually merits its appellation "City." As a Pueblo County planning official recently commented, "Their sales went real quick, but their development has been pretty slow."[6]

Regional Context

Colorado's Front Range region is a 150-mile urban corridor stretching along the eastern edge of the Rocky Mountains from Fort Collins to Pueblo City. This region, which includes the city of Denver, holds approximately 90% of Colorado's population. Yet it contains less than a third of the state's surface water, a major factor complicating its continued growth and expansion. Much of the region is dependent on water brought in from the western side of the Rockies to supplement existing supplies.

While Pueblo County, home of Colorado City, is still primarily a ranching area, it has participated in the economic growth of the Front Range communities over the past decade. The city of Pueblo, the county seat, has become a major industrial center in the state. The County's population has increasingly shifted from its rural areas to the city. Since 1950 the city's population has increased from 63,685 to over 100,000, although the population in the rest of the county has declined.

History

Colorado City is today the neglected stepchild of an irresponsible corporate parent. According to a Pueblo County realtor, the subdivision had its genesis in 1962, when Nathan Mendelsohn arranged with Holland Duell, a Pueblo County rancher, to jointly subdivide and develop Duell's 6,600-acre ranch.* Their

---

*Duell kept some acreage as a thoroughbred horse farm and family home, which has now been subdivided into a luxury residential community known as Hollydot. Although sales are just beginning, all utilities, including central water and sewer systems, have already been installed. A generous 45% of the acreage has been left as open recreational space, according to a Hollydot official, who said of the Colorado City and Hollydot projects, "They're two different animals. The Colorado City Water and Sanitation District can't provide for Colorado City's potential population, and their sales/use factor is very low."[7]

original agreement, sealed with just a handshake, incorporated Duell's desire to limit the project to his 6,600 acres and to subdivide the land into fully improved five-acre ranch-estate homesites. However, Duell was soon eased out of the project, although he retained ownership of slightly over 400 acres in the center of Mendelsohn's holdings.[8]

Mendelsohn promptly set about marketing lots at Colorado City in a manner contrary to Duell's wishes. Lots were sold unimproved. An additional 3,300 acres of contiguous rangeland were later incorporated into the project.[9]

Although Colorado City came under Great Western Cities' management in 1969, six years after sales had begun, all too little changed in the style of management. In early 1969, an aggressive young financier, William White, Jr., was eagerly searching for ways to buttress his newly formed but troubled conglomerate, Great Western United, Inc. In the course of his search, White encountered Mendelsohn. This seasoned land hustler sold his apparently profitable development corporation to Great Western United for $28.7 million worth of the latter's stock.[10] Only later did a change in corporate accounting rules reveal that Mendelsohn's land-sales schemes had put his company almost $900,000 in the red preceding Great Western United's purchase of it.[11]

According to a detailed history of Great Western Cities by Em Hall appearing in *The New Mexico Review and Legislative Journal* in 1970 and 1971:

> ...he [White] was buying by his own admission, the mammoth (and infamous) sales force that Nat K. Mendelsohn had built up over fifteen very profitable years of California subdividing. White told the Securities and Exchange Commission that he intended to use that sales force precisely as Mendelsohn had and told his stockholders that marketing land, Christmas trees, pizzas and sugar were really very similar. [From this point of view] sales were the goals, not cities.[12]

Unfortunately, according to *The New Mexico Review*, "Mendelsohn had sold out [to White]...just when start-up costs at Cochiti and Colorado City would be greatest."[13] Troubled with its own fiscal problems, Great Western Cities decided to concentrate its attention and resources on one subdivision, Cochiti Lake, at which sales began shortly after the GWC purchase. In consequence, the company initiated few changes to erase the Mendelsohn imprint at the older projects: California City, which started sales in 1958, and Colorado

City, which opened for sale in 1963. White's own colleagues had stated that he was "willing to sink the company's other 'new cities' to save Cochiti, if necessary."[14]

White left Great Western United in 1973 under pressure from its board of directors. In the intervening period, Great Western Cities' three land projects not only failed to improve the parent company's financial sheet, but added a considerable amount of red ink. The company's 1972 Form 10-K Report filed with the Securities and Exchange Commission reported:

> Historically, Great Western Cities has had to borrow substantial sums to meet its needs for operating capital, as operations have produced a negative cash flow...it is anticipated that Great Western Cities may require additional financing to meet its commitments for land improvements and community developments.[15]

In fact, Great Western Cities was having a hard time adjusting to the regulatory attention it had called forth. The same report states that "as a result of requests from certain state regulatory agencies, Great Western Cities has made various changes in its sales program which in the opinion of management have adversely affected its sales [during 1972]."[16] Two years later in its 1974 Prospectus the parent company echoed this complaint: "Management believes that legislation and regulation have had a materially adverse effect on its business in the past several years."[17]

Many of the company's problems resulted from legal actions initiated on the federal, state, and local levels. Great Western Cities never really modified Mendelsohn's marketing strategies. In 1972, the Federal Trade Commission issued a Cease and Desist Order against the company for various "practices which had the tendency to mislead and deceive customers as to the investment potential of lots...."[18]

The state Attorney General's Office has investigated complaints about Colorado City since 1973, although no action has ensued.[19] In 1974, the administrator of Colorado City's Water and Sanitation District was indicted by a Pueblo County Grand Jury for numerous criminal actions under Colorado's water statutes (see discussion under Water).

By 1974, net conditional sales at Colorado City had declined to $2.7 million from $14.1 million in 1971. An official of Great Western Cities interviewed by INFORM in 1974 bluntly explained why the marketing strategy which had worked so well for Mendelsohn had faltered under Great Western Cities' direction. "The days of selling a lot and a dream are over," he said. "You have to give people something when you sell to them now; you have to sell them a lot and reality."[20]

The combination of financial and regulatory problems besetting Great Western Cities resulted in its terminating the interstate sale of Colorado City lots on an installment-contract basis in February, 1975, although on-site sales to people intending to build immediately continued. By 1975, however, about 14,000 of the 16,000 lots marketed had been sold. In early 1976, Colorado City's project manager indicated that the company might begin an off-site sales program again, possibly "in the near future." However, he stated, "It won't be like the earlier days. The old fly-in approach* is a dinosaur that's dead."[21]

Great Western United announced in 1975 its intention to divest itself of its land-development subsidiary, having determined that "the long-range prospect of its land development businesses are not consistent with corporate objectives."[22] Should the development company change hands again, Colorado City could find itself with yet another foster parent. At this point, the consequences of such action to Colorado City lot purchasers cannot be anticipated.

THE OFFERING: LAND AND IMPROVEMENTS

LAND

Physical Characteristics

Colorado City is situated at an altitude of 5,770 to 6,450 feet in a grassy mountain valley within view of the Rockies. Its northeast corner abuts Interstate 25, which connects the communities along the state's Front Range. An intermittently flowing tributary of the Arkansas River, Greenhorn Creek, bisects the subdivision from east to west. The only other significant water body on the site is the 72-acre Lake Beckwith, which GWC created by enlarging a small pond.

Colorado City's attractive location, as well as its relative proximity to both the industrial center of Pueblo and the

---

*The "fly-in approach" involved flying prospective purchasers to the subdivision at company expense for a carefully guided sales tour and pitch.

Colorado City, in the foothills of the Rockies.

recreational lands in the 1 1/2-million-acre San Isabel National Forest eight miles east, suggest a desirable site for the "new community" promised purchasers in promotional material.

Status of development

Of Colorado City's total 9,900 acres, 8,270 were subdivided and recorded (i.e., platted) with Pueblo County between 1963 and February, 1975. This acreage was subdivided into approximately 16,642 lots, which were marketed throughout the country as "homesites" with good investment potential. By 1974, when approximately three-quarters of Colorado City's offered acreage had been sold, net conditional sales amounted to $62,879,000.[23] By the end of 1975, 14,108 (84%) of the lots offered—covering approximately 7,300 acres—had been sold. Of these lots, 7,392 (45% of the total) had been deeded to purchasers.*

According to an official with Pueblo County's Health Department, most of Colorado City lots are under one acre in size.[25] Great Western Cities data supplied to INFORM indicate that 67% of the subdivided acreage--5,541 acres--has been allocated to residential homesites, ranging in size from 1/4 to 2 1/2 acres. Lots were marketed at prices of $3,500 to $12,000. In addition, 870 of the subdivided acres have been allocated to multiple dwelling units, another 360 acres to commercial and industrial use, and 165 acres to community facilities. Natural open space and drainage areas comprise 1,250 acres—15% of the total—and 165 acres—2%—have been developed as recreational space.

Such as it is, development at Colorado City has proceeded haphazardly in four scattered units, one of which is a mobile-home park near Interstate 25. The other three units are located across the subdivision, near Lake Beckwith and the site's nine-hole golf course. These four disparate units serve as core development areas. Their lots are still being offered for sale; they are available for cash or on a standard mortgage basis, but not on an installment-contract basis, and they are sold only to those who plan to build immediately. All improvements— paved streets, utilities, underground electric lines—are provided, and FHA-VA home-building loans are available to builders

---

*According to the 1974 Great Western United Proxy Statement/Prospectus, 21,359 lots were sold at Colorado City between 1963 and 1974; however, 7,337 were returned to the company's inventory when purchasers defaulted on payments, leaving 14,022 still under contract as of August, 1974.[24] In the subsequent two years only 86 lots were sold!

in some of the units. Almost all of the several hundred homes at Colorado City are located in these units.

It is highly unlikely that Colorado City will ever achieve its projected population. In data sent to INFORM in mid-1976, Great Western Cities was still claiming an ultimate population of 35,000 to 70,000 people, but the project's manager stated privately, "We're not making population projections anymore."[26] A company sales official noted that the latest census, taken in July, 1975, showed a population of just 990 persons.[27]

Only two or three small light industries are currently located at Colorado City despite the fact that Great Western United's management undertook a policy of "incentive offerings of land to other businesses" designed to promote the "overall growth and development of the community...."[28] A half-acre shopping center with a few service businesses is located near Interstate 25.

Building has proceeded very slowly. About 20 new homes were added in 1975, bringing the total number of dwellings to only 370.[29] By contrast, McCulloch's slightly larger Arizona subdivision, Lake Havasu City (16,700 acres, 33,500 lots), begun in the same year as Colorado City, has by dint of real development, as well as heavy promotion efforts, acquired ten times as many houses as Colorado City and 10,000 inhabitants.

If development at Colorado City continues at its current pace, lot purchasers, whether they bought for investment or for future residential needs, will be sorely disappointed. At the subdivision's current average annual rate of increase, it will be 500 to 900 years (depending on the estimate) before its full projected population is achieved.

BASIC SERVICES

The 6,716 lot owners and 7,329 purchasers still making payments on contracts for Colorado City lots were sold property advertised as part of a new "planned community." "Colorado City," a promotional brochure read, "is not a dream of the future. It is a living vital reality today. People like you have bought land, have built homes and have found investment opportunities and employment in or near this modern and completely planned community."[30] Unfortunately, Great Western United took little responsibility for providing the services which make a lot suitable for a home and give land real value. Company shareholders were notified in the 1974 Proxy Statement/ Prospectus (a document not supplied to lot buyers) that Great Western Cities, Inc. was principally engaged in "the sale of previously acquired raw land in the form of subdivided *and unimproved lots* or larger parcels (...some with no off-site improvements, and others with only off-site improvements such as roads, drainage facilities and water distribution pipes, either installed or *to some degree* provided for...) [emphasis added]."[32]

Lot purchasers at Colorado City were led to believe they were buying homesites equipped with central water, roads, electricity, and telephone as well as recreational facilities.[32] However, no services are guaranteed in the purchase contract, and in 1976, thirteen years after sales began, services had been extended to only 10% to 15% of the lots. Worse still, there is not enough water legally available to the site to serve more that 1,377 lots, a tenth of those already sold.*

The legal and financial responsibility for providing water and sewerage service as well as recreational facilities for Colorado City does not fall on the "developer" who sold the land and promised the services and facilities. They are to be provided by two special districts--a Water and Sanitation District and a Recreation District--set up in early 1964 shortly after Mendelsohn began marketing Colorado City lots.

Under Colorado law, special districts are quasi-governmental legal entities authorized to issue tax-free general obligation bonds and thus to finance public improvements. Special districts are designed to raise large sums of money relatively quickly, money which can be repaid with interest in small increments over a ten- to twenty-year period. The repayment must be made by the landholders within the district's legally defined boundaries.

In a new subdivision, the developer is initially the largest landholder and generally controls the district's funding policies and development practices for many years. But by the time the bond debt must be repaid, there have generally been sufficient sales that the developer no longer owns most of the land. In fact, it is the new lot owners who bear the repayment responsibility.

Special districts can be a boon to a developer, but they present numerous hazards to an individual purchasing an unimproved lot on an installment-contract basis. The special service district's debt--the nature and extent of which the lot buyer may not fully understand--imposes a significant obligation on him. His lot and all the other property in the district serve as the ultimate collateral for the district's debt.

If the developer has erred in his original cost calculations, the district will have to expand its debt. If the

---

*Based on an average of three persons to a lot and a per capita water use of 150 gallons a day.

developer has erred in his population projections (so that income from "availability fees" for water, for instance, falls short of projections), the district may impose an ad valorem tax, which is unlimited unless otherwise stated by law, on lot owners in the district. This tax is used to repay the bondholders who originally lent their funds to the district.

In a developer-funded project, if the company does not have sufficient capital to continue development and goes into bankruptcy, a titled lot owner will still have his land. By contrast, if a special district is established to fund development and there are insufficient funds to pay its debt obligations, the lot owner can be required to forfeit his land to the district's bondholders.

At Colorado City, the Water and Sanitation District has been made responsible for installing and maintaining central water and sewerage systems; the Recreation District has been made responsible for developing and maintaining community recreation facilities. Lot purchasers have had to assume both a considerable extra cost and a legal risk for the sake of these basic improvements. Yet after thirteen years of operation, there is little assurance today that either district can provide sufficient improvements for Colorado City to grow into a viable community.

In explaining the current financial problems facing Colorado City, and particularly its Recreation District, the director of that District noted: "The long-range planning on growth and population [at Colorado City] was very liberal, while the cost of operating was figured very conservatively. The boards that set up the districts in 1963 were comprised mainly of company employees, and their revenue plan was too conservative--facilities were promised [by the company] that haven't been built and weren't financed, and now the districts are stuck with fulfilling old promises of the developer and his salesmen."[33] He mentioned as an example the nine-hole golf course, which was installed by Mendelsohn before Great Western United's acquisition of Colorado City. The cost of repairing and expanding the course, he said, represents "a $400,000 expenditure, and we haven't the money for that."[34]

Colorado City's advanced age and small population create special problems for the Recreation District, according to its director. "Recreation facilities draw residents to a community like this and the district is now caught in a ten-year funding plan arranged back in 1964. The plan just wasn't adequate to finance the development and maintenance over the years of all that the salesmen had originally promised."[35] The plan in question was devised by Mendelsohn. All lot purchasers were required to join the Recreation District, touted as MERBISC:

"Most Extraordinary Recreation Bargain in Southern Colorado."[36] The ten-year membership fee was initially set by the developer at $100 and was later increased by the District to $300. However, these fees, which were the District's principal source of revenue, were not adequate to fund its full responsibilities over the long term. Now, with more of these ten-year memberships expiring every year and the District in need of funds, Colorado City's absentee lot owners have to be pushed hard to undertake a second $300 ten-year membership. The Recreation District thus finds itself in the anomalous position of having to function as "a membership sales promotional office."[37] It also found it necessary in 1974 to levy an ad valorem tax of 4 mils against each lot. This is the maximum such tax allowed a recreation district under Colorado law.

The Water and Sanitation District has also increased its charges to lot purchasers, yet it can offer no assurance that all those paying these charges will receive water.

In 1964 the Water and Sanitation District was authorized by its "voters" (in effect, the development company) to issue $12 million in bonds. Of this total, $7 million was for construction of a central water system, $4.4 million was for sewers, and $850,000 was for storm sewers.[38] The District has actually issued only a small portion of the bond amount authorized, but a substantial debt burden has nonetheless been generated. As of June 1, 1976, the balance due on the District's bonded debt amounts to $2,889,815.[39] Since the District's assessed valuation (30% of actual value) amounts to approximately $4,139,000,[40] the ratio of outstanding debt to assessed valuation is thus a hefty 68%. (By contrast, Florida law limits this ratio to no more than 15% and New Mexico law to no more than 5%.)

In 1965, the District board, still company-controlled, decided on a mechanism for refunding its long-term debt. This involved a charge on all lots sold, but not on lots still held by the developer. When signing a sales contract, all lot purchasers were required to accept a Water and Sewer Availability Agreement. This agreement originally required purchasers to pay a "water availability" fee of $300 to $500, depending on the lot's front footage, for water service. In 1968, the District added a charge for sewerage service. By 1975 the District's charges to purchasers ranged from $1,100 to $1,500 for water service plus another $350 for sewer service. These amounts were to be paid in semi-annual installments "together with interest at the ANNUAL PERCENTAGE RATE of 7%...."*[41] Any default

---

*Since the lot buyer is giving the District the use of his money, the District might just as logically pay interest to the buyer.

COLORADO CITY 399

on payment constituted a default on the purchaser's sales contract with consequent forfeiture of the lot and of all payments. Beyond these substantial charges no taxes have been levied to date, and none are anticipated by the Water and Sanitation District, according to its current manager.[42]

Water

Colorado's Deputy State Engineer has asserted that water is "more valuable than gold"[43] in his state; the history of Colorado City's efforts to attain a sufficient water supply would support that assertion.

Despite its receipt of the above-mentioned fees, Colorado City's Water and Sanitation District has so far been unable to acquire a water supply for more than a small portion of the lots in the subdivision. Great Western Cities' advertising asserted that "as Colorado City develops, the water distribution system will expand according to a master plan administered by the property owners through their Colorado City Water and Sanitation District."[44] However, corporate planning for Colorado City's water supply was highly irresponsible and involved many misleading promotional claims.

By 1972, Great Western United's stockholders (though not lot purchasers) were notified in the Form 10-K Report filed with the Securities and Exchange Commission that "geological and hydrological reports to Great Western Cities have indicated that it is uncertain whether readily available water sources will be adequate to support the full contemplated population of the Colorado City area."[45] The company's 1975 Form 10-K reflected increased uncertainty:

> The present water needs of Colorado City are being met by surface water sources, the adequacy of which for the future is...disputed by the Federal Trade Commission and the Office of the Colorado State Attorney General.[46]

In July, 1976, the current manager of the District stated to INFORM personnel that to his knowledge no "master plan" for water delivery had ever been written up or published by Great Western Cities and that any such "plan" amounted to little more than good intentions.[47]

Colorado City is now legally entitled to 693.5 acre-feet of water a year for municipal use, the equivalent of 619,400 gallons per day. This is only enough water for 4,130 people at average rates of water use in dry climates (150 gallons per person per day). The 14,000 lots that have been sold could house 42,000 people (at 3 persons per lot), ten times the number for which there is water.

The central water system is in fact already extended to more lots than the District has water for. Water mains have been laid to 2,665 lots, about 16% of those in the subdivision. At average use rates* these lots would require over a million gallons of water a day. The delivery system, which is currently supplied by surface water from springs and the intermittently flowing Greenhorn Creek,† has a capacity of only 583,200 gallons per day. Colorado City's existing community uses about 100,000 gallons per day. According to a former employee of the State Health Department, Colorado City has already been "short of water several times,"[48] even with its limited population.

The current dilemma originated in Nathan Mendelsohn's early disregard for Colorado's water-appropriation doctrine. In Colorado, all surface water is controlled by the state. A special system of state water courts issues each user a legal right to a specified amount of water, to be withdrawn at a specified geographic point for a specified use. Users are given priority by category--i.e., agricultural, municipal, domestic--and by date of application. These "rights" are a kind of commodity which may be bought and sold. But the transference of rights from one use-category to another--e.g., from agricultural to municipal use--requires a legal procedure handled by the state's water court system.

Upon formation of its Water and Sanitation District in 1964, and over the subsequent years, Colorado City's development company did deed to the Water and Sanitation District the extensive water rights which it acquired with the ranch land it subdivided. These rights applied to a sizeable amount of water. However, they were legally defined as "irrigation rights." This designation limited the legal use of the water to agricultural purposes.

---

*Assumes three persons per lot and 150 gallons per person per day usage.

†An indication of the abuses perpetrated by Colorado City salesmen around this complex matter of water availability was related to INFORM by an employee of the Southeastern Colorado Water Conservancy District who visited Colorado City. Upon being asked about the water supply, a salesman pointed to the Greenhorn Creek. Not knowing his visitor was a local resident, he said definitively that the Greenhorn flowed all year long and would give the project all the water it could possibly need.[49]

As explained by an Acting Division Engineer of the State Water Resources Commission, "[Mendelsohn and his] Water and Sanitation District proceeded to design a water system that simply ignored the legal nature of the state's system of water priority."[50] Thus, the following announcement in Colorado City's promotional material suggesting a plentiful water supply for the community was strikingly deceptive:*

> The Colorado City Development Company deeded to the District all of its water assets. These include 72-acre Lake Beckwith, water wells and water rights of Hicklin Ditch. The water rights from Greenhorn Creek are among the earliest court-decreed rights in Colorado.[53]

The surface water used for municipal consumption during Colorado City's first ten years was available under an informal arrangement with downstream farmers. In 1973, however, the Administrator of the Water and Sanitation District diverted water, which legally belonged to the farmers, "out of priority," for Colorado City's municipal use, in order to maintain the water level of Lake Beckwith. The diversion depleted the downstream water supply, the pre-existing informal arrangement broke down, and the farmers obtained an injunction against the District Administrator. He was indicted by a Pueblo County Grand Jury "on counts of felony theft, embezzlement of public property, attempting to influence a public servant and a misdemeanor count of first degree official misconduct."[54] He was found guilty in 1974 on the minor charge.

After the injunction against the District Administrator was obtained, Colorado City's Water and Sanitation District was ordered by the State Water Commissioner to make its water rights conform to existing use practices. Toward this end the District requested in water court that its rights be transferred from agricultural to municipal use. In 1975, according to the present

---

*Also misleading is a statement in Great Western United's 1974 Prospectus which read: "A report to the District by its engineers indicates that [surface water] sources will serve a population of 26,000; the same report projects a total population at Colorado City in 1993 of approximately 5,000."[51] The current manager of Colorado City's Water and Sanitation District said of this "report": "If there was one, it's junk."[52] Furthermore, as explained above, no matter how many rights to surface water Colorado City had acquired before 1975, none of them were municipal rights.

Greenhorn Creek, Colorado City's much disputed water source.

District Administrator, the court granted the Water and Sanitation District the legal right to use 693.5 acre-feet per year of surface water for its municipal needs. The court calculated that this amount was sufficient to meet the needs of Colorado City's population for the next five years (using a 20%-per-year population-increase factor).[55] As of mid-1976, this supply is more than adequate for Colorado City's existing population, although it is entirely inadequate for the needs of all those who have purchased "homesites."

In order to obtain a legal right to more surface water, the District must return to court with another rights-transfer request. It cannot be assured of the court's favorable response. The District (i.e., the lot owners within the District) will again have to pay for the cost of the proceedings, and for any further municipal rights the court decrees.* Even if the District spends the money to go to court, it is doubtful whether all of Colorado City's irrigation rights could be transferred to allow municipal use. As the current manager of the District pointed out to INFORM personnel, Colorado law prohibits taking water from a stream when doing so adversely affects downstream users who have equal or senior water rights. In transferring its rights to Greenhorn Creek water from agricultural to municipal use, the District would still find itself with rights junior to those of many downstream users. Given the Creek's intermittent flow, if the District draws large amounts of water from it, downstream users with prior rights will surely be adversely affected.[57]

Mendelsohn's, and subsequently Great Western Cities', disregard for Colorado's complex water-rights system has so far nullified the real value of 90% of the 14,000 lots sold as "homesites" at Colorado City. Even as lot sales proceeded, Great Western United's 1972 Form 10-K Report acknowledged with respect to all three of the company's subdivisions: "...the extent to which the Projects can be developed in the future will depend upon the availability of water supplies...."[58]

In an effort to expand its functional water supply, the District has explored another water source whose use is not

---

*The cost problems now confronting the District in its efforts to enlarge its limited water supply are indicated by the fact that in 1973 it tried to purchase a neighboring ranch with its water rights for $2.5 million. However, after complicated legal proceedings, it rejected the purchase, according to a current member of the District's board, because of further costs involved in transferring the water rights from agricultural to municipal use.[56]

bound by the intricate legal restrictions placed on state surface flows. In Colorado, subsurface groundwater that is not tributary to rivers and streams may be mined by the owner of the land under which it lies, provided that the water be extracted at a rate which will not deplete the source for 100 years.* Colorado City does have a groundwater supply available to it, principally from the Dakota formation. However, problems with the water's quality and availability have prevented its effective use to date. Two developer-drilled wells into the Dakota Aquifer are no longer in operation. A former employee of the State Health Department stated that both wells went dry. He added that they extracted poor-quality water even when they were producing.[59] Extensive prior use has depleted the Aquifer sufficiently for the Bureau of Reclamation to state in an Environmental Impact Statement published in 1972 on the Fryingpan-Arkansas water-diversion project: "[It]...is unsuitable for obtaining substantial quantities of additional municipal and industrial water supplies."[60]

The 1974 Great Western United Proxy Statement/Prospectus brings up the further problem that "although it is possible that deep aquifers can yield a significant, but not fully adequate, amount of water for development needs, it is suspected that such aquifers may be contaminated by radium 226."[61] The Prospectus adds that dilution or filtration devices might eliminate this problem and notes: "The Health Department of Colorado has been monitoring radium 226 contamination in water from wells in Pueblo County, but has not yet determined the extent of potential harm from such water."[62]

Despite these groundwater problems, the District's manager responded optimistically to INFORM's 1976 queries about Colorado City's future water supply. He dismissed questions about the possibility of groundwater quality problems, saying, "If we hit an underground well of poor quality we can clean it up," but ultimately acknowledged that "the cost and quality of surface water make it more desirable."[63]

Even if lot purchasers at Colorado City were assured of a sufficient water supply, they would not all be able to assume that the District's delivery system would be extended to their lots. While the Water and Sewer Availability Agreement obligates each purchaser to pay the substantial "water availability" charges described previously before receiving title to his lot, the District's corresponding water-delivery obligations are vague and of dubious legal value. The Agreement states that:

---

*The rate of use of this groundwater is regulated under permit by Colorado's State Engineer.

> [The] District has undertaken to adopt an overall plan for the ultimate extension of water service to all of the subdivided lots in Colorado City....Extension of said system pursuant to the plan shall be made as need therefore appears on the basis of prudent management as determined in the reasonable discretion of the District....Notwithstanding anything set forth herein, the District shall not be bound or committed to any person or entity to furnish such water...to any particular lot or parcel at any particular time except in connection with its overall plan, or any segment thereof [emphasis added].*[64]

Less vague is the District's understandable refusal to provide any form of service to 947 of Colorado City's lots. Great Western United explains in its 1974 Proxy Statement/Prospectus that the Water and Sanitation District has declined to annex about 1,500 of Colorado City's 9,900 acres until Great Western Cities acquires "adequate quality water resources for transfer to the District to service the anticipated population of these lands."[65] In spite of the District's refusal to annex this acreage, acquired after the 1964 formation of the District, Great Western Cities has subdivided about 400 of the 1,500 acres into 947 lots, and platted them with the County as Colorado City Units 41 and 45. The company has marketed these lots right along with the lots included in the Water and Sanitation District.

As of May 31, 1974, 572 of the 947 lots located outside the District had been sold, and Great Western Cities had collected $82,165 in water- and sewerage-service availability charges. It anticipated receiving "as the remaining principal balance" another $490,000.[66] (The additional 7% per year interest charged on water and sewer availability fees considerably increases the total amount to be collected.)

The 1974 Proxy Statement/Prospectus claims that if the District will not annex Units 41 and 45, "Great Western Cities plans to form a separate water and sanitation district to serve

---

*Despite this wording, the company reported to INFORM that central water is *guaranteed* in the purchase contract to each lot "as part of the Water/Sewer Availability Agreement." However, it did admit that the completion of the central system is not guaranteed through either escrow accounts or surety bonding.

these lots."[67] Yet two years later the project manager at Colorado City told INFORM, "In another year or two the District will probably annex [those units] into its system [or]...wells can be put down if all else fails since our geological study indicates those units overlie the Dakota Aquifer."[68] (The problems of using this source have been discussed.)

Despite the large sums of money Great Western Cities and the District have collected in service charges from all of Colorado City's lot purchasers, the 1974 Proxy Statement/Prospectus states that water is currently available to lots not yet served by the District only "with the cost being borne by the owner."[69] A purchaser whose lot is not located along completed distribution lines "can receive water [but] only by tank truck delivery at costs substantially in excess of [water] charges to owners of lots lying along delivery lines."*[70]

As of August, 1975, according to the District's manager, the central water main had been extended to only 2,665 lots. Thus the 947 lots outside the District's boundaries and some 13,000† other lots within the district are presently subject to a double charge if they receive water service. Because of the community's small population, only 426 lots have been connected to the central system, 346 of which are residential lots, 25 of which are commercial/industrial, and 55 of which are multi-family. ▽[71]

The amended 1975 Property Report for Colorado City states that the tank-truck delivery rate for water is $5.00 per 1,000 gallons, and a water tank costs $350.∆ The 1976 charge to

---

*Tank-truck delivery of water rather than well use would be necessary because Pueblo County subdivision regulations restrict the use of wells to lots of at least one acre in size. Almost all the residentail lots at Colorado City are smaller than one acre.

†According to the District's manager there are a total of 15,759 lots in the District. However, available lot figures do not conform, since the additional 947 lots located outside the District give a total of 16,706, which is 64 more than Great Western Cities has marketed, according to data the company sent to INFORM in December, 1975.

▽Company data supplied to INFORM indicate that 350 lots were hooked up to the central water system as of December 31, 1975.

∆Since these same figures appear in the 1972 Colorado City federal Property Report, they probably err on the low side today.

District customers connected to the central system is much lower: $2.75 per month minimum for 2,000 gallons (or, $1.40 per 1,000 gallons).*

Given the small number of lots actually occupied at Colorado City, extension of the District's central water system is well ahead of physical need. As noted, however, if a greater portion of the lots sold were occupied, the District could not supply them with the required amount of water.

Sewage

Many of Colorado City's lots are just a quarter acre in size. Furthermore, much of the terrain is unsuitable for individual septic tanks because of clay soil and rock outcroppings. Yet originally no central sewage-disposal system was intended for the site. When Great Western Cities acquired the project in 1969, Pueblo County health officials encouraged the company to install a central sewage-disposal system, since the county had passed regulations in 1967 prohibiting septic tanks on lots smaller than one acre. According to a Pueblo County sanitarian, Great Western Cities agreed in 1970 to provide a central sewage-disposal system for the subdivision, although the company did not guarantee to do so in the purchaser's sales contract.[72] The U.S. Environmental Protection Agency helped Great Western Cities fulfill its agreement with the County Health Department by awarding the District a grant to cover 75% of the cost of a small sewage-treatment plant. The plant, built in 1972, has a design capacity of 560,000 gallons per day (sufficient to handle the sewage of 5,600 persons). It can be expanded as development increases.[73] It is currently processing 65,000 gallons of sewage per day.

District figures indicate that main sewer lines have been extended to 1,604 lots--about 10% of the total platted lots at Colorado City. Approximately 300 lots are currently hooked up to the system. A Pueblo County sanitarian stated that about 40 lots are still on individual septic systems, with permits for temporary use through 1978.[74] Since April 1, 1976, the District has charged a fee of $400 per lot for hookup to the central system.

---

*This sum may be put into clearer perspective by comparing it to the charge made by the nearby Pueblo West Metropolitan District at McCulloch Properties, Inc.'s Pueblo West subdivision. There water costs $0.85 per 1,000 gallons, which is considered high by its district officials.

Roads

While 160 miles of dirt roads provide access to all marketed lots at Colorado City, the site has only 17 miles of paved roads. Paved-road access was not guaranteed to purchasers, nor have funds for paving been assured through escrow accounts or surety bonding.

Negotiations have been underway for some time between the County and Great Western United over the question of road standards and the further question whether the County is willing to accept responsibility for road maintenance. When Colorado City was initially planned in 1963, Pueblo County had no standards for subdivision roads. At that time, according to Colorado City's project manager, the company and County worked out an agreement whereby the County would accept road-maintenance responsibility.[75] However, a County planning official told INFORM that at present "the roads out there are a big problem."[76] They do not meet the County's present drainage requirements and consequently the County does not want to accept them. Company maintenance thus far has been minimal, and, according to a local realtor, "Many of the dirt roads are overgrown."[77]

Drainage

As described by company data sent to INFORM in 1976, Colorado City's drainage system is poor. The company acknowledges that the existing system, which depends principally on natural swales and a few culverts, has a capacity to handle the runoff from no more than a five-year storm. Most planners advocate designing drainage systems to the much stricter standard of being able to handle the worst storm expected in a hundred years.

Located at the edge of mountains on terrain that includes steep slopes, the site is subject to infrequent but intense storms which generate large amounts of runoff. While company promotional material claims that many of the natural drainageways running through the site have been left as open space, a former county employee disagreed. He stated that much of the land was modified without taking "good drainage into account." Consequently, he noted, a bad storm in 1972 flooded Colorado City's sewer line (no storm sewage system existed) and nearly washed away the District's water tank.[78] Completion of the drainage system is not guaranteed in the purchase contract,* and funds

---

*While Great Western Cities stated the contrary in data submitted to INFORM in 1976, the Purchase Contract states only that the development company may enter a purchaser's land "in order to provide drainage patterns as may be necessary and beneficial...."[79]

for completion are not protected through escrow accounts or surety bonding.

Solid-Waste Disposal

There is no provision for solid-waste disposal on site at Colorado City. A private contractor collects refuse weekly and disposes of it at the Pueblo County sanitary landfill.

Utilities

Electricity will be available to all of the lots at Colorado City from the San Isabel Electric Company. An official with the utility company stated that the cost basis for line extension is averaged over a five-year period with minimum monthly bills of $35 to $40.[80] According to development-company figures, all 370 of the site's dwellings are served with electricity and 95% of the transmission lines are above ground.

Telephone service is available to all lots at costs based on applicable Public Utility Commission line-extension policies.

COMMUNITY AND RECREATIONAL FACILITIES

Thirteen years after its inception, the small Colorado City community has very few community facilities. Police protection is provided by the County Sheriff's office, which maintains a deputy office on the site. Fire protection is provided by a volunteer unit maintaining a fire station in Colorado City. Primary and secondary schools are located in the hamlet of Rye, five miles away. According to company data sent to INFORM, a middle school is under construction at Colorado City.

Medical facilities--doctors, dentists, and hospitals--are located in Pueblo, 24 miles from the site. A small shopping center with approximately nineteen service businesses is located on site.

Public transportation to the site from the north and south is provided by the Greyhound Bus Company, which makes a flag stop at Colorado City's entrance on Interstate 25.

According to the site's project manager, the development company has transferred title to 1,400 acres of land to the Colorado City Recreation District. However, the director of this District stated that less than 10% of the 1,400 acres had been improved.[81] The subdivision has a nine-hole golf course next to its artificial lake, and the District has constructed a baseball field, swimming pool, and tennis courts in one park area. Whether this constitutes the "Most Extraordinary Recreation Bargain in Southern Colorado," as the $300 "MERBISC" membership fee imports, is surely questionable.

ENVIRONMENTAL PROTECTION

In spite of the minimal amount of residential development at Colorado City—2% of its lots hold homes—the environmental effects of developing this mountain valley are not insignificant. A former County health official aptly noted: "Colorado City has a beautiful location, but lots of problems."[82] The problems—primarily erosion and flooding—can only get worse as housing construction continues. Relative both to INFORM's guidelines and to the practices followed at other subdivisions in this study, Great Western Cities' environmental-protection efforts are poor.

PLANNING

By and large, the company has not employed good site-planning practices. Although Great Western United's 1974 Proxy Statement/Prospectus described the amended master plan for Colorado City as "lots...in high-density cluster villages separated by open-space belts,"[83] a company-produced map of the site confirms no such site layout. Instead, it indicates a curvilinear road and lot design. This layout is preferable to a gridiron pattern in that it permits some fitting of roads and lots to the terrain. However, it is by no means as desirable as clustering would have been in these mountain foothills.

Only 17% of the site's total acreage has been allocated for open space, parkland, and recreational use, despite the fact that much of the land slopes steeply and thus may be better left undeveloped. This 17% allocation is considerably less than the 25% minimum many planners would recommend (see Guidelines).

The development process has not involved phasing sales with construction work, whereby installation of all services (and thus the physical alteration of the land) would be undertaken at one time in a particular section and would coincide with completion of installment contracts in that area. On the contrary, roads have been bladed throughout the entire subdivision many years before they will be needed. Many of these unpaved roads are overgrown. In the steeper areas where vegetation has not returned, the roads contribute to erosion.

No Environmental Impact Report was prepared for use in

planning and laying out the subdivision.

Colorado City includes no land areas of critical environmental concern, and thus its development will not disturb any such areas. However, it does include areas which are hazardous for building, land which Great Western has unfortunately subdivided and sold.

Development was not excluded from the 100-year floodplain. According to the engineers for the development company, the 25 or so arroyos which run through the site were all withheld from development and made part of the greenways.[85] However, Greenhorn Creek, which runs through Colorado City from its northeast corner down to its southwest corner, is prone to flooding from rapid snow melt in the spring and from seasonal storms. The 1974 report on the Hollydot development by the U.S. Department of Agriculture, Soil Conservation Service notes that "the major problem associated with the proposed development is the flood hazard from Greenhorn Creek...."[86] Although most of Colorado City's lots lie above the creek bed, some lots do abut the Creek. The District Conservationist for the Soil Conservation Service corroborated the flood risk to these lots.[87] As noted earlier, the five-year design for Colorado City's drainage system has already proven inadequate.

Very steeply sloped areas have been turned into lots. With proper engineering and architecture, buildings can be erected on such land relatively safely. But given the extra expense involved, the high erosion potential of such land, and, often, its aesthetic appeal, it is almost always better left for open-space uses in a new community. An examination of Great Western's map for the site indicates that many lots do in fact have slopes greater than 25%. Great Western's engineering firm told INFORM that some lots include areas with as much as a 40% slope but that such lots include some less steep land, which is reserved for building purposes.[88]

A final land-use problem is that the rolling foothill terrain of the Colorado City area is characterized by a wide variation in soil conditions, some of which pose construction problems for residential buildings. A 1974 Soil Conservation Service report on soil conditions at the Hollydot development within the Colorado City land area states: "Any dwelling with a basement could have additional problems. There could be foundation cracking due to the shrink-swell characteristics of the soils."[89] This may be true of portions of Colorado City as well.

WATER RESOURCES

Water-resource protection efforts are inadequate at Colorado City. The subdivision's rudimentary drainage system includes no sediment traps or retention ponds to keep dirt, chemicals, and other pollutants found in urban runoff from reaching Greenhorn Creek. No 100-foot open-space buffer zone has been established around the Creek, which zone would allow natural filtration of pollutants by the soil. Furthermore, the company has no program for revegetating such areas disturbed by building or road construction. Such a program would stop pollution at its source by controlling erosion.

While more is being done to control pollution from sewage than has been done to limit pollution from erosion and runoff, Great Western's measures are insufficient in the former category as well as in the latter.

The subdivision is now planned for central sewage disposal as a result of the County's insistence that Colorado City's quarter-acre lots were too small (and the soil in many areas unsuitable) for individual septic systems. While some "temporary" septic systems are still in use, the threat that failing leach fields will pollute groundwater has been minimized.

The existing central sewage plant, which is currently operating at below design capacity, provides secondary treatment. Two aerated holding ponds discharge under EPA permit into the Greenhorn Creek. In a report on the wasteload allocation for the Creek, the State Water Quality Control Division stated that "...wasteflows from Hollydot and Colorado City would enhance stream conditions provided they met present [1973] or 1978 effluent standards."[90] However, in 1973, the discharge failed to meet existing and 1978 state water-quality standards for ammonia.[91] Furthermore, the federal Water Pollution Control Act has set a goal of "no discharge" into the nation's waterways by 1983. Many new sewage-treatment systems, including most of those at subdivisions studied by INFORM, dispose of their effluent by spray irrigating a golf course or other land area. Percolating through the soil allows the sprayed effluent to be further purified before reaching a waterway.

Colorado City is one of the few subdivisions in the INFORM sample which obtains its water from surface water supplies rather than from groundwater. Thus, as of mid-1976 it had no impact on groundwater levels.

CONSUMER PROTECTION

As of mid-1976, Great Western Cities was only selling lots in the "core" development areas on a cash or conventional mortgage basis. However, its consumer practices when it was marketing lots on installment contracts were very poor relative to INFORM's guidelines and to the practices of other companies studied.

Sales

While one subdivider, Dart Resorts, conforms to as many as eight of INFORM's twelve guidelines for sound sales practices, at Colorado City Great Western Cities has followed none. (See Consumer Checklist.)

When Colorado City's quarter- to two-and-a-half acre lots were being marketed, they sold at prices of $3,500 to $12,000. The majority were sold on conventional installment contracts of 7 1/2 to 10 years' duration and with interest ranging from 5% to 8%. Originally purchasers had no rescission period and were offered no refund provisions. Under regulatory pressure the company was forced to abide by the requirements of the federal Office of Interstate Land Sales Registration,* under which a purchaser has three days after seeing the federal Property Report to cancel the contract and receive a refund; but it never offered a blanket fourteen-day rescission right as is required in California. Eventually, Great Western Cities initiated a one-year site inspection/cancellation privilege for out-of-state buyers as well as a lot-exchange program. Prospective buyers were also encouraged to visit the site before purchasing a lot. Like many other companies in this business, Great Western Cities would fly in prospective buyers for company-guided tours and a sales pitch. However, a pre-purchase site visit was not required. No credit check was conducted on prospective purchasers. No limitation was placed on the number of residential lots sold to an individual purchaser. No attorney or independent closer was encouraged to be present at the site during a sale, nor was a purchaser encouraged to review the sales con-

---

*The U.S. Department of Housing and Urban Development, Office of Interstate Land Sales Registration, requires the development company to issue a Property Report giving important consumer information on the lots offered for sale.

tract and federal Property Report with an attorney. Industrial, commercial, and multi-family lots as well as single-family lots were sold on installment contracts.

Title Protection

The approximately 6,500 people who are still paying installments on contracts for lots at Colorado City are not fully guaranteed receipt of title to their land. This could become a serious problem should Great Western Cities' tenuous financial position worsen and bankruptcy be declared (a phenomenon not unheard of among large subdivision companies).

Lots are platted with the County. Sales contracts were in recordable form but were not recorded for the purchaser by the company. Thus, unless a lot purchaser records the contract himself, there is no official record of his interest in the land. Title was not placed in trust or escrow when a purchaser signed his sales contract. Thus, it could become part of the company's general assets in a bankruptcy proceeding.

The developer's title to the land is encumbered by mortgages. However, lot purchasers are protected from losing title in the event of the mortgagor's foreclosure by clauses releasing individual lots from the terms of the mortgages..

According to the company, title to a lot is delivered, free and clear of all liens, upon the purchaser's full payment of his sales contract.

Additional Costs

The extra fees charged a Colorado City lot purchaser during the term of his contract payments are considerable. If any of these charges are not paid in full as due, the purchaser is held to be in default and all payments towards the lot under purchase are forfeited. These costs include the $300 Recreation District fee, $1,450 to $1,850 (plus 7% interest) due under the terms of the Water and Sewer Availability Agreement, and annual taxes. In 1975 taxes amounted to $93.46 per $1,000 of assessed value. As of 1976, assessed value will be based on 30% of the lot's full (improved) value, i.e., $280.38 on a $10,000 lot. Over the ten years of a contract, these fees and assessments will add at least $2,730 to $5,510 to the basic $3,500 to $12,000 price of a lot. Following receipt of title, a lot owner must pay another $825 in order to hook up to the central water and sewer systems.

Resale

According to a local real estate agent interviewed by INFORM in 1974, Colorado City lots have always had severely

limited resale value. This is because they were originally sold
at inflated prices based on improved values even though "many
lots were two miles from water and sewer lines" and were competing with lots still for sale by the developer.[92] However,
Great Western Cities did not warn prospective lot purchasers of
this fact in the federal Property Report, although the parent
company in its 1972 Form 10-K Report acknowledged that "there
presently are limited markets for resale of land at...Colorado
City...." The Report further stated, "...management believes
that such sales are made at prices substantially lower than
GWC's current offering prices."[93]

Disclosure

The 1975 amended Property Report filed with the federal
Office of Interstate Land Sales Registration (OILSR) by Great
Western Cities' subsidiary, the Colorado City Development Corporation, deserves special notice, as it is a particularly deficient document. It contains notably inadequate disclosure regarding the water supply for the subdivision and the availability of other basic services at the site. For instance, listed
under Existing and Proposed Improvements are roads, drainage
facilities, and water and sewer systems. Yet, under "date of
completion and responsibility for construction and maintenance
of existing and proposed improvements," the only item discussed
is road construction and maintenance. Tax data is given only
for the year 1972. Purchasers are not warned that a lot is apt
to have no resale value or that an individual owner would be
competing with the development company if he attempted to resell
his lot.

In sum, this four-page Report—which is in fact a State of
Hawaii Public Offering Statement filed there in 1972 and offered
to OILSR in lieu of a federal Property Report*—leaves the consumer ill-informed about Colorado City. The 1975 amended report consists of no more than the 1972 report with an added
page describing litigation underway between the developer and
the Federal Trade Commission. It is in sharp contrast to the
documents filed in accordance with OILSR's own requirements in
the last few years, documents which can give as many as twenty
to thirty pages of detailed information about services, financing, and physical characteristics of a subdivision as well
as financial data reflecting the fiscal stability of the development company.

---

*The Office of Interstate Land Sales Registration accepts Property Reports filed with the states of New York, California,
Florida, and Hawaii in lieu of federal Property Reports.

Legal Status

Great Western Cities has been the object of legal actions by the Federal Trade Commission since 1972 and was subject to an intensive investigation by the Colorado Attorney General's office in 1975.[94] Yet this attention has accomplished remarkably little to ensure that individuals who purchased Colorado City lots receive the improvements that would give their land value.

In 1972 Great Western United Corporation signed a Consent Order with the Federal Trade Commission (FTC) covering Great Western Cities' three land projects. According to data appended to a 1975 federal Property Report for Colorado City, the 1972 Complaint:

> ...alleged that the Developer and affiliates engaged in unfair trade practices which had the tendency to mislead and deceive customers as to the investment potential of lots, growth potential of areas in which subdivisions are located, cost to purchasers beyond purchase price of lots, income to be made by salesmen, and rescission rights under Regulation Z.[95]

However, in 1975, based on subsequent investigations, the FTC alleged that the developer and affiliated companies had violated the Consent Order. Negotiations were reopened which apparently dealt with the far broader issues of providing actual refunds and services to individuals who had already bought lots. As described in the 1975 Colorado City federal Property Report, a new settlement may entail the following:

> ...a cash payment of approximately $4,000,000 to certain "eligible" purchasers...who purchased property from the Developer and affiliated companies since October 20, 1972...further, the proposed settlement would require the Developer and affilated companies to spend or cause to be spent up to $16,000,000 on certain capital improvements in this development [i.e., Colorado City] and two other development projects [i.e., California City and Cochiti Lake]...over the next 10 years.[96]

The company, which has emphasized that the above-proposed settlement is tentative, stated in the same document, "...the Developer does estimate that [the settlement] will be adopted as described by December, 1975."[97] When queried in June, 1976, about the delay in finalizing this settlement, counsel to Great Western Cities stated that the matter had been resting with the Federal Trade Commission for several months.[98] The FTC acknowleged that negotiations had in fact ended.[99]

The FTC's Commissioners, however, have not yet formally ruled on the findings of the 1975 staff investigation. Should they rule that Great Western Cities did violate the 1972 Consent Order, the Commission may then recommend to the Department of Justice that civil court action against the company be taken by the federal government. Or, the FTC may instead settle with Great Western Cities out of court, i.e., adopt the settlement which has already been negotiated. As of October, 1976, INFORM was unable to determine why neither course of action had been taken.

In addition to this pending FTC action, Colorado City was the subject of a separate investigation initiated in the early part of 1975 by the Colorado State Attorney General's office. According to a source close to that investigation, Great Western Cities indicated that it wanted to settle out of court. Negotiations were well under way last year specifying the amount of funds to be designated for capital improvements and consumer redress at Colorado City.[100] Great Western United stated in its 1975 Annual Report: "It is anticipated that this complaint will be settled in connection with the FTC settlement; however, no assurances can be given."[101] According to INFORM's source, Great Western Cities is clearly in violation of the portions of Colorado's Consumer Protection Act which pertain to false and misleading advertising and to the delivery of goods and services, although this Act does not apply to real estate per se.[102]

However, for reasons that are unclear, the state Attorney General's office appears to have let the entire matter die. No evident action or settlement on behalf of the 14,045 lot purchasers at the site has resulted.

When queried about this matter in June, 1976, an attorney with the state Attorney General's Office explained:

> We have been investigating the complaints against Colorado City and are discussing these problems with Great Western Cities. There are statute of limitations problems, and there is a question of whether or not the Consumer Protection Act applies to real estate transactions. Our office tries to work through the Real Estate Commission's office.[103] (The latter is an administrative agency empowered only to suspend or revoke a developer's license.)

An attorney familiar with the case remarked in response:

> Why don't they go to Court and find out? Or do they think it is better to lose the issue by default?[104]

ENVIRONMENTAL CHECKLIST

Overall environmental protection record: POOR

Does the subdivider:

PLANS	Plan for complete basic services?	NO
	Phase lot sales and extension of services?	NO
	Get 80% build-out in 10 years of each section marketed?	NO
	Prepare an Environmental Impact Report?	NO
LAND	Use a curvilinear or cluster design?	YES
	Retain 25% or more open space?	NO
	Reserve from lot sale and development the following areas of critical concern:	
	wetlands?	--
	dunes and beaches?	--
	water sources?	--
	prime agricultural lands?	--
	habitats of endangered species?	--
	prime historical, archaeological, cultural, aesthetic, or recreational resources?	--
	Reserve from lot sale and development the following areas hazardous for building:	
	geological hazard areas (earthquake, landslide)?	--
	flood-prone areas (100-year floodplains, arroyos)?	NO
	areas of slope exceeding 25%?	NO
	Blade roads only in immediate development areas?	NO
	Clear only for buildings and roads?	YES
	Preserve existing topography?	YES
WATER RESOURCES	Design the drainage system to control erosion?	NO
	Retain 100-foot buffer zone around water bodies?	NO
	Replant disturbed land immediately?	NO
	Limit septic systems to one-acre or larger lots with adequate: percolation rates, slope, and distance from bedrock, water table and surface waters?	YES
	When utilizing central sewage disposal, provide tertiary treatment (or secondary and land disposal)?	NO
	Avoid major stream alteration?	YES
	Avoid major wetland dredging and filling?	--
	Use groundwater only up to the safe yield?	--

NOTE: See chapter on "Guidelines" for more complete explanation of items on Checklist.

COLORADO CITY

CONSUMER CHECKLIST

Overall consumer protection record: POOR*

Does the subdivider:

	Question	
SALES	Conduct a credit check on lot purchasers?	NO
	Limit lot sales to two per purchaser?	NO
	Sell only residential, i.e., no industrial, commercial or multi-family lots on installment contracts?	NO
	Require a cash downpayment of 20% on all sales?	NO
	Limit duration of installment contracts to 5 years?	NO
	Charge no interest on installment contracts?	NO
	Encourage attorney review of sales documents?	NO
	Require a pre-purchase site visit?	NO
	Allow a 14-day rescission period in which purchaser can obtain a refund for any reason?	NO
	Offer a partial refund if purchaser defaults?	NO
	Guarantee a refund, with interest, if promised services are not made available by date specified in contract?	NO
	Escrow contract payments, or provide equivalent surety bonding, for refund purposes?	NO
TITLE	Offer only platted lots?	YES
	Offer a recordable contract, and record the sale?	NO
	Offer unmortgaged land, or land mortgaged with a release clause, only?	YES
	Upon contract signing, deed title to purchaser, or place title in trust?	NO
BASIC SERVICES	Guarantee, or have available, to each lot:	
	central water, of adequate quantity and quality?	NO
	central sewage disposal, as necessary?	NO
	drainage system, adequate for 100-year storm?	NO
	solid waste disposal, via adequate method?	NO
	roads, paved, to county standards?	NO
	electricity and telephone?	NO
	Guarantee completion through escrowing or surety bonding?	NO
	If services are financed through special service district bonds, employ them only if:	
	initial governing body includes a county official?	NO
	elections include all landowners on one-man, one-vote basis?	NO
	sum of bonds is less than twice the developer's investment in basic services?	?
	sum of bonds is less than 15% of the assessed value of land in the district?	NO
	developer co-signs all bonds?	NO

*Evaluations reflect company policy when it was actively marketing lots on installment basis. As of mid-1976, GWC was only selling lots in the core area, on a cash or standard mortgage basis.

COST OF LOTS BOUGHT ON THE INSTALLMENT PLAN

LOT PRICE

basic price (¼ - 2½ acres)*	$3,500 - $12,000
finance charge (5% - 8%)	$859 - $4,924
Total	$4,359 - $16,924

ADDITIONAL ASSESSMENTS DURING TERM OF CONTRACT

Water & Sanitation District	$1,450 - $1,850
MERBISC fee (recreation)	$300
property taxes	$981 - $3,364
Total, 10 years	$2,731 - $5,514

ONE-TIME COSTS FOR SERVICES

lot survey		0
water		$425
well	-	
central extension	0	
central hook-up	$425	
sewage		$400
septic	-	
central extension	0	
central hook-up	$400	
electricity		0
telephone		0

*Includes industrial, commercial, and multi-family lots.

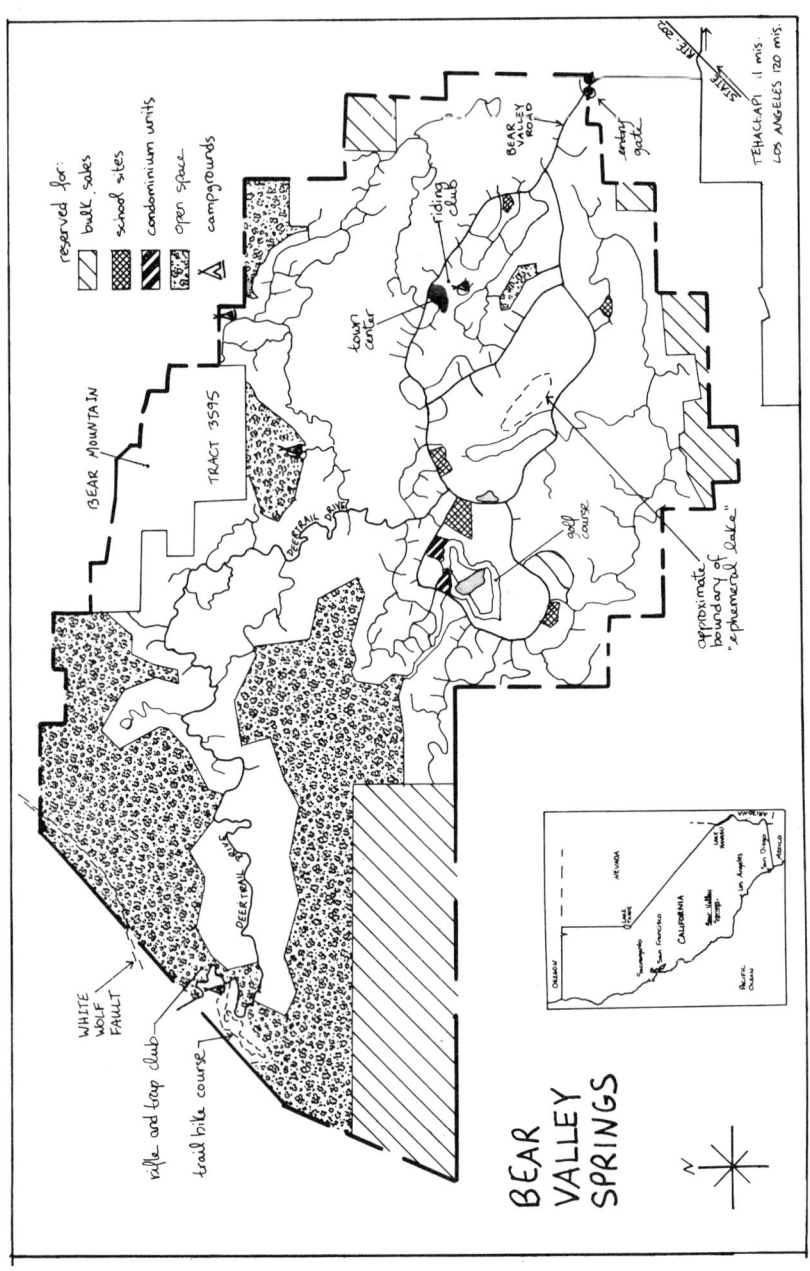

3

Bear Valley Springs

At Bear Valley Springs, the developer, Dart Resorts, a subsidiary of Dart Industries, Inc., offers the consumer as much as is offered at any other subdivision in the study. Yet there are still serious environmental and consumer problems at this subdivision.

In 1976, just five years after sales were initiated, all lots are already equipped with central water and, if under one acre, with central sewage. Site drainage is adequate, every lot is accessible by an oiled-surfaced road, and most have electricity and telephone. By contrast, seven of the nineteen* subdivisions in this study guarantee no more than a dirt road to most lots.

Dart's sales and title protection practices are the best of the nine† companies studied by INFORM. Its sales agreement gives the buyer title to his lot and allows him to start building a home on it as soon as he signs the contract, rather than waiting until he completes payments, as is the case at most of the subdivisions studied. However, despite the comparative quality of its consumer practices, in December, 1975, Dart settled two class-action suits, refunding approximately $1 million to purchasers who claimed that the lots were sold to them on the basis of investment value and resale potential they did not have.

Bear Valley Springs was Dart's first venture in the land-sales business. The company, better known for its Rexall, Westbend, and Tupperware products, acquired the land from a cattle rancher in 1969. The choice of the 26,000-acre site for a subdivision was a poor one. The land, located in Kern County, California, just 120

---

*Includes both the ten subdivisions in Volume I and the nine Florida subdivisions analyzed in Volume II.

†Includes the nine companies in Volumes I and II of this study.

miles northeast of Los Angeles, is extremely mountainous. There is over a mile difference in elevation between its lowest point at the bottom of Sycamore Canyon (about 900 feet above sea level) and its highest at the top of Bear Mountain (over 6000 feet).[1] About two-thirds of the land rises or falls precipitously, with slopes of over 30%.[2] The northwest corner of the site is traversed by an active earthquake fault and portions of the land are subject to landslides. The entire site is an important habitat for many wildlife species, including the endangered California condor, the largest and one of the rarest of North American birds.

Because of these environmental factors, perhaps only 20% of the site--in the area of the central valley floor on which Dart has in fact put its core development--is actually suitable for the type of recreational, second-home subdivision Dart is creating. Dart has taken some cognizance of slope and soil problems, trying to give each lot some land with a slope of less than 30%, and scaling the size and shape of lots to the terrain. Nevertheless, it has spread lots over about 70% of the site.

At present, with a population of approximately 100, the subdivision has had little environmental impact. However, some observers are concerned that as more of the subdivision's projected 12,000 to 15,000 occupants build homes, the potential for problems of erosion and groundwater pollution (from septic-tank failure) may increase.

Regional Context

While the subdivision of environmentally unsuitable land can sometimes be justified by population pressures, this is not the case for Bear Valley Springs. The site is located in the northeast region of the Tehachapi Mountains between the Mohave Desert to the east and the San Joaquin Valley to the west. There are minimal immediate-growth pressures from either direction. There are also at least four other large recreational subdivisions in the immediate vicinity and many more equally accessible to Los Angeles residents seeking a country home. The Kern County seat, Bakersfield, is fifty miles northwest of the Bear Valley Springs site. The nearby city of Tehachapi (population 4,370), eleven miles away is, according to the Chamber of Commerce, "poised on the threshold of a period of growth." At present, however, its economy is based on agriculture and cattle raising.

BEAR VALLEY SPRINGS   425

THE OFFERING: LAND AND IMPROVEMENTS

LAND

Physical Characteristics

In the 1972 Environmental Impact Report on the subdivision, required by California's Environmental Quality Act, the Bear Valley Springs site is described as having been "one of the areas least altered by man in the central Tehachapis, and in Kern County."[3] Until its acquisition by Dart in 1969, it was a working cattle ranch with no public access. The site is similar to many parts of Southern California; there are dry hills and deep ravines, covered with grasses and occasional stands of scrub oak and pine. The only natural water bodies on the site are a few small ponds, intermittent streams, and an "ephemeral lake" which appears in the rainy season. Dart has created two small artificial ponds.

Status of Development

Originally Dart planned to subdivide the 26,000-acre site into 4,500 homesites. It dedicated 5,950 acres of the steepest land to the Bear Valley Springs Community Services District as permanent open space.[4] However, its plan to subdivide 1,265 acres on the top of Bear Mountain was never implemented, so the actual number of lots in the project is 3,880. Since the project is planned as a second-home recreational community, Dart allocated only 10 acres for multiple-family dwellings and 25 acres for commercial space. There is no land allocated for industrial use. On the 18,785 acres scheduled for development, Dart plans an average density of roughly one dwelling unit per five acres. Lots range in size from a third of an acre to eighty acres; 10% are under an acre in size, 50% are one acre, 30% are from two to ten acres, and 10% are ten acres or larger.[5]

Lots of twenty acres or more may be further subdivided by their owners but resulting lots may be no smaller than ten acres. The Environmental Impact Report states that the project plans have provided for additional lots created in this manner.

At present, five years after sales began, 45% of the lots are sold and 200 fully paid for. Actual occupancy is proceeding slowly. The site has 245 structures (including 69 condominium units), but only 100 residents. If people continued to come to live at the project at the same rate they have in its first five years, it would not achieve its full projected population for approximately six hundred years. While this is a very long time, it is short in

Central saucer-shaped valley and surrounding mountains included in the Bear Valley Springs subdivision.

comparison to several even older subdivisions in this study, which would not be fully occupied at their present average rates of population growth for several thousand years.

BASIC SERVICES

Unlike every other company studied by INFORM, Dart not only promised to provide all lots with essential basic services, it actually made most of them available to site residents within the project's first five years.

Construction began in 1970 and was about 25% complete before sales began. In 1974, before even half the lots were sold, Bear Valley Springs was substantially finished, with its recreational facilities, streets, drainage, water system, and sewer system (where promised) in operation. The development is not totally problem-free, however, with regard to basic services. Given its soils and slope, at least the one-acre lots (50% of the total) probably should have been tied into the central sewage system. The widespread use of septic tanks increases the possibility that the site's water supply will become polluted. It is also conceivable that the supply of groundwater will prove inadequate to meet the demands of the projected population.

The mechanism for operating and maintaining site services and facilities is the Bear Valley Springs Community Services District. It subjects lot owners to certain financial liabilities, the extent of which may be misunderstood at the time of purchase. However, the liabilities are by no means as severe as those at a number of other subdivisions in this study, where special service districts have been used to finance major *capital* (not just operating) costs of improvements. The District will be responsible for operating and maintaining: the water supply system; the collection, treatment, and disposal of sewage and storm water; the collection and disposal of solid wastes; public recreation facilities; police protection; road improvements; utilities, and other public improvements. The District issues bonds and assesses property owners to finance these activities.[6]

According to Don Simpson, consulting engineer for the District, when Bear Valley Springs began, Dart, Kern County, and the District signed an agreement under which Dart would construct improvements in accordance with Kern County regulations and District specifications, and then turn them over to the District. Dart posted surety bonds to cover the costs of construction (labor and materials) of these improvements.[7] The only facility that the District would have to pay Dart for was the water system.

The District is run by a five-member board of directors. Elections are held every two years for staggered four-year terms. District voting membership is limited to registered-voter residents. Thus, as the California Subdivision Public Report* warns: "Until a purchaser becomes a resident of the district, he will have no control of taxes or bonding. The subdivider may be in complete control of the district."[8]

The voters established a bond limit of $8.3 million, and as of mid-1976, the District had issued and sold $3.5 million in bonds to finance portions of the water system. This exceeds the INFORM guideline that the bonds issued should not exceed 15% of the assessed value of the land in the district at time of issuance.† The District set a $130- to $360-a-year "water bond reduction charge" (depending on lot size) to cover the cost of debt service. In addition to this charge and District taxes (about $69 a year for an $8,000 lot),▽ lot owners must pay a $36-a-year water standby charge, and a $72-a-year sewer-system maintenance charge.

Bear Valley Springs also has a property-owners association which operates recreational facilities and enforces lot covenants and restrictions. All lot owners, rather than just site residents, are voting members of the Bear Valley Springs Association and must pay Association assessments. These are currently $65 a year, but would, according to the company, be $104 a year if the Association were not subsidized by Dart. The consulting engineer for the District told INFORM that Dart created the Association in part to compensate for the residency limitation on District membership. He cited the handling of Dart's proposal to add nine holes to the golf course as an example of how the Association has been used to foster more democratic procedures. Dart asked the District to submit the expansion proposal to the Bear Valley Springs Association for a vote. When the property owners decided that they did not want to pay for a golf course that would benefit only the small number of Bear Valley Springs residents, the District turned down the proposed expansion.[9]

---

*California requires the development company to issue a report disclosing pertinent consumer information on lots offered for sale.

†California law allows districts to issue bonds in amounts up to 200% of the assessed value of the property. This is the equivalent of 50% of the market value as assessed value is 25% of the market value.

▽$3.44/$100 assessed valuation in fiscal year 1975-76. Assessed valuation is 25% of the sales price.

Water

Although Bear Valley Springs is in a dry region of California, Dart has made more adequate provision for supplying its water than it has at its Tahoe Donner project. The central water system at the site is complete, with all mains installed and 250 lots hooked up. In addition to the monthly standby and water-reduction charges, residents must pay to have a lateral line extended from the main line to the house, and a $100 meter-installation charge.

The site's water presently comes from 28 wells Dart drilled on the site. These can supply 400 acre-feet of water a year (357,260 gallons per day) of acceptable quality. This amount is adequate for approximately 2,850 people at average rates of use in mountain areas (125 gallons per person per day). The Community Services District, which was incorporated into the Tehachapi Cummings Water District, also has an allocation of 3,600 acre-feet a year from the state water project. This additional water is adequate for approximately 25,700 people.

According to Walter Sandall, former Manager of the Community Services District, "eventually, with significant development or another nine holes on the golf course, we might have to draw on the Tehachapi Cummings water."[10] Dart designed the site's central water system for future hookup to the Tehachapi Cummings system, but the actual connection lines and necessary filtration plant will be built by the Community Services District when they are needed. Dart estimates that these hookup facilities will cost between $400,000 and $500,000: an amount that was budgeted for in the District's bonding capacity.

One danger for the current water supply is pollution. According to the Environmental Impact Report, because most of Bear Valley Springs' sewage will be disposed of by septic tank, "there always exists some potential for impairment of the groundwater...,"[11] A local U.S. Soil Conservation Service official stated, "There is definitely a potential for pollution from septics."[12]

Because of this possibility and a potential for depletion, the Community Services District tests well-water quality and levels every month. According to Sandall, the well levels have dropped during periods of drought. No impairment of quality has yet been noted.

Even if pollution or depletion of the groundwater resource were to occur, purchasers or residents at Bear Valley Springs would probably still be assured of a continued water supply since the subdivision's state water allocation is more than adequate to meet the needs of its projected population of 12,000 to 15,000.

The adequacy assumes, however, that the state water project can fulfill its commitments. According to Project Land Use, a Kern

County environmental organization, the state water project, although committed to deliver 4 million acre-feet, can only supply two and a half million acre-feet from present sources.[13] The California Water Resources Control Board confirms that it does not at present have the 4.3 million acre-feet annually needed to meet its commitments after the year 2000. But it hopes to discover new resources in the interim.[14]

Sewage

In contrast to its relatively conscientious effort to provide adequate basic services, Dart did not extend the central sewage system beyond its 460 one-third-acre and 69 condominium lots. Currently 72 lots are hooked up to the central sewage system. For the remaining lots, all of which are at least an acre in size, sewage will be disposed of by septic tanks or other individual systems. Although local regulatory agencies specified one acre as satisfactory for septic tanks at Bear Valley Springs, there are several indications that Dart also should have included at least the one-acre lots in the central system.

The primary problem with using septics at Bear Valley Springs is the slope of the land. On a steep slope, effluent leaching from the tank may run off too rapidly, before bacteria in the soil can digest it. It may then mix with groundwater in its unpurified state. According to the Soil Conservation Service, in much of the Bear Valley Springs development, soils are also rocky and shallow,[15] increasing the probability that inadequately treated sewage will leach into groundwater. (See Environmental Protection Guidelines.)

The Soil Conservation Service has classified five of the six types of soils found at the site as having "severe" limitations for septic-tank use. These soils cover about 80% of the site.[16] The central valley floor, where most of the development is now taking place and where the central sewage system is located, comprises the other 20%. This area contains the only soil at the site considered safe for septic-tank use.[17] There are many precedents for providing central sewage systems in areas with "severe" limitations. They include both the Soil Conservation Service's guidelines for Colorado's model subdivision regulations and New Mexico's Liquid Waste Disposal Regulations. Both state categorically that septic systems should not be put on land which the Soil Conservation Service classifies as having "severe" limitations for such use.

At present, the Kern County Health Department is insisting that septic tanks not be placed on any land with a slope greater than 30%. A representative of the Department stated that according to Dart engineers, each lot includes some land with less than a 30% slope.[18]

The County Health Department has also been concerned about areas in which the groundwater table is too close to the surface to install a septic tank. Dart states that this situation exists only at 37 lots in the valley floor.[19] Owners of these lots may have to install special "evaporation and transpiration" sewage-disposal systems. These cost more than the $1,200 needed for the installation of a standard septic system.* According to the Health Department, in one case Dart allowed a lot owner who faced this problem to trade his lot.

Because of concerns about the possible impact of septic-tank pollutants leaching into the groundwater, the Health Department required the Community Services District, as mentioned above, to conduct a monitoring program.[20] If the monitoring indicates that the groundwater is becoming polluted, the District may be required to expand the central sewage system to include all lots. Lot owners would then be liable for this new and considerable expense.

The Bear Valley Springs central sewage plant, serving condominiums and small lots, is being constructed in two stages. It is designed to treat liquid wastes from an ultimate population of 2,100 and the septic tank pumpage from the area not tied in to the central sewage system.[21] Because the population was not large enough to warrant a treatment plant until recently, a holding pond was used. According to Dart, as of February, 1976, the first part of the permanent facility (designed to treat 100,000 gallons per day) was operating at between 8,000 and 15,000 gallons per day.

Hookup to the central system costs lot owners $5 plus "a couple of hundred dollars" to install a lateral from the lot line to the house.[22] The Community Services District, as was mentioned earlier, charges a $72-a-year maintenance and operation fee.

About twenty lot owners, whose lots lie along a sewer line extended to the golf club, will have to pay the District $1,000 plus the cost of the lateral. This hookup charge--levied to cover the District's costs for this particular line--is about the same as the cost of the septic system they would otherwise have to install. Septic tank installation is at the lot owner's expense and dependent on health department regulations and permission.

Solid Waste

The Bear Valley Springs Community Services District is responsible for solid-waste disposal. It has contracted with a franchise collection and disposal service which uses the Tehachapi "landfill

---

*The $1,200 cost of a septic system at Bear Valley Springs is itself higher than that at other sites in this study, reflecting California's higher construction costs.

dump." There is a landfill site at Bear Valley Springs for future use if necessary, a precaution few other subdivisions in the INFORM sample have taken.

Roads

Dart has completed construction of the 100 miles of roads planned for Bear Valley Springs. The roads, which have oiled surfaces instead of asphalt paving, were built to Community Services District standards, not to county standards. Defined as "semi-public," the roads will be maintained by the District without County assistance--and thus the costs will be shared by only Bear Valley Springs lot owners.

According to the District consulting engineer, county design specifications for curves, sight distances, etc., were unnecessarily strict for mountain-subdivision roads. Building the roads to these standards would have required very large cuts and fills and a great deal of topographical alteration. Dart applied for and got County approval to build its roads according to special subdivision road standards which allowed tighter curves and shorter sights to fit the mountainous terrain. The County Board of Supervisors subsequently adopted, for health and safety reasons, a moratorium on this type of semi-public road.

The District engineer asserted that both the principle behind the special standards, and Dart's construction practices, which took the best features of those standards and improved on them, were good. However, he did acknowledge that there was room within the less stringent guidelines for abuse by unconscientious subdividers.[23]

Drainage

Bear Valley Springs' drainage system is more than adequate. It has not suffered from the severe erosion problems that have plagued Tahoe Donner, the other Dart Resorts subdivision profiled in this study. The system was built to handle the runoff from a 100-year storm. It includes gravel-lined channels, two ponds for impounding storm waters, and a sediment basin. Dart maintains the drainage (and roads) in each tract for one year after construction. The Community Services District then accepts maintenance responsibility. According to the former Manager of the District, "Dart has generally good drainage practices and has done its best to reduce erosion. We won't accept the roads or drainage system without adequate erosion control."[24]

Electricity and Telephone

The Southern California Edison Company has extended main electricity lines to all areas of the site except one 720-lot unit.

Dart has filed a letter of credit with the electric company to guarantee this extension. Secondary lines will be extended to lots when building plans are approved, but purchasers must pay a pole to house fee of $2.40 per foot if the house is more than 100 feet from the electricity line.

Pacific Telephone and Telegraph has installed telephone lines. There is no pole to house fee unless the distance is greater than 800 feet. All utility lines are above ground. They were put in, according to a Kern County planning official, before a state law requiring underground utilities was passed.

COMMUNITY AND RECREATIONAL FACILITIES

Bear Valley Springs, planned as a recreational second-home subdivision, has minimal community services: a fire station, a police force, a small general store and a snack bar. Dart has set aside five school sites and twenty-five acres for a town center. However, residents must now travel eleven miles to Tehachapi for all major facilities and services.

Access to Bear Valley Springs is strictly controlled. Police protection is provided by four full-time on-site policemen and four full-time gate attendants hired by the Community Services District.

Schools are the responsibility of the Tehachapi Unified School District. The nearest elementary schools are in Tehachapi and Cummings Valley; the nearest high school is in Tehachapi.

There are no major medical facilities near Bear Valley Springs, the lack of which concerned the Kern County Health Department. In commenting on the Environmental Impact Report (EIR), the Health Department staff suggested that the developer prepare for the eventual need to provide emergency health-care services for the development.[25] Dart has not yet done so. The only on-site emergency health care is first-aid training for the police.

Fire protection is furnished by the Tehachapi Substation of the Kern County Fire Department. According to the EIR, the Department recommended an on-site fire station, which Dart built and deeded to the County. The station is manned by a volunteer force. Emergency access roads and a fire-suppression water system have been installed, and fire hydrants are being added.

However, these provisions for fire protection may not be adequate. The California Subdivision Public Report warns purchasers that Bear Valley Springs is in a high-hazard grass- and brush-fire area. The EIR further reports that the area is susceptible to the phenomenon of "'dry lightning'...[which] creates a considerable fire hazard, since strikes may occur in remote [areas]...where they are hidden from the view of fire look-outs and access is difficult by overland fire fighting equipment."[26]

These warnings were reiterated by Project Land Use which reported to INFORM that the north slope of Bear Mountain is an area of extreme fire hazard. "The slope is heavily overgrown with brush and trees and is tinder dry in the summer. If a fire starts downslope and the winds are right, it could sweep up that face of the mountain in a matter of minutes. Without adequate warning, residents might not be able to evacuate in time."[27]

Recreational facilities at the project include: a nine-hole golf course, a recreation center, campgrounds, rifle and archery ranges, an equestrian center and trails, a trail-bike course, a park, and two man-made ponds. Dart constructed these facilities and deeded them to the Community Services District. The District then leased them to the property-owners association, which hired Dart to manage and operate them. By agreement, Dart will pay all golf-course maintenance and operation costs for four and a half years, and subsidize the association's operations. In an interview in 1974, the consulting engineer for the District stated that ultimately the development's recreation facilities might not be of adequate capacity in periods of peak use, although they seemed so during the project's planning phase, and are certainly so now.[28]

ENVIRONMENTAL PROTECTION

Dart used some environmentally sound planning and development techniques at Bear Valley Springs. There is a significant amount of open space, lots are scaled to the terrain, and there is adequate drainage and erosion control. However, the company ignored some of the intrinsically limiting aspects of the land when laying out the subdivision and planning for roads, water supply, and sewage disposal. These included geological hazards, slope, and groundwater. It was also rather insensitive to some of the site's special ecological resources. In comparison to other companies in this study, Dart's land-use and water-resource protection practices at Bear Valley Springs are fair.

PLANNING

Bear Valley Springs is laid out in a curvilinear pattern which conforms well to its precipitous topography. About 5,950 acres of the steepest, most rugged land--nearly 24% of the site--are being

preserved in their natural state.* This open-space allocation is
larger than that at most of the subdivisions studied by INFORM.
However, since approximately two-thirds of the Bear Valley Springs
site has very steep slopes, more land should have been set aside.
Dart has planned around the slope problem to a certain extent by
subdividing the steeper land into large lots. (About 40% of the
lots at Bear Valley Springs are two to ten acres or larger.)

The company has phased development and lot sales, but not development and occupancy. In what may be a nearly unique case of
over-diligence,† Dart installed all the site's basic services at
the outset. Since build-out is proceeding slowly, utility lines
may lie idle for many years.

Dart did prepare an Environmental Impact Report on Bear Valley
Springs. However, such reports were not required until 1972, when
California law changed. By that time most of the improvements for
the project had been completed. As the Report noted: "The question of adverse environmental effects which cannot be avoided is
somewhat out of phase, as the developer has basically completed the
project with the exception of two tracts."[29]

LAND

Despite its attempts to develop Bear Valley Springs as a natural, unspoiled weekend and vacation retreat, Dart failed to fully
protect the site's special ecological resources and characteristics.
More harmonious development practices could both have preserved
some areas of critical environmental concern, and avoided subjecting prospective lot owners to certain natural hazards.

Areas of Critical Environmental Concern

The site includes three types of areas of critical environmental concern. None has been adequately protected. Used previously
only as a cattle ranch, it contained the undisturbed habitats of
relatively uncommon flora and fauna. The western slopes of the
site are part of the range of the once plentiful California condor.
The condor, a huge vulture whose population has been reduced by

---

*As mentioned earlier, Dart has never followed up on its plan to
subdivide the 1,265-acre tract on the top of Bear Mountain. This
tract is presently undeveloped. If Dart preserves the land, the
site will have a 28% open-space allocation. If it sells the tract,
the 5,950 acres already allocated to open space will constitute 24%
of the remaining acreage.

†Dart also installed all services at its Tahoe Donner subdivision,
which is profiled in this book.

man's encroachment to about sixty birds, is on the Department of
the Interior's list of endangered species. The Mountain Quail,
also rare but not endangered, is found on the higher elevations of
Bear Mountain.[31]

The site contains a wide diversity of wildlife: birds, reptiles, and mammals. Larger mammals include California mule deer, fallow deer, black bear, coyotes, bobcats, and possibly ring-tailed cats and mountain lions. According to the EIR, this wildlife will in general suffer from "the physical removal of habitat for roads, homes, and facilities," and from the introduction of a new population: humans.[32]

The California Department of Fish and Game reported to INFORM that although Bear Valley Springs is not solely responsible for diminishing wildlife, it is yet another factor contributing to the urbanizing of the area. And while it is the cumulative effect of many subdivisions that threatens to displace the wildlife, Dart is at least individually responsible in two ways. The Kern County Health Department particularly criticized Dart's placement of a trail-bike course for motorcycles and a rifle range at the western edge of the site, the area the condor is most known to frequent. In its comments on Bear Valley Springs' Environmental Impact Statement, the Health Department stated, "We cannot expect that hunters and those utilizing the shooting area will automatically avoid taking a 'potshot' at such a conspicuous animal as the condor. Additionally, it would be expected that the trail bike course could be disruptive to these animals, which historically are noted to shy away from developed areas."[33]

Neither the Health Department nor the Department of Fish and Game was satisfied with Dart's general approach to wildlife management. Both agencies questioned the recommendations of Dart's ecological consultant that "a sportsmen's association be formed, and a hunting program established to control the deer and other populations."[34] Also questionable was the reference made in a Dart report to management programs for "removal" of bears if they become a nuisance, particularly around garbage cans. According to a Health Department comment on the EIR, "We wonder about the propriety of proposing the removal of bears from _Bear_ Mountain and _Bear_ Valley!"[35]

Bear Valley Springs is not only endowed with wildlife, but with special forms of vegetation. These exist in particular around an unusual "ephemeral lake," which appears in the rainy season in the central valley floor and becomes a marsh in the dry season. According to the County Health Department's comments on the EIR, this formation is a type of "vernal poolbed," which was "once common in the montane valleys in the Tehachapi region; with the exception of the remaining one in Bear Valley, most have been destroyed

by farming or other development.... To protect the unique flora
found there...development should not be allowed to destroy or significantly alter this unusual natural resource."[36] While Dart set
aside the area as a drainage easement, so that there would be no
building directly on it, some lots do include parts of the ephemeral lake. Development may thus obviously occur in such close proximity to it that damage or pollution of the resource could result.

A final area of special concern at Bear Valley Springs is its
archeological resources. A local archeologist is convinced from
the reports of hunters and others who have frequented the area that
it is rich in Indian remains, including pictographs.[37] The EIR
stated that, "Due to the probable archeological importance with regard to the potential archeological richness of Bear Valley, any
undue disturbance without an adequate site survey could result in
the loss of important antiquities."[38] However, no site survey or
inventory has been made, and the present Project Manager, when interviewed by INFORM, stated that he was "unaware" of archeological
sites.[39]

Areas Hazardous for Building

Beyond the threat to ecological resources, a potential resident will be concerned about hazards associated with the site.
There is an active earthquake fault. There are also landslide areas, extremely steep slopes, and areas subject to flooding. Dart
has adequately protected consumers against only one of these dangers. It has set aside as open space or classified as drainage
easements all areas subject to inundation in a 100-year storm.

The White Wolf Fault, a major earthquake fault (like the San
Andreas though not as long), cuts across the northwest corner of
the subdivision. Although there are no lots in this area, geological reports on the site show extensive faulting in areas where lots
have been mapped as well.[40]

The Environmental Impact Report on the site warns, "The Bear
Valley Springs area is part of a seismically active region."[41] It
continues, "While an exact prediction *cannot* be made, the probability of an earthquake occurring is felt by many to increase with
time.... It is generally felt that the area is within the region
where a maximum intensity earthquake of IX or X on the modified
Mercalli scale can be expected at some time in the future."[42] This
puts the site in one of the most severe earthquake areas in California (see Guidelines). Kern County's last earthquake, in 1952,
in which the White Wolf Fault was displaced vertically about three
to four feet, had a magnitude of 6.6 on the 10-point Richter scale.*[43]

---

*The Richter scale, a magnitude index, measures earthquake energy.
The Mercalli scale, an intensity index, measures actual ground
movement.

Steep cut with high erosion potential at Bear Valley Springs.

This earthquake danger at the site is not adequately disclosed to potential buyers. On the subject of site geology, the California Subdivision Public Report, quoting the state Division of Mines and Geology, states only that "'most of the area is underlain by relatively stable rock formations.'"[44]

Related to the problem of earthquakes is the one of landslides. Dart reported to INFORM that it has not subdivided any landslide areas. Project Land Use disagreed. "Much of the land on the northern portion of the subdivision is underlain by landslide features. Some of these moved during the 1952 earthquake on the White Wolf Fault and some did not. Some of the lots to be sold were located on these features, a very questionable practice if further earthquakes should occur. A seismic study commissioned by the Kern County Board of Supervisors stated that no conceivable use could be made of these areas as far as construction is concerned."[45]

Although California architects are trained in earthquake-proof construction, and California residents are used to the precarious geologic nature of their state, it is questionable whether a new subdivision for 12,000 to 15,000 people should be built in an active earthquake zone.

As was discussed earlier in this chapter, slope is also a problem on the mountainous Bear Valley Springs property. Many lots seem to have no level ground at all.[46] According to Project Land Use, most of the land on the north slope being left as natural open space "is so extremely steep and rugged that there is no way it could be built upon. Some of it is so steep that it is even dangerous to try and walk on. It is primarily an eroded fault scarp formed by the White Wolf Fault."[47] In fact, according to the EIR, "Category C slopes [31% or greater] comprise more than one-half of the project area, and a large percentage of these are 100% (1 horizontal unit to 1 vertical unit) or greater. As a result these areas tend toward instability and may under certain circumstances be subject to rapid erosion."[48]

According to the California Subdivision Public Report, the state Division of Mines and Geology "assume[s] that development will be concentrated on the more favorable sites, avoiding the steeper slopes."[49] However, construction may be planned on steep terrain. If it is, extensive erosion may become a very serious problem. Because of the expense, the engineering problems involved, and the possibility of erosion, slopes greater than 25% are widely considered to be unsuitable for building. (See Guidelines.)

There are two potential water-pollution problems at Bear Valley Springs: pollution of surface waters from erosion and runoff, and pollution of groundwater from sewage and septic-tank leaching. While Dart has controlled the former fairly well, it seems to be gambling with the latter.

Pollution from Erosion and Runoff

As noted, there is potential for serious erosion at Bear Vallay Springs. The shallow, coarse soils in parts of the site have been classified as "generally moderately to highly susceptible to erosion."[50] Lot development on steep slopes will exacerbate the problem since soils and vegetation will be disturbed. In addition, house construction will create impermeable surfaces, increasing runoff on land where it is particularly difficult to hold soils in place.

According to a Soil Conservation Service official, erosion has already resulted from construction of some house pads on steep slopes, and from some "pretty drastic cuts" which had to be made to put roads in on this mountainous terrain. Drainageways, clogged with silt, did overflow causing the land downslope to suffer siltation damage.[51] However, Dart has taken a number of precautions to lessen erosion. Its drainage system includes rock slope protection, siltation basins, and, wherever possible, natural channels with culverts under roads, rather than concrete storm sewers. Cuts are fertilized and reseeded, although reseeding has been difficult because of the dry climate. Dart has also tried to conserve natural vegetation and, apart from road construction, to avoid significantly altering the topography. Its roads have been built with permeable oiled surfaces, which are capable of absorbing water. In addition, it has platted large-size lots which leave more permeable ground than would smaller lots.

One step which has not been taken is the establishment of 100-foot buffer zones of natural land around the two artificial ponds and the ephemeral lake/marsh area. However, the former Bear Valley Springs Community Services District Manager, Walter Sandall, reported to INFORM that the two ponds have had no problems with siltation and sedimentation. In his view "Dart has done its best to reduce erosion."[52]

Pollution from Sewage

As was discussed earlier, Dart's sewage-disposal plans do not seem adequate to protect Bear Valley Springs' groundwater from pollution. Although its central sewage-treatment plant employs the

best available technology, only third-acre lots and condominiums--
10% of the site--will be connected to it. All lots one acre or
larger will rely on septic tanks or other individual disposal systems.

The site's soils have "severe" limitations for septic-tank
use. An official of the Soil Conservation Service predicted that
the septic systems will not function well. He noted the site's
slopes and the fact that in the lowest parts of the valley both
bedrock and the water table are very close to the surface. The official described the site as being like a dirt-filled saucer wherein water, running down the sides, forms a pool under the dirt at
the bottom. At Bear Valley Springs, this pool is the groundwater
from which Dart draws its water supply. He suggested that septic
effluent, running rapidly down from the higher slopes to the valley
floor, might pollute the groundwater, and that unless a central
sewage-collection and treatment system were built for the whole
site, there would be a health problem.[53] The EIR also mentioned the
potential for groundwater pollution.

As of 1976, the Community Services District monitoring program
had detected no significant impairment of groundwater quality. However, fewer than fifty families were then residing at the subdivision.

There is also the possibility that nutrients in the site's
treated sewage may indirectly cause one of the two artificial ponds
to become over-enriched. This potential results from what would
otherwise be sound environmental practice: spray irrigation of the
adjacent golf course with effluent from the sewage-treatment plant.
Unfortunately, the effluent may leach into the ponds too quickly
for the soil to adequately absorb its nutrients. The Health Department's recommendations to alleviate this problem included thorough treatment and chlorination of the effluent.[54] Dart followed
these recommendations.

The subdivision's central sewage plant will eventually have a
capacity for providing tertiary treatment to 225,000 gallons per
day of sewage. The first phase of the facility, which has a capacity of 100,000 gallons per day, is treating between 8,000 and
15,000 gallons per day depending upon the season. It is providing
treatment via activated sludge, aerobic digestion, sand filtration,
and chlorination. The second and final stage of construction will
increase the capacity by another 125,000 gallons per day.

As mentioned, the Bear Valley Springs project does have the
potential to deplete the groundwater resource by withdrawing too
much water. However, this eventuality should be avoided by the
Community Service District's monitoring program and by its option
to use 3,600 acre-feet per year of state water if there are any
signs of depletion.

CONSUMER PROTECTION

Dart has far better consumer practices than any other company studied by INFORM. Dr. K. Wayne Smith, President and Chief Executive Officer of Dart Resorts, indicated that because the company had no experience with land sales, it invented consumer policies according to what it considered good business practice. In a booklet designed to provide background on its 1969 entry into the land-development field, Dart explicitly stated that its land-development group's operating philosophy was to be "consistent with that of the Company's six other operating groups in developing consumer-oriented products of highest quality."[55] It translated this philosophy into specific guidelines which constitute, for the most part, model land-sales practices. Dart was also the most open, informative, and cooperative company of the nine studied by INFORM.

Sales

One of the most obvious differences between Dart and other large-scale land subdividers is that Dart appears genuinely concerned that lot buyers be well informed about their purchase, and that they buy for actual *use* rather than speculation. According to President Smith, "Purchasers must see the site before sales are final."[56] In addition, as required by California law, purchasers have fourteen days in which to reconsider their purchase and receive a full refund. The company claims that it encourages lot purchasers to talk with a lawyer during this period or before signing the sales agreement.

To promote real use, Dart made all basic services--central water, sewage disposal (to lots under one acre), paved roads, drainage, solid-waste disposal, electricity, and telephone--available within a few years after sales began. Because of soil limitations, the sewage system should probably have been extended to all lots in the subdivision. Nevertheless, no other subdivider in the INFORM sample guaranteed or even attempted to provide all necessary basic services at such an early stage of development.

Dart does not guarantee the purchaser a refund if promised services turn out to be impossible to obtain. However, according to President Smith, Dart has a standard complaint procedure whereby dissatisfied customers can petition for a refund or an exchange. Refunds or lot exchanges are granted "if the complaint is warranted." Dart exchanged a lot in one case where a septic system could not be installed because the water table was too high.

The company also promotes real use of lots by conducting a credit review of each purchaser. Lots between a third-acre and eighty acres in size cost $6,500 to $25,000. (Half of all lots are one acre and cost $10,000.) A prospective purchaser is "interviewed by a senior salesman or sales manager to assure that the terms and conditions of sale have been adequately explained and to confirm the purchaser's ability to pay."[57]

To discourage speculation, a single customer cannot purchase more than two homesite lots without formal management approval.[58] Dart even goes so far as to disavow the investment value of its lots. Customers are required to sign a statement verifying that salesmen did not promise or imply future appreciation of the lot at any specific rate. (Indeed, INFORM found from interviews with realtors in the town of Tehachapi that lots cannot even be sold for their original purchase price.) Only a salaried sales manager--not a commissioned salesman--can close a sale.

The company could take a few additional steps to further discourage speculation. It could require a cash downpayment of no less than 20% on all lots sold. (Downpayments now vary from 10% to 30%.) It could require a five-year payment period (a purchaser generally pays for a lot over ten years). A shorter payment period and a larger downpayment would, by requiring a greater financial commitment, serve to orient the purchaser even more toward real use of the lot.

The Purchase Agreement

Another outstanding difference between Dart and other land subdividers is the type of sales agreement it uses. Most land-sales companies sell lots on ten-year installment contracts, whereby purchasers pay approximately 4% to 8% interest on the unpaid balance annually. The consumer may neither use the lot, nor receive title until all payments are complete. Dart, by contrast, uses a sales agreement similar to a mortgage. While the purchaser still makes a downpayment, still pays for the lot over ten (or in a few cases even twenty) years, and is still charged interest (5.9% to 7.9%), he receives title to the lot, and permission to use it, immediately.* The purchaser also immediately becomes a member of the Bear Valley Springs Association and receives rights to use the common and camping areas.

If the lot buyer defaults on his payments, Dart institutes foreclosure proceedings, or, if the company and purchaser agree, a

---

*After making a downpayment, the purchaser signs a promissory note for the remainder, secured by a deed of trust. He then receives fee title. Permission to build may depend on Dart's subordinating its interest.

"deed in lieu" procedure by which the purchaser accepts a small payment for the deed.

Title Protection

Since the purchaser obtains title to the lot immediately, his interest in the land is fully protected in the event of the company's bankruptcy. All lots are platted with the County, and the company records the lot purchaser's deed with the County as well.

Costs

In addition to the basic lot price, a lot purchaser at Bear Valley Springs must pay a substantial collection of annual assessments. These include: property-owner association dues of $65; Community Service District taxes of $56 to $215, depending on lot size; a water-bond reduction charge of $130 to $360; a water-system standby charge of $36; a sewer standby charge (if the lot is one of the 10% under one acre) of $72; and property taxes of $203 to $782. These additional assessments total between $490 and $1,530 a year.

Besides paying these fees, a lot purchaser must also pay one-time charges of $100 for hookup to the central water system and approximately $1,200 for the installation of a septic system (provided the lot is not connected to the central sewage system) before actually building a home on the lot.

Dart indicated to INFORM that if it were not subsidizing the property-owners association, members' dues would be $104 a year. With regard to both this annual assessment and that of the Community Services District, the California Subdivision Report's usual warning is applicable: "Expenses of operation are difficult to estimate initially and...tend to increase substantially with price increases and the increased age of the facilities."[59]

Legal Status

Bear Valley Springs is one of the few subdivisions in the INFORM study against which there are currently no legal actions pending. However, in December, 1975, Dart settled two class-action suits, brought against it by dissatisfied purchasers who claimed that lots had been sold to them on the basis of an investment value which did not exist. The settlement provided refunds of 65% of paid principal and interest to those purchasers who owned lots; and of 58% of paid principal and interest to those purchasers who had stopped payments and had been foreclosed upon. About eighty purchasers who did not file a claim under these refund options are in an "arbitration class" and must testify before the court for individual relief. According to the attorneys for the plaintiffs, Dart has refunded approximately $1 million.[60]

COST OF LOTS BOUGHT ON THE INSTALLMENT PLAN

LOT PRICE

basic price (1/3 - 80 acres)	$6,500 - $25,000
finance charge (6% - 8%)	$1,943 - $10,258
Total	$8,443 - $35,258

ADDITIONAL ANNUAL ASSESSMENTS DURING TERM OF CONTRACT

property owners associations	$65
Community Services District	$57 - $215
water bond reduction charge	$130 - 360
water standby charge	$36
sewer standby charge (lots under 1 acre)	$72
property taxes	$203 - $782
Total, per year	$490 - 1,530
Total, 10 years	$4,900 - $15,300

ONE-TIME COSTS FOR SERVICES

lot survey		0
water		$100
well	—	
central extension	0	
central hookup	$100	
sewage		$5 - $1,200
septic system	$1,200	
central extension	0 - $1,000	
central hookup	$5	
electricity		0
telephone		0

---

*Includes industrial, commercial, and multi-family lots.

ENVIRONMENTAL CHECKLIST

Overall environmental protection record: FAIR

Does the subdivider:

PLANS	Plan for complete basic services?	YES
	Phase lot sales and extension of services?	YES
	Get 80% build-out in 10 years of each section marketed?	NO
	Prepare an Environmental Impact Report?	YES
LAND	Use a curvilinear or cluster design?	YES
	Retain 25% or more open space?	NO
	Reserve from lot sale and development the following areas of critical concern:	
	wetlands?	--
	dunes and beaches?	--
	water sources?	NO
	prime agricultural lands?	--
	habitats of endangered species?	NO
	prime historical, archaeological, cultural, aesthetic, or recreational resources?	NO
	Reserve from lot sale and development the following areas hazardous for building:	
	geological hazard areas (earthquake, landslide)?	NO
	flood-prone areas (100-year floodplains, arroyos)?	YES
	areas of slope exceeding 25%?	NO
	Blade roads only in immediate development areas?	YES
	Clear only for buildings and roads?	YES
	Preserve existing topography?	NO
WATER RESOURCES	Design the drainage system to control erosion?	YES
	Retain 100-foot buffer zone around water bodies?	NO
	Replant disturbed land immediately?	YES
	Limit septic systems to one-acre or larger lots with adequate: percolation rates, slope, and distance from bedrock, water table and surface waters?	NO
	When utilizing central sewage disposal, provide tertiary treatment (or secondary and land disposal)?	YES
	Avoid major stream alteration?	--
	Avoid major wetland dredging and filling?	--
	Use groundwater only up to the safe yield?	YES

*Floodways have been sold, but are covered by drainage easements on which owner cannot build.

†One acre limit but most of site classified by SCS as having "severe" limitations for septic tank use.

NOTE: See chapter on "Guidelines" for more complete explanation of items on Checklist.

BEAR VALLEY SPRINGS 447

CONSUMER CHECKLIST

Overall consumer protection record: GOOD

Does the subdivider:

<table>
<tr><td rowspan="12">SALES</td><td>Conduct a credit check on lot purchasers?</td><td>YES</td></tr>
<tr><td>Limit lot sales to two per purchaser?</td><td>YES</td></tr>
<tr><td>Sell only residential, i.e., no industrial, commercial or multi-family lots on installment contracts?</td><td>YES</td></tr>
<tr><td>Require a cash downpayment of 20% on all sales?</td><td>NO</td></tr>
<tr><td>Limit duration of installment contracts to 5 years?</td><td>NO</td></tr>
<tr><td>Charge no interest on installment contracts?</td><td>--</td></tr>
<tr><td>Encourage attorney review of sales documents?</td><td>YES</td></tr>
<tr><td>Require a pre-purchase site visit?</td><td>YES</td></tr>
<tr><td>Allow a 14-day rescission period in which purchaser can obtain a refund for any reason?</td><td>YES</td></tr>
<tr><td>Offer a partial refund if purchaser defaults?</td><td>NO</td></tr>
<tr><td>Guarantee a refund, with interest, if promised services are not made available by date specified in contract?</td><td>NO</td></tr>
<tr><td>Escrow contract payments, or provide equivalent surety bonding, for refund purposes?</td><td>YES</td></tr>
<tr><td rowspan="4">TITLE</td><td>Offer only platted lots?</td><td>YES</td></tr>
<tr><td>Offer a recordable contract, and record the sale?</td><td>YES</td></tr>
<tr><td>Offer unmortgaged land, or land mortgaged with a release clause, only?</td><td>YES</td></tr>
<tr><td>Upon contract signing, deed title to purchaser, or place title in trust?</td><td>YES</td></tr>
<tr><td rowspan="15">BASIC SERVICES</td><td>Guarantee, or have available, to each lot:</td><td></td></tr>
<tr><td>central water, of adequate quantity and quality?</td><td>YES</td></tr>
<tr><td>central sewage disposal, as necessary?</td><td>NO</td></tr>
<tr><td>drainage system, adequate for 100-year storm?</td><td>YES</td></tr>
<tr><td>solid waste disposal, via adequate method?</td><td>YES</td></tr>
<tr><td>roads, paved, to county standards?</td><td>NO</td></tr>
<tr><td>electricity and telephone?</td><td>YES</td></tr>
<tr><td>Guarantee completion through escrowing or surety bonding?</td><td>YES</td></tr>
<tr><td>If services are financed through special service district bonds, employ them only if:</td><td></td></tr>
<tr><td>initial governing body includes a county official?</td><td>?</td></tr>
<tr><td>elections include all landowners on one-man, one-vote basis?</td><td>NO</td></tr>
<tr><td>sum of bonds is less than twice the developer's investment in basic services?</td><td>YES</td></tr>
<tr><td>sum of bonds is less than 15% of the assessed value of land in the district?</td><td>NO</td></tr>
<tr><td>developer co-signs all bonds?</td><td>?</td></tr>
</table>

*Company forecloses or provides small payment to purchaser.

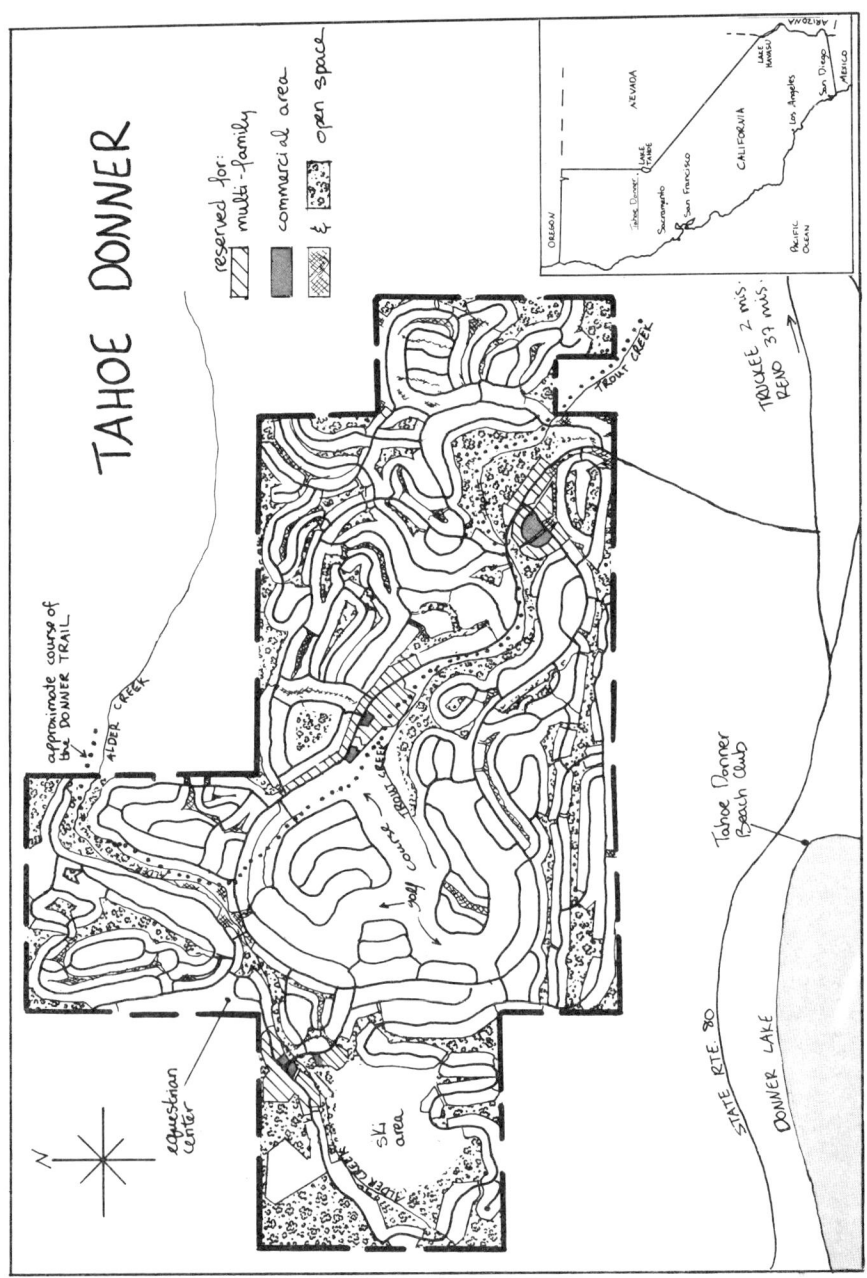

4
Tahoe Donner

> In the beginning...[there was] a tremendous mountain range...[next came] gorges, rivers, and lakes. Plants, animals, and birds moved in and made the Sierra their home. At Tahoe Donner, that's pretty much the way it is today.... If you like the way it is, you'll like the way it's going to be.[1]

Thus did Dart Industries, Inc., advertise its 4,020-acre recreational subdivision in California's Sierra Nevada Mountains. Tahoe Donner was as Dart described it. Located in the Lake Tahoe area, 38 miles from Reno, Nevada and 200 miles from San Francisco, Tahoe Donner is in a mountainous land of pine and fir forest interspersed with meadows and two mountain streams. Nearby is Donner Lake, "one of the most beautiful glacial lakes in the Sierra."[2] Prior to the start of construction, only dirt roads entered the area. Use was confined primarily to hunting, fishing, livestock grazing, and Christmas-tree farming.

Enthusiastic advertising copy notwithstanding, however, it is virtually impossible to maintain a wilderness while carving it into nearly 5,800 single-home lots of one-third to one-half acre in size designed to house a peak population of 19,545 people, as Dart has done at Tahoe Donner. Indeed, those natural characteristics of a mountain subdivision which make it most desirable and marketable--clear-running streams, quiet forests, unspoiled lakes, prevalence of trout, deer, and other wildlife--are often those most susceptible to degradation from development.

Dart, better known for its Rexall, Westbend, and Tupperware products, is, in terms of both environmental and consumer practices the most responsible developer of the nine studied by INFORM.* Yet serious problems in protecting water resources have been attributable to Dart's Tahoe Donner development activities.

Tahoe Donner is one of Dart's first land-development ventures. (The other is Bear Valley Springs, also profiled in this study.) It acquired the site, then called Tahoe Northwoods, when it purchased the two-year-old Lakeworld Development Company in December, 1970, and established a land-development subsidiary, Dart Resorts.

The benefits of Dart's being a newcomer to the land-development business are clear in the consumer area. It had an opportunity to start fresh, and its sales and title-protection practices are a radical departure from those of the other eight companies studied. The company conforms to a majority of INFORM's guidelines for adequate consumer protection. In contrast, the other eight developers conformed to the INFORM consumer-protection guidelines by and large only when state law required such policies.

In the environmental area, however, Dart has made serious mistakes. Its development methods initially caused severe erosion, though it appears to have considerably improved its practices over time. More importantly, Dart failed to take a sufficiently close look at the practicality and potential environmental impact of the plan agreed upon by Lakeworld and the county for providing the development with water and sewage disposal. The provision of both services has since spawned heated controversy. At present, the capacity of the water and sewage-disposal systems is insufficient to handle the needs of all lots sold. The California Department of Real Estate has halted lot sales at the subdivision, and a group of Tahoe Donner lot purchasers has filed a class-action suit against Dart Industries seeking $100 million in damages. The suit charges the company with fraud and misrepresentation as to the adequacy of sewer, water, and recreational facilities. (See discussion under Legal Status.)

Regional Context

Tahoe Donner is being built three miles northwest of the town of Truckee, California (population 1,400) in Nevada County. In 1970, 92% of the Truckee region's 23,500 acres was forest and open space. Only 8%--1,820 acres--was developed land. Tahoe Donner committed an additional 2,862 acres (not counting the 28.8% of the site to be left as open space) to development, more than doubling the land so used in the region.

The Dart project is not the only one in the area. The North Tahoe region has about 25 developments and has practically run out of large landholdings. Between 1964 and 1970, Nevada County acquired

---

*Includes the companies in Volumes I and II of this study.

an estimated 36,000 to 41,000 subdivision lots with a capacity for accommodating between 110,000 and 125,000 new residents.[4] As the population of the County was projected to be just 25,000 by 1970, there was clearly the potential for local resources to be overwhelmed.

Subdivision activity in the 1960s was already adversely affecting Nevada County's social and ecological environment. In July, 1970, California's Environmental Quality Study Council prepared a "memorandum of facts" on subdivisions within the state. Focusing on the impact of subdivision activity in the foothills and flatlands of the western part of the County, the Council commented:

> An estimated 160 miles of streams (37% of the stream mileage within Nevada County) have already been damaged by siltation, stream-bank alterations and domestic waste discharges resulting from subdivision development....
>
> The value of the land for wildlife is expected to diminish steadily as more homes are constructed. Some of the land now being subdivided is deer winter range which is already in critically short supply.
>
> Poorly designed subdivision roads are one of the biggest sources of silt pollution in Nevada County.[5]

The report pointed to the failure of California laws to cope with the situation:

> The subdivision questionnaire as issued by the State Department of Real Estate does not, for the most part, apply to the problems, and most of the control over environmental factors is relegated to the local agencies.[6]

By the late 1960s, subdivision was threatening to become a self-perpetuating phenomenon. A California Department of Fish and Game report found that the demand for land was greatly increasing the assessed valuations of adjacent lands. Rising taxes encouraged many larger agricultural and timberland owners to subdivide their holdings or sell to subdividers.[7]

Into this milieu came Lakeworld, with a plan for a new major recreational subdivision. It bought the land at Tahoe Donner for $3 million. The County Planning Commission approved the project in 1969, and Lakeworld submitted the first tentative subdivision map in March, 1970, nine months before Dart assumed responsibility for the project by acquiring Lakeworld.

The approval process involved a good deal of controversy. Local residents protested that considerable forest environment would be lost to urban development, and that if such a project had to be approved, other land was more suitable for the purpose. Approval of the tentative map was therefore made subject to a number of conditions designed to protect the environment and assure adequate facilities to support the new residential community. Some of these conditions instead were the seeds of Dart's subsequent problems. The conditions included:

- Annexation of the entire subdivision to the Truckee Sanitary District and construction of a complete sewer system in each unit.
- Agreement of the Truckee Donner Public Utility District to provide water to the subdivision.
- Provisions via deed restrictions for stabilization of soils during building and site-preparation work by future owners, regulation of tree cutting, and preservation of trees and open spaces on the rear 25 feet of all lots.
- Inclusion in subdivision-improvement work of soil-stabilization measures on cuts, fills, graded areas, and drainageways to be approved by the County Public Works Department based on recommendations of the Lahontan Regional Water Quality Control Board.
- Approval of drainage facilities by the Lahontan Board and the Public Works Department.
- Delineation in the final subdivision map of the limits of flooding caused by a 100-year storm, and prohibition of activity within this area which would degrade or threaten water quality.
- Widening of green belts to provide a deer corridor, in accordance with the requirements of the County Planning Director and with consideration of California Department of Fish and Game studies.[8]

These conditions have been met with varying degrees of success, as will be discussed below. What is now clear, however, is that while the County accurately foresaw many of the environmental problems inherent in Lakeworld's, and subsequently Dart's, subdivision plans, it was not skilled at devising solutions.

The County's most serious mistake, and one which has had disastrous consequences for many lot purchasers, was allowing a subdivision, potentially eight times the size of the local community, to rely on community resources for basic services. It was inevitable that these resources would be rapidly overtaxed, as indeed they now are. The local utility district has available from its present wells and springs only enough water to serve 1,324 additional connections at average rates of use.[9] Dart has already sold 2,200 Tahoe Donner lots, all of which will eventually require water.

Even worse, the Truckee Sanitary District's sewage-treatment facility, which processes Tahoe Donner's sewage, has already reached capacity. The Lahontan Regional Water Quality Control Board ordered a ban on new connections, including any at Tahoe Donner, on June 5, 1975. The California Department of Real Estate thereupon ordered a ban, which is still in effect, on further lot sales at Tahoe Donner.

THE OFFERING: LAND AND IMPROVEMENTS

LAND

Physical Characteristics

Tahoe Donner lies in a relatively level basin in a mountainous area about fifteen miles north of Lake Tahoe. It is close to that area's famous skiing and gambling resorts. Though most of the site is about 6,500 feet above sea level, the elevation of the land varies from a low of 6,200 feet to a high of 7,400 feet. Two mountain streams--Trout and Alder Creeks--cut across the development. While the area is green in the summer, it can be blanketed by many feet of snow in winter.

Status of Development

Of Dart's 4,020 acres, 52.5% has been divided, in a curvilinear pattern, into third- and half-acre single-family lots.* Another 1.9% (76.4 acres) is allocated to 469 multiple-family and condominium units; and over 5% (about 200 acres) is devoted to recreational, community, and commercial facilities. Dart has left a commendable 28.8% of the site--fully 1,158 acres--as natural open space. Since this is a recreational subdivision, there will be no industry on site.

Construction at Tahoe Donner began in 1970, and sales began in June of 1971. Work on facilities and amenities (roads, water and sewer mains, drainage system, ski complex and other recreational facilities) at the site is now virtually complete.

As of mid-1975, Dart had invested over $40 million in Tahoe Donner,[10] and there were 416 homes completed. According to the Draft Environmental Impact Report prepared by the Truckee Donner Public Utility District, Dart estimates that home construction and occupa-

---

*Dart also owns an additional 1,896-acre parcel, known as the Fibreboard acquisition, adjacent to the western boundary of the subdivision, but has announced no firm plans for development yet.

tion will occur at an annual rate of 2% during the first ten years
and 3% thereafter.

> At full use in 2008 the project is expected to
> have a maximum population of 19,545. The esti-
> mated average population is 14,854 including
> 10,945 seasonal and 3,909 permanent residents.
> In all probability the proportion of permanent
> residents will be much greater as the project
> moves toward full development. In such a case
> the peak population may approach the maximum
> population.[11]

All eleven units--consisting of 5,794 single-family lots and
469 multi-family and condominium lots--planned for Tahoe Donner
have been platted with Nevada County. As of mid-1976, only the
first seven of these units, covering 3,832 single-family lots and
160 condominiums, had been approved for sale by the California
Department of Real Estate, but sales have been suspended until the
settlement of the water and sewage situation described below.
While nearly half of the site's lots have been sold, only 47 homes
are occupied on a permanent basis. Occupancy is thus falling
far short of the 2% (120 units) a year anticipated. If growth
continues at its current pace it will be 500 to 600 years before
full occupancy occurs.

BASIC SERVICES

Dart has done more in the way of providing basic services than
any of the other subdividers studied by INFORM. At Tahoe Donner
it promised, in the sales agreement, central water, central sewage
disposal, an adequate drainage system, and paved roads, and guaranteed their completion through escrow accounts and surety bonding.
And, indeed, it completed construction of these facilities within
five years after lot sales began.

Unfortunately, as mentioned above, although water and sewer
mains are all in place, there is currently nowhere for the water to
come from and nowhere for the sewage to go.

Seven service districts and three property and condominium
owners' associations will operate and maintain all site facilities
and services. These districts* all include land and residents outside of Tahoe Donner. According to Dart, although the number of

---

*In addition to the Truckee Sanitary District and the Truckee Don-
ner Public Utility District, Tahoe Donner was annexed to the local
fire, school, airport, hospital, snow-removal and solid-waste disposal districts.

voting members (resident registered voters) varies depending on the district, the average is about 900. The districts have authority to tax Tahoe Donner lot owners and to issue bonds to pay for capital improvements. The amounts of both bonds and assessments are limited by state law. In the immediate future, only the Truckee Sanitary District (sewage) and Truckee Donner Public Utility District (water) are likely to have major capital expenditures.

The three property owners' associations* also have authority to assess the lot owners, although not to issue bonds. The associations' functions are to own, operate, and maintain common areas and facilities including parks, open space, and recreational amenities. Dart currently subsidizes the Tahoe Donner Owners' Association so yearly assessments are only $78. If lot owners were to pay the actual costs of operation and maintenance, Dart estimates that assessments would be $150 to $180. Since voting membership in the Association is based on lot ownership, Dart still has a controlling interest.

Water

In September, 1974, Dart Industries expressed its belief that "before any developer commits its funds to improvements, it must be assured of the availability of basic utilities.... Water is, of course, critical. Without it, there can be no development."[12] Dart may have learned this the hard way; for in the three-year period prior to the issuance of this statement, Tahoe Donner's water problems occasioned a suit against the company by the state of California; a five-month halt to sales; Dart's posting of a $5 million bond to cover possible consumer refunds; the abandonment of the subdivision's original million-dollar water intake-and-distribution facilities; the preparation of a 250-page Environmental Impact Report; and Dart's establishment of a $1.6 million letter of credit to cover possible costs of alternate water-supply facilities.

The site water problem, as Dart is quick to point out, originated in planning for which Lakeworld and local agencies were responsible. As mentioned, County subdivision approval was conditional upon Lakeworld's annexation to the Truckee Donner Public Utility District--the local water supplier. Yet in the late 1960s, the District was already concerned that the springs and wells upon which it relied might not be sufficient to meet the area's future water requirements. On the advice of a consulting firm (which could not find groundwater adequate to supply future needs) the

---

*The three associations are the Tahoe Donner Owners' Association, to which all owners belong, and the Ski Bowl Condominium Association and Golf Course Condominium Association, to which only condominium owners belong.

District applied to the California Water Resources Control Board in 1969 for permission to withdraw up to 4,000 acre-feet of water a year from Donner Lake.

According to a public statement issued by Dart, the District contracted with Lakeworld in March, 1970, to supply some of this Donner Lake water to the 5,800-lot Tahoe Donner subdivision. At the time, the District served just 517 domestic and 128 commercial connections. When Dart acquired Lakeworld, it agreed to pay for the pipeline and treatment facilities which the District would need to supply Tahoe Donner. These were completed, at a cost of $1 million, in 1973.

The pipeline and its potential effects promptly caused controversy. Homeowners already living around Donner Lake cited studies indicating that Dart's water use would lower the Lake's level one or two feet. They formed a "Plug the Pipeline Committee." One environmental advocate called Tahoe Donner's pipeline to the Lake the "vampire of the Sierras."[13]

On June 29, 1973, the California State Lands Commission sued Dart and the water district for installing the pipeline over the state-owned lake bed without proper permits.* Following the suit, Dart agreed with the California Department of Real Estate to halt lot sales for five months and to post a $5 million bond to cover refunds to lot purchasers should an adequate water supply not be found. The company also agreed to resume sales only in seven of the eleven units originally planned for the development. In addition, Dart extended a $1.6 million irrevocable letter of credit enabling the Truckee Donner Public Utility District to cover the costs of developing alternative water sources should that become necessary, and in 1974, hired a water-search consultant to find additional well sites.

The questions of where Tahoe Donner will obtain its water and what occupancy level the supply will support are still unanswered. As of late 1975, the Donner Lake pipeline, treatment, and pumping facilities lay idle. Dart and the District had withdrawn their request to use Donner Lake water.[14] Because it is involved in litigation over the water situation, Dart--the most cooperative company studied--would not discuss its future plans with INFORM. However, according to the County Public Works Department and others, Dart has done engineering surveys and test drilling, and has found a number of groundwater sources with a high probability of successful development. The final solution may cost Dart another million dollars, but few officials interviewed by INFORM questioned the company's commitment to fulfilling its obligation to lot owners.

As of the beginning of 1976, the 416 residences, including condominiums, using water at Tahoe Donner, together with the recrea-

---

*In California, all lake beds are under state jurisdiction.

tional facilities already operating, used 300 acre-feet annually (about 268,000 gallons per day). This represented almost half of the District's total usage and one third of its maximum capacity.* According to figures cited in the Truckee Donner Public Utility District Draft Environmental Impact Report (EIR), should *all* of the District's presently unused and reserve capacity--384 acre-feet per year--be allocated to Tahoe Donner, it could only supply, at present rates of use (0.29 acre-feet annually per connection), 1,324 additional homes. Yet a total of 2,200 homesites has already been sold to consumers. The needs of the entire subdivision were estimated in the EIR at 2,031 to 2,878 acre-feet per year.

The present cost of hookup to the central water system is not noted in the California Subdivision Public Report.† But according to Dart and the Truckee Donner Public Utility District, it is $150 plus the cost of extending a lateral line from the main line to the house.

Sewage

Tahoe Donner's difficulties in disposing of its sewage are even more acute than those it has experienced in obtaining water. The subdivision presently produces approximately 80,000 to 130,000 gallons a day of sewage. This is treated and disposed of at the 1.16 million-gallon-per-day Truckee Sanitary District sewage facility.

However, the plant exceeded its permitted capacity in 1975. In June of that year, the regional water pollution control agency, the Lahontan Regional Water Quality Control Board, accused the Truckee Sanitary District of bypassing overflow sewage to the nearby Truckee River. It issued a ban on any further sewer connections to the system, pending plant expansion and correction of severe infiltration/inflow problems. At the request of the Regional Board, the State Attorney General sued the District for injunctive and monetary relief.

The ban obviously left Dart with no method of sewage disposal for over 5,000 planned but unoccupied lots. It also left lot owners without permission to build. As a consequence, the California Department of Real Estate forbade further lot sales pending Dart's finding a way to remedy the situation. In an interim solution, the Truckee Sanitary District improved its facilities and cut back in-

---

*The Truckee Donner Public Utility District as a whole uses 700 acre-feet a year, has a maximum capacity of 847 acre-feet a year, and has known reserves of 237 acre-feet a year.[15]

†California requires the development company to issue a report disclosing pertinent information on the lots offered for sale.

filtration. As a result, on February 24, 1976, the Lahontan Board allowed the District 1,500 new connections, permitting current Tahoe Donner lot owners to build. However, the Department of Real Estate's prohibition on lot sales continues in effect.

Dart is not entirely to blame for this situation. According to a local realtor, Dart originally wanted to build its own treatment facility. However, the Lahontan Regional Water Quality Control Board required it to tie into the Truckee Sanitary District which would eventually tie into a regional plant. This regional facility, planned with a 12 million gallon-per-day capacity, was to provide high quality tertiary treatment for the sewage of the entire Tahoe-Truckee River Basin area.

The regional Tahoe-Truckee Sanitation Agency sought state and federal monies for the plant. These were only available based on population projections calculated from "bona fide 1970 census data." Proponents of the plant maintained that in the regional Tahoe-Truckee Sanitation Agency service area, census data tells only a small part of the story. Populations are seasonal, and the number of people expected in the future is much greater than the current population. Opponents, including the Sierra Club, do not contest these projections. However, they oppose expansion because the extra capacity would allow more growth than they feel the region can carry. The state of Nevada is opposed to a facility of any size because the site is upstream of Reno's water supply.[16]

The regional plant's design-capacity was reduced to 4.83 million gallons per day, adequate only for the existing population. EPA comments in the Environmental Impact Statement emphasize that sufficient federal funding for a larger treatment plant will not be forthcoming, and that any expansion of the facilities would have to be locally funded.

According to the Environmental Impact Statement, the population projection on which the 4.83 million gallon-per-day capacity is based "does not allow for the vacant lots now existing in established subdivisions which have building privileges (and outstanding sewage assessments)."[17] Thus, "the plant as proposed will be at or near capacity at startup,"[18] stated Roy C. Hampson, Executive Officer of the Lahontan Regional Water Quality Control Board. He estimates that within five years of the plant's opening, an additional capacity of 2.4 million gallons per day will probably be required.

Under current plans, the Truckee Sanitary District will be allowed to contribute only 1.16 million gallons per day to the proposed plant--an amount that is already processed by its present, inadequate facilities. Since full build-out of Tahoe Donner alone would generate nearly 2.0 million gallons of sewage per day, the District's allowable contribution would obviously not take care of the subdivision's wastes.

As was the case with its water supply, Dart would not discuss the sewage-disposal problem because of current litigation. However, its options seem relatively obvious. It and the other developers in the region can conserve water, go to court for permission to expand the regional plant, build their own treatment facilities, or upgrade the old Truckee Sanitary District facility to a tertiary treatment level (required by Nevada County). If the company cannot resolve the problem, it may have to refund payments to purchasers who have not yet built on their lots, and who may not be permitted, lacking adequate sewage-disposal facilities, to build in the future.

Hookup to Dart's sewage system costs homeowners $285 plus $5 per lineal foot for installation of lateral lines to the home. In addition, according to the California Subdivision Public Report, some lots in hollows require pumps costing an estimated $1,000. Besides these initial costs, lot owners pay assessments to the local Truckee Sanitary District and potentially also to the regional Tahoe-Truckee Sanitation Agency, even though they are not assured the right to tie in to either of these systems. The present sewage assessment for a $10,000 lot, levied by the Truckee Sanitary District, is about $20 per year. That assessment will increase with the expected hookup of the District into the regional sanitation system in 1977 or 1978, and may increase even more if Dart undertakes any of the aforementioned options.

Solid Waste

There is a local solid-waste district serving the Tahoe Donner and Truckee areas. The district provides regular trash pickup service for all residents and disposes of wastes at the Placer County sanitary landfill.

Roads

Roads at Tahoe Donner are paved, built to Nevada County standards, and dedicated to the County for maintenance. Bonds were posted for their completion. A County service district provides snow removal at a cost of $15 to $25 per year. At present, virtually all 62 miles of paved roads planned for the site are complete.

Drainage

Tahoe Donner's drainage system is complete and is adequate from a consumer perspective. One of the few subdivision drainage systems in INFORM's sample designed for a 100-year storm capacity, the system meets all County requirements and conforms with INFORM guidelines. All drainage is surface flow; ditches are rock-lined where high water velocities are expected, and grass- and soil-lined where velocities are expected to be less. Culverts run under the roads.

Maintenance of those parts of the drainage system which cross county-maintained roads is the County's responsibility. The rest of the system is the responsibility of the property owners' association.[19]

Utilities

Electricity and telephone lines have been extended to all Tahoe Donner lots and are connected to the 400 homes. Electricity is provided by the Truckee Donner Public Utility District at a connection charge of $350 for extension of wires from pole to house. Lot owners must pay an annual standby charge to the District of $15 for electricity and water. Telephone service is provided by Pacific Telephone & Telegraph. All utility lines are above ground.

COMMUNITY AND RECREATIONAL FACILITIES

Because Tahoe Donner is primarily a recreational, second-home development, its community facilities are minimal. Site residents must rely on the town of Truckee, three miles away, for schools, shopping facilities, medical and dental care, police protection, and public transportation.

The Truckee Fire District operates a station with a paid and volunteer force at the subdivision. However, the degree of fire protection it and the U.S. Forest Service can provide may be limited by water-storage facilities. According to a local realtor, the Truckee Fire District would like part of Tahoe Donner's idle water pipeline and pumping facilities to remain in place to protect Tahoe Donner and Donner Lake residents in the event of a major fire.

A school site has been reserved on the subdivision for future needs, and a gas station, a mini-market, and a four-acre shopping center are planned.

Recreation is a focus of Dart's sales effort at Tahoe Donner. While the site's recreational facilities are extensive compared to other subdivisions in this study, there is still some question as to whether they will be able to handle its peak population of 19,545 on a hot July afternoon.

As of mid-1976, Dart had completed construction of an eighteen-hole golf course; two clubhouses; an 11-acre equestrian center; a 220-acre ski area; a small beach on Donner Lake; two swimming pools; six tennis courts; and a campground.

As mentioned, the Tahoe Donner Owners' Association is responsible for operating and maintaining these facilities and Dart has turned over to it everything but the ski slopes and campground. It will continue to own and operate the ski day-lodge (restaurant, bar, equipment rentals, etc.) and a recreation building in the ski complex (with saunas, gym, and pool) which is for the exclusive use of condominium owners and hotel guests.

When the ski area is dedicated to the Association, the owners can decide if they want to operate it as a private facility or keep it open to the public. Dart agreed to indemnify the Association until it builds up a pool of money to operate the facilities. At present, the Association dues of $78 per year cover about half its actual operating costs. There are use fees for the golf course, ski lifts, and equestrian facilities.

Although the facilities at Tahoe Donner are more than adequate now, they may not always be. Usage is increasing; for example, average weekend attendance at the ski bowl increased from 300 people in 1974 to 2,000 people in 1975. Local residents also question the capacity of Tahoe Donner's small private beach, a 100-foot-long strip fronting on Donner Lake. They are concerned that, as the site's population increases, its residents may spill over onto the adjacent, also small, state-owned beach.

ENVIRONMENTAL PROTECTION

While Dart's environmental protection efforts at Tahoe Donner are among the better ones of the nineteen subdivisions studied, much of its good performance is due to the vigilance of concerned citizens and government agencies. There are also gaps in the company's policies. It has placed some homesites in hazardous areas. Erosion problems, though gradually being overcome, have been severe.

PLANNING

The basic layout of the site is environmentally sound. A significant amount of the land at Tahoe Donner has been reserved as open space: 28.8% of the site will be left in its natural state, and another 4.3% has been devoted to a golf course and ski area. The total amount alloted, 33.1%, puts Tahoe Donner among the small number of subdivisions in the INFORM study which exceed the INFORM guideline of 25% open space.

Lots and roads were laid out in a curvilinear rather than a grid pattern, which allows street alignment to conform to the terrain, reducing the need for grading and clearing.

However, according to the California Department of Fish and Game, the use of more advanced planning concepts could have helped mitigate Tahoe Donner's potential impact on the wildlife which is abundant in such mountainous areas. In 1970, the Department commented:

> It is tragically impossible to place large subdivisions such as...the proposed one north of Donner Lake in the wild lands of this State without [in] some degree--large or small--deteriorating the habitat of both fish and wildlife both on the site and in the adjacent area.[20]

The Department recommended that large subdivisions within wildlife-habitat areas not exceed an average density of one dwelling unit per two acres, or that lots be clustered so that at least 50% of the gross area is retained as permanent open space. This was not done at Tahoe Donner.

The Department of Fish and Game also recommended that Tahoe Donner reserve a corridor at least a quarter-mile (1,320 feet) wide to preserve the migration route used by deer going to and from their winter ranges. Tahoe Donner has a total width of 300 feet available for deer passage.[21]

Dart phased the installation of roads and utilities to coincide with lot sales. However, it did not time installation to coincide with projected *occupancy* of the subdivision. Its road, water, sewage, drainage, electricity, and telephone systems were constructed at the outset, at least thirty years before the project's scheduled build-out. While most of the other companies studied by INFORM ignored phasing, making minimal or no efforts to extend any services except roads by the time installment contract payments were completed, Dart erred in the opposite direction.

LAND

The Tahoe Donner site contains only one of INFORM's six types of areas of critical environmental concern: an area of prime historical interest. The Donner Trail, followed by the ill-fated pioneer party in the 1840s, crosses the property. It will be preserved, posted, and incorporated in the community trail system. Land lying in the 100-year floodplain is also reserved from development.

While Dart has employed these good land-allocation concepts, it has been less diligent about reserving from development lands not suited for building, including areas subject to geological hazards and areas of very steep slope. Although California architects and builders are familiar with techniques to mitigate such hazards, appropriate construction will be expensive for consumers and may still not fully prevent environmental damage.

One of the first considerations at any subdivision should be the ability of the land to support a building. The August, 1974, California Subdivision Public Report (California's lot sales disclosure document) for residential lots in Tahoe Donner's Unit I rather mildly states: "Most of this area is underlain by relatively stable rock formations. If construction is planned on steep terrain in the area, precautions should be taken during site development to minimize possible slope-stability problems."[22] The August, 1974, Public Report for the Golf Club Condominiums, however, includes a much stronger warning:

> The Uniform Building Code...provides for local building officials to exercise preventive measures during grading to eliminate or minimize damage from geologic hazards such as landslides, fault movements, earthquake shaking, rapid erosion or subsidence. This subdivision is located in an area where some of these hazards may exist. Some California counties and cities have adopted ordinances that may or may not be as effective in control of grading and site preparation.[23]

The Environmental Impact Report for the Truckee Donner Public Utility District, a document not readily available to purchasers at Tahoe Donner, is even more specific about geologic hazards. It states that, with a few exceptions, rocks and soils are stable and have no landslide potential. As for earthquakes, "The project area is located in a seismically active zone. Over 15 earthquakes of greater than magnitude 4 on the Richter Scale have been felt during the last 15 years." It predicts that "future seismic activity will probably occur near Truckee," and advises that "buildings and structures located on consolidated sediments or volcanics stand less chance of damage than those constructed on alluvium or glacial-fill areas." It describes glacial deposits as being concentrated in the western part of the site and alluvial deposits as covering "a small portion of the site generally adjacent to streams and meadows."[24]

The Environmental Impact Report also provides important information on the slope of land at Tahoe Donner:

> The ground slope, over most of Tahoe Donner, is from zero percent to 25 percent with one exception being the land near the ski area..., which has steep slopes from 25 to 40 percent....
> Ground slope from zero to 25 percent is considered satisfactory for residential development

while land with a slope greater than 26 percent
presents an unstable situation and is therefore
unsatisfactory for development.[25]

The Environmental Impact Report states (and an examination of a topographical map confirms) that a number of lots have been created on slopes of 25% to 40%. Besides involving the consumer in considerable expense for adequate and safe construction, subdividing such lots creates an enormous potential for erosion and loss of topsoil in the building process. Company practices in this area do not conform to INFORM's guideline of reserving from sale all land having a slope greater than 25%.

A final hazard not mentioned in the official documents cited above is that of excessive snow accumulations. According to a local realtor, Dart has allowed building in areas of potentially heavy snowdrifts and 100-mile-per-hour winds. He noted that in such areas it is impossible to keep roads plowed.

WATER RESOURCES

Virtually all of Dart's major environmental problems have had to do with water. In the course of development, the company caused, and had to correct, pollution from runoff and erosion in Trout Creek and Alder Creek, pollution from sewage infiltration of the Truckee River, and the potential drawdown of surface waters of Donner Lake.

Pollution from Erosion

Some soil erosion results from all land alteration and development. However, Dart made several mistakes in the initial phases of the project which produced serious erosion and siltation problems and necessitated major correction. To Dart's credit, it has worked to solve the problems and no one has faulted its cooperativeness. The Tahoe Donner ski slope was one initial problem area. It had been burned over in a forest fire and thus did not require clearing. However, Dart, in an effort to prolong the ski season, cleared away all the stumps and underbrush from the slope. (Leaving the stumps would have required waiting until enough snow had accumulated to cover them before opening the trails.)

The results of this diligence were horrifying. Dart executives watched the ski slopes slide away in the spring thaw, forming gullies big enough for toboggan runs. According to the Lahontan Regional Water Quality Control Board, the ski area was "a terrible mess" and the site's creeks were "badly muddied." Dart tried to correct the problem by reseeding the slopes and by building a siltation basin at the bottom. However, the basin was much too small, and even after being enlarged, it can handle only about half of the runoff.[26]

The revegetation effort was also only partially successful. Because of the dry summers and sandy soils, grasses did not take easily. Dart has had to construct contours and berms on the upper slopes to reduce erosion until natural revegetation can occur. It has also been necessary to irrigate the lower slopes to get grasses to grow. According to the Lahontan Board, these corrective measures have been "...all right. The slope is healing but there may be minor problems in the future. It will take two or three years to see if Dart's solutions will be effective over the long term."[27]

Another initial problem was the adverse impact on Trout Creek and Alder Creek of Dart's road-construction activities. Prior to the advent of the subdivision, the California Department of Fish and Game reported that these streams were excellent fish habitat. However, in November, 1971, the Department cited construction at Tahoe Donner as the cause of "quite turbid conditions" in these creeks. It reported that cinders used in road building were turning Trout Creek red. The Lahontan Board also found that excessively steep (more than 10%) road and drainage grades, large cuts and fills, and unlined drainage ditches were adding mud to the creeks. The problems were severe enough that the Truckee Outdoor Sportsmen's Club decided to stop stocking trout.

As with the ski slope, Dart took corrective action in conjunction with the Department of Fish and Game and the Lahontan Board. It now lines drainage ditches with either grass or gravel, depending on the velocities of the runoff flows. It uses jute matting and mulch until the reseeding season when it hydroseeds road cuts and excavations. It built several siltation basins in addition to the one at the base of the ski slope. And it submits its construction plans to the Lahontan Board for advice on siltation control.

According to Dr. Clarence Skau of the University of Nevada's Desert Research Institute in Reno, who has studied Trout and Alder since 1973, both creeks are now essentially healthy. He reiterated the Lahontan Board's opinion that Dart should have done better initial planning to avoid having to make costly and difficult corrections. However, he stated that trout production levels in Trout Creek are above average, probably because of nutrient enrichment. Dr. Skau also commented that Dart's contribution to Trout Creek water-quality problems is small, compared to those of a lumber mill, a California Highway Department maintenance yard, utility company cuts to lay cables, a gravel pit, and a county road--all of which cause sedimentation during rainstorms and snow melts.[28]

The California Department of Fish and Game concurs, though slightly more circumspectly. It believes the watershed has stabilized and reported that "loose" monitoring shows much improved water quality. "Trout seems to be running clear, while Alder has some cloudiness after a rainstorm. It's too early to say if Dart has done a good enough job. A subdivision is a massive environmental change."[29]

Dart has established open space buffer zones around the two creeks. However, in a number of places these are just barely of adequate width. Most environmental planners recommend a minimum 100 feet between a waterway and a building area to prevent polluting runoff from reaching the waterway. An examination of a topographical map of the Tahoe Donner subdivision indicates that as little as 50 feet has been left between certain homesite lots and the creeks; however, since building covenants prohibit building on the rear 25 feet of all lots, there will be at least 75 feet, and in most cases more distance, between actual buildings and stream banks.

Finally, Dart has established some good policies, dictated by lot covenants and restrictions, to preserve vegetative cover:

> Vegetation within any lot shall be planted and maintained in such a manner as to prevent or retard shifting or erosion and to encourage the growth of indigenous ground cover.

> The right of an Owner...to cut or remove any trees from his lot...shall be subject to...the approval thereof from the Environmental Control Committee.

> A rear yard...shall be the depth necessary to provide...an area equal to twenty percent (20%) of the gross area of such lot.[30]

Pollution from Sewage

As initially proposed, Lakeworld's Tahoe Northwoods project had one-acre lots with septic tanks for sewage disposal. However, the Lahontan Regional Water Quality Control Board discourages discharge of waste in heavily developed areas through individual underground disposal systems. The Board prevailed upon the Nevada County Planning Agency to require central sewage. As a result, Lakeworld reduced the minimum lot size and planned a sewage plant. This solution was not acceptable to the Board. It required Tahoe Donner to tie in with the Truckee Sanitary District's system, a decision which caused the site's current problems. (See discussion under Basic Services.)

Tahoe Donner's sewage presently receives only primary treatment, provided by the District's treatment facilities near Truckee.

The collection system discharges raw sewage into aeration lagoons where it decomposes by natural biological processes. The treated effluent is then disposed of in percolation and evaporation ponds, so that no waste is directly discharged into the Truckee River. Even with no direct discharge, a major portion of the untreated nutrients (nitrogen and phosphorus) in the sewage eventually reaches the River, threatening degradation of its recreational and aesthetic values.[31] This pollution problem was aggravated in 1975 when the plant reached maximum permitted capacity, and the Lahontan Board accused the Truckee Sanitary District of bypassing inadequately treated excess sewage directly to the River. The Board acted to limit such discharges until the District could tie into the regional sewage-treatment facility.

Groundwater and Surface Water Levels

Tahoe Donner originally posed a direct threat to Donner Lake, the beautiful "glacial lake" which adorns its advertising. The Lake is also the site of a state park. As was discussed earlier, the Truckee Donner Public Utility District applied for permission to draw as much as 4,000 acre-feet of water a year from Donner Lake. This withdrawal could have lowered the Lake level by up to two feet during the summer when both recreational and consumptive water uses are greatest. The Environmental Impact Report conceded that this could adversely affect recreational uses of the Lake, interfere with boat docks around the Lake, and disturb habitats for fish and aquatic organisms.

Water withdrawal from Donner Lake would also have diminished the amount of water the Lake released to Donner Creek and thence to the Truckee River. This would have reduced the ability of the Creek to maintain fish life. (The flow of the Creek is generally below the 15-cubic-feet-per-second rate that the Department of Fish and Game deems an optimum minimum.)

The Plug the Pipeline Committee, an offshoot of the Donner Lake Property Owners' Association, opposed the combined effort by the Truckee Donner Public Utility District and Dart to secure a water supply from the Lake. In a report citing various legal impediments and alternative measurements for the impact of the withdrawal, the Committee posed its basic question: "Why should the public [over half of the Donner Lake shoreline is public land] and owners of property near Donner Lake suffer ANY adverse effects for the sole purpose of producing dollars for Dart?!"[32] The Committee cited alternative sources of groundwater for foreseeable expansion within the District service area.

As of late 1975, Dart and the Truckee Donner Public Utility District had suspended their application for a permit to draw from the Lake and were investigating alternate water supplies for Tahoe Donner.

CONSUMER PROTECTION

Dart has by far the best sales practices of any company studied by INFORM. Dr. K. Wayne Smith, President and Chief Executive Officer of Dart Resorts, indicated that because the company had no experience with land sales, it invented consumer policies according to what it thought was good business practice. In a booklet designed to provide background on its entry into the land-development field, Dart explicitly stated that its land-development group's operating philosophy was to be "consistent with that of the Company's six other operating groups in developing consumer-oriented products of highest quality."[33] It translated this philosophy into specific operating guidelines which constitute, for the most part, model land-sales practices. Dart was also the most open, informative, and cooperative of the nine companies studied.

Sales Policies

One of the most obvious differences between Dart and other large-scale land subdividers is that Dart appears to be genuinely concerned that lot buyers be well informed about their purchase, and that they buy for actual use rather than speculation. According to Dr. Smith, "Purchasers must see the site before sales are final."[34] In addition, as required by California law, lot purchasers have fourteen days in which to reconsider their purchase and receive a full refund. The company claims that it encourages lot purchasers to talk with a lawyer during this period or before signing the sales agreement.*

To promote actual use of the lots, Dart has a policy of making all basic services--central water and sewage disposal, paved roads, drainage, solid-waste disposal, electricity, and telephone--available within a few years after sales have begun. As discussed earlier, while all mains are in place, there is still uncertainty about how the subdivision will obtain its water or dispose of its sewage. As a result, sales have been suspended. Still, there is no other subdivision in the INFORM sample where the developer guaranteed or even attempted to provide fully adequate basic services at such an early stage of development.

Dart does not guarantee a refund to the purchaser if promised services turn out to be impossible to obtain. However, according to Dr. Smith, Dart has a standard complaint procedure whereby dissatis-

---

*A local realtor thought the latter unlikely. He felt that unless a sale is closed on the spot, without an intervening trip to a lawyer, the sale is "95 percent lost."

fied customers can petition for a refund. Refunds are granted "if the complaint is warranted."

The company also promotes real use of lots by conducting a credit review of each purchaser. Lots, which are either a third- or a half-acre in size, cost between $9,000 and $30,000. Each prospective purchaser is "interviewed by a senior salesman or sales manager to assure that the terms and conditions of sale have been adequately explained and to confirm the purchaser's ability to pay."[35]

To discourage speculation, a customer cannot purchase more than two homesite lots without formal management approval.[36] Dart even goes so far as to disavow the investment value of its lots. Customers are required to sign a statement verifying that salesmen did not promise or imply future appreciation of the lot at any specific rate.

There are a few additional steps the company could take to further discourage speculation. Dart does not limit sales of the site's 16 commercial and 119 multi-family parcels to businesses which would utilize them immediately. It does not require a cash down payment of 20% on a lot (down payments vary from 10% to 30%). A purchaser generally pays for a lot over a ten-year rather than a five-year period. A shorter payment period and a larger downpayment would, by requiring a larger financial commitment, serve to orient the lot purchaser even more toward real use of the lot.

The Purchase Agreement

Another outstanding difference between Dart and other land subdividers is the type of sales agreement it uses. Most land-sales companies sell lots on ten-year installment contracts, whereby purchasers pay approximately 4% to 8% interest on the unpaid balance annually. The consumer may neither use the lot nor receive title until all payments are complete. Dart, by contrast, uses a sales agreement similar to a mortgage. While the purchaser still makes a downpayment, still pays for the lot over ten (or in a few cases even twenty) years, and is still charged interest (5.9% to 7.9%), he receives title to the lot, and permission to use it, immediately.* The purchaser also immediately becomes a member of the Tahoe Donner Owners' Association and receives rights to use the common areas. Dart is one of the few companies studied to provide purchasers with a method for using their lots during the payment period.

---

*After making a downpayment, the purchaser signs a promissory note for the remainder, secured by a Deed of Trust. He then receives fee title. Permission to build may depend on Dart's subordinating its interest.

If the lot buyer defaults on his payments, Dart institutes foreclosure proceedings, or, if the company and purchaser agree, a "deed in lieu" procedure by which the purchaser accepts a small payment for the deed. Most of the other companies studied by INFORM automatically cancel the sales agreement.

Title Protection

Since the purchaser obtains title to the lot immediately, his interest in the land is fully protected in the event of the company's bankruptcy. All lots are platted with the County, and the company records the lot purchaser's deed with the County as well.

Resales

There is currently a limited resale market for Tahoe Donner lots. A local real estate company, which handles many listings from Tahoe Donner owners, has only effected hardship resales. It will not take a listing from an owner who wishes to resell his lot for a price higher than that of competing lots because the supply is so much greater than the demand. According to the real estate company, "it is a buyer's market,...and a buyer is not willing to pay more than the original price. As lots become in shorter supply, this will change.... To say that the resale prices do not reflect a profit to the seller is true, at this time."[37]

Costs

Costs at Tahoe Donner are comparable to those at the other subdivisions in the INFORM sample which provide usable lots, i.e., lots with basic services. According to the 1974 California Subdivision Public Report, which describes the "estimated annual upkeep cost" for a $10,000 lot with no house and no water connection, annual costs would include $227 for Nevada County property taxes; $78 for the Tahoe Donner Owners' Association assessment; and $15 to $25 for a snow-removal district assessment. As mentioned, when Tahoe Donner ties into the new regional sewage-treatment plant, there will be additional monthly service charges. Lot owners also pay about $20 for sanitation-district assessments, and a $15 annual standby charge for water and electricity to the Truckee Donner Public Utility District. These extra costs total approximately $355 per year. In addition, hookup to basic services will cost at least $785.

Potentially, the most significant additional cost for purchasers of Tahoe Donner lots is property owners' association dues.*

---

*Condominium owners must belong to a condominium association as well as to the Tahoe Donner Owners' Association.

Membership in the Tahoe Donner Owners' Association--an integral part of lot ownership at Tahoe Donner--carries with it considerable financial responsibilities. Lot purchasers may use all recreational facilities, but the Association has the right to levy assessments against them for maintenance and operation of common areas and for other purposes. Members' control of operation and expenses is limited to the right to vote at meetings.

Because of the recreational orientation of the project, these expenses may be quite large. Property owners will be responsible for operating a golf course, beach and swimming pool, tennis club, campground, and ski slopes and lifts. (Dart will own and operate the ski day-lodge.)

In 1976, with Dart subsidizing the Association's expenses, each lot share was $78 per year. The company estimated that without subsidy, lot shares would be $150 to $180. The California Subdivision Public Report, however, warns prospective purchasers that "expenses of operation are difficult to estimate initially and even if accurately estimated, tend to increase substantially with price increases and the increased age of the facilities."[38] The cost of operating the ski slopes and lifts, when they are deeded to the property owners' association, will probably add $18 a year to Association assessments.

The impact of escalating costs on purchasers was made potentially more serious by reductions in the ultimate population. Dart originally planned Tahoe Donner for a total of 6,515 residential units (including condominiums). However, the project's water-supply and sewage-capacity problems may reduce the number of units by 40% to a total of 3,500. This would significantly raise per-lot shares of Association dues, forcing residents to pay much more than originally anticipated.

Legal Status

Because of its water and sewer problems at Tahoe Donner, Dart has had its sales suspended by the California Department of Real Estate and is involved in a class-action suit brought against it by a group of lot purchasers. The suit charges that Dart did not disclose its water and sewer problems to purchasers. It further charges that the site's recreational amenities are inadequate and under-funded. The attorneys for the plaintiffs, Harold Berliner and Richard Ellers, want Dart to furnish adequate water, a sewage-treatment facility, and additional recreational amenities. They are asking for $100 million in punitive damages for 2,000 lot owners who have been unable to build homes at Tahoe Donner.[39]

ENVIRONMENTAL CHECKLIST

Overall environmental protection record: GOOD

Does the subdivider:

Plan for complete basic services?	YES
Phase lot sales and extension of services?	YES
Get 80% build-out in 10 years of each section marketed?	NO
Prepare an Environmental Impact Report?	NO

Use a curvilinear or cluster design?	YES
Retain 25% or more open space?	YES
Reserve from lot sale and development the following areas of critical concern:	
wetlands?	--
dunes and beaches?	--
water sources?	--
prime agricultural lands?	--
habitats of endangered species?	--
prime historical, archaeological, cultural, aesthetic, or recreational resources?	YES
Reserve from lot sale and development the following areas hazardous for building:	
geological hazard areas (earthquake, landslide)?	NO
flood-prone areas (100-year floodplains, arroyos)?	YES
areas of slope exceeding 25%?	NO
Blade roads only in immediate development areas?	YES
Clear only for buildings and roads?	NO
Preserve existing topography?	YES

Design the drainage system to control erosion?	YES
Retain 100-foot buffer zone around water bodies?	YES
Replant disturbed land immediately?	YES
Limit septic systems to one-acre or larger lots with adequate: percolation rates, slope, and distance from bedrock, water table and surface waters?	YES
When utilizing central sewage disposal, provide tertiary treatment (or secondary and land disposal)?	NO
Avoid major stream alteration?	YES
Avoid major wetland dredging and filling?	--
Use groundwater only up to the safe yield?	YES

NOTE: See chapter on "Guidelines" for more complete explanation of items on Checklist.

CONSUMER CHECKLIST

Overall consumer protection record: GOOD

Does the subdivider:

<table>
<tr><td rowspan="12">SALES</td><td>Conduct a credit check on lot purchasers?</td><td>YES</td></tr>
<tr><td>Limit lot sales to two per purchaser?</td><td>YES</td></tr>
<tr><td>Sell only residential, i.e., no industrial, commercial or multi-family lots on installment contracts?</td><td>NO</td></tr>
<tr><td>Require a cash downpayment of 20% on all sales?</td><td>NO</td></tr>
<tr><td>Limit duration of installment contracts to 5 years?</td><td>NO</td></tr>
<tr><td>Charge no interest on installment contracts?</td><td>--</td></tr>
<tr><td>Encourage attorney review of sales documents?</td><td>YES</td></tr>
<tr><td>Require a pre-purchase site visit?</td><td>YES</td></tr>
<tr><td>Allow a 14-day rescission period in which purchaser can obtain a refund for any reason?</td><td>YES</td></tr>
<tr><td>Offer a partial refund if purchaser defaults?</td><td>NO*</td></tr>
<tr><td>Guarantee a refund, with interest, if promised services are not made available by date specified in contract?</td><td>NO</td></tr>
<tr><td>Escrow contract payments, or provide equivalent surety bonding, for refund purposes?</td><td>YES</td></tr>
<tr><td rowspan="4">TITLE</td><td>Offer only platted lots?</td><td>YES</td></tr>
<tr><td>Offer a recordable contract, and record the sale?</td><td>YES</td></tr>
<tr><td>Offer unmortgaged land, or land mortgaged with a release clause, only?</td><td>YES</td></tr>
<tr><td>Upon contract signing, deed title to purchaser, or place title in trust?</td><td>YES</td></tr>
<tr><td rowspan="13">BASIC SERVICES</td><td>Guarantee, or have available, to each lot:</td><td></td></tr>
<tr><td>central water, of adequate quantity and quality?</td><td>YES</td></tr>
<tr><td>central sewage disposal, as necessary?</td><td>YES</td></tr>
<tr><td>drainage system, adequate for 100-year storm?</td><td>YES</td></tr>
<tr><td>solid waste disposal, via adequate method?</td><td>NO</td></tr>
<tr><td>roads, paved, to county standards?</td><td>YES</td></tr>
<tr><td>electricity and telephone?</td><td>YES</td></tr>
<tr><td>Guarantee completion through escrowing or surety bonding?</td><td>YES</td></tr>
<tr><td>If services are financed through special service district bonds, employ them only if:</td><td></td></tr>
<tr><td>initial governing body includes a county official?</td><td>--</td></tr>
<tr><td>elections include all landowners on one-man, one-vote basis?</td><td>--</td></tr>
<tr><td>sum of bonds is less than twice the developer's investment in basic services?</td><td>--</td></tr>
<tr><td>sum of bonds is less than 15% of the assessed value of land in the district?</td><td>--</td></tr>
<tr><td></td><td>developer co-signs all bonds?</td><td>--</td></tr>
</table>

*Company forecloses or provides small payment to purchaser.

COST OF LOTS BOUGHT ON THE INSTALLMENT PLAN

LOT PRICE

    basic price (1/3 - 1/2 acre) $9,000 - $30,000
    finance charges (6% - 8%) $2,691 - $12,309

                                            Total $11,691 - $42,309

ADDITIONAL ANNUAL ASSESSMENTS DURING TERM OF CONTRACT

    property owners association $78
    districts $35
        sanitary $20
        snow removal $15
    water and electricity standby charge $15
    property taxes (on $10,000 lot) $227

                                  Total, per year $355
                                  Total, 10 years $3,550

ONE-TIME COSTS FOR SERVICES

    lot survey   0
    water $150
        well   -
        central extension   0
        central hookup $150
    sewage $285
        septic system   -
        central extension   0
        central hookup $285
    electricity $350
    telephone   0

---

*Includes industrial, commercial, and multi-family lots.

Methodology

INFORM's study of the retail land-sales industry, its impacts on consumers and the environment, and its regulation by government agencies, proceeded in five basic phases over a period of three and a half years.

Literature Search

Phase one, lasting nine months, involved background research to gather and review written materials and identify the experts in the country who have analyzed and focused attention on this industry and its performance.

In the area of consumer practices, the information compiled fell into two categories. The first included material published by dozens of retail land-sales companies: advertising and promotional pieces; Form 10-K Reports on file with the Securities and Exchange Commission; and federal Property Reports prepared for the Department of Housing and Urban Development, Office of Interstate Land Sales Registration (OILSR).

The second included material written about the consumer practices of land-sales companies: journalistic accounts in newspapers and magazines such as Robert Cahn's *Christian Science Monitor* series, "Land In Jeopardy"; books such as Anthony Wolff's *Unreal Estate*, Dorothy Tymon's *America is For Sale*, and Morton Paulson's *The Great Land Hustle*; letters of complaint sent to OILSR by dissatisfied consumers; testimony presented at the hearings OILSR conducted in seventeen U.S. cities; and legal suits filed against major land-sales companies for consumer abuses.

In the area of environmental practices, the information compiled also fell into two categories. The first included material describing and criticizing actual land-use and development practices of retail land-sales companies: reports by technical experts, journalists, environmental groups, and company officials. The second included material necessary to evaluate, from an environmental perspective, the appropriateness of the kinds of sites chosen for development. In this area of environmental practices, INFORM hired an outside consultant with expertise in the fields of land use planning and environmental control to develop an outline of the effects of alteration, construction, and occupation on land and water resources.

The broad range of technical and government reports, popular writing and expert opinions that surfaced during this initial phase of the study clearly indicated that there was more than adequate information available with which to define company sales approaches, compare them with actual company practices at subdivision sites, create detailed profiles of site operations, and define the extent of government regulation.

Field Work

During phase two, which covered a period of ten months, the scope of the study was defined in greater detail and plans for field work were drawn up and executed. The sample of companies to be studied in depth was established. This list comprises nine firms and nineteen sites in five states. The companies chosen are publicly held, and among the largest in the industry. The sample includes firms whose sole business is land sales and development and firms which are large conglomerates with land development subsidiaries. The sites selected are located in five of the six states where subdivision activities have been found to be most widespread. To illustrate the variety and extent of actual development under way, the sample included old (those begun in the early 1960s) and newer projects, and large and small sites (acreages range from 4,020 to 242,000 acres). The subdivisions are located in a variety of environments--mountains, wetlands, and desert grasslands--to show the range of environmental impacts resulting from such development.

After the sample was selected, an initial questionnaire was drawn up, delineating all the information that the initial research phase indicated would be required to evaluate site planning, company operations, and government regulation. This questionnaire was reviewed and criticized by two dozen planners, lawyers, developers, and regulators before being finalized.

The questionnaire was used as a basis for interviews and on-site observation conducted during the months of actual field work. Four months were spent by two of the project directors in Florida (where the eight sites included in Volume II are located). Another four months were spent traveling through four states in the Southwest and West where the other sites are situated.

The corporate headquarters of all the companies, and each of the nineteen sites, were visited. For all but three--AMREP's Rio Rancho, GAC's Rio Rico, and ITT's Palm Coast--company officials and/or site managers and engineers consented to be interviewed.

To provide background and perspective on the sites and their regional impacts, INFORM's study authors interviewed (and carried on months of follow-up correspondence) with hundreds of other people familiar with company or site practices. In the state capitals, INFORM interviewed officials and reviewed the files, wherever possible, of state agencies which had authority over subdivision activity. These agencies included: offices of state attorneys general, land-sales or real-estate commissions, water resource agencies, offices of state engineers, air pollution control agencies, departments of fish and game, and health departments. Where applicable, officials at the regional offices of federal agencies, including the United States Geological Survey (USGS) and the U.S. Army Corps of Engineers, were also interviewed.

In each county where there was a subdivision, INFORM interviewed the District Conservationist with the U.S. Department of Agriculture's Soil Conservation Service, and officials with the county departments of health, planning and zoning, and public works.

In addition to interviewing regulators on the state and local levels, INFORM reviewed materials in the files of public interest groups, such as New Mexico's Central Clearing House, and Southwest Research and Information Center, and The Florida Audubon Society. Hydrologists, ecologists, engineers, attorneys, journalists, local realtors and business people, service district administrators, and property owners' association officials, with particular knowledge about the sites, were also interviewed.

A massive amount of information was collected during this field research phase and in subsequent follow-up contact. This material includes: letters and reports from the files of individuals and organizations; drainage and soil studies; planning reports; environmental impact statements (on projects affecting the subdivisions, although not, except in one case, on the subdivisions themselves); actual and draft state legislation; permit applications such as those filed with the Florida Department of Environmental Regulation and the U.S. Army Corps of Engineers; magazine and newspaper articles; state land-sales registration filings; legal documents such as class action settlements, Federal Trade Commission complaints, and county and regional planning agency subdivision regulations.

Evaluation of Data and Definition of Guidelines

Phase three of the study, which involved twelve months of work, focused on identifying and organizing the information that was essential for evaluating the sites, and defining the evaluative criteria that should be used. This work resulted in two documents reproduced herein: the Site Fact Sheet which includes all the key facts that should be compiled on any site for evaluative purposes; and the Guidelines for Consumer and Environmental Protection Practices.

At the beginning of phase three, draft material on the key facts and the abuses identified at each site was prepared. This was followed by a review of the materials collected during all previous phases, including laws and technical opinion, for guidelines that could be applied to industry operations to prevent abuses in the future. The project authors analyzed the laws and regulations of six states which had particularly effective laws or which were a particular focus of subdivision activity, as well as the laws of other states and regions. Draft guidelines were prepared comprising standards which were felt to most directly and efficiently address each of the abuses identified. Where there were no legal precedents, INFORM sought the best technical advice on what kinds of guidelines might be used. The complete set of guidelines, with rationales and precedents, was then circulated to lawyers, land-use planners and developers, and real estate loan experts for review and comments before being finalized.

Final Writing and Editing

Phase four, entailing eight months of work, involved writing and editing the nineteen site profiles; evaluating each site's performance in light of the final guidelines; comparing site and company efforts; and preparing overall conclusions on the industry. It also included drafting chapters analyzing and evaluating the laws pertaining to subdivisions in six states--California, Colorado, New Mexico, Arizona, Florida, and New York--and preparing conclusions on the effectiveness of these regulatory programs.

A Site Fact Sheet was prepared for each subdivision including all the information deemed necessary to evaluate its performance. This was sent in each case to company headquarters and the project site manager for review. For all but two--GAC's Rio Rico and AMREP's Rio Rancho--either the site manager or company

METHODOLOGY

officials reviewed the Site Fact Sheet for accuracy. In a number of cases, companies which had previously been only minimally cooperative in supplying information answered all of INFORM's questions in detail. During this phase, additional telephone follow-up work was done to gather missing facts, verify information, and update data.

The study was organized for publication in three volumes: Volume I, Subdivisions in the Deserts and Mountains; Volume II, Subdivisions in the Wetlands; and Volume III, Subdivisions and the Law. The analyses of subdivisions in the West and Southwest were included in Volume I; those in Florida, in Volume II.

Manuscript Review

In the final three-month phase of the study, all chapters were circulated to outside reviewers for comment. Reviewers included local county planning officials, environmentalists, realtors, and many other individuals particularly conversant with the site. Changes and corrections based on this review were then incorporated into the final text.

SITE FACT SHEET

Name: _____

Development Company: _____

BASIC DESCRIPTION

Location: county _____
          state _____
          nearest major city (name) _____

Climate and terrain _____

Water bodies on site (name and type) _____

Prior use of the site _____

Size (total acres owned) _____

Year acquired _____

Sales: year began _____
        # acres subdivided (platted) _____
        # lots offered _____
        # lots sold _____
        # lots deeded (all payments complete) _____

Population: present _____
            final projected _____
            present number of dwelling units _____

METHODOLOGY

CONSUMER PROTECTION

Terms of Contract

    Size range of single-family lots (acres) _____

    Price range of single-family lots ($) _____

    Interest rate on contracts (range in %) _____

    Minimum downpayment (%) _____

    Duration of payment period (months) _____

    Rescission period (in which buyer may withdraw from contract and receive refund (days) _____

    Amount or terms of refund if purchaser defaults _____

    Other refund provisions (please describe) _____

Sales Policies

    Are prospective purchasers encouraged to visit the site before buying a lot? _____

    Is a credit check conducted on prospective lot purchasers? _____

    Is there any limitation on the number of residential lots sold to an individual purchaser? _____

    Is an independent closer or buyer's attorney required to be present at a sale? _____

    Is a prospective purchaser verbally encouraged to review the purchase contract and property report with his attorney? _____

    Are industrial, commercial or multi-family lots sold on an installment contract basis? _____

Title Protection

> Is the developer's title to the land encumbered by a mortgage or other financial obligation? _____
>
> If so, does the instrument contain a release clause guaranteeing that an individual lot purchaser will gain title to his lot upon full payment of all installments (regardless of developer's defaulting)? Or a release clause requiring additional payments for release? _____
>
> Are all lots offered for sale platted of record at the County Recorder's office? _____
>
> Is the lot buyer's contract recordable? _____
>
> Does the company record the contract for the buyer? _____
>
> Upon signing of a purchase contract, is title deeded to the purchaser, placed in trust or escrow? (specify) _____
>
> Are there any liens which might prevent a lot purchaser from obtaining title upon full payment? _____

Special Assessments

Amount which must be paid during term of contract and prior to lot purchaser's receiving permission to build:

> Special Service District fee ($ annually) _____
>
> property association dues ($ annually) _____
>
> property taxes ($ annually) _____
>
> lot survey ($) _____
>
> other (specify) ($) _____

BASIC SERVICES

Water: Availability

    # or % of lots planned for individual wells _____

    company testing procedure for well water quality _____

    # or % of lots planned for central water _____

    name of entity supplying central water _____

    # or % of lots to which water mains are extended _____

    # or % of lots hooked up to water system _____

    source of central water _____

    # acre/feet/year water rights owned _____

    current usage, central water (gals/day) _____

    capacity of central water system (gals/day) _____

    Is completion of central system guaranteed through either escrow accounts or surety bonding? _____

    Is availability of central water guaranteed in the purchase contract to each lot? _____

Costs

    drilling of individual well and pump (range in $) _____

    extension and hook-up to central system lines ($) _____

Sewage Disposal: Availability

    # or % of lots planned for septic systems _____

    company procedure to test lot soil suitability for septics _____

    minimum size of lots permitted to use septics _____

    # or % of lots planned for central system _____

    name of entity providing sewage system _____

    # or % of lots to which sewer lines are extended _____

    # or % of lots hooked up to sewer lines _____

    amount of sewage currently processed by treatment plant (gals/day) _____

    design capacity of sewage treatment plant (gals/day) _____

    Is completion of central system guaranteed through either escrow accounts or surety bonding? _____

    Is availability of central sewage disposal guaranteed in the purchase contract? _____

    Costs

    septic or individual package system (range in $) _____

    extension and hook-up to sewer lines ($) _____

Solid Waste Disposal: Availability

    disposal method (dump, sanitary landfill, incinerator, recycling system, etc.) _____

    entity responsible for maintenance (county, developer, homeowners association, etc.) _____

    Is regular pick-up service available? _____

METHODOLOGY

Roads

    paved (miles) _____

    unpaved (miles) _____

    construction standards (county, developer, other) _____

    entity providing maintenance (county, developer, other) _____

    Is road access to each lot offered for sale guaranteed through escrow accounts or surety bonding? _____

Drainage

    design storm capacity (100-year storm, etc.) _____

    entity responsible for maintenance _____

    Is completion of system guaranteed through escrow accounts or surety bonding? _____

    Is adequate drainage guaranteed, in the purchase contract, for each lot? _____

Utilities

    # of lots planned for service by electric & telephone lines at a standard cost _____

    # of lots currently served by existing electric & telephone lines _____

    Are lines above or below ground? _____

Costs

extension of electric lines to unserved lots ($ per mile) _____

extension of telephone lines to unserved lots ($ per mile) _____

Service Districts

If there are any special service districts on the site:

    What improvements may be financed? _____

On what voting basis is the district's
governing body elected? _____

When is the district's governing body
elected? _____

Are there any limits to the amount of bonds
that may be issued? _____

Community Services

Police protection: type of force (state police.
county sheriff, site) _____

                    location _____

Fire protection: type of force (paid,
volunteer) _____

                    location _____

Schools (distance to or on site)

        primary _____

        secondary _____

Medical care (distance to or on site)

        doctor _____

        dentist _____

        hospital _____

Shopping center (distance to or on site) _____

Public transportation (type)

        on site _____

        off site _____

ENVIRONMENTAL PROTECTION

Present (according to development plan in use 12/75)
allocation of sub-divided (platted) acreage to:

    lots--minimal improvements promised (i.e.,
roads) _____ %

    residential homesites--improved (i.e.,
roads & central water) _____ %

METHODOLOGY

       multiple dwelling units _____ %
       commercial use _____ %
       industrial use _____ %
       natural open space _____ %
       developed recreational space (golf
         courses, etc.) _____ %
       community facilities (schools, churches,
         etc.) _____ %

Present (12/75) development of subdivided (platted) acreage according to:

       gridiron pattern _____ %
       curvilinear pattern _____ %
       cluster pattern _____ %

If improvements (roads, water, sewers, etc.) are being installed according to a phased development plan, what are the time projections for completion of each phase?

	# acres	year improvements projected to be completed
phase 1	_____	_____
phase 2	_____	_____
phase 3	_____	_____
phase 4	_____	_____

Does any portion of the site include (yes or no):

       archeological ruins, historic or cultural
         resources _____
       tidal estuaries _____
       freshwater swamps or wetlands _____
       aquifer recharge areas _____
       dunes, beaches, or barrier islands _____
       habitats of endangered species _____
       100-year floodplains _____
       slopes exceeding 25% _____
       earthquake faults _____
       landslide areas _____
       arroyos _____
       recognized watersheds for drinking water _____
       prime agricultural lands (SCS Category I) _____

Does subdivided (platted) acreage *offered for sale* include (yes or no):

    archeological ruins, historic or cultural
        resources   _____
    tidal estuaries   _____
    freshwater swamps or wetlands   _____
    aquifer recharge areas   _____
    dunes, beaches, or barrier islands   _____
    habitats of endangered species   _____
    100-year floodplains   _____
    slopes exceeding 25%   _____
    earthquake faults   _____
    landslide areas   _____
    arroyos   _____
    recognized watersheds for drinking water   _____
    prime agricultural lands (SCS Category I)   _____

METHODOLOGY 489

Preparation of land--present subdivided (platted) acreage:

    cleared of vegetation (acres) _____
    dredged and filled wetlands (acres) _____
    significantly altered topography (acres) _____

Preparation of water bodies: (describe)

    creation of canals _____

    stream channelization _____

    draining of lakes _____

    creation of artificial lakes or ponds _____

Prevention of water pollution:

    from runoff

        size of buffer zone established between lots offered for sale and ocean, river, lake, canal, or any other water body shoreline _____ feet

        type of drainage system (use of swales, rip-rap, sediment traps, retention ponds, etc.) _____

        Are separate sanitary sewers and storm drainage systems employed? _____

        maximum period between devegetation & revegetation

    from sewage effluent

        type of treatment plant (holding pond, activated sludge, etc.) _____

        level of treatment provided (primary, secondary, (tertiary) _____

        effluent disposal method (describe) _____

Is there evidence that site use of groundwater is resulting in:
    depletion of water table _____
    saltwater intrusion _____
    increasing groundwater salinity _____
    land subsidence (sinkholes) _____

Glossary

acre: A measure of land equaling 43,560 square feet. There are 640 acres in a square mile.

acre-foot: The volume of water that would cover one acre to a depth of one foot: 326,000 gallons.

ad valorem tax: Tax imposed at a rate percent of the value of an item.

aeration lagoon: A basin in which secondary water-pollution treatment takes place; aerators force oxygen into waste water, feeding the bacteria which consume organic wastes.

agreement of sale: A written agreement or contract between seller and purchaser specifying the terms and conditions of sale.

alluvial fan: The soil deposit of a stream formed at the point where the stream issues from a gorge upon a plain; or forms another waterway.

alluvium: Clay, silt, gravel or similar detrital material deposited by running water.

amenities: Features conducive to increasing the value and attractiveness of real estate, such as recreational facilities.

amortization of debt: The process of retiring debt by a series of payments to a creditor or into a sinking fund.

appraisal: The establishment of the value of a specific property as of a specific date by systematic procedures that include physical examination, pricing, engineering estimates and comparison with known market values.

aquifer: A subsurface stratum of rock, sand or gravel that contains sufficient saturated permeable material to conduct groundwater and to yield economically significant quantities of it to wells and springs.

aquifer recharge area: An area in which water is absorbed and added to the groundwater reservoir.

arroyo: A usually dry gulley or channel carved by intermittently flowing creeks or streams in arid regions.

assessed value: The value placed on real estate by a governmental entity for tax purposes.

authorized debt: The maximum allowable debt determined by law, indenture or governing body.

berm: A narrow shelf, path, or ledge typically at the top or bottom of a slope; often created to reduce erosion.

biome: A major ecological community of all plant and animal life.

blading: The process of bulldozing a road.

blanket mortgage: A single mortgage that covers more than one piece of real property.

bond: A signed promise guaranteeing payment of a specified sum of money or guaranteeing a specific performance; an interest-bearing certificate of public or private indebtedness guaranteeing payment of face value on a specified date; an insurance agreement that pledges surety for financial loss caused to another by the act or default of a third person or by some contingency over which the third person may have no control.

broker: An agent acting as an intermediary between the buyer and seller of real or personal property.

buffer zone: An area extending from the banks or high water of the stream to some point landward. It protects the stream from adjacent developments which might increase runoff sedimentation or thermal pollution and creates a margin of safety from flood and erosion hazards.

build-out rate: The rate at which housing units are constructed, usually expressed as a percent of lots sold.

California Subdivision Public Report: California's version of a federal Property Report, a detailed description of property offered for sale to residents of the state of California.

class action suit: A legal proceeding brought about by several people with a similar complaint acting for an entire group in a court case.

closing: The procedure whereby ownership of a parcel of real estate is transferred from seller to buyer.

cluster pattern: A plan that groups housing units close together and utilizes the remaining land for common open space.

complaint: In a civil action, a document stating the cause of the action and the damages being sought; issued in order to inform the defendant of the reasons for the plaintiff's suit.

condominium ownership: A unique form of ownership wherein a multi-unit building is divided so that each owner has individual ownership of his unit and joint ownership in the common areas of the buildings and grounds. Condominiums are frequently used for residential housing and sometimes for office space. In addition to the initial purchase price, each owner in a condominium is liable on an annual basis for a predetermined portion of the expenses of maintaining the common areas.

contract: An oral or written agreement to carry out an act, the breach of which can be the basis for court action.

convey: To transfer the title of land from one owner to another.

covenant: A written assurance between two or more persons whereby one of the parties promises the performance or non-performance of certain acts or promises that a given state of events or physical conditions do or do not exist.

credit check: A procedure undertaken by lending institutions in mortgage applications and other requests for financing whereby the personal and financial history of an applicant is obtained and evaluated to determine the risk factor.

culvert: A drainage ditch or conduit to carry drainage under roads.

cut: An excavation such as that made in a hillside for house or road construction.

cut and fill: Excavating soil or rock from one location and depositing it as fill in another.

curvilinear pattern: A variation of the gridiron pattern which replaces parallel lines and right-angles with curves in street and lot layouts.

deed: A written instrument which, when properly executed and delivered, conveys an interest in real property.

deed restrictions: Limitations placed on the use of real property through deed covenants such as land coverage, setback requirement, architectural approval, or construction timing.

deed of trust: A conveyance of the title to property to a third party (trustee) as collateral security for the payment of a debt with the condition that the trustee shall return the title upon the payment of the debt. The trustee has the power to sell the property and pay the debt in the event of a default on the part of the debtor.

drainage district: A quasi-governmental entity the purpose of which is to construct, operate and maintain works necessary for drainage purposes. The district may issue bonds, and levy taxes and special assessments to fund these works.

drawdown: To deplete or lower a water level (in a reservoir or aquifer).

dredge and fill: Deepening a body of water by removing materials from its bottom and raising the elevation of adjacent land by depositing the dredged materials thereon.

easement: A right, privilege, or interest in a property recorded in a legal document granting a non-owner or occupier specific uses of the property. Easements may restrict the rights of the title holder or lessee insofar as they uphold the specific privileges and rights of the easement holder.

ecosystem: The sum total of relationships between living things and their non-living but supporting environment.

effluent: The liquid that comes out of a sewage treatment plant after completion of the treatment process; waste water.

encumbrance: Anything which affects or limits the title to property, including mortgages, easements, taxes, liens, or restrictions of any kind.

endangered species: Wildlife species whose populations are so reduced that their existence is threatened. These species, listed by the U.S. Department of Interior, are protected by federal law.

equity: The residual interest in a property or a business after satisfying the claims of all creditors; net worth; ownership interest.

erosion: The deterioration of land formations by the action of water, wind or construction activities.

escrow: A deed, bond, money or piece of property delivered to a third person to be held until the fulfillment of a condition; a fund or deposit designed to serve as an escrow.

GLOSSARY

eutrophication: The process by which bodies of water become enriched with mineral nutrients and organic materials, often causing algae growth. The decomposition of organic matter absorbs oxygen and leaves a residue of sediment which causes shallowing of the bottom. The process is often accelerated by discharge of sewage or overland runoff of fertilizers.

evaporation ponds: Shallow, artificial ponds into which sewage sludge is pumped, permitted to dry, and either removed or buried by more sludge. They are used in industry in connection with industrial waste water disposal.

evapotranspiration system: The combined amount of water released to the atmosphere in any area by both the transpiration of plants and the evaporation from the earth's surface.

federal Property Report: A mandatory detailed description of land offered for sale in subdivisions with over 50 lots by means of interstate commerce (telephone, newspaper, television, radio). A Property Report is written by the developer and registered with the Office of Interstate Land Sales Registration, Department of Housing and Urban Development. The developer is required to give every prospective customer a copy of the Property Report before a contract is signed.

Property Reports for any project may be obtained from HUD for a fee of $2.50 each by writing HUD/OILSR, 451 Seventh St., S.W., Washington, D.C. 20410 including the name of the developer and development, and the location of the subdivision.

floodplain: Level land that may be submerged by floodwaters.

foreclosure: A legal proceeding by which a lender seizes title to a property when the borrower/owner defaults on the mortgage.

Form 10-K Annual Report: A highly detailed financial report filed annually with the Securities and Exchange Commission by publicly-held corporations.

front-foot: Property measurement for sale or valuation purposes; the property is measured on its frontal line—each front-foot extends the depth of the lot.

General Improvement District: See Special Service district.

grading: Cutting through or otherwise disturbing the layers of the soil mantle so as to permanently change the existing landform.

gridiron pattern: A plan which simply breaks down survey sections into rectangular blocks and lots.

groundwater: Subsurface water that supplies wells and springs.

holding pond: A basin used primarily to detain runoff from impervious surfaces.

hydroseed: The process of replanting vegetative ground cover by spraying a combination of seeds and water to facilitate growth.

impervious surface: A surface such as paving or compacted clay, that does not allow water to penetrate into the ground.

improved land: Land which has been prepared for development (as distinguished from raw land) or which has been developed for use by the erection of buildings and other improvements.

infiltration: The penetration of water in soil or other material.

Irrigation district: A quasi-government entity the powers of which primarily relate to water rights and the distribution of water for irrigation purposes. The district may issue bonds, and levy taxes and special assessments to fund its work.

issued debt: The portion of authorized debt for which bonds have already been issued.

installment land contract: A land contract wherein the seller agrees to convey title to the purchaser at some future time when the contract payments have been met.

lease: A contract between an owner and a tenant setting forth conditions and terms of occupancy and of the use of the property.

lessee: One who contracts to rent property under a lease contract.

lessor: An owner who enters into a lease with a tenant.

leaching: The process by which septic-tank effluent seeps through and is filtered by the soil.

lien: A limited encumbrance on a property securing a specific indebtedness or obligation.

marginal land: Land which barely pays the cost of working or using.

marketable title: A title free and clear of objectionable liens or encumbrances.

market price: Price at which property sells on the open market.

market value: The price at which a willing seller would sell and a willing buyer would buy, neither being under abnormal pressure; as defined by the courts, it is the highest price estimated in terms of money which a property will bring if exposed for sale in the open market allowing a reasonable time to find a purchaser with knowledge of the property's use and capabilities for use.

mechanic's lien: A type of lien created by statute which exists in favor of persons who have performed work or furnished materials in the erection or repair of a building.

modified Mercalli index: A scale running from I to XII to measure the intensity of actual ground shaking during an earthquake.

metes and bounds: A description in a deed of a piece of land in which the boundaries are defined by directions and distances. This form of description is most commonly used in rural areas.

Metropolitan Service District: A quasi-governmental legal entity established by authority of State law to provide a range of municipal services. The district may issue bonds and levy taxes and assessments to fund its work.

mortgage: An instrument recognized by law in which property is pledged as security (without giving up possession) for payment of a debt or obligation.

mortgagee: One to whom a mortgagor gives a mortgage to secure a loan or performance of an obligation; a lender.

mortgagor: One who gives a mortgage on his property

mulch: A protective covering spread on ground to reduce evaporation, maintain even soil temperature, prevent erosion and enrich the soil.

negotiable: Assignable or transferable in the ordinary course of business.

note: A signed written instrument acknowledging a debt and promising payment.

Office of Interstate Land Sales Registration (OILSR): A division of the U.S. Department of Housing and Urban Development established in August, 1969 to administer the Interstate Land Sales Full Disclosure Act. All companies offering 50 or more unimproved lots for sale or lease by means of interstate commerce must file a Statement of Record with OILSR and provide all prospective buyers with a Property Report.

oxidation pond: A man-made lake or body of water in which wastes are consumed by bacteria; most frequently with other waste-treatment processes; a sewage lagoon.

percolation pond: A basin into which sewage-treatment plant effluent is pumped in order to percolate into the ground for disposal and further filtering.

plat: A map or chart of a piece of land delineating actual or proposed features such as lots; also the land represented.

primary treatment: The first stage in waste-water treatment, during which floating or settleable solids are mechanically removed by skimming or settling.

Property Report: See federal Property Report.

raw land: Land which is unimproved, i.e., no on-site or off-site development work has been done.

real property: Real property consists of land and, generally, whatever is erected or growing upon or affixed to it, including rights issuing out of, annexed to, and exercisable within or about the same.

recharge area: An area in which water is absorbed and added to the groundwater reservoir.

recording: The act of entering in a book of public record instruments affecting the title to real property.

release provision or clause: A clause found in a blanket mortgage which give the owner of the property the privilege of paying off a portion of the mortgage indebtedness and thus freeing a portion of the property from the mortgage — important when titles to small sections of land holdings are to be transferred.

rescission period: The period of time during which a contract may be canceled without cost. The Office of Interstate Land Sales Registration currently mandates a minimum three-day

GLOSSARY

rescission period after purchasers have received the federal Property Report.

retail land sale: The sale of parcels of land to the ultimate owner, in contrast to the sale of land to an intermediate owner such as a merchant builder.

retention basin: Permanent structures which store the peak runoff and release this storage at a controlled rate through an outlet.

Richter scale: A logarithmic scale for expressing the magnitude of an earthquake in terms of the energy dissipated; largest recorded earthquake to date registered 8.5.

right-of-way: The privilege one has to pass over the land of another; also that strip of land which railroad companies or other public utilities use for a roadbed; or as dedicated to public use for roadway, walk or other way.

rip-rap: A sustaining wall of stones used to strengthen, support, or prevent erosion of an embankment or slope.

runoff: Precipitation that flows overland to the nearest waterbody.

saltwater intrusion: The displacement of fresh surface water or groundwater by the advance of seawater, sometimes caused by drawdown.

sanitary landfill: A site for solid-waste disposal at which wastes are buried under a compacted earth cover thick enough to prevent insect, rodent, and vermin problems.

sanitary sewer: A sewer system that carries only domestic waste water. Stormwater runoff is taken care of by a separate system.

secondary treatment: The second step in most waste treatment systems, in which bacteria consume the organic parts of the wastes; sewage and bacteria are brought together in trickling filters or in the activated sludge process.

sedimentation: The settling of solids to the bottom of a water body.

sedimentation tanks: Chambers in which solids are removed from sewage. The waste water is pumped to the tanks, where the solids settle to the bottom or float on the top as scum. The scum is skimmed off the top, and solids on the bottom are pumped to incineration, digestion, filtration or other plants for disposal.

septic tank: A watertight container that settles out solids from raw sewage. The sludge and the scum are stored and processed anaerobically and/or chemically. The liquids are dissipated into the ground.

sheet-flooding: The flooding of large areas of land to shallow depths which occurs in areas with undefined drainage patterns.

slope: See groundslope.

sludge: Solid material removed from waste water by sewage-treatment systems.

soil stabilization: The use of various coverings and binders to shield soil surface from runoff, erosion or climatic conditons resulting in dispersed soil particles of a non-resistant nature. Control practices include mulches, chemical binders, gravel, concrete or metal retaining structures and energy dissipators to restrict downcutting of a channel.

Special Service districts: A quasi government entity typically formed to undertake either a single government function or a series of related functions. The major reason for formation of a Special Service district is financial as a Special Service district can be given the authority to tax and borrow money to carry out its functions.

storm sewer: A system of pipes that carries storm runoff from buildings and land.

subordination clause: A clause in a junior or second lien permitting retention of priority for prior liens. A subordination clause may also be used in a first deed of trust permitting it to be subordinated to subsequent liens as, for example, the liens of construction loans.

subdivision: A tract of land divided into smaller sections called lots; a housing project of primarily single-family dwellings.

subsidence: Gradual downward, local, mass movement of the earth's surface.

surety bond: An insurance agreement that pledges surety for financial loss caused to another by the act or default of a third person.

GLOSSARY

surface water: Waters falling upon, arising from, or naturally spreading over land; produced by rainfall, melting snow or springs.

swale: A low-lying or depressed, and often wet stretch of land; a natural drainage ditch.

tertiary treatment: A catch-all phrase for any sewage-treatment process beyond secondary waste-water treatment; involves the use of chemical methods and advanced physical techniques.

title: Evidence that the owner of land is in lawful possession of it.

topography: The nature of the surface of the land.

topsoil: Surface soil, usually including the organic layer in which plants have most of their roots.

tract: A defined area of land, which is generally subdivided into lots.

turbidity: The cloudy condition of a body of water that contains suspended material, such as clay or silt particles, dead organisms, or small living plants or animals.

watershed: The region drained by or contributing water to a stream, lake, or other body of water.

water table: The upper surface of free groundwater in a zone of saturation; also called groundwater table.

zone: An area set off by proper authorities for specific use subject to certain restrictions and limitations.

zoning: The act of city or county officials' specifying the type of use to which property may be put in specific areas.

Notes

I. THE LAND SUBDIVISION INDUSTRY

1. OVERVIEW OF THE INDUSTRY

1. Marion Clawson, *Man and Land in the United States* (Lincoln, Nebraska: University of Nebraska Press, 1964), pp.65-66.
2. Dorothy Tymon, *America is for Sale* (Rockville Centre, New York: Farnsworth Publishing Co., 1973), p.44.
3. "Corporate Giants That Soured on Real Estate," *Business Week,* Feb. 16, 1974, p.96.
4. The American Society of Planning Officials, Conservation Foundation, Urban Land Institute and Ragatz Associates, Inc., *Subdividing Rural America : Impacts of Recreational Lot and Second Home Development* (Washington, D.C.: Council on Environmental Quality, 1976), p.34.
5. "Corporate Giants That Soured on Real Estate," *op. cit.,* p.96.
6. Leonard Downie, Jr., "The Recreation Land Racket," *The Progressive,* May 1974, p.23.
7. *Ibid.,* p.24.
8. The American Society of Planning Officials, et al., *op. cit.,* p.97.
9. *Ibid.,* p.37
10. *Recreational Land and Leisure Housing Report,* July 30, 1973, Vol. 4, No. 13.

11. Grace Lichtenstein, "New Mexico and Arizona Suing Land Concerns Over Sales of Lots," *The New York Times,* Sept. 19, 1976.
12. INFORM telephone interview with Gary Terry, Executive Vice-President, American Land Developer's Association, Aug. 31, 1976.
13. The American Society of Planning Officials, et al., *op. cit.,* p.34.
14. The American Society of Planning Officials, Conservation Foundation, Urban Land Institute and Ragatz Associates, Inc., *Subdividing Rural America : Impacts of Recreational Lot and Second Home Development,* Executive Summary (Washington, D.C.: Council on Environmental Quality, Jan. 1976), p.6.
15. Richard Ragatz, "Location of Recreational Projects in U.S.," *American Land,* Jan./Feb. 1975, Vol. 4, No. 1, p.8.
16. INFORM telephone interview with official of Policy and Development Division, Office of Interstate Land Sales Registration, U.S. Dept. of Housing and Urban Development, Aug. 31, 1976.
17. INFORM telephone interview with Alan Kappelar, Acting Associate Deputy Assistant Secretary for Regulatory Functions, Office of Interstate Land Sales Registration, June 1, 1976.
18. Richard Ragatz, *op. cit.,* p.8.
19. *Ibid.,* pp.8, 27.
20. Richard Ragatz Assoc., Inc., *Recreational Properties : An Analysis of the Markets for Privately Owned Recreational Lots and Leisure Homes* (Washington, D.C.: National Technical Service, U.S. Dept. of Commerce, May 1974), "Errata."
21. Richard Ragatz, *op. cit.,* pp.25-26.
22. *Ibid.,* p.25.
23. "Commission Statistics," *Colorado Real Estate News,* official publication of Colorado Real Estate Commission, Denver, Sept. 1974, p.2.
24. California Dept. of Real Estate, "Subdivisions in California: Public Reports Issued and Lots and Acres by County, (Sacramento: California Dept. of Real Estate, June 1974).
25. Planning Division, Office of Economic Planning and Development, *Arizona's Remote Subdivisions* (Phoenix: State of Arizona, Jan. 1975), p.8.
26. INFORM telephone interview with official of Policy and Development Division, Office of Interstate Land Sales Registration, Aug. 31, 1976.

NOTES

27. Richard Ragatz, *op. cit.*, p.8.
28. Planning Division, Office of Economic Planning and Development, *op. cit.*, p.8.
29. *Ibid.*, p.1.
30. *Ibid.*, p.32, Table 9.
31. *Ibid.*, p.4.
32. *Ibid.*, p.32, Table 9.
33. *Ibid.*, p.4.
34. American Society of Planning Officials, et al., *op. cit.*, p.25.
35. *Ibid.*, p.26.
36. *Ibid.*
37. *Ibid.*
38. *Ibid.*, p.97.
39. *Ibid.*, p.107.
40. Richard Ragatz Assoc., Inc., *op. cit.*, p.29.
41. American Society of Planning Officials, et al., *op. cit.*, p.39, Note 4.
42. Richard Ragatz Assoc., Inc., *op. cit.*, p.37.
43. INFORM telephone interview with Carl Burlingame, publisher of *Recreational Development Today*, Sept. 1, 1976; and Richard Ragatz Assoc., Inc., *op. cit.*, p.37.
44. Leonard Downie, *op. cit.*, p.19.
45. INFORM telephone interview with official of Policy and Development Division, Office of Interstate Land Sales Registration, Aug. 31, 1976.
46. INFORM telephone interview with Gary Terry, Executive Vice-President, American Land Development Association, Aug. 31, 1976.
47. INFORM telephone interview with official of Policy and Development Division, Office of Interstate Land Sales Registration, Aug. 31, 1976.
48. Richard Ragatz Assoc., Inc., *op. cit.*, p.138.
49. The American Society of Planning Officials, et al., *op. cit.*, p.116.
50. *Ibid.*, pp.118-119.
51. "Beautiful Retirement Lot Just Could Be in Desert," *Mamaroneck Daily Times*, Aug. 15, 1973.
52. The American Society of Planning Officials, et al., *op. cit.*, p.119.
53. INFORM telephone interview with official of Policy and Development Division, Office of Interstate Land Sales Registration, Aug. 31, 1976.

54. INFORM telephone interview with Alan Kappelar, Acting Associate Deputy Assistant Secretary for Regulatory Functions, Oct. 1, 1976.
55. *Ibid.*
56. The American Society of Planning Officials, et al., *op. cit.*, p.98.
57. *Ibid.*, p.99.

4. GUIDELINES FOR CONSUMER AND ENVIRONMENTAL PROTECTION AT LARGE-SCALE SUBDIVISIONS

CONSUMER PROTECTION PRACTICES

1. The American Society of Planning Officials, Conservation Foundation, Urban Land Institute, and Ragatz Associates, Inc., *Subdividing Rural America: Impacts of Recreational and Second Home Development*, Executive Summary (Washington, D.C.: Council on Environmental Quality, Jan. 1976), p.2.
2. Great Western United Corp., *Proxy Statement/Prospectus* (Denver: Great Western United Corp., Aug. 28, 1974), p.154.
3. William C. Smith, "New Developments in Financing of Vacation Housing," *Vacation Housing and Recreation Land Development* (Ann Arbor, Michigan: Industrial Development Div., University of Michigan, 1973), p.64.
4. James J. Klink, and Carol A. White, "Accountants Reshape the Land Sales Industry," *Real Estate Review*, Spring 1973.
5. Robert Cahn, *Land in Jeopardy*, reprint from *Christian Science Monitor* (Boston: Christian Science Publishing Society, 1973), p.13.
6. The American Society of Planning Officials, Conservation Foundation, Urban Land Institute, and Ragatz Associates, Inc., *Subdividing Rural America: Impacts of Recreational Lot and Second Home Development* (Washington, D.C.: Council on Environmental Quality, 1976), p.25.
7. "Land Sales Boom: Let the Buyer Beware," *Consumer Reports*, Sept. 1972, p.606.
8. Robert Cahn, *op. cit.*, p.23.
9. William K. Reilly, ed., *The Use of Land* (New York: The Rockefeller Brothers Fund, 1973).
10. Federal Trade Commission, "Proposed Order in the Matter of Horizon Corporation," Docket No. 9017, Mar. 11, 1975, p.34, Sec. 13.

11. Robert Cahn, *op. cit.*, p.25.
12. James J. Klink, and Carol A. White, *op. cit.*
13. Donaldson, Lufkin and Jenrette, Inc., "Retail Land Development: Special Research Service, and Industry Analysis," Apr. 1972.
14. GAC Corp., *Form 10-K Annual Report* (Washington, D.C.: Securities and Exchange Commission, 1974).
15. INFORM telephone interview with Alan Kappelar, Acting Associate Deputy Assistant Secretary for Regulatory Functions, Office of Interstate Land Sales Registration, Dept. of Housing and Urban Development, Apr. 6, 1976.
16. "Securities Regulations of Interstate Land Sales—A Blue Sky Administrator's Viewpoint: Part 1," *Urban Lawyer* (1975), 7:215, p.404, Note 78.
17. *Federal Regulation of Land Sales: Full Disclosure Comes Down to Earth*, 21 Case Western Res. L. Rev. 5, (1969-1970), p.18.
18. Committee on the Office of Attorney General, National Association of Attorneys General, *Land and Condominium Sales Regulation* (Raleigh, North Carolina: National Association of Attorneys General, Nov. 1975), p.12.
19. *Ibid.*
20. *Ibid.*, p.9.
21. *Ibid.*, pp.8-9.
22. *Ibid.*, p.13.
23. *Ibid.*, pp.2-3.
24. William K. Reilly, ed., *op. cit.*, p.272.
25. The American Society of Planning Officials, Executive Summary, *op. cit.*, p.14.
26. Federal Trade Commission, "Decision and Order in the Matter of GAC Corporation," Docket No. C-2523 (Washington, D.C.: Federal Trade Commission, July 23, 1974).
27. The American Society of Planning Officials, et al., *op. cit.*, p.91.
28. Federal Trade Commission, "Decision and Order in the Matter of GAC Corporation," *op. cit.*
29. Federal Trade Commission, "Complaint and Proposed Order in the Matter of AMREP Corporation," Docket No. 9018 (Washington, D.C.: Federal Trade Commission, Mar. 11, 1975), p.26.
30. Federal Trade Commission, "Complaint and Proposed Order in the Matter of Horizon Corporation," Docket No. 9017 (Washington, D.C.: Federal Trade Commission, Mar. 11, 1975), p.36.
31. Federal Trade Commission, "Decision and Order in the Matter of GAC Corporation," *op. cit.*

32. William K. Reilly, ed., *op. cit.,* p.275.
33. *Ibid.,* p.292.
34. The American Society of Planning Officials, et al., Executive Summary, *op. cit.,* p.14.
35. Frank J. Popper, "Land Use Reform—Illusion or Reality," *Planning,* Sept. 1974, pp.14-19.
36. Committee on the Office of Attorney General, National Association of Attorneys General, *op. cit.,* p.12.
37. *Ibid.,* p.13.
38. Federal Trade Commission, "Complaint and Proposed Order in the Matter of AMREP Corporation," *op. cit.*
39. Federal Trade Commission, "Complaint and Proposed Order in the Matter of Horizon Corporation, *op. cit.,* p.35.
40. The American Society of Planning Officials, Executive Summary, *op. cit.,* p.12.
41. The American Society of Planning Officials, *op. cit.,* p.21-22.
42. *Ibid.,* p.22.
43. *Ibid.,* p.70.
44. William K. Reilly, ed., *op. cit.,* p.275.
45. The American Society of Planning Officials, Executive Summary, *op. cit.,* p.14.
46. INFORM telephone interview with Lawrence Mullrix, California Water Resources Control Board, May 11, 1976.
47. National Association of Homebuilders Research Foundation, *A Manual of Residential Water Supply Systems Development Demands* (Rockville, Maryland: National Association of Homebuilders, Aug. 1973).
48. INFORM telephone interview with Leonard Halpenny, hydrologist and President of The Water Development Company, Tucson, Arizona, Oct. 1974.
49. Colorado Environment Commission, *Colorado : Options for the Future* (Denver: Colorado Environment Commission, 1972),p.16.
50. D.A. Okun, *Water and Wastewater Engineering* (New York: John Wiley and Sons, 1966), Vol. 1.
51. U.S. Public Health Service, *Environmental Health Planning Guide* (Washington, D.C.: U.S. Public Health Service, 1973), p.37.
52. National Association of Home Builders, *op. cit.,* n.p.
53. National Association of Home Builders Research Foundation, *A Manual of Residential Sanitary Sewer System Development Standards,* Interim Copy (Rockville, Maryland: National Association of Home Builders, June 1973), Introduction.
54. The American Society of Planning Officials, et al., *op. cit.,* p.46.

55. The American Society of Planning Officials, Executive Summary, *op. cit.*, p.13.
56. New York State Dept. of Health, *Planning the Subdivision as Part of the Total Environment* (Albany: State of New York, 1970), p.42.
57. California Resources Agency and Division of Soil Conservation, *Environmental Impact of Urbanization on the Foothill and Mountainous Lands of California* (Sacramento: State of California, 1971), p.43.
58. Soil Conservation Service, *Guide for Reviewing Subdivision Plans in Colorado* (Denver: State of Colorado, 1974), n.p., Sec. 320.
59. U.S. Geological Survey, *Hydrologic Implications of Solid-Waste Disposal* (Washington, D.C.: Dept. of the Interior, 1970), n.p.
60. New York State Dept. of Health, *op. cit.*, p.50.
61. Federal Trade Commission, "Complaint in the Matter of AMREP Corporation," *op. cit.*, p.26.
62. Federal Trade Commission, "Decision and Order in the Matter of GAC Corporation, et al.," Docket No. C-2523 (Washington, D.C.: Federal Trade Commission, July 23, 1974), pp.21-22.
63. The American Society of Planning Officials, et al., *op. cit.*, p.24.
64. Committee on the Office of Attorney General, National Association of Attorneys General, *op. cit.*, p.31.
65. *Ibid.*, p.13.
66. Mancini, et al., Plaintiffs v. GAC Corporation, et al., "Agreement of Settlement," Case No. CIV 72-45-TUC-JAW (Tucson: Arizona District Court, 1974), p.5, Art. 10.
67. The American Society of Planning Officials, et al., Executive Summary, *op. cit.*, p.14.
68. Metropolitan District Act (1947), Title 32, Part 10, Art. 1, C.R.S. 1973
69. Hugh Mields, *Federally Assisted New Communities*, p.146.

ENVIRONMENTAL PROTECTION PRACTICES

1. Fred Bosselman and David Callies, *The Quiet Revolution in Land Use Controls* (Washington, D.C.: Council on Environmental Quality, 1971), p.1.
2. The Bureau Of National Affairs, Inc., *BNA Environment Reporter*, (1975), p.254.
3. The American Society of Planning Officials, Conservation Foundation, Urban Land Institute, and Ragatz Associates, Inc., *Subdividing Rural America: Impacts of Recreational Lot and Second Home Development*, (Washington: Council on Environmental Quality, 1976), p.20.
4. Stephen Sussna and Jack Kirchnoff, "The Problem of Premature Subdivision," *Appraisal Journal*, Oct. 1971.
5. William K. Reilly, ed., *The Use of Land* (New York: The Rockefeller Brothers Fund, 1973), p.292.
6. Dept. of Housing and Urban Development, "Assistance for New Communities," (Washington, D.C.: Dept. of Housing and Urban Development, 1972), Sec. 720, Art. 8, Par.(d).
7. James Clapp, *New Towns and Urban Policy* (New York: Dunellen Press, 1971), p.28.
8. Mancini, et al., Plaintiffs, v. GAC Corporation, et al., "Notice of Proposed Class Action Settlement," Case No. CIV-72-45-TUC-JAW (Tucson: United States District Court, District of Arizona, Aug. 1, 1974); and Weis, et al., Plaintiffs v. GAC Corporation, et al., "Notice of Proposed Class Action Settlement," Case No. 73-155-CIV-JE (Miami: United States District Court, Southern District of Florida, Aug. 1, 1974).
9. South Florida Regional Planning Council, "Amplification of Information Required for an Application for Development Approval," (Miami: South Florida Regional Planning Council, July 1974).
10. INFORM telephone interview with Thomas Jacobs, Governmental Affairs Coordinator, Tahoe Regional Planning Agency, Feb. 1976.
11. Paul Sears, "Planning and its Perversions," *The New Mexico Review*, Oct. 1972.
12. California Resources Agency and Division of Soil Conservation, *Environmental Impact of Urbanization of the Foothill and Mountainous Lands of California* (Sacramento: State of California, 1971), p.14.
13. Council on Environmental Quality, *The Fifth Annual Report* (Washington, D.C.: U.S. Government Printing Office, Dec. 1974), p.12.

NOTES 511

14. Bureau of Land Management, *Where Not to Build : Technical Bulletin Number 1* (Washington, D.C.: U.S. Dept. of the Interior, Apr. 1968), p.47.
15. N.Y. State Dept. of Health, *Planning the Subdivision as Part of the Total Environment* (Albany: State of New York, 1970), p.21.
16. Real Estate Research Corp., *The Costs of Sprawl* (Washington, D.C.: U.S. Government Printing Office, Apr. 1974), pp.21-22.
17. Bureau of Land Management, *op. cit.*
18. *Ibid.*, p.42.
19. *Ibid.*
20. Rocky Mountain Center on Environment, *Land Use Packet No. 1* (Denver: Rocky Mountain Center on Environment, Nov. 1971), p.44.
21. Eric Gerstung, "A Brief Survey of the Impact of Subdivision Activity on the Fish and Wildlife Resources of Nevada County," (Sacramento: California Dept. of fish and Game Resources Agency, Apr. 1970), p.9.
22. Fish and Wildlife Service, Dept. of Interior, *Federal Register* (Washington, D.C.: Dept. of Interior, Dec. 1, 1975), Vol. 40, Sect. IV, Art. 1, Par.(b).
23. John Clark, *Coastal Ecosystems* (Washington, D.C.: Conservation Foundation, 1974) p.101
24. *Ibid.*, pp.74-79.
25. John Clarke and Robb Turner, "Barrier Islands: A Threatened, Fragile Resource," *Conservation Foundation Newsletter*, Aug. 1975.
26. Florida Environmental Land Management Study Committee, *Environmental Land Management* (Tallahassee: State of Florida, Dec. 1973), p.98.
27. Office of Planning and Research, Governor's Office, *Summary Report : Environmental Goals and Policy* (Sacramento: State of California, June 1973), Appendix, p.3.
28. Ian McHarg, *Design with Nature* (Garden City, N.Y.: The Museum of Natural History Press, 1969), p.58.
29. *Ibid.*, pp.60-61.
30. William Reilly, ed., *op. cit.*, p.106.
31. Office of Planning and Research, Governor's Office, *op. cit.*, p.66.
32. Council on Environmental Quality, *The Fifth Annual Report, op. cit.*, p.66.
33. Adirondack Park Agency, *Model Land Use Controls Working Document #1* (Ray Brook, N.Y.: State of New York, Jan. 1975), p.83.
34. Office of Planning and Research, Governor's Office, *op. cit.*, Appendix, p.2.

35. The American Society of Planning Officials, et al., *op. cit.*, p.57.
36. Office of Planning and Research, Governor's Office, *op. cit.*, Appendix, p.2.
37. The American Society of Planning Officials, et al., *op. cit.*, p.109.
38. Office of Planning and Research, Governor's Office, *op. cit.*, Appendix, p.4.
39. Ian McHarg, *op. cit.*, p.60.
40. *Ibid.*, p.86.
41. Charles Howe, ed., *Residential Development in the Mountains of Colorado* (Denver: University of Colorado, 1972), pp.31-33.
42. California Resources Agency, and Division of Soil Conservation, *op. cit.*, p.19.
43. The American Society of Planning Officials, et al., *op. cit.*, p.53.
44. Soil Conservation Service, *Guide for Reviewing Subdivision Plans in Colorado* (Denver: State of Colorado, 1974), Sec. 440.
45. U.S. Environmental Protection Agency, *Processes, Procedures and Methods to Control Pollution Resulting from all Construction Activity* (Washington, D.C.: U.S. Environmental Protection Agency, Oct. 1973), p.32.
46. California Resources Agency and Division of Soil Conservation, *op. cit.*, p.19.
47. Adirondack Park Agency, *op. cit.*, p.78.
48. Tahoe Regional Planning Agency, "Subdivision Ordinance," (Adopted Mar. 22, 1972), Sec. VIII, Art. 21.
49. Tahoe Regional Planning Agency, "Grading Ordinance" (Adopted Feb. 10, 1972), Sec. VII, Art. 20, Par. 1.
50. Luna Leopold, *Hydrology of Urban Land Planning* (Washington, D.C.: U.S. Geological Service, 1968), p.1.
51. The American Society of Planning Officials, et al., *op. cit.*, p.50.
52. Luna Leopold, *op. cit.*
53. Eric Gerstung, *op. cit.*, p.6.
54. Luna Leopold, *op. cit.*, p.11.
55. Council on Environmental Quality, *The Fifth Annual Report*, *op. cit.*, p.13.
56. John Clarke, *Coastal Ecosystems*, *op. cit.*, p.162
57. Conservation Foundation, *Water Quality Training Institute Kit* (Washington, D.C.: Conservation Foundation, 1974), n.p.
58. U.S. Environmental Protection Agency, *op. cit.*, pp.75-78.
59. Ian McHarg, *op. cit.*, p.86.

NOTES 513

60. Charles Howe, ed., op. cit., p.84.
61. Eric Gerstung, op. cit., p.9.
62. Adirondack Park Agency, op. cit., p.60.
63. Soil Conservation Service, op. cit., n.p., Sec. 530.
64. California Resources Agency, and Division of Soil Conservation, op. cit., p.19.
65. U.S. Environmental Protection Agency, op. cit., p.46.
66. J.W. Patterson and R.A. Minear, Septic Tanks and the Environment (Chicago: Illinois Institute of Technology, June 1971), pp.1-4.
67. Luna Leopold, op. cit., p.17.
68. Conservation Foundation, op. cit., Chap. III, p.46.
69. William Reilly, ed., op. cit., p. 276.
70. Conservation Foundation, op. cit., Chap. III, p.46.
71. John Clarke, Coastal Ecosystems, op. cit., p.119
72. Charles Howe, ed., op. cit., p.87.
73. J.W. Patterson and R.A. Minear, op. cit., pp.3-27.
74. Eric Gerstung, op. cit., p.9.
75. Department of Public Health, Bureau of Sanitary Engineering, Sewage Disposal in Mountain Areas : A Summary Report (Sacramento: State of California, 1971), p.9.
76. Conservation Foundation, op. cit., Chap. III, p.33.
77. Ibid.
78. Trico Colorado, Inc., Pueblo West Metropolitan District Revised Service Plan (Pueblo West, Colorado: Trico Colorado, Inc., 1972).
79. John Dillion, "Unmaking A Florida Canal," Christian Science Monitor, Mar. 24, 1973.
80. John Clarke, Coastal Ecosystems, pp.129-130
81. Charles Wharton, "Statement for Congressional Hearings on Dredging, Modification and Channelization of Rivers and Streams," testimony given before U.S. Congress, Subcommittee on Conservation and Natural Resources, June 14, 1971.
82. Eric Gerstung, op. cit., p.10.
83. John Clarke, Coastal Ecosystems, p.152.
84. Harold Schmeck, "Land Subsidence Called A Threat," The New York Times, Oct. 13, 1975.
85. C.B. Sherwood and R.G. Grantham, Water Control vs. Sea-Water Intrusion, Broward County, Florida (Washington, D.C.: U.S. Geological Survey and Tallahassee Office, Florida Geological Survey, 1965), p.1.
86. Harold Schmeck, op. cit.

87. Applied Science and Resource Planning Inc., *Environmental Impact Report: Bear Valley Springs* (Sacramento: Applied Science and Resource Planning Inc., Nov. 1972), p.81.
88. Charles Howe, ed., *op. cit.*, p.51.
89. New York State Dept. of Health, *op. cit.*, p.36.
90. Southwest Florida Water Management District, "Rules and Regulations," adopted Sept. 11, 1974, Rule No. 16 CB 2.11.

II. SUBDIVISIONS IN DESERT GRASSLANDS

1. THE DESERT GRASSLAND ENVIRONMENT

1. *Encyclopedia Brittanica*, 1974 ed., s.v. "The North American Desert."
2. *Ibid.*
3. C.J. Hylander, *Wildlife Communities from the Tundra to the Tropics in North America*, (New York: Houghton Mifflin, 1966), p.96.
4. R.R. Humphrey, *The Desert Grasslands*, (Tucson: University of Arizona Press, 1958), p.3.
5. *Encyclopedia Brittanica*, 1974 ed., s.v. "Terrestrial Ecosystems."
6. C.J. Hylander, *op. cit.*, pp.244-245
7. *Encyclopedia Brittanica*, "Terrestrial Ecosystems," *op. cit.*
8. R.R. Humphrey and L.A. Mehinhoff, "Vegetation Changes on a Southern Arizona Grassland Range," in *Readings in Conservation Ecology*, ed. C.W. Cox, (New York: Appleton-Century Crofts, 1969), p.244-ff.
9. *Encyclopedia Brittanica*, "The North American Desert," *op. cit.*
10. R.R. Humphrey, *The Desert Grasslands*, *op. cit.*, p.6.
11. R.R. Humphrey, "Vegetation Changes on a Southern Arizona Grassland Range," in *Readings in Conservation Ecology, op. cit.*, p.244.
12. R.R. Humphrey, *The Desert Grasslands, op. cit.*, p.64.
13. Ruth Kirk, *The American Southwest Desert*, (Boston: Houghton, Mifflin & Co., 1973), p.128.
14. *Encyclopedia Brittanica*, 1974 ed., s.v. "Arizona."
15. Ruth Kirk, *op. cit.*, p.128.
16. California Resource Agency, Division of Soil Conservation, *Environmental Impact of Urbanization on the Foothills and Mountainous Lands of California*, (Sacramento: State of California, Nov. 1971), p.26.

NOTES 515

17. C.J. Hylander, *op. cit.*, p.245.
18. *Ibid.*, p.262.

2. RIO RANCHO ESTATES

1. AMREP Corp., *Form 10-K Annual Report* (Washington, D.C.: Securities and Exchange Commission, April 1975), p.5.
2. United States v. AMREP Corporation, et al., "Indictment," Case No. 75CR (New York: U.S. District Court, Southern District of New York, Oct. 28, 1975), Sec. II, Art. 18, Par. (e).
3. AMREP Corp., "How to Invest in a Better Life in the Sunny Southwest," Advertising Brochure, 1974, p.7.
4. AMREP Corp., *Status Report: Rio Rancho Estates, Inc.*, RR-822-8 (New York: AMREP Corp., Oct. 1, 1975), p.3.
5. AMREP Corp., *Offering Statement, Rio Rancho Estates* (New York: New York Dept. of State, Dec. 1974), pp.10-12.
6. AMREP Corp., *Status Report: Rio Rancho Estates, Inc., op. cit.*, p.3.
7. Federal Trade Commission, "Complaint in the Matter of AMREP Corporation," Docket No. 9018, (Washington, D.C.: Federal Track Commission, Mar. 11, 1975); and United States, Plaintiff v. AMREP Corporation, et al., "Indictment," *op. cit.*
8. INFORM telephone interview with official of the United States Census Bureau, Aug. 14, 1976.
9. Central Clearing House, *The Land of Enchantment*, (Santa Fe: Central Clearing House, 1972), pp.28-31.
10. AMREP Corp., *Form 10-K Annual Report, op. cit.*, p.5.
11. Stan Steiner and Ellen Souberman, "AMREP Finds Its Eldorado In Santa Fe," *The New Mexico Review*, Feb. 1971, p.2.
12. *Ibid.*
13. *Ibid.*
14. AMREP Corp., *Offering Statement, Rio Rancho Estates, op. cit.*, p.5.
15. United States v. AMREP Corporation, et al., "Indictment," *op. cit.*, Sec. II, Art. 18, Par. (d).
16. AMREP Corp., "Initial Statement of Record, Rio Rancho Estates," unpublished material from files (Washington, D.C.: Office of Interstate Land Sales Registration, n.d.), p.B-4.

17. AMREP Corp., "Consolidated Statement of Record, Rio Rancho Estates," unpublished material from files (Washington, D.C.: Office of Interstate Land Sales Registration, Aug. 18, 1969), p.B-4.
18. AMREP Corp., "Consolidated Statement of Record, Rio Rancho Estates," unpublished material from files (Washington, D.C.: Office of Interstate Land Sales Registration, Feb. 4, 1970), p.B-4.
19. AMREP Corp., *Form 10-K Annual Report* (Washington, D.C.: Securities and Exchange Commission, April 1974), p.6.
20. Charles Wood, "Amrep Steps Designed to Protect Environment, its President Says," *Albuquerque Tribune*, March 27, 1971.
21. Paul Sears, "Planning and Its Perversions," *The New Mexico Review*, Oct. 1972, p.6.
22. AMREP Corp., *Status Report: Rio Rancho Estates, op. cit.*, p.2.
23. *Ibid.*, p.3.
24. AMREP Corp., *Form 10-K Annual Report*, April 1975, *op cit.*, p.6.
25. AMREP Corp., *Offering Statement, Rio Rancho Estates, op. cit.*, p.11.
26. INFORM personal interview with Paul Sears, New Mexico journalist, Oct. 1974.
27. United States v. AMREP Corporation, et al., "Indictment," *op. cit.*, Sec. II, Art. 18, Par. (o)-ii.
28. *Ibid.*, Sec. II, Art. 18, Par. (o)-vii.
29. *Ibid.*, Sec. II, Art. 18, Par. (o)-xi.
30. *Ibid.*, Sec. II, Art. 18, Par. (o)-xiii, xi
31. Federal Trade Commission, "Proposed Order in the Matter of AMREP Corporation," Docket No. 9018 (Washington, D.C.: Federal Trade Commission, Mar. 11, 1975), Sec. III, Art. 2, Par. (e).
32. *Ibid.*, Sec. III, Art. 1.
33. AMREP Corp., *Offering Statement, Rio Rancho Estates* (New York: New York Dept. of State, June 20, 1973), p.6.
34. AMREP Corp., *Offering Statement, Rio Rancho Estates*, Dec. 1974, *op. cit.*, p.8.
35. *Ibid.*, p.10.
36. Written Communication from Philip Bishop, New Mexico State Engineer Office to INFORM, July 16, 1975.
37. New Mexico Environmental Improvement Agency, *Regulations Governing Liquid Waste Disposal* (Santa Fe: State of New Mexico, Sept. 14, 1973), p.5.
38. United States v. AMREP Corporation, et al., "Indictment," *op. cit.*, Sec. II, Art. 18, Par. (q)-xiv.

NOTES 517

39. AMREP Corp., *Offering Statement, Rio Rancho Estates*, Dec. 1974, *op. cit.*, p.10.
40. United States v. AMREP Corporation, et al., "Indictment," *op. cit.*, Sec. II, Art. 18, Par. (q)-x.
41. AMREP Corp., *Property Report, Rio Rancho Estates* (Washington, D.C.: Office of Interstate Land Sales Registration, Oct. 16, 1972), p.8.
42. United States v. AMREP Corporation, et al., "Indictment," *op. cit.*, Sec. II, Art. 18, Par. (p).
43. AMREP Corp., *Offering Statement, Rio Rancho Estates*, Dec. 1974, *op. cit.*, p.9.
44. INFORM personal interview with John Wright, Chief, Water Quality Section, New Mexico Environmental Improvement Agency, Oct. 1974.
45. Written Communication from Philip Bishop, New Mexico State Engineer Office, to INFORM, July 16, 1975.
46. INFORM telephone interview with David Stone, hydrologist, New Mexico State Engineer Office, Aug. 14, 1976.
47. INFORM personal interview with John Wright, Chief, Water Quality Section, New Mexico Environmental Improvement Agency, Oct. 1974.
48. New Mexico Environmental Improvement Agency, *Regulations Governing Liquid Waste Disposal*, *op. cit.*, p.5.
49. Horizon Corp., *Property Report, Canyon del Rio Estates (Rio Communities)*, (Washington, D.C.: Office of Interstate Land Sales Registration, May 20, 1975), p.14.
50. AMREP Corp., *Offering Statement, Rio Rancho Estates*, Dec. 1974, *op. cit.*, p.12.
51. *Ibid.*, p.11.
52. AMREP Corp., *Status Report: Rio Rancho Estates*, *op. cit.*, p.1.
53. Written Communication from Paul Sears, New Mexico journalist to INFORM, March 1976.
54. AMREP Corp., *Offering Statement, Rio Rancho Estates*, Dec. 1974, *op. cit.*, p.9.
55. *Ibid.*
56. *Ibid.*, p.12.
57. AMREP Corp., "Initial Statement of Record, Rio Rancho Estates," unpublished material from files, *op. cit.*, Part VIII, Section F.
58. Paul Sears, "How to Ignore A Flood," *The New Mexico Review*, Sept. 1972, p.3.
59. INFORM personal interview with Paul Sears, New Mexico journalist, Oct. 1974.
60. *Ibid.*

61. Written Communication from Paul Sears, New Mexico journalist, March 1976.
62. AMREP Corp., *Offering Statement, Rio Rancho Estates*, Dec. 1974, *op. cit.*, pp.10-12.
63. *Ibid.*, p.10.
64. *Ibid.*, p.11.
65. INFORM telephone interview with official of the Public Service Company of New Mexico, n.d.
66. AMREP Corp., *AMREP Corporation Annual Report*, (New York: AMREP Corp., 1972), p.1; and AMREP Corp., "Rio Rancho Estates: Your Investment in the Future," Advertising Brochure, April 1965, p.1.
67. Paul Sears, "Planning and Its Perversions," *The New Mexico Review*, Oct. 19742, p.6.
68. *Ibid.*, p.20.
69. *Ibid.*, p.7.
70. INFORM personal interview with Paul Sears, New Mexico journalist, Oct. 1974.
71. Paul Sears, "How to Ignore A Flood," *op. cit.*, pp.4-5.
72. INFORM telephone interview with Joseph Pierce, New Mexico Environmental Improvement Agency, Mar. 30, 1976.
73. Arlene Cinelli, "County Commentary: Let Us Not Forget the Flood," *Sandoval County Times Independent*, Nov. 28, 1975.
74. Paul Sears, "How to Ignore a Flood," *op. cit.*, pp.4-5.
75. *Ibid.*
76. INFORM personal interview with John Wright, Chief, Water Quality Section, New Mexico Environmental Improvement Agency, Oct. 1974.
77. AMREP Corp., Consolidated Statement of Record, Rio Rancho Estates, Section VIII, Exhibit, Unpublished material from files, (Washington, D.C.: Office of Interstate Land Sales Registration, Apr. 21, 1971).
78. *Ibid.*, n.p.
79. *Ibid.*, n.p.
80. New Mexico Environmental Improvement Agency, *Regulations Governing Liquid Waste Disposal, op. cit.*, p.5.
81. INFORM telephone interview with Philip Bishop, New Mexico State Engineer Office, Aug. 13, 1976.
82. AMREP Corp., *Offering Statement, Rio Rancho Estates*, Dec. 1974, *op. cit.*, pp.4-5.
83. *Ibid.*p.5.
84. *Ibid.*
85. AMREP Corp., *AMREP Corporation Annual Report* (New York: AMREP Corp., July 15, 1975), p.17.

NOTES 519

86. United States v. AMREP Corporation, et al., "Indictment," op. cit., Sec. II; and Federal Trade Commission, "Complaint in the Matter of AMREP Corporation," op. cit., Par. 32-56.
87. AMREP Corp., Offering Statement, Rio Rancho Estates, Dec. 1974, op. cit., pp.4-5.
88. Federal Trade Commission, "Complaint in the Matter of AMREP Corporation," op. cit., Par. 47.
89. INFORM personal interview with AMREP sales representative, New York City, Fall 1973.
90. INFORM telephone interview with New Mexico Tourist Bureau, Aug. 13, 1976.
91. Federal Trade Commission, "Proposed Order in the Matter of AMREP Corporation," op. cit., Sec. II, Art. 7.
92. Federal Trade Commission, "Complaint in the Matter of AMREP Corporation," Sec. II, Art. 18, Par. (g)-xv.
93. Federal Trade Commission, "Decision and Order in the Matter of GAC Corporation, et al.," Docket No. C-2523, (Washington, D.C.: Federal Trade Commission, July 23, 1974), Part II, Sections A-F.
94. Federal Trade Commission, "Complaint in the Matter of AMREP Corporation," op. cit., Par. 42.
95. AMREP Corp., Offering Statement, Rio Rancho Estates, Dec. 1974, op. cit., p.7.
96. Federal Trade Commission, "Proposed Order in the Matter of AMREP Corp.," op. cit., Sec. I, Art. 9, Par. (b).
97. Ibid., Sec. III.
98. AMREP Corp., Offering Statement, Rio Rancho Estates, Dec. 1974, op. cit., pp.3, 8.
99. AMREP Corp., Property Report, Rio Rancho Estates, Oct. 16, 1972, op. cit., p.2.
100. Horizon Corp., Property Report, Rio del Oro (Rio Communities), (Washington, D.C.: Office of Interstate Land Sales Registration, May 20, 1975), p.4.
101. AMREP Corp., Offering Statement, Rio Rancho Estates, Dec. 1974, op. cit., p.7.
102. Ibid., pp.10-12.
103. "Rio Rancho Land Auction, 'Success'," Albuquerque Journal, Aug. 27, 1975.
104. Letter from The Better Business Bureau of New Mexico, to INFORM, Oct. 10, 1973.
105. AMREP Corp., Offering Statement, Rio Rancho Estates, Dec. 1974, op. cit., p.3.
106. United States v. AMREP Corporation, et al., "Indictment," op. cit., Sec. I, Art. 16.

107. AMREP Corp., *Offering Statement, Rio Rancho Estates*, Dec. 1974, *op. cit.*, p.9.
108. *Ibid.*, p.8.
109. Federal Trade Commission, "Proposed Order in the Matter of AMREP Corporation," *op. cit.*, Sec. III, Art. 10.
110. AMREP Corp., *Offering Statement, Rio Rancho Estates*, Dec. 1974, *op. cit.*, p.8.

3. COCHITI LAKE

1. Great Western United Corp., *Form 10-K Annual Report* (Washington, D.C.: U.S. Securities and Exchange Commission, May 31, 1975), p.14.
2. U.S. Army Corps of Engineers, Albuquerque District, *Final Environmental Statement: Cochiti Lake, Rio Grande, New Mexico* (Albuquerque: U.S. Army Corps of Engineers, Feb. 1974), p.II-29.
3. Em Hall and Jim Bensfield, "Cochiti Lake - The Making of the Seven-Day Weekend," *The New Mexico Review and Legislative Journal*, Vol. 2, No. 11 (Nov. 1970), pp.6-8.
4. *Ibid.*
5. U.S. Army Corps of Engineers, *Final Environmental Statement, op. cit.*, p.I-4.
6. Em Hall, "An Expose of 'Great Western Cities'," *The New Mexico Review and Legislative Journal*, Vol. 2, No. 10 (Oct. 1970), p.8.
7. Great Western United Corp., *Proxy Statement/Prospectus* (Denver: Great Western United Corporation, Aug. 28, 1974) p.112.
8. U.S. Army Corps of Engineers, *Final Environmental Statement, op. cit.*, p.I-2, I-6, V-3.
9. *Ibid.*, p.VIII-6.
10. *Ibid.*p.I-3.
11. Great Western United Corp., *Proxy Statement/Prospectus, op. cit.*, p.177.
12. U.S. Army Corps of Engineers, *Final Environmental Statement, op. cit.*, p.III-5, III-6.
13. *Ibid.*, p.III-4.
14. *Ibid.*, p.III-6.
15. U.S. Army Corps of Engineers, *Final Environmental Statement, op. cit.*, Appendix.
16. John Soper, "Questions on Cochiti Lake," *The New Mexican*, Oct. 24, 1971.

17. Master Lease between the Pueblo de Cochiti and California City Development Company, entered into April 15, 1969.
18. U.S. Army Corps of Engineers, *Final Environmental Statement, op. cit.*, p.III-14.
19. W. Wilson Cliff, "Plans for Cochiti Lake Community Unveiled," *Albuquerque Journal*, July 31, 1970, p.A-1, A-6.
20. Lease Between the Pueblo de Cochiti and California City Development Company, "Exhibit A; Plan of Business Operation," *op. cit.*
21. David Duran, "$1.1 Million Invested at Cochiti," *Albuquerque Tribune*, Sept. 4, 1971, p.A-7.
22. Great Western United Corp., *Proxy Statement/Prospectus, op. cit.*, p.177.
23. *Ibid.*, p.154, 157.
24. Great Western United Corp., *Form 10-K Annual Report, op. cit.*, p.12.
25. "Cochiti Lake: What Do You Get for Your Cash?" *The Albuquerque News Chieftain*, Nov. 20, 1970, p.1.
26. Acuff, "Off the Cuff," *Albuquerque News*, Dec. 3, 1970.
27. Pueblo de Cochiti, "Charter of the Town of Cochiti Lake, Cochiti, New Mexico, Aug. 18, 1970.
28. "Cochiti Lake: What Do You Get for Your Cash?," *op. cit.*, p.1.
29. State of New Mexico ex rel. James A. Mahoney, Attorney General v. Fred J. Russell, Acting Secretary of the Interior, et al., "First Amended Complaint," Civil Case No. 8754, (Albuquerque: United States District Court, District of New Mexico, December 31, 1970).
30. David L. Norvell, Attorney General of the State of New Mexico, et al., Plaintiffs, v. Sangre de Cristo Development Company, Inc., "Memorandum of Opinion," Civil Case No. 9106, (Albuquerque: United States District Court, District of New Mexico, February 20, 1974).
31. Great Western United Corp., *Proxy Statement/Prospectus, op. cit.*, p.168.
32. *Ibid.*, p.178.
33. Great Western Cities, Inc., *Property Report, Cochiti Lake*, (Washington, D.C.: U.S. Dept. of Housing and Urban Development, Office of Interstate Land Sales Registration, Oct. 28, 1975), p.2.
34. Great Western United Corp., *Proxy Statement/Prospectus, op. cit.*, p.159.
35. Great Western Cities, Inc., *Property Report, Cochiti Lake, op. cit.*
36. *Ibid.*, p.3.

37. Great Western United Corp., *Proxy Statement/Prospectus, op. cit.*, p.179.
38. Great Western Cities, Inc., *Property Report, Cochiti Lake, op. cit.*, p.13.
39. *Ibid.*, p.15
40. *Ibid.*, p.12
41. *Ibid.*, p.19.
42. *Ibid.*, p.16.
43. Great Western United Corp., *Proxy Statement/Prospectus, op. cit.*, p.179.
44. Great Western Cities, Inc., *Property Report, Cochiti Lake, op. cit.*, p.17.
45. U.S. Army Corps of Engineers, *Final Environmental Statement, op. cit.*
46. "Memorandum of Unterstanding Between Corps of Engineers and Pueblo of Cochiti," Contract No. A-29005-CIV ENG-66-17, (Albuquerque: The State of New Mexico, Nov. 16, 1975).
47. Great Western Cities, Inc., *Property Report, Cochiti Lake, op. cit.*, p.10.
48. U.S. Army Corps of Engineers, *Final Environmental Statement, op. cit.*, p.III-1.
49. *Ibid.*, p.VI-3.
50. INFORM telephone interview with an Official at the Albuquerque Area Office Bureau of Indian Affairs, U.S. Department of the Interior, July 23, 1975.
51. INFORM telephone interview with S.W.A. Group (formerly Sasaki-Walker), Master Planner, Jan. 26, 1976.
52. Great Western Cities, Inc., *Property Report, op. cit.*, p.8.
53. U.S. Army Corps of Engineers, *Final Environmental Statement, op. cit.*
54. *Ibid.*, pp.III-23-34.
55. *Ibid.*, p.II-12.
56. INFORM telephone interview with David Lloyd, Great Western Cities, Inc., June 24, 1976.
57. Great Western United Corp., *Proxy Statement /Prospectus, op. cit.* p.158.
58. *Ibid.*
59. Great Western Cities, Inc., *Property Report, Cochiti Lake, op. cit.*, Supplement.
60. Federal Trade Commission, *Decision and Order In the Matter of Great Western United Corporation, et al.*, Docket No. C-2306 (Washington, D.C.: U.S. Federal Trade Commission, Oct. 20, 1974), Sec. I-B.
61. Great Western Cities, Inc., *Property Report, Cochiti Lake, op. cit.*, Supplement.

NOTES 523

4. RIO COMMUNITIES

1. Horizon Corp., *New Mexico's Rio Grande Valley*, Advertising Brochure (Tucson: Horizon Corp., Aug. 1974), p.1.
2. Horizon Corp., *Property Report, Rio del Oro (Rio Communities)*, P-C-3282, (Washington, D.C.: U.S. Dept. of Housing and Urban Development, Office of Interstate Land Sales Registration, May 20, 1975), pp.11-14.
3. Federal Trade Commission, "Complaint and Proposed Order in the matter of Horizon Corporation," Docket Number 9017, (Washington, D.C., March 11, 1975); and O'Neil and Beeman, Plaintiffs v. Horizon Corp., et al., "Notice of Proposed Class Action Settlement," Case no. CIV-75-133 TUC JAW (Tucson: Arizona District Court, Aug. 15, 1975).
4. Federal Trade Commission, "Complaint and Proposed Order," Docket Number 9017, *op. cit.*, p.21, Part XXII, Section 81.
5. Horizon Corp., *Form 10-K Annual Report*, (Washington, D.C.: Securities and Exchange Commission, April 1975), p.2.
6. Unauthored, *How to Successfully Invest in Real Estate*, (Englewood Cliffs, N.J.: Prentice Hall, Inc., April 1970), pp.4-7.
7. Horizon Corp., *What You Should Know Before You Buy Land*, Advertising Brochure (Tucson: Horizon Corp., 1972), pp.7-8.
8. Horizon Corp., "Rio Communities," Advertising Brochure (Tucson: Horizon Corp., Aug. 1974).
9. Horizon Corp., "Population and Industrial Growth of the Albuquerque Area," Advertising Brochure (Tucson: Horizon Corp., Aug. 1974), p.3.
10. Horizon Corp., *Property Report, Rio del Oro (Rio Communities)*, May 20, 1975, *op. cit.*, p.2.
11. *Ibid.*, p.5.
12. Federal Trade Commission, "Complaint and Proposed Order," Docket Number 9017, *op. cit.*, p.5, Part III, Section 16, ¶(c).
13. O'Neil and Beeman v. Horizon Corporation, et al.,No. CIV-75-133 TUC JAW, "Notice of Proposed Class Action Settlement," *op. cit.*, p.5.
14. *Ibid.*, p.4.
15. "Horizon Corp. Agrees to Settle Class Suit in Land-Fraud Case," *Wall Street Journal*, Aug. 12, 1975.
16. Horizon Corp., "Report to INFORM," unpublished survey prepared for this study, June 1976, Appendix D.
17. *Ibid.*
18. *Ibid.*, Supplementary Questions.
19. INFORM personal interview with Horizon Sales Representative, Oct. 1974.
20. Horizon Corp., "Report to INFORM," *op. cit.*, Social Responsibility.

21. *Ibid.*
22. "Update: Address by Horizon President Sidney Nelson," *New Horizons*, Summer, 1974.
23. Horizon Corp., *Property Report; Rio del Oro (Rio Communities)*, May 20, 1975, *op. cit.*, p.8.
24. Horizon Corp., *Form 10-K Annual Report* (Washington, D.C.: Securities and Exchange Commission, April 1972), p.1.
25. Horizon Corp., "Report to INFORM," *op. cit.*, Fact Sheet.
26. Horizon Corp., *Property Report; Tierra Grande (Rio Communities)*, P-C-2462, (Washington, D.C.: U.S. Dept. of Housing and Urban Development, Office of Interstate Land Sales Registration, May 20, 1975); *Property Report; Canyon del Rio Estates (Rio Communities)*, P-C-2678, (Washington, D.C.: U.S. Dept. of Housing and Urban Development, Office of Interstate Land Sales Registration, May 20, 1975); *Property Report; Rio del Oro (Rio Communities)*, May 20, 1975, *op. cit.*
27. Horizon Corp., *Property Report, Canyon del Rio Estates*, May 20, 1975, *op. cit.*, pp.11-13.
28. Federal Trade Commission, "Complaint and Proposed Order," Docket No. 9017, *op. cit.*, p.28, Order, Section 3, ¶(b).
29. Horizon Corp., *Property Report, Rio del Oro (Rio Communities)*, May 20, 1975, *op. cit.*, p.7.
30. INFORM personal interview with Richard Marshall, Public Affairs, Horizon Corporation, Oct. 1974.
31. Federal Trade Commission, "Complaint and Proposed Order," Docket No. 9017, *op. cit.*, p.19, Part XXVII, Section 71.
32. *Ibid.*, p.43, (Order, Section 42).
33. Horizon Corp., *Property Report, Rio Grande Estates*, P-C-1014RC, (Washington, D.C.: U.S. Dept. of Housing and Urban Development, Office of Interstate Land Sales Registration, Aug. 23, 1973), p.23.
34. Financial statements for Horizon Communities Improvement Association, Inc., and Tierra Grande Improvement Association, Inc., prepared by Coopers and Lybrand, Certified Public Accountants, Phoenix, Ariz., April 3, 1975.
35. Art Bouffard, "Horizon Land Owners Pay for Improvements," *Albuquerque Journal*, Dec. 15, 1974.
36. *Ibid.*
37. "Editorial: Some Basis for Complaint," *Albuquerque Journal*, Dec. 19, 1974.
38. Horizon Corp., *Property Report, Tierra Grande*, May 20, 1975, *op. cit.*, p.16; Horizon Corp., *Property Report, Rio del Oro*, May 20, 1975, *op. cit.*, p.15; Horizon Corp., *Property Report, Canyon del Rio Estates*, May 20, 1975, *op. cit.*, p.15.

39. *Ibid.*, p.12.
40. Letter to INFORM from Philip Bishop, Office of the New Mexico State Engineer, July 16, 1975.
41. Greater Belen Chamber of Commerce, *Community Audit* (Belen, N.M.: Greater Belen Chamber of Commerce, undated), p.2.
43. Horizon Corp., *Property Report, Rio del Oro,* May 20, 1975, *op. cit.*, p.12.
44. *Ibid.*
45. Horizon Corp., "Rio Communities Use Plan," Advertising Brochure (Tucson: Horizon Corp., Feb. 1972).
46. Horizon Corp., *Property Report, Rio del Oro,* May 20, 1975, *op. cit.*, pp.13-14.
47. Horizon Corp., "Rio Communities Use Plan," *op. cit.*
48. New Mexico Environmental Improvement Agency, *Regulations Governing Liquid Waste Disposal, op. cit.*, p.5.
49. Horizon Corp., *Property Report, Tierra Grande*, May 20, 1975, *op. cit.*, p.14; Horizon Corp., *Property Report, Rio del Oro,* May 20, 1975, *op. cit.*, p.14; Horizon Corp., *Property Report, Canyon del Rio Estates,* May 20, 1975, *op. cit.*, p.14.
50. Horizon Corp., "Report to INFORM," *op. cit.*, Fact Sheet.
51. Horizon Corp., "Rio Communities Use Plan," *op. cit.*
52. Horizon Corp., *Property Report, Canyon del Rio Estates,* P-C-2678 (Washington, D.C.: U.S. Dept. of Housing and Urban Development, Office of Interstate and Sales Registration, June 19, 1973), p.14.
53. Horizon Corp., *Property Report, Tierra Grande,* May 20, 1975, *op. cit.*, p.17; Horizon Corp., *Property Report, Rio del Oro,* May 20, 1975, *op. cit.*, p.17; Horizon Corp., *Property Report, Canyon del Rio Estates,* May 20, 1975, *op. cit.*, p.17.
54. Horizon Corp., "Report to INFORM," *op. cit.*, Supplementary Questions.
55. Horizon Corp., *Update '75: Horizon Corporation's Rio Communities* (Tucson: Horizon Corp., March 1, 1975), p.12.
56. Horizon Corp., *Property Report, Canyon del Rio Estates,* May 20, 1975, *op. cit.*, pp.11-14.
57. Horizon Corp., "Report to INFORM," *op. cit.*, Fact Sheet.
58. INFORM personal interview with Lamar Hanson, Rio Communities Manager, Oct. 1974.
59. Horizon Corp., "Report to INFORM," *op. cit.*, Fact Sheet.
60. *Ibid.*
61. Horizon Corp., "Tierra Grande," Adversiting Brochure (Tucson: Horizon Corp., Oct. 1974).

62. Horizon Corp., *Property Report, Tierra Grande,* May 20, 1975, *op. cit.,* p.17; Horizon Corp., *Property Report, Rio del Oro,* May 20, 1975, *op. cit.,* p.17; Horizon Corp., *Property Report, Canyon del Rio Estates,* May 20, 1975, *op. cit.,* p.17.
63. Paul Sears, "How to Ignore a Flood," *The New Mexico Review,* Sept. 1972.
64. *Ibid.*
65. *Ibid.*
66. Horizon Corp., "Contract for Purchase of Land in Rio Communities," FC-3413RC, Jan. 1976, p.3.
67. Federal Trade Commission, "Complaint and Proposed Order," Docket No. 9017, *op. cit.*
68. INFORM personal interview with Horizon Corp. Sales Representative, Oct. 1974.
69. Horizon Corp., *Property Report, Tierra Grande,* May 20, 1975, *op. cit.,* p.5-A; Horizon Corp., *Property Report, Rio del Oro,* May 20, 1975, *op. cit.,* p.5-A; Horizon Corp., *Property Report, Canyon del Rio Estates,* May 20, 1975, *op. cit.,* p.5-A.
70. Horizon Corp., *Form 10-K Annual Report,* April 1975, *op. cit.,* p.2.
71. Horizon Corp., "Report to INFORM," *op. cit.,* Fact Sheet.
72. Federal Trade Commission, "Complaint and Proposed Order," Docket No. 9017, *op. cit.,* Part XXXIII, Sections 83, 84.
73. INFORM personal interview with Horizon Corp. Sales Representative, Oct. 1974.
74. Horizon Corp., "Contract for Purchase of Land in Rio Communities," *op. cit.,* p.2.
75. Horizon Corp., "Report to INFORM," *op. cit.,* p.2.
76. *Ibid.,* Fact Sheet.
77. *Ibid.,* Supplementary Questions.
78. O'Neil and Beeman v. Horizon Corporation, et al., No. CIV-75-133 TUC JAW, "Notice of Proposed Class Action Settlement," *op. cit.,* p.2.
79. Federal Trade Commission, "Complaint and Proposed Order, Docket No. 9017, *op. cit.,* p.26, Order, Section 3(a).
80. O'Neil and Beeman v. Horizon Corporation, et al., No. CIV-75-133 TUC JAW, "Notice of Proposed Class Action Settlement," *op. cit.,* p.13.

5. ARIZONA SUNSITES

1. Horizon Corp., *Form 10-K Annual Report*, (Washington, D.C.: Securities and Exchange Commission, 1972), p.4.
2. Horizon Corp., *Form 10-K Annual Report*, (Washington, D.C.: Securities and Exchange Commission, 1973), p.5.
3. Horizon Corp., "When You Buy Land, Know About the Company You Buy It From," Advertising Brochure (Tucson: Horizon Corp., Nov. 1972).
4. Planning Division, Arizona Dept. of Economic Planning and Development, *Environmental Services Needs Study: 1970-1990, Cochise County*, (Phoenix: State of Arizona, Nov. 1971), p.29.
5. *Ibid.*, p.18.
6. *Ibid.*
7. *Ibid.*, p.30.
8. *Ibid.*, p.28.
9. Planning Division, Arizona Dept. of Economic Planning and Development, *Arizona's Remote Subdivisions*, (Phoenix: State of Arizona, Jan. 1975), p.10.
10. *Ibid.*, p.32.
11. *Arizona Daily Star*, Oct. 9, 1974.
12. INFORM telephone interview with James Altenstadter, Director of Cochise County Planning Dept., Oct. 15, 1975.
13. *Ibid.*
14. INFORM telephone interview with James Altenstadter, Director of Cochise County Planning Dept., Feb. 1976.
15. Horizon Corp., *Form 10-K Annual Report*, 1973, *op. cit.*, p.2.
16. *Ibid.*, p.1.
17. INFORM personal interview with Richard Marshall, Public Affairs, Horizon Corp., Oct. 1974.
18. INFORM personal interview with Lucky Bradshaw, project official at Arizona Sunsites, Oct. 1974.
19. *Ibid.*
20. Personal communication to INFORM from James Altenstadter, Director of Cochise County Planning Dept., Spring 1976.
21. Horizon Corp., "Arizona Sunsites Land Use Plan," Advertising Brochure (Tucson: Horizon Corp., Aug. 1974).
22. *Ibid.*
23. INFORM personal interview with Richard Marshall, Public Affairs, Horizon Corp., Oct. 1974.
24. Horizon Corp., *Property Report: Arizona Sunsites*, (Washington, D.C.: U.S. Dept. of Housing and Urban Development, Office of Interstate Land Sales Registration, May 20, 1975), p.2.

25. *Ibid.*, p.11.
26. Horizon Corp., *Property Report: Arizona Sunsites*, (Washington, D.C.: U.S. Dept. of Hsusing and Urban Development, Office of Interstate Land Sales Registration, Oct. 1975), p.12.
27. Horizon Corp., *Property Report*, May 20, 1975, *op. cit.*, p.11
28. *Ibid.*
29. Horizon Corp., *Property Report*, Oct. 1975, *op. cit.*, p.12.
30. Planning Division, Arizona Dept. of Economic Planning and Development, *Environmental Services Needs Study, 1970-1990, op. cit.*, p.16.
31. INFORM telephone interview with Cochise County Sanitarian, Oct. 14, 1975.
32. Horizon Corp., *Form 10-K Annual Report*, (Washington, D.C.: Securities and Exchange Commission, 1974), p.1.
33. INFORM telephone interview with James Altenstadter, Director of Cochise County Planning Dept., Nov. 1975.
34. Horizon Corp., *Property Report*, Oct. 1975, *op. cit.*, pp.15&18.
35. INFORM telephone interview with James Altenstadter, Director of Cochise County Planning Dept., Nov. 1975.
36. U.S. Dept. of Agriculture, Soil Conservation Service, "Preliminary Investigation Report: Black Diamond Peak Watershed, Cochise County, Arizona." Unpublished paper, Willcox-San Simon Soil Conservation District and Cochise County, Arizona, March 1971.
37. *Ibid.*, p.2.
38. *Ibid.*, p.3.
39. Horizon Corp., *Property Report*, May 20, 1975, *op. cit.*, p.12.
40. *Ibid.*, p.13.
41. *Ibid.*, p.9.
42. "Preliminary Investigation Report: Black Diamond Peak Watershed," *op. cit.*, p.19.
43. *Ibid.*
44. *Ibid.*
45. *Ibid.*, p.20.
46. *Ibid.*, p.5.
47. *Ibid.*, p.19 and INFORM telephone interview with James Altenstadter, Director of Cochise County Planning Dept., Nov. 1975.
48. INFORM telephone interview with James Altenstadter, Director of Cochise County Planning Dept., Nov. 1975.
49. "Preliminary Investigation Report: Black Diamond Peak Watershed," *op. cit.*, p.18.
50. INFORM telephone interview with James Altenstadter, Director of Cochise County Planning Dept., Oct. 15, 1975.
51. Arizona Water Commission, *Summary: Phase 1 - Arizona State Water Plan Inventory of Resources and Uses*, (Phoenix: State of Arizona, July 1975), p.28.

52. *Ibid.*, "Table 16," p.31.
53. *Ibid.*, "Table 13," p.26.
54. *Ibid.*
55. Planning Division, Arizona Dept. of Economic Planning and Development, *Environmental Services Needs Study, 1970-1990, op. cit.*, p. 13.
56. Arizona Water Commission, *Summary: Phase 1 - Arizona State Water Plan Inventory of Resources and Uses, op. cit.*, p.32.
57. Horizon Corp., *Property Report*, May 20, 1975, *op. cit.*, p.5.
58. INFORM personal interview with Leonard Halpenny, hydrologist and President of The Water Development Company, Tucson, Oct. 1974.
59. INFORM telephone interview with Cochise County Sanitarian, Nov. 1975.
60. Personal communication from Charles Schoenecke, former employee of Horizon Corp., to Richard Heidermann, U.S. Dept. of Housing and Urban Development, Office of Interstate Land Sales Registration, June 16, 1972.
61. Horizon Corp., *Property Report*, May 20, 1975, *op. cit.*, p.6.
62. *Ibid.*
63. Horizon Corp., "Subsidiaries Receipt of Deposit," 1974.
64. Horizon Corp., *New York Property Report, Arizona Sunsites* (New York Dept. of State, Aug. 1975), p.5.
65. Horizon Corp., *Property Report*, Oct. 1975, *op. cit.*, p.2
66. *Ibid.*, p.22.
67. INFORM telephone interview with local real estate agent, Oct. 8, 1975.
68. O'Neil and Beeman, Plaintiffs v. Horizon Corporation, et al., "Notice of Proposed Class Action Settlement," Case No. CIV. 75-133 TUC JAW, (Tucson: Arizona District Court, Aug. 15, 1975), p.5.

6. RIO RICO

1. Arizona State Office of Economic Planning and Development, *Rio Rico, Arizona Community Profile* (Phoenix: State of Arizona, 1974).
2. James Russell, "GAC Back On Track," *Miami Herald*, July 25, 1976.
3. *Ibid.*
4. *Ibid.*
5. INFORM telephone interview with Ronald Lovitt, Attorney for Plaintiffs in Mancini, et al. v. GAC Corporation, et al., July 16, 1976.

6. "Arizona's Beauty Big Sales Pitch with Developers," *Arizona Daily Star*, Dec. 29, 1971.
7. GAC Corporation, *GAC Corporation Fact Book* (Miami: GAC Corp., n.d.), p.2.
8. Thomas Pew, "Peddling the Great West," *Saturday Review*, Sept. 4, 1971, p.48.
9. *Ibid.*, p.119.
10. INFORM personal interview with Robert Hathaway, Santa Cruz County Tax Assessor, Oct. 1974.
11. Thomas Pew, "GAC Property 'Overpriced,' Underdeveloped," *Troy Daily News*, April 26, 1972.
12. Steven Auslander, "$100 Million Suit Filed Against GAC in Arizona," *Tucson Star*, Apr. 21, 1972.
13. GAC Corp., *GAC Corporation Annual Report*, (Miami: GAC Corp., 1974), p.22.
14. "Arizona's Beauty Big Sales Pitch with Developers," *op. cit.*
15. GAC Properties, Inc., Petition for Review of Full Cash Value, submitted to Arizona State Board of Property Tax Appeals, (Phoenix, Arizona, Dec. 25, 1970).
16. *Ibid.*
17. Thomas Pew, "Peddling the Great West," *op. cit.*, p.50.
18. "Arizona's Beauty Big Sales Pitch with Developers," *op. cit.*
19. GAC Properties, Inc., *Property Report, Rio Rico Estates*, (Units 3, 4, 6, 7, 8, 9, 10, 11, 12, 13 and 16), No. 0-0825-02-117, (Washington, D.C.: U.S. Dept. of Housing and Urban Development, Office of Interstate Land Sales Registration, Oct. 28, 1975), p.22.
20. INFORM personal interview with H.C. Soto Realty Company, Nogales, Arizona, Oct. 1974.
21. INFORM personal interview with Nogales Realty Company, Nogales, Arizona, Oct. 1974.
22. Gary Soucie, "Subdividing and Conquering the Desert," *Audubon*, July 1973, p.34.
23. Thomas Pew, "Peddling the Great West," *op. cit.*, p.50.
24. *Ibid.*
25. U.S. Dept. of Housing and Urban Development, *HUD News*, No. 74-100, (Washington, D.C.: U.S. Dept. of Housing and Urban Development, March 28, 1974), p.2.
26. INFORM personal interview with Randolph Gaines, Planning Director, Santa Cruz County Planning and Zoning Department, Oct. 1974.
27. "HUD Moves to Halt Land Sales by GAC," *The Wall Street Journal*, Oct. 15, 1975.

NOTES 531

28. INFORM telephone interview with Murray Epstein, supervising Attorney for the bankruptcy Settlement Committee, July 1976.
29. INFORM telephone interview with William Baffert, Santa Cruz County Supervisor, April 14, 1976.
30. INFORM personal interview with Randolph Gaines, Planning Director, Santa Cruz County Planning and Zoning Department, Oct. 1974.
31. Thomas Pew, "Peddling the Great West," *op. cit.*, p.23.
32. Arizona State Office of Economic Planning and Development, *Environmental Needs Study: Santa Cruz County*, (Phoenix: State of Arizona, Sept. 1971), p.23.
33. *Ibid.*, p.15.
34. *Ibid.*, p.7.
35. Arizona State Office of Economic Planning and Development, *Rio Rico, Arizona Community Profile, op. cit.*
36. INFORM personal interview with Nogales Sanitarian, Oct. 1974.
37. Mancini, et al., Plaintiffs v. GAC Corporation, et al., "Notice of Proposed Class Action Settlement," Case No. CIV 72-45-TUC-JAW (Tucson: Arizona District Court, Aug 1, 1974), p.8.
38. GAC Corp., "Fact Sheet: Rio Rico," (Miami: GAC Corp., Aug. 30, 1973), p.8.
39. Mancini, et al., Plaintiffs, v. GAC Corporation, et al., "Notice of Proposed Class Action Settlement," *op. cit.*, p.7.
40. INFORM telephone interview with Louis Doyle, Santa Cruz County Tax Assessor, Apr. 9, 1976.
41. INFORM telephone interview with David Hughes, Court-appointed Trustee for GAC Corporation, July 14, 1976.
42. James Russell, *op. cit.*
43. INFORM telephone interview with Paul, Landy, Baily and Yacos, Attorneys for GAC Corporation, July 1976.
44. INFORM telephone interview with David Hughes, Court-appointed Trustee for GAC Corporation, July 14, 1976.
45. James Russell, *op. cit.*
46. GAC Properties, Inc., *Deeds of Reservation and Restrictions: Rio Rico Subdivision*, "Amendments for Rio Rico Villas Units 5, 12 and 13," (Tucson: GAC Properties, Inc., July 28, 1971), n.p.
47. Mancini, et al., Plaintiffs v. GAC Corporation, et al., "Agreement of Settlement," Case No. CIV 72-45-TUC-JAW, (Tucson: Arizona District Court, 1974).

48. *Ibid.*, p.12
49. *Ibid.*
50. *Ibid.*, p.10.
51. INFORM telephone interview with Ronald Lovitt, Attorney for Plaintiffs in Mancini, et al. v. GAC Corporation, et al., July 16, 1976.
52. Mancini, et al., Plaintiffs, v. GAC Corporation, et al., "Agreement of Settlement," *op. cit.*, p.6.
53. INFORM telephone interview with Ronald Lovitt and J. Thomas Hannan, Attorneys for Plaintiffs in Mancini, et al. v. GAC Corporation, et al., April 1976.
54. GAC Properties, Inc., *Deeds of Reservation and Restrictions: Rio Rico Subdivision*, "Amendments for Rio Rico Villas," *op. cit.*, n.p.
55. *Ibid.*
56. Letter to INFORM from Randolph Gaines, Planning Director, Santa Cruz County Planning and Zoning Department, July 1976.
57. *Ibid.*
58. GAC Properties, Inc., *Property Report, Rio Rico Estates*, Oct. 28, 1975, *op. cit.*, p.12.
59. Arizona Water Commission, *Arizona State Water Plan: Inventory of Resources and Uses*, (Phoenix: State of Arizona, July 1975), p.21, Table 12.
60. *Ibid.*, p.24.
61. *Ibid.*, pp.25-26, Table 13.
62. INFORM personal interview with Edgar Condes, Deputy Director, Santa Cruz County Environmental Health Department, Oct. 1974.
63. Mancini, et al., Plaintiffs v. GAC Corporation, et al., "Agreement of Settlement," *op. cit.*, p.8.
64. *Ibid.*
65. INFORM telephone interview with Mr. Petty, Citizens Utilities Corporation, April 20, 1976.
66. *Ibid.*
67. INFORM telephone interview with Juan Alegria, Santa Cruz County Health Department, April 22, 1976.
68. INFORM personal interview with Edgar Condes, Deputy Director, Santa Cruz County Environmental Health Department, Oct. 1974.
69. *Ibid.*
70. INFORM telephone interview with Juan Alegria, Santa Cruz County Environmental Health Department, April 22, 1976.

71. INFORM telephone interview with Gene R. Fontes, Santa Cruz County Engineer, April 20, 1976.
72. INFORM telephone interview with Mr. Petty, Citizens Utilities Company, April 20, 1976.
73. INFORM telephone interview with Randolph Gaines, Planning Director, Santa Cruz County Planning and Zoning Department, May 6, 1976.
74. *Ibid.*, April 8, 1976.
75. Agreement between Walter Wetten, Santa Cruz County Planning and Zoning Director, and GAC Properties, Inc. of Arizona, Aug. 7, 1969; as per correspondence from Gene R. Fontes, Santa Cruz County Engineer, to INFORM, April 20, 1976.
76. INFORM telephone interview with Gene R. Fontes, Santa Cruz County Engineer, April 20, 1976.
77. *Ibid.*
78. *Ibid.*
79. INFORM telephone interview with Randolph Gaines, Planning Director, Santa Cruz County Planning and Zoning Department, April 22, 1976.
80. INFORM telephone interview with Louis Doyle, Santa Cruz County Tax Assessor, April 9, 1976.
81. Arizona Real Estate Dept., *Final Subdivision Report (Amended)*, "Rio Rico Ranchettes: Unit No. 18," (Phoenix: State of Arizona, 1971), p.1.
82. *Ibid.*, "Unit No. 16."
83. INFORM telephone interview with Gene R. Fontes, Santa Cruz County Engineer, April 20, 1976.
84. INFORM personal interview with Edgar Condes, Deputy Director, Santa Cruz County Environmental Health Department, Oct. 1974.
85. INFORM personal interview with Charles Fowler, Director of Public Relations at Rio Rico, GAC Corporation, Oct. 19, 1974.
86. INFORM personal interview with Edgar Condes, Deputy Director, Santa Cruz County Environmental Health Department, Oct. 1974.
87. INFORM personal interview with Charles Fowler, Director of Public Relations at Rio Rico, GAC Corporation, Oct. 19, 1974.
88. INFORM personal interview with William Schaeffer, Water Quality Control Division, Arizona Dept. of Health, Oct. 1974.

89. Arizona State Board of Health, *Bulletin Number 12* (Tucson: State of Arizona, 1974).
90. INFORM personal interview with Edgar Condes, Deputy Director, Santa Cruz County Environmental Health Department, Oct. 1974.
91. GAC Properties, Inc., *Property Report, Rio Rico Villas*, (Units 9, 10, 14 and 16), (Washington, D.C.: U.S. Dept. of Housing and Urban Development, Office of Interstate Land Sales Registration, July 1, 1975), p.17.
92. Federal Trade Commission, "Decision and Order, in the Matter of GAC Corporation," Docket No. C-2523, (Washington, D.C.: Federal Trade Commission, July 23, 1974), Summary, p.17.
93. *Ibid.*, Part II, Section C.
94. *Ibid.*, Summary, p.20.
95. Mancini, et al., Plaintiffs v. GAC Corporation, et al., "Agreement of Settlement," *op. cit.*, p.3.
96. *Ibid.*, p.4.
97. *Ibid.*, p.14.
98. GAC Corp., *Form 10-K Annual Report*, (Washington, D.C.: Securities and Exchange Commission, 1975), p.5.
99. Mancini, et al., Plaintiffs v. GAC Corporation, et al., "Agreement of Settlement," *op. cit.*
100. *Ibid.*, p.17.
101. *Ibid.*, p.7.
102. *Ibid.*, p.11.
103. *Ibid.*, p.12.
104. *Ibid.*, p.14.
105. *Ibid.*, p.2.

7. LAKE HAVASU CITY

1. David Hamernick, *Mohave County's Land Subdivisions in Unincorporated Areas* (Phoenix Office of Economic Planning and Development, n.d.), p.2.
2. Arizona State Office of Economic Planning and Development and Office of the Governor, *Arizona's Remote Subdivisions: An Inventory* (Phoenix: State of Arizona, Jan. 1975), p.32.
3. Division of Planning, Arizona State Office of Economic Planning and Development, *Environmental Needs Study 1970-1990: Mohave County* (Phoenix: State of Arizona, March 1974), p.26.

4. McCulloch Properties, Inc., "Today's Story of Lake Havasu City," Advertising Brochure, 1972, p.25.
5. *Ibid.*, p.3.
6. INFORM telephone interview with Robert Delany, U.S. Fish and Wildlife Service, Needles, Calif., Feb. 15, 1976.
7. Milton R. Schroeder, *The Public Control of Private Land in Arizona* (Phoenix: Office of Economic Planning and Development, July 1973), p.62.
8. *Ibid.*
9. "Adolescent 'New Town' Grows in Arizona," *New York Times*, July 12, 1976.
10. *Ibid.*
11. INFORM personal interview with Edward Olivier, Vice President and Treasurer, McCulloch Oil Corp., Oct. 1974.
12. INFORM telephone interview with Benjamin Avery, former reporter for *Arizona Republic*, Feb. 23, 1976.
13. McCulloch Properties, Inc., "Today's Story of Lake Havasu City," *op. cit.*, p.24.
14. *Ibid.*, p.25.
15. *Ibid.*
16. Community Development Division, Arizona State Office of Economic Planning and Development, *Lake Havasu City, Arizona Community Prospectus* (Phoenix: State of Arizona, Oct. 1973), p.1.
17. McCulloch Properties, Inc., "Today's Story of Lake Havasu City," *op. cit.*, p.11.
18. INFORM telephone interview with Russell Brant, Holly Corp., Scottsdale, Arizona, March 1976.
19. "SARA Becoming A Reality," *Lake Havasu City Herald*, July-Aug. 1974, p.3.
20. McCulloch Oil Corp., *McCulloch Oil Corporation Annual Report* (Denver: Jeppensen & Co., 1972 Report), p.18.
21. McCulloch Properties, Inc., "Today's Story of Lake Havasu City," *op. cit.*, p.10.
22. D.H. Yergin, "Your Own Little Place in the Sun," *Harper's Magazine*, March 1974, p.32.
23. INFORM telephone interview with Edward Olivier, Vice-President and Treasurer, McCulloch Oil Corp., March 1976.
24. California State Department of Real Estate, *Subdivision Public Report and Permit*, File No. 254 (Sacramento, California: State of California, Aug. 30, 1974), p.3.
25. INFORM telephone interview with Pat Duncan, Trico Western Corp., Lake Havasu City, July 21, 1975.

26. INFORM telephone interview with Russell Brant, Holly Corp., Scottsdale, Arizona, March 1976.
27. INFORM telephone interview with E. R. Lemmon, Lake Havasu City Project Manager, March 1976.
28. Community Development Division, Office of Economic Planning and Development, *Lake Havasu City, Arizona Community Prospectus,* op. cit., p.2.
29. Trico Western Corp., *Lake Havasu City Statistical Data Report* (Lake Havasu City, Arizona: Trico Western Corp., Aug. 1974), n.p.
30. INFORM telephone interview with Leonard Halpenny, hydrologist and President of Water Development Company, Tucson, Arizona, Feb. 1976.
31. INFORM telephone interview with Benjamin Avery, former reporter for *Arizona Republic,* Feb. 1976.
32. Ralph Nader Study Group, *Politics of Land* (New York: Grossman Publishers, 1973), p.316.
33. INFORM telephone interview with Benjamin Avery, former reporter for *Arizona Republic,* Feb. 1976.
34. INFORM telephone interview with Charles Royall, General Manager, Lake Havasu Irrigation and Drainage District, July 10, 1975.
35. McCulloch Properties, Inc., "Today's Story of Lake Havasu City," op. cit., p.20.
36. Community Development Division, Arizona State Office of Economic Planning and Development, *Lake Havasu City, Arizona Community Prospectus,* op. cit., p.4.
37. McCulloch Properties, Inc., *Property Report, Lake Havasu City* (Washington, D.C.: U.S. Dept. of Housing and Urban Development, Office of Interstate Land Sales Registration, Nov. 28, 1975), p.20.
38. INFORM telephone interview with Charles Royall, General Manager, Lake Havasu Irrigation and Drainage District, Feb. 1976.
39. *Ibid.*
40. Trico Western Corp., op. cit., n.p.
41. INFORM telephone interview with Charles Royall, General Manager, Lake Havasu Irrigation and Drainage District, July 10, 1975.
42. INFORM telephone interview with staff member, Bureau of Reclamation, Boulder City, Nevada, Feb. 1976.
43. INFORM telephone interview with Charles Royall, General Manager, Lake Havasu Irrigation and Drainage District, Feb. 1976.

44. Community Development Division, Arizona State Office of Economic Planning and Development, *Lake Havasu City, Arizona Community Prospectus, op. cit.*, p.6.
45. California State Department of Real Estate, *op. cit.*, p.4.
46. INFORM personal interview with Leonard Halpenny, hydrologist and President of Water Development Company, Tucson, Arizona, Oct. 1974.
47. INFORM personal interview with Neil Adams, Chief Sanitarian, Mohave County Dept. of Health, Oct. 1974.
48. INFORM telephone interview with employee of Soil Conservation Service, Kingman, Arizona, Feb. 1976.
49. INFORM personal interview with E. R. Lemmon, Lake Havasu City Project Manager, Oct. 1974.
50. INFORM personal interview with James Allan, Soil Conservation Service, Oct. 1974.
51. INFORM telephone interview with Patricia Duncan, Trico Western Corp., Feb. 1976.
52. INFORM telephone interview with Mr. Young, U.S. Army Corps of Engineers, Los Angeles, Calif., Feb. 1976.
53. INFORM telephone interview with employee of Soil Conservation Service, Kingman, Arizona, Feb. 1976.
54. McCulloch Properties, Inc., *Property Report, Lake Havasu City*, Nov. 28, 1975, *op. cit.*, p.9.
55. *Ibid.*, p.19.
56. *Ibid.*, p.19.
57. McCulloch Corp., *1964-1974 Lake Havasu City Growth Report* (Phoenix: McCulloch Corp., 1974).
58. D. H. Yergin, "Your Own Little Place in the Sun," *op. cit.*, p.40.
59. INFORM personal interview with E. R. Lemmon, Lake Havasu City Project Manager, Oct. 1974.
60. INFORM telephone interview with Mr. Young, U.S. Army Corps of Engineers, Los Angeles, Calif., Feb. 1976.
61 INFORM telephone interview with Thomas Staley, Soil Conservation Service, Feb. 15, 1976.
62. INFORM telephone interview with Mr. Young, U.S. Army Corps of Engineers, Los Angeles, Calif., Feb. 1976.
63. INFORM telephone interview with Charles Royal, General Manager, Lake Havasu Irrigation and Drainage District, March 1976.
64. INFORM telephone interview with Mr. Mills, official of Lake Havasu Sanitary District, Feb. 1976.
65. McCulloch Properties, Inc., *Property Report, Lake Havasu City, op. cit.*, p.5.

66. Memorandum from R. L. Stevenson, California Real Estate Commission, to Thomas J. Nolan, Nov. 2, 1970.
67. *Ibid.*
68. INFORM personal interview with local real estate agent, Oct. 1974.
69. *Ibid.*
70. California Real Estate Commission, "Appraisal of Lake Havasu City Lots," ed. R. L. Stevenson, File No. 248, State of California, Sept. 29, 1972.
71. Community Development Section, Arizona State Office of Economic Planning and Development, *Lake Havasu City, Arizona Community Prospectus, op. cit.*, p.1.
72. California State Department of Real Estate, *op. cit.*, p.9.
73. Robert D. Hershey, "Filing With S.E.C. Tags McCulloch Oil As Inquiry Target," *New York Times*, Sept. 15, 1976.

8. PUEBLO WEST

1. Colorado Land Use Commission, *A Handbook on Senate Bill 35*, (Denver: State of Colorado, June 1972), p.9.
2. INFORM personal interview with Jeris Danielson, Colorado State Deputy Engineer, Colorado State Division of Water Resources, Dept. of Natural Resources, Oct. 15, 1974.
3. Colorado Geological Survey, Dept. of Natural Resources, *Geology of Ground Water Resources in Colorado*, (Denver: State of Colorado, 1974), p.6.
4. *Ibid.*, p.2.
5. Colorado Environmental Commission, *Colorado: Options for the Future*, (Denver: Colorado Environmental Commission, Mar. 1972), p.7.
6. *Ibid.*, p.14.
7. Bureau of Reclamation, U.S. Dept. of the Interior, *Final Environmental Statement: Pueblo Dam and Reservoir Fryingpan - Arkansas Project, Colorado*, (Washington, D.C.: U.S. Dept. of the Interior, June 2, 1972), p.(i).
8. McCulloch Properties Inc., *Pueblo West*, (Los Angeles: McCulloch Properties, Inc., 1972), p.9.
9. Bureau of Reclamation, U.S. Dept. of the Interior, *Draft Environmental Statement: Pueblo Dam and Reservoir Fryingpan - Arkansas Project, Colorado*, (Washington, D.C.: Department of the Interior, Mar. 18, 1974), Vol. 1, Part II, pp.5-9.

10. *Ibid.*, Vol. 2, Part III, p.225.
11. *Ibid.*, Vol. 1, Part II, p.4.
12. Bureau of Reclamation, U.S. Dept. of the Interior, *Final Environmental Statement, op. cit.*, p.3.
13. *Ibid.*, p.13.
14. Bureau of Reclamation, U.S. Dept. of the Interior, *Draft Environmental Statement, op. cit.*, Vol. 2, Part IV, p.7.
15. McCulloch Properties, Inc., *Pueblo West, op. cit.*
16. Bureau of Reclamation, U.S. Dept. of the Interior, *Final Environmental Statement, op. cit.*, pp.19, 40, 52, 73
17. *Ibid.*, Attachment 3.
18. *Ibid.*, p.65.
19. INFORM telephone interview with Alan Bloomquist, former Regional Planning Director for Pueblo County, Apr. 1976.
20. McCulloch Properties, Inc., *Pueblo West, op. cit.*, p.21.
21. INFORM telephone interview with Charles L. Thomson, General Manager, Southeastern Colorado Water Conservancy District, Apr. 1976.
22. Government of Local Affairs Study Committee, "Interim Reports on Local Government," Attachments B and C, Memorandum from Dodie Gale, Division of Local Government, to The Legislative Council, Sept. 3, 1975.
23. Metropolitan Districts Acts (1947), as Amended, Chap. 89, Art. 3, Sec. 5, C.R.S. 1963.
24. Letter from Carl F. Eiberger, Attorney, Law Offices of Akolt, Shepherd, Dick and Rovira, Denver, Colorado, to Robert Krechter, McCulloch Properties, Inc., Los Angeles, California, Feb. 13, 1969.
25. *Ibid.*
26. *Ibid.*
27. INFORM telephone interview with former board member of Pueblo West Metropolitan District, Oct. 15, 1975, and Ken Gepfert, "Farley Defends Land Use Record," *Rocky Mountain News*, Aug. 4, 1974.
28. *Ibid.*
29. Ralph Nader Study Group, *Politics of Land*, (New York: Grossman Publishers, 1973), pp.316-320.
30. Letter from Carl F. Eiberger, Attorney, Law Offices of Akolt, Shepherd, Dick and Rovira, Denver, Colorado, to Robert Krechter, McCulloch Properties, Inc., Los Angeles, California, May 7, 1969.
31. Ken Gepfert, *op. cit.*
32. Written communication from former board member of Pueblo West Metropolitan District to INFORM, July 1976.

33. Metropolitan Districts Act (1947), as Amended, Chap. 89, Art. 3, Sec. 5, , Par. 1(a), C.R.S. 1963.
34. Written communication from former board member of Pueblo West Metropolitan District to INFORM, July 1976.
35. *Ibid.*
36. Wilson, Jones, Morton and Lynch, *Official Statement Relating to Pueblo West Metropolitan District: $37,075,000 District Bonds of 1969*, Series 1976A, (San Mateo, California: Wilson, Jones, Morton and Lynch, Mar. 9, 1976), p.3.
37. Written communication from former board member of Pueblo West Metropolitan District to INFORM, July 1976.
38. Trico Colorado, Inc., *Pueblo West Metropolitan District Revised Service Plan*, (Pueblo West, Colorado: Trico Colorado Inc., Apr. 1972), p.2.
39. Wilson, Jones, Morton and Lynch, *op. cit.*, p.14.
40. *Ibid.*, p.9.
41. INFORM telephone interview with Wayne Berry, Samuel Jones Real Estate Agency, Apr. 1976.
42. INFORM telephone interview with Robert Gustad, local utility contractor, Jan. 30, 1976.
43. McCulloch Properties, Inc., *Property Report: Pueblo West*, (Washington, D.C.: U.S. Dept. of Housing and Urban Development, Office of Interstate Land Sales Registration, Amended June 14, 1974), p.19.
44. INFORM telephone interview with Wayne Berry, Samuel Jones Real Estate Agency, Apr. 1976.
45. Wilson, Jones, Morton and Lynch, *op. cit.*, p.11; Trico Colorado, Inc., *op. cit.*, p.1; McCulloch Properties Credit Corp., *Prospectus*, (Los Angeles: McCulloch Properties Credit Corp., Apr. 11, 1972), p.8; and McCulloch Properties Credit Corp., *Offering Circular*, (Los Angeles: McCulloch Properties Credit Corp., May 15, 1975), p.19.
46. McCulloch Properties Credit Corp., *Offering Circular, op. cit.*, p.19.
47. Wilson, Jones, Morton and Lynch, *op. cit.*, p.11.
48. *Ibid.*, p.12
49. Wilson, Jones, Morton and Lynch, *Official Statement Relating to Pueblo West Metropolitan District: $37,075,000 District Bonds of 1969*, Series 1974C, (San Mateo, Calif.: Wilson, Jones, Morton and Lynch, July 23, 1974), p.22.
50. Trico Colorado, Inc., *op. cit.*, p.1.
51. INFORM telephone interview with former board member of Pueblo West Metropolitan District, Oct. 15, 1975.

52. Trico International, Inc., *Service Plan for the Pueblo West Metropolitan District,* (Scottsdale, Arizona: Trico International Inc., May 1969), Sec. III, p.2.
53. *Ibid.*
54. *Ibid.*
55. INFORM telephone interview with former board member of Pueblo West Metropolitan District, Oct. 15, 1975.
56. Trico Colorado, Inc., *op. cit.,* p.1.
57. INFORM personal interview with a resident of Pueblo West, Oct. 1974.
58. INFORM telephone interview with Thomas Jagger, General Counsel for Pueblo West Metropolitan District, Mar. 24, 1976.
59. McCulloch Properties, Inc., *Property Report: Pueblo West, op. cit.,* p.11.
60. INFORM personal interview with former board member of Pueblo West Metropolitan District, Oct. 1974.
61. Wilson, Jones, Morton and Lynch, *Official Statement Relating to Pueblo West Metropolitan District,* Series 1976A, *op. cit.,* p.20.
62. *Ibid.,* pp.19-20.
63. INFORM personal interview with former board member of Pueblo West Metropolitan District, Oct. 1974.
64. INFORM personal interview with a resident of Pueblo West, Oct. 1974.
65. Wilson, Jones, Morton and Lynch, *Official Statement Relating to Pueblo West Metropolitan District,* Series 1976A, *op. cit.,* p.11ff., Note 5 to Financial Statements.
66. *Ibid.*
67. *Ibid.,* Note 6 to Financial Statements.
68. INFORM telephone interview with former board member of Pueblo West Metropolitan District, Oct. 15, 1975.
69. Wilson, Jones, Morton and Lynch, *Official Statement Relating to Pueblo West Metropolitan District,* Series 1976A, *op. cit.,* p.11ff., Notes to Financial Statements.
70. *Ibid.,* p.6.
71. INFORM personal interview with former board member of Pueblo West Metropolitan District, Oct. 1974.

72. INFORM telephone interview with Edward Olivier, Vice President and Treasurer, McCulloch Oil Corp., Mar. 21, 1976.
73. McCulloch Properties, Inc., *Property Report, Pueblo West, op. cit.,* pp.21ff., Note 9 to Consolidated Financial Statements.

74. Bureau of Reclamation, U.S. Dept. of the Interior, *Draft Environmental Statement, op. cit.*, Vol. 2, Part IV, p.7.
75. INFORM telephone interview with Charles L. Thomson, General Manager, Southeastern Colorado Water Conservancy District, Mar. 18, 1976.
76. Trico Colorado, Inc., *op. cit.*, p.2.
77. *Ibid.*
78. INFORM telephone interview with Charles L. Thomson, General Manager, Southeastern Colorado Water Conservancy District, Mar. 18, 1976.
79. Bureau of Reclamation, U.S. Dept. of the Interior, *Draft Environmental Statement, op. cit.*, Vol. 3, Part IX, pp.27-28.
80. INFORM telephone interview with Charles Roberts, Water Resources Engineer, Colorado State Division of Water Resources, Dept. of Natural Resources, Sept. 27, 1976.
81. Trico Colorado, Inc., *op. cit.*, p.7.
82. INFORM telephone interview with Gerald Novac, General Manager, Trico Colorado, Inc., Mar. 22, 1976.
83. *Ibid.*
84. INFORM telephone interview with Charles Roberts, Water Resources Engineer, Colorado State Division of Water Resources, Dept. of Natural Resources, Sept. 27, 1976.
85. INFORM telephone interview with Gerald Novac, General Manager, Trico Colorado Inc., Mar. 22, 1976.
86. Wilson, Jones, Morton and Lynch, *Official Statement Relating to Pueblo West Metropolitan District*, Series 1976A, *op. cit.*, p.17.
87. INFORM telephone interview with Gerald Novac, General Manager, Trico Colorado, Inc., Mar. 22, 1976.
88. Kenneth Gepfert, *op. cit.*
89. Written communication from former board member of Pueblo West Metropolitan District to INFORM, July 1976.
90. Trico Colorado, Inc., *op. cit.*, pp.1-2
91. *Ibid.*, p.2.
92. Wilson, Jones, Morton and Lynch, *Official Statement Relating to Pueblo West Metropolitan District*, Series 1976A, *op. cit.*, p.11ff., Note 5 to Financial Statements.
93. INFORM telephone interview with assistant to Thomas McCurdy, Twinlakes Reservoir and Canal Co., Mar. 24, 1976.
94. *Ibid.*
95. McCulloch Properties, Inc., *Property Report, Pueblo West, op. cit.*, p.21ff., Note 9 to Consolidated Financial Statements.

NOTES 543

96. Trico Colorado Inc., *op. cit.*, p.7.
97. INFORM telephone interview with Donald Theobold, Engineer, Trico Colorado, Inc., May 2, 1976.
98. INFORM telephone interview with Charles L. Thomson, General Manager, Southeastern Colorado Water Conservancy District, Mar. 18, 1976.
99. INFORM telephone interview with Joseph Marcot, Project Manager, North Shore Recreation Area, Bureau of Reclamation, Pueblo, Colorado, Apr. 21, 1976.
100. INFORM telephone interview with assistant to Charles Thomson, Southeastern Colorado Water Conservancy District, Mar. 22, 1976.
101. INFORM telephone interview with Charles Thomson, General Manager, Southeastern Colorado Water Conservancy District, Mar. 18, 1976.
102. INFORM telephone interview with Joseph Marcot, Project Manager, North Shore Recreation Area, Bureau of Reclamation, Pueblo, Colorado, Apr. 21, 1976.
103. INFORM telephone interview with former board member of Pueblo West Metropolitan District, Apr. 1976.
104. Trico Colorado, Inc., *Pueblo West Metropolitan District Revised Service Plan, op. cit.*, p.13.
105. Wilson, Jones, Morton and Lynch, *Official Statement Relating to Pueblo West Metropolitan District*, Series 1976A, *op. cit.*, p.24.
106. INFORM telephone interview with Joseph Marcot, Project Manager, North Shore Recreation ARea, Bureau of Reclamation, Pueblo, Colorado, Apr. 21, 1976.
107. INFORM telephone interview with former board member of Pueblo West Metropolitan District, Mar. 1976.
108. INFORM telephone interview with Joseph Marcot, Project Manager, Bureau of Reclamation, Pueblo, Colorado, Mar. 23, 1976.
109. *Ibid.*
110. McCulloch Properties, Inc., *Property Report: Pueblo West, op. cit.*, p. 18.
111. INFORM telephone interview with assistant to Charles Thomson, Southeastern Colorado Water Conservancy District, Mar. 22, 1976.
112. INFORM telephone interview with official of the Pueblo County Health Department, Mar. 26, 1976.
113. Trico Colorado, Inc., *op. cit.*, p.58ff., Exhibit 2.
114. *Ibid.*, p.8.
115. *Ibid.*

116. McCulloch Properties, Inc., *Pueblo West, op. cit.*, p.17.
117. INFORM telephone interview with official of Pueblo County Air Pollution Control Division, Mar. 27, 1976.
118. INFORM telephone interview with former board member of Pueblo West Metropolitan District, Apr. 1976.
119. *Ibid.*
120. INFORM telephone interview with Allan Hayden, Pueblo County Commissioner, Mar. 27, 1976.
121. INFORM telephone interview with Joseph Marcot, Project Manager, North Shore Recreation Area, Bureau of Reclamation, Pueblo, Colorado, Mar. 23, 1976.
122. *Ibid.*
123. INFORM telephone interview with Robert Carlson, Bureau of Reclamation, Mar. 18, 1976.
124. McCulloch Properties, Inc., *Property Report, Pueblo West, op. cit.*, p.14.
125. INFORM telephone interview with Barbara Kochevar, journalist for *Pueblo Star Journal*, Mar. 24, 1976.
126. Wilson, Jones, Morton and Lynch, *Official Statement Relating to Pueblo West Metropolitan District*, Series 1976A, *op. cit.*, p.18.
127. Bureau of Reclamation, U.S. Dept. of the Interior, *Final Environmental Statement, op. cit.*, p.8ff., Exhibit 9, (Letter from William Horton, Acting District Engineer, Albuquerque District, Army Corps of Engineers to Ellis Armstrong, Commissioner, Bureau of Reclamation, Mar. 20, 1972).
128. *Ibid.*, p.73.
129. INFORM telephone interview with official of Pueblo County Air Pollution Control Division, Mar. 27, 1976.
130. INFORM telephone interview with official of Soil Conservation Service, Pueblo Office, Apr. 13, 1976.
131. INFORM telephone interview with official of the Pueblo County Health Department, Mar. 26, 1976.
132. *Ibid.*
133. Letter from Mr. R. Pearl, Groundwater Geologist, Pueblo County Health Dept., to Paul Weiss, Colorado State Dept. of Health, July 29, 1971.
134. INFORM personal interview with Dennis Anderson, Colorado State Dept. of Health, Oct. 1974.
135. Written communication from McCulloch Properties, Inc., to INFORM, Dec. 1975.
136. McCulloch Properties, Inc., *Property Report, Pueblo West, op. cit.*, p.7.

137. INFORM telephone interview with official of Pueblo County Tax Assessors Office, Mar. 23, 1976.
138. INFORM personal interview with realty agent, Kelly Realty Agency, Oct. 22, 1974.
139. McCulloch Properties, Inc., *Property Report, Pueblo West*, op. cit., p.20.
140. INFORM personal interview with realty agent, Kelly Realty Agency, Oct. 22, 1974.
141. McCulloch Properties Credit Corp., *Offering Circular, op. cit.*, p.22.

III. SUBDIVISIONS IN MOUNTAINS

1. THE MOUNTAIN ENVIRONMENT

1. David F. Costello, *The Mountain World* (New York: Thomas Crowell Co., 1975), p.149.
2. C.J. Hylander, *Wildlife Communities from the Tundra to the Tropics* (New York: Houghton Mifflin, 1966), p.104.
3. Charles W. Howe, ed., *Residential Development in the Mountains of Colorado* (Denver: University of Colorado, 1972), p.77.
4. David F. Costello, *op. cit.*, p.92.
5. Charles Thurow, William Toner and Duncan Erley, *Performance Controls for Sensitive Lands* (Chicago: American Society of Planning Officials, 1975), p.71.
6. Colorado Environmental Commission, *Colorado : Options for the Future* (Denver: Colorado Environmental Commission, State of Colorado, Mar. 1972), p.5.
7. David F. Costello, *op. cit.*, p.86.
8. Colorado Environmental Commission, *op. cit.*, p.15.
9. *Ibid.*, p.14.
10. *Ibid.*
11. Charles Thurow, William Toner and Duncan Erley, *op. cit.*, p.4.
12. William K. Reilly, ed., *The Use of Land* (New York: Rockefeller Brothers Fund, 1973), pp.107-108.
13. California Resources Agency and Division of Soil Conservation, *Environmental Impact of Urbanization of the Foothill and Mountainous Lands of California* (Sacramento: State of California, 1971), p.6.

2. COLORADO CITY

1. Colorado City Development Co., "Colorado City," Advertising Brochure, Colorado City Development Co., 1973, n.p.
2. Em Hall, "An Expose of 'Great Western Cities'," *The New Mexico Review and Legislative Journal,* Oct. 1970, p.6.
3. Great Western United Corp., *Proxy Statement/Prospectus,* (Denver: Great Western United Corp., Aug. 28, 1974), p.169.
4. Ralph Nader Study Group, *Politics of Land,* (New York: Grossman Publishers, 1973), pp.321-343.
5. Colorado City Development Co., *op. cit.,* n.p.
6. INFORM telephone interview with Ronald Simpson, official of Pueblo County Regional Planning Commission, Jan. 30, 1976.
7. INFORM telephone interview with Robert Price, official of Hollydot, Inc., May 24, 1976.
8. INFORM personal interview with Kenneth L. Richardson, Vice-President, Ab Duell Realty, Inc., Oct. 21, 1975.
9. INFORM telephone interview with Ronald Simpson, official of Pueblo County Regional Planning Commission, Jan. 30, 1976.
10. Great Western United Corp., *Proxy Statement/Prospectus, op. cit.,* p.112.
11. Em Hall, "An Expose of 'Great Western Cities'," *The New Mexico Review and Legislative Journal,* Oct. 1970, p.2.
12. Em Hall, "Cochiti Lake Revisited," *The New Mexico Review and Legislative Journal,* Nov. 1971, p.3.
13. *Ibid.*
14. *Ibid.*
15. Great Western United Corp., *Form 10-K Annual Report,* (Washington, D.C.: Securities and Exchange Commission, 1972), p.9.
16. *Ibid.,* p.8.
17. Great Western United Corp., *Proxy Statement/Prospectus, op. cit.,* p.165.
18. Great Western United Corp., *Property Report, Colorado City,* (Washington, D.C.: Dept. of Housing and Urban Development, Office of Interstate Land Sales Registration, Aug. 1975), Supplement.
19. INFORM telephone interview with staff attorney, Colorado State Attorney General's Office, June 23, 1976.
20. INFORM personal interview with Richard Levenberg, former counsel with Great Western Cities, Oct. 25, 1974.

NOTES 547

21. INFORM telephone interview with Lawrence Knopf, Project Manager at Colorado City, Mar. 1, 1976.
22. Great Western United Corp., *Annual Report*, (Denver: Great Western United Cities, 1975), p.38.
23. Great Western United Corp., *Proxy Statement/Prospectus, op. cit.*
24. *Ibid.*
25. INFORM telephone interview with an official of Pueblo County Health Dept., Jan. 30, 1976.
26. INFORM telephone interview with Lawrence Knopf, Project Manager at Colorado City, Mar. 1, 1976.
27. INFORM telephone interview with Great Western Cities sales representative at Colorado City, Jan. 30, 1976.
28. Great Western United Corp., *Proxy Statement/Prospectus, op. cit.*, p.174.
29. INFORM telephone interview with Roger Smades, District Engineer, Colorado State Health Department, Jan. 30, 1976.
30. Colorado City Development Co., *op. cit.*, n.p.
31. Great Western United Corp., *Proxy Statement/Prospectus, op. cit.*, p.152.
32. Colorado City Development Co., *op. cit.*, n.p.
33. INFORM telephone interview with Dean Anderson, Administrator, Colorado City Recreation District, Feb. 2, 1976.
34. *Ibid.*
35. *Ibid.*
36. Colorado City Development Co., *op. cit.*, n.p.
37. INFORM telephone interview with Dean Anderson, Administrator, Colorado City Recreation District, Feb. 2, 1976.
38. Colorado City Development Co., *op. cit.*, n.p.
39. Boettcher and Company, "General Obligation Refunding Water Bonds, Colorado City Water and Sanitation District, $2,815,000," (Pueblo County, Colorado: Boettcher and Company, July 1, 1974).
40. *Ibid.*
41. Colorado City Realty Company, "Agreement for Sale and Purchase of Real Estate," Oct. 1974, Water and Sewer Availability Agreement.
42. INFORM personal interview with William Hambrick, Manager, Colorado City Water and Sanitation District, Oct. 15, 1975.
43. INFORM telephone interview with Jeris Danielson, Colorado State Deputy Engineer, Colorado State Division of Water Resources, Dept. of Natural Resources, Oct. 15, 1974.
44. Colorado City Development Co., *op. cit.*, n.p.

45. Great Western United Corp., *Form 10-K Annual Report*, (Washington, D.C.: Securities and Exchange Commission, April 1972), p.17.
46. Great Western United Corp., *Form 10-K Annual Report*, (Washington, D.C.: Securities and Exchange Commission, April 1975), p.32.
47. INFORM telephone interview with William Hambrick, Manager, Colorado City Water and Sanitation District, July 1976.
48. INFORM personal interview with former official of Pueblo County Health Dept., Oct. 1974.
49. INFORM telephone interview with assistant to Charles Thomson, Southeastern Colorado Water Conservancy District, Mar. 22, 1976.
50. INFORM personal interview with Robert Jesse, Acting Division Engineer, State Water Resources Commission, Oct. 1974.
51. Great Western United Corp., *Proxy Statement/Prospectus, op. cit.*, p.175.
52. INFORM telephone interview with William Hambrick, Manager, Colorado City Water and Sanitation District, July 1976.
53. Colorado City Development Co., *op. cit.*, n.p.
54. Great Western United Corp., *Proxy Statement/Prospectus, op. cit.*, p.176.
55. INFORM telephone interview with William Hambrick, Manager, Colorado City Water and Sanitation District, Oct. 1975.
56. INFORM telephone interview with Frank Svarc, board member of Colorado City Water and Sanitation District, June 1976.
57. INFORM telephone interview with William Hambrick, Manager, Colorado City Water and Sanitation District, May 1, 1976.
58. Great Western United Corp., *Form 10-K Annual Report*, 1972, *op. cit.*, p.17.
59. INFORM personal interview with former official of Pueblo County Health Dept., Oct. 1974.
60. Bureau of Reclamation, U.S. Dept. of the Interior, *Final Environmental Statement : Pueblo Dam and Reservoir Fryingpan-Arkansas Project*, (Washington, D.C.: U.S. Dept. of the Interior, June 2, 1972), p.32.
61. Great Western United Corp., *Proxy Statement/Prospectus, op. cit.*, p.176.
62. *Ibid.*
63. INFORM telephone interview with William Hambrick, Manager, Colorado City Water and Sanitation District, Mar. 1, 1976.
64. Colorado City Realty Co., "Agreement for Sale and Purchase of Real Estate," Oct. 1974, Water and Sewer Availability Agreement.

NOTES 549

65. Great Western United Corp., *Proxy Statement/Prospectus,* op. cit., p.175.
66. Great Western United Corp., *Proxy Statement/Prospectus,* op. cit., p.175.
67. *Ibid.*
68. INFORM telephone interview with Lawrence Knopf, Project Manager at Colorado City, Mar. 1, 1976.
69. Great Western United Corp., *Proxy Statement/Prospectus,* op. cit., p.175.
70. *Ibid.*
71. INFORM telephone interview with William Hambrick, Manager, Colorado City Water and Sanitation District, Oct. 1975.
72. INFORM telephone interview with a Pueblo County Sanitarian, Pueblo County Health Dept., Jan. 30, 1976.
73. INFORM telephone interview with William Hambrick, Manager, Colorado City Water and Sanitation District, Mar. 1, 1976.
74. INFORM telephone interview with a Pueblo County Sanitarian, Pueblo County Health Dept., Jan. 30, 1976.
75. INFORM telephone interview with Lawrence Knopf, Project Manager at Colorado City, Mar. 1, 1976.
76. INFORM telephone interview with Ronald Simpson, official of Pueblo County Regional Planning Commission, Jan. 30, 1976.
77. INFORM personal interview with local realtor, Ab Duell Realty Co., Oct. 1974.
78. INFORM personal interview with former official of Pueblo County Health Dept., Oct. 1974.
79. Colorado City Realty Co., "Agreement for Sale and Purchase of Real Estate," Oct. 1974, n.p.
80. INFORM telephone interview with Robert Gustad, San Isabel Electric Company, Jan. 30, 1976.
81. INFORM telephone interview with Dean Anderson, Administrator, Colorado City Recreation District, Feb. 2, 1976.
82. INFORM personal interview with former official of Pueblo County Health Dept., Oct. 1974.
83. Great Western United Corp., *Proxy Statement/Prospectus,* op. cit., p.174.
84. INFORM personal interview with Ross Campbell, District Conservationist, Soil Conservation Service, U.S. Dept. of Agriculture, Oct. 1974.
85. INFORM telephone interview with official of McIntire and Quiros of Colorado, Inc., engineers for Colorado City, May 1976.

86. Letter from the Soil Conservation Service, U.S. Dept. of Agriculture, Pueblo, Colorado to Richard Simpson, McIntire and Quiros of Colorado, Inc., engineers for Colorado City, Feb. 22, 1974.
87. INFORM personal interview with Ross Campbell, District Conservationist, Soil Conservation Service, U.S. Dept. of Agriculture, Oct. 1974.
88. INFORM telephone interview with official of McIntire and Quiros of Colorado, Inc., engineers for Colorado City, Sept. 17, 1976.
89. Letter from the Soil Conservation Service, U.S. Dept. of Agriculture to Richard Simpson, McIntire and Quiros of Colorado, Inc., Feb. 22, 1974.
90. Water Quality Division, Colorado Dept. of Public Health, *Waste Load Allocation for the Arkansas River, Monument Creek, Fountain Creek, Greenhorn Creek, and the Cucharas River*, (Denver: State of Colorado, Apr. 1974), p.6.
91. *Ibid.*
92. INFORM personal interview with local realtor, Ab Duell Realty Co., Oct. 1974.
93. Great Western United Corp., *Form 10-K Annual Report*, 1972, *op. cit.*, p.13.
94. INFORM telephone interview with an attorney, formerly with Colorado State Attorney General's Office, Sept. 1976.
95. Great Western United Corp., *Property Report, Colorado City*, (Washington, D.C.: U.S. Dept. of Housing and Urban Development, Office of Interstate Land Sales Registration, Aug. 1975), Supplement.
96. *Ibid.*
97. *Ibid.*
98. INFORM telephone interview with David Lloyd, Counsel to Great Western Cities, July 7, 1976.
99. INFORM telephone interview with a staff attorney, Los Angeles Office, Federal Trade Commission, July 6, 1976.
100. INFORM telephone interview with an attorney, formerly with Colorado State Attorney General's Office, June 23, 1976.
101. Great Western United Corp., *Annual Report*, (Denver: Great Western United Corp., 1975), p.57.
102. INFORM telephone interview with an attorney, formerly with Colorado State Attorney General's Office, June 23, 1976.
103. INFORM telephone interview with staff attorney, Colorado State Attorney General's Office, June 1976.

NOTES 551

104. INFORM telephone interview with an attorney, formerly with Colorado State Attorney General's Office, June 23, 1976.

3. BEAR VALLEY SPRINGS

1. Applied Science and Resource Planning, Inc., *Environmental Impact Report: Bear Valley Springs*, (Sacramento: Applied Science and Resource Planning, Inc., Nov. 27, 1972), p.6.
2. *Ibid.*, p.8, Slope Map.
3. *Ibid.* p.35.
4. McIntire and Quiros, Planning and Engineering Division, *Bear Valley Springs Development* (Monterey Park, Calif.: McIntire & Quiros, Nov. 1972), p.2.
5. *Ibid.*, p.66.
6. *Ibid.*, p.65.
7. INFORM personal interview with Donald Simpson, Consulting Engineer, Bear Valley Springs Community Services District, Oct. 1, 1974.
8. California Department of Real Estate, *Final Subdivision Public Report*, File No. 9327 SAC, Fifth Amendment (Sacramento, Calif.: Sept. 13, 1972).
9. INFORM personal interview with Donald Simpson, Consulting Engineer, Bear Valley Springs Community Services District, Oct. 1, 1974.
10. INFORM telephone interview with Walter Sandall, former Manager, Bear Valley Springs Community Services District, Spring 1976.
11. Applied Science and Resource Planning, Inc., *Environmental Impact Report, op. cit.*, p.81.
12. INFORM telephone interview with Hal Hill, U.S. Soil Conservation Service, May 20, 1976.
13. Written communication to INFORM from Project Land Use, Inc., Mar. 22, 1976.
14. INFORM telephone interview with Lawrence Mullrix, California Water Resources Control Board, May 11, 1976.
15. Applied Science and Resource Planning, Inc., *Environmental Impact Report, op. cit.*, pp.17-18.
16. *Ibid.*, pp.19-20, Table 1 and Soils Map.
17. *Ibid.*, pp.18, 20, Soils Map.

18. INFORM telephone interview with Arthur Richards, Kern County Health Department, May 21, 1976.
19. INFORM telephone interview with Walter Sandall, former Manager, Bear Valley Springs Community Services District, Spring 1976.
20. California Dept. of Real Estate, *Final Subdivision Public Report, op. cit.*, p.5.
21. California Regional Water Quality Control Board, Central Valley Region, "Waste Discharge Requirements for Bear Valley Community Services District, Bear Valley Springs Association, and Dart Industries, Inc.," Order No. 72-34 (Fresno, Calif.: Aug. 27, 1971.
22. INFORM telephone interview with Walter Sandall, former Manager, Bear Valley Springs Community Services District, Spring 1976.
23. INFORM personal interview with Donald Simpson, Consulting Engineer, Bear Valley Springs Community Services District, Oct. 1, 1974.
24. INFORM telephone interview with Walter Sandall, former Manager, Bear Valley Springs Community Services District, Spring 1976.
25. Kern County Health Dept., Environmental Health Division, *Bear Valley Springs Specific Plan and EIR, Environmental Survey Report* (Bakersfield, Calif.: Kern County Environmental Health Dept., Mar. 2, 1973), p.4.
26. Applied Science and Resource Planning, Inc., *Environmental Impact Report, op. cit.*, p.26.
27. Written communication to INFORM from Project Land Use, Inc., Mar. 1976.
28. INFORM personal interview with Donald Simpson, Consulting Engineer, Bear Valley Springs Community Services District, Oct. 1, 1974.
29. Applied Science and Resource Planning, Inc., *Environmental Impact Report, op. cit.*, p.106.
30. *Ibid.*, p.97.
31. Written communication to INFORM from Project Land Use, Inc., Mar. 1976.
32. Applied Science and Resource Planning, Inc., *Environmental Impact Report, op. cit.*, p.94.
33. Kern County Health Dept., Division of Environmental Health, *Bear Valley Springs Specific Plan and EIR, Environmental Survey Report, op. cit.*, p.2.
34. Applied Science and Resource Planning, Inc., *Environmental Impact Report, op. cit.*, p.98.

NOTES 553

35. Kern County Health Dept., Division of Environmental Health, *Bear Valley Springs, Specific Plan and EIR, Environmental Survey Report, op. cit.*, p.3.
36. *Ibid.*, p.1.
37. INFORM telephone interview with Robert Schiffman, Professor of Archeology, Bakersfield College, Spring 1976.
38. Applied Science and Resource Planning, Inc., *Environmental Impact Report, op. cit.*, p.102.
39. INFORM telephone interview with Buzz Cordoza, Project Manager, Bear Valley Springs, May 25, 1976.
40. Applied Science and Resource Planning, Inc., *Environmental Impact Report, op. cit.*, pp.13-14, Geology Map.
41. *Ibid.*, p.15.
42. *Ibid.*, p.16.
43. *Ibid.*, p.15.
44. California Dept. of Real Estate, *Final Subdivision Public Report, op. cit.*, p.4.
45. Written communication to INFORM from Project Land Use, Inc., Mar. 1976.
46. Applied Science and Resource Planning, Inc., *Environmental Impact Report, op. cit.*, p.8, Slope Map.
47. Written communication to INFORM from Project Land Use, Inc., Mar. 1976.
48. Applied Science and Resource Planning, Inc., *Environmental Impact Report, op. cit.*, p.7.
49. California Dept. of Real Estate, *Final Subdivision Public Report, op. cit.*, p.4.
50. Applied Science and Resource Planning, Inc., *Environmental Impact Report, op. cit.*, p.78.
51. INFORM telephone interview with Robert Roan, U.S. Soil Conservation Service, May 21, 1976.
52. INFORM telephone interview with Walter Sandall, former Manager, Bear Valley Springs Community Services District, Spring 1976.
53. INFORM personal interview with Hal Hill, U.S. Soil Conservation Service, Oct. 1, 1974; INFORM telephone interview with same, May 20, 1976.
54. California Regional Water Quality Control Board, Central Valley Region, Order No. 72-34, *op. cit.*
55. Dart Industries, Inc., *Land Development at Dart Industries, Inc., op. cit.*
56. INFORM telephone interview with Dr. K. Wayne Smith, President and Chief Executive Officer, Dart Resorts, Feb. 24, 1976.

57. Dart Industries, Inc., *Land Development at Dart Industries, Inc., op. cit.*
58. INFORM telephone interview with John Banker, Attorney, San Francisco, Aug. 12, 1976.

4. TAHOE DONNER

1. Lakeworld, Division of Dart Industries, Inc., "The Beginning," Advertising supplement to *San Francisco Examiner/Chronicle, Contra Costa Times, Sacramento Bee, et al.*, 1971.
2. Dart Industries, Inc., "Summer Loves Tahoe Donner," Advertising brochure.
3. Jones & Stokes Associates, Inc., *Draft Environmental Impact Report: Application by Truckee Donner Public Utility District to Lease State Land and Divert Water from Donner Lake*, prepared for State of California State Lands Commission and State Water Resources Control Board (Sacramento: Jones & Stokes Associates, Inc., Aug. 8, 1974), p.143.
4. Eric Gerstung, "A Brief Survey of the Impact of Subdivision Activity on the Fish and Wildlife Resources of Nevada County," (California Department of Fish and Game Resources, Apr. 1970), p.1.
5. Robert C. Fellmeth, Project Director, *Politics of Land: Nader Study Group Report on Land Use in California*, (New York: Grossman Publishers, 1973), p.184.
6. *Ibid.*, p.185.
7. Eric Gerstung, *op. cit.*, p.2.
8. Memorandum from Nevada County Planning Department to Lakewood Company, Re: Tentative Map Approval, Tahoe Northwoods M70-1.0, April 6, 1970.
9. INFORM calculation based on *Draft Environmental Impact Report, op. cit.*, p.11.
10. Memorandum from Roy C. Hampson, Executive Officer, California Regional Water Quality Control Board, Lahontan Region, to Regional Board Members, July 11, 1975.
11. Jones & Stokes Associates, Inc., *Draft Environmental Impact Report, op. cit.*, p.61.
12. Untitled statement by Dart Resorts with respect to the pipeline issue (Los Angeles: Dart Resorts, Sept. 24, 1974), p.4.

13. INFORM personal interview with Harold Berliner, Attorney, Nevada County, Oct. 1974.
14. Letter to INFORM from James F. Trout, Manager of Land Operations, California State Lands Division, Sacramento, Calif., Aug. 4, 1975.
15. Jones & Stokes Associates, Inc., *Draft Environmental Impact Report, op. cit.*, p.11.
16. Written communication to INFORM from California Regional Water Quality Control Board, Lahontan Region, Spring 1976.
17. U.S. Environmental Protection Agency, Region IX, *Final Environmental Impact Statement: Wastewater Treatment and Conveyance System, North Lake Tahoe-Truckee River Basin Sanitation Agency*, F-EPA-24005-CA (San Francisco: U.S. Environmental Protection Agency, Sept. 17, 1974), p.148.
18. U.S. Environmental Protection Agency, *Final Environmental Impact Statement, op. cit.*, p.249.
19. INFORM telephone interview with Wesley Zachary, Nevada County Public Works Department, Mar. 5, 1976.
20. Memorandum from Benjamin Glading, Regional Manager, Region II, California Department of Fish and Game Resources, to Chief of Operations, Division of Soil Conservation, Re: Urban Development on California's Watershed Lands, Aug. 28, 1970, p.2.
21. *Ibid.*, p.4.
22. California Dept. of Real Estate, *Final Subdivision Public Report*, File No. 9290 SAC, Fourth Amendment (Sacramento: State of California, Aug. 2, 1974), p.6.
23. California Dept. of Real Estate, *Final Subdivision Public Report (Amended)*, File No. 11,756 SAC (Sacramento: State of California, Aug. 2, 1974), p.3.
24. Jones & Stokes Associates, Inc., *Draft Environmental Impact Report, op. cit.*, pp.73-74.
25. *Ibid.*, pp.67, 69.
26. INFORM telephone interview with David Dubois, California Regional Water Quality Control, Lahontan Region, Mar. 5, 1976.
27. *Ibid.*
28. INFORM telephone interview with Dr. Clarence Skau, Department of Renewable Resources, Desert Research Institute, University of Nevada, Mar. 8, 1976.
29. INFORM telephone interview with James Ryan, Fishery Biologist, California Department of Fish and Game Resources, Mar. 5, 1976.
30. Dart Industries, Inc., *Covenants and Restrictions: Tahoe Donner Association* (Los Angeles, Dart Industries, Inc., May 18, 1971), pp.5, 8, 10.

31. U.S. Environmental Protection Agency, *Final Environmental Impact Statement, op. cit.*, pp.98, 100.
32. Plug the Pipeline Committee, "Response to Draft Environmental Impact Report, Application by Truckee Donner Public Utility District to Lease State Land and Divert Water from Donner Lake," prepared for California State Land Commission and California State Water Resources Control Board (Truckee, Calif.: Plug the Pipeline Committee, Sept. 23, 1974), p.VI-1.
33. Dart Industries, Inc., *Land Development at Dart Industries, Inc.*, (Los Angeles: Dart Industries, Inc., 1971).
34. INFORM telephone interview with Dr. K. Wayne Smith, President and Chief Executive Officer, Dart Resorts, Feb. 24, 1976.
35. Dart Industries, Inc., *Land Development at Dart Industries, Inc., op. cit.*
36. INFORM telephone interview with Dr. K. Wayne Smith, President and Chief Executive Officer, Dart Resorts, Feb. 24, 1976.
37. Written communication to INFORM from a Truckee, Ca., real estate agent, April 1976.
38. California Dept. of Real Estate, *Final Subdivision Public Report*, File No. 9290 SAC, *op. cit.*, p.3.
39. INFORM telephone interview with Richard Ellers, Attorney, Aug. 12, 1976.

Afterword

U.S. corporations produce and sell most of the goods and services used in this country. In the process, they determine the nature of work and working conditions for over 40 million people (almost half the total work force); they control one third of the nation's tangible wealth; they make major decisions as to the consumption of natural resources and the generation of air and water pollution; they establish needs and requirements for many public services and substantively shape American values and buying patterns. The corporation, while functioning as an economic entity, thus plays a significant role in forming public policy.

INFORM, a non-profit, tax-exempt organization, was set up in 1973 to study the social role and impact of U.S. industries, particularly on the environment, on employees, and on consumers. The organization's focus is not only on assessing the extent of corporate social impacts but also on defining the kinds and costs of programs and practices available to industries to improve their performance.

INFORM's research is published in books and reports. These publications clarify for concerned Americans--government officials, business managers, investors, workers, public interest groups--some of today's most serious corporate problems and the options for change. Some INFORM publications also provide citizens with tools they can use to study and evaluate industry practices themselves.

INFORM's first book, *A Clear View: Guide to Industrial Pollution Control,* was published in July 1975, and is now commercially available from Rodale Press. It is a manual which provides citizens with a sound methodology to conduct their own research into industrial pollution problems.

INFORM's second book, *Energy Futures,* published in June 1976, provides data that clarify the state of new energy-technology development and the nature of corporate participation in R&D efforts.

Two other studies are currently under way at INFORM:

- An analysis of occupational safety and health problems at smelting operations in the non-ferrous metals industry and of the adequacy of governmental and corporate efforts to control them.

- A study of corporate involvement in urban preservation work: profiles of projects aimed at restoration and reuse of the man-made environment; a review of business and government incentives to encourage conservation activities.

During its first three years, INFORM has been supported mainly by grants from foundations and contracts or grants from several government agencies. A growing percentage of funding for INFORM's program comes from a third source: individual and institutional subscribers, who receive books, abstracts of in-depth reports, and INFORM's newsletter. (See subscription form below.)

INFORM STAFF AND ADVISORS

INFORM Staff: Director, Joanna Underwood; Editor, Jean M. Halloran; Administrator, Margaret Reinfeld; Director of Development, Anne Alexander; Research Associates: Leslie Allan, James Cannon, Manuel Gomez, Stewart Herman, Beryl Kuder, Alfred J. Malefatto, Sarah L. Oakes, Ranne Warner, Raynor Warner; Research Consultants: Mary Roman, Jean Schreier; Research Assistants: Elizabeth Hillyer, Vincent Trivelli, Margaret Vaillancourt; Production Editor, Dan Smullyan; Administrative Assistants: Mary Ferguson, Heidi Marquis, Alice Schiller, Judy Zuckerman.

Steering Committee: Robert Alexander, consultant, McKinsey & Co.; Marshall Beil, lawyer, Karpatkin, Pollet & LeMoult; Susan Butler, fund-raising consultant; William Butler, marketing consultant; Albert K. Butzel, partner, Butzel & Kass; Timothy Hogen, Resource Recovery Program Manager, SCA Services, Inc.; Lewis Kruger, partner, Krause, Hirsch & Gross; Raymond Maurice, sociologist; John P. Milton, Chairman, Threshold International Center for Environmental Research; Charles P. Noyes, environmental writer and photographer; Herschel E. Post, Assistant Vice President, Morgan Guaranty Trust Co.; Martha Stuart, President, Communications for Change; Edward H. Tuck, partner, Shearman &

Sterling; Ranne Warner, Research Associate, Harvard Business School; Anthony Wolff, environmental writer.

Advisory Council: Fred S. Dubin, President, Dubin, Mindell, Bloome Associates, Consulting Engineers; LaDonna Harris, President, Americans for Indian Opportunity; Hon. Paul N. McCloskey, Jr., Congressman, Calif.; Stewart Udall, Chairman, Overview.

INFORM SUBSCRIPTIONS

For institutions, organizations and individuals interested in INFORM's program, we offer a subscription service through which books, newsletters, and abstracts of INFORM findings may be received.

I would like to receive an annual subscription to INFORM.

	Annual rate
____Corporate and Financial Institutions Newsletter 2 copies of each book and abstract of findings	$500
____Government agencies, Universities, Libraries Newsletter 1 copy of each book and abstract of findings	$125
____Individuals, Non-profit groups Newsletter 1 abstract of findings for each book	$ 25
____Sustaining subscribers	$100

BOOK ORDERS

I would like to order:

Promised Lands

($20 per volume)

____copies of Vol. 1, *Subdivisions in Deserts and Mountains*

____copies of Vol. 2, *Subdivisions in Wetlands*

____copies of Vol. 3, *Subdivisions and the Law*

A Clear View: Guide to Industrial Pollution Control
(Rodale Press)

___ hardcover copies at $6.95 each

___ softcover copies at $3.95 each

Energy Futures: Industry and the New Technologies

___ copies of Full Report at $265
(bulk, government, library and public interest discounts available)

___ copies of Abstract at $5.00 each

INFORM News

___ copies of "Regulation of Occupational Safety and Health: Perspective from Palmerton," January, 1976, 8 pages, at $1.00 each

___ copies of "Trash to Energy," August, 1976, 8 pages, at $1.00 each

___ Please bill me.   ___ Payment enclosed.

Mail my subscription/books to: _____

_____

_____

Return to: INFORM, 25 Broad St., N.Y.C., N.Y.   10004
            (212) 425-3550

            Donations to INFORM are tax-deductible.